C000050211

1 MONTH OF
FREE
READING

at

www.ForgottenBooks.com

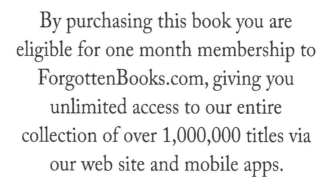

By purchasing this book you are eligible for one month membership to ForgottenBooks.com, giving you unlimited access to our entire collection of over 1,000,000 titles via our web site and mobile apps.

To claim your free month visit:

www.forgottenbooks.com/free990099

* Offer is valid for 45 days from date of purchase. Terms and conditions apply.

ISBN 978-0-260-93366-9
PIBN 10990099

This book is a reproduction of an important historical work. Forgotten Books uses
state-of-the-art technology to digitally reconstruct the work, preserving the original format
whilst repairing imperfections present in the aged copy. In rare cases, an imperfection in
the original, such as a blemish or missing page, may be replicated in our edition. We do,
however, repair the vast majority of imperfections successfully; any imperfections that
remain are intentionally left to preserve the state of such historical works.

Forgotten Books is a registered trademark of FB &c Ltd.
Copyright © 2018 FB &c Ltd.
FB &c Ltd, Dalton House, 60 Windsor Avenue, London, SW19 2RR.
Company number 08720141. Registered in England and Wales.

For support please visit www.forgottenbooks.com

SIXTY-THIRD

ANNUAL REPORT

OF THE

TOWN OFFICERS

OF THE

Town of Rockland

For The Year Ending December 31

1936

THE DOUGLAS PRINT
ROCKLAND, MASS.

Officers of the Town of Rockland

1936

Town Clerk (elected annually)
RALPH L. BELCHER

Town Treasurer (elected annually)
CHARLES J. HIGGINS

Tax Collector (elected annually)
JAMES A. DONOVAN

Selectmen, Board of Public Welfare and Fence Viewers
(elected annually)
HARRY S. TORREY
JOHN J. BOWLER   NORMAN S. WHITING

Bureau of Old Age Assistance
(appointed by the Board of Public Welfare)
HARRY S. TORREY
JOHN J. BOWLER   NORMAN S. WHITING

Assessors
(one elected annually for three years)
DENNIS L. O'CONNOR   Term expires 1939
JOSEPH B. ESTES   Term expires 1938
NORMAN J. BEALS   Term expires 1937

School Committee
(for term of three years)
HELEN M. HAYDEN   Term expires 1939
M. AGNES KELLEHER   Term expires 1938
E. STUART WOODWARD   Term expires 1938
WILLIAM A. LOUD   Term expires 1937
BENJAMIN LELYVELD   Term expires 1937

Park Commissioners
(one elected annually for three years)
PATRICK H. MAHONEY   Term expires 1939
DANIEL H. BURKE   Term expires 1938
CHARLES T. WALLS   Term expires 1937

Water Commissioners
(one elected annually for three years)
RALPH FUCILLO   Term expires 1939
SAMUEL W. BAKER   Term expires 1938
EVERETT S. DAMON   Term expires 1937

Board of Health
(one elected annually for three years)
MICHAEL J. FITZGIBBONS   Term expires 1939
JOSEPH FRAME M. D.   Term expires 1938
JOSEPH H. DUNN M. D.   Term expires 1937

Sewerage Commissioners
(one elected annually for three years)
FREDERIC HALL   Term expires 1939
GILES W. HOWLAND   Term expires 1938
CHARLES M. HINES   Term expires 1937

Trustees of the Memorial Library
(two elected annually for three years)
BURTON L. CUSHING   Term expires 1939
JOHN B. FITZGERALD   Term expires 1939
EMILY CRAWFORD   Term expires 1938
ANNIE McILVENE   Term expires 1938
EMMA W. GLEASON   Term expires 1937
FRANCIS J. GEOGAN   Term expires 1937

Auditors
(elected annually)
HAROLD C. SMITH   LEO E. DOWNEY
C. ELMER ASKLUND

Tree Warden
(elected annually
ALFRED T. METIVIER

Highway Surveyor
(elected annually
RODERICK MacKENZIE

Constables
(elected annually
CORNELIUS J. McHUGH   JOHN J. MURPHY
ADOLPH L. W. JOHNSON   ROBERT J. DRAKE
GEORGE J. POPP

Moderator
(chosen by Town Meeting)
MAGORISK L. WALLS

APPOINTMENTS
(by Selectmen)

Chief of Police
GEORGE J. POPP

Police Officers
CORNELIUS J. McHUGH   JOHN J. MURPHY
ADOLPH L. W. JOHNSON   ROBERT J. DRAKE

Special Police Officers
EDWARD J. CULLINAN   JOSEPH J. L. DeCOSTA
MAURICE MULLEN   EARL WYATT
JOHN J. DWYER JR.   CARL BENHAM
CHARLES M. HINES   ELMER DUNN
FORREST L. PARTCH   CHARLES METIVIER
RALPH WHEELER   ALDEN BLANCHARD
THOMAS MAHONEY   JOHN GORMAN
CHARLES BOUDREAU   ARTHER E. OLIVER
BERNARD DELORY   HAROLD MORSE

MICHAEL J. O'BRIEN	JOHN F. HANNON
W. ALTON WHITING	THOMAS FITZGERALD
HENRY ROCHE SR.	FREDERICK J. PERRY
THOMAS MAHON	LEE RHODENIZER
WILLIAM C. NICHOLS	GEORGE MANLEY
LEO E. DOWNEY	WILLIAM F. SHARPE

Keeper of the Lock-Up
GEORGE J. POPP

Election Officers

Precinct One   Precinct Two

Wardens
WILLIAM J. FLYNN   JOHN A. WINSLOW

Deputy Wardens
ROBERT PARKER   HAROLD C. POOLE

Clerks
IRVIN E. EMERY   FRED RYAN

Deputy Clerks
CARL FASS   J. LOCKE LANNIN

Inspectors
JOHN J. PAULIN   ELLIS BLAKE
MATTHEW O'GRADY   CHARLES F. SHIELDS

Deputy Inspectors

ROBERT D. ESTES	FRANCIS L. GAMMON
TIMOTHY WHITE	E. BURTON RAMSDELL
ANNIE GARRITY	OLIVE C. WHEELER
HELENA W. HUNT	MARY E. LYNCH

Registrars of Voters
(one appointed annually for three years)
*ESTHER H. RAWSON   Term expires 1939

THOMAS MORRISSEY   Term expires 1938
JOHN D. CARNEY   Term expires 1937
* To fill vacancy OLIVE H. CRAWFORD deceased,
Aug. 6, 1936.

Sealer of Weights and Measures
HAROLD J. INKLEY

Measurer of Wood and Bark
GILES W. HOWLAND

Weighers of Hay and Coal—Also Public Weighers

RALPH KEENE   EDITH PETRELL
ELIZABETH DONOVAN   ARTHUR PETRELL
PERCY JACOBS   DOMINICK PETRELL

Agent for Burial of Indigent Soldiers and Care of
Soldiers' Graves
LOUIS B. GILBRIDE

Inspector of Animals and Stables
WILLIAM T. CONDON

Town Physicians for poor and Soldiers' Relief
FREDERICK H. COREY, M. D.
JOSEPH H. DUNN, M. D.

Superintendent Gypsy Moth
ALFRED T. METIVIER

Forest Fire Warden
CLYSON P. INKLEY

APPOINTMENTS
(by School Committee)
Superintendent of Schools
R. STEWART ESTEN

APPOINTMENTS
(by Water Commissioners)
Superintendent of Water Works
JAMES B. STUDLEY

APPOINTMENTS
(by Board of Health)
Inspectors of Plumbing
FREDERIC HALL   J. STUART McCALLUM

Milk Inspectors
BOARD OF HEALTH

APPOINTMENTS
(by Moderator)
Finance Committee

MARION MANSFIELD DONOVAN	
	Term expires 1939
FLORENCE DUDLEY	Term expires 1939
JAMES P. KANE	Term expires 1939
BERNARD MONAHAN	Term expires 1939
ARTHUR S. WYMAN	Term expires 1939
MARY L. SHAW	Term expires 1938
ALTON F. LYONS	Term expires 1938
EVA HUBLEY	Term expires 1938
RALPH W. BINGHAM	Term expires 1938
WILLIAM J. SWIFT	Term expires 1938
HERBERT S. GARDNER	Term expires 1937
MATTHEW D. GAY	Term expires 1937
MARY CLANCY	Term expires 1937
EDMUND F. HARNEY	Term expires 1937
CHARLES P. HOWLAND	Term expires 1937

Chief of Fire Department
CLYSON P. INKLEY   Tenure of Office

Report of the Town Clerk

MARRIAGES REGISTERED IN THE TOWN OF ROCKLAND FOR THE YEAR 1936

January 3.   Jospeh Diliddo and Antoinette Delida both of Rockland.

January 8.   Alfred T. Metivier and Darthea L. Smith both of Rockland.

January 17.   Thomas James Larkin and Eleanor Louise Stoddard both of Rockland

January 26.   Earl F. Thompson Jr., and Mildred F. Condon both of Rockland.

February 7.   Arthur Vincent Smith of Rockland and Ellen Elizabeth Manley of North Abington.

February 13.   Frank Mezzetti Jr., of Quincy and Lillian Eaniri of Rockland.

February 15.   Alfred Morehouse of Rockland and Etta Lucy Unwin of Grafton, Vermont.

February 22.   Norman Thornton Gilman and Mary Alice Mayhew both of Rockland.

February 23.   Edward Cull of Rockland and Mary McMahon of Brockton.

Mar 1.   Edward N. Anderson and Ada I. Franke both of South Boston.

March 5. Harry Badmington and Eleanor Marie Dorr both of Rockland.

April 5. Warren Harry Barstow of Rockland and Helen Olga Schreeder of Halifax.

April 11. John Petrell Jr., of Rockland and Dorothy Beatrice Wilmot of Whitman.

April 12. Joseph DelPrete and Antoinette Josephine Umbrianna both of Rockland.

April 12. Alfred Joseph Pignatalli of Randolph and Teresa Spano of Rockland.

April 16. J. Norman Delory of Rockland and Helen Fisk Barrett of Springfield.

April 19. Harold Rushwick of North Abington and Mary Flaherty of Rockland.

April 19. Armand C. Bolduc of Lewiston, Maine and Carmeline Mastrodomenico of Rockland.

April 25. Bradford Dexter Whiting of Rockland and Dorothy Gertrude Daley of South Hanson.

April 29. Clifton Earle Nightingale of Marshfield and Julia Marie Ferron of Rockland.

May 2. Turner Wright Gilman of Chicago, Illinois and Barbara Earl Starbard of Rockland.

May 2. John Francis Mahoney of Hanson and Florence Mary Bowen of Rockland.

May 3. Donald Brooks Alden of Avon and Martha Emily Brilliant of Rockland.

May 9. John Francis Connor of Quincy and Margaret Anne McHugh of Rockland. /

May 15. Ewart Henry Spafford of Rockland and Mary Florence Dubrelle of East Bridgewater.

May 16. John Tedeschi of Rockland and Angelina Fasci (Pratico) of South Weymouth.

May 23. Walter Edwin Loring of South Weymouth and Geraldine Elizabeth Appleford of Rockland.

May 23. Alphonse Grant of East Weymouth and Emily Theresa Mariani of Rockland.

May 27. Raymond Elbridge Ewell of Rockland and Marian Eleanora Zeoli of East Weymouth.

May 27. John Frances McGrath of South Weymouth and Vivian Noren of Rockland.

May 28. Andrew Michael Walsh of Holbrook and Ruth Elizabeth Ford of Rockland.

May 29. William Peter Lioy and Rachel Catherine Wheeler both of Rockland.

June 1. James Francis Keane and Marguerite Louise Hussey both of Rockland.

June 1. William Joseph Phillips of Taunton and Josephine Gladys Perry of Rockland.

June 2. Raymond Lambert Garland of Rockland and Ethel Antoinette Morse of East Weymouth.

June 6. Harry Wellington Nichols of Whitman and Ida Leavitt of Rockland.

June 7. John Oliver Donovan of Rockland and Mary Josephine Glancy of Dorchester.

June 9. George Henry Paquette and Barbara Lincoln Poole both of Rockland.

June 12. Edward Leslie Pike of Whitman and Viola Mary Duhamel of Rockland.

June 12. Roger Tafton Ransom of Rockland and Florence Isabel Wheeler of Pembroke.

June 14. Harold Leslie Tilden and Marjorie Elizabeth Chandler both of Rockland.

June 16. Joseph William Pennini and Eleanor Margaret Wyman both of Rockland.

June 17. Alton Francis Lyon and Villa May Webber both of Rockland.

June 21. Louis Robert Crocker of Rockland and Dorothy Cora Leach of East Weymouth.

June 25. Harold Richard Whitman and Mary Grace Anderson both of Hingham.

June 28. James Patrick DiMestico of Whitman and Frances Olive Coit of Rockland.

June 28. George Donald Jacob of Abington and Josephine Mildred Brown of Rockland.

June 28. Charles Henry Buckley of Wollaston and Eva Mae Benoit of Rockland.

July 2. John Arthur Fihelly of Rockland and Mary Gilday of Brockton.

July 3. Frederick Francis Fontaine and Evelyn Mc-Phee both of Rockland.

July 10. Arthur Sumner Hammond and Ruth Marie Field (Josselyn) both of Rockland.

July 12. Herbert George Corliss and Elizabeth Annie Swift (Taylor) both of Rockland.

July 18. Arthur Lawrence FitzGerald of Rockland and Julia Elizabeth Lenehan of Dorchester.

July 29. Patrick Herbert Groom of Brockton and Gertrude Lyons Bowen of Rockland.

August 1. Harold William Cunningham and Mary Grace Kelley both of Rockland.

August 2. Edward C. Pilote of San Francisco, Cal., and Kathryn M. Hickey of Rockland.

August 8. Roy Henderson Pendleton of Quincy and Rose Katherine Flaherty of Roxbury.

August 15. Millard F. Manning of Norwich, Conn., and Charlotte M. Baker of Rockland.

August 15. Lawrence Damon and Lillian Wyatt both of Rockland.

August 16. M. Edward Reardon of Rockland and Margaret C. Fisher of Braintree.

August 21. Frederick Dold of Jamaica Plain and Esther M. Elliott of Rockland.

August 22. Merton Y. Clement and Gertrude Shaw (McLaughlin) both of Rockland.

September 3. James B. Smith and Dorothea H. Roberts both of Rockland.

September 5. Eugene Stanley Sozzi of Brooklyn, New York and Amelia Therese Lioy of Rockland.

September 6. George Raphael Ronka and Marjorie Farnsworth both of Rockland.

September 18. Lawrence Webster Birnie and Helen Louise Benton both of Brockton.

September 26. Jeremiah John Lyons of Brockton and Annie Teresa Mahoney of Rockland.

September 27. Charles Spencer Carr of Boston and Miriam Warshaw of Rockland.

October 1. Richard Hussey and Louise A. Caplice both of Rockland.

October 1. Wallace Dana Vogell of Rockland and Evelyn Marie Quinn of Hingham.

October 9. Ronald J. L. Rowe of Quincy and Marion L. Blake of Rockland.

October 10. Oakley Ashton Seaman and Gertrude Agnes McHugh both of Rockland.

October 11. Joseph P. Garbacauskas and Anna Balonis both of Rockland.

October 11. Harry Sidney Webster of Rockland and Madeline Vida Silvia of South Hanover.

October 12. William Harold Friary of Rockland and Anne Theresa Sullivan of Jamaica Plain.

October 16. Alison Lantz of Marshfield and Hazel Benton of Rockland.

October 17. Charles Herbert Low of Brockton and Ethyl Arlene Oliver of Rockland.

October 24. Clyde F. Greene of Rockland and Mary Carmen Uberti (Freitas) of West Bridgewater.

October 25. Paul John McDonnell and Jennie Marie Fransosa both of Rockland.

October 28. Amadeo Angelo Giberti of Whitman and Gertrude Katherine Hickey of Rockland.

November 7. Willis William MaCaulay of Somerville and Theo Emery Brown of Rockland.

November 9. Fred Weston Wentworth and Rena Loranger both of Rockland.

November 14. Nelson William St. Jean of Rockland and Anita Cartier of Sanford, Maine.

November 26. Anthony Robert Engino and Marie Rose Houle both of Rockland.

November 28. Joseph Daniel Galinis and Ruth E. Harrington both of Rockland.

November 28. Raymond Otis Scott and Eleanor Arlene Richards both of Hanover.

December 13. John A. Lamb of Rockland and Mary Ann Nehubian, (Skeahan) of Newton.

December 18. Albert Thomas Orrall of Abington and Doris Esther Mahoney of Rockland.

December 19. Charles H. Eastman Jr. of Beechwood and Blanche Louise Plouffe of Rockland.

December 24. Walter Clifton Molander and Grace Helen Earle both of Rockland.

December 24. Arthur William Earle of Rockland and Anita Mary Anctil of Pembroke.

BIRTHS REGISTERED IN THE ...WN OF ROCKLAND FOR THE YEAR 1936

Date of Birth	Name	Name of Parents and Name of Mother	Birthplace of Parents
Jan 1	Shirley Mae Atkinson	George E. and Gertrude M. Wood	Whitman / Bridgewater
Jan 6	Barbara Marcia ...	... and Sarah P. Shyavitz	Russia / Poland
Jan 17	... Mia Ferguson	Aus R. and Sara A.	... / Rockland
Jan 19	... Deborah ...	...ld H. and Ade M.	P. E. I. / ...
Jan 20	Richard Arthur Benoit	Arthur A. and ...	...
Jan 21	Nancy Lee ...	Lelland and ...n A. ...	No. ... / W ...
Jan 22	Clinton Thomas Bliss	...h F. and Mel ...	Lawrence / ...
Jan 22	Virginia Mae ...	...m C. and ...e M. Hyland	...a / ...
Jan 28	Robert Henry Fortin	...o P. and Mildred A. Reed	... / Boston
Jan 30	Laura Louise Adamson	David F. and Ruth A. Bowman	Maine / Lawrence
Feb 1	(Male) Heath	William C. and ... M. Talbot	Boston / ...
Feb 5	...ia Karen Green	Charles E. and ...ry A. Keegan	Rockland / New York
Feb 12	George Edward Stringer	Charles F. and Marion E. Philbrick	...
Feb 13	Barbara Ann Umbrianna	George John and Agnes E. ...	...
Feb 15	... Lewis Cass	Donald L. and Ella M. ...	...m / N. Al...
Feb 16	Stillborn		
Feb 18	... Charles Tarbox	Elbridge A. and Alberta E. Milburn	Lynn / Lynn
Feb 22	Rosella Katherine	...rd A. and Bernice Pike	Russia / Abington
Feb 25	...a Sarah Shafter	Samuel and Diena Rossman	Scituate / Russia
Feb 29	... Damon	George H. and Evelyn L.	... / Norwell
Mar 5	...	...es F. Jr., and Grace G.	...ge / ...
Mar 6	Elizabeth ...	Anthony and Annie ...	Italy / Rhode
Mar 9	Frank Stychynsky	...o and Dorothy Pierce	...nd / Ro...
Mar 10	(Me) Botto	...m M. and ...e M. McCue	Ro... / Duxbury
Mar 10	Maurice Joseph Dalton	...ld W. and ...a C. Sundell	Brockton / Abington
Mar 14	George Sundell ...	...	Rockland / Conn.
Mar 20	David ... Donovan	Daniel DeC. and ...	Rockland / ...

BIRTHS REGISTERED IN THE WN OF ROCKLAND FOR THE YEAR 1936

Date of Birth	Name	Name of Parents and Name of Mother	Place of Birth	arts
Mar 21	Neil	Daniel J. and Mary J.		
Mar 29		John E. and Mad E.		
Apr 2		Wes and Mary L.		
Apr 8	Edward William	Edw N. and Rith L. Hie		Brockton
Apr 12	Alice Jane Wyatt	Earl W. and He		
Apr 15		Thos V. and Pearl V.	Bridgewater	
Apr 17	Beverly	J aas E. and Ma L.		
Apr 18	Melvin	John W. Bryson and	Nova Scotia	
Apr 28		ails F. and Dorothy	Boston	N.
May 3		rehr F. and Roy L.	Braintree	
May 5	Alfred D. and Doris E.		all	
May 5	Anne Gilmartin	Er E. and Hilda H.	Boston	
May 12		Fir L. and Gea E. Bacon		
May 13		alk H. and Gee A.		Illinois
May 17		Thomas H. and Ken L.	Conn.	
May 17		Ed and Lillian Snow	Nw Yk	
May 24	Aaa Botto	Diic and Gm	Swampscott	P. E. I.
May 26	Gr	Ar E. and Mary J. McCarvell	He	
May 27	William Derochea	ah W. and My Banus	N.	
June 3		ed J. and	Me	
June 5		Ed and Ken V.		
June 16		Leo A. and Roy T.	Wpton	
June 17	J	J ph and He	By	
June 21		ee S. and Gee C.		
June 29	Ivar G. and Gertrude A. J			N.
June 30		Ek G. and in E. Downey	Boston	

BIRTHS REGISTERED IN THE TOWN OF ROCKLAND FOR THE YEAR 1936

Date of Birth	Name	Name of Parents and Maiden Name of Mother	Birthplace of Parents
July 5	Helen Frances Mock	▒ld H. and Helen F. Byrnes	Boston ▒▒d
July 18	Lela Elizabeth ▒y	Thomas B. ▒rd ▒la D. Collyer	Rhode Island Hingham
July 25	▒r Dean Sargent	Arthur J. Jr., ▒rd ▒ice D. Hawes	Rockland Braintree
July 30	Beverly Joyce Djerf	Hugo A. ▒rd ▒lura J. ▒ie	Quincy Rhode Island
Aug 2	Sally Rolien Lewis	▒e R. ▒rd ▒na R. Gallagher	Rockland Abington
Aug 5	Katherine ▒e Schatz	▒st and Marie ▒er	Germany Germany
Aug 7	Kenneth Robert Bowser	Kenneth S. ▒rd Lillian M. Davis	New Brunswick Brockton
Aug 6	J▒es Norris Redgate	▒es A. ▒rd I▒e M. Norris	Rockland ▒cy
Aug 10	Leslie Carleton Damon	Henry C. ▒rd Dorothy H. Derby	Abington 1 ▒n
Aug 14	Joseph Twomey	Maurice ▒rd Mildred F. Corcoran	Lynn Boston
Aug 15	Judith Am ▒ry	▒ur C. and Evelyn Cheney	Everett Rockland
Aug 19	▒ur ▒n Baker	Alton F. ▒rd 1 ▒a ▒te	S. Hanover t ▒n
Aug 19	▒y Ellen h▒se	John P. ▒rd Alice Josephine Flynn	Blue Hill, Me. Rockland
Aug 21	Carol Ann ▒n	Earl F. Jr., and Mildred F. ▒in	▒n Brockton
Aug 23	Gail ▒ie Gelinas	George O. ▒rd Gertrude B. Stanley	Boston Scituate
Aug 24	Ann Rose ▒ry Holway	Lowell H. ▒rd ▒n C. Donohew	Hyde Park Kansas C. Mo.
Aug 24	Robert Alvin ▒r	G▒s A. and Ruth E. Robinson	Hingham Tewksbury
Aug 25	Norman Wilfred ▒ps	Wilfred J. ▒rd Eleanor Little	Fall River Hanover
Aug 29	▒rd ▒s Larkin	T▒s J. ▒rd Eleanor L. Stoddard	Alberton, P.E.I. Rockland
Aug 29	Sheila L▒e MacLeod	▒t M. ▒rd Marie L. Holbrook	Holbrook N. Abington
Sept 5	▒ce ▒ne Ryan	Raymond E. ▒rd Marion Redfield	Rockland ▒th
Sept 13	▒y Jean Williams	Henry G. ▒rd Gladys C. Patt	Rockland E. Bridgewater
Sept 14	Shirley Louise Walton	Donald C. ▒rd Ebba L. ▒n	▒e Bristol, ▒.
Sept 18	Frederick ▒r Robinson	Robert A. ▒rd Helen L. Tibbetts	1 ▒n, Eng. Dorchester
Sept 19	▒d Monahan	Arthur L. ▒rd ▒d J. Jordan	Norwell E. Hampton
Sept 21	Dorcas Ann ▒y	Norman S. ▒rd ▒th Stringer	Osterville Rockland
Sept 22	▒h ▒h Mitchell	▒ld W. ▒rd Ruth E. Delano	▒a Scotia Rockland

BIRTHS REGISTERED IN THE TOWN OF ROCKLAND FOR THE YEAR 1936

Date of Birth	Name	Name of Parents Maiden Name of Mother	Birthplace of Parents
Oct 24	Richard Gordan Morehouse Jr.	Richard G.	Athens, Vt.	Rockland
Sept 25	Edward	A. Jr.	Italy	
Sept 25				
Oct 18			Italy	Italy
Oct 20	Maureen	E. and		
Oct 21	Mary	Gordon		Norwell
Oct 30		George M. and Margaret M. Thib		Nova Scotia
Nov 3		George H. and Evelyn Crocker	Scituate	
Nov 4		Weston B.	Holbrook	
Nov 8	Edward	Richard E.	Syria	Ireland
Nov 12		Charles B. and Lillian H.		
Nov 13	William			
Nov 13	Alfred Thomas			
Nov 16	Leo	Otto A.	N.	No.
Nov 16	Wright			S.
Nov 24		and Beatrice R.		
Nov 25	Illegitimate			
Nov 30	Sandra	William E. and C. Hammell	N.	New
Dec 6		H. and Barbara Poole		
Dec 13	Mary	E. and Ila M.		Ro
Dec 15	Slinger	H. and Margaret C. Littlefield		Abington
Dec 15		B.		
Dec 20		William R. and F.		
Dec 20		T.		
Dec 21				
Dec 30	Sue	B. and Carolin E.		

DEATHS REGISTERED IN THE TOWN OF ROCKLAND FOR THE YEAR 1936

Date	Name	Yrs	Ms	Ds	Cause of Death	Birthplace
Jan 1	Edith ... Mra	80	1	28	... nia	Rd
Jan 1	Alice E. ... han	33	8	5	... te Colitis	Rd
Jan 3	... F. Vargus	61	2	1	bar ... na	an
Jan 9	... I ... in	72			... s	Mass.
Jan 10	... s A. ... Wd	88	10	15	... ly Salis	Avon
Jan 13	Php Bliss Sheldon	50	4	8	Lobar ... nia	Maine
Jan 17	... ns ... Rd	81	1	2	... to ... ts	N. Ab
Jan 18	Mr. C. ... Hint	66	6	6	bar ... na	...
Jan 20	Lucy A. Ames	66		4	... rrhage	Ms.
Jan 26	Ed ... ny ... kett	66	1		... c ... his	...
Jan 27	Ed ... in ...	63	11	10	... al Ob ... ton	Norwell
Jan 30	... ret B. Anold	79		16	... er of Li ver	...
Feb 3	... s ... Gs	86	5		... phy of Estate	Nova
Feb 3	... el ... ley	68	7	17	... l ... ter	Ro l
Feb 4	l ... d ... n Poole	55	6	10	... itis	Ro l
Feb 5	... e ... Nd	71	2	24	... nary Occlusion	P. E. I.
Feb 6	... he ... ds	77	4	1	... nary Occlusion	R
Feb 6	My ... h Siley	71	7	17	... nary sclerosis	... he
Feb 8	Serena P. ... Rk	90	8	28	Nardosis	...
Feb 8	... e H. Everson	73	9	20	Suicide	Ro l
Feb 10	... s D. ... My	81	4	12	... to sclerosis	Rockl
Feb 13	... he ... Rs ... Py	74	4	20	... l ... morrhage	Rd
Feb 14	Grace ... a ... De	61	5	1	bar ... monia	...
Feb 16	J. ... Rd ... As	81	8		... s	... er
Feb 17	Stillborn					Me
Feb 18	... h A. ... ocker	10	6	8	... l ... cus	...
Feb 20	... Rs ... ds ... in	50	5	17	... s ... de	... n

DEATHS REGISTERED IN THE ▉N OF ▉ ▉D ▉R THE YEAR 1936

De	Name	Yrs	Mos	Ds	Cause of Death	Birthpl ae
Feb 27	▉e ▉s Cl ▉nt	66	9	17	Influenza	Rockland
Mar 2	▉k ▉e	81	3	14	Arterio sclerosis	Iowa
Mar 3	Ada Ma Beal	81	6	4	Arterio sclerosis	▉d
Mar 3	Annie B. ▉ell	52	8	26	Cerebral ▉orhage N.	▉ld
Apr 12	▉ze F. ▉h	77	5	2	Chronic Myocarditis	Illinois
Apr 13	▉Bs ▉Fhn Dominic Petrell	65	3	20	Arterio sclerosis	▉d
Mar 21	▉e ▉Man	79	1		Infectious ▉s ▉h	▉th
Mar 21	▉Bs ▉Bs	82	8	24	▉y	Rockland
Mar 24	▉e M. ▉n	71	4	12	Arterio sclerosis	▉d
Mar 30	▉s	67	10		Coronary Occlusion	Rockland
Apr 11	Augusta F. Rolli ▉h	58	8	11	Pyemia ▉m	It ▉y
Apr 16	▉k ▉w	54	5	25	Suicide	Rhode ▉d
Apr 22	J. Norman DeLory	63			Coronary sclerosis	▉th
Mar 30	Elsie ▉h Bacon	68	10	2	Angina Pectoris	Norwell
May 5	Mary ▉l eth DeWitt	21	6	7	▉s	Newburyport
May 7	Doris ▉tt Momenico	77	2	4	Abscessed glands neck ▉e gastro enteritis	Brockton
May 13	Catherine ▉y ▉a	61			Coronary ▉s	Ireland
May 13	Margaret ▉tz	75	6	24	▉y	▉d
May 21	Leta ▉es A. ▉ell	55	5	8	▉s	Nova ; ▉a
May 21	▉w J. O'Connor	65	8	19	▉y	Maryland
May 25	▉a W. Carville	66	10	19	Chronic Nephritis	▉d
May 26	William ▉n ▉s ▉s McManus	43	9	17	Cerebral ▉orhage ▉m	▉d
May 27	▉e B. Clark	30	9	3	Pulmonary ▉a Pancreas	Lawrence
June 2	▉a ▉e Weatherbee	76	5	20	▉y	Nova Scotia
June 3	John H. Flynn					Rockland

DEATHS REGISTERED IN THE TOWN OF ROCKLAND FOR THE YEAR 1936

Date	Name	Age Yrs	Mos	Ds	Cause of Death	Birthplace
June 4	Jlia Helena Strefska	24	3	20	...osis	Rockland
June 5	Elsie Josephine Grdner	20	2	18	Hodgkins Disease	Rockland
June 7	Arthur W. Stringer	60	5	21	Suicide	England
June 12	Albert C. ...ell	68	8	19	Cancer of Th yoid gland	Rhode Island
June 14	Ina Belle Colburn	68	9	11	Chronic Myocarditis	Me
June 18	Olivia Chiarlo	73	8	15	Chronic Endocarditis	Italy
June 27	Margaret F. Sullivan	78	8	12	Arterio ...sis	R
July 6	Elmon J. ...n	85	9	21	Pernicious Amia	Me
July 7	John Andrew Martin	84	6	2	...ry ...sis	
July 9	Philias A. Martel	73	3		...a of Prostate	England
July 10	...a Ball	78		14	Cerebral Hemmorrhage	Boston
July 11	Annie Maloney	54			Cirrhosis of ...er	Ireland
July 11	...e Frances Byrnes	45	5	1	Carcinoma of Signoid	Hanover
July 18	Edgar Wilfred Howland	58	9	5	Coronary sclerosis	Rockland
July 24	Thero n W. Swain	68			Uremia	New York
July 28	Edward D. ...n	76	11		...r of Prostate	R
Aug 3	...les H. Smith	20			Embryonal carcinoma	Poland
Aug 4	Stanislaw Dziekenski	54	9	22	Broncho pneumonia	R
Aug 14	G...r Allen Poole	63	10	8	Cerebral hemorrhage	R
Aug 14	...as L. Stoddard	82	11	19	Chronic Endocarditis	Boston
Aug 20	Albert Raymond Garland	27	5	19	Suicide	
Aug 22	Aubrey De West Faunce	65	9	16	Hypertrophiel Postate	N. Grafton
Aug 28	...r J. ...u	66	5	11	Coronary ...h	Rockland
Sept 5	James F. White	61	9		Cardio-Renal Disease	Wellfleet
Sept 6	Lewis F. Doane	79	5	13	Myocarditis	Rockland
Sept 8	Henry Herbert Arnold	81			Myocarditis	...
Sept 10	Edith M. Patterson	35			Septicemia	

DEATHS REGISTERED IN THE TOWN OF ... D FOR THE ... R 1936

Date	Name	Yrs	Ms	Ds	Cause of Death	Bipl ae
St 15	Ruth ...	18	1	9	...ic Fever	...
St 15	Samuel Ellis ...ole	85	3	2	...s ... E.	...
St 16	...n ...t ...ay	70	1	10	...r of Prostate	Holb ...
St 18	...a Leola ...o	47	2	3	...l ...rrhage	Taunton
St 18	...t C. Burbank	56	4	8	...c Dilation	...
St 18	...r J. ...l ...t	50	2	19	...e ...sis	M ...
St 21	...s Everett Ewell	73	1	2	...y ...s	Brockton
St 21	...l ...n ...n				Congenital ...t Disease	...
St 29	...k Burton	57			...l ...orrhage	...
Oct 3	Ida Ella ...n	86	10	25	...o ...s	Ro ...
Oct 4	...s L. Finnegan ...s	36			...za	Me
Ot 7	...h A.	70	6		Diabetes ...o sclerosis	Nova Scotia
Oct 8	...a Burrell	85	11	4	...rditis	Ro ...
Oct 13	Ella My ...y	70			...o sclerosis	Carver
Ot 19	...a F. Hallett	85		2	...ation bile ducts	R ...
Oct 20	...y ...Momenico				Broncho pneumonia	B ...
Oct 21	Edgar Baker	75			...in. Pem ...y	Ro ...
Nov 3	...t ...) Damon	71	11	15	Struck by ...o	Ro ...
Nov 4	...s J. Gaines	78	6	12	...oma of Uterus	Nova Scotia
Nov 4	Ma ...e ...y	75	7	14	...nary sclerosis	Sto ...
Nov 7	...n ...h Oiver	70	10	24	...t block	Attleb ...
Nov 8	...r C. M. Brainerd	84		7	...a	...
Nov 10	...n ...e ...t	51	9	21	...y ...bosis	...
Nov 10	...a A.	24	6	12	Pulmonary ...losis	...
Nov 21	...n My Doane Barstow	46	4	6	...c ...s	...
Nov 22	...s S. Burke	65	1	9	Broncho ...a	...
Nov 28	George A. Dunn					...

DEATHS REGISTERED IN THE [W]N OF [R]L[ND] FOR THE YEAR 1936

Date	Name	Age Yrs	Mos	Ds	Cause of Death	Birthplace
Dec 3	An W. Stetson	46	6	2	Pulmonary Oedema	Brockton
Dec 8	Ay. Dondero	79	5	—	Mis	tay
Dec 13	Ren M. ll	62	—	22	Broncho pa	id
Dec 14	By Aa Perry	73	5	5	Diabetes tds	igh
Dec 15	Gs le Stetson	33	9	21	Chr. Val tr rt Disease	Wil
Dec 18	Ra Wm Shurtleff	85	9	13	Broncho pa	Wil
Dec 24	Uth An Bray	77	4	—	Gil age	Ay
Dec 25	On K. Bs	55	—	—	Burned to dh	id
Dec 30	Ellen J. Keavy	79	6	12	Wc Ws	Rh

REPORT OF THE RECORDS FOR THE YEAR 1936

ANNUAL TOWN MEETING, MARCH 2, 1936

Pursuant to the warrant a meeting was held March 2, 1936 at the Rockland Opera House, beginning at 7:30 o'clock P. M., and the following votes were passed and action taken.

Article 1. Magorisk L. Walls was chosen Moderator and sworn to the faithful discharge of his duties.

The Moderator appointed the following tellers for the meeting: Myra Burke, Mary Clancey, Joseph Lelyveld, John Ransom, Nelson Gardner.

Article 2. Voted to accept the reports of the various town officers and committees. as published in the town report with the exception of paragraph 2, page 171, of the Police report which was deleted.

Article 3. Voted to raise and appropriate the following amounts for the purposes named.

School Department	$ 102 673 00
State Aid	900 00
Soldier's Relief	8 000 00
Military Aid	50 00
Care of Soldier's Graves	150 00
Burial of Indigent Soldiers	100 00
Soldier's Memorial Library & Dog Fund	3 832 68
Street Lighting	8 810 00
Highway Surveyor	1 350 00
Tarvia & Road Binder	6 000 00
Highway Repair	7 000 00

Sidewalks	1 000 00
Cleaning Union Street	1 100 00
Clean Up Week	100 00
Guide Boards and Signs	100 00
Fire Department	10 400 00
Police Department	8 846 00
Forest Fires	700 00
Board of Health	6 000 00
Inspecting Animals & Stables	100 00
Parks	1 851 00
Old Age Assistance	25 000 00
Moth	300 00
Tree Warden	500 00
Office Rent	1 160 00
Town Officers	6 600 00
Sealer Weights & Measures	400 00
Elections	1 500 00
Compensation Insurance	2 250 00
Mass. Hospital School	800 00
Mass. Industrial School	1 600 00
Town Report & Poll Book	700 00
Support Outside Poor & Infirmary	50 000 00
Mother's Aid	6 000 00
Town Notes & Interest	26 000 00
Assessors	2 500 00
Snow Removal	23 500 00
Reserve Fund	1 000 00
Miscellaneous Assessors	850 00
Miscellaneous Treasurer	500 00
Miscellaneous Clerk	350 00
Miscellaneous Selectmen	120 00
Miscellaneous Collector	1 275 00
Miscellaneous Registrars	200 00
Miscellaneous Sealer	105 00
Miscellaneous Unclassified	1 150 00

Total amount raised and appropriated
Under this article $323 422 68

Under Article 3.

The appropriation for the School Department was raised to $102,673.00 to provide the sum of $400.00 for the employment of an assistant to the janitor of the McKinley School at the expense of the School Dept.

Article 4. Voted to raise and appropriate the sum of Eighteen thousand seven hundred ten dollars and sixty-six cents ($18,710.66) to be paid in to the town treasury on account of overlays in the following departments.

Soldiers' Relief	$ 1	362 30
Forest Fires		189 92
Fire Department	1	128 74
Board of Health	1	111 66
Miscellaneous	1	930 04
Beacons		3 00
Snow		936 34
Outside Poor & Infirmary	7	741 05
Old Age Assistance	4	307 61
	$18	710 66

Article 5. Voted to authorize the Town Treasurer with the approval of the Selectmen, to borrow money from time to time in anticipation of the revenue of the financial year beginning January 1, 1937, and to issue a note or notes therefor, payable within one year, and to renew such note or notes as may be given for a period of less than one year in accordance with Section 17, Chapter 44, General Laws.

Article 6. Voted to raise and appropriate the sum of one thousand dollars, ($1,000.) to be spent under the direction of the Selectmen for the part payment of a Visiting Nurse.

Article 7. Voted to appropriate the sum of thirty-two thousand dollars ($32,000.00) for use of the Water Department the same to be taken from the Water Revenue.

Article 8. Voted to raise and appropriate the sum of two hundred eighty-eight dollars ($288.00) to be spent under the direction of the Selectmen for the purpose of renting quarters for the use of the Veterans of the Spanish-American War.

Article 9. Voted to raise and appropriate the sum of four hundred dollars ($400.00) to be spent under the direction of the Selectmen for the observance of Memorial Day.

Article 10. Voted to raise and appropriate the sum of sixty dollars ($60.00) for the care of the Town Cemetery.

Article 11. Voted to raise and appropriate the sum of nine hundred dollars ($900.00) to be spent under the direction of the Selectmen for the purpose of renting quarters for the use of the Rockland Post No. 147 of the American Legion.

Article 12. Voted to raise and appropriate the sum of one hundred fifty dollars ($150.00) for the use of the Plymouth County trustees for County Aid to Agriculture and to choose James D. Mahoney as town director as provided in Sections 41 and 45 of Chapter 126, General Laws.

Article 13. Voted to raise and appropriate the sum of three thousand eight hundred six dollars and thirteen cents ($3,806.13) for the maintenance of the Plymouth County Hospital.

Article 14. Voted to raise and appropriate the sum of six hundred dollars ($600.00) for the maintenance of Traffic Beacons and Signals.

Article 15. Voted to raise and appropriate the sum of one hundred dollars ($100.00) to be used by the School Committee to pay the expense of heating, lighting and casualty insurance of the Jr.-Sr. High School and McKinley

School buildings as well as additional expenses for janitors and supervision when the buildings are used by individuals and associations for educational, recreational and like
purposes under provision of Chapter 71, Section 71 of the
General Laws.

Article 16.   Voted to raise and appropriate the sum of
two hundred ninety-two dollars and fifty cents ($292.50)
to insure the Firemen of the Town of Rockland that they
might receive compensation in case of accident when on
duty.

Article 17.   Voted to build an elevated water tank, with a
capacity of about 1,000,000 gallons.

Under Article 17.
Mr. Lindbergh, Engineer, of the National Gunite Contracting Co. was given unanimous consent of the meeting
to speak from the floor.

Article 18.   Voted to instruct the water commissioners
to purchase or take by eminent domain a suitable site in
Rice Park, so called, for the location of an elevated tank,
to be paid for from water revenue or water bonds.
        Affirmative 300   Negative 88

Article 19.   Voted: That, for the purpose of financing
the construction of a water tank, and the purchase and laying of pipe, and to enable the Town to secure the benefits of
the Emergency Relief Appropriation Act of 1935, there
be raised and appropriated the sum of $70,000.00 and the
treasurer, with the approval of the selectmen, be and hereby
is authorized to borrow the sum of $40,000.00 and to issue
bonds or notes of the Town therefor, under authority of and
in accordance with the provisions of Chapter 404 of the
Acts of 1935, said bonds or notes to be payable in not more
than twenty years at such term and maximum rate of interest as may be fixed by the Emergency Finance Board.

All moneys received by way of grant from the Federal Government on account of this project shall be applied first to meet the cost of construction thereof (including preliminary expenses), and any balance thereof shall be applied to payment of the loan herein authorized.

The selectmen are hereby authorized and directed to accept on behalf of the town, for use in carrying out such project a Federal Grant of money pursuant to the Emergency Relief Appropriation Act of 1935, and the water commissioners are authorized to proceed with the construction of said project and enter into all necessary and proper contracts and agreements in respect thereto, all subject to applicable Federal regulations; and the selectmen and the water commissioners are authorized to do all other acts and things necessary or convenient for obtaining said grant, for making said loan, and for construction of said project.

Affirmative 290   Negative 23

Necessary two thirds affirmative votes required for the adoption of the article being 209 votes.

Article 20. Voted to raise and appropriate the sum of nine hundred thirty-six dollars and fifty-five cents ($936.55) to be paid as land damage to various persons for the taking of land in East Water Street as laid out by the County Commissioners.

Article 21. Voted to lay a drain pipe on Rice Avenue with catch basin at 26 Rice Avenue the necessary amount for cost of material to be taken from the appropration of Article 6, Special Town Meeting of October 23, 1935, the labor to be furnished by the Works Progress Administration.

Article 22. Voted to raise and appropriate the sum of five thousand seven hundred thirty-seven dollars ($5,737.) to be spent under the direction of the Park Commissioners for the completion of the Athletic field in Memorial Park, the labor to be furnished by the Works Progress Administration.

Article 23.   Voted to maintain the road which leads to the Jefferson School from Market Street.

Article 24.   Voted a committee of five be appointed by the Moderator to work in conjunction with the school and park departments to devise ways and means for disposal of sewage, from Rockland Jr. Sr. High School through a W. P A. project or emergency overlay, and to pass over the raising and appropriating of $6,000.00.

Committee appointed: Norman Beals, Chairman; Thomas Reardon, Giles Howland, Dr. Jos. H. Dunn, Harold Fihelly.

Article 25.   Voted to raise and appropriate the sum of seven hundred fifty dollars ($750.00) to pay cost of material and other general expenses of the W. P. A.

Article 26.   Voted to pass over the raising and appropriating of a sum of money to install a street light in front of 128 Belmont Street.

Article 27.   Voted to instruct the Board of Selectmen to provide, without cost to the town, an occasional State Police Patrol over the roads of the town.

Article 28.   Voted to transfer the sum of $698.50 from the special appropriation for repairs on the Library roof and to appropriate it to the following purposes:

For balance due on heater in Library	$ 301 18
For new radiators in stack room in Library	150 00
For brass pipes in Library	80 00

Balance added to regular Library appropriation   167 32

Total $ 698 50

Article 29. Voted to pass over instructing the moderator to appoint a committee of five citizens, to serve without compensation, and to be known as the Highway Committee, whose duties shall be to plan and make recommendations relative to repairs, building and rebuilding of sidewalks and streets; and to instruct the highway surveyor to co-operate and advise with said committee in the carrying out of his duties.

        Affirmative 232   Negative 178

Article 30. Voted to raise and appropriate the sum of five hundred dollars ($500.00) to be spent under the direction of the Selectmen for the purchase of furnishings and equipment for the Town Offices.

Article 31. Voted that the moderator appoint a committee of 15 to act in connection with the Tri-Town observance of Armistice Day and to raise and appropriate three hundred dollars ($300.00) for same.

Committee appointed: Fred Martin, Chairman; John R. Parker, J. Edward Kane, Linwood Capen, Harold Anderson, Rufus Chilton, Ellis Rome, Ashley Beals, Augustus Ledwell, Mary Mullen, Annie Carey, Allen Howland, Ralph Wheeler, Elizabeth Casey, Esther McGrath.

Article 32. Voted to raise and appropriate the sum of $1,300.00 to re-tube the two boilers in the McKinley School and make a pit and lower the grates in one as recommended by the special committee.

Article 33. Voted to pass over the raising and appropriating of a sum of money to build a sidewalk and curb on the west side of Howard Street from Webster Street to Park Street a distance of about 200 feet.

Article 34.   Voted to lay a drain with catch basins from 19 Payson Avenue to Arlington street and the amount of two hundred dollars ($200.) be taken from the appropriation under Article 6, Special Town Meeting of October 23, 1935 for materials, the labor to be furnished by the W. P. A.

Article 35.   Voted to raise and appropriate the sum of two hundred twenty-two dollars and thirty-six cents ($222.36) to keep street lights on all night service.

Article 36.   Voted to build a drain and catch basins in westerly side of Liberty Street from East Water to Custer Street a distance of 625 feet and the amount of two hundred seventy-five dollars ($275.00) be taken from the appropriation under Article 6, Special Town Meeting of October 23, 1935 for materials, the labor to be furnished by the W. P. A.

Article 37.   Voted to pass over the raising and appropriating of a sum of money to purchase land and erect a suitable fire-proof building to house town equiment.

Article 38.   Voted to repair the bridge on Old Market Street and to raise and appropriate the sum of one hundred dollars ($100.00) for the same.

Article 39.   Voted to pass over the raising and appropriating of the sum of ten hundred fifty dollars ($1,050.00) for the purchase of a Power Sprayer.

Article 40.   Voted to pass over the raising and appropriating of the sum of four hundred fifty dollars ($450.00) for planting new trees on the Highway the Labor to be done under the W. P. A.

Article 41.   Voted to accept a town way known as Beal Street Extension, as laid out by the Selectmen and filed with the Town Clerk from East Water Street running easterly a distance of about 430 feet.

Meeting adjourned to Monday, March 9, 1936 at 7:30 P. M.

Article 42. Voted to accept a town way, known as George Street Extension, as laid out by the Selectmen and filed with the Town Clerk from the corner of George Street and Crescent Street running south a distance of 200 feet.

Article 43. Voted to raise and appropriate the sum of five thousand dollars ($5,000.00) to be spent in conjunction with the State and County to rebuild East Water Street from where the rebuilding ended in 1935 to Liberty Street and drainage to Cushing Pond.

Article 44. Voted to pass over the raising and appropriating of a sum of money to purchase a new tractor or repair the present tractor.

Article 45. Voted to pass over the raising and appropriating of a sum of money for the collection of garbage in accordance with rules and regulations to be made by the Board of Health.

Article 46. Voted to raise and appropriate the sum of thirty dollars ($30.00) to install two street lights on Forest Street between the corner of Pleasant and Hingham Streets.

Article 47. Voted to elect the Moderator for a term of one year and beginning with the Annual meeting for the election of Town Officers in the year 1937 the office of Moderator be placed upon the Official Ballot.

Article 48. Voted to build a sidewalk and curb in the Easterly side of Howard Street from Custer Street to Vernon Street and the amount of one hundred twenty-five dollars ($125.00) be taken from the appropriation under Article 6, Special Town Meeting of October 23, 1935 for materials, the labor to be furnished by the W. P. A.

Article 49. Voted that the laying of a water pipe and hydrant on private way known as Carey Court be referred to the Selectmen and the work be done as a future W. P. A. project provided this is possible.

Article 50. Voted to raise and appropriate the sum of five hundred fifty dollars ($550.00) to purchase a new cruising automobile with radio for the use of the police Department and to trade in the present automobile.

Article 51. Voted to pass over the raising and appropriating of a sum of money to install an electric light on Webster Street between East Water Street and Hingham Street.

Article 52. Voted to extend the sidewalk on the north side of Crescent Street from the residence of James B. Studley to the corner of George Street and distance of 350 feet and the amount of one hundred fifty dollars ($150.00) be taken from the appropriation under Article 6, Special Town Meeting of October 23, 1935 for materials, the labor to be furnished by the W. P. A.

Article 53. Voted to pass over the raising and appropriating of a sum of money to build a sidewalk and curb on the west side of Concord Street from the north line of the residence of William Cunningham southerly to the residence of Ernest M. Locke but referred to the Selectmen for consideration as a future W. P. A. project.

Article 54. Voted to pass over the raising and appropriating of a sum of money to build a cement curb and asphalt sidewalk on the west side of Howard Street beginning at Market Street to Vernon Street.

Article 55. Voted to build an asphalt sidewalk with cement curb on easterly side of Howard Street from Vernon Street to Crescent Street, a distance of approximately five hundred and fifty (550) running feet and the amount of one hundred seventy-five dollars (175.00) be taken from the appropriation under Article 6, Special Town Meeting of October 23, 1935 for materials, the labor to be furnished by the W. P. A.

Article 56. Voted to raise and appropriate the sum of two hundred dollars ($200.00) to build a sidewalk and curb on west side of Liberty Street from Mrs. Boyle's Store to Webster Street.

Article 57. Voted to build a sidewalk and curb on the south side of Bigelow Avenue from Union Street to Myrtle street and the amount of five hundred and fifty dollars ($550.00) be taken from the appropriation under Article No. 6, Special Town Meeting of October 23, 1935 for materials, the labor to be furnished by the W. P. A.

Article 58. Voted to build a fence on the north side of Salem Street near the residence of Hiram Babcock the necessary funds to be taken from the Highway appropriation.

Article 59. Voted to build a sidewalk and curb on the west side of Myrtle Street from Exchange Street to the residence of Timothy Ryan and the amount of five hundred and fifty dollars ($550.00) be taken from the appropriation under Article No. 6, Special Town Meeting of October 23, 1935 for materials, the labor to be furnished by the W. P. A.

Article 60. Voted to pass over the raising and appropriating of a sum of money to build a sidewalk on the north side of Exchange Street from Union to Myrtle Street.

Article 61. Voted to rebuild Division Street and the amount of seven hundred dollars ($700.00) be taken from the appropriation under Article No. 6, Special Town Meeting of October 23, 1935 for materials, the labor to be furnished by the W. P. A.

Article 62. Voted to raise and appropriate the sum of one hundred dollars ($100.00) to retop with asphalt a sidewalk on the south side of Rice Avenue.

Article 63. Voted to pass over the making of a parking area on the town lot in front of the Police Station and the appropriating of a sum of money for grading and lighting said lot.

Article 64. Voted to pass over the raising and appropriating of a sum of money to place the grounds of the School Street lot in condition for parking, and to provide suitable lighting for same.

Article 65. Voted to authorize the Selectmen to appoint a committee of five (5) to study parking facilities in the business area and to determine available space adjacent thereto suitable for parking lots and to report with recommendations at a future town meeting.

Committee appointed: Joseph Lelyveld, Chairman; Warren Woodward, George Popp, Lawrence Blanchard, Lee Rhodenizer.

Article 66. Voted to pass over the raising and appropriating of a sum of money for placing trees along sidewalk borders, the work to be done under the direction of the Tree Warden.

Article 67. Voted that the Moderator appoint a committee of five (5) to investigate the need of playgrounds in the North, East, South and West sections of the town, said committee to present a report of recommendations at a future town meeting.

Committee appointed: Park Commissioners, Joseph Cogan, Albert Sullivan.

Article 68. Voted to pass over the changing of the location of the fire whistle at the Engine House and the raising and appropriating of a sum of money for the same.

Article 69. Voted to raise and appropriate the sum of fifteen dollars ($15.00) to install an electric light on Market Street in the area between the light nearest the Market Street Garage and the residence of Arthur E. Torrey.

Article 70. Voted to pass over the raising and appropriating of a sum of money for lighting the location of fire alarm boxes throughout the town.

Article 71. Voted to pass over the appointing of a committee of seven (7) to consider the advisability of the town opening a factory for the manufacture of shoes to employ men and women now on welfare.

Article 72. Voted to authorize the Selectmen to appoint a committee of five (5) to work with local civic organizations in their activities to bring new industries to Rockland, and to assist in the security of existing business whenever required but to pass over the raising and appropriating of a sum of money to defray advertising and other expenses of said committee.

Committee appointed: Abram Lelyveld, Chairman; Joseph Lelyveld, John Dillon, Herbert G. Perry, Joseph B. Estes.

Article 73. Voted to pass over the erection of two (2) Neon signs to direct traffic to the Rockland shopping area, one to be placed at the junction of Market and Union Street on Route 123, the other at the junction of Union and Liberty Street and the raising and appropriating of a sum of money for the purchase and lighting of these signs.

Article 74. Voted to raise and appropriate the sum of five hundred dollars ($500.00) for an Assessors' Map.

Article 75. Voted to raise and appropriate the sum of one hundred dollars ($100.00) to prosecute Criminal Cases in Court.

Article 76. Voted to pass over the separating of the office of Selectmen and the Board of Public Welfare, and to provide for the election of a Board of Public Welfare of three members, and at the annual town meeting of 1937 that one member be elected for three years and two members for on year each; at the 1938 town meeting that one member be elected for three years and one member for one year, and thereafter at each annual meeting to elect one member of the Board of Public Welfare for three years.

Article 77. Voted to pass over the electing of the Selectmen to serve for terms of three years in the following manner: At the 1937 town meeting to elect one Selectman for a term of three years and two Selectmen for terms of one year each; at the 1938 town meeting to elect one Selectman for a term of three years and one Selectman for a term of one year, and thereafter at each town meeting to elect one Selectman for a term of three years.

Article 78. Voted to pass over the raising and appropriating of a sum of money to be spent under the direction of the Park Commissioners for the complete construction of six tennis courts and their equipment in Memorial Park, the labor from W. P. A.

Article 79. Voted to pass over the raising and appropriating of a sum of money to be spent under the direction of the Park Commissioners for the construction of walks in Memorial Park, the labor from the W. P. A.

Article 80. Voted to raised and appropriate the sum of forty-five dollars ($45.00) for the installation of three street lights on Pond Street and Wilson Street.

Article 81. Voted to repair the sidewalk on the south

side of Church Street from Blanchard Street to Franklin
Avenue the cost of the same to be taken out of the regular
sidewalk appropriation.

Voted to pay Moderator, clerks, and tellers the usual fees.

A motion to return to Article No. 27 not agreed to.

Voted that the Finance Committee be extended a vote
of thanks of the meeting for their untiring efforts in investigating the matters to be brought before the town meeting
and the able manner in which the information was placed
before the meeting.

Unanimous vote.

Article 82.   A Subsequent Meeting for the Election of
Town Officers was held in the Rockland Opera House, Savings Bank Building, on Monday, March 9th, 1936.   The
polls opened at 5:45 A. M. and closed at 4:00 P. M.   The
result was as follows:

Total number of ballots cast   3693

TOWN CLERK—ONE YEAR

Ralph L. Belcher	3016
Blanks	677

TOWN TREASURER—ONE YEAR

Charles J. Higgins	2975
Blanks	718

TAX COLLECTOR—ONE YEAR

James A. Donovan	2952
Blanks	741

SELECTMEN, BOARD OF PUBLIC WELFARE
AND FENCE VIEWERS—ONE YEAR

John J. Bowler	1788
Elmer C. Cobb	1726
William A. Lannin	1316
Harry S. Torrey	1741
Norman S. Whiting	1779
Arthur S. Wyman	430
Blanks	2299

(see recount March 14, 1936)

HIGHWAY SURVEYOR—ONE YEAR

John J. Dwyer	31
William H. Friary	1451
Toiva Jarvinen	77
Roderick MacKenzie	1935
Curtis C. Toothaker	164
Blanks	35

ASSESSOR—THREE YEARS

Dennis L. O'Connor	2153
James F. O'Connor	376
Charles C. Pinson	856
Blanks	308

AUDITORS—ONE YEAR

C. Elmer Asklund	2181
Leo E. Downey	2279
Harold C. Smith	2183
Curtis C. Toothaker	1
Blanks	4435

SCHOOL COMMITTEE—THREE YEARS

Helen M. Hayden	2068

Nellie K. Lonergan 1259
Blanks 366

WATER COMMISSIONER—THREE YEARS

Ralph Fucillo 1722
John J. McCarthy 1717
Blanks 254
(see recount March 14, 1936)

BOARD OF HEALTH—THREE YEARS

James M. Feeney 941
Michael J. Fitzgibbons 2093
Blanks 659

LIBRARY TRUSTEES—THREE YEARS

Burton L. Cushing 2331
John B. Fitzgerald 2343
Blanks 2712

PARK COMMISSIONER—THREE YEARS

Patrick H. Mahoney 2507
Blanks 1186

SEWER COMMISSIONER—THREE YEARS

Frederic Hall 2332
Blanks 1361

TREE WARDEN—ONE YEAR

William W. Brown 291
Stanley P. Cushing 211
Edward B. Farrar 83
Charles L. Hunt 861
Alfred T. Metivier 1867
Blanks 380

CONSTABLES—ONE YEAR

Austin Beale	719
Norman S. Crosby	767
Robert J. Drake	2617
Adolph L. W. Johnson	2823
Cornelius J. McHugh	2494
John H. Murphy	2605
George J. Popp	2540
Blanks	3900

A true copy.   Attest:

RALPH L. BELCHER,
Town Clerk

AMOUNTS RAISED AND APPROPRIATED
ANNUAL MEETING, MARCH 1936

School Department	$102	673 00
State Aid		900 00
Soldiers' Relief	8	000 00
Military Aid		50 00
Care of Soldiers' Graves		150 00
Burial Indigent Soldiers		100 00
Soldiers' Memorial Library & Dog Fund	3	832 68
Street Lighting	8	810 00
Highway Surveyor	1	350 00
Tarvia & Road Binder	6	000 00
Highway Repair	7	000 00
Sidewalks	1	000 00
Cleaning Union Street	1	100 00
Clean Up Week		100 00
Guide Boards and Signs		100 00
Fire Department	10	400 00
Police Department	8	846 00

Forest Fires	700	00
Board of Health	6 000	00
Inspecting Animals and Stables	100	00
Parks	1 851	00
Old Age Assistance	25 000	00
Moth	300	00
Tree Warden	500	00
Office Rent	1 160	00
Town Officers	6 600	00
Sealer Weights & Measures	400	00
Elections	1 500	00
Compensation Insurance	2 250	00
Mass Hospital School	800	00
Mass Industrial School	1 600	00
Town Report & Poll Book	700	00
Support Outside Poor & Infirmary	50 000	00
Mothers' Aid	6 000	00
Town Notes and Interest	26 000	00
Assessors	2 500	00
Snow Removal	23 500	00
Reserve Fund	1 000	00
Miscellaneous Assessors	850	00
Miscellaneous Treasurer	500	00
Miscellaneous Clerk	350	00
Miscellaneous Selectmen	120	00
Miscellaneous Collector	1 275	00
Miscellaneous Registrars	200	00
Miscellaneous Sealer	105	00
Miscellaneous Unclassified	1 150	00
Overlays	18 710	66
Part Payment Visiting Nurse	1 000	00
Quarters Veterans Spanish-American War	288	00
Observance Memorial Day	400	00
Care Town Cemetery	60	00
Quarters American Legion	900	00
County Aid to Agriculture	150	00
Maintenance Plymouth County Hospital	3 806	13
Traffic Beacons & Signals	600	00

Heating, Light & Casualty Ins. Jr.-Sr.

High & McKinley School	100	00
Insurance for Firemen	292	50
**Financing construction of Water Tank and		
Laying Pipe	70 000	00
Land damages East Water Street	936	55
Completion Athletic Field Memorial Park	5 737	00
Cost of Material & General Expense W. P. A.	750	00
Purchase furnishings & equipment for Town Office	500	00
Tri-Town observance Armistice Day	300	00
Re-tube two boilers McKinley School	1 300	00
All Night service street lights	222	36
Repair bridge Old Market Street	100	00
Rebuild East Water Street	5 000	00
Two street lights Forest Street -	30	00
Purchase new cruising automobile with Radio		
for Police department	550	00
Build sidewalk and curb west side of Liberty St		
From Mrs. Boyle's store to Webster St.	200	00
Retop with asphalt sidewalk south side		
Rice Ave.	100	00
Install electric light on Market St.	15	00
Assessors Map	500	00
Criminal cases in court	100	00
Three electric lights on Pond & Wilson Sts.	45	00

	$436 115	88
Appropriation from Water Revenue	32 000	00

** Provided Federal grant is received.
  Authorized borrowing $40,000.00
  (Bonds or notes issued expected to be amortized
  from Water Revenue.)

A true copy.   Attest:

RALPH L. BELCHER,

Town Clerk

SPECIAL TOWN MEETING, MARCH 9, 1936

Pursuant to the warrant a meeting was held held March 9, 1936 at the Rockland Opera House, beginning at 7:00 P. M., and the following votes were passed and action taken.

Article 1. Magorisk L. Walls was chosen Moderator and sworn to the faithful discharge of his duties.

Article 2. Voted, to instruct the Selectmen to petition the P. W. A. to amend the application on Project Number Mass. 1143 for the widening and rebuilding of Union Street and laying sewer pipes therein, by eliminating the laying of sewer pipes and to approve the use of the proceeds of the loan for street purposes.

Under Article 2. The Moderator read a communication from the J. R. W_orcester & Co., Engineers, for the town on the above project relative to elimination of sewer pipe and the advisability of changing the type of roadway surface.

Then at 7:25 P. M. voted to adjourn.

A true copy. Attest:

RALPH L. BELCHER,
Town Clerk

RECOUNT
Rockland, Mass., March 14, 1936

This is to certify that:

Upon petition of William J. O'Hayre and others recount of the ballots cast at the Town Election held March 9, 1936 for the office of Selectmen, Board of Public Welfare and Fence Viewers was made at the Rockland Opera House, Saturday, March 14, 1936, beginning at 9:00 A. M.

The result was as follows:

John J. Bowler	1786
Elmer C. Cobb	1726
William A. Lannin	1310
Harry S. Torrey	1745
Norman S. Whiting	1779
Arthur S. Wyman	438
Blanks	2295

JOHN D. CARNEY,
OLIVE H .CRAWFORD,
THOMAS MORRISSEY,
RALPH L. BELCHER,

Registrars of Voters

RECOUNT

Rockland, Mass., March 14, 1936

This is to certify that:

Upon petition of James F. O'Connor and others a recount of the ballots cast at the Town Election held March 9, 1936 for the office of Water Commissioner for three years was made at the Rockland Opera House, Saturday, March 14, 1936 beginning at 9:00 A. M.

The result was as follows:

Ralph Fucillo   1722

John J. McCarthy   1719
Blanks   252

JOHN D. CARNEY,
OLIVE H. CRAWFORD,
THOMAS MORRISSEY,
RALPH L. BELCHER,
    Registrars of Voters

Total Vote, Rockland
PARTY PRIMARY, APRIL 28, 1936

Total number ballots cast   601

Precinct 1		Precinct 2		Total
Democratic Ballots Cast				
Men	137	Men	125	262
Women	72	Women	62	134
	209		187	396
Republican Ballots cast				
Men	52	Men	84	136
Women	25	Women	44	69
	77		128	205

DEMOCRATIC PARTY TOTALS

Delegates at Large to National Convention
Eight to be elected
Group

	P-1	P-2	Total
David I. Walsh	131	93	224
Marcus A. Coolidge	98	70	168
James M. Curley	130	92	222

William J. Granfield	96	65.	161
Joseph McGrath	100	67	167
Margaret M. O'Riordan	104	67	171
Elizabeth L. McNamara	96	66	162
Grace Hartley Howe	93	65	158

Not grouped

Timothy E. Carroll	8	5	13
Alexander F. Sullivan	14	10	24
Blanks	802	896	1698

Alternate Delegates at Large to National Convention
Eight to be elected
Group

Clementina Langone	97	69	166
Mary Maliotis	93	66	159
Golda R. Walters	94	63	157
Sadie H. Mulrone	96	65	161
Louise B. Clark	99	67	166
H. Oscar Rocheleau	91	65	156
Stanley W. Wisnioski	91	64	155
Julian D. Rainey	93	65	158
Blanks	918	972	1890

District Delegates to National Convention, 15th Dist.
Two to be elected
Group

Helen L. Buckley	138	92	230
Lawrence W. Caton	86	74	160

Not grouped

Frank Tigue	14	9	23
Blanks	180	199	379

Alternate District Delegates to National Convention
15th, Dist., Two to be elected
Group

George Helford	90	69	159
Charles C. Paine	87	74	161
Blanks	241	231	472

Presidential Preference

Franklin D. Roosevelt	54	48	102
Rev. C. E. Coughlin	4	1	5
Alfred E. Smith	1		1
Paul Dever	1		1
Landon		4	4
Blanks	149	134	283

State Committee, Norfolk and Plymouth District
One to be elected

Thomas H. Buckley	134	96	230
Clyde Green		1	1
Blanks	75	90	125

Delegate To State Convention, Rockland
One to be elected

James M. Feeney	91	70	161
Neal J. Lioy	44	41	85
James F. Shanahan	63	72	135
Blanks	11	4	15

Town Committee, Rockland
Twenty-five to be elected

William H. Friary	124	90	214
Hugh Walls	96	75	171
Margorisk L. Walls	113	96	209
James T. Shea	113	71	184
Neal Lioy	106	70	176
Dennis L. O'Connor	102	78	180
Thomas Morrissey	100	69	169
Robert W. Norris	80	59	139
Elizabeth Casey	92	60	152
Elizabeth A. Walsh	105	65	170
Annie G. Garrity	107	69	176
James F. Shanahan	118	84	202
J. Edward Kane	105	65	170
Robert N. Parker	102	70	172
Daniel DeC. Donovan	104	79	183

Arthur S. Wyman	91	73	164
Alfred T. Metivier	86	64	150
Charles L. Callanan	92	66	158
Norman J. Beal	83	70	153
Marguerite M. Parker	99	73	172
M. Agnes Kelleher	100	77	177
Leo E. Downey	91	67	158
George E. Mansfield	95	79	174
Frank D. Orvitt	109	77	186
Francis P. Rubino	83	56	139
Blanks	2729	2873	5602

REPUBLICAN PARTY TOTALS

Delegates At Large to National Convention
   Four to be elected
      Group

Charles F. Adams	50	102	152
George F. Booth	50	100	150
Joseph W. Martin	51	101	152
Allen T. Treadway	51	99	150
Blanks	106	110	216

Alternate Delegates at Large to National Convention
   Four to be elected
      Group

Mary Phillips Bailey	52	98	150
Florence H. LeFevre	53	98	151
Wallace Stearns	52	97	149
Anna C. M. Tillinghast	52	99	151
Blanks	99	120	219

District Delegates to National Convention,
   15th District, Two to be elected
      Group

John W. Beal	60	113	173
Joseph F. Francis	42	89	131

Not Grouped
Charles M. Carroll	3	8	11
Donald W. Nicholson	5	6	11
Blanks	44	40	84

'Alternate Dist. Delegates to National Convention
15th District, Two to be elected
Group
Isabel K. Winsper	48	91	139
Carrie L. Wade	53	100	153
Blanks	53	65	118

Presidential Preference
Landon	37	86	123
Borah	3	5	8
Vandenberg	3		3
Hoover	1	3	4
Alfred E. Smith		1	1
Blanks	33	33	66

State Committee, Norfolk and Plymouth District
One to be elected
Vernon W. Marr	52	93	145
Blanks	25	35	60

Delegate to State Convention, Rockland
One to be elected
Frank S. Alger	26	25	51
Norman S. Whiting	40	93	133
Blanks	11	10	21

Town Committee, Rockland
Twenty to be elected
Lawrence E. Blanchard	53	87	140
Matthew F. O'Grady	53	80	133
Joseph B. Estes	52	95	147
Norman S. Whiting	57	99	156
Dana S. Collins	52	97	149

Olive H. Crawford	48	89	137
Jessie B. MacConney	47	88	135
Elsie B. Studley	46	85	131
Harold C. Poole	53	87	140
Charles E. Orr	49	84	133
Harry S. Torrey	50	95	145
Esther H. Rawson	51	81	132
Archie F. Minnis	51	85	136
Paul F. O'Donnell	47	75	122
Frank S. Alger	49	80	129
J. Thomas Condon	49	81	130
Bliss M. Ranney	48	85	133
Charles P. Howland	47	85	132
E. Curtis Brewster	52	90	142
M. Warren Wright	49	83	132
Richard K. Morton		1	1
Ray Purnelle		1	1
Blanks	537	827	1364

SPECIAL TOWN MEETING

Pursuant to the warrant a meeting was held Meeting was held in the Rockland Opera House on Wednesday, June 3, 1936 beginning at 7:30 P. M. and the following votes were passed and action taken.

Article 1. Magorisk L. Walls was chosen Moderator and sworn to the faithful discharge of his duties.

Article 2. Voted to instruct the Selectmen to petition the P. W. A. to extend the scope of the Project Number Mass. 1143-R for the widening and rebuilding of Union Street from North Avenue to Union Square to include the rebuilding, and laying drainage pipes, and alteration of sidewalks, and improving of Union Square, and the replacing of water services where needed, from the end of present pro-

ject to Market Street and authorize the Selectmen and Highway Surveyor to construct said project and contract with
respect thereto; and to authorize and instruct the treasurer
to pay the town's proportion of the expense thereof from
the sale of bonds as authorized at the meeting of October
23rd, 1935.

At 7:40 P. M. the following were appointed tellers for
the meeting, Abram Lelyveld, James Shea, and Ralph Fucillo and a count of the voters present was made. There
were 286 voters present.

The Moderator ruled that as there was not 300 voters
present no action could be taken on articles asking for an
appropriation of money.

Voted to lay articles number 3, 4, 5, 6, 8, 9, 10, 11 and 12
on the table until articles 7 and 13 were disposed of.

Article 7. Voted to rescind the vote passed at the Town
Meeting of March 7, 1927 where it was:

"Voted that whenever a limited and determinable area
desires the extension of a water main other than of general advantage to the community the Board of Water Commissioners are authorized in so far as funds will permit to
furnish and lay the water mains, gates and hydrants, provided the person or persons receiving such benefit or advantage shall do the excavating and filling of the trench for
said mains satisfactory to the Water Commissioners."

Article 13. Voted not to reduce the salary of the Tax
Collector by the amount of the fees collected by him or instruct said tax collector to turn all fees collected by him over
to the town treasurer.

At 8:00 o'clock P. M. the Moderator ruled that it being evident that more than 300 voters were present at the

meeting action could be taken on the articles calling for appropriation of money.

Article 3. Voted to raise and appropriate the sum of Six thousand five hundred dollars ($6500.00) to defray expenses of W. P. A. work.

Article 4. Voted to raise and appropriate the sum of three hundred eighty-one dollars ($381.00) to reimburse Edward J. Rourke the balance due for the use of his roller used for the rebuilding of North Avenue in 1934.

Article 5. Voted to appropriate one hundred forty-three dollars ($143.00) to be paid out of the appropriation made for Parks under article 3 at the Annual Town Meeting of March 2nd, 1936, to pay E. F. Benson Inc., for the use of steam shovel.

Article 6. Voted to pass over the raising and appropriating of a sum of money to be spent under the direction of the Park commissioners to pay for materials and services on W. P. A. projects in Memorial Park.

Article 8. Voted to pass over the raising and appropriating of the sum of Four hundred dollars ($400.00) to be used for Highway Repairs in addition to the amount raised at the March meeting.

Article 9. Voted to pass over the raising and appropriating of the sum of one hundred fifty dollars ($150.00) for striping streets and putting up caution signs.

Article 10. Voted to instruct the Water Department to lay a pipe on Pleasant Street, west, and to raise and appropriate the sum of two hundred fify dollars ($250.00) and that an additional two hundred fifty dollars ($250.00) be appropriated from Water Revenue to pay for the cost of same and provided further that no Welfare or W. P. A. labor be used on this job.

Article 11. Voted to raise and appropriate a sum of four hundred twenty-five dollars ($425.00) for an Assessors map.

Article 12. Voted to raise and appropriate the sum of two thousand dollars ($2000.00) for work at Reed's Pond, the labor to be furnished by the Works Progress Administration provided an easment is secured from the Trustees of the Spring Lake Cemetery to allow the use of their land which borders on said pond, and when proposed project is open to public bathing that the local Board of Health make weekly tests as to the purity of the water for bathing purposes.

Voted to pay the Moderator ten dollars for his services.

Voted to adjourn.

A true copy.   Attest:
                        RALPH L. BELCHER,
                                Town Clerk

AMOUNTS RAISED AND APPROPRIATED,
SPECIAL TOWN MEETING, JUNE 3rd, 1936

Raised and appropriated
Defray Expenses of W. P. A. work $ 6 500 00
Reimburse Edward J. Rourke, bal due
    from 1934   381 00
Laying water pipe on Pleasant St., west   250 00
Assessors' Map   425 00
For work at Reed's Pond (providing easment
    to land is secured from Trustees of
    Spring Lake Cemtery)   2 000 00
                                          _____
                                          $ 9 556 00

Appropriated
From amount raised under Article No. 3
Town Meeting of March 2, 1936, For Parks,
to pay E. F. Benson Inc., for use of steam
shovel $ 143 00
From Water Revenue, as additional amount
for laying of water pipe on Pleasant
St., west $ 250 00

A true copy.   Attest:

RALPH L. BELCHER
Town Clerk

SPECIAL TOWN MEETING,
SEPTEMBER 10, 1936

Pursuant to a warrant a Special Town Meeting was held
in the Rockland Opera House, Thursday, September 10,
1936, beginning at 7:30 P. M. and the following votes
were passed and action taken.

Article 1.   Magorisk L. Walls was chosen Moderator
and sworn to the faithful discharge of his duties.

Article 2.   Voted to PASS OVER the instructing of the
Board of Water Commissioners and Selectmen to locate the
water tank in Rice Park a distance of 1200 feet or more
from the nearest dwelling house.

Article 3.   Voted to PASS OVER the instructing of
the Board of Water Commissioners to locate the water
tank in Rice Park, so called, a distance of 1200 feet or more
from the nearest dwelling house on Rice Avenue, and the
raising and appropriating of an additional sum of money
to construct a water tank with necessary pipe connections.

Article 4. Voted that the town approve of a location for the water tank at a distance of 486 feet from the nearest dwelling on Rice Avenue.

A motion to return to Article No. 3 was not agreed to.

Voted to adjourn.

A true copy. Attest:

RALPH L. BELCHER,
Town Clerk

Total Vote, Rockland
STATE PRIMARY, SEPT. 15, 1936

	P-1	P-2	Total
Republican ballots cast	422	454	876
Democratic ballots cast	202	205	407
	624	659	1283
Total number ballots cast			1283

REPUBLICAN PARTY

GOVERNOR

John W. Haigis	298	340	638
Blanks	124	114	238

LIEUTENENT GOVERNOR

Leverett Saltonstall	291	331	622
Blanks	131	123	254

SECRETARY

Frederick W. Cook	289	331	620
Blanks	133	123	256

TREASURER

William E. Hurley	246	249	495
William G. Andrew	12	25	37
Fred Jefferson Burrell	59	80	139
Blanks	105	100	205

AUDITOR

Richard Darby	101	90	191
Russell A. Wood	147	175	322
Blanks	174	189	363

. ATTORNEY GENERAL

Felix Forte	272	288	560
Blanks	150	166	316

SENATOR IN CONGRESS

Henry Cabot Lodge, Jr.	252	288	540
Alonzo B. Cook	31	23	54
Guy M. Gray	5	9	14
Thomas C. O'Brien	55	55	110
Blanks	79	79	158

CONGRESSMAN—15th District

Charles L. Gifford	186	238	424
John Henry McNeece	178	146	324
Blanks	58	70	128

COUNCILLOR—2nd District

Harrison H. Atwood	69	74	143
Joseph B. Grossman	90	145	235
Clayton L. Havey	137	112	249
Blanks	126	123	249

SENATOR, Norfolk and Plymouth Dist.

Newland H. Holmes	105	137	242
Warren B. Woodward	250	251	501
Thomas C. O'Brien		9	9
Blanks	67	57	124

REPRESENTATIVE IN GENERAL COURT
4th Plymouth District

Frederick M. Barnicoat	189	239	428
Archie F. Minnis	207	181	388
Blanks	26	34	60

REGISTER OF PROBATE AND
INSOLVENCY—Plymouth County

Sumner A. Chapman	225	270	495
Dexter Winfield Wilbar	63	47	110
Blanks	134	137	271

COUNTY COMMISSIONERS,
Plymouth County

Frederic T. Bailey	244	284	528
Harold D. Bent	227	235	462
James A. White	81	77	158
Blanks	292	312	604

COUNTY TREASURER

Avis A. Ewell	228	255	483
Francis T. Kane	106	99	205
Blanks	88	100	188

ASSOCIATE COUNTY COMMISSIONER
Plymouth County

Frank L. Sinnott	276	296	572
Blanks	146	158	304

DEMOCRATIC PARTY

GOVERNOR

Charles F. Hurley	168	171	339
Blanks	34	34	68

LIEUTENENT GOVERNOR

Philip J. Philbin	66	77	143
Thomas F. Galvin	15	28	43

Francis E. Kelly	78	51	129
Blanks	43	49	92

SECRETARY

Joseph Santosuosso	75	76	151
William J. Ahearne	12	17	29
John J. Buckley	16	22	38
John D. O'Brien	21	15	36
Edward W. O'Hearn	21	20	41
William F. Sullivan	11	9	20
Blanks	46	46	92

TREASURER

James C. Scanlan	71	81	152
James M. Hurley	90	80	170
Blanks	41	44	85

AUDITOR

Thomas H. Buckley	155	160	315
Leo D. Walsh	28	22	50
Blanks	19	23	42

ATTORNEY GENERAL

Paul A. Dever	143	149	292
Blanks	59	56	115

SENATOR IN CONGRESS

James M. Curley	99	95	194
Robert E. Greenwood	34	50	84
Thomas C. O'Brien	48	36	84
Blanks	21	24	45

CONGRESSMAN—15th District

John D. W. Bodfish	88	100	188
Albert Crossley	6	7	13
Edward C. Peirce	6	6	12
James M. Quinn	49	38	87
Blanks	53	54	107

COUNCILLOR—2nd District

John Joseph Cheever	28	26	54
Charles J. Fitzgerald	29	30	59
Thomas F. Galvin	16	18	34
John J. Gillis	10	12	22
James F. Hickey	8	5	13
William H. McDonald	24	21	45
Thomas P. O'Donnell	19	7	26
Blanks	68	86	154

SENATOR, Norfolk and Plymouth Dist.

William M. Bergan	131	111	242
Thomas C. O'Brien		1	1
Blanks	71	93	164

REPRESENTATIVE IN GENERAL COURT
4th Plymouth District

Daniel DeC. Donovan	163	158	321
Arthur S. Wyman	1		1
Archie Minnis		1	1
Blanks	38	46	84

REGISTER OF PROBATE AND
INSOLVENCY—Plymouth County

Alfred G. Malagodi	130	114	244
Blanks	72	91	163

COUNTY COMMISSIONERS,
Plymouth County

Louis A. Reardon	141	140	281
William B. Carey	1		1
Albert M. Heath	2		2
Arthur Wyman	1		1
Blanks	259	270	529

COUNTY TREASURER
Plymouth County

James P. Fitzgerald	140	137	277
Blanks	62	68	130

ASSOCIATE COUNTY COMMISSIONER

Plymouth County

James Campbell			1
Leo Downey		1	1
Blanks	201	204	405

SPECIAL TOWN MEETING

Pursuant to the warrant a meeting was held in the Rockland Opera House, Monday, October 26, 1936 beginning at 7:30 P. M. and the following votes were passed and action taken:

Article 1. Magorisk L. Walls was chosen Moderator and sworn to the faithful discharge of his duties.

Voted to recess until 8:00 o'clock P. M. it being evident that a quorum was not present.

At 8:00 o'clock P. M. the Moderator ruled that it being evident that there were not three hundred (300) voters present as provided by By-Law of the town no action could be taken under articles two and three of the warrant which called for appropriations of money.

Upon motion of Dr. Joseph Lelyveld it was:

VOTED that it be the sense of the meeting that the Water Commissioners be instructed to construct a water tank, within the limit of the amount of money available, as raised and appropriated under Article No. 19 of the An nual Town Meeting held Mach 2nd, 1936.

Then at 8:20 o'clock P. M. VOTED to adjourn.

A true copy of the record. Attest:

RALPH L. BELCHER,

Town Clerk

Total Vote
STATE AND NATIONAL ELECTION
Rockland, Mass., November 3, 1936

Number of ballots cast

Precinct One	2053
Precinct Two	2261
Total	4314

ELECTORS OF PRESIDENT AND VICE PRESIDENT

	P-1	P-2	Total
Aiken and Teichert, Socialist Labor. Party	1	4	5
Browder and Ford, Communist Party	2	0	2
Colvin and Watson, Prohibition	0	0	0
Landon and Knox, Republican	852	1053	1905
Lemke and O'Brien, The Union Party	208	202	410
Roosevelt and Garner, Democratic	944	935	1875
Thomas and Nelson, Socialist Party	7	19	26
Blanks	39	48	87

GOVERNOR

Fred G. Bushold, Union-Coughlin-Townsend	37	39	76
Alfred H. Evans, Phohibition	2	4	6
John W. Haigis, Republican	853	1045	1898
Horace I. Hillis, Socialist Labor party	1	3	4
Otis Archer Hood, Communist Party	4	2	6
Charles F. Hurley, Democratic	998	983	1981
Alfred Baker Lewis, Socialist party	7	9	16
William H. McMasters, The Union Party	116	115	231
Blanks	35	61	96

LIEUTENENT GOVERNOR

Henning A. Bloman, Socialist Labor Party	15	10	25

Freeman W. Follett, Prohibition	9	2	11
Walter S. Hutchins, Socialist Party	15	23	38
Francis E. Kelly, Democratic	989	999	1988
Leverett Saltonstall, Republican	924	1121	2045
Paul C. Wicks, Communist Party	2	1	3
Blanks	99	105	204

SECRETARY

Frederic W. Cook, Republican	953	1150	2103
Ralph Dow, Socialist Party	13	23	36
George L. McGlynn, Socialist Labor Party	10	14	24
Mary E. Moore, Communist Party	15	3	18
Joseph Santosuosso, Democratic	927	902	1829
Blanks	135	169	304

TREASURER

Thomas Gilmartin, Socialist Labor Party	8	11	19
Mabelle M. Groves, Prohibition	9	5	14
Harold J. Hatfield, Independent Progressive	7	10	17
Eva Hoffman, Communist Party	4	0	4
James M. Hurley, Democratic	938	943	1881
William E. Hurley, Republican	953	1149	2102
Sylvester J. McBride, Socialist Party	22	22	44
Blanks	112	121	233

AUDITOR

Lyman M. Aldrich, Prohibition	9	5	14
Thomas H. Buckley, Democrat	1084	1062	2146
Richard Darby, Independent	6	18	24
Elizabeth Donovan, Socialist Party	15	23	38
Alfred Haase, Communist Party	5		5
Walter J. Hogan, Socialist Labor	8	10	18
Russell A. Wood, Republican	818	1021	1839
Blanks	108	122	230

ATTORNEY GENERAL

Morris Berzon, Socialist Party	12	16	28
Paul A. Dever, Democratic	1033	1038	2071
Felix Forte, Republican	839	1036	1875
George F. Hogan, prohibition	7	9	16
Fred E. Oelcher, Socialist Labor			
Party	10	9	19
Michael Tuysuzian, Communist Party	4	3	7
Blanks	148	150	298

SENATOR IN CONGRESS

Alonzo B. Cook, Townsendite-			
Prohibition-Economy	6	13	19
Albert Sprague Coolidge, Socialist			
Party	5	13	18
James M. Curley, Democratic	806	767	1573
Ernest L. Dodge, Socialist Labor party	4	7	11
Charles Flaherty, Communist Party	4	1	5
Guy M. Gray, Townsend-Social Justice	20	17	37
Moses H. Gulesian, Townsend Plan	12	28	40
Henry Cabot Lodge, Jr., Republican	916	1103	2019
Wilbur D. Moon, Prohibition	1	3	4
Thomas C. O'Brien, The Union Party	229	239	468
Blanks	50	70	120

CONGRESSMAN—15th District

John D. W. Bodfish, Democratic	729	720	1449
Nora Ouimette Duprey, Socialist party	12	13	25
Charles L. Gifford, Republican	785	1000	1785
William McAuliffe, The Union Party	67	63	130
John Henry McNeece, Social Justice-			
Townsend	354	337	691
Blanks	106	128	234

COUNCILLOR—2nd District

Charles J. Fitzgerald, Democratic	956	962	1918
Joseph B. Grossman, Republican	888	1066	1954
Fred H. Lord, Socialist Party	47	55	102
Blanks	162	178	340

SENATOR, Norfolk and Plymouth Dist.

William M. Bergan, Democratic	1041	1025	2066
Newland H. Holmes, Republican	834	1042	1876
Blanks	178	194	372

REPRESENTATIVE IN GENERAL COURT
4th Plymouth District

Frederick M. Barnicoat, Republican	857	1069	1926
Daniel DeC. Donovan, Democratic	1140	1129	2269
Blanks	56	63	119

REGISTER OF PROBATE AND
INSOLVENCY—Plymouth County

Rufus E. Blair, Independent	27	45	72
Sumner A. Chapman, Republican	906	1099	2005
Alfred G. Malagodi, Democratic	909	896	1805
Blanks	211	221	432

COUNTY COMMISSIONERS,
Plymouth County

Frederic T. Bailey, Republican	754	930	1684
Harold D. Bent, Republican	861	1022	1883
George M. Kane, Democratic	702	665	1367
Louis A. Reardon, Democratic	926	928	1854
Blanks	863	977	1840

COUNTY TREASURER
Plymouth County

Avis A. Ewell, Republican	911	1094	2005
James P. Fitzgerald, Democratic	982	980	1962
Blanks	160	187	347

ASSOCIATE COUNTY COMMISSIONER
Plymouth County
(To fill vacancy)

Frank L. Sinnott, Republican	1149	1370	2519
Blanks	904	891	1795

Question No. 1. All Alcoholic Beverages

Yes	1221	1232	2453
No	461	596	1057
Blanks	371	433	804

Question No. 2. Beers and Wines

Yes	1205	1208	2413
No	415	557	972
Blanks	433	496	929

Question No. 3. All Alcoholic Beverages in Packages

Yes	1246	1266	2512
No	387	511	898
Blanks	420	484	904

FOURTH PLYMOUTH REPRESENTATIVE DISTRICT

At a meeting of the Town Clerks of the Fourth Plymouth Representative District held in the Town Clerk's office, Rockland, Mass., on Friday, November 13, 1936 at 12:00 o'clock noon, the records of votes cast in each precinct and town, for Representative in General Court, Fourth Plymouth District, were duly examined and Frederick M. Barnicoat of Hanover appeared to be elected.

The following is a schedule of the votes cast in said district.

Frederick M. Barnicoat of Hanover, (R) three thousand seven hundred and sixty-two (3762).

Daniel DeC. Donovan of Rockland (D), two thousand seven hundred and ninety-four (2794).

Blanks, two hundred and two (202).

Whole number of ballots cast, six thousand seven hundred and fifty-eight (6758).

BERNARD L. STETSON,
Town Clerk, Hanover
WARREN T. HOWARD,
Town Clerk, Hanson
RALPH L. BELCHER,
Town Clerk, Rockland

DETAIL OF VOTE BY TOWNS

	Rockland	Hanover	Hanson	Total
Frederick M. Barnicoat	1926	1058	778	3762
Daniel DeC. Donovan	2269	201	324	2794
Blanks	119	24	59	202
	4314	1283	1161	6758

RECOUNT

Rockland, Mass., December 5, 1936

Pursuant to an order from the Secretary of the Commonweath, dated November 27, 1936, the Board of Registrars of Voters met at the Town Office, Saturday, December 5, 1936 at 9:00 A. M. and recounted the ballots cast, at the State and National Election of November 3rd, 1936, for the office of LIEUTENANT GOVERNOR. The result was declared as follows:

LIEUTENANT GOVERNOR

	P-1	P-2	Total
Henning A. Blomen, Socialist Labor Party	15	10	25
Freeman W. Follett, Prohibition	6	2	8
Walter S. Hutchins, Socialist Party	17	21	38
Francis E. Kelly, Democratic	989	996	1985
Leverett Saltonstall, Republican	926	1125	2051
Paul C. Wicks, Communist Party	2	2	4
Blanks	98	105	203
Whole number ballots cast	2053	2261	4314

JOHN D. CARNEY,
THOMAS MORRISSEY,
ESTHER H. RAWSON,
RALPH L. BELCHER,

Board of Registrars of Voters

Sixty-Third Annual Report
Of The Selectmen

STATE AID 1936

Paid under Chapter 19, Revised Laws and Amendments thereto.

Total amount of State Aid Paid			$	650 00
Appropriation	$	900 00		
Under appropriation	$	250 00		

CARE OF SOLDIERS' GRAVES
Paid:—

C. S. Tilden, care of graves	$	50 00		
W. A. Whiting, care of grave		15 00		
W. F. Hunt, care of grave		15 00		
James Maguire, care of grave		5 00		
Louis Gilbride, agent		50 00		
Expended			$	135 00
Appropriation	$	150 00		
Under appropriation		15 00		

HIGHWAY SURVEYOR
Paid:—

William H. Friary, Salary	$	258 30		
Roderick MacKenzie, Salary	1	091 70		
Expended			$	1 350 00
Appropriation	$ 1	350 00		

ANIMALS AND STABLES
Paid:—

William T. Condon, Services as Inspector			$	100 00
Appropriation	$	100 00		

SEALER OF WEIGHTS AND MEASURES

Paid:—

Harold J. Inkley, Salary		$ 400 00
Appropriation	$ 400 00	

RESERVE FUND

Transfers:

Tree Warden	$ 400 00	
Striping Streets	150 00	
Police Dept. Cornelius McHugh accident	126 20	
Police Dept. Purchase Police Car	74 00	
Highway Dept. Repairs	249 80	
		$ 1 000 00
Appropriation	$ 1 000 00	

CARE OF TOWN CEMETERY

Paid:—

William E. Vining		$ 60 00
Appropriation	$ 60 00	

MILITARY AID 1936

Appropriation	$ 50 00	
Nothing expended		
Under		$ 50 00

BURIAL OF INDIGENT SOLDIERS

Appropriation		$ 100 00
Nothing expended		
Under	$ 100 00	

CLEAN UP WEEK

Paid:—

Rockland Standard Pub. Co.		
Adv. and Notice	$ 3 75	

John J. Dwyer, Collection of rubbish   83 50

Expended		$ 87 25
Appropriation	$ 100 00	
Under	12 75	

COMPENSATION INSURANCE
Paid:—

Amos A. Phelps, premium on policy		$ 1 931 46
Appropriation	$2 250 00	
Under appropriation	$ 318 54	

COMPENSATION INSURANCE FOR FIREMEN
Paid:—

Charles E. Torrey, Premium on Policy		$ 292 50
Appropriation	$ 292 50	

PURCHASE OF POLICE CAR
Piad:—

George N. Beal, Purchase of Car	$ 525 00
United Bosch Corp., Radio for car	59 50
George J. Popp, Express	81
E. B. Adams, Generator	38 69

Expended		$ 624 00
Appropriation	$ 550 00	
Transfer from Reserve Fund	74 00	
		$ 624 00

SOLDIERS' MEMORIAL LIBRARY

Natalie F. Holbrook, salary	$ 600 00
Elida Butler, salary	600 00
N. E. Tel & Tel Co., services	39 96
Edison Electric Ill. Co., service	96 46
Lida A. Clark, salary	1 200 00
Lida A. Clark, supplies	7 40
W. G. Holbrook, salary	900 00
Rockland Water Dept., service	5 00

Rome Bros., supplies		39
Brockton Public Market, supplies		90
A. S. Peterson, supplies	14	77
Hall & Torrey, supplies	19	61
F. J. Barnard, binding books	87	14
Library Book House, books	351	75
The Savogran Co., supplies	3	00
H. R. Huntting Co., supplies	7	67
Douglas Print, cards	7	75
Am. Library Asso., books	4	00
Charles Scribner & Sons, books	25	00
McGraw-Hill Book Co., books	11	65
Junior Literary Guild, books	28	84
Beckley Cardy Co., books	3	58
Murray Bros., repairs	6	00
Rockland Coal & Grain, coal	103	00
A. A. Phelps, Insurance	143	39
Jean Karr, book	9	49
A. I. Randall Inc., printing	8	60
The Personal Book Shop, books	16	66
Funk & Wagnalls Co., books	7	60
Florence M. Howland, books	7	50
John H. Wyatt, supplies		75
The Library Guild, book	3	50
Joseph Thibeault, repair lawn mower	2	75
A. Culver Co., coal	85	00
Rockland Standard Pub. Co., printing	7	65
Norman H. Henly Co., book	1	21
Beacon Press Inc., book	1	60
Moore Cothell, subscriptions	100	60
H. J. Hemmett Co., repairs		73
Gaylord Bros., supplies	1	48
Chapman & Grimes, supplies	2	08
Am. Rescue League, subscription		60
Gordon Conant, repair clock	2	00
Howland's Ins. Office, insurance	44	87
H. W. Wilson Co., subscription	21	20

———————$ 4 593 13

Appropriation $ 3 832 68
Dog Fund   593 61
Transfer   167 35
Total available   ————$ 4 593 61
Under   48

REPAIRS AT PUBLIC LIBRARY

Paid:—
Hall & Torrey, bal. on boiler $ 301 18
J. S. McCallum, radiator and pipes   186 25
                                  ——————
Expended $ 487 43
Transfered under Art. 28 $ 531 18
Unexpended Bal.   43 75

TOWN OFFICERS

Paid as Salary:—
Harry S. Torrey, Selectman, Board
  of Public Welfare, Fence Viewer and
  Old Age Assistance $ 1 980 00
Norman S. Whiting, Selectman, Board
  of Public Welfare, Fence Viewer
  and Old Age Assistance   300 00
John J. Bowler, Selectman, Board
  of Public Welfare, Fence Viewer
  and Old Age Assistance   300 00
Charles J. Higgins, Treasurer   1 350 00
James A. Donovan, Tax Collector 1 350 00
Ralph L. Belcher, Town Clerk   700 00
Ralph L. Belcher, Registrar of Voters   75 00
Heirs of Olive Crawford,
  Registrar of Voters   45 00
Esther Rawson, Registrar of Voters   30 00
Thomas Morrissey, Registrar of Voters   75 00
John Carney, Registrar of Voters   75 00
Elmer Asklund, Auditor   100 00

Leo Downey, Auditor   100 00
Harold Smith, Auditor   110 00

Expended $ 6 590 00
Appropriation $ 6 600 00
Under appropriation   10 00

BOARD OF HEALTH

Paid:—

Patrick Mahoney, trucking $	3 75
Plymouth County Hospital	
Care of patients	3 060 30
Payroll, Labor	672 76
Evelyn Delory, salary	1 200 00
J. A. Carriuolo, M.D., special service	66 00
Burying Cats and Dogs	34 00
Dr. Joseph H. Dunn, service	
on contagious cases	81 00
Thomas Welsh, sharpening tools	19 90
Dr. Joseph H. Dunn, supplies and express	16 46
H. Gelinas, services	15 00
John J. Dwyer, work at town dump	18 00
Dr. F. H. Corey, service	5 00
Dr. H. J. Hulse, service	5 00
Dr. N. F. Lough, service	5 00
Rockland Standard Pub. Co., cards	3 50
Thomas W. Reed Co., supplies	10 79
Everyready Supply Co., towels	18 48
George E. Bolling, services	7 00
Dr. Joseph H. Frame, salary	100 00
Dr. Joseph H. Frame, visits and	
fumigation	93 50
Mrs. David Gaines, services	15 00
Hall & Torrey, tile pipe and supplies	152 93
A. Culver, Co., cement	65
Dr. A. H. Barron, service	5 00
A. Wainshalbaum, trucking	2 00
Rome Bros., supplies	4 38

Michael Fitzgibbons, salary	50	00
Rockland Coal & Grain, cement	1	30
Mrs. Ed. Hennigan, gravel	3	75
Dr. Joseph Dunn, Salary	50	00
Henry T. Roche Sr., care of		
Town Dump	150	00
A. I. Randall Inc., printing	9	60
John Hood Co., supplies	24	80
Mass. Memorial Hospital,		
Care of patients	42	00
Dr. J. B. Gallagher, dental work	10	00
Dr. D. H. Burke, dental work	10	00
Dr. M. J. Dunn, dental work	10	00
Dr. Frederic Billings, dental work	10	00
Dr. H. P. Russell, services	5	00
G. W. S. Hyde, sharpening tools	3	90

Expended		$ 5 995	75
Appropriation	$ 6 000	00	
Under appropriation		4	25

LIST OF PAYROLL, BOARD OF HEALTH

Paid:—

Thomas Kelley	$ 39	38
Michael J. Fitzgibbons	246	95
Joseph Meade	90	00
Charles McGonagle	2	25
Michael Murphy	18	00
Wesley Sears	6	75
James Smith	9	00
Daniel Hines	2	25
William Fox	9	00
Martin Keough	6	75
Raymond Rainsford	6	75
Leon Ignatowicz	86	62
Henry Roche	15	75
William Santry	56	25
Maurice Caplice	15	75

Michael Bowen		2 25
Thomas McDonald		2 25
Albert Callahan		7 31
Joseph Melnoski		4 50
Ralph Fisher		4 50
Samuel Cannaway		15 75
William Cannaway		2 25
Charles Hines		2 25
John Gorman		2 25
Stanley Fisher		9 00
Arthur C. Smith		9 00

Total $ 672 76

TREE WARDEN

Paid:—

Payroll, Labor	$	599 18
Forrest Partch, repairs		3 23
Rome Bros., tools and supplies		146 33
Rockland Standard Pub. Co., 100 cards		4 25
A. S. Peterson, supplies		1 80
G. W. S. Hyde, hooks		3 00
Doyle Gas Co., gas		5 30
West Side Grocery, gas		1 50
Hickey Bros., gas		25 79
Elliot F. Magoun, supplies		7 84
E. P. Reed Lumber Co., supplies		1 13
Rockland Coal & Grain Co., supplies		36
Sherwin & Williams, Arsenate of lead		140 97

Expended	$	940 68
Appropriation	$500 00	
Transfer from Reserve Fund	400 00	
	—$	900 00
Over available funds		40 68

List of Payroll—Tree Warden
Alfred Metivier $ 235 41

James Sullivan	25 87	
John White	9 28	
Herbert Brown	9 00	
Maurice Caplice	11 25	
Chester Curtis	16 03	
Charles McGonagle	50 63	
Frank Hammond	39 39	
Arthur Casey	114 00	
Henry Shelly	40 51	
Charles Rose	4 50	
Albert Finegan	14 63	
John Kelley	4 50	
Stanley Cushing	5 34	
John Lonergan	5 34	
James McDonald	5 34	
Ed Lonergan	8 16	
Total	$	599 18

MOTH DEPT. 1936

Paid:—

Payroll, Labor	$ 264 92	
Rockland Water Dept., service	10 00	
Frank H. Shaw, storage	11 66	
Rome Bros., supplies	29	
Crawford service, supplies	4 80	
Expended	$	291 67
Appropriation	$ 300 00	
Under appropriation	8 33	

List of payroll—Moth Dept.

Frank Hammond	$ 67 50
James Mahoney	40 50
Harold Hickey	9 00
Alfred Metivier	69 16
Edward Metivier	4 50
James Sullivan	6 75

Jeremiah Shea   45 00
Roderick MacKenzie   4 50
Charles McGonagle   6 75
Albert Finnegan   5 63
Henry Shelly   5 63

    Total $ 264 92

POLICE DEPARTMENT
Expenditures for 1936

N. E. T. & T. Co., service $ 95 11
Edison Electric Light, service   55 10
Chief of Police, service   1 924 00
Use of Auto   260 00
John H. Murphy, service   1 434 40
Cornelius J. McHugh, service   1 424 80
Robert J. Drake, service   1 424 80
Adolph Johnson, service   1 424 80
John J. Dwyer, service   113 22
Maurice Mullen, service   152 36
Michael O'Brien, service   31 91
Charles Hines, service   5 00
Fred Sharp, service   2 00
Alton Whiting, service   1 00
Thomas Fitzgerald, service   3 91
John F. Hannon, service   5 00
Rockland Coal & Grain Co., coal   59 00
A. Wainshilbaum, repairs and supples   48 26
Bailey Motors Co., gasoline
    and supplies   248 49
M. Linsky, school badges   4 50
Edmund Beary, labor   12 00
U. S. Post Office, stamped envelopes   16 92
Lannins Lunch, food for prisoners   46 50
Lawrence Lovell, labor   3 60
Olympia Confectionery, food for
    prisoners   4 05

Ralph Measures, labor	11	33
Amos Phelps, insurance, police car	4	50
Dr. Leavitt, injury to McHugh	19	00
Goddard Hospital, injury to McHugh	25	00
William McCarthy, lettering police car	8	00
Becker & Co., supplies	11	56
George N. Beal, supplies to police car	16	80
Mat's Lab., installation police radio	10	00
Iver Johnson Co., supplies	27	96
Charles Vaughn, supplies	6	70
Hancock Paint Co., traffic paint	1	85
Mann Auto Sales, supplies, repairs	14	70
E. B. Atmus Co., supplies	6	31
Rome Brothers, supplies	7	55

Total		$ 8 972 04
Appropriation	$ 8 846 00	
Transfer Reserve Fund	126 20	
	$ 8 972 20	
Expended	8 972 04	
Under		16

FIRE DEPARTMENT MAINTENANCE

Hallamore Machine Co., repairing $	5	00
Edison Electric Light Co.,		
Material for fire alarm	53	66
Capen & Lane, soda and acid	6	72
Maynard & Childs, oil	40	70
J. Henderson, labor	21	15
A. Golemme, trucking, WPA	7	00
Ames Electric Co., bulbs and repairs	17	00
Rockland Trans. Co., express		60
Rockland Welting Co., labor	1	00
Jenkins & Simmons, express	2	85
Damon Electric Co., material	1	60

W. Fyffe Electric Co., wire	78	56
W. Woodward, insurance	54	13
J. Riordan, supplies	5	40
Atlas Products Co., supplies	14	60
Douglas Print, printing	3	50
Standard Oil Co., supplies	6	95
J. A. Rice Co., supplies	5	40
Woodward Spring Co., brake lining	14	89
Bailey Motor Sales Co., battery	30	77
J. J. Dwyer, truck	7	00
A. L. Paulding & Sons, work on brakes	2	50
E. F. Magoun, oil	2	00
Stop Fire Company, extinguisher	10	00
Jack's Auto Glass Co., repairing radiator	20	00
Crandall Packing Co.. new hose	400	00
Hunt-Marquadt, battery charger	18	20
E. L. LaBaron, material	6	22
P. Oulette, labor	15	00
Brewer & Co., acid	5	77
A. Culver Co., cement	1	95
E. P. Reed Co., lumber	11	25
E. E. Lane, supplies	5	00
H. Cook, labor	50	00
F. Metivier, labor	50	00
A. Clark, labor	4	00
Electric Light Co.,	175	32
A. J. Vargus, supplies	92	70
Old Colony Gas Co.	44	66
Telephone Co.	68	05
Hall & Torrey, labor and material	111	00
American LaFrance Co., labor and . supplies	377	25
Gorham Fire Equipment Co., supplies	360	36
Brockton Public Market, supplies	6	08
Rockland Coal & Grain Co.	288	01
Rockland Water Dept.	21	35
M. F. Ellis & Co., supplies	33	00
Rome Bros., supplies	16	97

C. P. Inkley, expense	82	90
Engine Co. No. 1, payroll	1 587	50
Ladder Co. No. 1, payroll	1 506	50
J. Fitzgibbons, chauffeur	1 731	60
W. Parker, chauffeur	1 638	00
J. Mulready, substitute	120	00
George W. Clark, Supt. Fire Alarm	400	00
J. P. Barry, Deputy Chief	200	00
C. P. Inkley, Chief	1 500	00
C. P. Inkley, Use of Auto	250	00

Total	$11 691	62
Appropriation	10 400	00
Over appropriation	$ 1 291	62

FOREST FIRE DEPARTMENT

Howe & French, Soda	$ 8	96
Capen & Lane, Soda	8	96
Brewer & Co., Acid	6	47
Payroll	631	00

Total	$ 655	39
Appropriation	700	00
Under appropriation	$ 44	61

MEMORIAL PARK

Paid:—

Payroll, labor	$ 1 429	02
Payroll, truck and horse	28	25
A. Wainshilbaum, supplies	7	63
Rome Bros., supplies	32	40
Rockland Standard Pub. Co., letterheads	2	00
Hall & Torrey, supplies	4	85
Stuart McCallum, repair water pipe		85
Hickey Bros., supplies	2	29
Lester Wyman, loam	77	00

G. W. S. Hyde, repairs	40
Rockland Hardware & Paint Co.,	
Tools and fertilizer	53 62
M. Vincent Fitzgibbons, Ins. on grand	
stand	26 20
James D. Mahoney, supplies	7 00
Rockland Water Dept., service	1 25
James E. Kemp, sharpening law mower	1 60
E. F. Benson, services	143 00
Edward Breen, supplies	23 00
A. J. Vargus, supplies	1 70
Rockland Coal & Grain Co., cement	8 28

Expended		$ 1 850 34
Appropriation	$ 1 851 00	
Under appropriation	66	

List of Payroll—Memorial Park

Peter Hickey	$ 487 38
Joseph Meade	461 82
James Mahoney	479 82

Total	$ 1 429 02

AMERICAN LEGION POST NO. 147

Paid:—

American Legion Building Association Rent	$ 900 00
Appropriation	$ 900 00

PETER A. BOWLER CAMP NO. 63
Spanish War Veterans

Paid:—

Old Colony Post Building Association Rent	$ 288 00
Appropriation	$ 288 00

PLYMOUTH COUNTY EXTENSION SERVICE

Paid:—

Treas. Plymouth County Aid to Agriculture		$ 150 00
Appropriation	$ 150 00	

PLYMOUTH COUNTY HOSPITAL MAINTENANCE

Paid:—

Treasurer of Plymouth County		$ 3 806 13
Appropriation	$ 3 806 13	

RENT OF TOWN OFFICES

Paid:—

Rockland Savings Bank		$ 1 140 00
Appropriation	$1 160 00	
Under appropriation	20 00	

ELECTIONS 1936

Paid:—

Payroll, Tellers and Moderator	$	983 00
Rockland Standard Pub Co., printing		378 25
Bemis Drug Co., dinners		18 20
Rockland Lunch, dinners		1 60
Alice Lee Restaurant, dinners		35 75
George Foulas, dinners		27 45
Mrs. J. J. Lannin, dinners		6 00
Roman Garden, dinners		2 25
Becker & Co., supplies		4 00
John J. Bowler, rent of Opera House		
7 times		470 00

Expended		$ 1 926 50
Appropriation	$ 1 500 00	
Over appropriation	426 50	

TOWN REPORT AND POLL BOOK

Paid:—

A. I. Randall, Inc.

2500 Town Reports	$ 756 40

Rockland Standard Pub. Co.
650 Poll Books   353 75
Russell Chandler, delivering
Town Reports   20 00
N. S. Whiting Jr., delivering
Town Reports   9 00
Earl Wallace, delivery town reports   9 00

Expended $ 1 148 15
Appropriation $ 700 00
Over appropriation   448 15

BEACONS 1936

Paid:—
Edison Electric Ill. Co., services $ 115 80
Damon Electric Co., service   197 85
Traffic Equipment Co., service   280 00
Charles Hines, resetting beacon   3 00

Expended $ 596 65
Appropriation $ 600 00
Under appropriation   3 35

VISITING NURSE

Paid:—
Mrs. Harry W. Burrell, Treasurer
Visiting Nurse Association $ 1 000 00
Appropration $ 1 000 00

MASS. HOSPITAL SCHOOL

Paid:—
Commonwealth of Massachusetts $ 677 94
Appropriation $ 800 00
Under appropriation   122 06

MASS. INDUSTRIAL SCHOOL

Paid:—
Town of Weymouth, Mass. $ 1 002 16

City of Quincy, Mass.   477 80
Norfolk County Agri. school   16 00
City of Boston, Mass.   101 74

Expended $ 1 597 70
Appropriation $ 1 600 00
Under appropriation   2 30

STREET LIGHTING 1936
Paid:—
Edison Electric Ill. Co., service $ 9 007 11
Install Electric Light, Market St.   15 00
Install Electric Light, Forest St.   30 00
Install Electric Light, Pond and
  Wilson Place   45 00

Expended $ 9 097 11
Appropriation $ 9 122 36
Under appropriation   25 25

MEMORIAL DAY OBSERVANCE
Paid:—
Warshaw Market, flowers $ 6 00
Allen B. Howland, miscellaneous   5 88
S. P. Bruinsma, 490 wreaths   58 80
James M. Feeney, 300 dinners   165 00
Hartsuff Post Mem. Asso., wreathe   3 00
Elbert L. Chamberlain, 6 1-2
  gross flags   50 38
Mrs. Annie Carey, postage   58
Old Colony Post Drum Corps, services   33 33
Rockland High School Band, services   33 33
Rockland Post Am. Legion Drum
  Corps, services   33 33

Expended $ 389 63
Appropriation   . $ 400 00
Under appropriation   10 37

REFURNISHING TOWN OFFICES

Paid:—

Paul Ouilette, Labor	$	25 00
Yawman & Erbe, office furniture		266 37
E. T. Ryan Iron Works, grill work		165 80
Harry L. Rome, shades and desk top		8 67
Fred Stevenson, labor		30 25
Hall & Torrey, supplies		1 79

Expended			$ 497 88
Appropriation	$	500 00	
Under appropriation		2 12	

EAST WATER STREET CONSTRUCTION
1935 Appropriation

Paid:—

Payroll, Labor	$	82 93
Nelson Cement Stone Co., curbing		165 40
Hall & Torrey, iron fence		15 08

Expended			$ 263 41
Unexpended Bal. 1935	$	487 99	
Expended		263 41	
Unexpended Balance			$ 224 58

List of Payroll:

George Beverely	$	6 80
William Condon		1 50
George Tyler		19 50
Frank O'Hara		9 00
Fred Cormier		25 31
George Clarke		7 32
Frank Ciffello		2 25
Raymond LaComb		11 25
Total	$	82 93

CRIMINAL CASES IN COURT

Paid :—

Jared Gardner, Photo criminals	$	12 00
John J. Dwyer, Storage of car		10 00
Robert J. Jackson, services		33 75
Leroy Phinney, services		22 50
George J. Popp, services		12 00

Expended		$	90 25
Appropriation	$	100 00	
Under appropriation		9 75	

CLEANING UNION STREET

Paid :—

Thomas Higgins, Labor	$ 1	089 00
Michael Tedeschi, Labor		4 50

Expended		$ 1	093 50
Appropriation	$ 1	100 00	
Under appropriation		6 50	

GUIDE BOARDS AND SIGNS

Paid :—

M. J. Fitzgibbons, setting signs	$	31 00
Charles E. Meara, signs		2 00
Rockland Coal & Grain, 1 post		68
Nat. Colortype Co., 2 signs		6 85
N. Y., N. H. & H. R. R., freight		1 00
Traffic Equip. Co., 5 signs, 9 posts		57 25

Expended		$	98 78
Appropriation	$	100 00	
Under appropriation		1 22	

TOWN NOTES AND INTEREST

Paid :—

Director of Accounts, certifying notes	54 00
Payment School Bonds	16 000 00

Interest School Bonds	5 225 00
Plymouth County Hospital Note	1 000 00
Discount on Notes	626 89
Interest on Notes	457 11

Expended		$23 763 00
Appropriation	$26 000 00	
Under appropriation	2 237 00	

PAYMENT TO E. J. ROURKE

Paid :—

| Ed. J. Rourke, balance use of steam Roller, 1934 | | $ 381 00 |
| Appropriation | $ 381 00 | |

ARMISTICE DAY OBSERVANCE 1936

Paid :—

Italian Woman's Club, 1st prize float	$ 25 00
Tri Town Woman's Club 2nd prize float	15 00
American Red Cross, 1st prize car	10 00
Marshall's Car, 2nd prize car	5 00
Rockland Post American Legion 1st prize marching	15 00
Rockland High School, 2nd prize marching	5 00
Rockland Auxiliary, American Legion 1st prize marching	15 00
Rockland Girl Scouts 2nd prize marching	5 00
Whitman Legion Post 1st prize Band	10 00
Whitman High School, 2nd prize Band	10 00
Rockland High School, prize	10 00
Abington High School, prize	10 00
V. F. W. Junior Drum Corps, prize	10 00

Mrs. Mildred Rome, postage and Printing etc.	22 65	
John J. Dwyer, hire of car	9 00	
Stanley Ames, use of amplifier	4 00	
Bay State Dec. Co., dec. High school	3 00	
William F. McCarthy, sign	3 25	
Alice Lee Restaurant, dinners	19 00	
Mrs. J. J. Lannin, Refreshments at school	76 35	
Doris M. Strong, supplies	60	
Mrs. Annie Carey, Judges	6 00	
M. Mullen, janitor cleaning school	5 00	
Charles Metevier, janitor cleaning school	5 00	

Expended		$ 298 85
Appropriation	$ 300 00	
Under appropriation	1 15	

ASSESSORS 1936

Paid as Salary:

Joseph B. Estes	$ 1 440 00	
Norman J. Beal	530 00	
Dennis L. O'Connor	530 00	

Expended		$ 2 500 00
Appropriation	$ 2 500 00	

MISCELLANEOUS SELECTMEN

Paid:—

Rockland Trans. Co., express	35
A. S. Peterson, supplies	5 08
Douglas Print, letterheads	9 50
U. S. Post Office, envelopes	79 60
H. C. Metcalf, cleaning typewriter	1 00
Dues to Selectmen's Asso'n.	6 00
Becker & Co., supplies	5 70

L..E. Muran Co., supplies 6 00

Expended		$ 113 23
Appropriation	$ 120 00	
Under appropriation	6 77	

MISCELLANEOUS SEALER OF WEIGHTS

Paid:—

N. & L. E. Gurley, supplies	$ 16 16	
A. A. Phelps, insurance	19 50	
Harold J. Inkley, expense sealers meeting	10 00	
Harold J. Inkley, use of auto	50 00	
Harold J. Inkley, paid for use of tester	7 00	
Harold J. Inkley, expenses	2 00	

Expended	104 66	
Appropriation	$ 105 00	
Under appropriation	34	

MISCELLANEOUS TOWN CLERK

Paid:—

A. S. Peterson, supplies	$	5 00
Charles H. Goss, Cushion		1 75
J. Emmett Sullivan & Son 17 Death Returns		4 25
J. J. Sheppard & Sons, 2 Death Returns		50
George E. Mansfield 12 Death Returns		3 00
C. L. Rice & Son, 39 Death Returns		9 75
Ralph L. Belcher, vital statistics		224 85
Joseph Frame M. D., 2 birth returns		50
N. F. Lough M. D., 2 birth returns		50
F. H. Corey M. D., 5 birth returns		1 25
A. H. Barron M. D., 7 birth returns		1 75

J. F. Curtin M. D., 3 birth returns		75
H. P. Russell M. D., 4 birth returns	1	00
R. B. Rand M. D., 3 birth returns		75
H. J. Hulse M. D., 9 birth returns	2	25
Rockland Standard Pub. Co.,		
Adv. & Binding Standard	12	50
W. B. Woodward, Bond	5	00
Murray Bros. Co., binding books	4	50
H. C. Metcalf, supplies	3	00
Becker & Co., metal guides and		
supplies	15	54
A. L. Dixon, supplies	3	50
Ralph L. Belcher, expense Town Clerk's		
meeting	5	50
Fidelity Spec. Co., supplies	2	00
Stone's Express, express		35
U. S. Post Office, envelopes	14	10
Walton Trunk Co., 2 filing cases	10	50
Ralph L. Belcher, postage and mailing	7	75

Expended			$ 345 09
Appropriation	$	350 00	
Under appropriation		4 91	

MISCELLANEOUS TREASURER

Paid:—

U. S. Post Office, envelopes	$	97 04
A. S. Peterson, supplies		2 43
Becker & Co., Check register		3 12
C. J. Higgins, Expense to Boston		30 43
The Todd Co., checks		43 79
L. E. Muran Co., file case		6 00
C. J. Higgins, Postage and mailing		47 60
Amos A. Phelps, Bonds		247 86
Ward's Stationer, supplies		75
C. J. Higgins, 250 envelopes		5 70

C. J. Higgins, Stationery   13 25

Expended $ 497 97
Appropriation $ 500 00
Under appropriation   2 03

MISCELLANEOUS REGISTRARS OF VOTERS

Paid:—
Rockland Standard Pub. Co.,
    Adv. and check lists   154 25
Robinson Envelope Seal Co., seals   3 50
Austin Print, 500 blanks   5 75
Secretary Com. of Mass., Reg. of voters   3 50
R. L. Belcher, postage   3 72
Payroll Nov. 3, recount   24 00
John J. Bowler, rent of Opera
    House, recount   3 00

Expended $ 197 72
Appropriation $ 200 00
Under Appropriation   2 28

MISCELLANEOUS ASSESSORS

Paid:—
Hobbs & Warren, supplies   4 57
L. E. Muran Co., supplies   88 43
A. A. Phelps, insurance   10 00
Hall & Torrey, supplies   18 63
L. E. Muran Co., cards and poll sheets   78 45
E. A. Studley, abstract deeds   12 00
Rockland Standard Pub. Co. cards   11 25
N. E. Tel. & Tel. Co., service   71 14
L. E. Muran Co., loose binders   74 51
Alton F. Lyons, transfer cards and
    service   55 00
Douglas Print, cards   25 50
A. S. Peterson, supplies   28 26

A. I. Randall Inc., census cards and
  printing   60 85
George H. Barnstead Co., printing cards 1 00
H. C. Metcalf, Cleaning Typewriter
  and supplies   5 00
Brockton Trans. Co., express   2 35
Edison Electric Ill. Co., lamps   1 20
U. S. Post Office, envelopes   30 00
Banker & Tradesman, Manual and
  subscription   11 75
Jenkins &' Simmons, express   35
Joseph B. Estes, School in instruction 12 00
Dennis L. O'Connor, School
  of Instruction   12 00
Joseph B. Estes, auto expense   89 65
Dennis L. O'Connor, auto expense   40 35
Spaulding Moss Co., supplies   5 57
S. W. Baker, magnifying glass   2 00
W. B. Woodward, insurance   12 48
Norman J. Beal, auto expense   60 75
Norman J. Beal, School of instruction 12 00
Joseph B. Estes, postage and
  mailing   9 97

Expended $ 847 01
Appropriation $ 850 00
Under appropriation   2 99

MISCELLANEOUS UNCLASSIFIED
Paid:—
Mason L. Loring, running
  town lines $ 4 00
Joseph W. Lincoln, running
  town lines   3 00
Edison Electric Ill. Co., service
  and lamps   107 27
John B. Mahar, Settlement
  Damage Suit   250 00

Harry S. Torrey, expenses Boston and postage	15	94
N. E. Tel. & Tel. Co., service	106	13
Charles S. Hines, Cleaning town Offices	260	00
N. S. Whiting, services	102	02
Rockland Standard Pub. Co., Adv. and printing	15	00
Damon Electric Co., repairs	12	51
Becker & Co., supplies	21	24
Howland & Howland, Survey Beal St.	7	00
Douglas Print, License Blank	7	25
Comm. Public Safety, License Blanks		85
Postal Telegraph Co., Telegram		32
F. J. Geogan, Service Town Counsel and Court Cases	391	30
U. S. Post Office, stamps	2	00
Hobbs & Warren, License Blanks	9	29
Hall & Torrey, supplies	5	91
John J. Dwyer, putting out flags	60	00
James A. Donovan, No Trespassing sign	1	50
Russell Chandler, Repairs	2	25
Payroll, Guarding Fire Boxes	176	00
Mrs. David C. Duniford, damage on clothes	20	00
Harry L. Rome, 9 shades	12	15
Payroll, Removing trees Union St.	36	32
H. C. Metcalf, repair adding machine	1	75
Joseph A. Frame, repair on desk	4	40
Alton F. Lyon, Settlement Damage Suit	50	00
Harold H. Capen, Damage Auto Tire	9	33
Bay State Flag Co., Dec. Town Office Armistice Day	10	00
Nathan Ames, Damage to Auto	3	50
Expended	$ 1 708	23

Appropriation $ 1 150 00
Over appropriation   558 23

MISCELLANEOUS TAX COLLECTOR

Paid:—

A. S. Peterson, supplies	5 15
A. A. Phelps, Bonds	422 00
James A. Donovan, expenses to Boston	12 00
Hobbs & Warren, supplies	24 35
Douglas Print, Excise Bills	43 00
James A. Donovan, Postage mailing	22 07
U. S. Post Office, envelopes	154 30
Austin Print, letterheads and bills	39 25
A. I. Randall Inc., Tax bills	57 45
Ralph L. Belcher, assistance on Tax bills	65 00
L. E. Muran, 2 cash books	38 46
Rockland Standard Pub. Co., Adv. and Tax sale	143 25
Francis J. Geogan, Recording deeds and service	228 00
Brockton Enterprise, Adv. notice	2 63

Expended $ 1 256 91
Appropriation $ 1 275 00
Under appropriation   18 09

SUMMARY

Miscellaneous Clerk	$ 345 09
Miscellanous Selectmen	113 23
Miscellaneous Sealer	104 66
Miscellanous Treasurer	497 97
Miscellaeous Registrars of Voters	197 72
Miscellaneous Assessors	847 01
Miscellaneous Unclassified	1 708 23

Miscellaneous Collector   1 256 91

Expended $ 5 070 82
Appropriation $ 4 550 00
Over appropriation   520 82

ASSESSORS MAP, W. P. A.

Paid:—

J. Thomas Condon, auto expense	$	55 56
Charles L. Baxter, auto expense		21 54
Curtis Toothaker, auto expense		42 12
Carl Fass, auto expense		3 00
John J. Bowler, rent of office		90 00
Quincy Oil Co., oil		40
Charles Morgan, auto expense		334 80
L. E. Muran, tracing cloth and paper		73 54
Hall & Torrey, supplies		13 85
Rome Bros., supplies		37 33
Buff & Buff, repairs and hire of instrument		118 75
G. W. S. Hyde, supplies		75
A. S. Peterson, supplies		5 25
Spaulding Moss Co., supplies		6 61
Edison Electric Ill Co., lamps		60

Expended $ 804 10
Bal. 1935 Appropriation $ 139 12
Appropriation March   500 00
Appropriation June   425 00

Total amount available $ 1 064 12
Unexpended Bal.   260 02

W. P. A. ADMINISTRATION

Paid:—
N. E. Tel. & Tel. Co., service $ 188 28

John J. Bowler, use of car	323	00
Dion-Hafford, supplies W. P. A.		
Sewing	1	10
Fred M. Ryan, service	1 232	50
M. Warren Wright, service	481	50
Hall & Torrey, supplies	24	78
J. A. Rice Co., supplies W. P. A.		
Sewing	13	17
E. L. Chamberlain, paper, rat' project	7	80
Dr. Joseph H. Dunn, accident case	2	00
Rome Bros., Tools	4	10
A. S. Peterson, supplies	15	82
John J. Bowler, rent of offices		
W. P. A.	435	00
Spaulding Moss Co., supplies	9	42
H. C. Metcalf, 2 typewriters and		
repairs	60	25
Damon Electric, Electric work		
W. P. À. Sewing	31	90
John J. Dwyer, trucking commodity		
supplies	84	50
W. T. Grant Co., supplies	1	00
Stimpson & Co., Bags, commodity		
supplies	28	91
Harry S. Torrey, expense to Boston		
on Projects	5	45
Hancock Paint & Varnish Co., paint	60	20
Rockland Standard Pub. Co., 1000 cards	13	00
Rockland Coal & Grain, supplies	10	12
Fred S. Delay, Med. supplies WPA	36	91
Joseph B. Estes, expenses Fall		
River W. P. A.	47	30
Howland & Howland, surveyors stakes	5	65
Jenkins & Simmons, express		35
B. O. Estes, supplies sewing WPA	2	00
J. Thomas Condon, use of		
auto, W. P. A.	67	65

Franklin & Perkins, bags, commodity
  supplies   39 70
Stall & Dean, supplies W. P. A.
  Project   60 91
Edison Electric Ill. Co. Lamps   6 08
Milton Bradley Co., supplies   4 52
Payroll, Nurse Project   88 30
Ella F. Lovewell, Nurse Project   22 47
Mary Keene, Nurse Project   12 00
L. E. Muran, supplies   4 50
Payroll, Tree Dept. W. P. A.   12 07
Union Market Co., supplies sewing
  W. P. A.   86
John J. Dwyer, trans. Kindergarten
  Project   175 00

Expended $ 3 620 07
Bal appropriation 1935 $ 1 671 73
Appropriation March   750 00
Appropriation June   1 500 00

Total $ 3 921 73
Unexpended Bal.   301 66

PARK, W. P. A.

Paid:—

George O'Donnell, Labor $ 564 30
Payroll, Trucks and labor   808 88
Abe Wainshalbaum, gas and supplies   43 98
Thomas Walsh, sharpening tools   7 20
C. H. Thornhill, cinders   1 949 50
A. J. Vargus, gas   13 30
Rome Bros., supplies   109 21
G. W. S. Hyde, sharpening tools   5 95
Boston Pipe Co., gate valve   9 75
Corcoran Supply Co., pipe and supplies 149 33
Rockland Coal & Grain Co., supplies 300 63
Hall & Torrey, supplies   101 24

Darcy Trans Co., express		75
F. Beauregard, gravel	20	40
Lester M. Wyman, Loam	1 779	35
Rockland Hardware & Paint Co.,		
Grass Seed and supplies	328	13
Edward P. Breen, use of roller	20	00
A. Culver Co., Lime	8	45
Hickey Bros., gas	2	27
Geo. E. Bolling, service	5	00
James D. Mahoney, repairs	16	70
Waldo Bros. Co., supplies	4	35
Bemis Drug Co., Photo of Park	1	26
Wm. T. McCarthy, Board Signs	8	70
Rockland Welding Co., repairs		
on tractor	90	81
Spaulding Moss Co., Blue Prints	4	14
Rockland Water Dept. service	2	50
Market St. Garage, 1-3 cost of repairs		
on Tractor	35	95
P. I. Perkins, 1-3 cost of repairs		
on tractor	14	49

Expended			$ 6 406	52
Bal. Appropriation 1935	$	826 02		
Appropriation 1936	5	737 00		

Total	$ 6 563	02
Bal unexpended	156	50

IMPROVEMENT AT REID'S POND
Paid:—

Payroll, Horses and trucks	$ 734	49
Hall & Torrey, supplies	75	15
Hobart's Auto Supply, gas	4	00
C. H. Swift, gas	45	64
A. Culver Co., supplies	142	85
Rockland Welding Co., repairs	2	00
Rockland Coal and Grain, Supplies	12	28

C. A. Paulding, oil	2 00	
Rome Bros., supplies	4 56	
Thomas Murrell, sand	1 50	
E. F. Benson, Fill for pond	199 35	
G. W. S. Hyde, sharpening tools	1 00	
Jenkins & Simmons, express	60	
P. I. Perkins, repairs	14 49	
Market St. Garage, repairs	35 95	
Fred Webster, gravel	80	
Otis Mann, gravel	3 60	
Bay State Nurseries, shrubs	299 00	
Fred S. Delay, Med. supplies	9 00	
Expended		1 588 26
Appropriation	$ 2 000 00	
Unexpended Bal.	411 74	

HIGHWAY REPAIRS

Paid:—

Gordon Mann, Rent of pit	$ 112 50	
Wm. Friary, use of auto	214 46	
Payroll, Labor	3 695 81	
E. L. LeBarron Foundry, Catch Basin, grates and covers	63 00	
Southeastern Cons. Co., catch basin	90 70	
Berger Metal Culvert Co., metal pipe	30 03	
Chas. J. McCarthy, tools	46 79	
Tylers Garage, repairs and storage	182 19	
Jenkins & Simmons, express	2 85	
Rockland Trans. Co., express	72	
Curry Bros. Oil Co., oil	35 20	
Rome Bros., supplies	74 01	
Hedge & Matthews Co., supplies	1 40	
A. Wainshalbaum, repairs	10 00	
Rockland Disposal Co., removal of Rubbish	126 00	
Weymouth Asphalt Co., patching	1 353 50	
Rockland Welding Co., repairs	12 75	

M. F. Ellis Co., supplies	111	92
Ed. Howland, Cleaning catch basin	6	75
Hobart Auto Supply Co., supplies	3	30
Doyle Tire & Battery Co., supplies	1	66
Lannin Garage, gas and storage	152	28
Roderick MacKenzie, use of auto	202	14
A. Culver Co., supplies	6	93
Hall & Torrey, supplies	82	20
Bradford Weston, material	83	45
The Barrett Co., Tarvia	75	00
Comm. of Public Safety, inspection of Roller	10	00
George N. Beal, supplies	20	50
Buffalo-Springfield Co., Repairs on Roller	38	75
Roderick MacKenzie, loam	7	00
Rockland Coal & Grain, supplies	34	28
C. H. Swift, supplies	1	62
P. I. Perkins, repairs	152	82
Traffic Equipment Co., steel broom	42	00
C. A. Paulding, supplies	1	54
Paulding & Magoun, repairs	31	00
C. Engino, lanterns	10	00
E. P. Reed Lumber Co., supplies	3	30
Market St. Garage, repairs	52	01
A. J. Vargus, supplies	6	10
Foxwell & Marble, supplies	17	00
Rockland Hardware & Paint Co., supplies	21	70
Rockland Water Dept., service	22	50

Expended			$ 7 249	64
Appropriation	$ 7 000	00		
Trans. from Reserve fund	249	80		
Total available			$ 7 249	80
Under				16

List of Payroll, Highway Repairs

Paid :—

Gerald Grant	18	00
Omer Gelinas	141	75
Chas. Brennick	27	00
Domenic DelPrete	21	66
John Martin	47	53
C. W. Lincoln	30	66
A. W. Clarke	25	88
Melvin Gay	54	90
Frank I. Shaw	2	25
Joseph Hillsher	9	00
Leo Haggerty	11	53
Ronald Greene	9	00
Thomas Murrell	7	03
Albert Norman	28	69
Donald Baker	14	06
Fred Wheeler	70	04
Patrick Mahoney	42	00
Joseph Meade	13	50
Maurice Mahoney	37	40
Henry Roche	76	50
Robert Morrissette	110	25
George Beverly	62	31
Earl Wallace	5	34
John Shoughrow	14	06
Harry McKinnon	5	06
Michael Bowen	3	38
William Bell	3	75
Thomas Bailey	1	41
Edward Coffey	4	50
Percy Simmons	9	00
Peter Hickey	4	50
Elmer Harrington	17	16
Wm. H. Friary	169	50
Michael Haggerty	14	06
Timothy Mahoney	1	12

Harold Corcoran	58 50
John Arkel	3 94
Alfred Benoit Jr.	9 60
Leo Banville	4 50
Joseph Costello	9 60
William Green	24 00
Peter Gilmartin Jr.	24 00
Peter Gilmarten Sr.	4 50
James Horan	4 50
Paul McDonald	3 94
John McEnelly	9 00
Robert Mulready	9 00
Thomas O'Connor	3 94
John Ricca	3 94
Charles Shalgian	3 94
James Twomey	3 94
Wm. Cannaway	25 88
Frank Cifello	16 88
Thomas Higgins	18 00
Fred Thibeault	14 63
Philip Murphy	139 51
Raymond LaComb	91 98
Joseph DelPrete	16 88
Chas. Fucillo	32 63
Donald Owens	36 29
Henry Gizer	32 63
Fred Finch	14 63
Michael Mastro	30 38
Lawrence Cull	13 78
Michael Murphy	108 57
Chas. DeCenzo	4 50
Irving Turner	10 13
Henry Cook	21 38
Lawrence McAuliffe	3 38
Arthur Casey	238 50
Lyle Tibbetts	29 82
George Tyler	577 50
J. J. Dwyer	174 75

James Umbrianna	25 88
Arvid Noren	29 54
A. W. Ross	27 29
James Smith	26 16
Louis Roche	118 41
Myron Bacon	34 88
Linus Hackett	151 88
Harry Roberts	5 63
Joseph Daley	31 79
Charles Hunt	23 63
John White	19 13
Abe Wainshalbaum	15 00
Wm. Condon	106 50
Clifford Rose	6 00
Leo Cull	56 81
Chas. Shoughrow	37 41
Willard Grant	18 00
Harold Keene	5 62
Harold Rainsford	9 00

Total	$ 3 695 81

EAST WATER STREET CONSTRUCTION 1936

Paid:—

Payroll, Labor	$ 8 307 66
R. V. Blanchard, sand	58 80
N. E. Concrete Pipe Co., tile pipe	1 599 06
Bradford Weston, Blasting and	
use of shovel	835 40
A. Culver Co., cement	44 85
Hall & Torrey, supplies	42 97
Rockland Coal & Grain,	
coal and lumber	101 18
N. E. Metal Culvert Co.	
1 paved insert	10 99
De Equipment Co., rent of pump	6 00
Southeastern Cons. Co., catch basin	229 95
A. J. Vargus, supplies	3 30

E. L. LeBarron Foundry, frames and
grates   132 00
Rockland Trans. Co., express   1 00
Rockland Water Dept. use of compressor 60 00
Wetmore Savage, conduct   52 32
Homelite Corp., rent of pump   47 50
Bemis Drug Co., 1st aid kit   1 23
Dolby's Filling Station, gas and oil   5 48
Crystal Concrete Corp. Concrete   56 68
M. F. Ellis Co., Twine   1 14
C. H. Swift, oil for roller   2 00
Rome Bros., supplies   1 09
Bradford Weston, stone   1 748 52
H. H. Arnold Co., 2 posts   6 00
Warren Bros. Roads Co., Pemolethis
Oil   416 19
John H. Lamb, gas and oil   43 15
C. Thompkins, gravel   85 00
Expended $13 899 46

Appropriation $ 5 000 00
Received Comm. of Mass.   6 242 53
Received Plymouth County   3 121 79

Total to date $ 14 363 79
Unexpended Bal   464 33
Final payments not received from State and County.

List of Payroll East Water Street
Leo Cull $ 531 68
Waldo McPhee   334 41
Michael Murphy   247 57
Lawrence Cull   342 39
Kenneth Kemp   225 12
Gilman Paulding   118 48
Ed Casey   249 18
Gordon Hammond   110 59
Lyle Tibbetts   1 41

Louis Roche	84 65
Frank Cifello	356 21
Maxwell Flint	29 82
Frank O'Hara	314 20
James Winslow	95 90
Harold Rainsford	29 29
Wm Foley	20 81
Robert Morrisette	94 22
Kenneth Bowser	29 82
John Morrison	81 27
Chas. Lincoln	29 82
Ed. Condon	29 82
Norman Weeks	29 82
Paul McDonald .	19 72
Henry Lombard	120 09
Francis Hamilton	106 07
John Ricca	273 52
Wesley Richardson	104 39
Henry Giza	29 82
Wm. Cannaway	14 90
Wilbar Adams	29 82
Arthur Ricca	19 12
Herbert Brown	169 09
Timothy Twomey	10 12
Frank Hussey	75 95
John McAuliffe	180 58
Fred Cormier	250 93
Harry Barstow	282 57
Arthur Ross	15 20
Randall Green	4 50
Timothy Mahoney	179 85
Thomas Fitzgerald	113 08
John Hannon	103 54
John J. Dwyer	196 50
Geo. Beverly	276 14
Linus Hackett	293 37
Geo. Tyler	209 25
Wm. T. Condon	476 25

Patrick Mahoney	274 75
A. DelPrete	132 00
George Umbrianna	193 98
Thomas Murrill	144 75
Arthur Casey	38 25
Abe Wainshalbaum	123 00
Harry McKenna	32 34
Roy Blanchard	63 00
William Bell	16 50
Michael Bowen	48 75
Melvin Gay	177 50
Joseph Sullivan	18 00
Albee Richards	24 00
Chas. Conlon	37 50
Omar Gelinas	32 34
W. Alton Whiting	10 14

Total $ 8 307 66

LIBERTY STREET DRAIN

Paid:—

Payroll, trucks	$	32 40
Rome Bros., tile		95 20
Hall & Torrey, supplies and tile		68 07
Rockland Water Dept.,		
Use of compressor		13 75
Rockland Coal & Grain, cement		1 30
E. Le LeBarron Foundry Co.,		
Catch basin		12 50

Expended $ 223 22
Transferred from W. P. A. Streets $ 275 00
Unexpended bal.   51 78

CRESCENT STREET SIDEWALK

Paid:—

Payroll, Labor	$	24 07
Bradford Weston, Bit. concrete		65 60

A. Culver Co., cement	33 80	
Quincy Oil Co., oil	1 44	
Expended		$ 124 91
Trans. from W. P. A. Streets	$ 150 00	
Unexpended Bal.	25 09	

PAYSON AVENUE DRAIN

Paid:—

Payroll, labor	14 00	
Hall & Torrey, supplies and tile	150 98	
E. L. LeBarron Foundry, Catch Basin covers	10 50	
Southeastern Cons. Co., gate and frame	19 53	
Thomas Walsh, sharpening tools	4 99	
Expended		$ 200 00
Trans. from W. P. A. Streets	$ 200 00	

RICE AVENUE SIDEWALK

Paid:—

Payroll, Labor	$ 92 73	
A. Culver Co., cement	65	
Market St. Garage, supplies	6 12	
Expended		$ 99 50
Appropriation	$ 100 00	
Under appropriation	50	

List of Payroll		
Elmer Harrington	$ 31 50	
Geo. Umbrianna	3 94	
Thomas McWilliams	4 50	
Robert Badger	3 94	
Philip Murphy	11 25	
George Beverly	85	
Albert Clark	2 25	
George Tyler	34 50	
Total		$ 92 73

LIBERTY STREET SIDEWALK

Paid:—
Payroll, Labor	$	164 76
A. Culver Co., cement		16 25
Bradford Weston, Bit. concrete		18 20

Expended			$	199 21
Appropriation	$	200 00		
Under appropriation		79		

List of Payroll:
Linus Hackett	$	13 50
Omer Gelinas		13 50
Henry Roche		16 03
George Beverly		24 23
Edward Coffey		13 50
Michael Murphy		9 00
Frank Cifello		13 50
Robert Morrisette		13 50
Arthur Casey		36 00
Geo. Tyler		12 00

Total	$	164 76

PLEASANT STREET

Appropriation	$	250 00
Nothing Expended		

BRIDGE OLD MARKET STREET

Paid:
Payroll, Labor	$	60 75
Berger Metal Culvert Co., pipe		38 48

Expended			$	99 23
Appropriation	$	100 00		
Under appropriation		77		

List of Payroll:

Linus Hackett	$	13 50
Omer Gelinas		13 50
Henry Roche		13 50
George Tyler		20 25
Total	$	60 75

STRIPING UNION AND OTHER STREETS

Paid:—

Ralph Measures, Labor	$	115 13
Tyler's Garage, gas		1 60
Hall & Torrey, Paint		33 06
Expended	$	149 79
Amt. Trans. from Reserve Fund	$ 150 00	
Under		21

DIVISION STREET

Paid:—

Payroll, trucks	$	43 88
Trans. from W.P.A. Streets	$ 700 00	
Unexpended Bal.		656 12

MYRTLE STREET SIDEWALK

Paid:—

Rome Bros., supplies	$	11 18
Thomas Fox, sand		6 00
Payroll, trucks		333 41
Pearl Murrill, sand		39 50
Hall & Torrey, tools		8 07
Bradford Weston, Bit concrete		141 21
Rockland Coal & Grain, supplies		8 38
P. T. Manter, supplies		2 25
Expended	$	550 00
Trans. from W.P.A. Streets	$ 550 00	

BIGELOW AVENUE SIDEWALK

Paid:—
A. Culver Co., cement	$ 3	90
Rockland Coal & Grain, supplies	124	28
Payroll, trucks	207	29
Pearl Murrill, sand	9	50
G. W. S. Hyde, sharpening tools	4	05
Bradford Weston, Bit. concrete	195	39
Hall & Torrey, supplies	4	75

Expended		$ 549	16
Trans. from W. P. A. Streets	$ 550	00	
Unexpended Bal.		84	

HOWARD STREET TO CUSTER, ART. 48

Paid:—
E. F. Benson, sand	3	48
Hall & Torrey, supplies	8	03
Dolby's Gas Station, gas	1	10
Rockland Coal & Grain, supplies	40	24
Payroll, truck	8	75
Bradford Weston, Bit. concrete	63	00

Expended		$ 124	60
Trans. from W.P.A. Streets	$ 125	00	
Unexpended Bal.		40	

HOWARD STREET, ART. 55

Paid:—
Payroll, trucks		$ 42	88
E. F. Benson, sand		13	84
Rockland Coal & Grain, supplies		55	92
Bradford Weston, Bit. concrete		61	90
Expended		$ 174	54
Trans. from W.P.A. Streets	$ 175	00	
Unexpended Bal.		46	

REBUILDING UNION STREET, P. W. A.

Paid:—

American Bank Note Co., Coupon on Bonds	$	74 77
N. England Road Building Ass'n. Adv.		48 40
Brockton Enterprise, Adv.		16 50
Boston Globe Pub. Co., Adv		24 75
Payroll, Police		847 76
Bradford Weston, Construction of Street	46	568 76
J. R. Worcester Co., Eng. services	2	950 00
Addison F. Holmes, testing clay pipe		12 00
Director of Accounts, Certifying notes		34 00
Rockland Standard Pub. Co., Cuts		18 25
Francis J. Geogan, Legal services		19 00
Merchants Nat. Bank, Interest on notes		117 89
Warren Tech. Co., Testing material		250 00

Amount expended $51 005 33

Total amount not received from Federal Gov't.

EAST WATER STREET LAND DAMAGE

Paid:—

Heirs Frederick Lewis, land damage	$	132 00
Ethel McCallum, land damage		113 00
Charles W. Poole land damage		175 75
Mrs. Mabel Whiting, land damage		47 50
Frank H. Shaw, land damage		133 80
Charles H. Mason land damage		59 00
H. Waldo Cushing, land damage		132 80
Florence C. Dudley, land damage		100 00

Expended			$	893 85
Appropriation	$	936 55		
Left to be paid on damages		42 70		

SNOW REMOVAL

Paid:—

Payroll, Labor	$23 071	27
N. E. Roads Mach. Co., new plow	255	00
N. E. Roads Mach. Co., repairs on plows	34	00
Rockland Welding Co., Repairs on Plows	202	77
Thomas Fox, sand	86	00
Hall & Torrey, tools and supplies	3	45
Henry J. Condon, repairs on plows	16	00
G. W. S. Hyde, repairs	14	75
H. H. Arnold, 2 pcs. Steel	2	00
George N. Beal, repairs on tractors	60	78
Boston Sand & Gravel Co., sand	26	81
Mrs. F. B. Southworth, damage to fence	6	00
A. Wainshalbaum, supplies	2	80
E. F. Benson, sand	16	04
A. N. Boynton, repair plows	16	00
Crystal Concrete Co., sand	67	07
Walter S. Wheeler, repairs Cushing Pond fence	127	34
Market St., Garage, Repairs Reed's Pond fence	45	18
Mann's Auto Service, repairs	29	71
Gideon Studley, storage of sand	75	00

Expended			$24	157 97
Appropriation	$23	500 00		
Over appropriation		657 97		

TARVIA AND ROAD BINDER

Paid:—

Payroll, Labor	$ 2 918	37
The Barrett Co., Tarvia	2 562	73
Mrs. Thomas Murrill, sand	17	00
A. Culver Co., supplies	4	15

Bradford Weston, stone		474 09
Douglas Print, printing cards		2 50
Rockland Coal & Grain, supplies		23 11
Expended		$ 6 001 95
Appropriation	$ 6 000 00	
Over appropriation		1 95

List of Payroll:—

Fred Wheeler	$	99 84
Raymond LaComb		34 31
Joseph Daley		90 84
John Shoughrow		81 28
Donald Baker		84 09
Harry McKennon		36 00
Frank Cifello		107 16
Patrick Mahoney		92 25
Domenic DelPrete		139 50
Albert Norman		54 28
Harry Roberts		41 92
Lyle Tibbetts		25 31
Leo Cull		27 56
Harold Garfield		36 98
Myron Bacon		41 06
Michael Haggerty		30 09
Stephen McNamara		6 75
K. Badmington		10 69
Michael Murphy		62 58
Earl Corcoran		26 59
John Ricca		4 50
Robert Thompson		4 50
Paul McDonald		4 50
Daniel Ewell		24 89
Lawrence McAuliffe		15 61
Paul Lincoln		4 50
Melvin Gay		78 75
Arthur Casey		201 75
Abe N Wainshalbaum		60 00

John J. Dwyer	154 50
Austin Beale	11 49
Burrell Dill	10 26
John Martin	99 84
Chas. Fucillo	2 95
Joseph Kelliher	5 76
Arthur Leary	5 76
Ed. Thornill	5 76
Fred Dunn	10 26
Henry Roche	41 20
Aldo Bolto	2 11
Earl Costello	4 92
Michael Mastro	23 06
Irving Turner	9 00
Albert Callahan	2 53
Peter Hickey	47 81
Joseph Meade	40 78
Thomas Bailey	4 50
Wesley Richardson	10 24
Seymore Neiforth	21 24
Louis Crocker	18 42
Wilson Condon	25 45
John Morrison	15 05
Ralph Lincoln	31 64
Kenneth Bowser	20 96
Ernest Shores	18 72
Thomas McDonald	8 58
Leo Condon	21 25
Frank Blake	13 64
Elwin Gould	5 77
Chas. Hyland	8 02
Meyer Marcus	20 67
Harold Rainsford	4 50
Arthur Najarian	13 08
Ralph Fisher	6 33
Timothy Mahoney	6 33
Herbert Brown	26 72
Leon Owens	4 06

Fred Fisher	2 95
John Costello	5 76
Wm. Condon	99 00
Michael Bowen	20 25
Linus Hackett	46 69
Omer Gelinas	46 69
Frank Morrison	7 31
Edward Dill	7 31
Eugene Norman	7 89
Fred Kane	2 81
Harold Haggerty	2 81
Timothy Twomey	2 81
Leo McAuliffe	5 06
Arthur Senecal	2 81
Philip Murphy	4 50
Wm. Bell	12 00
George Tyler	213 75
Oakley Seaman	2 25
Robert Morrisette	72 84
C. W. Lincoln	18 00
Geo. Hamilton	3 94
Wm. Cannaway	3 94
Robert Quinlan	3 94
Allen Badger	3 94
John Curtis	3 94
Arthur Doherty	3 94

Total $ 2 918 37

SIDEWALKS 1936

Paid:—

Crystall Concrete & Gravel Co. sand $	47 45
Rockland Coal & Grain, cement	38 34
Payroll, Labor	415 27
Rockland Welding Co., Repairs	18 25
Bradford Weston, Bit. concrete	295 40
A. Culver Co., cement	40 30
Hall & Torrey, supplies	11 05

Rockland Water Dept., use of
compressor   25 75
C. H. Swift, supplies   1 40
George N. Beal, repairs   2 70

Expended $ 895 91
Appropriation $ 1 000 00
Under appropriation   104 09

List of Payroll:
George Tyler $ 51 56
George Beverly   58 65
Arthur Casey   90 70
Linus Hackett   36 00
Henry Roche   36 00
Omer Gelinas   36 00
Fred Wheeler   18 00
Myron Bacon   18 00
Frank Cifello   25 31
Wm. Bell   9 00
Earl Wallace   9 00
Robert Morrisette   18 00
Edward Coffey   9 00

Total $ 415 27

W. P. A. STREETS

Paid:—
A. Wainshalbaum, use of crane and
supplies $ 65 93
Patrick Mahoney, sand   5 50
Southeastern Cons. Co., catch basin   354 67
E. L. LeBarron Foundry Co.,
grates and frames   78 70
Payroll, trucks and horses 1 768 94
Harvey Bowser, care of lanterns   106 00
A. Culver Co., supplies   354 77
E. F. Benson, sand   206 25

John Lonergan, care of lanterns   10 00
Rockland Coal & Grain, supplies   673 32
Hall & Torrey, supplies and tile   444 65
Rockland Welding Co., repairs   4 25
Rome Bros., supplies   28 89
G. W. S. Hyde, sharpening tools   86 15
C. A. Paulding, gas   3 12
Norman J. Beal
    Use of equipment   39 75
Mrs. Emma Stoddard, gravel   32 15
N. England Iron & Steel Co., supplies   73 23
C. A. Pinson, material   44 34
C. A. Pinson, use of garage   80 00
M. F. Ellis, supplies   5 92
John H. Lamb, gas   26 36
Fletcher Beauregard, gravel   192 20
Ryan Market, supplies   5 59
Thomas Welsh, sharpening tools   110 96
Albert Norman, care of lanterns   61 00
Thomas Whalen & Son, blasting   297 68
James G. Lamb, gas   7 58
Fearing & Walker, gas   4 25
Elliot Poole, gas   2 16
The Barrett Co., Tarvia   319 82
Bradford Weston, stone   490 38
Rockland Standard Pub. Co., cards   6 50
Samuel Wainshalbaum, iron pipe   12 00
K. Peters, supplies   70
Howland & Howland, stakes   4 10
Dolby Filling Station, gas   5 20
Rockland Water Dept., use of
    compressor   14 75
C. E. Thompkins, gravel   2 60
Lester M. Wyman, gravel   8 50
C. H. Swift, gas   2 25
Fred S. Delay, 1st Aid Kit   10 52

    Expended $ 6 050 63

Bal. appropriation 1935 $ 6 307 99
Part appropriation 1936   5 000 00

Total available $11 307 99
Trans. by vote of town to different streets   2 725 00
Unexpended Bal.   2 532 36

RECAPITULATION OF AMOUNTS AVAILABLE AND EXPENDITURES

(*)—Denotes Unexpended Dec. 31st, But Available for use.

	Raised	Expended	Over	Under	Reserve Fund
Soldiers Relief	$ 6 000 00	$ 7 510 95	$	$ 489 05	$
School Department	102 673 00	102 673 00			
My Aid	50 00			50 00	
State Aid	900 00	650 00		250 00	
Care of Town Cemetery	60 00	60 00			
Care of Soldiers' Graves	150 00	135 00		15 00	
Burial of Indigent Soldiers	100 00			100 00	
Clean Up Week	100 00	87 25		12 75	
Plymouth Cy. Hosp. Maint.	3 806 13	3 806 13			
Criminal Cases in Court	100 00	90 25		9 75	
Street Lighting	9 122 36	9 097 11		25 25	
Highway Surveyor	1 350 00	1 350 00			
Tia and Road Binding	6 000 00	6 001 95	1 95		
Highway Repairs	7 000 00	7 249 64		16	249 80
Soldiers' Burial Library	4 593 61	4 593 13		48	
Sidewalks	1 000 00	895 91		104 09	
Rent to American Legion	900 00	900 00			
Memorial Day Observance	400 00	389 63		10 37	
Cleaning Union Street	1 100 00	1 093 50		6 50	
Signs and Guide Boards	100 00	98 78		1 22	

RECAPITULATION OF AMOUNTS AVAILABLE AND EXPENDITURES

(*)—Denotes Unexpended Dec. 31st, But Available for use.

	Raised	Expended	Over	Under	Reserve Fund
Spanish War Veterans	288 00	288 00			
Fire Department	10 400 00	11 691 62	1 291 62		
Forest Fires	700 00	655 39		44 61	
Police Department	8 846 00	8 972 04		16	126 20
Inspector of Animals and Stables	100 00	100 00			
Sealer Weights and Measures	400 00	400 00			
Board of Health	6 000 00	5 995 75		4 25	
Park Department	1 851 00	1 850 34		66	
Mth Department	300 00	291 67		8 33	
Plymouth Cty. Ext. Service	150 00	150 00			
Fire Warden	500 00	940 68	40 68		400 00
Plymouth Cty. Hospital	3 806 13	3 806 13			
Rent of Town fees	1 160 00	1 140 00		20 00	
Town fees	6 600 00	6 590 00		10 00	
Elections	1 500 00	1 926 50	426 50		
Mass. Hospital School	800 00	677 94		122 06	
Mass. Industrial School	1 600 00	1 597 70		2 30	
Town Report and Poll Book	700 00	1 148 15	448 15		
Town Notes and interest	26 000 00	23 763 00		2 237 00	
Snow 1936	23 500 00	24 157 97	657 97		

RECAPITULATION OF AMOUNTS AVAILABLE AND EXPENDITURES

(*)—Denotes Unexpended Dec. 31st, But Available for use.

	Raised	Expended	Over	Under	Reserve Fund
sars	2 500 00	2 500 00			
Misc. Clerk	350 00	345 09		4 91	
Msc. Selectmen	120 00	113 23		6 77	
Misc. Sealer	105 00	104 66		34	
Misc. Treasurer	500 00	497 97		2 03	
Misc. Registrars of &Hs	200 00	197 72		2 28	
Misc. Collector	1 275 00	1 256 91		18 09	
Msc. Assessors	850 00	847 01		2 99	
Misc. Unclassified	1 150 00	1 708 23	558 23		
Reserve Fund	1 000 00	1 000 00			
Beacons	600 00	596 65		3 35	
Visiting Nse	1 000 00	1 000 00			
sation Ins	2 250 00	1 931 46		318 54	
sation Ins, Firemen	292 50	292 50			
W. P. A. Administration	3 921 73	3 620 07		301 66	
Old Age Assistance	25 000 00	31 660 22	6 666 22		
Public Welfare	56 000 00	58 643 78	2 643 78		
W. P. A. Assessors' Map	1 064 12	804 10		(*)260 02	
W. P. A. Public Parks	6 563 02	6 406 52		(*)156 50	
Repairs at Public Library	531 18	487 43		(*) 43 75	

RECAPITULATION OF AMOUNTS AVAILABLE AND EXPENDITURES

(*)—Denotes Unexpended Dec. 31st, But ... for use.

	Raised	Expended	Over	Under	Reserve Fund
E. Water St., ... Damage	936 55	883 85		(*) 42 70	
Purchase of Police Auto	550 00	624 00			74 00
Rebuilding Union St. PWA		51 005 33			
W. P. A. Myrtle Street	550 00	550 00			
W. P. A. Division Street	700 00	43 88		(*)656 12	
Refurnishing	500 00	497 88		2 12	
Payment to E. J. Rourke	381 00	381 00			
Striping Union and ... Streets		149 79		21	150 00
W. P. A. Howard St. to ...	125 00	124 60		40	
W. P. A. Howard St. to Crescent	175 00	174 54		46	
W. P. A. Bigelow Avenue	550 00	549 16		84	
Improvements Reed's Pond	2 000 00	1 588 26		(*)411 74	
Pleasant St, laying	250 00			(*)250 00	
Bridge Old Market St.	100 00	99 23		77	
W. P. A. Payson ... Drain	200 00	200 00			
... St, Sidewalk	150 00	124 91		25 09	
Liberty St., Sidewalk	200 00	199 21		79	
Rice ..., Sidewalk	100 00	99 50		50	
East ... St., Const.	14 363 79	13 899 46		(*)464 33	
Highway Repairs	7 000 00	7 249 66		16	249 80

RECAPITULATION OF AMOUNTS AVAILABLE AND EXPENDITURES

(*).—Denotes Unexpended Dec. 31st, But Av il alle for use.

	Raised	Expended	Over	Under	Reserve Fund
Liberty St., Drain	275 00	223 22		51 78	
I le Day ance	300 00	298 85		1 15	
East Water St. st.	487 99	263 41		(*)224 58	
W. P .A. Streets	8 582 99	6 050 63		(*)2 532 36	
Overlays	18 710 66	18 710 66			
Retubing Boilers, School Dept.	1 300 00	1 295 40		4 60	
Light, Heating, McKinley School	100 00	62 00		38 00	

Report of Board of Public Welfare

The Board of Public Welfare herewith submits its annual report, covering the period from January 1 to December 1, 1936 inclusive.

The requests for aid in the Department of Public Welfare for the year 1936, varied greatly in the different months of the year. During the summer and fall our aid showed a decided improvement due in part to the labor created by the P. W. A. project for the rebuilding of Union Street, the employment by the W. P. A., and the State Sidewalk projects, and the transferring of cases of recipients reaching the age of sixty-five to the Bureau of Old Age Assistance.

In the latter part of the year the aid again increased, due to the cutting of our quota by the W. P. A., and State Sidewalk project, also the closing of the Apt Shoe Co. in November, which caused many of their employees to request relief.

At the end of the year the Board of Public Welfare can see no lessening of relief for the coming year, unless some means can be found to get new business for our town.

The distribution of clothing and food under the W. P. A. is being handled the same as last year. The project is under the supervision of the W. P. A., where needy families may receive supplies of food and clothing. We wish to thank the different Churches, the Red Cross, and Fraternal societies for their helpfulness and co-operation given us in our Social Service work.

Special mention should also be made to our Visiting Nurse who has had charge of our Practical Nurse project and the Town Physicians who have given so liberally their time for the care of our needy sick.

We have at the present time on our Relief Rolls:

11 Mother's Aid Cases
3 Child Boarded Cases
90 Families, Outside Poor
62 Single Persons, Outside Poor
20 Families, Soldiers Relief
16 Single Persons, Soldiers Relief
210 Old Age Assistance Cases
23 At Infirmary

OLD AGE ASSISTANCE

The number of Old Age Assistance cases for 1936 has increased from 106 to 210 persons. The large increase is the result of lowering, by the State, to conform with the Federal Social Security Act, the age limit from seventy to sixty-five years of age, for those eligible to receive this assistance.

This act came into operation on September 1, 1936 although the Federal Government reimbursed the towns for their share from February 1, 1936.

As the Federal Government reimburses the town to the extent of 50% up to $30.00 per month and the State reimburses 2/3 of the remainder of the expenditure given, the recipient; the cost to the town should be very much less than at present although the annual appropriation will be more.

HARRY S. TORREY,
NORMAN S. WHITING,
JOHN J. BOWLER

The report of the Board of Public Welfare for the year
1936 is hereby submitted:

BUREAU OF OLD AGE ASSISTANCE

Town Physicians, services $ 250 00
Paid Other Towns, Relief   1 096 72
Administration:
  Norman S. Whiting, services   100 00
  Hobbs & Warren, supplies   2 86
    Total Expended $43 223 74
    Expended from Federal Funds 11 557 52

                               31 666 22
Appropriation   25 000 00

Over $ 6 666 22

Balance on hand Dec. 31, 1936 from
  Federal Allotment $ 1 993 39
Expended for Administration from Federal
  Funds $ 400 00
Balance on hand for Administration from
  Federal Fund $ 51 66

MOTHER'S AID

Expended under Chapter 118, General Laws.

Expended $ 5 172 94

INFIRMARY

Paid:—

Earl and Blanche Wyatt, salary $ 1 020 00
Annie Stewart, maid   490 00
Kate Kelly, maid   308 00

Harriet Martin, maid	30	00
Carolyn Geary, maid	49	00
Celia Derosie, services	14	00
A. Culver Co., feed	233	95
Edison Electric Ill. Co., lighting	134	55
New Eng. Tel. & Tel. Co., services	50	88
W. F. Barnes, fish	255	13
Carey's Home Bakery, bread	169	20
Harold Gelinas, butter	203	90
John F. Mahoney, butter	109	55
McIver's Home Bakery, bread	117	90
Alice Holbrook, supplies	7	00
A. S. Peterson, tobacco	319	68
Reformatory for Women, clothing	23	62
Commonwealth of Mass., supplies	95	80
Edison Electric Ill. Co., supplies	5	90
Rockland Water Dept., service	91	59
Rome Bros., supplies	19	98
E. L. Murrill, meats	280	77
Harold Capen, meats	273	49
McManus Box Co., sawdust	18	40
Hall & Torrey, supplies and repairs	92	80
J. A. Rice Co., supplies	40	77
Lot Phillips Co., slabs and sawdust	53	50
A. Culver Co., supplies	27	35
W. E. Trufant, supplies	29	95
Monument Mills, supplies	26	80
Rockland Hardware Co., supplies	31	49
N. H. Ranney, clothing	90	30
Warshaw's Market, provisions	263	20
Rockland Pharmacy, medicines	81	08
Herbert F. Gardner, provisions	118	37
A. Culver Co., coal	265	00
Ryan's Market, provisions	209	59
Annie Caplice, provisions	103	85
James G. Lamb, provisions	130	76
Geo. W. S. Hyde, shoeing	27	00
Roderick McKenzie, plowing	53	13

Boynes Service, repairs	18	00
Fred S. Delay, medicines	203	87
Antonio Fiaschetti, provisions	79	60
New Eng. Cedar Bedding Co., sawdust	1	30
Charles V. Blanchard, killing hogs	7	00
Burrell & DeLory, shoes	14	15
O. R. Cummings, repairs	43	10
Roland S. Poole, glasses	13	50
Rockland Standard, cards	1	50
Railway Express, express		59
Nemasket Trans. Co., express		50
Benjamin Ford, services	4	00
G. Lioy, rep. shoes	13	50
William Tracey, supplies	104	81
M. Y. Clement, meats	400	31
Elbert Chamberlin, supplies	84	88
Harry Rome, supplies	50	79
Handschumacker & Co., supplies	8	20
Rockland Coal & Grain, supplies	37	80
Mrs. Charles E. Gifford, clothing	6	00
Old Colony Appliance Corp., repairs	4	50
John H. Lamb, supplies	157	33
Rockland Coal & Grain, coal	420	70
William Sanborn. supplies	2	25
Market St. Grocery, provisions	105	06
John F. Donovan, 2 pigs	11	00
Hatherly Market, supplies	62	64
I. Rome, clothing	12	00
H. I. Stickney, sharpening mower	1	50
A. Tedeschi, supplies	156	39
Dennis L. O'Connor, shoes	3	50
Everett C. Ford, 55 chicks	8	25
W. H. Clayton, shoeing horse	3	00
Forrest L. Partch, repairs	2	85
Sunbeam Gardens, plants	1	00
Howland Ins. Co., insurance	43	65
Joseph Thibeault, repairing mower	3	50
John A. Lamb, provisions	180	79

Fred M. Blanchard, horse collar	2 00
Arthur G. Wills, papering	6 35
The Leonard Co., repairs	4 24
A. J. Vargus, supplies	1 50
John J. Dwyer, transportation	2 00
Emil Kelstrand, rep. shoes	5 25
Dr. Benjamin Lelyveld, medical	12 00
Damon Electric, repairs	7 31
Geo. Tyler, cesspool	12 00
W. H. Deal, plants	3 00
Wainshilbaum Bros., repairs	4 78

Total $ 8 301 07

EXPENSES OF OUTSIDE POOR

Hospitals :-

Brockton Hospital	$ 1 327 00
N. E. Deaconess Hospital	43 50
Holbrook Hospital	21 42
Moore Hospital	91 00
Weymouth Hospital	248 09
Pondville Hospital	207 50
Mass. Eye and Ear Inf.	67 20
Goddard Hospital	508 05
Childrens Hospital	74 50
Mass. General Hospital	108 48

Total $ 2 696 74

Administration :-

Harriet Anderson	$ 644 00
Becker & Co.	5 25
John J. D'wyer, commodity transportation	97 00
John J. Dwyer, trans. to hospital	27 00
John J. Dwyer, trans. to C.C.C. Boys	8 00
Yawman & Erbe, supplies	38 64

Yawman & Erbe, filing cabinet	37 83	
First National Stores, bags	4 16	
Hobbs & Warren, supplies	23 28	
N. E. Tel. & Tel. Co., service	3 63	
Harry S. Torrey, paid C.C.C. Boys Exp.	8 50	
A. L. Dixon, rep. typewriter	3 50	
Hall & Torrey Co., supplies	5 15	
A. I. Randall, Inc., printing	18 45	
U. S. Post Office, postage	3 00	
Total		$ 927 39
Town Physicians		350 00
Paid Other Towns		1 786 76
Cash	$ 21 833 90	
Provisions	6 530 21	
Fuel	1 766 25	
Rent	4 790 00	
Medical	2 210 13	
Clothing	216 44	
Burials	655 00	
Boarded	1 275 00	
Miscellaneous	131 95	
		$39 408 88
Total		$53 470 84 ·

SUMMARY OF BOARD OF PUBLIC WELFARE

Expended in Infirmary	$ 8 301 07
Expended Mother's Aid	5 172 94
Expended Outside Poor	45 169 77
Total	$58 643 78

Expended on Public Welfare, Mother's
   Aid and Infirmary $58 643 78

Appropriation   56 000 00

Over $ 2 643 78

CREDITS

Received from State, Old Age Assistance	$ 16 817 98
Received from other Towns,	
Old Age Assistance	1 694 63
Received from State, Mother's Aid	2 922 14
Received from Other Towns, Mother's Aid	130 58
Received from State, Temporary Aid	1 086 06
Received from Other Towns, Temporary Aid	3 916 34
Received from persons, Temporary Aid	45 80
Received from Board at Infirmary	2 527 10
Received from Sick State Poor	78 80
Total	$ 29 219 43

Due from Other Towns for Board	
At Infirmary	$ 1 772 00
Due from State, Temporary Aid	10 377 32
Due from Other Towns Temporary Aid	6 057 64
Due from State, Mother's Aid	4 613 27
Due from Other Towns, Mother's Aid	181 34
Due from State, Old Age Assistance	7 620 00
Due from Other Towns, Old Age Assistance	898 34
	$ 31 519 91

Signed,

HARRY S. TORREY,
NORMAN S. WHITING,
JOHN J. BOWLER,

Board of Public Welfare and
Bureau of Old Age Assistance

ESTIMATES OF APPROPRIATIONS FOR THE
YEAR 1937 BY HEADS OF THE DIFFERENT
DEPARTMENTS AND AMOUNTS RAISED IN 1936

	Raised 1936	Est. 1937
School Department	$102 673 00	$111 640 00
State Aid	900 00	800 00
Soldier's Relief	8 000 00	8 000 00
Military Aid	50 00	50 00
Care of Soldiers' Graves	150 00	150 00
Burial Indigent Soldiers	100 00	100 00
Soldiers' Memorial Library and Dog Fund	3 832 68	4 200 00
Street Lighting	8 810 00	9 234 00
Highway Surveyor	1 350 00	1 500 00
Tarvia & Road Binder	6 000 00	8 000 00
Highway Repair	7 000 00	7 000 00
Sidewalks	1 000 00	1 000 00
Cleaning Union Street	1 100 00.	1 100 00
Clean Up Week	100 00	100 00
Guide Boards and Signs	100 00	150 00
Fire Department	10 400 00	10 800 00
Police Department	8 846 00	9 668 00.
Forest Fires	700 00	700 00
Board of Health	6 000 00	6 000 00
Inspecting Animals and Stables	100 00	150 00
Parks	1 851 00	3 115 20
Old Age Assistance	25 000 00	35 000 00
Moth	300 00	300 00
Tree Warden	500 00	500 00
Office Rent	1 160 00	1 240 00
Town Officers	6 600 00	7 360 00
Sealer Weights & Measures	400 00	400 00
Elections	1 500 00	850 00
Compensation Insurance	2 250 00	2 250 00
Mass. Hospital School	800 00	500 00

Mass. Industrial School	1 600 00	3 500 00
Town Report & Poll Book		
($756.40 and $353.75)	700 00	1 200 00
Support Outside Poor		
and Infirmary	50 000 00	50 000 00
Mothers' Aid	6 000 00	8 000 00
Town Notes and Interest	26 000 00	28 000 00
Assessors `	2 500 00	2 750 00
Snow Removal	23 500 00	10 000 00
Reserve Fund	1 000 00	5 000 00
Misc. Assessors	850 00	1 100 00
Misc. Treasurer	500 00	800 00
Misc. Clerk	350 00	350 00
Misc. Selectmen ·	120 00	200 00
Misc. Collector	1 275 00	1 400 00
Misc. Registrars ·	200 00	100 00
Misc. Sealer	105 00	175 00
Misc. Unclassified	1 150 00	2 000 00

REBUILDING OF UNION STREET

The rebuilding of Union Street is of sufficient importance for the Selectmen to give a brief outline of the work accomplished on our main thoroughfare.

The rebuilding was made possible through the co-operation of the Federal Government granting to the town, through a Public Works Administration project, a 45% grant to the town up to the estimated cost of $63,500.00 or a grant of $28,575.00.

The original project called for widening the street two feet on the east side from North Avenue to Union Square and two feet on the west side from Pacific Street to Union Square. It also called for rebuilding the road bed; laying a larger size water main from Exchange Street to North Ave.; installing new hydrants of an improved type, in the business district; new service connections, to connect with water mains; laying of drainage, with suitable catch basins for the entire length of construction.

Before starting the work the J. R. Worcester Co. of Milk Street, Boston was engaged to have charge of the engineering part of the work. Bradford Weston Inc. being the lowest bidder was awarded the contract for rebuilding.

The road was constructed with a twelve inch gravel foundation with stone and bituminous concrete for the road surface, making a durable and easy riding surface, and one that can be easily repaired when necessity requires.

The Old Colony Gas Co. also laid a new gas main the entire length of the construction and the New England Telephone Co. extended their underground service over part of the work.

As the work neared completion we realized there were

ample funds to extend the scope of the project. At a special town meeting, the town voted to proceed with the same type of construction from Union Square to Market Street, provided the Public Works Administration would contribute its share of the funds. This contribution we were able to obtain.

The road was rebuilt full width from Union Square to Market Street with some additions of granite curbing and replacing concrete sidewalk near Union Square. New services connecting with water mains were put in. Other improvements consisted of widening the corner at Market Street, and building a quarter round bituminous curb on the edge of the street, and when advisable, loaming and seeding the shoulders between street and sidewalk.

An immense amount of time and effort was spent in completing the details, to further this project, and the Board of Selectmen feel that the town has been greatly improved. The entrance from the side streets to Union Street is one of the outstanding accomplishments.

At this time the Board wishes to thank, besides the Federal Government, Mr. Thomas Worcester, of the J. R. Worcester Co. consulting engineers; Messrs. Turner, Ransom and Baxter, who were field engineers; Mr. Lowney, who was inspector of the work from the W. P. A. office; Mr. Bradford Weston and his foreman Fred Strother, who had charge of the building of the road; for their fullest cooperation at all times in the rebuilding of Union Street.

Signed,

HARRY S. TORREY,
JOHN J. BOWLER,
NORMAN S. WHITING

List of Jurors

As prepared by the Selectmen of the Town of Rockland
Under General Laws of Massachusetts, Acts of 1921, Chapter 234, Section 4.

Rockland Mass., July 1, 1936

Name Street and Number	Occupation
Altsman, Harry J., 849 Union	Poultry Man
Ames, Stanley, 34 Prospect	Engineer
Bacon, Paul, 48 Williams	Salesman
Baxter, Charles L., 487 Market	Civil Engineer
Beals, Ashley, 44 George	Carpenter
Bell, William, 558 Liberty	Truck Driver
Bowler, John J., 99 Hingham	Manager
Bowser, James, 62 Concord	Carpenter
Brassill, Francis J., 99 North Ave.	Barber
Briggs, George E., 139 Exchange	Machinist
Burns, James L., 159 Union	Shoe Operative
Burrell, H. Chester, 340 Liberty	Shoe Operative
Capelice, James H., 108 Howard	Shoe Operative
Chandler, Russell, 1138 Union	Shoe Operative
Coffey, Dennis F., 134 Liberty	Flagman
Crowley, Timothy J., 58 Park	Shoe Operative
Daley, Daniel J., 42 Plain	Shoe Operative
Damon, Archer W., 43 Munroe	Shoe Operative
Damon, Frank W., 50 Reed	Electrician
DeLory, Bernard, 54 Stanton	Clerk
Dill, Percey E., 136 North Avenue	Shoe Operative
Dillon, John, 989 Union	Agent
Dondero, Joseph, 412 Webster	Shoe Operative
Donovan, Daniel H., 117 Liberty	Machinist
Dyer, Bertrand A., 329 North Ave.	Shoe Repairer
Eaniri, Gerald, 22 Pacific	Shoe Operative

Easton, Carrol, 858 Union .... Salesman
Ednie, John, 520 Market .... Painter
Estes, Joseph B., 305 Liberty .... Town Assessor
Fass, Carl G., 377 North Ave. .... Draftsman
Fearing, Charles L., 436 East Water .... Mechanic
Fihelly, Harold, 206 Vernon .... Insurance Agent
Fitzgerald, Thomas F., 51 North Ave. .... Shoe Operative
Flavell, Paul I., 193 Crescent .... Draftsman
Gammon, Frank L., 135 Union .... Manager
Garrity, Peter, 162 North Ave. .... Janitor
Gelinas, George O., 99 Exchange .... Asst. Manager
Harney, Edmund F., 66 Church .... Shoe Operative
Higgins, Thomas S., 32 Belmont .... Laborer
Hobart, Albert C., 57 School .... Civil Engineer
Holmes, Harry O., 248 Central .... Meter Reader
Hunt, Lester A., 224 Myrtle .... Shoe Operative
Inglis, Wilbur T., 66 Prospect .... Boxmaker
Jacobs, S. Percy, 137 East Water .... Clerk
Johnson, Clarence B., 266 Plain .... Teamster
Kelley, Arthur B., 40 North Ave. .... Clerk
Kelsey, Carl, 173 Crescent .... Shoe Operative
Kramer, Charles F., 39 Grove .... Shoe Operative
Lambert, Arthur J., 17 Custer .... Shoe Operative
Lelyveld, Benjamin, 129 Pacific .... Podiatrist
Lewis, Willard A., 69 Hartsuff .... Shoe Operative
Locke, Louis F., 30 Reed .... Webbing
Loud, Fred, 28 Myrtle .... Bookkeeper
Lovell, Jasper, 4 Maple .... Box Cutter
Mahon, Thomas, 31 Summit .... Janitor
Mahoney, Patrick H., 35 Cary Court .... Teamster
Marks, Austin, 477 Webster .... Farmer
Mastrodomenico, Joseph, 355 Union .... Sheo Operative
McCarthy, Michael J., 22 School .... Shoe Operative
McKeever, James, 199 Webster .... Clerk
McVein, Ralph, 142 Concord .... Clerk
McKim, George, 570 Webster .... Tinsmith
Meade, Joseph, 203 North Ave. .... Shoe Operative
Mullen, Daniel J., 1126 Union .... Clerk

Muti, Louis, 317 North Ave. .... Shoe Operative
Phillips, Roland P., 196 East Water .... Manager
O'Grady, Matthew, 108 Belmont .... Laboror
O'Hayre, Bernard F., 278 Reed .... Shoe Operative
Orr, Charles E., 67 Stanton .... Salesman
Partch, Forest L., 57 Taunton Ave. .... Electrician
Patterson, Henry E. L., 889 Union .... Florist
Poole, Norman C., 580 W. Water .... Halesman
Ransom, Roger T., 31 Hartsuff ....Engineer
Reardon, Thomas, 101 Summit .... Clerk
Richards, Theodore, 104 Reed .... Shoe Operative
Ryan, Patrick C., 122 Myrtle .... Shoe Operative
Shanahan, James, 83 Pacific .... Real Estate
Sheehan, Maurice, 101 Prospect .... Shoe Operative
Shields, Charles T., 42 Franklin Ave. .... Shoe Operative
Shurtliff, Alton E., 40 East Water .... Retired
Smith, Bartholomew J., 35 Stanton ......Shoe Operative
Sylvia, John E., 76 Albion .... Cigar Maker
Thompson, Earl F., 273 Howard .... Manager
Umbrianna, Michael, 35 Salem .... Shoe Operative
Vargus, Antone J., 215 Crescent .... Auto Supplies
Wallace, Earl, 231 Myrtle .... Truck Driver
Whiting, W. Alton. 455 Webster ...... Shoe Operative

HARRY S. TORREY,
NORMAN S. WHITING,
JOHN J. BOWLER,

Selectmen of Rockland

Works Progress Administration

To the Board of Selectmen:

For the first time the Federal Emergency Relief Administration has gone through a complete calendar year under one alphabetical designation—the W. P. A.

In the Town of Rockland during the fiscal year 1936 activities have progressed upon a predetermined plan and all the special projects voted in town meeting have been completed with the exception of repairing Division Street. For some unknown reason the W. P. A. powers that be, refrained from granting the project during the year. However, presidential approval has now been received upon the project and work should start upon Division Street as soon as the man quota is available.

Other projects not started but which have received presidential approval include Extension of Rice Ave., Rebuilding of Douglas Street, Rebuilding of Plain St., from Reed St., to North Ave., Extension of Water Mains on Carey Court, Installing Water Holes, Development of Cushing's Pond, Federal Department of Commerce Approved Airway Marker, Tennis Courts in Memorial Park, Relocating Water Gate Boxes and Installing 7,000 lineal feet of Cement Curb and Sidewalks. Additional project proposals have been forwarded through proper channels upon which presidential approval is expected and which cover a wide range of subjects.

Projects in operation, approved and applied for, should be sufficient to keep three times as many at work as the present man quota will permit up to June 30th which date terminates the Emergency Act unless Congress votes an extention or new plans.

At the beginning of the municipal fiscal year there were 254 local people upon the W. P. A. pay roll and at the close of the year this number had been reduced to 178. This curtailment of quota is nation wide and the Fall River district office is continuing individual investigation and ordering further curtailments. It is assumed that a definite program and man quota will be established very soon. There has been in operation during the municipal year twenty-nine different direct Town of Rockland projects. Upon these projects Federal paid labor totaling $195,058.05 has been paid. For the operation of these projects, the Town has expended $26,480.92 for materials, truck hire, administration, etc. This is approximately 13 per cent of the Federal expenditure.

In addition to the foregoing a number of Rockland persons have been at work upon State supervised projects which include Traffic Research, Auto Census, Pre-School Unit, National Youth Administration, Commodity Distribution and Market Street Sidewalks. Market Street Sidewalks was taken over from the State Bond Issue the middle of September and gave employment to approximately 100 persons. A fair estimate for Federal labor expenditure on state projects would exceed $30,000 which added to the local project expenditure would make a total of Federal labor expended in Rockland during 1936 of over $225,000.

Under the Rockland sidewalk project, nine thousand, three hundred and seven running feet of cement curbing has been installed.

Four thousand four hundred and twenty-seven feet has bituminous top, one thousand one hundred feet has one coat of bituminous and three thousand seven hundred and eighty has gravel top. On account of lack of available local funds it was considered advisable to place the concrete curbing without the black top and keep the men employed which was the intent of the W. P. A.

\ A tabulation of Federal and local expenditures in Rockland by projects follows:

Rockland Projects

	Amount Paid Federal Labor	Town Paid For Materials etc.
*Sewing Unit	$43 678 82	$ 64 52
Assessors' Map	16 639 02	868 42
Painting Caution & Parking Lines	201 45	60 20
Wild Cherry Tree Removal	1 740 00	4 10
Locating Street Bounds	5 296 78	12 25
Removing Dead Trees	5 197 00	
Clean Open Drains	2 618 00	
Gravel Walks Reed Park	5 848 50	
Athletic Field Memoral Park	19 106 46	6 406 02
*Gravel Walks Memorial Park	7 953 66	
Stanton Street Extension	2 846 28	258 08
*Household Aides	3 393 16	122 77
Rebuild Plain Street	6 921 20	1 232 11
Rebuild Wilson, Colby Curry Streets	4 896 00	654 68
Webster and Liberty Street Sidewalks	3 268 40	194 66
Paint High School Rooms	6 569 20	334 86
Water Main Salem St.	4 358 08	3 547 70
Cut and Trim Shade Trees	2 037 00	12 07
Covered Drain Liberty and Stanton Street	2 014 28	649 90
Covered Drains, Payson and Rice Ave. and Grove St.	2 458 35	220 60
*Assessors' Index	250 16	
Dry Hydrant, Accord Pond	897 19	44 01
*Permanent Sidewalks	14 353 22	2 790 16
*Reed's Pond Development	17 391 61	1 039 22
*Forest St. Water Mains	5 294 43	3 281 31
*Public Recreation	2 672 28	71 51
*Paint High School Halls	2 192 69	890 16

*Covered Drains, Liberty St.
   at Custer St.   1 692 09   217 09
*Grantee-Grantor Index   1 825 23

   * Project in operation at close of municipal year.

               Respectfully submitted,

                           FRED M. RYAN,

                           Local Coordinator

Highway Surveyor's Report

To the Honorable Board of Selectmen:

I wish to report that all of the work covered by the various highway appropriations for the year 1936 has been completed.

This included sidewalks on Church Street, Liberty Street, Crescent Street, Howard Street, Plain Street, West Water Street, and Rice Avenue. New sidewalks were also built on Bigelow Avenue, and on Myrtle Street, between Exchange Street and Bigelow Avenue.

A section of East Water Street, between John Lamb's store and the Rice and Hutchins factory was rebuilt under Chapter 90 in co-operation with the State and County.

New drains were put in on Liberty Street, from East Water Street to Vernon Street, also on Plain Street from Payson Avenue to Market Street. A drain was put in also on East Water Street from Everett Street to Cushing's Pond, and one on Rice Avenue.

New curbing was built on Liberty Street from Market Street to Vernon Street and on Webster Street from East Water Street to the Hanover line.

Respectfully submitted,

RODERICK MacKENZIE,

Highway Surveyor

Sealer of Weights and Measures

To the Honorable Board of Selectmen:

Gentlemen:

I have, with my standards, weights and measures, tested and sealed all weighing and measuring devices which I have jurisdiction over, also several scales for private use.

Inspections and weighing of merchandise which is put up for sale and delivery were also made, also all gas meters were retested. The inspection and resealing of these measuring devices is an important item after sealing.

Frequently, inspection of all stores in town that have measuring devices are made. Computing scales need attention as in many cases they are found to be incorrect. Peddlars increase yearly and I make sure all have proper licenses. The town receives the fund from these licenses.

The oil meters on oil trucks are another item which have to be checked more carefully on account of the increasing sale of oil. At this time I am asking for an appropriation of seventy dollars ($70.00) for the purchase of a fifty gallon test can.

The duties of a Sealer of Weights and measures increase yearly and I am on call at all times. My duties are under State and Town regulations.

Below is an itemized account of the work I have performed for 1936.

	Adjusted	Sealed	Not Sealed	Condemned
Platform over 5,000 lbs	1	4		
Platform under 100 to 5,000 lbs.	10	39		
Counter 100 lbs. or over		2		
Counter under 100 lbs.	3	38		
Beam over 100 lbs.			1	
Beam under 100 lbs.		2	1	
Spring over 100 lbs.	2	8	2	
Spring Under 100 lbs.	19	62		
Computing under 100 lbs.	13	56	2	
Personal Weighing		8		
Prescription		4		

WEIGHTS

	Adjusted	Sealed	Not Sealed	Condemned
Avoirdupois	6	323		2
Apothecary		55		
Metric		36		

CAPACITY MEASURES

	Adjusted	Sealed	Not Sealed	Condemned
Liquid		102		1
Dry		6		

AUTOMATIC MEASURING DEVICES

	Adjusted	Sealed	Not Sealed	Condemned
Oil Meters	1	6	3	
Gasoline Pumps		28	8	
Gasoline Meters	9	35	7	
Kerosine Pumps		14		
Oil Measuring Pumps		35	4	
Quantity Measure on Pumps	13	191		
Cloth Measuring devices		1		
Yard Sticks		38		

TOTAL UNITS SEALED

Total Units Sealed   1093
Weighing and measuring devices
   Adjusted   77
Weighing and measuring devices
   Condemned   4
Weighing and measuring devices
   Not Sealed   28
Sealing fees returned to Town Treasurer $108 55

REWEIGHING AND REMEASURING

Number Tested   291
Number Correct   213
Over Weight   58
Under Weight   20

Respectfully submitted,

HAROLD J. INKLEY

Park Commissioners' Report

Your Park Department expenditures under the regular appropriation amounted to $1,850.46, most of which was expended in Memorial Park for general upkeep, insurance repairs and supplies with labor receiving over eighty-five percent of the entire sum appropriated.

The Federal Government Project on the new major athletic field in Memorial Park on which work was suspended during the Spring was completed during the Summer and Fall with the exception of some final touching up and rolling of the running track, parking area and seeded ground.

The Federal Government Project at Major Reed Park was completed in the early Summer and we would encourage everyone to visit this beautiful area where an outdoor fireplace and drinking water is available for picnicers.

The Federal Government provided several recreational supervisors under the direction of Mr. Norman Crosby so that we were able to have an entire Summer of supervised play for children and adults. More boys played baseball then ever before and soft ball, a new game to Rockland, became popular among adults. It appears now that the project will continue throughout 1937.

Plans for all Federal projects in your Parks will be presented to the Finance Committee and to the town for their approval or rejection.

We are indebted to Mr. Christopher Murphy for the care of the area adjoining his home on Plain Street and to all men and women who have worked on the various Federal projects in our Parks.

> DANIEL H. BURKE,
> PATRICK H. MAHONEY,
> CHARLES T. WALLS

Report of Fire Department

To the Honorable Board of Selectmen:

Gentlemen:

I hereby submit my report as Chief of the Fire Department for the year 1936.

The Fire Department answered a total of 173 Alarms during the year, of which 114 were Still Alarms and 56 Bell Alarms, and 3 A. D. T. Calls; one to the Rockland Welt Co., and two to the E. T. Wright Co. We had 15 False Alarms, but the Alarms on July the 4th showed a decrease. 14 of the Alarms were taken care of by the Chief's Car.

The Department used 8250 feet of 2 1-2 inch hose; 1850 feet of 1 1-2 and 7800 feet of Chemical hose. Also 825 gallons of Soda and Acid, 4 quarts of Pyrene; 2 1-2 gallons of Foam; 10 packages of Chimney Compound, besides the Pump Cans which were used 222 times. The Light equipment was used for 8 1-2 hours.

Engine Co. No. 1 and the Chief's Car with the Light unit was sent to aid Brockton; and the Chief's Car with the Light unit was also sent to help Abington, also aid was sent to Hanover. Our Cellar Syphon was loaned to Northampton during the flood period. The Inhalator was used three times during the year. Twice in Hanover and once in Rockland. In two cases the person recovered but the third case was hopeless at the start.

FIRE ALARM SYSTEM

On account of rebuilding the road on Union Street the

Fire Alarm was rebuilt from Pool's Corner to Union Square. It was also necessary to rebuild or change over the larger part of the System on Market Street from Lane's Corner to Spring Street, and also on Center Avenue. This was caused by the building over of the sidewalks and the moving of the poles to the opposite side of the street.

Some of our Fire Alarm boxes have about outlived their usefullness and they should be replaced with new ones.

APPARATUS

As the Apparatus has not been inspected for some time I believe that it should be done although everything appears to be in good condition. The Triple Combination should be repainted this year and the tires on the Combination should be replaced with new ones on the front.

The new Relief Valve which was installed on the Pump is a great improvement over the old one.

RECOMMENDATIONS AND REMARKS

For the year 1937 I recommend an appropriation of $10,800.00 which includes a new boiler for the heating system, the painting of the Triple Combination and the restoration of pay cuts if approved by the town.

The appropriation of 1936 was overdrawn about $1,200.00 which is accounted for by the payroll of Call men of about $700.00 over the amount estimated, the rebuilding of Fire Alarm on Union and Market Street of $300.00; insurance of $55.00; Oxygen and Testing of Tanks of $75.00; all of which no allowance was made for in the 1936 appropriation.

We are still trying to maintain the Fire Department on a smaller appropriation than was allowed when the Town had only 85 fires instead of 170 as at present.

CONCLUSION

In concluding this report I wish to thank the Board of Selectmen, Board of Water Commissioners and their employees, also the Chief and members of the Police Department, for the help and co-operation given the Fire Department. I also wish to express my appreciation to the Officers and Members of the Fire Department and to all others who have assisted me in the performance of my duty as Chief of the Fire Department.

Respectfully submitted,

CLYSON P. INKLEY,

Chief Rockland Fire Department

REPORT OF FOREST FIRE WARDEN

To the Honorable Board of Selectmen:
Gentlemen:

I hereby submit my report as Forest Fire Warden for the year 1936.

This department answered 40 calls for Woods and Grass Fires during the year 1936, which was a decrease of 18 over the previous year.

None of the fires were of a serious nature and we were able to keep within the appropriation.

For the year 1937 I recommend an appropriation of $700.00.

Respectfully submitted,

CLYSON P. INKLEY,

Forest Fire Warden

Plymouth County Extension Service

To the Honorable Board of Selectmen:

During the last year Plymouth County spent $18,511. in assisting those engaged in various forms of Agriculture, the towns contributing a toal of $3,450.00 of this sum. Rockland's appropriation was $150.00.

As a clearing house for up to date knowledge of Agricultural production practice, The Plymouth County Extension service takes a prominent part in maintaining taxable and investment values in the land, buildings, stock and equipment used in the industry.

In addition to its standard program of Farm and home advice and assistance, including 4-H Club work with the boys and girls of the county, The Extension service handled the federal soil conservation and resettlement work here.

I believe we should continue to co-operate with the other towns of the county in maintaining and increasing the efficiency of this public service.

I recommend an appropriation of $150.00.

JAMES D. MAHONEY,

Town Director

Report of Infirmary

To the Honorable Board of Selectmen:
Gentlemen:

I wish to present to you a report of activities and improvements which have taken place during the year 1936.

We have taken care of thirty-six inmates during the entire year, five women and thirty-one men.

Two deaths have occurred, both being males. We have had six in the hospital room.

Repainted the women's hallway and bed rooms. Also grained the wood work.

Raised one hundred and twenty-five bushels of potatoes, raised squash, milk, eggs and other small vegetables.

Placed new curtains where needed.

Respectfully submitted,

EARL WYATT,

Supt. of Infirmary

Report of Inspector of Animals

To the Honorable Board of Selectmen:

Gentlemen:

I herewith submit my report as Inspector of Animals and Stables for the year ending December 31, 1936.

Number of Stables inspected	35
Number of Cows inspected	110
Number of Swine inspected	160
Number of Goats inspected	10
Number of visits made in Inspections	84
Number of Dogs quarantined	11
Number of Cows quarantined	9
Number of visits made to premises of quarantined animals	91
Number of animals sent to Divisions of Livestock Disease Control for Laboratory Test	

I recommend an appropriation of $150.00

Respectfully submitted,

WILLIAM T. CONDON,

Inspector of Animals and Stables

Report of Trustees of Memorial Library

The Trustees of the Memorial Library submit the following report for the year 1936.

Several improvements were made in the building. The floors were shellaced, the work being done by Mr. Holbrook. The waterpipes, which were worn out, were replaced by brass pipes at a cost of $72. As the stack room was never adequately heated, two additional radiators were installed. The expense was $114.25.

For nearly nineteen years, Mr. John A. Martin was janitor of the building. That his interest in the library never ceased, even after his retirement, was shown by a legacy of $100 to the library. This was deposited in the Rockland Savings Bank as a trust fund, the interest to be used, according to instructions, for the purchase of books.

Other gifts received were $5 from the Rockland Woman's Club and $6.55 from the Junior Mothers' Club. The Trustees are appreciative of these gifts and thank the donors.

Withdrawals of interest from the trust funds were:

Hattie Curtis Fund	$ 15 59
Alice L. French Fund	6 82
Zenas M. Lane Fund	14 14
Everett Lane Fund	4 50
Mary A. Spence Fund	15 44
Sarah J. Spence Fund	8 91
John W. Rice Fund	1 00

Charles Edwin Vinal Fund   29 01
Mothers' Mutual Improvement Society Fund   1 32

                                                 $ 96 73

The Trustees take pleasure in testifying to the interested
and capable service rendered by the librarian and her assistants, and by the janitor in the care of the building and
grounds. For information regarding the circulation of
books and magazines, exhibits, and special service, the citizens are referred to Mrs. Clark's report which follows this
one.

Owing to the decrease in the dog refund from $593.61 to
$447.34, the Trustees advise for 1937 besides the dog refund
an appropriation of $4200.

The terms of Francis J. Geogan and Emma W. Gleason
expire in 1937.

FRANCIS J. GEOGAN,
JOHN B. FITZGERALD,
BURTON L. CUSHING,
ANNIE E. McILVENE,
EMILY F. CRAWFORD,
EMMA W. GLEASON,
                                                 Trustees

Librarian's Report

To the Trustees of the Rockland Memorial Library:

The fifty-eighth report of this library is herewith submitted.

A total of 58,907 books and magazines have been loaned for home use.

The average monthly circulation, 4,909. The average daily circulation, 200. Largest number delivered in one day, 431. Smallest number delivered in one day, 75.

Received for fines, reserved books, subscriptions from non-residents, sale of cook books, old magazines and books, $303.00.

Number of books added by purchase (including replacements), 384. Number of books presented, 39. Number of books worn out and missing, 142. Number of books rebound 141. Number of books in library on December 31, 1936, 20,278.

Character of books loaned: literature, 4 per cent; history and travel, 4 per cent; biography, 3 per cent; miscellaneous (adult), 5 per cent; fiction (adult), 53 per cent; fiction (juvenile) 13 per cent; miscellaneous (juvenile) 6 per cent; magazines, 12 per cent.

Our town reflects the present economic conditions, more work, less time for the companionship of books. It is a normal reaction, and all public libraries have been losing in circulation as the world began to recover from the depression. The largest increase in the use of books has always come during the years when business activities have been lowest. Another factor, no doubt, for changed statistics, is the place the commercial rental library has come to play in the community.

However, a brief analysis of the figues of our circulation shows interesting growth in the case of certain classes of books, and these figures are very useful in directing where the emphasis should be placed in book buying in general.

The library cannot begin to supply the demand for the latest technical books, nor the latest discoveries in science, business, the theatre, or even government.

We note an increase in quiet recreational and serious reading with a more critical attitude in the choice of material. The demand is marked for books about public issues and public personalities, for new social and industrial ideas, and for opinions of the leading minds of the day. There is a noticeable increase in the use of reserved books and of the magazine collection.

Workers in various projects consulted the children's books for ideas, and reference books are continually in use by high school and college students, with an increasing indication of adult use, stimulated by adult activities.

Parents and teachers are aided in selecting educational and recreational reading and we have done our best in suggesting the "next best" when the book called for is not available. When this proves unsatisfactory we refer the patrons to larger libraries, or make use of the inter-library Loan System, and borrow from the Boston Public Library and the Massachusetts Division of Public Libraries.

Classroom libraries are still sent to our graded schools, upon request, and early in the year books that were considered hard to read were sent to the High school where they were introduced to the students through their English instructor.

A new and revised certificate list has been compiled and circulated by the Division of Public Libraries. This reading for certificate has been revived somewhat this year and is active in the lower grades. It is a great step towards making better citizens when we get children to read more and better books. The broader the interest of an individual, the better he fits into society. Books that have been most successfully filmed are most frequently asked for in the children's room.

More books were rebound by commercial binders this year, and the staff has given "first aid" treatment to a larger number than usual.

Many minor exhibits have proved attractive to our public, and seasonable books were displayed, in connection with these exhibits.

Many gifts have been of real practical help in providing reading matter at a time when funds have been somewhat decreased and demands often increased. Special mention should be made of the generous gifts of money from the Rockland Woman's Club and the Mothers' Club of Rockland.

The improvement in the radiation of heat from the newly installed radiators in the stack room is greatly appreciated. The amount expended is offset by comfort and enjoyment.

Upon request from the C. C. C. Camp at Fort Ethan Allen, Vermont, where many Rockland young men are stationed, popular books of fiction were collected and sent to them. A very gratifying letter of appreciation was received in return and an earnest hope that more books might be forwarded later, as the need is great where so many are congregated.

Our thanks are extended to the editor of the local paper and the correspondent for the Brockton paper for their courtesies.

The achievement of the staff deserves hearty thanks, and the librarian takes pleasure in acknowledging constant support of the Trustees.

Our hope is to gain friends for the library each year. Through the willingness to give ever increasing service, may we build up a capital of good will.

There remains much to anticipate and to accomplish.

Respectfully submitted,

LIDA A. CLARK,

Librarian

Assessors' Report 1936

The Assessors have assessed the sum of $338.969.75 upon the Polls and Property subject to taxation in the Town of Rockland and have committed said sum to the Collector for collection.

Number polls assessed		2585
Value real estate assessed	$5 725 669 00	
Value land assessed	1 542 980 00	

Total values real estate including land $7 268 649 00

VALUE PERSONAL PROPERTY

Value of stock in trade	$177 140 00
Value of live stock	13 800 00
Value of machinery	205 895 00
Value of all other personal	425 158 00

Total value tangible personal property $ 821 993 00

Total valuation real and personal property 8 090 642 00

Town appropriations	$510 314 38
County Tax	14 871 58
State Tax	13 100 00
State Parks & Reservations	143 51
Water Department (used in Estimated receipts)	32 000 00
Overlay	· 9 334 54

$579 764 01

ESTIMATED RECEIPTS

Income Tax	$ 21	240	60
Corporation Tax	7	013	98
Race Track Distribution		524	00
Motor Vehicle Excise	8	925	09
Licenses		680	00
Fines		1	75
Federal Grant Rebuilding			
Union Street	28	500	00
Notes or Bonds Rebuilding			
Union Street	35	000	00
Water Tank Federal Grant	30	000	00
Notes or Bonds Water Tank	40	000	00
General Government		358	88
State Aid		920	00
Health and Sanitation	1	129	27
Beverage Licenses	4	565	08
Charities	18	571	77
Old Age Assistance	10	833	20
Soldiers Benefits		247	03
Schools	1	311	08
Libraries		298	00
Vocational Training		644	66
Water Department	32	000	00
Refund Dog Damages		105	00
Interest	9	609	92
Tax Costs		215	60
Transfer from repairs on			
Library Roof		698	50
Poll Tax	5	170	00

Total Estimated Receipts	$258 563	41

Total amount to be raised on property	$321 200	60
Tax rate per thousand	39	70
Number of automobiles assessed		2197
Value of automobiles	$472 985	00

Number of persons, partnerships and
corporations assessed for real estate   1905
Number on personal estate   310
Number of dwellings   1872
Number of cows   - 85
Number of Horses   19
Number of swine   63
Number of fowl   6050
Value of fowl $6 470 00
Number of acres   5704

AMOUNTS COMMITTED TO COLLECTOR

Real and Personal $321 200 60
Poll Taxes   5 170 00
Excise Tax   12 513 36
December assessment on Polls   58 00
December assessment on property   27 79
                                   _____

    Total $338 969 75

            Respectfully submitted,
                    NORMAN J. BEALS,
                    JOSEPH B. ESTES,
                    DENNIS L. O'CONNOR

Report of Chief of Police

Honorable Board of Selectmen,
Town of Rockland,
Gentlemen :—

I herewith submit my report for the Police Department
of the Town of Rockland for the year ending December
31, 1936.

NUMBER OF ARRESTS

Year 1936 213

	Male	Female	Total
Assault and Battery	12	3	15
Adultery	1	0	1
Bastardy	2	0	2
Breaking and entering	7	0	7
Concealing leased property	1	0	1
Circulating False Alarm of fire	2	0	2
Capias	2	0	2
Disturbance	0	1	1
Drunkenness	115	1	116
Fish and Game Law violation	1	0	1
Indecent exposure	1	0	1
Insane persons	5	1	6
Larceny	11	0	11
Lewdness	2	0	2
Motor Vehicle violations	28	0	28
Manslaughter	1	0	1
Non-Support	15	0	15
National Motor Vehicle Theft Act	1	0	1
Trespassing	1	0	1
Totals	207	6	213

Males 207

Females 6
Total 213

MISCELLANEOUS

Automobile thefts investigated 10
Automobiles recovered 14
Auto Accidents investigated 54
Complaints investigated 584
Miles traveled by Police Cruiser 12,994
Persons reported missing 8
Persons located out of town and local 12
Number of arrests for out of town police 10
Red light calls answered 312
Store doors found unlocked 28
Summones served for out of town Depts. 42
Telegrams (emergencies) persons notified 18

Last April the Police Dept. purchased a new Cruising Car, radio equipped; and since then this department has been able to receive latest police items transmitted by the Mass. State Police. This department also has a radio at the police station and is tuned to the same frequency which affords service when the cruising car is on patrol. This department wishes to acknowledge our gratitude to the State Police for their services the past year. This addition to this department has added increased efficiency; and has enabled the patroling of the entire Town with immediate contact of a police officer. This service was made possible by the co-operation of the local telephone exchange, whom we wish to thank for their assistance.

Correction is hereby acknowledged from the report of this department relative to "No fatal accident" during 1935. This paragraph was unintentionally misstated in my report and was an oversight which I regret. For the year 1936 three (3) fatal accidents occurred; all persons responsible were summoned to Court and a conviction was made in one case, the other two were adjudged unavoidable.

Crimes in the Town of Rockland for the year 1936 were of a minor nature, and most of the complaints were disposed. As stated in previous Town report issues of this department, all emergency calls can be answered by requesting the local telephone operator to "put on the red light" which is a signal to the officer or officers on patrol and the call will be answered immediately. I make mention of this fact here, as I know that many citizens are not conversant of this system. This department urges the citizens to take advantage of this system especially during the night and early morning hours; this system has been in force many years and has proven very satisfactory, together with the innovation of radio in the police cruiser.

Widening of Union Street has added consirerable space beween rear of parked cars which is used as the traveled way and it is expected that painted parking spaces will be available after the weather permits. Complaints of excessive speed on Union St., was considered and has been greatly curtailed.

Request that Rockland citizens who operate motor vehicles comply with traffic regulations such as; unreasonable rate of speed; double parking; parking in driveways; and parking at proper angle, by strict obedience of these regulations this department believes would be setting a splendid example to visiting motorists.

Again I take pleasure in giving the thanks of the entire department to Town and County officials and to the many other citizens who have given valuable assistance when given the opportunity. As Chief of the department I am appreciative of the fine work of the regular and special officers, all of whom have labored to give the finest service.

Respectfully submitted,
GEORGE J. POPP,
Chief of Police

Board of Health Report

The Board of Health herewith submits its annual report for 1936.

Number of cases of Scarlet Fever reported	11
Number of cases Lobar Pnuemonia	13
Number of cases Cerebral Spinal Meningitis	1
Tuberculosis	3
Chicken Pox	6
Whooping Cough	12
Measles	14'
Dog Bites	6

There is nothing remarkable to report in regard to the health of the town.

Many complaints of people dumping waste and rubbish any place except on their own premises are received.

Dumping old autos, especially on Salem Street is very Common. If the people of the town wish to go on, they must report such incidents to the Board of Health.

JOSEPH H. DUNN,
M. J. FITZGIBBONS,
JOSEPH FRAME,

Board of Health

Report of Tree Warden

To the Board of Selectmen:

There was a considerable amount of work done on the trees of the town and those overhanging the road.

Most of this work was through labor supplied by the W. P. A.

The elm trees were sprayed for the elm leaf beetle to some extent, but more was needed. These trees should be sprayed at least twice, to keep them under control.

Owing to storms with a high wind velocity, several trees were blown over, and others were badly damaged.

For the coming year, I recommend an appropriation of $1000.

Respectfully submitted,

ALFRED T. METIVIER

Tree Warden

Report of Gypsy Moth Superintendent

To the Board of Selectmen:

The most infested area of the town was canvassed for Gypsy Moth and Brown Tail Moth.

The Gypsy Moth infestation has started to spread throughout the town the last few years and should be checked before it gets out of control. A larger amount should be appropriated for this work.

I recommend an appropriation of $500.

Respectfully submitted,

ALFRED T. METIVIER

Gypsy Moth Supt.

In Memoriam

Olive H. Crawford

Born, September 20, 1859 - Died, August 6, 1936

Member of
Board of Registrars of Voters
Town of Rockland
1924 - 1936

Collector of Taxes

Taxes of 1934

Outstanding January 1, 1936	$ 67 329 62
Collected during year	˙66 536 81
Outstanding January 1, 1937	792 81

1934 Motor Vehicle Excise

Outstanding January 1, 1936	$ 2 037 97
Collected during year	. 1 967 62
Ontstanding January 1, 1937	70 35

Taxes of 1935

Outstanding January 1, 1936	$132 431 29
Collected during year.	61 764 82
Outstanding January 1, 1937	70 666 47

1935 Motor Vehicle Excise

Outstanding January 1, 1936	$ 4 182 72
Collected during year	2 378 04
Outstanding January 1, 1937	1 804 68

Taxes of 1936

˙ Amount committed to Collector	$326 456 39
Collected during year	202 527 48
Outstanding January 1, 1937	$123 928 91

1936 Motor Vehicle Excise

Amount committed to Collector	$ 12 513 36
Collected during year	7 396 82
Outstanding January 1, 1937	$ 5 116 54

JAMES A. DONOVAN,

Collector of Taxes

Report of Town Treasurer

TREASURER'S REPORT OF THE RECEIPTS AND
DISBURSEMENTS FOR THE YEAR ENDING
DECEMBER 31, 1936

January 1, 1936, Cash on hand $ 47 229 13

RECEIPTS

Anticipation Tax Notes	$225 000 00	
Taxes—Real Estate, Poll, Old		
Age, Personal	306 293 30	
Taxes, Excise	9 632 39	
Interest on Taxes	8 999 36	
Tax Titles Redeemed	6 318 21	
Tax, Costs	137 60	
Liquor Licenses	4 310 00	
Licenses, Miscellaneous	673 00	
Trust Funds	1 479 33	
Dog Licenses	545 00	
Water Department Receipts	28 146 98	
Joint Water Dept. Receipts	8 282 06	
Memorial Library	303 00	
City of Boston, Tuition	419 40	
Unearned Comp. Ins. Premium	516 13	
A. Culver Co., Reeds Pond	50 00	
		$601 105 76
		$648 334 89
Sealer of Weights	109 35	
Court Fines	126 00	
		235 35

Miscellaneous Receipts
Board of Health 294 52
School Department 99 40
Sale Materials 136 48

530 40

County Treasurer
Dog Dividend 593 61
E. Water St. Construction 3 121 26

3 714 87

Welfare and Old Age Assistance Refunds
Other Towns and Cities 8 324 45

8 324 45

Union St. Construction
Notes Issued 35 000 00
Premium 45 00
Acc. Interest 117 89
Federal Grant 16 434 24

51 597 13

Water Tank Construction
Notes Issued 40 000 00
Acc. Interest 48 89

40 048 89

State Treasurer
Aiding Mothers 2 922 14
Temporary Aid 1 086 06
Indigent Persons 78 80
O. A. Federal Grant 14 002 57
Old Age Assistance 16 817 98
E. Water Construction 6 242 53
Income Tax 24 006 38
Business Tax 555 54
Corporation Tax 5 290 42
Electric Light and Gas 2 693 31

Race Track Distribution	632 46	
Industrial School	535 02	
Tuition	1 198 62	
Public Health	787 86	
State Aid	676 00	
Burial Indigent Soldiers	100 00	
Veterans Exemption	252 76	

77 878 45

$830 664 43

PAYMENTS

Selectmen's Warrants		$237 096 22	
Public Welfare Warrants		58 643 78	
School Warrants		102 673 00	
Old Age Assistance Warrants		31 646 22	
Old Age Assistance, U. S. Grant		11 957 52	
Water Warrants		23 907 16	
Joint Water Warrants		11 500 14	
Town of Abington, Joint Rates		1 321 94	
Anticipation Tax Notes		225 000 00	
Tax Refunds		235 95	
County Treasurer			
County Tax	14 653 59		
Dog Licenses	567 80		

15 221 39

Water Tank Project No. 1343RS		2 765 00	
Trust Funds		1 479 33	
Special School Appropriation		1 932 25	
Commonwealth of Massachusetts			
State Tax	13 100 00		
State Parks and Reservation	108 46		

13 208 46

Cash on Hand December 31, 1936   92 076 07

                                        $830 664 43

OUTSTANDING INDEBTEDNESS

Anticipation Tax Notes $125 000 00

PERMANENT LOANS

Junion-Senior Schools Bonds
   Outside Debt Limit   70 000 00
   Inside Debt Limit   72 000 00

                                        142 000 00

Plymouth County Hospital
   Outside Debt Limit   4 000 00
Union Street Construction
   2% Coupon Notes, 1937-1946   35 000 00
Water Tank Construction
   2% Coupon Notes, 1937-1956   40 000 00

                                        $346 000 00

JOINT WATER DEPARTMENT

Receipts:
   From Joint Rates $ 2 531 98
   From Rockland 1-2 Maintenance   5 750 06
   From Abington 1-2 Maintenance   5 750 08
   Due Abington 1935   55 95

                                        $ 14 088 07

Payments:
   Warrants $11 500 14
   1-2 Joint Rates, Abington   1 265 99
   Balance due, Abington 1935   55 95
   1-2 Joint Rates, Rockland   1 265 99

                                        $ 14 088 07

WATER DEPARTMENT

Payments:

Warrants	$ 23 907 16
1-2 Cost Joint Maintenance	5 750 06
	$ 29 657 22

Receipts:

Water Rates, Construction, etc	28 146 98
1-2 Joint Rates	1 265 99
Pleasant St. Appropriation, Due	244 25
	$ 29 657 22

BALANCE SHEET

ASSETS

Cash		$ 92 076 07
Accounts receivable		
Taxes		
Levy 1934	944 35	
Levy 1935	70 666 47	
Levy 1936	123 928 91	
		195 539 73
Motor Excise		
1934	70 35	
1935	1 804 68	
1936	5 116 54	
		6 991 57
Tax Titles		8 212 25
Overdrawn Accounts		
Tarvia and road binding	1 95	
Fire department	1 291 62	
Tree Warden	40 68	
Elections	426 50	
Town report and Poll book	448 15	

Snow	657 94	
Miscellaneous	558 23	
Old Age Assistance	6 666 22	
Public Welfare	2 643 78	

	12 735 07

	$315 554 69

LIABILITIES

Anticipation Tax Notes	$125 000 00
Special Accounts	8 411 70
Unexpended Balances	6 135 56
Water Tank Project	37 283 89
Surplus Revenue	138 723 54

	$315 554 69

CEMETERY TRUST FUNDS

Bequest	Cemetery	Balance Jan. 1. 1936	Deposited During 1936	Income	Expended	Balance Dec. 31, 1936
Jeremiah Leahy	St. Patricks	D1 54		$3 05	$3 05	$101 54
Mary Spence	St. Patricks	406 21		12 27	12 30	406 18
Margaret Smith	St. Patricks	101 54		3 05	3 05	D1 54
Patrick McCaffrey	St. Patricks	108 75		3 27	3 27	D8 75
James H. O'Connell	St. Patricks	101 54		3 05	3 05	D1 54
Gallaher-Driscoll	St. Patricks	239 85		7 22	7 24	239 83
Chester Ford	St. Patricks	471 28		14 23	10 00	475 51
Mary Gallagher	St. Patricks	D1 54		3 05	3 05	101 54
Catherine lyre	St. Patricks	203 10		6 13	6 14	203 09
Daniel Sullivan	St. Patricks	D1 54		3 05	3 05	D1 54
Patrick Cullinane	St. Patricks	76 15		2 29	2 29	76 15
George Hatch	St. Patricks	101 54		3 05	3 05	101 54
James Crowley	St. Patricks	101 54		3 05	3 05	101 54
Margaret D. Ilan	St. Patricks	203 10		6 13	6 14	203 09
Daniel Crowley	St. Patricks	101 54		3 05	3 05	101 54
Bridget Conway	St. Patricks	115 95		3 47	5 00	114 42
Patrick O'Hearn	St. Patricks	50 76		1 51	1 51	50 76
Daniel H. Jah	St. Patricks	D1 54		3 05	3 05	D1 54
las riDell	St. Patricks	D1 54		3 05	3 05	101 54
James Maguire	St. Patricks	D1 54		3 05	3 05	101 54

CEMETERY TRUST FUNDS—Continued

Bequest	Cemetery	Balance Jan. 1. 1936	Deposited During 1936	Income	Expended	Balance Dec. 31, 1936
Ellen Sullivan	St. Patricks	50 76		1 51	1 51	50 76
Mary J. Coughlin	St. Patricks		100 00			100 00
Katherine E. Rowley	St. Patricks	203 10		6 13	6 14	203 09
Michael Sullivan	St. Patricks	101 54		3 05	3 05	101 54
William Kth	St. Patricks	101 50		4 11	3 02	102 59
James Tangney	St. Patricks	200 00		6 04	3 00	203 04
Catherine E. O'Brien	St. Patricks	101 54		3 05	3 05	101 54
Thos Russell	St. Patricks	101 54		3 05	3 05	101 54
Timothy Kelliher	St. Patricks	152 32		4 59	4 60	152 31
Mary J. Samuels	St. Patricks	203 10		6 13	6 14	203 09
William B. Burke	St. Patricks	50 76		1 51	1 51	50 76
Henry Lyons	St. Patricks	101 54		3 05	3 05	101 54
Sarah J. Spence	St. Patricks	406 21		12 27	12 30	406 18
William Fitzgerald	St. Patricks	101 54		3 05	3 05	101 54
Thos J. Flynn	St. Patricks	101 54		3 05	3 05	101 54
John Leahy	St. Patricks	203 09		6 13	6 13	203 09
John Parker	St. Patricks	86 29		2 59	2 58	86 30
Thos J. Ash	Holy Family	126 93		3 81	3 82	126 92
Jeremiah Santry	Holy Family	203 10		6 13	6 14	203 09
Ana B. Rogers	Holy Family	101 55		3 05	3 06	101 54

CEMETERY TRUST FUNDS—Continued

Bequest	Cemetery	Balance Jan. 1 1936	Deposited During 1936	Income	Expended	Balance Dec. 31, 1936
John W. [?]	Holy Family	126 93		3 81	3 82	126 92
Mary E. [?]	Holy Family	101 55		3 05	3 06	101 54
Frederic Dill	Mt. Pleasant	108 32		3 25	4 00	107 57
Ernest M. Paine	Mt. Pleasant		100 00			100 00
Guy L. [?]	Mt. Pleasant		100 00			100 00
Wallace Damon	Mt. Pleasant		100 00			100 00
Collins-Branson	Mt. Pleasant	217 68		6 55		224 23
Elra S. [?]	Mt. [?]	137 65		6 24		143 89
C. A. Johnston	Mt. Pleasant	82 47		2 47	2 00	82 94
Henry [?]se	Mt. Pleasant	233 11		7 03	4 00	236 14
[?]ha Hutchinson	Mt. [?]	61 34		1 84	2 00	61 18
A. Hilton Studley	Mt. [?]	250 65		7 48	9 00	249 13
[?]m G. Perry	Mt. Pleasant	117 32		3 53	4 00	116 85
Gardner-Damon	Mt. Pleasant	100 00		3 01	3 00	100 01
Gles H. [?]le	Mt. Pleasant	100 00		3 01	3 00	100 01
Howard [?]r	Mt. Pleasant	137 08		4 13	4 00	137 21
Charles G. Turner	Mt. Pleasant	118 77		3 57	3 00	119 34
Frederic Shaw	Mt. Pleasant	103 21		4 69	4 00	103 90
Ltie [?]n	Mt. [?]	101 15		3 04	3 00	101 19
McManus-Horne	Mt. Pleasant	50 00		3 01	1 00	52 01

CEMETERY TRUST FUNDS—Continued

Bequest	Cemetery	Balance Jan. 1, 1936	Paid During 1936	Income	Expended	Balance Dec. 31, 1936
A. A. Crocker	Mt. Pleasant	132 42		3 99	4 00	132 41
Frank P. Lewis	Mt. Pleasant	54 55		1 63	2 00	54 18
Jas J. Donaldson	Mt. Pleasant	312 89		9 43	4 00	318 32
Henry G. Mn	Mt. Pleasant	521 43		15 74	4 00	533 17
Marsena Hrs	Mt. Pleasant	127 83		3 83	3 00	128 66
E. W. Whiting	Mt. Pleasant	155 39		4 67	4 00	156 06
Fidelia Estes	Mt. Pleasant	310 77		9 33	10 00	310 10
Emma L. Williams	Mt. Pleasant		100 00			100 00
Abbie F. Merrill	Mt. Pleasant		200 00			200 00
Eben P. Everett	Mt. Pleasant	86 63		2 59	2 00	87 22
Geor. Lawrence	Mt. Pleasant	175 43		7 90	6 00	177 33
Andrew McIlvene	Mt. Pleasant	240 44		7 20	11 00	236 64
Edward Crane	Mt. Pleasant	113 60		3 41	3 00	114 01
L. Evelyn Dill	Mt. Pleasant	176 38		5 32	3 00	178 70
Ellis	Mt. Pleasant	122 22		5 56		127 78
H. J.	Mt. Pleasant	106 76		3 21	2 00	107 97
Harold B. Vesper	Mt. Pleasant	106 48		3 21	4 00	105 69
ie H.	Mt. Pleasant	100 26		3 01	3 00	100 27
Easton Lot No. 249	Mt. Pleasant	211 98	100 00	6 38	4 00	314 36
	Mt. Pleasant	104 59		3 15	2 00	105 74

CEMETERY TRUST FUNDS—Continued

Bequest	Cemetery	Balance Jan. 1, 1936	Deposited During 1936	Income	Expended	Balance Dec. 31, 1936
George T. Poole	Mt. Pleasant	313 05		9 44	8 00	314 49
Dill-Lothrop	Mt. Pleasant	206 82		6 22	3 00	210 04
Elias A. Burrell	Mt. Pleasant	101 32		3 04	3 00	101 36
John Stoddard	Mt. Pleasant	75 00		1 68		76 68
Emma M. Coy	Mt. Pleasant	100 00		4 55	2 00	102 55
L. Wilfred Pole	Mt. Pleasant	103 97		3 11	3 00	104 08
Mary H. Breck	Mt. Pleasant	103 24		3 10	2 00	104 34
Lucie Linton	Mt. Pleasant	103 43		3 10	2 00	104 53
Thompson-Whiting	Maplewood	119 10		3 58	2 25	120 43
J. W. &-C. Hobart	Maplewood	330 59		9 97	4 50	336 06
Phillips-Goodspeed	Maplewood		100 00			100 00
Adna Burrell	Maplewood	125 64		3 77	2 25	127 16
Flora Thurlough	Maplewood	50 16		1 50	1 66	50 00
John W. This	Maplewood	128 30		3 87	2 25	129 92
Leander Torrey	Maplewood	121 62		3 65	2 25	123 02
N. A. Beal	Maplewood	102 45		3 07	4 25	101 27
Hopkins-Damon	Maplewood	104 82		3 15	4 25	103 72
David J. Lantz	Maplewood	50 97		1 51	2 25	50 23
Henrietta Stetson	Maplewood	566 28		17 10	27 90	555 48
William T. Mr	Maplewood	106 35		3 19	2 25	107 29

CEMETERY TRUST FUNDS—Continued

Bequest	Cemetery	Balance Jan. 1. 1936	Deposited During 1936	Income	Exp ended	Balance Dec. 31, 1936
Albert Phillips	Maplewood	52 72		1 57	2 25	52 04
?ah Davis	Maplewood	325 81		9 82	3 00	332 63
Mrs.	?dge Whiting	Maplewood	116 94		3 51	2 25	118 20
D. W. ?abs	Maplewood	168 16		5 07	11 45	161 78
a?cy ?ing	Maplewood	71 10		2 14	2 25	70 99
?iel Phillips	?od	158 67		4 78	3 00	160 45
s?ac Everson	Maplewood	100 45		3 01	3 00	100 46
Henry A. Baker	Spring Lake	100 75		6 35	7 00	100 10
?os A. ?ed	Spring Lake	157 10		4 64	9 50	152 24
Jessie Doane	Spring Lake	105 83		6 65	8 00	104 48
Z?s Jenkins	Spring Lake	113 59		7 16	8 00	112 75
Irving Arnold	Spring ?ke	150 00		8 15	6 00	152 15
Joseph J. Burgess	Spring Lake		125 00			125 00
Edbridge Payne	Mill Hill	322 47		9 73	6 00	326 20
B?ey Battles	Beal	257 27		7 70	10 00	254 97
William J. ?den	Assinippi	1?4 39		1 56	4 00	101 95

CHARLES J. HIGGINS,
Town Treasurer

Annual Report

of the

WATER COMMISSIONERS

of the

Town of Rockland

for the

Year Ending December 31, 1936

JOINT WATER BOARD OF ABINGTON
AND ROCKLAND

H. C. WITHERELL   S. W. BAKER
Chairman   Secretary

GEORGE GRAY   E. S. DAMON
F. L. MERRILL   R. FUCILLO

LEWIS E. WHEELER
Water Registrar

————————

WATER BOARD OF ROCKLAND

S. W. BAKER, Chairman

E. S. DAMON   R. FUCILLO

JAMES B. STUDLEY, Superintendent

Regular meetings of the Board every Thursday evening
at 7:30.

Main and Superintendent's Office,   96 E. Water Street
Open 8-12 A. M.   1-5 P. M.   Telephone 901

Collection Office, Room 2 Savings Bank Block.

Open 9-12 A. M.   2-5 P. M.
Friday Evenings 7-9 P. M.
Saturday 9-12 A. M.
Telephone 940

Water Commissioners' Report

The Water Commissioners herewith submit their fifty-first annual report.

Mr. William Brown, Engineer at the Pumping Station was also appointed Superintendent of Joint Works.

The Centrifugal Pump purchased in 1923 was shipped to the factory and thoroughly over hauled, and is now in good working condition.

A new Pardee Chlorinator was installed in place of the old one that was at the station.

Services in Rockland	1 938
Services in Abington	1 428
Services in Joint Works	125
New services in Rockland	10
New Services in Abington	13

Water rates received by Abington	$25 405 62
Water rates received by Rockland	25 803 81
Water rates received by Joint Works	2 891 92
	$54 101 35

JOINT REPORT 1936

Edison Electric Ill. Co., service	$ 3 331 29
William Brown, Salary and remittance	1 880 46
Lewis Wheeler, Salary and remittance	1 676 50
Abington Coal Corp., coal for station	763 48
Lunt Moss Co., Centrifugal pump repairs	612 24

Hayes Pump & Machinery Co., Chlorinator	589	19
Rockland Water Department, leak and services	345	39
Merrimac Chemical Co., Chlorine and Ammonia	228	35
Town of Pembroke, Taxes	211	38
N. E. T. & T. Co., service	175	76
C. J. Higgins, Services as treasurer	100	00
S. W. Baker, Services as secretary	100	00
Harrison Witherell, Services as chairman	100	00
A. W. Chesterton Co., Packing and supplies	84	97
Walworth Co., Pipe fittings	79	12
National Carloading Corp., Freight	63	61
Rose the Mover, Freight	60	00
Crandell Packing Co., supplies	57	71
Edward Winslow, labor	57	09
George Gray, Services as Commissioner	50	00
Frank Merrill, Services as Commissioner	50	00
E. S. Damon, Services as Commissioner	50	00
Tony Sasso, labor	48	94
Joseph Sims, labor	47	27
Socony Vacuum Oil Co., gas and oil	43	77
Ralph Fucillo, Services as Commissioner	39	60
Douglas Print, Printing	38	27
E. I. Dupont DeMemores Co., Ammonia	37	68
Abington Water Department, services and repairs	36	93
George Lang Co., supplies	35	08
Edson Corp., Pump	33	50
Jenkins Brothers, Gate Valves	31	72
Leslie Brown, labor	27	58
Howe & French Inc., Chlorine	27	10
Curry Brothers Oil Co., oil and supplies	26	37
Robert Porter, labor	25	33
Elof Nelson, labor	22	00
Harry Arena, labor	20	25
Robert Wheeler, labor	18	57
Edward Whitmarsh, labor	18	00
W. V. Irving, sign painting	18	00
Wallace & Tiernan Co., Chemical supplies	17	20
John Foster Lumber Co., supplies	15	43

Edward Johnson, labor	15	19
Stearn's Express, express	11	09
Ralph Stetson, labor	10	69
J. J. McCarthy, Services as Commissioner	10	40
Dodge-Haley Co., supplies	10	16
Builders Iron Foundry, charts	10	16
Amos Phelps, Bond	10	00
Commissioner Public Safety, Inspection at station	10	00
John Keith, labor	9	00
E. M. White, supplies	8	61
Garlock Packing Co., supplies	8	59
Sears, Roebuck Co., supplies	8	23
Benson's Cafe, food for laborers	8	20
Alden Merrill, labor	7	88
John Titchen, labor	7	31
Herford Damon, labor	7	31
Edwin Richardson, labor	6	19
Crosby Steam Gage Co., Charts	5	83
A. Culver Co., Paint	5	25
Roger Ranson, labor	4	78
Rockland Transportation Co., express	4	74
Phillip Murphy, labor	4	50
Damon Electric, Switches	3	50
Donald McPhelmy, labor	3	38
F. H. Hovey, supplies	2	50
Joseph Thibeault, repairing lawn mower	2	50
A. J. Vargus, supplies	2	40
Railway Express, express	2	39
Industrial Lock Nut, supplies	2	23
Boston Pipe & Fittings Co., supplies	1	40
Welch Co. Inc., lumber		60

Total	$	11 500	14
Rockland one-half	$	5 750	07

REPORT OF SUPERINTENDENT

Joint Board of Water Commissioners of
Abington and Rockland.

Gentlemen:

I herewith submit my report as Superintendent for the
year ending December 31, 1936.

The usual analysis of water from Big Sandy Pond and
Little Sandy Pond has been made by the State Board of
Health.

Three new services were installed and two service leaks
repaired, a new By Pass installed at Main gate at Pumping Station, also renewal of bolts on flanges of suction
pipe in well house.

All the hydrants have been painted and three renewals
were installed.

The two pumping units and the outside trimmings on
station and well house have been painted and all the sashes
have been puttied and drawn.

I would recommend that the residence at Pumping Station and the iron stand pipe at Beach Hill have one coat
of paint.

Cleaning of shores of pond should be continued.

The financial report of the Joint Works will be found
under the report of the Water Registrar.

Respectfully submitted,
WILLIAM H. BROWN,
Superintendent

SUPERINTENDENT'S REPORT

To the Board of Water Commissioners:
Gentlemen:

I herewith submit my report of the Water Department
for the year ending December 31, 1936.

Receipts from Water Rates	$	25 803	81
Receipts from Installation of services		1 121	41
Receipts from small jobs		1 175	36
Receipts from Meter Repairs		45	95
Excess cash turned in			45
	$	28 146	98

COLLECTIONS

On January 1, 1936 there was an outstanding indebtedness to the Department of $14,575.20. This has been re-
duced to $11,688.84 as of Dec. 31, 1936. The Town ac-
cepted Chapter 391 of the Acts of 1923, in 1927. Upon
advice of Mr. Theodore N. Waddell, Director of Accounts,
this law was put into effect during the year. This act pro-
vides that unpaid water bills become a lien on property. An
additional fee of $1.50 is charged for looking up the title
to the property and recording the same in the Registry at
Plymouth. While this places an additional hardship on
water takers, who are in arrears, it is the only insurance
the Town has, to collect outstanding water accounts.

SERVICES

New service installations	10
Renewals of services	29
Renewals to property line	7
Services lowered	3
Services discontinued	6

HYDRANTS - GATES

Main gates new and replaced	6
Hydrant gates added	5
Hydrants raised to grade	2
Hydrants repaired	6
Hydrants relocated inside curb	4
New hydrants added to system	2

Under the P. W. A. Union Street rebuilding 10 new hydrants were installed to replace the ten old hydrants that were removed.

10 main gates raised.

90 Boxes raised.

1 Privately owned hydrant was discontinued.

LEAKS

10 Leaks were repaired during the year.

UNION STREET REBUILDING

A part of the rebuilding of Union Street from North Avenue to Market Street, the existing 10 inch Main was replaced by a 12 inch Main from North Avenue to Exchange Street, under the road contract and was further extended to Webster Street by the Water Department.

All services from North Avenue to Market Street were renewed under the road contract.

10 New hydrants of five inch design were installed. Three with 8 inch feeders.

A new section gate was cut in at the head of Taunton Avenue making it possible to shut off a portion of the Town in case of a break without disrupting the service over a large area.

MAINS

Salem Street Construction

Following the policy of the Department instituted a few years ago, the dead end between Greenwood Street and near Spruce Street on Salem Street was connected. The labor was furnished by the W. P. A. the Department furnishing the material. The work was carried on in a very efficient manner under the supervision of foreman in charge of the project.

The tieup of this dead end will give residents of the Hatherly section additional water pressure which was badly needed in case of fire and will also improve the quality of water for consumers on the street.

West Pleasant Street Construction

By vote of the special town meeting held June 3 the main on Pleasant Street was extended a distance of 270 feet. $250.00 was appropriated by the Town, and the balance from the Water Department revenue.

Forest Street Construction

On petition of residents of Forest Street for water service an application was submitted to the Works Progress Administration for an allotment of funds for labor, which was granted, providing the department furnished the material. Material was furnished and the work is still in progress of construction. Transite pipe was furnished for this project at a saving to the Town. This pipe has an advantage over cast iron pipe, in that it is not subject to corrosion.

GENERAL

The compressor rented for the Salem Street Construction was purchased by the Department. The rental due on the compressor at the completion of the work, was applied towards the purchase price. The equipment has proven to be beneficial and a saving to the Town.

LOCAL REPORT OF EXPENSES

The following expenditures are included in the total expenditures of $23,907.16.

Forest Street Water Main Extension

Pipe	$ 2 523	05
Freight	225	87
Tees, and sleeves	75	00
Blasting labor	21	38
Dynamite	10	05
Trucks	147	96
Gasoline	150	00
Kerosene	4	00
Gates	43	80
Hydrant	35	00
Lumber	17	00
Coal	1	35
Bits	17	85
Gate Boxes	9	00
	$ 3 281	31

Salem Street Water Main Extension

Labor	$ 369	23
Truck	159	81
Pipe	1 434	63
Bits	294	06
Dynamite	109	28
Gasoline	109	80
Lumber	46	80
Hydrotite	44	00
Tools	30	00

Lanterns	38	00
Gate Boxes	26	70
Hardware	12	75
Parts for Gas hammer	9	43
Gravel	7	00
Damage to Compressor	5	05
Kerosene	4	50
Oil	2	50
Express	2	05
Battery	2	76
Clay	1	00
Coal		90
Merclor	1	10
	$ 2 711	35
Compressor rental	836	35
	$ 3 547	70

West Pleasant Street Extension

Labor	$ 196	83
Dynamite	1	50
Pipe, 270 ft. at 84c	226	80
Tees	16	80
Sleeve	3	30
1-8th Bend	5	00
Hydrant	60	00
Gates	43	80
Gate Boxes	9	00
Hydrotite	8	00
Jute	1	50
Kerosene	1	00
	$ 573	53

Town Appropriation	$250	00

Balance paid from water receipts.

Union Street Extension

465 ft. 12 inch Pipe in place	$ 2 388 19
Paid on Account	1 000 00
Due	$ 1 388 19

Respectfully submitted,

JAMES B. STUDLEY,

Superintendent

LOCAL REPORT 1936

Johns-Manville, Transit Pipe	$ 2 523 05
James Studley, Salary	2 080 00
Warren Pipe Co., Pipe for Salem Street	1 434 63
P. I. Perkins Co., Compressor and Tools	1 431 37
Harry Holmes, Salary	1 404 00
Lewis Litchfield, Salary	1 404 00
Bradford Weston, 12 inch pipe for Union Street Extension	1 000 00
Tony Sasso, Labor	938 25
Henry Harris, Labor and remittances	902 40
Alice Gammon, Office	858 00
Edward Winslow, Labor	735 48
A. B. Reed, Engineering fee	500 00
Socony-Vacuum Oil Co., Gasoline and Oil	448 88
Industrial Lock Nut, Fittings and repair parts	430 43
Edwin Richardson, Labor	379 63
S. W. Baker, Services as Commissioner	300 00
E. S. Damon, Services as Commissioner	300 00
Cambridge Machine & Tool Co., Hydrants and Valves	289 60
McAuliffe & Burke Co., Pipe and fittings	252 95
Ralph Fucillo, Services as Commissioner	237 50

N. Y., N. H. & H. R. R., Freight on Pipe	226	95
William Bell, Use of truck and labor	224	85
N. E. T. & T. Co., Service	212	62
Thomas DeYoung, Labor	206	68
Corcoran Supply Co., Pipe and fittings	193	71
National Meter Co., Meters and parts	184	32
R. C. Sullivan Co., Pipe and fittings	181	46
Red Hed Mfg. Co., Fittings	174	32
Sears, Roebuck Co., Tools	159	06
Rockland Coal & Grain Co., Coal and lumber	153	29
John R. Parker P. M., Postages and Box rent	140	37
W. J. Dunn Co., Resharpening bits and points	135	78
Raymond Martell, Labor and supplies	132	90
Howland and Howland, Surveying tank site Rice Avenue	118	50
A. Wainshalbaum, Use of truck and labor	121	68
Chase, Parker Co., Hoist-chuck-chains	109	67
Bradford Weston, Asphalt & Dynamite for Union Street	104	86
Kelton Bates, Labor	102	26
Warren Woodward, Insurance	94	34
Amos Phelps, Bond and Insurance	93	80
A. Culver Co., Coal and Kerosene	90	15
E. S. Damon, Insurance	87	58
Phoenix Meter Co., Meters and parts	87	55
Fred Kane, Labor	86	85
Charles McGonnigle, Labor	80	46
E. L. LeBaron Foundry Co., Gate Boxes	78	79
Roger Ransom, Labor	72	85
Michael Bowen, Labor and Truck	71	96
Searafino Gentile, Dynamiting	71	29
Springfield Commercial Body Co., Body for Ford Truck	65	00
J. J. McCarthy, Services as Commissioner	62	50
John Washburn, Registering water liens	62	20
Hall & Torrey, Paint and Supplies	59	10
Builders Iron Foundry, Tees	55	86
Dunlop Tire Co., Tires for truck	54	92

J. Thomas Condon, Surveyor's Map, Used for Union St., Job	53	00
Peter DeSimone, Labor	52	90
Charles Fucillo, Labor	53	31
Damon Electric, Labor and supplies	44	81
Louis Wade, Labor	44	73
Edison Electric Ill. Co., Services	42	68
Director of Accounts, Certifying bonds for tank	40	00
Gulf Refining Co., Oil	39	90
Howland Insurance, Insurance	38	45
Mueller Co., Supplies	34	63
Dodge & Haley Co., Trolley and Track	32	54
Harwood Stoddard, Labor on carpenter work	32	15
Douglas Print, Printing and Stock	31	76
Felix Carreaux, Labor	30	67
Charles McCarty Co., Joint Runners	29	88
Vulcan Tool Co., Points	27	37
Jenkins & Simmons Express, express	27	32
Tovia Jarvinin, Labor and truck	27	19
National Foundry Co., Boxes	27	18
Weymouth Asphalt & Concrete Co., Asphalt	26	46
Thomas Bailey, Labor	25	87
Carl Mahn, Labor	25	26
Chandler & Farquar Co., Supplies	25	15
Brown Wales & Co., Supplies	24	88
Lester Rose, Labor	24	46
Jenkins Brothers, Gate Valves	23	90
Dolby's Filling Station, Service and supplies	23	00
Phillip Murphy, Labor	22	89
Darling Valve Mfg. Co., Supplies	22	19
C. A. Baker, Gas and Torch	21	97
Waldo Brothers, Sewer Pipe	21	93
Southeastern Construction Co., Cement blocks	21	80
M. F. Ellis Co., Picks	21	17
Harvey Sales & Service Co., Rims	20	58
William Berry, Labor	20	53
George Ryan, Labor	20	53
Lawrence O'Connor, Labor	20	53

Albee Richards, Truck and Labor	20	24
Hydraulic Development Corps., Hydrotite	20	00
Charles Briggs, Blacksmith work	19	19
Austin Print, Printing and Stock	18	75
Boston Pipe & Fitting Co., Supplies	18	18
D. Delprete, Truck and labor	18	00
Brockton Building Wrecking Co., Lumber	17	88
Joseph Melewski, Labor	17	25
Vincent Geloran, Labor	17	16
Henry Shelly, Labor	17	10
Perrin & Seamans, Screen and Tamp	16	32
Earl Wallace, Labor	16	00
Thomas Welsh, Blacksmith work	15	35
A. J. Vargus, Batteries and Supplies	15	16
F. W. Webb Co., Drinking fountain	15	00
Sinclair Refining Co., Gasoline	15	00
Walworth Co., Valves	15	00
John Henderson, Labor	13	50
West Side Grocery, Charcoal and wood	13	00
Aldo Botto, Labor	12	94
Edward Whitmarsh, Labor	12	60
A. I. Randall, Printing water reports	12	80
Rockland Standard Publishing Co., Printing and advertising	12	75
Thomas Murrell, Truck and labor	12	00
Roy Blanchard, Truck and labor	12	00
General Electric Supply Corp., Motor	11	97
Bettridge Service, Supplies	11	95
Rockland Hardware Co., Supplies	11	85
George Caldwell, Boxes	11	80
Kenneth Bowser, Labor	11	40
Al. Stella, Labor	11	20
Mann Auto Sales, Supplies	10	46
Merrimac Chemical Co., Merclor	10	38
No Pee Trading Co., Box Finder	10	00
Thomas Cosgrove, Sale of Meter	10	00
Edson Corporation, Supplies	9	28
Henry Finch, Labor	9	28

Percy Simmons, Labor	8	44
Clifford Elliott, Labor	8	40
Joseph Arena, Use of trailer	8	00
Lewis Wheeler, Torch	8	00
James Haggerty, Labor	8	00
Martin Keough, Labor	7	88
J. C. Moore Corp., Book	7	80
Brown Instrument Co., Pens and Charts	7	77
H. G. Bolster Mfg. Co., Wiping Cloths	7	72
J. E. Kemp, Tail board for truck	7	50
Rockland Transportation, Express	7	04
Roderick MacKenzie, Sand	7	00
Patrick Mahoney, Use of Truck	7	00
Edward Metivier, Labor	6	75
Blake & Rebhan Co., Supplies	6	70
E. P. Reed Lumber Co., Lumber	6	15
Lawrence Lovell, Labor	5	63
Fred Chamberlain, Labor	5	63
Becker Co., Cash Book	5	58
A. S. Peterson, Supplies	5	47
Manifold Supply Co., Paper and Ribbons	5	25
Jack's Radiator Shop, Radiator	5	00
Jesse Davis, Labor	4	50
Michael Haggerty, Labor	4	50
Peter Gilmartin, Labor	4	50
Basil Murray, Labor	4	50
Charles Hyland, Labor	4	50
John Arthur, Labor	4	50
Frank Riley, Labor	4	50
Robert Wheeler, Labor	4	22
Crawford Machine Works, Brake and Repairs	4	00
George Stoddard, Use of Horses		75
George N. Beal, Repairs and supplies		80
H. C. Metcalf, Repairs to Typewriters	3	75
Patrick Burton, Labor		66
A. B. Dick Co., Stencils		60
A. W. Chesterton Co., Pens		50
Charles Gibbons, Labor		38

John Sullivan, Labor	3	09
Brockton Garage, Muffler	3	00
Water Works Engineering, Magazine	3	00
Fred Thibeault, Labor	3	00
Crawford Service Station, Alcohol	2	52
Old Colony Plumbing Supply, Oil	2	50
L. Josselyn & Son., Cleaner	2	23
Brockton Transportation Co., Express	1	86
Hill & Magoun, Bearing and spring	1	75
G. R. Bradley, Office supplies	1	65
E. M. Gowell, Cement blocks	1	62
Bostitch Boston Co., Ink Pad	1	50
Jannell Motor, Springs	1	35
Llyle Tibbetts, Labor	1	13
Mathewson Machine Works, Map tracing	1	05
Bridgewater Brick Co., Clay	1	00
Bemis Drug Co., Supplies		84
Underwood Elliot Fisher, Ribbon		75
Anthony Fiachetti, Food for Laborers		60
Rome Brothers, Buzzers		40
Market Street Garage, Gasoline		34
H. H. Arnold Inc., Wrench		15

$ 23 907 16

S. W. BAKER,

E. S. DAMON,

R. FUCILLO,

Water Commissioners of Rockland

REPORT OF WATER REGISTRAR

To the Joint Board of Commissioners of
Abington and Rockland

Gentlemen:

I herewith submit my report as Water Registrar for the
year ending December 31, 1936.

Water Rates	$ 2 891 92
New Services	55 29
Total Amount Collected	$ 2 947 21
Water Rates Due	$ 310 54

Three new accounts added this year.

Respectfully submitted,

LEWIS E. WHEELER,

Water Register

Month 1936	Hours Pumping h. m.	Daily Average h. m.	Gallons Pumped	Daily Gallons	lbs al consumed	Daily average lbs	Ave. height reservoir	Gals pumped per lbs coal	Gals pumped per k. w. h.	Gals. pumped per gal. gas
January	252 35	8 09	18 561 000	598 742	72 690	2345	96	354	735	4 550
February	281 00	9 42	18 638 000	642 688	34 110	1176	97	353	735	4 549
March	298 35	9 38	18 915 000	610 161	15 652	505	97	353	733	4 545
April	297 30	9 55	19 305 000	624 500	14 129	471	97	355	745	4 550
May	338 40	10 56	21 472 000	692 645	9 020	291	98	357	745	4 547
June	376 35	12 33	23 818 000	793 933	5 435	247	97	356	741	4 549
July	367 30	11 52	23 057 000	743 774	1 050	350	98		741	4 551
A*gst	399 45	12 53	25 251 000	814 580	None		97		746	4 549
September	345 00	11 30	21 675 000	722 500	9 330	311	97	352	736	4 547
O*er	324 00	10 27	20 230 000	648 226	10 465	338	97	356	733	4 550
*ber	285 00	9 30	17 770 000	592 333	12 90	433	97	352	733	4 545
December	290 50	9 23	18 264 000	589 51	15 85	511	97	353	732	4 549
*tl	3 857		246 956 000		200 716					
Average	321 25		20 579 666		16 726		97	354	738	4 548

Average Stc Hd 216. Average Dynamic Head 281.3. Maximum weekly Oct, June 2 to June 8
7,033,000 gals. Min daily O*, daily, June 8, 1,139,000 gals. Coal used 1936, 227,480 lbs. Gal
on hand, January 1, 1937, 156,222 lbs. Gallons pumped via Stm 24,543,000 gals. Gallons pumped via
1,319,000 gals. Gallons pumped via electricty, 221,094,000 gals. Gas on hand *ry 1, 1937, 320 gals.
Duty done in foot lbs. per 110 lbs. al, 87,089,173.

WILLIAM H. BROWN, *gr

ELEVATED TANK

PWA Project No. 1343 RS Addition To Water System

At our annual meeting it was voted to instruct the Water Commissioners to purchase a lot of land on Rice Avenue for the purpose of erecting a 1,000,000 gallon elevated tank and $70,000.00 was appropriated. The Government's offer was received August 24, 1936 and accepted September 21, 1936. Bids were immediately advertised. When the bids were opened they were in excess of our appropriation on account of the increase cost of material and labor that had taken place between our March meeting and October. On October 26, 1936 at a special town meeting it was voted to instruct the Commissioners to erect the largest size tank possible within the March appropriation of $70,000.00.

On December 2, 1936, proposals were received from the Chicago Bridge & Iron Co., and Pittsburgh-DesMoines Steel Co., for furnishing and erecting a 500,000-gallon elevated steel water tank, steel tower, foundations, underground piping and auxiliary equipment, and an alternate and furnishing a tank of 600,000-gallon capacity.

The following bids were received for the tank, tower, foundations, piping and equipment.

	500,000 Gal. Tank	600,000 Gal. Tank
Chicago Bridge & Iron Co.	$62,480	$67,180
Pittsburgh DesMoines Steel Co.	$63,962	$69,462

Contract for 500,000 gal. tank awarded to
Chicago Bridge & Iron Co.

Total cost of projects is as follows:

Advertising	$200
Land	500
500,000 gal. Steel tank & 120 ft. tower	45,200
Foundations, piping, street surfacing etc.	17,280
Contingencies	1,820
Engineering Fee	3,200
Clerk of the Works	1,200
Tests of steel, concrete & pipe	600
	$70,000

U. S. Grant $31,500.00   Rockland $38,500.00

Work is now in progress and is to be completed by July, 1, 1937.

Auditors' Report

We have audited the books of the various departments of the town and have found them to be correct. The audit included the books of the treasurer, tax collector, school department, water department, town clerk and sealer of weights and measures.

The balance reported by the treasurer has been reconciled with the statements furnished by the various banks used as depositories of the town funds.

Respectfully submitted,

HAROLD C. SMITH, Chairman
C. ELMER ASKLUND,
LEO E. DOWNEY

::

Annual Report

of the

SCHOOL DEPARTMENT

of the

Town of Rockland

❖❖❖❖❖❖❖❖❖

For the Year Ending December 31, 1936

::

SCHOOL CALENDAR 1937

WINTER TERM

Begins Monday, January 4, 1937, seven weeks; ends Friday, February 19, 1937.

SPRING TERM

Begins Monday, March 1, 1937, seven weeks; ends Friday, April 16, 1937.

SUMMER TERM

Begins Monday, April 26, 1937, nine weeks, ends Wednesday, June 23, 1937. Teachers return Thursday and Friday, June 24 and 25 for year-end duties and organization work.

HOLIDAYS

March 26, 1937, Good Friday.
May 31, 1937, Memorial Day Celebration.
October 29, 1937, Teachers' Convention.
November 11, 1937, Armistice Day.
November 24, 1937, schools close at noon for remainder of week, Thanksgiving Recess.

SIGNALS FOR NO SESSIONS OF SCHOOL

Fire Station Siren

A. M.

7:30—2 2 repeated: No session of High School.

8:15—2 2 repeated: No forenoon session for first six grades.

P. M.

12:45—2 2 repeated: No afternoon session for first six grades.

The "No School Signal" is used only in extremely stormy weather. The school bus starts on its first trip in the morning ten minutes after seven o'clock in order to collect the children in time for the opening of high school at 8:30 A. M. and the elementary schools at 9:00 A. M. Unless the signal is used before 7:00 o'clock many of the children are already on their way by bus. It is very difficult to determine weather conditions for the day as early as 7:00 o'clock except in cases of severe storms.

People in the outskirts of our town often cannot hear the signal, in which case children appearing in school are disappointed to learn that they must cover the long distance back to their homes, while they may be chilled or wet.

We wish each parent to use his or her best judgment as to whether or not the weather is auspicious for sending their children to school. No penalty is inflicted upon any child for non-attendance on account of severe weather.

Since our teachers are in school and many of the pupils do not hear the signal, it seems wise to use the time to good advantage in warm buildings, whereas during days when the signal may be used many children are out of doors, becoming wet and contracting colds.

Is it not wiser to have them in warm school rooms under supervision, receiving beneficial instruction?

R. STEWART ESTEN,

Superintendent of Schools

January 1, 1937.

School Directory 1936-1937

SCHOOL COMMITTEE

DR. WILLIAM A. LOUD, Chairman   327 Salem Street
Tel. 430. Term expires March, 1937.

DR. BENJAMIN LELYVELD,   320-A Union Street
Tel. 16-W. Term expires March, 1937

E. STUART WOODWARD   385 Market Street
Tel. 115-W. Term expires March, 1938

MISS M. AGNES KELLEHER   297 Howard Street
Tel. 1484-W. Term expires March, 1938

MRS. HELEN M. HAYDEN,   429 Liberty Street
Tel. 454-R. Term expires March, 1939

SUPERINTENDENT OF SCHOOLS

R. STEWART ESTEN   111 Payson Avenue
Office Tel. 1540. Residence Tel. 1250
Office hours every school day from 8:30 to 9:00 A. M.
and on Wednesday evenings from 7:00 to 8:00 o'clock.

SCHOOL DEPARTMENT SECRETARY

HARRIET E. GELINAS   241 Myrtle Street
Office Tel. 1540. Residence Tel. 1244.

PRINCIPAL OF HIGH SCHOOL

GEORGE A. J. FROBERGER   28 Exchange Street
Office Tel. 1540. Residence Tel. 1302-W.
Office hours every school day from 8 to 9 A. M., Mon-

days and Thursdays from 3 to 4 P. M., and Wednesday
evening from 7 to 8 o'clock.

ATTENDANCE OFFICER AND SCHOOL NURSE

LOUISE A. CONSIDINE   69 Webster Street
Office Tel. 1540
Office hours at the high school every school day from
8:30 to 9:30 A. M.

SCHOOL PHYSICIANS

JOSEPH H. DUNN, M. D.   319 Union Street
Office Tel. 836-W.   Residence Tel. 836-R
Office Hours: 2 to 3 and 7 to 8 P. M.

JOSEPH FRAME, M. D.   144 Webster Street
Office Tel. 38-W
Office Hours: 12:30 to 2 and 6:30 to 8 P. M.

DENTAL HYGIENIST

EVELYN DELORY   323 Market Street
Office hours at the McKinley School daily when schools
are in session from 9:00 A. M. to 12 M., and from 1:30 to
3:30 P. M.

DIGEST OF LAWS AND REGULATIONS RELATING TO SCHOOL ATTENDANCE

Children who are five years and six months of age by the
opening of school in September, 1937, shall be admitted to
the first grade. Those who become five years of age after
March 1, 1937, may be admitted after passing a satisfactory
mental examination.

Children, otherwise eligible to enter school in September
for the first time, are required by law to present at time of

entrance either a certificate of vaccination or a certificate of unfitness for vaccination. The school committee and board of health have ruled that certificates of unfitness for vaccination must be renewed each year. Children coming into the school system from other places, whether at the opening of the year in September or during the school year, will be required to produce satisfactory evidence regarding vaccination.

Pupils desiring to enter the first grade must enroll on or before October 1. Otherwise they will not be admitted.

The school hours for the first grade children, shall be from 9 until 11:30 A. M. The afternoon session shall correspond with other grades, 1:30 P. M. until 3:30 P. M. The ruling, took effect March 6, 1933.

Pupils who have been absent from school on account of contagious disease must secure a permit from a school physician before re-entering. In cases of doubt, or in cases where there exists a suspicion of contagion, the parents should advise, and the teachers should require that the pupils consult the school nurse, who may refer the case to a school physician for further examination.

Any pupil having a contagious disease or showing symptoms of such a disease may be temporarily excluded from school by the teacher on her own initiative or at the direction of the school nurse or school physician.

Sickness is the only legal excuse for absence from school.

All children between the ages of fourteen and sixteen years must be in school unless they are actually employed under the authority of an employment certificate, a home permit or a special certificate permitting farm or domestic employment.

Any pupil who habitually violates rules of the schools, or otherwise seriously interferes with the proper and orderly operation of the school which he attends, may be temporarily excluded by the teacher or the superintendent of schools or may be permanently expelled by the school committee.

Pupils under seven years of age or over sixteen who elect to attend school must conform to the same rules and regulations as those pupils who are within the compulsory age—from seven to fourteen.

Teachers may require a written excuse signed by a parent or guardian covering any case of absence, tardiness or dismissal.

Whenever a pupil is suspended by a teacher or prinicpal, for any cause for any length of time, an immediate report must be made to the superintendent's office.

Those pupils attending the first eight grades will be transported to and from school if they live in the town of Rockland and reside more than one mile and a quarter from the school where they are authorized to attend.

Those pupils attending the high school, grades nine to twelve, inclusive, will be transported to and from school it they live in the town of Rockland and reside more than two miles from the high school.

RECENT RULINGS PERTAINING TO OUR SCHOOLS

There shall be a Supervisor of Buildings who shall represent the School Committee in charge of all school buildings when they are used by outside organizations (other than school organizations.)

The Supervisor's duties shall be to prevent any damage

to school property and to be responsible for proper conduct in and on school property. (prevent smoking, drinking and unbecoming conduct in the buildings).

The organization using the building shall be responsible for the expense of such a supervisor.

The supervisor shall receive his instructions from the Superintendent of schools.

The supervisor shall receive remuneration at the rate of $2.50 until 10:30 P. M.; $4.00 if the function continues until 11:30 P. M.; $5.00 after 11:30 P. M.; 75c per hour will be the charge for the building if used before 6:00 P. M. This ruling took effect December 1, 1934.

All work performed by the School Committee shall be awarded to native born citizens, naturalized citizens, or those who have taken out their first naturalization papers.

The tuition for pupils whose parents reside out of town and wishing to attend the Rockland Schools shall be established as follows: Senior High, $100 per year; Junior High, $80; elementary grades, $60.

Post-Graduates who are admitted to the Rockland High School September 4, 1935 or thereafter, shall take a minimum of twenty hours of work per week; shall be satisfactory in conduct; shall be regular in full day's attendance and maintain satisfactory averages in all subjects.

RULES REGARDING PAYMENT OF SALARIES.

The teachers of the Rockland schools shall receive their salaries bi-weekly after two weeks of actual classroom teaching from the opening of school in September until the close of schools in June. During July and August one salary check monthly will be paid, not later than the fifteenth of the month.

All teachers who are absent on account of personal illness shall receive the difference between the substitute's pay or its equivalent and the teacher's regular pay. This became effective September 1, 1935.

All regular appointed teachers who are absent on account of personal reasons other than sickness shall have 1-200 of the yearly salary deducted for each school day's absence.

A teacher will continue to receive full pay for five calendar days on account of death in the immediate family.

Visiting school authorized by the superintendent of schools or work pertaining to the schools may be allowed without loss of salary.

The superintendent, principals, special teachers, teachers and janitors shall receive their salaries beginning with the opening of school in September 1933 on a twelve months' basis rather than on a ten months' basis as formerly.

Substitute teachers shall be paid at the rate of $4.50 per day beginning with the opening of schools in September, 1933.

After September 1, 1933, the janitors shall be allowed no "sick leave" but five calendar days will be allowed with full pay for death in the immediate family.

REPORT OF ROCKLAND SCHOOL COMMITTEE

To the Citizens of Rockland:

The School Commitee again expresses its gratitude to those organizations who give help to deserving pupils in the form of annual scholarships; also to the Kiwanis Club for taking over the responsibility of providing free milk for needy children.

The practice of the Chamber of Commerce in giving an annual prize could well be emulated by other groups as a method of encouraging good scholarship.

We commend the interest and endeavor of the Superintendent, teachers, and all employees as indicative of their loyalty to the school system, and now that business is showing a definite upward trend we hope the town will soon restore the cut in salaries which has been in effect since 1932.

The loss of some good teachers during the past year because of low salaries is worth your careful consideration.

It has always been the policy of the School Committee to buy supplies locally, if possible, even though in some cases we are obliged to pay top prices. In regard to coal, however, we became convinced that a large saving could and should be made since we are very heavy buyers of this commodity. We therefore made the fact plain when we advertised for bids that the lowest bidder, whether local or out of town, would receive the contract if he could supply the quality desired. The lowest local bid was $7.75 per ton for soft coal and $12.50 for hard coal, but the lowest out of town bid was $6.64 for soft coal and $10.00 for hard coal. Since we buy approximately 500 tons of soft coal and 100 tons of hard coal the saving to the town by buying outside of Rockland was $805. The coal delivered to us has been entirely satisfactory.

Respectfully submitted,

WILLIAM A. LOUD, Chairman,
M. AGNES KELLEHER,
HELEN M. HAYDEN,
BENJAMIN LELYVELD,
E. STUART WOODWARD.

FINANCIAL STATEMENT
RESOURCES 1936

General Appropriation $102 673 00

EXPENDITURES

General Expenses $ 5 099 15
Expense of Instruction   73 265 78
Operation and Maintenance   18 380 73
Auxiliary Agencies   5 682 05
New Equipment   245 29

Total Expenditures $102 673 00

TOWN TREASURER'S RECEIPTS ON ACCOUNT OF SCHOOLS

State Reimbursements:
Teachers' Salaries $10 350 00
Tuition and Transportation
  of Wards   1 198 62
City of Boston for Tuition and
  and Transportation of Wards   419 40
Materials sold in high
  school shop   34 20
Sale of boiler junk   2 20

Total Receipts $ 12 004 42

Net cost of schools to town $ 90 668 58

RENTAL OF McKINLEY HALL AND SENIOR HIGH GYMNASIUM

Town Appropriation to offset expenses $100 00

Receipts (turned over to Town
    Treasurer) $ 63 00
Expenditures:
J. J. L. DeCosta $10 50
L. M. Glover Co.   49 50
Cambosco Scientific Co.   2 00

    Total Expenditures $ 62 00

    Balance $ 1 00
Unexpended Appropriation $38 00

APPROPRIATION FOR RETUBING McKINLEY SCHOOL BOILERS

Town Appropriation $ 1 300 00
Expenditures:
   International Engineering Works, Inc.   1 295 40

Unexpended Balance $ 4 60

ALLOWANCE FOR PLASTERING AT JUNIOR-SENIOR HIGH

Allowance (Granted by Finance Committee,
   November 1935) $ 100 00
Expenditures:
   O. R. Cummings $ 99 80

Unexpended balance of allowance $ 20

DETAIL OF 1936 EXPENDITURES

Total Resources $102 673 00

GENERAL EXPENSES

Superintendent's Salary $3 600 00
Other Administrative Expense   1 499 15

EXPENSE OF INSTRUCTION .

Supervisors' Salaries	3 399 19
Principals' Salaries	6 921 00
Teachers' Salaries	58 985 86
Text Books	1 224 97
Stationery, Supplies and Miscellaneous	2 734 76

OPERATION AND MAINTENANCE

Janitors' Wages	8 041 53
Fuel	4 509 58
Miscellaneous	2 446 15
Repairs	3 383 47

AUXILIARY AGENCIES

Libraries	65 73
Health	1 863 54
Transportation	1 181 69
Sundries	2 571 09

OUTLAY

New Equipment	245 29
Total Expenditures	$102 673 00

FINANCIAL STATEMENT ITEMIZED
SUPERINTENDENT OF SCHOOLS

R. Stewart Esten, Salary	$ 3 600 00

OTHER ADMINISTRATIVE EXPENSES

Co-operative Test Service, Sample copies	55
Louise A. Considine, mileage	99 33

Graphic Duplicator Co.,
Ink remover   60
Harriet E. Gelinas, salary   1 125 00
Kee Lox Mfg. Co., typewriter ribbons   1 04
John C. Moore, bkkg forms   3 22
N. E. Tel. & Tel. Co., service   107 04
National Education Association,
bulletins   97
John R. Parker, P. M., stamped
envelopes, stamps   141 04
A. I. Randall, labor certifictae
envelopes   14 80
Wright & Potter Printing Co.,
ledger blanks   2 08
Yawman Erbe Mfg. Co., file guides   3 48

Total $ 1 499 15

EXPENSE OF INSTRUCTION

Supervisors' Salaries $ 3 399 19
Principals' Salaries   6 921 00
Teachers' Salaries   58 985 86

TEXT BOOKS

D. Appleton Century Co. $ 14 15
American Education Press   12 25
American Book Co.   50 14
Allyn & Bacon   83 78
Acorn Publishing Co.   7 44
The Baker Taylor Co.   3 08
Bobbs-Merrill Co.   35 08
C. C. Birchard & Co.   1 90
E. P. Dutton & Co., Inc.   1 71
Follett Book Co.   1 16
Ginn & Co.   567 20
Houghton Mifflin Co.   7 61
Henry Holt & Co., Inc.   6 51

D. C. Heath Co.	51	49
Harcourt Brace & Co., Inc.	24	36
Hall & McCreary	10	50
The Inor Publishing Co.	3	14
Lyons & Carnahan	15	73
Little, Brown & Co.		82
Laidlaw Bros.	7	50
Charles E. Merrill Co.	5	80
Macmillan Co.	79	77
McGraw-Hill Book Co.	30	40
Noble & Noble	15	26
Newson & Co.	3	26
National Geographic Society	3	50
Prentice-Hall, Inc.	13	49
Edward Stern & Co.	1	95
Silver Burdett & Co.	22	33
Charles Scribner's Sons	4	43
Scott, Foresman & Co.	68	05
Benj. H. Sanborn & Co.	22	94
University of Chicago Press	2	17
World Book Company	16	39
John C. Winston Co.	28	68
Webster Publishing Co.	1	00

Total $ 1 224 97

SUPPLIES

Am. Type Founders Sales Corp. Shop materials	$ 8	45
Burroughs Adding Machine Co., pamphlets		48
Brodhead-Garrett Co., shop materials	111	04
The Boston Music Co., music	48	26
C. C. Bichard Co., music	28	50
Beaudette & Co., stencils	2	05
E. E. Babb & Co., Inc., misc. Schoolroom supplies	284	51

P. & F. Corbin, replacing keys	2	39
Co-operative Test Service, tests	1	00
The Classroom Teacher, seatwork	30	52
John S. Cheever Co., paper	662	84
Central Scientific Co., science		
materials	63	64
Cambosco Scientific Co., micropticon	47	50
Dowling School Supply Co., paper	42	86
A. B. Dick Co., stencils	9	55
Franklin Publishing Co., flash cards	12	74
F. C. Ford & Co., Inc.		
shop materials	7	50
Carl Fischer, Inc., music	12	01
Gregg Publishing Co., notebooks	2	16
Gledhill Bros., schoolroom supplies	21	02
Houghton Mifflin Co., tests	3	29
Hickey Bros., 2 bottles noxon		40
Harvard University Press ,tests	1	54
J. L. Hammett Co., misc.,		
schoolroom supplies	299	28
Iroquois Publishing Co., lab. books	12	29
Milton Bradley Co., schoolroom		
supplies	78	85
H. B. McArdle, schoolroom supplies	16	20
McKinley Publishing Co., maps	4	86
Oliver Ditson Co., music	16	24
Osgood-Globe Corps., press rollers	10	04
Phillips Ribbon & Carbon Co., carbon	5	00
Phillips Paper Co., paper	43	48
George T. Pascoe, paper	27	50
Rome Bros., shop supplies	2	59
Rockland Standard, printing supplies	1	60
Rockland Hardware & Paint Co.		
shop supplies	16	37
R. H. S., Cafeteria, allowance		
for food classes	25	27
Rockland Coal & Grain Co.,		
lumber for shop	65	67

J. A. Rice Co., Inc., supplies		
for sewing classes	10	36
Remington, Rand, Inc., H. S. per-		
manent record cards	50	51
Reformatory for Women, flags	26	66
A. I. Randall, Inc., stock for printing	5	55
Royal Typewriter Co., replacing		
typewriters	120	00
South Western Publishing Co.,		
Acct. materials	129	23
L. C. Smith & Corona Type Co.,		
replacing Typewriters	96	00
Simonds Saw & Steel Co., saw for shop	3	28
Shakun Printing Machinery Co.,		
shop supplies	6	07
Sengbusch Self-closing Inkstand		
Co., inkwells	15	53
O. H. Toothaker, globes	10	00
Talens School Products, Inc.,		
drawing supplies	97	49
Underwood Elliott Fisher Co., re-		
placing typewriter	37	50
John H. Wyatt Co., stencils, ink,		
ribbons	28	02
World Book Co., tests	40	18
Henry J. Winde Co., lumber for shop	13	64
Percy D. Wells, cards	10	07
C. B. Webb Co., basketballs for grades	5	18

Total $ 2 734 76

JANITORS' WAGES

Elmer Dunn, Junior-Senior High	$1 293	16
Charles Metevier, Junior-Senior high	1 405	37
Maurice Mullen, sub. at		
Junior-Senior High	272	00
Joseph DeCosta, McKinley School	1 305	00
Mary Davis, McKinley School	360	00

Joseph Thibeault, Helper at McKinley School	126	00
Andrew Leck, Jefferson School	950	00
Frank Hammond, Gleason School	450	00
Ardelle Cushing, Market St. School	350	00
Frank Curtis, Webster St. School	350	00
Elizabeth Casey, Central St. School	180	00
Thomas Gallagher, Lincoln School	1 000	00

Total $ 8 041 53

FUEL

Abington Coal Corporation, coal	$2 856	42
The Albert Culver Co., coal	742	67
M. J. Fitzgibbons, wood	33	00
Lot Phillips & Co., Corp., wood	12	00
Charles T. Leavitt, Inc., coal	623	65
Roderick MacKenzie, wood	20	00
Rockland Coal & Grain Co., coal	221	84

Total $ 4 509 58

MISCELLANEOUS OPERATING EXPENSES

A. P. W. Paper Co., paper toweling and toilet paper	95	00
Brockton Public Market, janitors' supplies	3	63
Bartlett, Coppinger, Maloon Co., cheesecloth	13	91
P. & F. Corbin, keys	7	33
The Continental Chemical Co., floor materials	37	50
Charlestown State Prison, brushes, mop pails	84	33
Dominic DelPrete, removal of garbage	3	00
Lester Edwards, labor at high school	3	22
Edison Electric Ill. Co., service	1 211	87

Thomas Fox, labor at Lincoln school   20 25
The Floor Treatment Co., floor wax   48 60
L. M. Glover Co., janitors' supplies   118 56
William M. Horner, wax and floor oil   109 50
A. C. Horn Co., floor materials   73 00
The Holmerden Co., janitors supplies   29 25
Hickey Bros., kerosene for cleaning   1 70
Edwin P. Kershaw, dust cloths   7 00
John R. Lyman, cleaning cloths   16 60
John H. Lamb, brushes   2 50
Market St. Garage, gas for cleaning   2 79
Masury-Young Co., misc. janitors'
    supplies   41 60
Old Colony Gas Co., service   30 46
Rockland Water Dept., service   311 56
Rockland New System Laundry,
    laundering gym curtains   51
Leon W. Reynolds, sawdust   18 00
So. Weymouth Laundry, cleansing
    auditorium curtains   50 00
George Tyler, pumping out cesspool   53 00
Taunton Lumber Co., floor wax   39 00
C. Van Blarcom, mops   4 80
West Disinfecting Co., wax   2 74
Young Broom Co., Inc., brooms   4 94

        Total $ 2 446 15

REPAIRS

' H. H. Arnold Co., Inc., belt
    laced, supplies $ 2 95
Stanley R. Ames, victrola repaired   4 90
American Type Founders Sales Corp.,
    supplies   1 75
American Fire Equipment Co., Inc.,
    fire extinguishers   11 85
Burroughs Adding Machine Co.,
    service contract   5 00

Brockton Welding Shop, H. S.
heating apparatus repaired   65 68
Bristol County House of Cor-
rection, mats   11 88
Boston Plate & Window Glass Co.,
glass and putty   42 05
Norman J. Beals, flag pole repaired   6 65
Bay State Belting Co., covering
iron pulley   6 25
J. H. Baker, clock repaired   2 00
Edward E. Babb & Co., Inc., window
shade pulleys   7 58
O. R. Cummings, plastering at high
school   94 95
P. & F. Corbin, door checks
repaired   9 05
Elbert L. Chamberlin, replacing 2
shovels   1 50
W. D. Cashin Co., heating appartus
at high school   233 53
Carbon Solvents Laboratories, mdse   9 00
Earl C. Damon, saw repaired   1 00
Damon Electric, electrical repairs   16 88
Thomas Fox, Jefferson School walk
and McKinley school cesspools   103 00
Grand Specialties Co., two door
stops   1 54
Gilbert, Howe, Gleason & Co., Adjust-
ment of Jefferson pump   11 80
General Electric Co., motor repairs   19 08
George W. S. Hyde, tools sharpened   1 75
A. C. Horn Co., paint   185 89
Hall & Torrey, misc. repairs   459 44
Int. Engineering Works, Inc.,
Paint, lockers repaired   80 89
Johnson Service Co., thermostat repairs   16 44
Lot Phillips & Co., Corp., brazing and
filing saw   75

Liberty Electric Co., glue heater
repaired 3 82
Mass. Division of Blind, pianos tuned
and repaired 19 50
J. S. McCallum, plumbing repairs 94 66
Old Colony Appliance Corp., frigidaire
overhauled 42 50
Herman A. Poole, setting glass 1 50
Forrest L. Partch, electric repairs · 9 03
Rome Brothers, paint and misc.
materials for repairs 1 077 59
Harry L. Rome, replacing curtains 5 75
Rockland Welding & Eng. Co.,
misc. repairs 28 00
Rockland Hardware & Paint Co.,
misc. repairs 4 00
Rockland Coal & Grain Co., materials
for repairs 56 77
E. P. Reed Lumber Co., materials
for repairs 1 28
Stone Hardware Co., Inc., lock set 6 30
Standard Electric Time Co., clock
repairs 194 69
Sloan Valve Co., 12 diaphragm sets 5 02
Edwin Schutt, misc. repairs 218 91
Fred Thibeault, steam fitting repairs 41 25
Vega Plumbing & Heating Co., H. S.
heating apparatus 128 47
John H. Wyatt Co., typewriters
repaired 29 40

Total $ 3 383 47

LIBRARIES

Acorn Publishing Co., encyclopedias $ 15 83
Beckley-Cardy Co., books 20 38
Eldridge Entertainment House, Inc.,
book 1 50

Funk & Wagnalls Co., book	1 71
Follett Puplishing Co., books	11 85
Macmillan Co., book	2 11
Albert Najarian, magazine subscriptions	12 35

Total $ 65 73

HEALTH

Bemis Drug Co., supplies		4 62
Louise A. Considine, salary	1	391 51
Louise A. Considine, Mileage		99 33
Narrangansett Machine Co., gym equipment		2 16
Plymouth County Health Association, loan of audiometer		3 00
Thomas W. Reed Co., tongue depressors	12	92
Joseph H. Dunn, M. D., salary		175 00
Joseph Frame, M. D., salary		175 00

Total $ 1 863 54

TRANSPORTATION

John J. Dwyer, use of bus	$ 1	154 19
Howland's Insurance Office Bond for J. Dwyer		15 00
Eastern Mass., Street Railway, bus tickets		12 50

Total $ 1 181 69

NEW EQUIPMENT

E. E. Babb & Co., Inc., cafeteria table	9 60
Albert Culver Co., shovel	2 25
Carl Fischer, Inc., drum	4 95

E. B. Gray, program board	10 62	
J. L. Hammett Co., chair	4 24	
George T. Hoyt Co., 2 flag poles	70 00	
Massachusetts Reformatory, cafeteria		
stools	99 92	
Old Colony Piano Co., piano	15 00	
Rockland Coal & Grain Co.,		
lumber for cabinet	28 71	
Total		$245 29

SUNDRIES

Ames Radio Service, rental of		
amplifier	$ 10 00	
Frank S. Alger, paper adds	6 00	
Buck Printing Co., tickets	6 63	
Brockton Transportation Co.,		
expressage	3 94	
The Beal Press, engrossing diploma	30	
Babson Institute, poster service	15 85	
Commissioner of Public Safety,		
boiler inspection	5 00	
Phillip S. Collins, insurance premium	271 87	
John J. Dwyer, expressage	1 50	
Everett S. Damon, insurance premium	88 00	
Emerson & Co., rubber stamps	2 99	
Howland's Insurance Co., premiums	288 45	
Hemingway Bros., expressage	60	
J. L. Hammett Co., diplomas, covers,		
engrossing	61 89	
Jenkins & Simmons Express,		
expressage	28 29	
Edward A. Lincoln, Binet		
Examinations	48 00	
Murray Bros., Co., rebinding band		
books, school books	89 70	
Nemasket Transportation Co., express	35	
National Ticket Co., tickets		
for auditorium	25 77	

Albert Najarian, census enumeration   65 30
James F. O'Connor, insurance
   premiums   122 92
Pro Merito Society, pins   19 77
Amos A. Phelps, insurance
   premiums   1 095 01
Rockland Transportation Co.,
   expressage   1 23
Rockland Standard, advertising   4 50
A. I. Randall Inc., school
   reports, stock   112 55
Charles Elliott Torrey, insurance
   premium   92 24
Warren B. Woodward, insurance
   premiums   102 44

     Total $ 2 571 09

REPORT OF SUPERINTENDENT OF SCHOOLS

To the School Committee of Rockland:

The eighth annual report of my work as Superintendent of Schools is submitted herewith:

In endeavoring to train our school children for effective citizenship we are teaching not only printed subject matter but the social qualities that increase the power and influence of the individual and of the group, essential to the welfare of any progressive community. It is very gratifying to state that it is my belief that each year a finer school spirit is noticeable. This ability to work and play together in harmony and loyalty creates a strong foundation for purposeful endeavor as each student becomes an active participant in the up building of his community.

Our teachers both through professional meetings and sports activities are developing to a marked degree, enthussiasm in their common interest, the education of the children entrusted to them.

OMISSION OF REPORTS

Following last year's suggestion of the finance committee, only noteworthy results and requirements included in the reports submitted annually by the high school department heads to the Superintendent, will be stated herein. This is done to reduce the expense of printing.

SPECIFIC REQUESTS FROM DEPARTMENTS

Not only the English Department, but each class in high school recognizes the need of a better equipped library. Annual gifts of books, magazines and money for their purchase are acknowledged gratefully but until a teacher-librarian can be engaged, the benefits of our library are greatly curtailed.

The Cooking Department needs additional utensils for classroom instruction while new bench tops and vises will aid the work of Industrial Arts.

Our present first year Latin textbook which has been in use for a long period should be replaced by some modern edition, one which offers more reading in story form.

DEVELOPMENT OF PROJECTS

Supervision of penmanship in the elementary schools, instituted last year under the instruction of Mrs. Mary Costello, is being continued with considerable improvement achieved. The reconstructed courses in English, History and Geography for the elementary grades were adopted and became effective last September.

TEACHER REPLACEMENT

Miss Dorothy Giles, for the past year and a half French teacher in the high school resigned in December to be married. Miss Myrtle Graves of Norwell, a graduate of Radcliffe with a Master's degree from Harvard, majoring in the foreign languages, was appointed as a substitute to fill the vacancy. Miss Graves has had more than six years of teaching experience in the high schools of Norwell, Concord and Quincy, Massachusetts.

Miss Rose T. Magadini who has taught in our Commermericial Department for the past seven years was granted a leave of absence for one year without pay to pursue graduate work in Education at Boston University. Her position was filled by the appointment for a year of Mr. Earl I. Komarin a graduate of the Commercial department of the

Salem State Teachers' College. Mr. Komarin had formerly substituted in the Peabody, Mass. Schools.

Mr. William P. Earley, teacher and coach in the high school for the past six years resigned to go into business. Mr. Chester J. Poliks of Gardner, Mass. a graduate of Connecticut State College with advanced work at Fitchburg State Teachers' College, Clark and Columbia Universities was appointed to take Mr. Earley's place. Mr. Poliks had taught the past two years in the Templeton High school where he coached a state championship team in baseball and a football team that had an enviable record. Mr. Poliks has had considerable experience in the field of Biology.

Miss Constance Tobey who had served as a substitute teacher in Sewing and Social Science in our high school the previous year was appointed as a regular teacher.

Miss Margaret McHugh, a grade teacher in our elementary schools since September 1926 resigned to be married. Her place was filled by the transfer of Miss Mildred Healey from the first to the third grade in the McKinley Building. Miss Healey's position was filled by Miss Marjorie Smith of Rockland, a graduate of the Bridgewater State Teachers' College, as a substitute teacher.

Miss Alyce O'Brien, teacher of one of the sixth grades in the McKinley School since September 1933 resigned to accept a position in the Wilmington Junior High School. For some time we have felt the need of a man in the building to assist in organizing the boys on the playground, so Paul Casey of Rockland, a graduate of the Bridgewater State Teachers' College was appointed as a substitute in the sixth grade made vacant by the resignation of Miss O'Brien.

Miss Kathryn M. Hickey teacher of the fourth grade in the McKinley School resigned to be married. Miss R. Louise Cone, teacher of the same grade in the Lincoln

School was given that grade upon request. Miss Miriam Roberts, a teacher of the fourth and fifth grades in the Webster Street School was transferred to the fourth grade at the Lincoln School. The vacancy in the Webster Street School was filled by the transfer of Miss Josephine Lannin who has taught at the Central Street School since September 1932. The vacancy there was filled by the appointment of Miss Helen Kovalchuk of Rockland as a substiute teacher. Miss Kovalchuk graduated from Bridgewater State Teachers' College in June 1936.

NURSERY SCHOOL.

/ A unit of the nursery schools which constitutes a part of the Emergency Educational Program authorized by the Works Progress Administration has been in operation continuously in the McKinley School gymnasium since last January with four teachers employed for 2, 3 or 4 year old children. The unit accommodates the children of parents who are on W. P. A. rolls or are those with low income. We have had more than 40 enrolled with an average attendance of 25. The session of the school is from nine o'clock until two with a luncheon served at noon. In December the State gave us permission to add a cook to our staff of workers in the unit.

WORKS PROGRESS ADMINISTRATION
ACT AS IT AFFECTS SCHOOLS

Our department has continued its plan to co-operate with the town officials in providing suitable quarters for the sewing project which is housed on the third floor of the McKinley school. The expense of heating and lighting these rooms has been taken from the school budget. This has amounted to several hundred dollars for annual operation.

This fall the School Committee gave permission to the Recreation Project to use the McKinley School gymnasium for its games and recreational projects. The building is in use several afternoons and evenings each week. The expense of heat, light and janitor service has been defrayed from school budget funds. It seems that if these worthwhile projects are to continue that a sum of money should be raised and appropriated by the town for the continuance of them rather than to use the funds appropriated for the schools.

We have availed ourselves of the opportunity of the National Youth Administration as it operates in schools and colleges throughout the United States. Boys and girls 16 years of age and over whose parents are on low income may apply for this financial assistance. Our quota in Rockland is set at $84 per month. At present we have 14 boys and girls who are receiving this financial aid of $6.00 per month for which they render twenty hours of service to the schools. In some cases it is clerical work and in some janitor service. This financial help is given them to pay for school lunches or to purchase necessary clothing or transportation in order to continue their work in high school.

SCHOOL BUILDINGS AND GROUNDS

Junior-Senior High

The redecoration of the walls and ceilings of the building have been in process of renovation the past year with the work not fully completed at this time. This was undertaken as a W. P. A. project and a very creditable piece of work has been accomplished. The School Department furnishes the material cost from its budget and the federal government pays the labor costs. It was necessary for our department to have the plastering done. A special committee appointed by the town at its March meeting in 1936 met with the School Committee to consider the advisability of changes in our present drainage system. A plan was prepared, but to date the work has not been started. It is highly desirable that this be done that sewage odors will not enter the building nor water back up in our gymnasium as formerly.

The Western Waterproofing Company who undertook the task of making the building water-tight five years ago has been called back several times due to the recurring leaks in the walls. At present it will be necessary to repack the staff beads with oakum and white lead if the remaining leaks are to be stopped. The window shades are badly stained and are beyond repairs in some instances. There are several bad settlement cracks in the foundation walls which must be repaired this year to prevent water entering the building.

The mastic floors in the corridors and toilets have been repaired by the janitors. It will be necessary this year to have several layers of the mastic floor renewed, this expense occuring every three or four years or to replace them with asphalt or rubber tile which is much more durable and in the long run less expensive to maintain. The gravel walks and drives to the building, if covered with a hard surface would prevent tracking our floors with dirt and gravel and thus prolong the life of the mastic corridors.

Through the efforts of our woodworking department and the drawing department a set of scenery was made for the auditorium stage. This was very much needed for our dramatic productions and entertainments. We have had a cabinet constructed on the second floor back of the stage to store the musical instruments which are used by our orchestra and band members.

The acoustic properties of our auditorium are not good so that an amplifier has been rented for our graduation exercises the past two years. When it is possible this condition should be changed by installing absorbent material in the walls and ceilings of the room. A cyclorama for the stage would add greatly to dramatic productions. A moving picture projector is very much needed in the building.

With Memorial Park enlarged and with a fine track it is

highly desirable that the high school should sponsor a track program this year. There are many students who are not qualified to play football, basketball or baseball who would benefit by having a track program. A member of our faculty is well qualified to give track instruction. This is a healthful type of sport and benefiicial exercise for many, both boys and girls. If our athletic program is to continue and be fnancially self-supporting it is imperative that we have an enclosed field so that admission fees may be obtained. With this is mind the School Committee has gone on record as favoring such a project.

It is my belief that our building will be much more efficiently heated when oil units are installed in our boilers. The heat will be more constant. With the installation of oil heat we shall release the services of a janitor at least half time. This help is very much needed in the high school. From estimates which have been submitted we believe that there will be quite a financial saving after the first cost if oil heat is installed. The saving quoted is $365 per year.

It will be necessary to replace several exit doors in the building this year as well as some rotten window sashes.

We have a flag staff on the high school building which now makes it possible for the flag to wave throughout the winter during pleasant weather.

On account of the loss of a vacuum in our heating equipment it was necessary to repack the pipes in our heating and ventilating rooms. This was a big undertaking, but the work has improved the heating of the building.

McKinley School
This past summer the two boilers were retubed and the grates lowered in one to provide a larger combustion chamber. These repairs were made upon the recommendation

of a special committee appointed by the moderator upon request of the town meeting. The work was awarded to the International Engineering Works of Framingham.

The drainage of the school yard has been a problem for several years as the contour of the surface is such that water stands in the rear of the yard for some time. Considerable adjoining property on Belmont Street drains into the school yard. Because the school cesspools were constantly overflowing we had an additional drain installed which has remedied that situation. Nevertheless, water continues in the yard making it unsanitary.

It is imperative that the cement walks at the north and south ends of the building be repaired and the cement and brick work of the building repointed.

Several leaks have developed in the building since the interior was redecorated last year so stains have appeared in several rooms. Additional roof repairs will be necessary to prevent these leaks. Snow rails are quite necessary on the building since those already there are inadequate.

Lincoln

Water enters this building whenever we have had rain storms and makes it difficult to operate the furnaces on account of flooded conditions. Either a pump should be installed to remove this water when it enters the building or a cement shoulder should be placed around the structure.

The school yard should be improved by having it hard surfaced. The dust and gravel which now enters the building are a menace to the pupils. As soon as a walk on the east side of the building is put in this work should be done. We anticipate its completion this summer.

Minor repairs have been made in the plumbing and heating apparatus of the building. Some rotten window sash has been replaced.

Jefferson

Minor repairs of locks and other hardware have been made. More than 20 panes of glass have been broken in the windows. This matter was called to the attention of the police department. These damages occur week-ends and during vacation periods.

Webster Street

Repairs to the furnace and locks have been made. A wire fence on the east side of the school property has been installed. The heating equipment is very old in this building and it will be necessary to replace it within a few years.

Market Street

The small stove in the heating stack has been repaired and is used in very cold weather. The heating equipment in this building is very old and will need replacement before many years.

Gleason

Repairs to the veranda of this building will be necessary this year. Many of the timbers have become unsound and must be replaced. Minor repairs to the plumbing have been made and new water bubblers installed.

Central Street

Repairs have been made to clapboards on the front of the building to prevent leaks inside. A new water bubbler was installed.

CONCLUSION

Education may be defined as the acquisition of knowledge, skill and the development of character.

Children are under the instruction of teachers only one fourth of each twenty-four hour day. Because continually higher requirements are demanded throughout the teaching profession, teachers are better equipped each year to do their part in the mental and social development of children under their guidance. If parents more and more will help to share this splendid opportunity of developing children's minds and character, teachers and parents together will be rewarded by a future peace loving, law abiding and progressive citizenry.

As always, I acknowledge with gratitude the helpful cooperation of teachers, parents, principals and Rockland School Committee members.

Respectfully submitted,

R. STEWART ESTEN.
Superintendent of Schools

December 31, 1936

REPORT OF JUNIOR-SENIOR HIGH SCHOOL
PRINCIPAL

Mr. R. Stewart Esten
Superintendent of Schools
Rockland, Massachusetts

My Dear Mr. Esten

My annual report as Principal of Junior-Senior High
School is presented herewith for your consideration.

On October 1, 1935, the enrollment of the school was
634, and on October 1, 1936, it was 670, an increase of 36
pupils.   This increase, together with the unequal division
of pupils in the various courses of study, has caused our
study rooms to be over-crowded at certain periods of the
day.   The seventh grade rooms are filled to capacity due
to the large enrollment in that grade.   Otherwise, this increase has offered no serious problem.

The average attendance for the past year has been very
good.   There has been some improvement in the matter
of punctuality.   With the co-operation of all parents, I feel
certain that the number of cases of tardiness can be steadily
decreased.

Our testing program was too limited in scope to allow for
any definite conclusions relative to the standard of work
accomplished.   Only in English were we able to give diagnostic and achievement tests in every grade of the school,
and then only one division in each grade had this opportunity.   For the most part our scores on these standard
tests compared favorably with those of other Class A high
schools in the country.   It is essential that a definite testing program be worked out at an early moment for until

there is some yardstick by which achievement can be measured, the success óf our school program is a matter of conjecture.

Seventeen seniors, having met the requirements in scholarship and character, were inducted into Pro Merito last June. Other seniors, who will have met the requirements through good work during the first half year, will be eligible for membership in Pro Merito after the mid-year. As Pro Merito becomes more thoroughly established at the school, it will increasingly become a great incentive for high scholarship.

A class in Household Arts has been formed this fall for the girls of the school. This course deals with certain essentials for successful homemaking. Units of study pertaining to home economics, insurance, budgeting, home nursing, child care, and the like, are contained therein. This is a practical subject and one, in my opinion, which should be taken by all girls at some time before they leave high school.

There has been a marked improvement in school spirit during the fall term. The good influence of this growing school loyalty has made itself felt in many ways about the school. Surely it helped materially during the football season. I venture to repeat what some years experience has led me to believe—school work is done better, school life is more enjoyable, and success comes more often in athletics or the other extra-curriculum activities in the school possessing a fine school spirit. I am confident that this same degree of progress will continue throughout the year.

Now that the fine running track is nearly completed, we should give serious consideration to the establishment of track as a part of our athletic program. In the various activities of this sport, many boys of the school who have not the interest or ability in other forms of athletics, may have the advantages of participating. As we have a member of our faculty who is qualified to coach track, I hope that arrangements can be made so that this activity may be started in the spring.

Certain outstanding events of the year merit brief mention. We entered the state-wide oratorical contest last year and the representative from our school won third place at the district finals held at Brockton. In view of the fact that this was our first attempt, the result was noteworthy. During the year a set of scenery for the stage in the auditorium was built by our Industrial Arts department. This will prove to be invaluable in staging the various school shows. Last spring a fine gymnasium exhibit was put on by the Physical Education departments. I hope more parents and friends of the school will be able to witness our next exhibition which will be held in the spring. All of the above were helpful and of educational value.

A word of appreciation for the painting project at the school should be included in this report. The recently painted interior has restored the original fine appearance of the building. It is to be hoped that all who use the building will co-operate in keeping it in its present fine condition.

We regret the loss of two fine teachers, Miss Giles and Mr. Earley. Miss Murphy is also leaving soon in order to accept a better position. All of these teachers have accomplished much for the good of Rockland High, and will be greatly missed. However they go with our best wishes for continued success.

The Rockland Woman's Club again presented the school with a donation of some money with which to purchase needed books for the library. We also received for the library two sets of books from Mrs. Starbard. Both of these gifts ae appreciated for they help to fill one of the real needs of the school. Gradually library equipment is being obtained, but there remains the need of a teacher-librarian so that the library may be efficiently used.

Knowledge in itself is not sufficient. To know what to do requires knowledge: to do it takes character. Unless knowledge is rightfully used, society is the loser for having educated an individual. Therefore the school can and should assist the church and the home in that most important function of character training. We will continue to stress this matter in all of the school's activities.

I conclude this report by expressing my sincere thanks for the co-operation and assistance which I have received from the school committee, the Superintendent of Schools, the faculty and the young people of the school.

Respectfully submitted,

GEORGE A. J. FROBERGER,
Principal

Report of School Physicians and School Nurse

Mr. R. Stewart Esten
Superintendent of Schools
Rockland, Massachusetts

My dear Mr. Esten:

Below are the reports of the School Physicians and School Nurse.

A physical examination was made of all the pupils of the elementary grades. The players on the high school teams, both boys and girls, were given a careful examination before being allowed to participate in athletics.

We carried out our annual program of Diphtheria Immunization and we wish to urge all parents to avail themselves of this opportunity to protect their children.

We feel that the Milk Fund is a very worthwhile project and hope that it may continue as a benefit to the children.

Following is the list of defects found:

Cases of enlarged tonsils and adenoids	90
Cases of enlarged cervical glands	14
Cases of defective hearing	23
Cases of defective vision	41
Cases under care of the Chadwick Clinic	22
Number given Toxoid innoculations	161

ACTIVITIES OF SCHOOL NURSE

Classrooms in the elementary schools are visited twice weekly, oftener if the occasion demands it. High school classes are visited whenever requested. Elementary grade pupils are weighed four times during the school year. Special inspections are made in each classroom monthly, and daily if the children have been exposed to contagion. An office hour is maintained by the nurse each school morning from 8:30 to 9:30 o'clock and she may be reached by telephoning the school office.

Number of visits to schools	1782
Number of visits to homes	659
Number of dressings to minor wounds	107
Number of emergency treatments	31
Number taken home ill	69
Number sent to school physician	3
Number sent to family physician	19
Number of pupils weighed and measured	2042
Number of inspections	4007
Number taken to hospital clinics	16
Number taken for x-rays	12
Number of visits to Nursery school	95
Number of examinations of Nursery school children	2223

All cases of non-attendance which have been reported have been investigated.

Respectfully submitted,

JOSEPH H. DUNN, M. D.,
JOSEPH FRAME, M. D.,
LOUISE A. CONSIDINE, R. N.

FINANCIAL REPORT OF CAFETERIA

MISS ELEANOR LOUD

January 1, 1936 — December 31, 1936

RECEIPTS:

Balance January 1, 1936	$ 25	62
Sale of Food	4 292	55

Total Cash	$ 4 318	17

EXPENDITURES:

Meats and Provisions:

William F. Barnes	17	15
John Mahoney	150	38
Hickey Brothers	612	89
Paul Tranniello	2	00
Angelo Umbrianna	1	50

Wholesale Groceries:

E. V. Fitts & Co.	235	54
H. F. Ellis Co.	108	88
Hunt Potato Chip Co.	40	11
Standard Brands Inc.	6	15
Som Won Co.	2	00
H. Primack	9	40
R. C. Williams & Co., Inc.	39	52
S. Gumpert Co., Inc.	16	00

Milk:

A. C. Stoddard	264	75
Whiting Milk Co.	61	02

Bread and Rolls:

Berwick Cake Co.	231	84
Carey's Home Bakery	33	16
Wonder Bread Co.	216	26
Continental Baking Co.	5	28
Hathaway Baking Co.	2	84
Hostess Baking Co.	29	08

Cushman's Bakery	35	34
Crackers and Cookies:		
Loose-Wiles Biscuit Co.	110	44
National Biscuit Co.	19	53
Felber Biscuit Co.	3	26
Ice Cream:		
Plymouth Rock Ice Cream Co.	812	85
Candies and Miscellaneous:		
A. S. Peterson	433	72
Eleanor Loud (Reimbursement for Groceries purchased for Cafeteria)	16	11
Operating Expenses:		
Arthur Casey	10	00
Dominic DelPrete	5	00
Globe Ticket Co.	28	00
Malcolm Pratt (Reimbursement for glasses purchased for kitchen)	3	00
Old Colony Gas Co.	77	60
Edison Electric Illuminating Co.	88	00
Old Colony Appliance Corp.	4	75
Student Activities	3	00
Margaret Quinn, Help	560	00
Rockland Water Dept.	10	00
Rockland New System Laundry	2	44
Service Charges	4	20

Total expenditures		$ 4 312	99
Balance		5	18
		$ 4 318	17

ROCKLAND HIGH SCHOOL
GRADUATION EXERCISES
CLASS OF 1936

Wednesday Evening, June Seventeenth
Rockland High School Auditorium

PROGRAM

Processional "Zouave March"   *Jackson*
        R. H. S. Orchestra

Invocation   Rev. Richard K. Morton

Honor Essay   "Personality Through Life"
        Elinor Goddard Baker

Song (a) "Where My Caravan Has Rested"   *Lohr*
    (b) "Sylvia"   *Speaks*
        Girls' Glee Club

Honor Essay   ·   "Our Supreme Objective"
        Charlotte Evelyn Hammond

Chamber of Commerce Prize Essay   "Our Community"
        Merilyn Walker Studley

Music, "Maritana" Selection   *Wallace*
        R. H. S. Orchestra

Honor Essay   "The Conquering Faith"
        Maxine Woodrow Sheldon

Song "The Beautiful Blue Danube" (requested)   *Strauss*
        Rockland High Chorus

Honor Essay   "The Essence of Friendship"
                    Elizabeth Guild Studley

Chamber of Commerce Scholarship Award
                    Dr. Joseph Lelyveld
                    President of Chamber of Commerce

Woman's Club Scholarship Award, Mrs. Ernest A. Studley
                    Chairman of Scholarship Committee

Awarding of other prizes and Presentation of Diplomas
                    Dr. William A. Loud, Chairman
                    Rockland School Committee

Class Song   Words and Music by Mildred Alden Dill

Song, "America"   Chorus and Audience

Benediction   Rev. Richard K. Morton

Director of the Chorus   Miss Blanche G. Maguire
Director of the Orchestra   Mr. Michael Cassano
Accompanists, Mary Asklund, '38, and Ruth Southard, '37

GRADUATES

*Elinor Goddard Baker
Ruth Eleanor Baker
Katherine Frances Bell
Louise Gertrude Benoit
Marjorie Ernestine Benton
Ardelle Mae Bowser
*Willard Alden Burrell
Mary Frances Cella
William Ralph Chadwick
Edward Thomas Corcoran
*Mildred Alden Dill
*Lurana Eileen Egan
Donald Anthony Fange
Mildred Elizabeth Fiaschetti
Edward Minton Frame
Ralph John Fucillo
Edward Arthur Gibbons
Harry Joseph Giblin

Kathryn Lucy McGee
Elizabeth Agnes McMorrow
Gertrude Elaine Mahoney
*Grace Elizabeth Mastrodo-
    menico
Mary Clara Mastrodomenico
Helen Marie Metevier
Joseph William Nihill
*Edith Victoria Olson
Alyce Louise Reagan
Thomas A. Reardon, Jr.
Virginia Evelyn Reed
*Ruth Richards
Eleanor Marie Rose
Cecilia Lillian Schleiff
*Helen Edith Schofield
*Maxine Woodrow Sheldon
Daniel Frederick Smith

*Phyllis Eleanor Goodfellow
Ruth Emma Grant
*Donald Howard Gurney
Myles Vincent Haggerty
*Charlotte Evelyn Hammond
Willard Harney
*Eleanor Christine Harrington
John Sheridan Hickey
*Rose Lorraine Jasper
Joseph William Kelley
John Lawrence Kennedy
*Mark Lelyveld
Sarah Veronica LeMotte
Dorothy Burton Lovewell
Delma Marie McEnroe

Loverna Bell Stetson
*Stuart Vernon Stoddard
*Elizabeth Guild Studley
Merilvn Walker Studley
Josephine Gertrude Tracey
Frederick George Verdone
Elfrida Maxine Von Beidel·
Wendell Earl Weeks
Raymond Francis Whiting
Adlare Joseph Wilmot
Francis Leslie Woodward
Ruth Leslie Wvatt
Richard John Young
Augustine Charles Yourell

*Pro Merito — Honor Society. Average of 85 per cent or over
    for 4 years.

CLASS OFFICERS

DONALD GURNEY   President
ROSE JASPER   Vice President
LURANA EAGAN   Secretary
JOHN KENNEDY   Treasurer

SOCIAL COMMITTEE

Merilyn Studley,   Daniel Smith,   Joseph Wilmot

CLASS COLORS
Blue and Silver

CLASS MOTTO
"Facta Non Verba"

CLASS FLOWER
Supreme Rose

AGE GRADE TABLE AS OF OCTOBER 1, 1936

									AGE								
Grade	5	6	7	8	9	10	11	12	13	14	15	16	17	18	19	20	Total
1	57	55	6														118
2		45	56	12	5												118
3			55	52	15	9	1										132
4				49	65	11	6	1									132
5				1	48	42	24	7	2	1							125
6						44	55	19	12	1							131
7							54	62	11	6	2						135
8								35	54	8	3	3					103
9									40	70	15	8					133
10									2	43	40	28	2				115
11										3	26	67	3	1			100
12												25	42	14	2	1	84
Ungraded					4	1		4	2		4	2			1		18
Total	57	100	117	114	137	107	140	128	123	132	90	133	47	15	3	1	1444

SCHOOL ENROLLMENT

As of December 23, 1936

Teacher	School	Grade	Number of Pupils
Marjorie Smith	McKinley	1	40
Mary H. Greenan	McKinley	2	38
Mildred E. Healey	McKinley	3	35
R. Louise Cone	McKinley	4	44*
Elva M. Shea	McKinley	5	24
Margaret Shortall	McKinley	5	29
Paul Casey	McKinley	6	32
Nellie M. Ford	McKinley	6	32
Eleanor L. Birch	McKinley	Special Class	16
Catherine Coen	Lincoln	1	26
Blanche Thacher	Lincoln	2	30
Harriette E. Cragin	Lincoln	3	36
Miriam Roberts	Lincoln	4	36
Eileen Fitzgibbons	Lincoln	5	31
Margaret McDermott	Lincoln	6	34
W. Louise Flannery	Jefferson	1 and 2	31
Bertha Campbell	Jefferson	2 and 3	35
Blanche Crowell	Jefferson	4 and 5	33
Annie A. Shirley	Jefferson	5 and 6	32
Lillian G. Murdock	Webster Street	1, 2 and 3	28
Josephine Lannin	Webster Street	4 and 5	28
Ethel Wetherbee	Market Street	1, 2 and 3	19
Margaret Blake	Market Street	4, 5 and 6	24
Madeline Lannin	Gleason	1 and 2	25
Dorothy Ellershaw	Gleason	3 and 4	30
Helen Kovalchuk	Central Street	1, 2 and 3	19

Total		787
Junior-Senior High school enrollment December 23, 1936		659
Grand Total		1 446

TEACHERS UNDER APPOINTMENT DECEMBER 31, 1936

Teacher	Grade or subject	Educational and Professional Training	Date of First Appointment in Town	Salary
SUPERINTENDENT OF SCHOOLS				
R. Stewart Esten		Middlebury Col., Columbia Univ.	Sept. 1929	$3,600.00
JUNIOR - SENIOR HIGH				
George A. J. Froberger, Principal		Uni. of Maine	Sept. 1935	2,880.00
Robert C. Healey, Sub-master, Latin		Boston College, B. U.,	Sept. 1919	2,430.00
Katherine S. Burke, Geog., Science		Bridgewater Tea. Col.	Sept. 1906	1,260.00
Joseph Cogan, Sciences		Bates College	Sept. 1929	1,755.00
Mary D. Costello, English, Penmanship		Quincy Training School	Sept. 1898	1,260.00
Marguerite Croak, Commercial		Boston University	Sept. 1933	1,250.00
Dorothy Giles, French		Tufts College	Sept. 1935	1,350.00
John B. Haggerty, Manual Training		Fitchburg Tea. C.	Sept. 1934	1,200.00
Ellen M. Hayes, English		Univ. of Wisconsin	Sept. 1927	1,620.00
Victoria Howarth, English		Radcliffe College	Sept. 1925	1,800.00
Emma S. Jewett, History		Hyannis Tea. College	Sept. 1908	1,260.00
Eleanor Loud, Household Arts		Simmons College	Sept. 1935	1,000.00
Olive H. Mayer, English		Boston University	Sept. 1935	1,200.00
Esther McGrath, History, Literature		Bridgewater Tea. Col.	Sept. 1918	1,260.00
Helen Molloy, Junior Bus. Training		Keene Normal	Sept. 1930	1,170.00
Evelyn Murphy, Commercial		Salem Normal	May 1933	1,100.00
John B. O'Hayre, History		Boston College	Jan. 1931	1,485.00
Malcolm Pratt, Mathematics		Dartmouth College	Jan. 1933	1,450.00
Chester Poliks, Phys. Ed., Biology			Dec. 1936	1,710.00
Frances L. Squarey, English, Lit.		Bridgewater Tea. C.	Sept. 1921	1,260.00
Robert A. Studley, History		Univ. of N. H.	Sept. 1927	1,575.00
Bertha L. Tenney, Arithmetic		Farmington Normal	Sept. 1927	1,260.00

TEACHERS UNDER APPOINTMENT DECEMBER 31, 1936

Name	Institution	Date	Salary
Constance Tobey, Sewing, History	Univ. of N. H.	Sept. 1936	1,100.00
Earl I. Komarin, Commercial	Salem Tea. College	Sept. 1936	1, 2000
John Ryan, History	Boston College and Bridgewater Tea. Col.	S bstitute	$4.50 per day

McKINLEY SCHOOL

Name	Institution	Date	Salary
Eleanor Birch, Special Class	Salem Tea. College	Sept. 1935	1,150.00
Nellie M. Ford, Prin., Grade 6	High School, Special Courses	Sept. 1896	1,440.00
Mary H. Greenan, Grade 2	Added B. U., Hyannis Tea. Col.	Sept. 1930	1,260.00
Mildred E. Healey, Grade 3	Lesley Normal	Sept. 1930	1,000.00
R. Louise Cone, Grade 4	Wheelock, Boston Univ.	Sept. 1930	1,215.00
Elva M. Shea, Grade 5	Bridgewater Tea. Col.	Sept. 1928	1,057.50
Margaret Shortall, Grade 5	Bridgewater Tea. Col	Oct. 1932	1,000.00
Marjorie Smith, Grade 1	Bridgeawter Tea. Col.	Sbtitute	$4.50 per day
Paul Casey, Grade 6	Bridgeawter Tea. Col.	Sbtitute	$4.50 per day

LINCOLN SCHOOL

Name	Institution	Date	Salary
Eileen Fitzgibbons, Prin., Grade 5	Bridgewater Tea. Col.	Sept. 1925	1,260.00
Catherine Coen, Grade 1	Salem Teachers' Col.	Sept. 1930	1,170.00
Blanche Thacher, Grade 2	Wheelock Ktg. School	Jan. 1930	1,125.00
Harriette E. Cragin, Grade 3	High School, Sp. Courses	Sept. 1910	1,260.00
Miriam E. Roberts, Grade 4	Bridgewater Tea. Col.	Sept. 1934	1,000.00
Margaret McDermott, Grade 6	Hyannis Tea. College	Sept. 1925	1,260.00

JEFFERSON SCHOOL

Name	Institution	Date	Salary
Annie A. Shirley, Grades 5 and 6	Bridgewater Tea. Col.	Sept. 1912	1,350.00
Bertha Campbell, Grades 2 and 3	Mass State, Hyannis Tea. Col.	Sept. 1923	1,260.00
Blanche Crowell, Grades 4 and 5	Framingham Tea. Col.	Sept. 1931	1,170.00
Louise Flannery, Grades 1 and 2	Lesley Normal	Sept. 1926	1,102.50

TEACHERS UNDER APPOINTMENT DECEMBER 31, 1936

GLEASON SCHOOL

Dorothy Ellershaw, Grades 3 and 4	Bridgewater Tea. Col.	Sept. 1935	1,000.00
Madeline Lannin, Grades 1 and 2	Lesley Normal	Jan. 1935	1,000.00

WEBSTER STREET SCHOOL

Lillian G. Murdock, Grades 1, 2 and 3	Quincy Training School	Sept. 1922	1,260.00
Josephine Lannin, Grades 4 and 5	Bridgewater Tea. Cl	Sept. 1932	1,000.00

MARKET STREET SCHOOL

Margaret Blake, Grades 4, 5 and 6	Hyannis Tea. Col.	Sept. 1929	1,000.00
Ethel Wetherbee, Grades 1, 2 and 3	Symonds Ktg. Shol	Sept. 1928	1,260.00

CENTRAL STREET SCHOOL

Helen Kovalchuk, Grades 1, 2, and 3	Bridgewater Tea. Col.		Substitute $4.50 per day

SPECIAL TEACHERS

*Blanche Maguire, Music	Attended B. U. and Northampton School of Pedagogy	March 1929	837.00
**Michael Cassano	Virtuoso Music School Private Study in Music	Sept. 1928	1,125.00
Louise A. Considine, Nurse	St. Eliz. Hosp. Training School	Sept. 1922	1,395.00
Josephine Fitzgibbons, Phys. Education for Girls	Posse-Nisson	Sept. 1929	1,125.00
Marian S. Whiting, Drawing	Mass. School of At	Sept. 1930	1,440.00

< Two days each week
** Three days each week.

APPOINTMENTS 1936

Earl I. Komarin, High School
Constance Tbey, High School
Chester Poliks, High School

TEACHERS UNDER APPOINTMENT DECEMBER 31, 1936

RESIGNATIONS 1936

William P. Earley, High School
Kathryn Hickey, McKinley School
Margaret McHugh, McKinley School
Alyce O'Brien, McKinley School

INDEX

CKLAND
N REPORT

1937

SIXTY-FOURTH

ANNUAL REPORT

OF THE

TOWN OFFICERS

OF THE

Town of Rockland

FOR THE YEAR ENDING DECEMBER 31

1937

ROCKLAND STANDARD PUBLISHING CO.

Rockland, Massachusetts

Officers of the Town of Rockland 1937

Town Clerk (elected annually)
RALPH L. BELCHER

Town Treasurer (elected annually)
CHARLES J. HIGGINS

Tax Collector (elected annually)
JAMES A. DONOVAN

Moderator (elected annually)
MAGORISK L. WALLS

Selectmen, Board of Public Welfare and Fence Viewers
(elected annually)
HARRY S. TORREY
JOHN J. BOWLER   NORMAN S. WHITING

Bureau of Old Age Assistance
(appointed by Board of Public Welfare)
HARRY S. TORREY
JOHN J. BOWLER   NORMAN S. WHITING

Supervisor of Old Age Assistance
(appointed by Board of Public Welfare)
MARY L. O'BRIEN

Assessors
(one elected annually for three years)
NORMAN J. BEALS   Term expires 1940
DENNIS L. O'CONNOR   Term expires 1939
JOSEPH B. ESTES   Term expires 1938

School Committee
(for term of three years)

WILLIAM A. LOUD   Term expires 1940
BENJAMIN LELYVELD   Term expires 1940
HELEN M. HAYDEN   Term expires 1939
M. AGNES KELLEHER   Term expires 1938
E. STUART WOODWARD   Term expires 1938

Park Commissioners
(one elected annually for three years)

CHARLES T. WALLS   Term expires 1940
PATRICK H. MAHONEY   Term expires 1939
DANIEL H. BURKE   Term expires 1938

Water Commissioners
(one elected annually for three years)

EVERETT S. DAMON   Term expires 1940
RALPH FUCILLO   Term expires 1939
SAMUEL W. BAKER   Term expires 1938

Board of Health
(one elected annually for three years)

JOSEPH H. DUNN, M. D.   Term expires 1940
JOSEPH FRAME, M. D.   Term expires 1938
*EDWARD J. CULLINAN   Term expires 1938
  * Appointed to fill vacancy MICHAEL J. FITZGIB-
  BONS, deceased June 14, 1937

Sewerage Commissioners
(one elected annually for three years)

CHARLES M. HINES   Term expires 1940
FREDERIC HALL   Term expires 1939
GILES W. HOWLAND   Term expires 1938

Trustees of the Memorial Library
(two elected annually for three years)

EMMA W. GLEASON   Term expires 1940
FRANCIS J. GEOGAN   Term expires 1940
BURTON L. CUSHING   Term expires 1939
JOHN B. FITZGERALD   Term expires 1939
EMILY CRAWFORD   Term expires 1938
ANNIE McILVENE   Term expires 1938

Auditors
(elected annually)
HAROLD C. SMITH   LEO E. DOWNEY
C. ELMER ASKLUND

Tree Warden
(elected annually)
ALFRED T. METIVIER

Highway-Surveyor
(elected annually)
RODERICK MacKENZIE

Constables
(elected annually)
CORNELIUS J. McHUGH   JOHN J. MURPHY
ADOLPH L. W. JOHNSON   ROBERT J. DRAKE
GEORGE J. POPP

APPOINTMENTS

(by Selectmen)

Chief of Police
GEORGE J. POPP

Police Officers
CORNELIUS J. McHUGH   JOHN J. MURPHY
ADOLPH L. W. JOHNSON   ROBERT J. DRAKE

Special Police Officers

EDWARD J. CULLINAN   JOSEPH J. L. DeCOSTA
MAURICE MULLEN   EARL WYATT
JOHN J. DWYER JR.   CARL BENHAM
CHARLES M. HINES   ELMER DUNN
FORREST L. PARTCH   CHARLES METIVIER
RALPH WHEELER   HAROLD MORSE
THOMAS MAHONEY   SAMUEL J. CANNAWAY
CHARLES BOUDREAU   JAMES McKEEVER
BERNARD DELORY   JOHN DOYLE
MICHAEL J. O'BRIEN   JOHN F. HANNON
W. ALTON WHITING   THOMAS FITZGERALD
HENRY ROCHE SR.   FREDERICK J. PERRY
THOMAS MAHON   LEE RHODENIZER
WILLIAM C. NICHOLS   GEORGE MANLEY
              LEO E. DOWNEY

Keeper of the Lock-Up
GEORGE J. POPP

Election Officers
Precinct One   Precinct Two

Wardens
WILLIAM J. FLYNN   JOHN A. WINSLOW

Deputy Wardens
ROBERT PARKER   HAROLD C. POOLE

Clerks
IRVIN E. EMERY   FRED RYAN

Deputy Clerks
CARL FASS   J. LOCKE LANNIN

Inspectors
JOHN J. PAULIN   ELLIS BLAKE
MATTHEW O'GRADY   CHARLES F. SHIELDS

Deputy Inspectors
ROBERT D. ESTES   FRANCIS L. GAMMON
TIMOTHY WHITE   E. BURTON RAMSDELL
ANNIE GARRITY   OLIVE C. WHEELER
HELENA W. HUNT   MARY E. LYNCH

Registrars of Voters
(one appointed annually for three years)
JOHN D. CARNEY   Term expires 1940
ESTHER H. RAWSON   Term expires 1939
THOMAS MORRISSEY   Term expires 1938

Sealer of Weights and Measures
HAROLD J. INKLEY

Measurer of Wood and Bark
GILES W. HOWLAND

Weighers of Hay and Coal — Also Public Weighers
RALPH KEENE   EDITH PETRELL
ELIZABETH DONOVAN   ARTHUR PETRELL
PERCY JACOBS   DOMINICK PETRELL

Agent for Burial of Indigent Soldiers and Care
of Soldiers' Graves
LOUIS B. GILBRIDE

Inspector of Animals and Stables
WILLIAM T. CONDON

Town Physicians for poor and Soldiers' Relief
FREDERICK H. COREY, M. D.
JOSEPH H. DUNN, M. D.

Superintendent Gypsy Moth
ALFRED T. METIVIER

Forest Fire Warden
CLYSON P. INKLEY

APPOINTMENTS
(by School Committee)

Superintendent of Schools
R. STEWART ESTEN

APPOINTMENTS
(by Water Commissioners)

Superintendent of Water Works
JAMES B. STUDLEY

APPOINTMENTS
(by Board of Health)

Inspectors of Plumbing
FREDERIC HALL   J. STUART McCALLUM

Milk Inspectors
BOARD OF HEALTH

APPOINTMENTS
(by Moderator)
Finance Committee

WILLIAM KANE	Term expires 1940
WESLEY PIERCE	Term expires 1940
EDWARD RYAN	Term expires 1940
MARY CLANCEY	Term expires 1940
JAMES APPLEFORD	Term expires 1940
MARION MANSFIELD DONOVAN	Term expires 1939
FLORENCE DUDLEY	Term expires 1939
JAMES P. KANE	Term expires 1939
BERNARD MONAHAN	Term expires 1939
ARTHUR W. WYMAN	Term expires 1939

MARY L. SHAW   Term expires 1938
ALTON F. LYONS   Term expires 1938
EVA HUBLEY   Term expires 1938
RALPH W. BINGHAM   Term expires 1938
WILLIAM J. SWIFT   Term expires 1938

Chief of Fire Department

CLYSON P. INKLEY   Tenure of Office

Report of the Town Clerk

MARRIAGES REGISTERED IN THE TOWN OF
ROCKLAND FOR THE YEAR 1937

January 1. Leopoldo P. Sicuranza of South Weymouth and Katherine F. Holbrook of Rockland.

January 2. Lewis W. Bennett of Rockland and Katherine M. Welch of Brockton.

January 10. Robert C. Wyatt of Rockland and Esther Hefler of Whitman.

January 21. Lawrence L. Smith of Rockland and Clara E. Fritz of North Abington.

January 31. Harry C. Vail and Hazel F. Johnson both of Braintree.

February 7. Charles E. Petrosevich of Hanover and Helen A. Glinsky of Rockland.

February 11. George W. Bennett of Rockland and Mary Cullinan of Lowell.

February 11. Kenneth T. Smith of Rockland and Dorothy Finch of Weymouth.

February 14. William H. McIver of Rockland and Barbara E. Clapp of Whitman.

February 14. Allen B. Howland of Rockland and Doris F. Adams of Abington.

February 20. Harold C. Poole of Rockland and Thelma F. Gardner of Cohasset.

March 7. Leslie M. Hibberd and Louise V. Paulding both of Rockland.

March 27. Harold E. Peterson of Brockton and Elsie Muti of Rockland.

March 28. John F. Bailey of Rockland and Ruth L. Fagan of Avon.

March 28. Lester R. Bowles of Rockland and Dagmar E. Johnson of Brockton.

March 28. John W. MacDonald and Marguerite E. Coit both of Rockland.

April 2. Carl Conte of Brockton and Janet Angie of Rockland.

April 3. Frederick A. Leary of Hanover and Mary M. Flavell of Rockland.

April 4. Matthew S. Ajeman of Rockland and Elizabeth R. Lincoln of Norwell.

April 9. William F .Tenney of Braintree and Elizabeth M. Essery of Rockland.

April 10. Elmer Jacques Bloom of Illinois and Mariesta Dodge Howland of Rockland.

April 10. Wilfred T. Magoun of Rockland and Anna R. Hunt of Marshfield.

April 16. Ray L. Hutchinson and Dorothy L. Hollis both of Rockland.

April 17. William M. Campbell of Rockland and Myra E. Tamblin of Nashua, N. H.

April 18. Rosiario Provenzano of South Boston and Helen Crea of Rockland.

April 18. Peter J. Chiminiello of Quincy and Mary E. Ingeno of Rockland.

April 24. Shirley A. Peterson of Rockland and Annie J. Capen of Stoughton.

April 24. Felix F. Welcome of Brockton and Florence A. Whiting of Rockland.

April 25. Leonard R. Mastrodomenico of Rockland and Angela L. Maurea of Brockton.

April 30. Arthur S. Josselyn of Rockland and Martha L. Johnson of North Abington.

May 16. Curtis E. Sayce and Mary R. Benson both of Hanson.

May 16. Leon F. Brady and Geraldine E. Felix both of Rockland.

May 19. Edgar Sargent of Cohasset and Blanche L. Beal of Rockland.

May 23. James F. Hart and Esther L. Rudkin both of Rockland.

May 25. Raymon H. MacNeil of Middleboro and Jeanette M. Whitman of Bourne.

June 2. William S. Young Jr., of Hanover and Elwilda Stoddard of Rockland.

June 3. Theo G. Morss of North Abington and Dorothy C. Delory of Rockland.

June 14. Joseph H. Bourque of Rockland and Alice C. Defossis of Lynn.

June 19. Francis T. Dwyer of Rockland and Mary P. Everson of Brighton.

June 20. William M. Brady of Haverhill and Regina C. McDonnell of Rockland.

June 20. George Early of Brockton and Dorothy Williams of Rockland.

June 22. Joseph A. Dulac of Laconia, N. H., and Norma B. Packard of Rockland.

June 27. Karl H. Benner and Dorothy Louise Hall both of Whitman.

June 27. Michael Cassano of Rockland and Jeanette P. Vergona of Everett.

June 27. John J. Franey of North Abington and Ella E. McCarthy of Rockland.

June 27. Gordon R. Quindley and Anona W. Bearce both of Rockland.

July 1. John W. McCarthy and Helen M. O'Brien both of Rockland.

July 1. Gordon L. Blake and Teresa V. Lawless both of Rockland.

July 2. Paul H. Chase and Helen M. Erickson both of Brockton.

July 3. William B. Drayton of South Hanson and Doris V. Sanville of Boston.

July 3. Charles N. Weatherbee of Rockland and Dorothy E. Ellershaw of Brockton.

July 3. Francis M. Hill of Cohasset and Florence M. Beal of Rockland.

July 4. Alfred D. R. Cormier of Brockton and Verda R. Barry of Rockland.

July 14. Byron C. Swift of East Braintree and Clara N. Brayton of Rockland.

July 17. Robert L. Blaisdell of W. Hanover and Eleanor A. Somers of Rockland.

July 24. William E. Hickey and Mary E. Burton both of Rockland.

July 25. David C. Gray of Brockton and Cynthia V. Moore of Rockland.

July 26. Donald C. Dunbar of Whitman and Hazel M. Brown of Halifax.

August 7. Marshall B. Stetson and Alice Gaudet both of Winooski, Vt.

August 7. Franklin R. Hickey and Helen G. McCarthy both of Rockland.

August 8. James F. Yourell and Myrtle G. Courtnell both of Rockland.

August 10. Joseph F. McHugh of Rockland and Grace D. Donovan of Boston.

August 11. William F. F. Hussey of Rockland and Miriam F. Packard of Whitman.

August 19. William H. Pratt and Lucretia R. Mason both of Rockland.

August 20. Waldo L. MacPherson and Lillian H. Tower both of Abington.

August 23. Louis W. Dearth of Rockland and Phyllis Hinglebine of Brockton.

August 26. George L. O'Brien of Rockland and Dorothea MacDonald of South Weymouth.

August 29. Nelson S. Ewell and Rose E. Everett both of Rockland.

September 3. Frederick M. Chase of Rockland and Elizabeth A. Clark of South Easton.

September 4. Matthew D. Gay and Esther T. Smith both of Rockland.

September 5. Warren I. Ware and Pauline E. Lescault both of Rockland.

September 11. Albert P. Ruprecht of Kingston and Alberta A. Cannon of Rockland.

September 12. John W. McHugh of Pawtucket, R. I., and Winifred L. Dugan of Rockland.

September 17. Lawrence A. Nichols of Hanover and Gertrude T. Strachan of Norwell.

September 18.   Paul Fontaine of Brockton and Abbie Ellis of Rockland.

September 25.   Thomas E. McNutt of Rockland and Mary E. Kenneally of E. Bridgewater.

September 27.   John R. Perchard of Hyde Park and Elizabeth P. Cullinan of Rockland.

September 30.   John Cameron Weir of Rockland and and Florence M. Cushing of No. Abington.

October 2.   Richard Knowles Morton of Rockland and Dorothy Gertrude Dixon of Wollaston.

October 9.   Gilbert F. Forrand of Rockland and Jennie Lind of Brockton.

October 10.   Janero Eoniri and Doris H. Swain both of Rockland.

October 12.   Bernard V. Delory of Rockland and Helena M. Burns of Whitman.

October 16.   Walter Melville of So. Weymouth and Margaret Shortall of Rockland.

October 16.   Elmore C. Brewster of Rockland and Helen R. Stoddard of Stoughton.

October 21.   Stanley B. Bowman Jr. asd Eleanor M. Finegan both of Rockland.

October 21.   Harold F. Sheehan and Catherine L. Gammon both of Rockland.

October 27.   Herbert F. Ellis of Abington and Emma M. Allison of Rockland.

October 29. Thomas E. Brides of Brockton and Rose. H. Walsh of Rockland.

October 30. Earle E. Felix of Rockland and Mary C. Tower of Hanover.

November 7. Elias T. Nokes of Cambridge and Erma M. Whitman of Rockland.

November 8. John V. Noland of Rockland and Lillie L. Hatch of Hanover.

November 11. Anthony C. Rubino and Margaret E. Skehan both of Rockland.

November 14. Albert F. DelPrete of Rockland and Christine M. Carpenter of So. Weymouth.

November 20. Douglas A. Guthrie of Norwell and Frances E. Chaponis of Hanover.

November 25. Paul H. Dotton of Allston and Mary H. Twomey of Rockland.

November 25. Eldridge Abbot Stuart of Taunton and Bessie Mary Carreaux of Rockland.

November 25. Ulric White of Rockland and Helen Luise of E. Braintree.

November 25. Burton H. Smith of Whitman and Ida P. Blanchard of Rockland.

November 25. William A. Mullins of Rockland and Marjorie Bonney of Brockton.

November 27. Herman B. Hicks of Rockland and Helen Nowelle of Brockton.

November 29. Edward Goodwin of Brockton and Louise Holbrook of Rockland.

December 3. Wesley Mitchell of Wollaston and Irene Ricca of Rockland.

December 4. Doyle A. New of Laredo, Texas and Sylvia H. Clark of Hanover.

BIRTHS REGISTERED IN THE TOWN OF ROCKLAND FOR THE YEAR 1937

Date of Birth	Name	Name of Parents with Maiden Name of Mother	Birthplace of Parents
Jan 3	Helen Marie Metivier	Edward J. and Dorothy M. Shaw	Rockland Vermont
Jan 16	Mary Umbrianna	Joseph W. and Rose M. Sinopli	Rockland Cohasset
Jan 17	James Chames	John and Geneva A. Martin	Greece Westboro
Jan 19	Robert Edwin Peabody	John L. and Rita W. Cannon	Maine Brockton
Jan 21	Julia Ann Blanchard	Fred E. and Hazel E. Carrier	Vermont Vermont
Jan 23	Norbert Francis Lough Jr.	Norbert F and Gertrude A. Riley	Boston Hinsdale
Jan 29	Ronald Lester Benoit	Edward J. and Lillian Gardner	Rockland Rockland
Feb 2	Patricia Louise Doherty	John J. and Alberta Rowell	N. Abington Brockton
Feb 6	Mary Louise Smith	Alfred and Grace Damon	N. Easton Ashby
Feb 8	Stillborn		
Feb 13	William Arthur Bryant	Lloyd C. and Ellen P. Rutkin	Rockland Rockland
Feb 15	Josephine Mary Aretino	George and Mary Umbriano	Italy Rockland
Feb 17	Elaine Ann Benton	Earl C. and Anna Thompson	E. Taunton Idbro
Feb 21	Mary Elizabeth Eamon	Wm. A. and Elizabeth M. Connors	Whitman Rockland
Feb 23	Richard Edward Driscoll	Edward J. and Katherine A. Bailey	Abington Fland
Feb 23	Paul Metcalf	Edward J. ard Margaret V Turley	S. Boston N. Hampshire
Feb 25	Charles Frederick Brown	William W. and Alice E. Binney	Rockland Abington
Feb 26	Fredrick Eugene Damon	Owen C. and Hazel G. Lewis	S. Weymouth Brockton
Feb 26	James Edward Hayden	Robert E. and Hermina M. Morehouse	S. Braintree Vermont
Mar 9	Patricia Ann Damon	Lawrence A. and Lillian M. Wyatt	Whitman Brockton
Mar 12	Mitchell Chuckran	Mitchell and Doris Bendell	Peabody Brockton
Mar 22	Daniel Monahan	Harold B. and Mary J. Donoghue	Norwell Brockton
Mar 29	Nancy Jane Morehouse	Robert W. and Marion Chamberlain	Vermont Watertown
Mar 30	Robert Lee Tower	Eldrew N. and Mary L. Cannon	Cohasset Whitman
Apr 4	Carole Marie Hawley	Archie S. and Rolande M. Beauregard	Malden Canada
Apr 6	Bruce Ferguson	John and Alice Cushman	Fall River Kingston

BIRTHS REGISTERED IN THE TOWN OF ROCKLAND FOR THE YEAR 1937

Date of Birth	Name	Name of Parents with Maiden Name of Mother	Birthplace of Parents
Apr. 7	Helen Frances Schofield	Ralph E. [and] Florence A. Mann [ar]k P. [ard] Alice Jeffers	Abington Rockland; Rockland E. Bridgewater
Apr. 8	Philip Francis M [garbled]		Rockland Rockland
Apr. 8	Stillborn		
Apr. 12	Rosemary I [garbled]	Paul J. [and] Jennie [garbled]	Rockland Rockland
Apr. 19	Barl [ana] [garbled] Ok	Harold O. [ard] Margaret C. Morrison	[garbled]; Brockton
Apr. 21	Ralph William [garbled] Bger	[Ral]ph H. [and] Muriel V. Sow	[W]er Brockton; Rockland
Apr. 22	[Mn] Frances Tilden [garbled]	Harold L. [ard] Marjorie E. Chandler	[garbled]; Quincy
Apr. 25	David Irving [garbled]	Leo J. [ard] [axel] G. Dunham	Brockton Rhode Island
Apr. 27	Helen Elizabeth Stella	Paul I. [ard] [Mne] A.	Sicily Abington
Apr. 28	Jane [garbled]	Alton F. [ard] [Ma] M. [Wer]	Hanover Me
Apr. 29	Jane [garbled]	Ell[ert] L. [ard] Margaret M. Hartshorn	Rockland Virginia
Apr. 30	Cynthia Jean Chamberlin	John N. [ard] [Van] M. Brown	Brockton Rockland
May 4	John Fredric Madden	[Evi] R. [ard] Margaret G. Hurtin	Norwell Hingham
May 6	[Mas] Edward Olson	[Wn] H. [and] Helen Schreeder	[Vale] Taunton
May 12	Elizabeth Ann Barstow		
May 18	Stillborn	[Mo] [ard] Dorothy Pierce	Rockland Duxbury
May 21	[Be] Dorothy Botto	Karl F [and] [Elie] G. [Irin]	[aCa] Rockland
May 21	[My My] Treen	[Sir] [and] [Me] R. Vinton	N. Hampshire Braintree
May 23	[Wm] [Ber] Bowman	Samuel [ard] Josephine Costa	Italy [Kut]
May 25	Joseph Samuel [Wasi]	Clifford J. [and] Fanny E. [Kley]	[Ga] Rockland
May 25	Rol[ert] Edward Bombardier	Robert E. [ard] [Barl ana] N. Donnelly	Barnstable Rockland
May 26	Barry [garbled] Delano	Emil M. [ard] Ellen M. Wisser	N. Y. City Halifax
May 27	Alfred Maxmillian Pistoresi	Scott W. [and] [Isie] R. [Wfe]	Maine Boston
June 7	Robert Warren [Nls]	[Ma] M. [ard] Dorothy F. Corcoran	Rockland [Kd]
June 14	Sandra Mae [garbled]	[ye] F. [ard] [My] C. Freitas	[ad] Portugal
June 23	Donald Leo		

BIRTHS REGISTERED IN THE TOWN OF ROC ... D FOR THE YEAR 1937

Date of Birth	Name	Name of Parents with ... Maiden Name of Mother	Birthplace of Parents
July 5			Texas
July 6	Richard	... R. and ... Me E.	
July 8		... S. ard ... L.	Hanover N.
July 9	... ert	... L. ard Margaret	
July 14	Barbara	... S. ard Marion H.	N. Abin
July 17	William	... L. ard ... E.	R. ... N.
July 18		... A. ard Margaret O.	
July 19		... J. ard ... I	
July 21		... R. ad	
July 22		... E. and ... F. Burrell	
Aug 3	Ann Rita	... A. ad ... Bellan	
Aug 3	Henry	... F. ard	
Aug 3	... Louis	Edward L. ad Mildred A. Burke	
Aug 4	... Joseph	... ard ... J.	
Aug 9		Robert C. ad Mary F.	
Aug 12		Antonio ard	S. Weymouth Italy
Aug 17	Lorraine	... S. ard ... T.	Scotland
Aug 19		... S. ard ... C. Holbrook	
Aug 21	Ann Davis	... R. ard ... F.	
Aug 29		... E. and ... E. Smith	
Sept. 2		Howard H. ard ... S. Patterson	Norwell
Sept 4		Edgar S. ard	S.
Sept 5		George E. ard ... I. Mer	
Sept 7	... Parker	William R. ard Barbara	

BIRTHS REGISTERED IN ㅐE TOWN OF ROCKLAND FOR THE ㅐR 1937

ㅐe of Birth	Name	Name of Parents with Maiden Name of Mother	Birthplace of Parents
St 9	1 ㅐm	Wm F. ad ㅐs E. iㅐy	ㅐm N. Abington
St 16	ㅐy ㅐe ㅐy	ㅐe G. ad Lillian E. ㅐh	ㅐn Taunton
St 16	ㅐe ㅐe Smith	ㅐy J. ad ㅐy ㅐr	ㅐd Everett
St 17	N ㅐy ㅐr Smith	ㅐh ad Helen A. ㅐy	ㅐd ㅐn
St 21	ㅐs ㅐt	ㅐtt I. ad ㅐa D. ㅐr	ㅐe ㅐd ㅐm
St 22	ㅐl ㅐs ㅐh	ㅐy B. and ㅐn G. ㅐby	Peabody ㅐn
St 24	ㅐie ㅐa ㅐa	ㅐd E. ad ㅐe E. ㅐa	N. ㅐn ㅐnt
St 25	ㅐe ㅐa ㅐa ㅐglioli	ㅐa ad ㅐe ㅐpi	ㅐy Italy
St 27	William ㅐ ㅐe	M. B. ad ㅐl E. ㅐia	ㅐe rㅐp ㅐn
Ot 1	Joseph Edward ㅐa	ㅐh E. ad ㅐn L. ㅐs	ㅐe ㅐd S. W ㅐh
Ot 8	ㅐa Ann Hussey	ㅐd W. ad ㅐe A. ㅐe	Rockland
Ot 11	J ㅐne ㅐe ㅐll	ㅐd E. ad ㅐn E. Zioli	ㅐd ㅐh
Oct 15	ㅐr Allan ㅐe	) ㅐh P. ㅐz	ㅐd ㅐd
Oct 17	ㅐd ㅐn ㅐk	Gervace G. ad Agnes E. ㅐy	ㅐa ㅐer
Ot 17	ㅐn Evans ㅐr	ㅐn W. and ㅐa M. ㅐn	N. Abington E. ㅐd
Ot 19	Betsey ㅐe Sargent	ㅐk C. ad ㅐge	ㅐn ㅐe
Oct 20	Beverly ㅐs ㅐn	ㅐr L. J., ad ㅐe E. ㅐs	ㅐd Brooklyn, N. Y.
Ot 23	ㅐl Warren Cifello	William ㅐk ad Ruth ㅐll	ㅐd ㅐr
Ot 23	ㅐe William ㅐtt	ㅐk ㅐy M. ㅐan	ㅐd ㅐr
Ot 30	ㅐn ㅐs ㅐd	George W. ad My L. ㅐo	ㅐd ㅐd
Oct 30	ㅐy ㅐn ㅐi	ㅐh I. ad ㅐa C. ㅐh	ㅐa ㅐ.
Ot 30	ㅐe ㅐa ㅐtt	Albert R. ad ㅐr A. ㅐn	W. ㅐd ㅐn
Nov 5	ㅐn ㅐh ㅐe	ㅐn A. ad ㅐie I. ㅐe	ㅐd Attleboro
ㅐv 10	ㅐn ㅐa ㅐr	ㅐs S. ad ㅐr ㅐn	ㅐn ㅐa
ㅐv 12	ㅐe ㅐl ㅐs	Walter G. ad ㅐl M. ㅐn	ada. S. ㅐn
ㅐv 14	Donald ㅐd Menard	ㅐl F. ad ㅐe A.	ㅐn Abington ㅐd

BIRTHS REGISTERED IN THE TOWN OF ROCKLAND FOR THE YEAR 1937

Date of Birth	Name	Name of Parents with Maiden Name of Mother	Birthplace of Parents	
Nov 15	Margaret Ann Petrell	Frank and Louisa M. Cox	Braintree	Holbrook
Nov 18	Jean Louise Hutchinson	Ray L. and Dorothy L. Hollis	N. H.	S. Brantree
Nov 18	Jessie Patricia Wis	John and Jessie MacLennan	Nva Scotia	Nva Scotia
Nov 20	Dorothy Ann Thompson	Earle F Thompson Jr. & Mildred Condon	Brockton	Brockton
Nov 21	Catherine Spinale	James S. and Hortense E. Roberts	Boston	Boston
Nov 29	Frederick Francis Fontaine	Frederick F. and Evelyn Mee	Rockland	S. Weymouth
Nov 30	Carolyn Joan Rushwick	Joseph and Ana Fiaschetti	N. Abington	Italy
Nov 30	Carol Ann Riley	Charles F. and Marion L. Giles	Quincy	Pike, N. H.
Dec 1	Giles Mr Lincoln	Giles W. and Evelyn E. Doherty	Norwell	Abington
Dec 10	Marceline Diane Conley	James M. ard Beatrice Beauregard	Rhode Island	Fall River
Dec 10	Joseph Golemme Jr.	Joseph and Antoinette Lanzillotto	Italy	Italy
Dec 11	Dorothy Joan Reidy	John F. and Dorothy L. Barry	New York	Pembroke
Dec 22	Walter Eric Colby	Eric V. and Edith E. Pier	England	Merrimac
Dec 30	Thas Leo Wls	Magorisk L. and Elsie V. Thas	Rockland	Rockland
Dec 30	Margaret Elizabeth Melly	James L. and Ruth M. McDonnell	Abington	Rockland

DEATHS REGISTERED IN THE TOWN OF ROCKLAND FOR THE YEAR 1937

Date	Name	Age Y	M	D	Cause of Death	Birthplace
Jan 3	Margaret E. Burke	80	5	29	Bates	Win
Jan 7	Catherine Frances Lane	68	1	4	Coronary	Hld
Jan 16	Joseph Wm Bryant	77	11	4	Protate	Me
Jan 28	Irene Delano Ellis	56	10	12	Gastric	Qy
Feb 5	Emma ... me	75	6	—	Chronic	Oro n, M.
Feb 8	Stillborn					
Feb 10	James ... do	75	2	18		...er
Feb 14		79	10	25		Hld
Feb 15	Burton Well Poole	61	9	23	Angina	Hld
Feb 17	... Shea	73	—	—		in
Feb 17	Lois M. Bates	72	8	3	Vascular	
Feb 19	Elizabeth V. Downey	80	—	27	...ension	
Feb 19	Julia ... Campbell				sclerosis	
Feb 25	... Snell	64	1	26	Cerebral hemorrhage	Rockland
Feb 28	Ellen M. Hurley	80			Chronic Myocarditis	Hld
Mar 1	James H.	61	5	15		b...n
Mar 5	Margaret ... Huggan	91	2	19	Broncho	M.
Mar 8	Mary E. Leslie	94	1	17	Myocarditis	New Jersey
Mar 11		1	11	20	Broncho	Nova Scotia
Mar 16	George ... Wal	74	1	13	Myocarditis	Ireland
Mar 25	Mary True Smith	79	11			Brockton
Mar 27	Daniel ...	39	2	5	Appendicitis	Scituate
Mar 28	James H.	68	3	28		N. H.
Mar 30	Kathryn F. Riordan	76	4	16	Pyloric Stenosis	B...
Apr 2	... Sherwood Hayes	68	—	8	Prostate	Everett
Apr 2	Patrick J. Delaney	78	—	11	Myocarditis	Ireland

DEATHS REGISTERED IN THE TOWN OF ROCKLAND FOR THE YEAR 1937

Date	Name	Age Y	Age M	Age D	Cause of Death	
Apr 5	Mel L Money	81	6	7	Arterio Sclerosis	Ill
Apr 8	Elin (Baby) Snyder		3½		City	Mass
Apr 12	Chas elirt Fle Mer	88	6	11	Cerebral hemorrhage	Me
Apr 13	Florence Elvira Batson	86	8	11	Myocarditis	Ill
Apr 16	In eat Ill	79	7	5	Ms	Mass
Apr 18	Christian St. Germaine	87	2	20	Ms	New York
Apr 19	ohn W. Ivers	53		8	Age	N. Brookfield
Apr 24	Mia M. Newton	65			Hart	Ill
May 2	Mry L. Sh	89	9		Cerebral hemorrhage	Me
May 3	Me Sylvester	76			Cerebral his	Min
May 4	Dorothy Rhda Hicks	21	11	16	Nec titis	Italy
May 13	Mary Teresa Frino	88	8	8	Clry This lgs	Oat
May 14	Orsena Tribou	79	2	2	ute Nephritis	Ms
May 16	J rns I Barry	72	7	7	Clry Thrombosis	gh
May 17	Sin					
May 18	aES F. Me	86	11		Arerio eis	A
May 25	Eugene Een Brown	31	1	2	Mitral Regurgitation	Me
May 26	ella dMa	66	6	5	Ma Reix	Ill
May 27	dla M. Sena	58	6	8	Coronary eis	B
May 28	Wm after nHl	67	11	16	Cerebral dage	Italy
June 1	eeln	75	3	27	Protate	Ill
June 4	Alfred I Courtney	56	3		Nia	Ill
June 5	Mel J Eons	77	4		eto Bladder	Me
June 14	In M. Me	89	8	9	eto eis	Ill
June 29	In A. Lamb Te	62	8	17	dla nl	3th.
July 15	Mry Es Te	72	1	12	Cler of Liver	Scotland
July 16						Ireland

DEATHS REGISTERED IN THE TOWN OF ROC[KLAND] FOR THE YEAR 1937

Date	Name	Y	M	D	Cause of Death	Birthplace
Jly 17	Julia Lynch	82	2	12	Arterio ...	Ireland
July 26	Patrick J. Luddy	71	4	10	A..o ...	E. Bridgewater
Ag 1	Sarah ... ilton	85	11	27	Chronic ...sis	Nova Scotia
Aug 9	... Shoughrow	48	2	11	Pyonephrosis	Marlboro
Aug 14	...n Sullivan	27		14	Edema of the Brain	Rockland
Aug 20	David W. ...	78	7		A..o ...	Qncy
Aug 29	John J. McCarthy	81	1	11	...io vascular disease	Rockl ...
Aug 31	Sylvia ...	4	10	28	Septicemia	Rockl ...
...t 7	...	83	4	23	Chronic nephritis	Rockl ...
...t 11	...ne	65		24	A..io sclerosis	
Spt 15	Sophia Sampson Ford	93	8	27	Senile s ...	N. S
...t 16	Mry Gertrude Smith	40			M.. ...rrhage	
e.t 19	...	53	3		C ...itis	
e.t 20	...w Henderson	80	3	1	Cerebral hemorrhage	
Spt 21	Willis ...	71	7	1	Arterio s ...	
...t 22	... Burrell	96	1	10	A..o ...	
...t 23	Mry ...on	82		12	...ll r..hage	Hanover
e.t 28	Mry ...ey	64	8	4	...s ...	Boston
Oct 4	Benjamin ...	76			...o ...erosis	...
Oct 5	Jhn T. ...lyn	72			...y Tuberculosis	E. Bridg
Oct 13	...s Shalgian	27	1	15	...to accident	Mass.
Oct 19	...d	59		21	...to acc ...nt	Webster
Oct 20	... B. ...d	63	1	18	Coronary ...	Irel ..
Oct 28	Daisy ...ton	63	4	7	Cerebral ...age	With..
Oct 30	... Sr.	64	5	12	Carcinoma of ...eas	...
Oct 30	...t M. ...bell	51		15	Cardio ...ar	...d
Nov 1	Effie ...n Doherty	3	4	22	Hit by Auto	Brockton

DEATHS REGISTERED IN THE TOWN OF ROCKLAND FOR THE YEAR 1937

Date	Name	Age Y	M	D	Cause of Death	Birthplace
Nov 5	Stillborn					Bnd
Nov 6	Charlotte Ann Arnold	74	5	20	Aortic regurgitation	Ch own
Nov 11	Elizal eth Louise Pratt	74	6	29	Myocarditis	nd
Nov 16	Frances L. Roche	44	4	7	Heart Disease	Rland
Nov 16	Patrick Joseph Foley	74	2	4	Arterio sclerosis	kdland
Nov 19	John O'Brien	71	11	13	Bronchiectasis	
Nov 20	Adelbert hes Davis	67	10	28	Coronary Thrombosis	Me
Dec 6	Joseph Moss	81	10	16	etio sclerosis	England
Dec 8	Vito ho	57	5	22	General Paresis	Italy
Dec 10	Stephen W. Sherman	80			ida Prostate	Marshfield
Dec 11	Frederick A. Shaw	86	5	4	Arterio sclerosis	Rockland
Dec 12	Charles Robert Maloney		2	21	1 Gt'l ifa Aorta	Rockland
Dec 13	Nellie G. ord F.	51	11	14	ifa Pancreas	Ireland
Dec 17	Roger Moulton	3	5	21	Cerebro-spinal Meningitis	Brockton
Dec 23	Everett Valentine Alley	66	10	9	Mitral regurgitation	Maine
Dec 24	Amanda Lisette Poole	80	10	7	Myocarditis	Hanover
Dec 25	Ellen M. Condon	78	8	30	Myocarditis	Rockland
Dec 25	Elberta Forest Heald	63	11	1	Coronary Thrombosis	New York
Dec 27	Bertha M. agre	59		23	Cerebral hemorrhage	New Bedford

Report of the Records for the Year 1937

Pursuant to the warrant a meeting was held in the Rockland Opera House, beginning at 7:30 o'clock P. M. and the following votes were passed and action taken.

Article 1. Magorisk L. Walls was chosen Moderator and sworn to the faithful discharge of his duties.

The Moderator appointed the following tellers for the meeting: Esther Rawson, Madeline Lannin, Elizabeth Walsh, Myra Burke, Nelson Gardner, Alonzo Ford, Paul Trainor, Elmer Cobb, and Charles Callanan.

Article 2. Voted to accept the reports of the various Town Officers and Committees as published in the Town Report.

Article 3. Voted to raise and appropriate the following amounts for the purposes named:

Schools	$104	423	00
State Aid		700	00
Soldiers' Relief	8	000	00
Military Aid		50	00
Care Soldiers' Graves		150	00
Memorial Library and Dog Fund	4	200	00
Street Lighting	9	234	00
Highway Surveyor	1	350	00
Tarvia and Road Binder	7	000	00
Highway Repairs	7	000	00

Sidewalks	2 500	00
Cleaning Union Street	1 100	00
Clean Up Week	100	00
Guide Boards and Signs	100	00
Fire Department	10 062	00
Police Department	8 800	00
Forest Fires	700	00
Board of Health	6 000	00
Inspecting of Animals	150	00
Park Department	3 115	00
Old Age Assistance	35 000	00
Moth Department	300	00
Tree Warden	900	00
Town Officers	6 800	00
Office Rent	1 240	00
Sealer of Weight and Measures	400	00
Elections	850	00
Compensation Insurance	2 250	00
Mass. Hospital School	500	00
Mass. Industrial School	3 000	00
Town Report and Poll Book	1 200	00
Support of Poor and Infirmary	45 000	00
Mothers' Aid	8 000	00
Town Notes and Interest	25 000	00
Assessors	2 500	00
Snow Removal	1 000	00
Reserve Fund	1 000	00
Miscellaneous Assessors	1 100	00
Miscellaneous Treasurer	800	00
Miscellaneous Clerk	350	00
Miscellaneous Selectmen	120	00
Miscellaneous Collector	1 400	00
Miscellaneous Registrars	200	00
Miscellaneous Sealer	105	00
Miscellaneous Unclassified	1 150	00
Total amount raised under this article	$314 899	00

Under Article No. 3. Meeting of March 1, 1937:

Voted to Pass over appropriation for Burial of Indigent Soldiers.

A motion by the Chief of the Fire Department that the amount of $10,462.00 be raised and appropriated for the Fire Department was not agreed to.

Affirmative vote 165   Negative vote 174

Voted that it be the sense of the meeting that the town report and poll book be put out to open competitive bids.

Under Article No. 3. Adjourned meeting, March 8, 1937

Voted to reconsider Article No. 3.

Voted to reconsider the sense of meeting vote whereby it was voted that the printing of the town reports and poll book be put out to open competitive bidding.

Voted to instruct the Board of Selectmen to advertise for competitive bids, from the Rockland Printers only, for printing Town report and Poll book.

Voted to reconsider appropriation for town notes and interest.

A motion by the Town Treasurer to raise and appropriate $28,000.00 for Town Notes and Interest was not agreed to.

Affirmative votes 84   Negative vote 92

Article 4. Voted to raise and appropriate the sum of twelve thousand seven hundred thirty-five 7/100 dollars

($12,735.07) to be paid into the Town Treasury on account of overlays in the following departments:

Tarvia and Road Binder	1	95
Fire Department	1 291	62
Tree Warden	40	68
Elections	426	50
Town Report and Poll Book	448	15
Snow	657	94
Miscellaneous Unclassified	558	23
Old Age Assistance	6 666	22
Public Welfare	2 643	78

$ 12 735 07

Article 5. Voted to authorize the Town Treasurer, with the approval of the Selectmen, to borrow money from time to time in anticipation of the revenue of the financial year beginning January 1, 1938, and to issue a note or notes therefor, payable within one year, and to renew such note or notes as may be given for a period of less than one year in accordance with Section 17, Chapter 44, General Laws.

Article 6. Voted to raise and appropriate the sum of fifteen hundred dollars ($1,500.00) to be spent under the direction of the Selectmen for the part payment of a Visiting Nurse.

Article 7. Voted to appropriate the sum of thirty-two thousand dollars ($32,000.00) for the use of the Water Department the same to be taken from the Water Revenue.

Article 8. Voted to raise and appropriate the sum of two hundred eighty-eight dollars ($288.00) to be spent under the direction of the Selectmen for the purpose of renting quarters for the use of the Veterans of the Spanish-American War.

Article 9. Voted to raise and appropriate the sum of four hundred dollars ($400.00) to be spent under the direction of the Selectmen for the observance of Memorial Day.

Article 10. Voted to raise and appropriate the sum of sixty dollars ($60.00) for the care of the Town Cemetery.

Article 11. Voted to raise and appropriate the sum of nine hundred dollars ($900.00) to be spent under the direction of the Selectmen for the purpose of renting quarters for the use of the Rockland Post No. 147 of the American Legion.

Article 12. Voted to raise and appropriate the sum of one hundred and fifty dollars ($150.00) for the use of the Plymouth County Trustees for County Aid to Agriculture and to choose James D. Mahoney as Town Director as provided in Sections 41 and 45 of Chapter 128, General Laws. Unanimous vote.

Article 13. Voted to raise and appropriate the sum of three thousand six hundred thirty-three dollars and twelve cents ($3,633.12) for maintenance of the Plymouth County Hospital.

Article 14. Voted to raise and appropriate the sum of six hundred dollars ($600.00) for the maintenance of traffic beacons and signals.

Article 15. Voted to raise and appropriate the sum of two hundred and ninety-two dollars and fifty cents ($292.50) to insure the Firemen of the Town of Rockland that they might receive compensation in case of accident when on duty.

Article 16. Voted to raise and appropriate the sum of five thousand dollars ($5,000.00) to be spent in conjunction with the State and County to rebuild East Water Street from where the rebuilding ended in 1936 to Webster Street.

Article 17. Voted to raise and appropriate the sum of -six hundred forty dollars and eighty-seven cents ($640.87) to pay for the overlay on the construction of Union Street.

Article 18. Voted to pass over the raising and appropriating of the sum of Eight hundred thirty-eight dollars and twenty-seven cents ($838.27) to reimburse the J. R. Worcester Co. for actual loss in the contract with the town in the construction of Union Street.

Article 19. Voted to raise and appropriate the sum of five hundred ten dollars ($510.00) to pay Bradford Westin Inc., for extras claimed in the construction of Union Street.

Article 20. Voted to raise and appropriate the sum of three thousand fifty-three dollars and eighty cents ($3,053.80) to be spent under the direction of the Park Commissioners to pay for materials and services on Federal projects, the labor to be furnished by the Federal Government.

Voted to take up Article No. 34.

Article 34. Voted to raise and appropriate the sum of Five thousand dollars ($5,000.00) to be spent for the cost of materials and general expenses under the W. P. A.

Article 21. Voted to appropriate from the sum raised under article No. 34 the amount of fifteen hundred dollars ($1,500.00) to rebuild Plain Street from the Railroad Crossing to North Avenue, and to include drainage from the Railroad Crossing to the residence of John Kelleher, the labor to be paid for under the W. P. A.

Article 22.   Voted to raise and appropriate the sum of one hundred and fifty dollars to pay for striping streets of the town.

Article 23.   Voted to raise and appropriate the sum of one hundred dollars ($100.00) for criminal cases in court.

Article 24.   Voted to raise and appropriate the sum of seventy dollars ($70.00) for the purchase of a fifty gallon test can to be used by the Sealer of Weights and Measures.

Article 25.   Voted to pass over the allowing of home owners who are behind in their taxes to work them out in the highway or other departments.

Article 26.   Voted to pass over the granting of power to the Selectmen to intervene in any labor disputes which may arise in town.

Article 27.   Voted to accept a town way, known as Smith Road, as laid out by the Selectmen and filed with the Town Clerk, from Liberty Street running westerly a distance of three hundred and forty-four feet.

Article 28.   Voted to gravel Smith Road from Liberty Street a distance of three hundred forty-four (344) feet and that the amount of three hundred and fifty dollars ($350.00) to be taken from the appropriation for Highway repairs raised under Article No. 3 to pay for the cost of same.

Article 29.   Voted to accept a town way, known as Douglas Street, as laid out by the Selectmen and filed with the Town Clerk, from Rice Avenue southerly a distance of three hundred seventy 45/100 (370.45) feet.

Article 30.   Voted to pass over the raising and appropriating of the sum of forty-two hundred dollars

($4,200.00) for the erection of a building for the housing of town equipment on the lot opposite Reed's Pond owned by the town, but that the Moderator be instructed to ap- . point a committee of three to secure suitable housing quarters for all town equipment.

Committee appointed: Roderick MacKenzie, J. Edward Kane and Fred M. Ryan.

Article 31. Voted to raise and appropriate the sum of five hundred dollars ($500.00) for an Assessor's Map.

Article 32. Voted to appropriate from the sum raised under article No. 34 the amount of two hundred seventy-fice dollars ($275.00) for materials for a drain and two catch basins on the easterly side of Salem Street starting at 420 Salem Street and running to number 468, a distance of approximately 480 feet, the labor to be furished by the W. P. A.

Article 33. Voted to raise and appropriate the sum of one hundred dollars ($100.00) to be used by the School Committee to pay for the expenses of heating, lighting and for Casualty Insurance of Junior-Senior High School and McKinley School Buildings as well as additional expense for janitors when the buildings are used by individuals and associations for educational, recreational, and like purposes under the provision of Chapter 71, Section 71 of the General Laws.

Article 35. Voted to appropriate from the sum raised under article No. 34, the amount of two hundred twenty-five dollars ($225.00) for materials to install a covered drain with catch basin on the East side of Howard Street from Custer Street to Vernon Street and the labor to be furnished by the W. P. A.

Article 36. Voted to appropriate from the sum raised under article No. 34, the amount of one hundred fifty dollars ($150.00) for materials to place a catch basin and drainage near the residence of John Parker on Belmont Street, the labor to be furnished by the W. P. A.

Voted to take up Article No. 38.

Article 38. Voted to raise and appropriate the sum of Five hundred dollars ($500.00) to purchase the lot of land southwest of the railroad at the corner of Plain and Grove Streets, known as the Washington Reed Lot, consisting of four (4) acres more or less.
Unanimous vote.

Article 37. Voted to raise and appropriate the sum of Two thousand dollars ($2,000.00) for cost of materials for the construction of a seepage bed on the Washington Reed Lot, southwest of the railroad track, to take care of the requirements of the Junior-Senior High School, the labor to be furnished by the W. P. A.

Article 39. Voted to raise and appropriate the sum of Five hundred dollars ($500.00) to take care of the catch basions and gutters on various streets of the town.

Article 40. Voted to appropriate from the sum raised under article No. 34 the amount of Four hundred dollars ($400.00) for materials to build a sidewalk and curb on the west side of Highland Street from Market Street to Plain Street, the labor to be furnished by the W. P. A.

Article 41. Voted to pass over the raising and appropriating of the sum of eight hundred fifty dollars ($850.00) to build a sidewalk and curb on the west side of Plain Street from Market Street to Payson Avenue.

Article 42. Voted to pass over the raising and appropriating of the sum of eleven hundred dollars ($1,100.00) to build a sidewalk and curb on Myrtle Street (west side) from Bigelow Avenue to Summit Street.

Article 43. Voted to appropriate from the sum raised under article No. 34 the sum of Five hundred dollars ($500.00) for materials to build a sidewalk and curb on the south side of Summit Street from Union Street to Myrtle Street, the labor to be furnished by the W. P. A.

Article 44. Voted to appropriate from the sum raised under article No. 34 the amount of Three hundred fifty dollars ($350.00) to be used for materials to build a sidewalk and curb on the west side of Plain Street from West Water Street to Emerson Street, the labor to be furnished by the W. P. A.

Article 45. Voted to appropriate from the sum raised for Sidewalks under Article No. 3 the amount of seven hundred twenty-five dollars ($725.00) to build a sidewalk and curb on the south side of East Water Street from Union Square to Howard Street.

Article 46. Voted to pass over the raising and appropriating of the sum of twelve hundred dollars ($1200.00) to build a sidewalk and curb on the west side of Liberty Street from East Water Street to Vernon Street.

Article 47. Voted to build a sidewalk and curb on the west side of Everett Street from East Water Street to Stanton Street and that the amount of six hundred dollars ($600.00) be appropriated from the sum raised for Sidewalks under article No. 3 to pay for the cost of same.

Article 48. Voted to raise and appropriate the sum of One thousand dollars ($1,000.00) for materials to build a sidewalk and curb on the west side of Spring Street from Market Street to the Infirmary the labor to be furnished by the W. P. A.

Article 49. Voted to appropriate from the sum raised under article No. 34, the amount of Four Hundred dollars

($400.00) for materials to build a sidewalk and curb on Cliff Street (North side) from Myrtle Street to Liberty Street, the labor to be furnished by the W. P. A.

Article 50.   Voted to appropriate from the sum raised under article No. 34 the amount of Four hundred twenty-five dollars ($425.00) for materials to build a sidewalk and curb on the east side of Arlington Street from Market Street to Payson Avenue, the labor to be furnished by the W. P. A.

Article 51.   Voted to raise and appropriate the sum of Nine hundred dollars ($900.00) for materials to build a sidewalk and curb on the westerly side of Union Street from Liberty Street to Oregon Avenue, the labor to be furnished by the W. P. A.

Article 52.   Voted to raise and appropriate the sum of Six hundred twenty-five dollars ($625.00) for materials to build a sidewalk and curb on the northerly side of Prospect Street from Highland Street to West Water Street, the labor to be furnished by the W. P. A.

Article 53.   Voted to pass over the raising and appropriating of One thousand dollars ($1,000.00) to build a sidewalk and curb on the southerly side of Williams Street from Plain Street to Prospect Street.

Article 54.   Voted to raise and appropriate the sum of Eleven hundred dollars ($1,100.00) to build a sidewalk and curb on the northerly side of Webster Street from Union Street to Wall Street.

Article 55.   Voted to pass over the raising and appropriating of a sum of money to repair the bridge on Liberty Street near Liberty Court.

Article 56. Voted to raise and appropriate the sum of One thousand dollars ($1,000.00) for materials for improvements of the grounds at Reed's Pond, the labor to be furnished by the W. P. A.

Article 57. Voted to pass over the raising and appropriating of Eleven hundred fifty dollars ($1,150.00) to build an asphalt sidewalk with curb on the east side of Union Street from the residence of Dr. Frederick Corey to Bigelow avenue, approximately 1000 feet.

Article 58. Voted to build an asphalt sidewalk with curb on the west side of Howard Street from Webster Street to Park Street, a distance of approximately 250 feet and the amount of Two hundred and fifty dollars ($250.00) be appropriated from the amount raised for Sidewalks under article No. 3 to pay for the cost of same.

Article 59. Voted to pass over the raising and appropriating of a sum of money for materials for a curb on the westerly side of Salem Street running from Spruce Street to North Avenue, the labor to be furnished by the W. P. A.

Article 60. Voted to raise and appropriate the sum of Seven hundred dollars ($700.00) for materials to build a sidewalk on the north side of Salem Street from Union Street to Greenwood Street, a distance of about 1300 feet, the labor to be furnished by the W. P. A.

Article 61. Voted to raise and appropriate the sum of Three hundred dollars ($300.00) for materials to build an asphalt sidewalk and curb on the south side of Blossom Street from Liberty Street to Everett Street, a distance of approximately 600 feet, the labor to be furnished by the W. P. A.

Article 62. Voted to pass over the raising and appropriating of a sum of money to build a sidewalk with asphalt top and curb on the west side of Concord Street from Market Street southerly to the residence of Ernest M. Locke.

Article 63. Voted to build a tarvia sidewalk with curb on the southerly side of North Avenue from Union Street to the residence of Arthur Barry, a distance of 630 feet, and that the amount of Seven hundred dollars ($700.00) be appropriated from the sum raised for Sidewalks under article No. 3 to pay for the cost of same.

Article 64. Voted to pass over the raising and appropriating of a sum of money to rebuild a sidewalk and curb on the north side of Pacific Street from Union Street to Division Street, a distance of approximately 1500 feet.

Voted to adjourn until March 8, 1937, 7:30 P. M.

Article 65. Voted to raise and appropriate the sum of Five hundred thirteen dollars and sixty cents ($513.60) to take care of the overlay on East Water Street Construction.

Article 66. Voted to raise and appropriate the sum of three hundred dollars ($300.00) to be used to employ a Supervisor of Bureau of Old Age Assistance, this sum to be used in conjunction with the grant received from the Federal Government.

Article 67. Voted to accept a town way, known as Wilson Street, as laid out by the Selectmen and filed with the Town Clerk, from Pond Street westerly a distance of eight hundred and eight (808) feet.

Article 68. Voted to appropriate, as it accrues from Water Revenue, the sum of Nineteen hundred and fifty dollars ($1,950.00) for the purchase of 2550 feet of pipe to complete installation of water mains on Forest Street where work is now in progress by W. P. A.

Article 69. Voted to pass over the establishing of a planning board under the provisions of General Laws, Chapter 41, Section 81A, as amended by Chapter 211 of 1936; the board to consist of five members, the first elections to be for one to five year terms, and thereafter one each year for a five year term; and the directing of the Moderator to appoint a temporary board to serve until the regular board was duly elected.

Article 70. Voted to pass over. the acceptance of the provisions of General Laws, Chapter 41, Section 81F to 81J, inclusive, as amended by Chapter 211 of 1936.

Article 71. Voted to pass over the raising and appropriating of the sum of Eleven hundred dollars ($1,100.00) for the preparation of a zoning plan under the direction of the planning board.

Article 72. Voted to pass over the authorizing of the Fire Department to place a colored light over each fire alarm box throughout the town, for identification of location at night, and the raising and appropriating of a sum of money for the same.

Article 73. Voted to build catch basins on the west side of Everett Street from East Water Street to Blossom Street, a distance of 200 feet, and that the amount of Two hundred fifty dollars ($250.00) be appropriated from the sum raised for Highway Repairs under article No. 3 to pay for the cost of same.

Article 74. Voted to appropriate from the sum raised under article No. 34 the amount of One hundred six dollars ($106.00) to reimburse for an overdraft for labor performed under W. P. A. poject for painting warning signs in 1936.

Article 75. Voted NOT to elect the Selectmen and Board of Public Welfare to serve for terms of three years.

Article 76. Voted NOT to discontinue the Stop and Go lights at the corner of Howard and East Water Street.

Article 77. Voted to raise and appropriate the sum of Four hundred dollars ($400.00) to pay for the expense of heating, lighting, gas and removal of garbage in the Mc-Kinley School Building when the building is used by the Nursery, Sewing and Recreational projects of the Works Progress Administration.

Under article 77. Voted to request School Department to have intsalled separate meters to measure light used by Nursery, Sewing and Recreational projects at McKinley School.

A motion to reconsider Article No. 18 was not agreed to.

Sense of meeting votes:

Voted that, when work is finished, all plans and specifications used in the construction of seepage bed and attachments to the sewage disposal plant of the Junior-Senior High School, shall be filed in the office of the School Department.

Voted that the Finance Committee be extended a vote of thanks of the meeting for their untiring efforts in investigating the matters to be brought before the town meeting and the able manner in which the information was placed before the meeting. Unanimous vote.

Voted to pay Election Officials the usual fees.

Article 78. A Subsequent Meeting for the Election of Town Officers was held in the Rockland Opera House, Savings Bank Building, on Monday, March 8th, 1937. The polls opened at 5:45 A. M. and closed at 4:00 P. M. The result was as follows:

Total number of ballots Cast   3556

MODERATOR—One Year

  Magorisk L. Walls   2663
    Blanks   893

TOWN CLERK—One Year

  Ralph L. Belcher   2959
    Blanks   597

TOWN TREASURER—One Year

  Charles J. Higgins   2916
    Blanks   640

TAX COLLECTOR—One Year

  James A. Donovan   2934
    Blanks   622

SELECTMEN, BOARD OF PUBLIC WELFARE
AND FENCE VIEWERS—One Year

  John J. Bowler   1955
  Elmer C. Cobb   1797
  Archie F. Minnis   857
  Harry S. Torrey   1816
  Norman S. Whiting   1856
    Blanks   2387

HIGHWAY SURVEYOR—One Year

  Toiva M. Jarvinen   867
  Roderick MacKenzie   2510
    Blanks   179

ASSESSOR—Three Years

George Beal	731
Norman J. Beals	2323
Blanks	502

AUDITORS—One Year

C. Elmer Asklund	2251
Leo E. Downey	2364
Harold C. Smith	2291
Blanks	3762

SCHOOL COMMITTEE—Three Years

William B. Carey	1574
Benjamin Lelyveld	1787
William A. Loud	1700
Myrtle Prescott	437
Blanks	1614

WATER COMMISSIONER—Three Years

Everett S. Damon	2013
Charles P. Howland	822
Eugene P. Sheehan	591
Blanks	130

BOARD OF HEALTH—Three Years

Arthur W. Casey	552
Joseph H. Dunn	2664
Blanks	340

LIBRARY TRUSTEES—Three Years

Francis J. Geogan	2566
Emma W. Gleason	2386
Blanks	2160

PARK COMMISSIONER—Three Years

Charles T. Walls	2573
Blanks	983

SEWER COMMISSIONER—Three Years

Charles M. Hines	2475
Blanks	1081

TREE WARDEN—One Year

William C. Greene	153
Charles L. Hunt	1029
Alfred T. Metivier	2004
Blanks	370

CONSTABLES—One Year

Austin Beale	582
Robert J. Drake	2388
John Fucillo	1216
Adolph L. W. Johnson	2585
Cornelius J. McHugh	2301
John H. Murphy	2380
George J. Popp	2301
Blanks	4027

A true copy, ATTEST:

RALPH L. BELCHER,
Town Clerk

AMOUNTS RAISED AND APPROPRIATED
ANNUAL MEETING, MARCH 1, 1937

Schools	$104 423 00
State Aid	700 00
Soldiers' Relief	8 000 00

Military Aid	50	00
Care Soldiers' Graves	150	00
Memorial Library and Dog Fund	4 200	00
Street Lighting	9 234	00
Highway Surveyor	1 350	00
Tarvia and Road Binder	7 000	00
Highway Repairs	7 000	00
Sidewalks	2 500	00
Cleaning Union Street	1 100	00
Clean Up Week	100	00
Guide Boards and Signs	100	00
Fire Department	10 062	00
Police Department	8 800	00
Forest Fires	700	00
Board of Health	6 000	00
Inspecting of Animals	150	00
Park Department	3 115	00
Old Age Assistance	35 000	00
Moth Department	300	00
Tree Warden	900	00
Town Officers	6 800	00
Office Rent	1 240	00
Sealer of Weight and Measures	400	00
Elections	850	00
Compensation Insurance	2 250	00
Mass. Hospital School	500	00
Mass. Industrial School	3 000	00
Town Report and Poll Book	1 200	00
Support of Poor and Infirmary	45 000	00
Mothers' Aid	8 000	00
Town Notes and Interest	25 000	00
Assessors	2 500	00
Snow Removal	1 000	00
Reserve Fund	1 000	00
Miscellaneous Assessors	1 100	00
Miscellaneous Treasurer	800	00
Miscellaneous Clerk	350	00
Miscellaneous Selectmen	120	00
Miscellaneous Collector	1 400	00

Miscellaneous Registrars	200	00
Miscellaneous Sealer	105	00
Miscellaneous Unclassified	1 150	00
Overdrafts 1936:		
Tarvia and Road Binder	1	95
Fire Department	1 291	62
Tree Warden	40	68
Elections	426	50
Town Report and Poll Book	448	15
Snow	657	94
Miscellaneous Unclassified	558	23
Old Age Assistance	6 666	22
Public Welfare	2 643	78
Part payment Visiting Nurse	1 500	00
Rent Quarters Veterans Spanish-American War	288	00
Observance Memorial Day	400	00
Care Town Cemetery	60	00
Quarters, Post No. 147, American Legion	900	00
County Aid to Agriculture	150	00
Maintenance Plymouth County Hospital	3 633	12
Traffic Beacons and Signals	600	00
Insure Firemen	292	50
Rebuild East Water Street	5 000	00
Overlay Construction Union Street	640	87
Extras claimed Construction Union Street		
(Bradford Weston)	510	00
Parks, materials and services Federal		
projects	3 053	80
Cost of Materials and General Expenses		
W. P. A.	5 000	00
Striping Streets	150	00
Criminal cases in Court	100	00
Purchase 50 gal Test Can	70	00
Assessors Map	500	00
Heat, light, casualty Ins., Jr.-Sr. High		
and McKinley Schools	100	00
Purchase Washington Reed Lot	500	00
Materials for construction seepage bed		
Washington Reed Lot	2 000	00

Clean catch basins and gutters	500	00
Materials for sidewalks and curb west side Spring Street	1 000	00
Materials for sidewalks and curb west side Union St., from Liberty St. to Oregon Av.	900	00
Materials for sidewalk and curb north side Prospect St., from Highland to West Water Street	625	00
Sidewalk and curb north side Webster St., from Union to Wall Street	1 100	00
Materials for improvements at Reeds Pond	1 000	00
Materials for sidewalk on north side Salem St. from Union to Greenwood Streets	700	00
Materials for asphalt sidewalk and curb south side Blossom St., from Liberty St. to to Everett Street	300	00
Overlay East Water Street construction	513	60
Supervisor Bureau Old Age Assistance	300	00
Heat, light, gas, and removal garbage McKinley School when used by Nursery, Sewing, Recreational projects W. P. A.	400	00
	$360 420	96

Appropriations, from Water Revenue General Expense and Maintenance Water Dept.	32 000	00
Purchase 2550 ft. pipe to complete installation water mains Forest St.	1 950	00
	$394 370	96

A true copy Attest:

RALPH L. BELCHER,

Town Clerk

SPECIAL TOWN MEETING
SEPTEMBER 9, 1937

Pursuant to the warrant a meeting was held in the Rockland Opera House, Thursday, Sept. 9, 1937, beginning at 7:30 o'clock P. M. and the following votes were passed and action taken.

The meeting was called to order at 7:30 P. M. by the Moderator.

The warrant and Constables return of service thereof was read by the Town Clerk.

Upon question of a quorum the Moderator appointed the following tellers to count the number of voters present and they were sworn by the Town Clerk.

Tellers appointed: Archie F. Minnis, Alton Lyon and Norman J. Beals.

The tellers reported that there were 211 voters present at the meeting.

The Moderator ruled that in conformity with a by-law of the town no appropriation of money could be made unless 300 voters were present.

Voted to recess until 8:00 o'clock P. M.

At 8 P. M. the meeting was again called to order and a count of the voters present made by the tellers. They reported 238 voters present.

Voted to recess until 8:25 o'clock P. M.

At 8:25 P. M. the meeting was again called to order and a count of the voters present made by the tellers and they reported 262 voters present.

Then at 8:30 o'clock P. M. it was voted that the meeting be adjourned until 7:30 o'clock P. M., Tuesday, September 14, 1937.

ADJOURNED MEETING, SEPT. 14, 1937

The meeting was called to order at 7:30 P. M. by the Moderator.

A count of the voters present was made by the tellers and they reported 340 voters present.

The Moderator ruled a quorum was present and action called for under the articles in the warrant could be taken.

Article 1.   Voted to raise and appropriate the sum of Sixteen Hundred Fifty-Six Dollars ($1,656.00) as part payment for material to be used in the Sewing Project of the W. P. A.

Article 2.   Voted to raise and appropriate the sum of Four Thousand Dollars ($4,000.00) to pay for the cost of materials and overhead expense of the W. P. A.

Article 3.   Voted to raise and appropriate the sum of Thirty-Five Hundred Dollars ($3,500.00) for the payment of town notes and interest.

Then at 8:00 o'clock P. M. Voted to adjourn.

At true copy of the record.
ATTEST:

RALPH L. BELCHER,
Town Clerk

AMOUNTS RAISED AND APPROPRIATED
SPECIAL TOWN MEETING

September 14th, by adjournment from September 9, 1937

For part payment for materials to be used in W. P. A. Sewing Project	$ 1 656 00
For cost of materials and overhead expense of the W. P. A.	4 000 00
Town Notes and Interest	3 500 00
	$ 9 156 00

Attest:

RALPH L. BELCHER,
Town Clerk

FISH AND GAME LICENSES ISSUED DURING YEAR 1937

Resident Fishing	86 at $2.00	$172 00
Resident Hunting	110 at $2.00	220 00
Resident Sporting	34 at $3.25	110 50
Resident Minor and Female Fishing	19 at $1.25	23 75
Resident Minor Trapping	1 at $2.25	2 25
Resident Trapping	6 at $5.25	31 50
Non-Resident Fishing (3 day)	1 at $1.50	1 50
	257	$561 50
Less Clerk's Fees 257 at 25c		64 25
		$497 25

Duplicates	7 at 50c	3 50
Resident Sporting (Free)		
(over 70 yrs of age)	27	

Paid to Division of Fisheries and Game $500 75

DOG LICENSES ISSUED DURING YEAR 1937

Male	177 at $ 2.00	$354 00
Female	24 at $ 5.00	120 00
Spayed Female	74 at $ 2.00	148 00
$25 Kennel	1 at $25 00	25 00
	276	$647 00
Less Clerk's Fees 267 at 20c		55 20
Paid to Town Treasurer		$591 80

Sixty-Fourth Annual Report Of the Selectmen

STATE AID 1937

Paid under Chapter 19, Revised Laws and Amendments thereto.

Total Amount of State Aid Paid		$ 643 00
Appropriation	$ 700 00	
Under appropriation	$ 57 00	

MILITARY AID 1937

Expended		$ 10 00
Appropriation	$ 50 00	
Under appropriation	$ 40 00	

CARE OF TOWN CEMETERY

Paid:

William E. Vining, services		$ 60 00
Appropriation	$ 60 00	

CARE OF SOLDIERS' GRAVES

Paid:—

C. S. Tilden, labor	$ 50 00	
W. A. Whiting, labor	15 00	
W. F. Hunt, labor	15 00	
James Maguire, labor	5 00	
Louis B. Gilbride, labor	50 00	
Expended	————$	135 00
Appropriation	$ 150 00	
Under appropriation	$ 15 00	

BURIAL OF INDIGENT SOLDIERS

Paid:—
C. L. Rice & Sons $ 100 00
Expended $ 100 00
No appropriation

CLEAN-UP WEEK

Paid:—
Dominico DelPrete, removing rubbish $68 49
Rockland Standard, Advertising   2 00
Expended $ 70 49
Appropriation $ 100 00
Under appropriation   29 51

CRIMINAL CASES IN COURT

Paid:—
George J. Popp, services $ 34 00
John J. Dwyer, services   4 00
Adolph Johnson, services   3 00
Robert J. Jackson, services   16 40
Leroy L. Phinney, services   38 20

Expended $ 95 60
Appropriation $ 100 00
Under appropriation   4 40

STREET LIGHTING 1937

Paid:—
Edison Electric Ill. Co., services $ 9 200 92

Expended $ 9 200 92
Appropriation $ 9 234 00
Under appropriation   33 08

HIGHWAY SURVEYOR

Paid:—
Roderick MacKenzie, salary $ 1 350 00

Expended $ 1 350 00
Appropriation $1 350 00

TARVIA AND ROAD BINDER

Paid:—
Payroll, labor	$ 3 076 44
Thomas Murrill, sand	68 00
The Barrett Co., tarvia	3 465 21
Lester Wyman, sand	51 50
Bradford Weston, stone	238 74
Chris Tompkins, sand	29 00
Rockland Coal and Grain, coal	14 00
McRae-Ouderkirk, supplies	35 00

Expended $ 6 977 89
Appropriation $ 7 000 00
Under Appropriation   22 11
List of Payroll Tarvia and Road Binder
George Ford	$ 83 25
Patrick Mahoney	124 50
Gordon Hammond	36 56
Lyle Tibbetts	82 72
Wilbur Adams	71 43
William Cannaway	65 25
Joseph Daley	41 63
Kenneth Kemp	36 85
George Artino	29 25
Philip Murphy	82 12
George Blake	61 88
John Ricca	18 00
Wm. McGarry	53 72
Michael Haggerty	18 00

Thomas McDonald	1	69
Frank Cifello	19	50
Earl Dunham	1	69
Harry Roberts	10	97
Eugene McKenna	1	69
Seymour Neiforth	1	69
Raymond Rainsford	1	69
Donald Baker	31	78
Emery Gould	1	69
Meyer Marcus	1	69
John Dwyer	162	00
A. Wainshalbaum	19	50
Raymond LaComb	19	13
Thomas McEnelly	54	56
Omer Gelinas	16	31
Walter Morrissette	9	00
Irving Turner	50	06
Wm. Green	121	47
Henry Cook	48	37
Domenic DelPrete	228	00
Arthur Casey	335	25
Wm. Condon	274	50
Samuel Williams	23	62
Fred Cormier	48	09
Eugene Green	27	56
Edward Gibbons	11	81
John Tedeschi	28	69
Louis Roche	74	25
Leo McAuliffe	18	56
Donald Owen	43	31
Joseph Sullivan	33	19
John Costello	50	62
Burrell Dill	66	94
Chas. Hunt	7	31
Frank Hibberd	13	50
Vincent Lee	47	81
Melvin Gay	96	75
Edward Casey	1	13

Paul McDonald	1 13
Leo Cull	0 00
Eugene Norman	9 00
Arthur Najarian	23 06
Aldo Botto	4 50
Thomas Bailey	28 68
Ed. Condon	9 56
Ed. Dill	2 25
Michael Bowen	22 50
Irving Torrey	7 31
Fred Smith	7 31
Henry Lombard	7 31
Chas. V. Shalgian	7 31
John Troy	7 31
Alfred Davis	7 31
C. H. Curtis	7 31
Maurice Mahoney	7 31
John Martin	4 50
Maurice Caplice	3 94
M. Hopigian	1 97
Ed. Farrar	1 97
Ernest Shores	2 25
Russell McNevin	5 06
Richard Kane	5 06
Herbert Brown	18 56
Lawrence Cull	3 94
Ralph Tedeschi	13 50
Geo. Tyler	36 00

———————$ 3 076 44

HIGHWAY REPAIRS

Paid:—

Gordon Mann, rent of pit	$ 75 00
Rome Bros., supplies	112 47
Payroll, labor	3 673 17
P. I. Perkins, supplies	12 90
E. L. LeBarron Foundary, grates	96 53

New England Concrete Pipe Co. pipe   232 65
R. L. Files and others, 2 sets tracks
   for tractor   125 00
Geo. L. Fairbain, rent of mixer   80 00
Tyler's Garage, storage of tractor   93 16
Roderick MacKenzie, sand and gravel   47 50
Rockland Welding Co., welding   10 00
Geo. W. S. Hyde, sharpening tools
   and supplies   125 45
Rockland Coal & Grain Co., lumber   48 14
E. P. Reed Lumber Co., 12-8 inch tile   3 36
Bradford Weston Inc., bit. concrete   927 89
Market Street Garage, rebuilding
   tractor   436 60
Southeastern Cons. Co., catch basin   90 92
Lelyveld Shoe Store, rubber boots   16 50
Buffalo-Springfield Roller Co.
   parts for roller   58 35
Rockland Auto Parts, supplies   6 00
M. F. Ellis Co., supplies   78 64
Comm. Public Safety, ins. of boiler   10 00
Chas. J. McCarthy, shovel spoon   67 80
American Brush Co., street brooms   17 23
Hall & Torrey Co. Inc., supplies   53 55
Rockland Disposal Co., removal of
   rubbish   45 00
Rockland Trans. Co., express   1 75
A. Wainshalbaum, gas, oil and storage   70 01
N. E. Iron & Steel Co., steel   25 92
Church Street Garage, storage, small
   tractor   24 00
Lester Wyman, gravel   10 20
Traffic Equip. Co., 24 dray brooms   42 00
Berger Metel Culvert Co., metal pipe   31 04
Standard Oil Co., oil   1 30
A. Culver Co., coal   37 15
Jenkins & Simmons, express   35
Bailey Motors Co., supplies   10 18

Thomas Welch, sharpening tools 13 20
Roderick MacKenzie, use of car 187 47

Expended		$ 6 998 38
Appropriation	$ 7 000 00	
Under appropriation	1 62	

HIGHWAY REPAIR PAYROLL
August 31, 1937

Paid:—

George Tyler	$ 606 93
William Meekin	10 97
James Sullivan	12 94
Thomas Bailey	9 00
John Ricca	96 75
Elmer Harrington	6 75
Harold Rainsford	26 44
Omer Gelinas	69 75
Myron Bacon	27 47
Joseph DelPrete	7 88
Fred Cormier	87 75
Leo Cull	49 75
Peter Hickey	14 63
Dominic DelPrete	210 00
Michael Bowen	36 75
Raymond LaCombe	98 26
Linus Hackett	65 25
Thomas Higgins	81 00
John J. Dwyer	90 00
William Bell	32 12
Lawrence Cull	79 32
William Condon	114 00
George Beverly	43 35
Thomas McDonald	6 75
Donald Baker	12 94
Philip Murphy	49 50
Lyle Tibbetts	85 22

Louis Roche	51 75
Gordon Hammond	47 25
George Artino	78 75
Melvin Gay	40 50
William Cannaway	101 25
Gerald Hammond	27 00
Joseph Daley	45 00
Arthur Ross	36 00
Arvid Noren	31 50
Wilbur Adams	64 13
Irving Turner	57 38
Kenneth Kemp	36 00
Maurice Mahoney	31 50
Fred Smith	31 50
Antonio Spozianni	22 50
Frank Cifello	22 80
Henry Fraser	29 25
Sam Williams	56 25
Patrick Mahoney	154 50
Fred Cheney	9 00
Joseph Kerski	28 13
William Green	42 38
Michael Murphy	45 00
Vincent Martin	27 00
John Tedeschi	31 50
Thomas Murrill	78 00
Arthur Casey	93 00
Willard Grant	13 50
Thomas Callahan	22 50
Henry Cook	38 25
James Thibeault	9 00
Earl Corcoran	9 00
George Ford	22 50
Michael Haggerty	13 50
Antonio Tedeschi	4 50
Joseph Tedeschi	9 00
Thomas McEnelly	18 00
Thomas Morton	11 25

A. Wainshilbaum	36 00	
Gene Green	25 88	
George Blake	29 25	
Donald Owens	29 25	
Charles Hunt	13 50	
Vincent Lee	4 50	
Burrell Dill	4 50	
Joseph Sullivan	4 50	
Arthur Najarian	4 50	
		$ 3 673 17

SOLDIERS' MEMORIAL LIBRARY

Paid:—

Natalie F. Holbrook, salary	$ 600 00
Elida Butler, salary	600 00
Lida A. Clark, salary	1 200 00
Lida A. Clark, supplies	8 56
Winifred G. Holbrook, salary	900 00
Edison Electric Ill. Co., service	100 24
Rockland Water Dept., service	5 10
N. E. Tel. & Tel. Co., service	39 96
Chas. Scribner & Sons, books	12 50
A. S. Peterson, supplies	20 11
Hall & Torrey Inc., supplies	82 10
Library Book House, books	353 38
Junior Literary Guild, supplies	27 27
Howard Diersch, repairs	12 85
Forrest Partch, repairs	2 90
Amos A. Phelps, insurance	168 55
Howlands Ins. Office, insurance	14 31
American Library Asso., books	5 00
Demco Library Asso., books	50
F. J. Barnard Co., supplies	29 37
International Library Asso., books	11 62
Filing Equip. Bureau, cards	19 34
Rockland Coal & Grain Co., coal	201 40

O. H. Toothaker, books   2 16
Ida A. Totman, book   5 00
Rockland Standard Pub. Co., printing   3 50
New England News Co., books   41 92
Frank E. Fitts, labor   4 74
Social Justice Pub. Co., subscription   2 00
Douglas Print, cards   15 00
G. R. Niles, setting glass   1 35
Funk & Wagnalls, year book   7 60
Bemis Drug Co., Electric fan   3 98
McManus Box Co., slabs   13 00
A. I. Randall Inc., printing   4 75
Gaylord Bros., supplies   3 90
Christian Science Pub. Co., subscription 2 25
American News Co., subscription   90 50
D. R. Hunting Co., supplies   3 05
L. A. Wells, binding   5 78
H. W. Wilson, subscription   21 20
American Rescue League, subscription   60

Expended $ 4 647 34
Appropriation $4 200 00
Dog Fund   447 34
Total Available   ———$ 4 647 34

SIDEWALKS 1937

Paid:—
Weymouth Asphalt Co., material $ 90 77
Chris Tompkins, gravel   3 20
Hedge & Matthews, supplies   11 09
A. Culver Co., supplies   26 40
Rockland Coal & Grain Co., supplies   29 99
Bradford Weston Inc., bit. concrete   76 13
George W. Beal, gas and oil   3 62
Payroll, labor and Trucks   492 25

Expended $ 733 45

Transferred to Howard St.	$	250	00
Transferred to North Avenue		700	00
Transferred to E. Water St.		725	00

Total of Transfers				$ 1 675	00
Appropriation	$ 2 500	00			
Ámount of Transfers and					
Sidewalks	2 408	45			
Under Appropriation	91	55			

AMERICAN LEGION POST No. 147

Paid:—

American Legion Building Association, rent	$ 900	00
Appropriation	$ 900	00

CLEANING UNION STREET

Paid:—

Thomas J. Higgins, labor	$ 1 195	50	
Archie Flynn, labor	4	50	

Expended			$1 200	00
Appropriation	$ 1 100	00		
Transfer Reserve Fund	100	00		
			$ 1 200	00

SIGNS AND GUIDE BOARDS

Paid:—

M. J. Fitzgibbons, putting up signs	$	24	65
Bay State Motor. Exp. Co., express			90
Charles A. Vaughan, 9 signs, 6 posts		64	50
Rome Bros., paint for R. R. signs			95
Robert Hayden, paint and putting			
up sign		9	00

Expended			$ 100	00
Appropriation	$100	00		

PETER A. BOWLER CAMP No. 63

SPANISH WAR VETERANS

Paid:—

Old Colony Post Building Association, rent		$ 288 00
Appropriation	$ 288 00	

FIRE DEPARTMENT MAINTENANCE

Payrolls:—

C. P. Inkley, Chief	$ 1 500 00	
J. P. Barry, Dep. Chief	200 00	
G. W. Clark, Supt. Fire Alarm	400 00	
J. Fitzgibbons, driver	1 731 60	
W. Parker, driver	1 638 00	
J. Mulready, sub. driver	120 00	
Engine Company No. 1, payroll	1 470 00	
Ladder Company No. 1, payroll	1 253 50	
		$ 8 313 10

Department Expense		
A. Culver Company, fuel	$ 166 97	
Rockland Coal & Grain Co., fuel	104 47	
Telephone Co.	69 73	
Edison Light Co.	165 04	
Old Colony Gas Co.	43 40	
Water Department	24 21	
Damon Electric Co.	6 75	
A. J. Vargus	151 74	
American La France Co.,		
Labor and materials	186 88	
Boston Coupling Co., supplies	80 21	
Rome Bros., supplies	9 05	
Hall & Torrey, supplies	15 98	
J. Riordon, supplies	7 05	
J. Dwyer, truck hire	7 00	
Douglas Print	7 50	
Union Market	5 57	
Gorham Fire Equipment Co.	309 10	
Hyle Cook, labor	62 00	

Francis Metivier, labor	62 00
Albert Clark, labor	45 00
C. P. Inkley, use of auto	250 00
E. E. Lane, supplies	4 00
Stanley Ames, repairing	5 00
Brewer & Co., soda and acid	17 92
N. J. Beals, boiler room	412 50
Hallamore Machine Co., repairing	3 00
Lester Pratt, labor	7 00
J. S. McCallum, labor and material	18 00
A. A. Phelps, insurance	1 36
Edison Light Co., material	10 48
Chelsea Wrecking Co.	13 00
H. C. Metcalf	34 00
Standard Oil Co.	5 86
Chester Bandon, repairers tanks	5 75
Justin J. McCarthy Co., nozzle	43 14
Fred Yelland, supplies	7 00
Maxim Motor Co., ladder rounds	6 00
Simmons Express Co.	1 75
Fred Moore, oil	41 25
A. Hemmings, extinguisher	5 00
M. F. Ellis & Co., supplies	4 50
J. A. Rice Co., supplies	1 20
Rockland Transportation Company	50
Boston Mill Remnant, wiping cloths	12 25
Walter Killiam, jack	12 50
Gamewell Company	2 63
C. P. Inkley, Telephone and expense	90 70
Remedy Co., Inc.	2 09
P. Ouelette, labor	32 00
J. E. Kemp, repairing windshield	4 25
G. W. Hyde	2 50
Bemis Drug Co.	50
A. H. Blanchard Co.	10 71

	$ 2 598 49
Total Expense	$10 911 59

| Appropriation | $10 062 00 |
| Over appropriation | $ 849 59 |

FOREST FIRE DEPARTMENT

Payrolls	$ 569 00
Chester Bandon, repairing tanks	16 25
Boston Coupling Co., hose	44 00

Total Expenses	$ 629 25
Appropriation	700 00
Under Appropriation	70 75

POLICE DEPARTMENT

Paid:—

Cornelius J. McHugh,	
patrol services	$ 1 424 80
Robert J. Drake, patrol services	$ 1 424 80
Adolph Johnson, patrol services	1 424 80
John H. Murphy, patrol services	1 434 40
George J. Popp, service as chief	1 924 00
George J. Popp, use of auto	260 00
Maurice J. Mullen, police service	114 70
John J. Dwyer, Jr., police service	112 35
Charles Hines, police service	19 00
Samuel Canaway, police service	18 00
Michael O'Brien, police service	14 50
John H. Hannon, police service	8 00
N. E. Tel. Co., service	86 06
Brockton Edison, service,	
station and Webster street	73 09
Bailey Motors, gasoline, supplies	
police car	212 79
George N. Beals, supplies,	
repairs police car	33 14
A. Wainshilbaum, supplies, police car	36 50
Olympia Confectionery, food for	
prisoners	28 30

Rockland Coal & Grain, coal
for police station 88 40
John Cheever, supplies police station 13 25
Rome Bros., supplies 6 82
Ralph Measures, labor at station 6 00
Hall & Torrey, supplies 5 10
Dr. Norbert Lough, treating prisoner 5 00
Leroy Hutchins, supplies 4 00
Amos Phelps, insurance police car 3 90
Matt Radio, repairs to police radio 4 00
A. S. Peterson, supplies 2 25
Percy Albee, cleansing blankets police
station 1 70
Jenkins & Simmons, express 35
John Dwyer, carting rubbish from
station 8 00
A. Wainshilbaum, supplies, repairs, etc 73 16
S. S. S. Co., markers for street 58 80
————————$ 8 929 96
Appropriation $ 8 800 00
Received from Reserve Fund 139 16

$ 8 939 16
Expended 8 929 96

Under $ 9 20

ANIMALS AND STABLES

Paid:—
William T. Condon, services as inspector $ 150 00
Appropriation $ 150 00

SEALER OF WEIGHTS AND MEASURES

Paid:—
Harold J. Inkley, salary $ 400 00
Appropriation $ 400 00

BOARD OF HEALTH

Paid:—

Payroll, labor	$ 1 944 62
Plymouth County Hospital, care of patients	1 468 70
Burying cats and dogs	16 50
Joseph H. Dunn, M. D. services of contagious cases	74 00
J. A. Caninolo, M. D., special service	68 00
Evelyn Delory, salary	1 250 00
M. J. Fitzgibbons, salary	25 00
Bemis Drug Co., supplies	23 23
Henry Roach Sr., service at dump	159 00
Geo. E. Bolling, analysis of water Reeds pond	7 00
John J. Dwyer, truck	3 00
Rockland Standard Pub. Co. Milk license	3 75
Joseph Frame, M. D. salary	100 00
Joseph Frame, M. D., visits and fumigation	56 00
Rockland Coal & Grain Co., tile pipe	39 47
F. H. Corey, M. D., service	6 00
Rome Bros., tile pipe	14 00
Geo. W. S. Hyde, repairs	8 20
Southeastern Cons. Co., cement blocks	20 00
Hall & Torrey Co. Inc., tile pipe	390 66
Rockland Water Dept., supplies	17 30
A. Culver Co., supplies	2 40
Rockland Hardware Co., tile pipe	81 00
Dr. M. J. Dunn, dental work	10 00
Dr. J. H. Burke, dental work	10 00
Dr. J. B. Gallagher, dental work	10 00
Everready Supply Co., towels	13 54
McGregor Inst. Co., supplies	50 92
John Hood Co., supplies	21 68
Chris Tompkins, gravel	4 40

Dr. J. H. Dunn, salary   50 00
Thomas Murrell, sand   6 25
Edward Cullinan, salary   25 00

Expended $ 5 979 62
Appropriation   · $ 6 000 00
Under appropriation   20 38

LIST OF PAYROLL, BOARD OF HEALTH

Paid:—
Thomas McDonald $ 9 00
Harry Roberts   9 00
Seymore Neiforth   4 50
Michael Bowen   15 50
Wesley Richardson   3 38
Joseph P. Meade   36 00
M. J. Fitzgibbons   81 00
William Santry   9 00
Robert Hayden   48 38
Daniel Riley   18 00
Emory Gould   3 94
William Fox   24 75
Maurice Mahoney   9 00
Joseph Flannery   9 00
Charles McGonagle   22 50
James F. Maloney   9 00
Robert Casey   4 50
Edward Cullinan   369 56
Samuel Cannaway   266 63
Harold Corcoran   306 00
Michael Haggerty   15 20
John J. Dwyer   103 50
Thomas Bailey   121 50
Joseph Shoughrow   24 75
John Flynn   24 47
Samuel Williams   20 25
George Blake   22 50

Charles Descenzo	22 50
Edward Metivier	24 75
Stephen Whiting	6 75
David Mahoney	24 25
James Flannery	9 00
John Owens	4 50
Ralph Badger	22 50
Paul Golemme	18 00
John Kelley	22 50
Lester Pratt	13 50
Florence Corkery	13 50
Leon Owens	4 50
Felix Carreaux	18 56
Angus MacLeod	9 00
James Thibeault	9 00
John Gammon	4 50
Charles Gibbons	15 75
Charles Lincoln	27 00
Leon Ignatowicz	11 25
Austin Marks	9 00
James Carreaux	13 50
Earl Corcoran	9 00
Michael Murphy	13 50
James Tippins	9 00
W. Alton Whiting	9 00
Joseph Sullivan	9 00
Total	$ 1 944 62

PARK DEPT. 1937

Paid:—

Payroll, labor	$ 2 585 26
Rockland Water Dept., service	10 00
A. Culver Co., lime	9 75
Robert Hayden, sharpening tools	2 10
Rockland Standard Pub. Co., cards	50
A. J. Vargus, supplies	11 27

Rome Bros., supplies	7 38	
George O'Donnell, Tel. calls	65	
Hall & Torrey Co. Inc., supplies	7 33	
Rockland Hardware Co., grass		
seed and supplies	40 10	
Abe Wainshilbaum, supplies	21 31	
Rockland Coal & Grain Co., posts	5 11	
James E. Kemp, sharpening mower	3 00	
James D. Mahoney, power mower		
and supplies	335 70	
M. Vincent Fitzgibbons, insurance	35 00	
Patrick H. Mahoney, truck	31 00	

Expended		$ 3105 46
Appropriation	$ 3 115 00	
Under Appropriation	9 54	

LIST OF PAYROLL, PARK DEPT.

George O'Donnell	$ 537 14	
Peter Hickey	681 96	
Joseph P. Meade	666 01	
James Mahoney	697 76	
Abe Wainshilbaum	2 39	

Total		$ 2 585 26

MOTH DEPT. 1937

Paid:—

Amos A. Phelps, insurance	$	5 00
Payroll, labor		160 22
Rome Bros., supplies		5 65
Sherwin & Williams, arsenate of lead		95 76
Rockland Hardware Co., supplies		5 74
Hickey Bros., gas and oil		13 20
Spurr & Tedeschi, gas and oil		6 05
James G. Lamb, gas and oil		1 60

Crawford Gas Station, gas and oil   6 78

| Expended | | $ | 300 00 |
| Appropriation | $ 300 00 | | |

LIST OF PAYROLL, MOTH DEPT.

Alfred Metivier	$ 139 94
Frank Hammond	5 07
Joseph Cull	5 07
Henry Whiting	5 07
Albert Finnegan	5 07

Total $ 160 22

PLYMOUTH COUNTY EXTENSION SERVICE

Paid:—
Plymouth County $150 00

| Expended | | $ | 150 00 |
| Appropriation | $ 150 00 | | |

PLYMOUTH COUNTY HOSPITAL

Paid:—
Treasurer Plymouth County
maintenance of Plymouth County
Hospital $ 3 633 12

| Expended | | $ 3 633 12 |
| Appropriation | $ 3 633 12 | |

FIRE DEPT. HEATER APP. 1933

Paid:—
J. S. McCallum, installing heater $500 00

| Expended | | $ | 500 00 |
| Appropriation | $ 500 00 | | |

TREE WARDEN 1937

Paid:—

John J. Dwyer, truck	$ 5	00
A. Culver Co., supplies	1	60
Elliot F. Magoun, supplies	48	11
Payroll, labor	498	83
Rome Bros., supplies	46	28
Rockland Standard Pub. Co., cards	12	50
FitzHenry-Guptill, repair sprayer	90	15
Geo. W. S. Hyde, repairs	6	00
Sherwin-Williams Co., Arsenate lead	159	12
Crawford Service Station, supplies	3	75
Pete Hart, supplies	1	18
A. L. Paulding, supplies	1	00
E. P. Reed Lumber Co., supplies	6	90
William Bell, truck	45	94
Hickey Bros., supplies	13	58
J. S. McCallum, repairs	4	60
Frank Shaw, supplies	5	76
A. Wainshilbaum, supplies	3	00

Expended		$	953 30
Appropriation	$ 900	00	
Trans from Reserve Fund	53	30	
Total		$	953 30

LIST OF PAYROLL, TREE WARDEN

Alfred Metivier	$ 311	83
Joseph Shoughrow	4	50
William Bell	117	25
Frank Hammond	18	00
Albert Finnegan	40	50
Robert Austin	2	25
Edward Metivier	4	50
Total	$ 498	83

RENT OF TOWN OFFICES

Paid:—
Rockland Savings Bank, rent $1 240 00
Appropriation $ 1 240 00

EAST WATER STREET LAND DAMAGE

Paid:—
Edith J. Lamb, payment of damages $9 20
John H. Lamb, payment of damages   22 80
Samuel Walker, award for damages   3 20

Expended $ 35 20
Appropriation $ 42 70
Under appropriation   7 50

SEALER OF WEIGHTS AND MEASURES TEST CAN

Paid:—
Rockland Weld. Eng. Co., test cans $70 00

Expended $ 70 00
Appropriation $70 00

TOWN OFFICERS

Harry S. Torrey, Selectman
Board of Public Welfare
Fence Viewer and Old
Age Assistance $ 1 980 00
Norman S. Whiting, Selectman
Board of Public Welfare
Fence Viewer and Old
Age Assistance   300 00
John J. Bowler, Selectman,
Board of Public Welfare
Fence Viewer and Old
Age Assistance   300 00

Charles J. Higgins, treasurer	1 350 00	
James A. Donovan, tax collector	1 500 00	
Ralph L. Belcher, town clerk	700 00	
Ralph L. Belcher, Registrar of voters	75 00	
Esther Rawson, Registrar of voters	75 00	
John Carney, Registrar of voters	75 00	
Thomas Morrissey, Registrar of voters	75 00	
C. Elmer Asklund, auditor	100 00	
Leo Downey, auditor	100 00	
Harold Smith, auditor	110 00	
Magorisk L. Walls, Moderator	50 00	

Expended		$ 6 790 00
Appropriation	$ 6 800 00	
Under appropriation	10 00	

ELECTION 1937

Paid:—

Bemis Drug Co., dinners	$ 26 05	
Payroll, tellers and moderator	346 00	
Warren B. Hamilton, dinners	2 25	
John J. Bowler, rent of Opera House	220 00	
Rockland Standard Pub. Co., printing	280 10	
George Foulas, dinners	18 40	
Mrs. E. B. Lannin, dinners	9 00	

Expended		$ 901 80
Appropriation	$ 850 00	
Trans Reserve Fund	51 80	
Total		$ 901 80

PURCHASE WASHINGTON REED LOT

Paid:—

Howland & Howland, one half cost of survey	$ 29 82

| Appropriation | $ 500 00 |
| Bal. unexpended | $ 470 18 |

MASS. HOSPITAL SCHOOL

| Appropriation | $ 500 00 |

Nothing expended

MASS. INDUSTRIAL SCHOOL

Paid:—

Town of Weymouth, Mass.	$ 1 624 51
City of Quincy, Mass.	199 40
Norfolk County Agri. school	118 00
City of Boston, Mass.	309 24
City of Brockton, Mass.	13 20

Expended		$ 2 264 35
Appropriation	$ 3 000 00	
Under Appropriation	735 65	

TOWN REPORT AND POLL BOOK

Paid:—

Earl Wallace, delivering town reports	$ 9 00
Ralph Measures, delivering town reports	9 00
Russell Chandler, delivering town reports and car	20 00
Douglas Print, printing report	789 00
Douglas Print, poll book	343 44

Expended		$ 1 170 44
Appropriation	$ 1 200 00	
Under appropriation	29 56	

TOWN NOTES AND INTEREST

Paid:—

| Director of Accounts Certifying Notes | $ 22 00 |

Payment School Bonds	16 000 00
Interest on School Bond	5 025 00 -
Plymouth County Hospital Note	1 000 00
Discount on Notes	1 347 95
Interest on Notes	485 00
Payment Union Street Bond	4 000 00
Interest on Union Street Bond	350 00

Expended		$28 229 95
Appropriation	$25 000 00	
Appropriation, Sept 9.	3 500 00	

| Total appropriation | $28 500 00 |
| Under appropriation | 270 05 |

SNOW REMOVAL

Paid:—

Rockland Welding Co., 2 new plows	$ 431 00
Rockland Welding Co., repairs on plows	9 50 -
Solvay Sales Corp., calcin chloride	46 50
Payroll, labor	302 55
E. P. Reed Co., lumber	50
Market Street Garage, repairs on tractors	81 82
G. W. S. Hyde, repairs	21 60
Pearl Murrill, sand	43 50
Gideon Studley, storage of sand	75 00
P. I. Perkins, supplies	53 03
Church St., Garage, storage	12 00
Lester Wyman, sand	6 00

Expended		$ 1 083 00
Appropriation	$1 000 00	
Over appropriation	83 00	

ASSESSORS

| Paid as Salary | |
| Joseph B. Estes | $ 1 440 00 |

Dennis L. O'Connor	530 00	
Norman J. Beal	530 00	
Expended		$ 2 500 00
Appropriation	$ 2 500 00	

MISCELLANEOUS CLERK

Paid:—

Rockland Trans. Co., express	$	35
Douglas Print, Birth Certificates		12 00
Murray Bros. Co., binding record		9 55
Ralph L. Belcher, vital statistics		199 50
Joseph Frame, M. D., 2 birth returns		50
N. F. Lough, M. D., 6 birth returns		1 50
J. F. Curtin, M. D., 4 birth returns		1 00
A. H. Barron M. D., 2 birth returns		50
H. J. Hulse, M. D., 6 birth returns		1 50
F. H. Corey, M. D., 14 birth returns		3 50
C. L. Rice & Son Inc.		
46 Death returns		11 50
Geo. E. Mansfield, 8 death returns		2 00
Emmett Sullivan 17 death returns		4 25
D. C. Metcalf, repair typewriter		4 00
Warren B. Woodward, bond		5 00
Rockland Standard Pub. Co.		
Dog notice		7 50
Ralph L. Belcher, postage		
and mailing		3 19
Becker & Co., desk and supplies		74 50
A. S. Peterson, supplies		1 95
Ralph L. Belcher, expense		
Town Clerk's meeting		5 50

Expended		$ 349 29
Appropriation	$ 350 00	
Under appropriation	71	

MISCELLANEOUS SELECTMEN

Paid:—

A. S. Peterson, supplies	$	95
W. W. Lydstone, repair ink wells	4	25
Plymouth County Selectmen's Asso. Dues	6	00
Hobbs & Warren, blanks	5	02
Paul Eisenhart, staples	1	50
U. S. Post Office, envelopes	86	32

Expended	$	104 04
Appropriation	$ 120 00	
Under appropriation	15 96	

MISCELLANEOUS SEALER WEIGHTS AND MEASURES

Paid:—

Hobbs & Warren, books	$	55
Robinson Seal Co., seals	6	86
Amos A. Phelps, insurance	16	38
W. E. L. E. Gurley, supplies	8	13
Rockland Welding Co., supplies	10	00
Harold J. Inkley, use of auto	60	00

Expended	$	104 92
Appropriation	$ 105 00	
Under Appropriation	08	

MISCELLANEOUS TREASURER

Paid:—

L. E. Moran Co., check reg.	$	29 65
Todd Sales Co., check writer	102	00
Charles J. Higgins, postage and mailing	68	05
Amos A. Phelps, burglary insurance	18	08
U. S. Post Office, envelopes	81	44

Annette White, services	150	00
Hobbs & Warren, supplies	10	56
Robinson Seal Co., blanks	1	45
Todd Co., 20,000 checks	93	10
H. C. Metcalf, typewriter repairs	1	00
Ward's Stationers, supplies	2	05
Amos A. Phelps, bond	202	50
Douglas Print, supplies	3	00
The Austin Print, letter heads	4	00
Charles J. Higgins, expenses to Boston	30	80

Expended		$	797	68
Appropriation	$ 800	00		
Under Appropriation	2	32		

MISCELLANEOUS ASSESSORS

Paid:—

Hobbs & Warren, blanks	$	3	20
L. E. Muran, supplies		86	08
A. I. Randall Inc., cards		23	60
James F. O'Connor, insurance		23	58
Davol Printing House, notices		2	00
L. E. Muran, Cards and poll sheets		79	56
A. S. Peterson, supplies		14	63
N. E. Tel. & Tel. Co., services		72	41
Edison Electric Ill. Co., lamps		2	80
Geo. N. Barnstead, cards		1	00
U. S. Post Office, envelopes		62	00
Prentise Hall Inc., manual		5	08
Alton F. Lyon, transfer cards and service		114	75
L. E. Muran, loose binders		77	44
Donald Baker, map frames		4	00
Hall & Torrey Inc., supplies		3	50
Amos A. Phelps, insurance		10	00
Dennis L. O'Connor, auto expense		61	20
Banker & Tradesman, subscription		10	00

Brockton Trans. Co., express	1 30
Douglas Print, letterheads and cards	23 00
H. C. Metcalf, cleaning typewriter and supplies	4 10
Joseph B. Estes, auto expense	110 11
Norman J. Beal, auto expense	76 55
Spaulding Moss Co., scales and blue prints	4 27
Ernest A. Studley, abstracts	9 75
Dennis L. O'Connor, school of instruction	12 00
Joseph B. Estes, school of instruction	12 00
Norman J. Beal, school of instruction	12 00
Jenkins & Simmons, express	1 15
Mary E. Twomey, services	116 00
Warren B. Woodward, insurance	10 48
Rockland Standard Pub. Co. cards	24 00
Norman J. Beal, repairs on furniture	5 52

Expended		$ 1 079 06
Appropriation	$ 1 100 00	
Under appropriation	20 94	

MISCELLANEOUS COLLECTOR

Paid:—

U. S. Post Office, envelopes	$ 191 48
Amos A. Phelps, burglary and Robbery insurance	18 09
James A. Donovan, postage and mailing	22 07
Ralph L. Belcher, clerical assistance on tax	200 00
A. S. Peterson, supplies	3 85
Hobbs & Warren, supplies	35 37

Amos A. Phelps, bond	415 00	
James A. Donovan, expenses to Boston	12 00	
A. I. Randall Inc. tax bills	36 45	
The Austin Print, notices	12 25	
Rockland Standard Pub. Co.		
Adv. Tax Sale	146 50	
Francis J. Geogan, legal		
service on tax sale	282 00	
Becker & Co., supplies	3 40	

Expended		$ 1 413 96
Appropriation	$ 1 400 00	
Trans. from Reserve Fund	13 96	

Total Expended	$ 1 413 96

MISCELLANEOUS REGISTRARS OF VOTERS

Paid:—

Rockland Standard Pub. Co.		
advertisement	$ 14 00	
R. Dexter Tohman, ballot box	70 75	
U. S. Post Office, envelopes	28 20	
John H. Wyatt Co., adding machine	65 00	

Expended		$ 177 95
Appropriation	$ 200 00	
Under appropriation	22 50	

MISCELLANEOUS UNCLASSIFIED

Paid:—

Emma W. Gleason, storage of flags $	48 00
Dr. Joseph H. Dunn, examination	
injuries	8 00
R. Robert Torrey, numbering houses	27 00
Geo. Gelinas, damage to car	21 25
N. E. Tel. & Tel. Co., services	105 53

Edison Electric Ill. Co., service	121	54
Edison Electric Ill. Co., lamps for town clock	7	80
Paul Eisherhart, staples	1	50
Harry S. Torrey, expense to Boston and postages	10	00
Chas. Hines, cleaning town office	265	00
Damon Electric Co., wiring bell and supplies	12	00
Howland & Howland, layout new streets and services	117	31
Becker & Co., supplies	8	40
John J. Dwyer, putting out flags	82	50
Frances J. Geogan, legal services	270	15
N. S. Whiting, services	110	50
Ralph L. Belcher, expenses recording new streets	8	24
L. E. Muran, filing cases	13	80
U. S. Post Office, envelopes	19	23
H. C. Metcalf, repairs and supplies	3	00
Roland S. Poole, care of town clock	53	25
Comm. Public Safety, License blanks		95
Jared Gardner, photo stone Prospect St	3	00
N. Y., N. H. & H. R. R., expense Plain street	10	54
Rockland Standard Pub. Co. Posters and Jury list	13	75
Hobbs & Warren, license blanks	3	38
Michael Fitzgibbons, setting R. R. signs	9	00
Chas. J. Higgins, no trespass signs	2	00
Nemasket Trans. Co., express		90
Payroll, guarding fire alarms	344	00
Rome Bros., supplies		35
A. I. Randall Inc., payroll sheets	22	65
Franklin & Perkins, paper towels	4	50
The Douglas Print, letterheads	5	50

Traffic Equipment Co., signs
East Water street,   16 40
Harry L. Rome, rubber flooring   2 25
Hall & Torrey Inc., supplies   3 60
Alton F. Lyon, settlement damage
suit   75 00
                                          _____

Expended $ 1 834 77
Appropriation $ 1 150 00
Over appropriation   684 77

BEACONS 1937

Paid:—
Edison Electric Ill. Co., service $ 146 61
Damon Electric, care of Stop and
Go lights   100 00
Traffic Equipment Co. care of
Beacons   340 00
Damon Electric, repairs   9 35
                                     _____

Expended $ 595 96
Appropriation $ 600 00
Under appropriation   4 04

EAST WATER STREET CONSTRUCTION
APPROPRIATION 1935

Paid:—
Warren Bros., settlement on
concrete surface $ 125 00
Chris Tompkins, gravel   10 00
Rockland Coal & Grain, supplies   15 84
A. Culver Co., Cement   1 30
Bradford Weston, stone   49 69
Crystal Concrete Co., concrete   22 75
                                     _____

Expended $ 224 58
Bal. of 1935 Appropriation $ 224 58

REFURNISHING ASSESSORS OFFICE
Article 52, 1934 appropriation from Surplus

Paid:—
L. E. Muran Co., 1 counter file
.. and shelves $ 180 00

Expended		$ 180 00
Appropriation	$ 180 00	

VISITING NURSE

Paid:—
Mrs. Harry W. Burrell, Treasurer

Visiting Nurse Association		$ 1 500 00
Appropriation	$ 1 500 00	

LIBERTY STREET DRAIN
Balance from Appropriation 1936

Paid:—
Southeastern Cons., Co.,
2 catch basins $ 41 22

Expended		$ 41 22
Appropriation	$ 51 78	
Under appropriation	10 56	

W. P. A. PLAIN STREET

Paid:—

Payroll, trucks	$ 538 39
Rockland Coal and Grain Co., cement	7 15
Rockland Hardware Co., supplies	20 24
N. E. Concrete Pipe Co., pipe	253 35
C. L. Baxter, labor and supplies	21 00
E. L. Baron Foundry, 7 basin frames	83 90

Southeastern Cons. Co.,

basin blocks	133	52
Rome Bros., supplies	14	03
A. Culver Co., cement	2	50
A. Wainshilbaum, gas, etc.	72	41
Thomas Walsh, sharp tools	19	00
Hall & Torrey Co., supplies	4	95
Melvin Gay, use of car	18	00
Fred S. Delay, supplies first aid	2	54
The Barret Co., Tarvia		
at 115 gal.	309	02

Expended		$ 1 500 00
Appropriation	$1 500 00	

PARK W. P. A.

Paid:—

Payroll, trucks and labor	$	468 57
Fred S. Delay, medical supplies		45
A. J. Vargus, supplies		1 60
Rome Bros., supplies		1 26
C. L. Baxter, service		8 00
A. Wainshilbaum, supplies		1 00
Louise Roberts, shed		15 00
Rockland Hardware, supplies		79 34
Rose & Shaw, moving shed		10 00
Hall & Torrey Co., supplies		1 88
Quincy Sand & Gravel Co., gravel		2 20
Daniel Riley, gravel		8 00
Otis Mann, gravel		2 25
Guy Benner, gravel		12 15
Donald Wyman, gravel		35 90
Joseph Mileski, supplies		2 00
C. H. Thornhill, cinders		658 80
Patrick Mahoney, loam		120 00

Expended	$ 1 428 40

Trans. 1936 appropriation   156 50
Appropriation   3 053 80

Total appropriation $ 3 210 30
Under appropriation   1 781 90

W. P. A. STREETS

Paid:—

Rockland Coal & Grain Co., supplies	$138 51
John Manville, material	129 92
C. E. Tompkins, gravel	5 80
A. Wainshilbaum, truck	33 70
Hall & Torrey Co. Inc., supplies	92 20
E. L. LeBarron Foundry Co., grate and frame	18 00
Trucks, Douglas Street	291 01
Thomas Welch, sharpen tools	41 70
A. Culver Co., cement and supplies	124 29
No. Abington Coop. Bank rent of garage	60 00
Rockland Welding Co., repairs	2 25
Lester Wyman, sand	26 08
J. S. McCullam, supplies	15 28
John H. Lamb, supplies	2 50
E. F. Benson, sand	74 74
Rockland Water Dept. use of compressor	19 00
Ryan's Market, supplies	1 20
Bradford Weston, material Church street	143 01
Chas. F. Tilden, supplies	5 00
Sears-Roebuck Co., forge	10 20
Trucks on various streets	28 44

Expended $ 1 260 83
Trans. from 1936 appropriation $ 2 532 36

Part of appropriation	3 500 00	
Cost of Union St. Curb	238 00	
Total amount available		$ 6 270 36

SUMMARY OF TRANSFERS

Striping Streets	$ 106 00	
Plain Street	1 500 00	
Howard Street drain	225 00	
Salem Street drain	275 00	
Belmont Street drain	150 00	
Arlington Street sidewalk	425 00	
Plain Street sidewalk	350 00	
Cliff Street sidewalk	400 00	
Highland Street, sidewalk	400 00	
Summit Street sidewalk	500 00	
Expended on transfers		$ 4 331 00
Expended on W. P. A. Streets		1 260 83
Total expended		5 591 83
Balance unexpended		$ 678 53

IMPROVEMENT AT REED'S POND

Paid:—

Payroll, horses and trucks	$ 255 21
Hall & Torrey Co. Inc., supplies	361 72
Rome Bros., supplies	24 24
A. Culver Co., supplies	85 70
Otis Mann, gravel	7 70
Fred S. Delay, medical supplies	3 61
Lester Wyman, sand	30 00
H. J. Hulse, M. D., service on injury	37 00
Austin Mark's, stone	2 00

Charles S. Beal, cedar posts	15 00	
Quincy Sand & Gravel Co., filling	193 00	
C. H. Swift, gas	4 52	
Crystal Concrete Corp., concrete	250 00	
G. W. S. Hyde, repairs	7 00	
Corcoran Supply Co., bubbler and supplies	6 50	
Bradford Weston Inc., stone dust	22 81	
Wm. Emmon, labor	12 00	
Thomas Fox, sand	1 40	
A. J. Vargus, supplies	3 52	
N. E. Iron & Steel Co., steel	3 00	
Market Street Garage, supplies	1 93	
E. L. LeBarron Foundry, supplies	5 74	
A. Wainshilbaum, supplies	17 70	
F. L. Partch, install lights	47 83	
Plymouth Cordage Co., rope	14 87	
A. I. Randall Inc., signs	5 90	
Charles W. Banclon, repairs	5 00	
Rockland Standard Pub. Co., signs	5 50	
Edison Electric Ill. Co., service	5 60	
Rockland Coal & Grain Co., supplies	68 48	
Expended		$ 1 504 58
Appropriation	$ 1 000 00	
Trans. from 1936	411 74	
Trans from Reserve Fund	150 00	
		$ 1 561 74
Under appropriation		57 16

W. P. A. ADMINISTRATION

Paid:—

Fred M. Ryan, services	$ 1 272 00
M. Warren Wright, services	645 50
John J. Bowler, use of car	318 00
John J. Bowler, tel. extension	12 00

Franklin & Perkins, bags	78	89
A. S. Peterson, supplies	25	90
John J. Dwyer, trucking commodity		
supplies	236	50
John J. Bowler, rent of offices		
W. P. A.	360	00
Rockland School Dept.		
use of hall	9	50
N. E. Tel. & Tel. Co., service	128	65
Singer Sewing Mach. Co., repairs	2	15
Rockland Standard Pub. Co., cards	8	20
Stall & Dean, supplies recreation		
project	65	28
J. A. Rice Co., supplies	9	37
H. C. Metcalf, repairs	6	00
American Red Cross., first aid books		
and outfits	11	40
Rome Bros., supplies		90
Fred S. Delay, medical supplies	17	46
Haywood & Haywood, blue prints	5	61
A. Culver Co., Egg boxes	22	00
Charles Bowler, repairs on Sewing		
machine	4	50
Fred M. Ryan, use of car	28	00
Bemis Drug Co., supplies	10	62
John J. Dwyer, trans., kindergarten		
project	280	00
Hall & Torrey Co. Inc., supplies	45	07
M. F. Ellis Co., supplies	9	00
Irene Crehan, swimming		
instructor	171	00
The Sport Shop, supplies		
recreational	26	70
John S. Cheever, supplies	10	50
Ryan's Market, supplies	3	00
John Campbell, repairs	7	33
Archer Adv. service, cards	3	00

Harry S. Torrey, expense to
Boston   5 00
Rockland Pharmacy, supplies   3 44
Rockland Coal & Grain, supplies   25 47

- Expended $ 3 867 94
Bal. appropriation 1936 $ 301 66
Part appropriation   1 500 00
Appropriation   4 000 00

Total $ 5 801 66
Unexpended balance   1 933 72

DIVISION STREET, W. P. A.

Paid:—

Payroll, trucks $ 605 80
Rockland Hardware Co., 6 shovels   8 70
Chas. L. Baxter, surveying   32 00
A. Culver Co., cement   5 85
A. Wainshilbaum, oil   3 05

Expended $ 655 40
Trans. W. P. A. $ 656 12
Unexpended Balance   72

W. P. A. UNION STREET SIDEWALK

Paid:—

Rockland Coal & Grain Co., supplies $ 11 47
Bradford Weston Inc. bit concrete   370 97
Trans. Pre Cast Curb., 850' curb   238 00
Lester Wyman, sand   5 02
Warren Vinton, supplies   2 00
A. Wainshilbaum, use of crane   13 63
Payroll, trucks   255 11

Expended $ 896 20
Appropriation $ 900 00
Unexpended balance   3 80

BRADFORD WESTON CONSTRUCTION OF UNION STREET

Paid:—
Bradford Weston, Union Street
Article 17 $ 510 00

Expended $ 510 00
Appropriation $ 510 00

EAST WATER STREET CONSTRUCTION BALANCE 1936

Paid:—
N. E. Concrete Corp., tile pipe $ 370 80
Jenkins & Simmons, express   2 00
Rockland Coal & Grain, coal   109 76
Standard Oil Co., asphalt   790 65
Nelson Cement Stone Co., curbing   678 70
Bradford Weston Inc., bit. concrete   446 89

Expended $ 2 398 80
Bal. appropriation 1936 $ 1 652 53
Appropriation 1937   513 60
Payment by County of
Plymouth   232 67

Total   2 398 80

COMPENSATION INSURANCE FOR FIREMEN

Paid:—
Phillip S. Collins, insurance $ 292 50

Expended $ 292 50
Appropriation $ 292 50

WORKMEN'S COMPENSATION

Paid:—

Amos A. Phelps, insurance	$ 1 979 93	
Expended		$ 1 979 93
Appropriation	$ 2 250 00	
Under appropriation	270 07	

STRIPING UNION STREET
(Article 74 Trans. W. P. A. Amt. $106.00)

Paid:—

James Sullivan, labor	$ 26 50	
William Dunham, labor	26 50	
Ralph Measures, labor	26 50	
Frank Dixon, labor	26 50	
Expended		$ 106 00
Appropriation	$ 106 00	

ASSESSORS MAP W. P. A.

Paid:—

Rome Bros., supplies	$ 18 14	
Spaulding Moss. Co., supplies	6 83	
Expended		$ 24 97
Bal. 1936 appropriation	$ 260 00	
Appropriation	500 00	
Total amount available		$ 760 02
Unexpended balance		735 05

SEEPAGE BED JUNIOR SENIOR HIGH SCHOOL

Paid:—

Howland & Howland, plans	$ 159 73
Spaulding Moss. Co., blue prints	6 45

Ralph Belcher, recording plans   2 00

Expended $ 168 18
Appropriation $2 000 00
Balance unexpended   1 831 82

STRIPING STREETS

Paid:—
Ralph L. Measures $ 146 14
Hancock Paint & Varnish Co.   3 70

Expended $ 149 84
Appropriation $ 150 00
Under appropriation   16

MEMORIAL DAY OBSERVANCE

Paid:—
Rockland High School Band $ 35 00
American Legion Drum Corps   35 00
Old Colony Post Junior
    Drum Corps   35 00
Annie Carey, postage   75
Peter Bowler Camp No. 63 lunches   23 00
Hartsuff Post Mem. Asso. drivers   73 00
Mass. State Guard Veterans   23 00
American Legion Post No. 147   23 00
H. L. Tilden, flowers   9 00
S. P. Bruinsma, 500 wreaths   60 00
Eagle Toy and Fireworks Co.,
    7 gross flags   54 25
Old Colony Post No. 1788, dinners   23 00

Expended $ 394 00
Appropriation $ 400 00
Under appropriation   6 00

WEBSTER STREET SIDEWALK

Paid:—

Labor	$ 884 23	
Chas. L. Baxter, surveying	6 00	
Chris, Tompkins, gravel	3 00	
A. Culver Co., cement	67 00	
Rockland Coal & Grain Co., supplies	7 98	
Bradford Weston Inc., bit. concrete	131 79	
Expended		$ 1 100 00
Appropriation	$ 1 100 00	

LIST OF PAYROLL

Geo. Beverly	$ 86 70
Lyle Tibbetts	78 75
Leo Cull	27 00
Wm. Cannaway	85 50
Harry Roberts	13 78
Herbert Brown	4 50
Wm. Condon	88 50
George Tyler	208 50
Louis Roche	38 25
Wilbur Adams	60 75
Fred Cormier	56 25
Donald Owen	58 50
Thomas McDonald	4 50
Burrill Dill	24 75
Patrick Mahoney	48 00
Total	$ 884 23

HOWARD STREET DRAIN

Paid:—

E. L. LeBarron Foundry Co., Catch basin	$ 11 90
N. E. Concrete Pipe Corp. tile pipe	117 48

Labor, trucks	25 13	
G. W. S. Hyde, sharpening tools	1 60	
Hall & Torrey Co., supplies	2 49	
Southeastern Cons. Corp. concrete		
blocks	32 71	
N. Menoli, supplies	90	
Rockland Coal and Grain Co.		
supplies	24 64	
Chris Tompkins gravel	5 00	

Expended	$	221 85
Trans. from W. P. A.	$ 225 00	
Under	3 15	

SALEM STREET DRAIN W. P. A.

Paid:—

E. L. LeBarron Foundry		
catch basin cover	$ 11 90	
N. E. Concrete Corp., concrete pipe	102 96	
A. Culver Co., supplies	4 80	
Southeastern Cons. Co., blocks	25 83	
A. Wainshilbaum, gas,	2 20	
Rockland Coal & Grain Co.,		
supplies	3 60	

Expended	$	151 29
Trans. from W. P. A.	$ 275 00	
Unexpended balance	123 71	

HOWARD STREET SIDEWALK
From Webster St. to Park St.

Paid:—

Payroll, labor	$ 250	

Expended	$	250 00
Appropriation	$ 250 00	

NORTH AVENUE SIDEWALK

Paid:—
Rockland Coal and Grain Co.
cement $ 33 80
Market Street Garage, service and
supplies   33 24
Bradford Weston Inc. bit concrete   170 10
Payroll, labor   462 43

Expended $ 699 57
Trans from Sidewalk appropriation   700 00
Under appropriation   43

LIST OF PAYROLL

Leo Cull	$ 24 75
Lyle Tibbetts	36 56
Donald Owen	34 03
George Beverly	65 03
Wilbur Adams	29 53
Fred Cormier	13 50
Ralph Tedesci	20 25
William Condon	2 25
George Tyler	90 75
Arthur Casey	66 00
Patrick Mahoney	30 00
William Cannaway	9 00
Herbert Brown	25 03
Edward Casey	11 25
Vincent Piasecki	4 50

Total $ 462 43

BELMONT STREET DRAIN W. P. A.

Paid:—
E. L. LeBarron Foundry, grates $ 23 80
Southeastern Cons. Co., blocks   11 88

N. E. Concrete Pipe Co. tile Pipe	57 86	
A. Tedeschi, supplies	1 43	
Hall & Torrey Co., supplies	1 50	
Thomas Walsh, sharpening tools	8 40	
Lester Wyman, gravel	2 00	
Payroll, trucks	41 57	
Expended		$ 148 44
Trans. from W. P. A.	$ 150 00	
Unexpended Balance	1 56	

CLEANING CATCH BASINS AND DRAINS

Paid:—

Rockland Disposal Co., service	$ 78 00	
Payroll, labor	448 35	
E. L. LeBarron Foundry Co., cover	11 90	
Expended		$ 538 25
Appropriation	$ 500 00	
Trans. Reserve Fund	38 25	
Total		$ 538 25

LIST OF PAYROLL CATCH BASINS AND DRAINS

Lawrence Cull	$ 27 00
Kenneth Kemp	37 13
George Ford	1 69
Edward Casey	1 69
Robert Casey	1 69
George Ingles	6 19
Paul McDonald	1 69
Leo Cull	48 38
Donald Owen	2 25
Wm. Condon	84 00
Geo. Tyler	52 50
Chas. Roberts	30 94

Louis Roche	24 75
Herbert Brown	9 00
Melvin Gay	9 90
Thomas Bailey	29 07
Raymond LaCombe	7 88
Lyle Tibbetts	16 60
Arthur Casey	27 00
Daniel Riley	2 00
Geo. Atlina	27 00

Total	$ 448 35

EAST WATER STREET SIDEWALK

Paid:—

Rockland Coal and Grain Co. cement	$ 45 60	
Bradford Weston Inc., bit concrete	19 09	
A. Culver Co., supplies	58 44	
Payroll, labor	601 87	
Expended		$ 725 00
Appropriation	$ 725 00	

LIST OF PAYROLL
EAST WATER STREET SIDEWALK

George Beverly	$ 85 00
Ralph Tedeschi	65 25
Louis Roche	38 25
Vincent Lee	56 25
Chas. Descenzo	29 25
Vincent Pearecki	38 25
Fred Cormier	43 31
William Green	83 73
William Bell	12 00
Arthur Casey	18 00

Lyle Tibbetts	31 50	
Herbert Brown	5 06	
Patrick Mahoney	96 00	
Total	$	601 87

NURSERY PROJECT W. P. A.

Paid:—

James G. Lamb, supplies	$ 72 90	
Roderick MacKenzie, ice	5 60	
Expended	$	78 50
Trans. from Reserve Fund	$ 150 00	
Under	71 50	

EAST WATER STREET CONSTRUCTION 1937

Paid:—

Payroll, labor	$ 5 519 71
Edward T. Dwyer, use of steam shovel	949 00
Mass. State Prison, grates and frames	137 03
F. W. Carey, dynamiting	19 92
Wyman Poultry Ranch, gravel	1 25
Crystal Concrete Corp. concrete	524 75
Bradford Weston Inc., stone and bit mixture	2 648 93
Trimount Bit. Products, asphalt	771 01
Roy V. Blanchard, sand	21 00
Charles Tompkins, gravel	125 00
John H. Lamb, gas and oil	48 20
Rockland Coal & Grain Co., supplies	250 28
Comm. of Mass., concrete curb	70 65
Scully Steel Products Co., Supplies	49 14
Southeastern Cons. Co., catch basins	94 99
Bay State Nurseries, supplies	27 25

New England Cons. Pipe Corp. pipe   220 31
M. F. Ellis, supplies   4 61
A. Culver Co., cement   31 80
Hall & Torrey Co. Inc., supplies   56 12

Expended $11 570 95
Appropriation $ 5 000 00
Received from Comm. of Mass.   5 489 31
Received from County of
  Plymouth   2 744 65

Total $13 233 96
Unexpended balance $ 1 663 01

LIST OF PAYROLL
EAST WATER STREET CONSTRUCTION

Leo Cull	$ 316 63
Waldo McPhee	288 29
Wm. Condon	512 51
Burrill Dill	102 31
Chas Fucillo	190 45
Kenneth Kemp	4 50
Wilbur Adams	319 64
Geo. Ingles	163 39
Edward Casey	255 96
Louis Crocker	26 15
Lawrence Cull	203 96
Ralph Tedeschi	166 49
Fred Cormier	184 52
Joseph Flannery	217 13
Russell McNevin	9 00
Geo. Beverly	408 94
Arthur Casey	97 50
D. DelPrete	174 37
Thomas Murrill	84 00
Frank Cifello	63 96
Thomas Fitzgerald	45 00

Samuel Cannaway	27 00
Louis Roach	82 61
Patrick McKenna	138 03
Ernest McNutt	138 01
Wm. Cannaway	5 92
Henry Cook	18 00
Melvin Gay	208 50
Joseph Casey	39 94
John J. Dwyer	78 00
Joseph Golemme	66 00
Geo. Tyler	84 00
Abe Wainshilbaum	54 75
Roy V. Blanchard	60 00
Patrick Mahoney	96 00
Tovia Jarvinen	36 00
Wm. C. Green	84 00
Francis Hamilton	102 94
Ed. Metivier	16 20
John Flynn	38 25
Webster Robbins	11 25
Michael Bowen	52 66
Robert Casey	106 19
Clarence Damon	34 60
Wm. H. Friary	18 00
John Ricca	83 66
W. Alton Whiting	4 50

Total $ 5 519 71

MATERIAL FOR SEWING PROJECT W. P. A.

Paid:—

Treasurer of United States, part payment		$ 828 00
Appropriation	$ 1 656 00	
Under appropriation	828 00	

ARLINGTON STREET SIDEWALK W. P. A.

Paid:—

Lester Wyman, gravel	$ 2	00
Rockland Coal & Grain, supplies	18	45
Bradford Weston Inc., bit. concrete	224	77
Joseph R. Reardon, supplies	5	65
A. Culver Co., supplies	46	20
Hall & Torrey Co., supplies	6	89
Payroll, trucks	65	53

Expended		$	369 49
Trans. from W. P. A.	$ 425	00	
Under	55	51	

PLAIN STREET SIDEWALK W. P. A.

Paid:—

Warren A. Vinton, supplies	$ 1	00
A. Culver Co., cement	6	00
Bradford Weston Inc., bit. concrete	261	29
Chris. Tompkins, gravel	2	20
Payroll, trucks	17	74

Expended		$	288 23
Trans. from W. P. A.	$ 350	00	
Under	61	77	

PROSPECT STREET SIDEWALK W. P. A.

Paid:—

Lester Wyman, gravel	$ 7	00
Abe Wainshilbaum, supplies	2	55
A. J. Vargus, gas		50
Rockland Coal & Grain, supplies	8	38
Chris Tompkins, gravel	4	00
Rome Bros., supplies	3	70
Bradford Weston Inc., bit. concrete	239	92

A. Culver Co., supplies	52 80	
Payroll, trucks	205 92	
Expended		$ ‒ 524 77
Appropriation	$ 625 00	
Under appropriation	100 23	

CLIFF STREET SIDEWALK W. P. A.

Paid:—

Bradford Weston Inc., bit. concrete	99 48
Peters Grocery, oil	1 40
George L. Fairbain, rent of mixer	13 75
Rockland Coal & Grain Co., supplies	60 16
Lester Wyman, gravel	3 50
Rockland Motor Co., supplies	2 02
Payroll, trucks	110 96

Expended		$ 291 27
Trans. from W. P. A.	$ 400 00	
Under	108 73	

REPAIRS TO STEAM ROLLER

Paid:—

Clyde Everett, 1 set rear rollers		$ 225 00
Trans. from Reserve Fund	$ 225 00	

W. P. A. HIGHLAND STREET SIDEWALK

Paid:—

Lester Wyman, gravel	$ 4 00
Rockland Coal & Grain, supplies	74 53
C. W. Briggs, supplies	75
Bradford Weston Inc., bit. concrete	113 40
Chris Tompkins, gravel	6 60
Payroll, trucks	112 89

Expended	$ 312 17

Trans. from W. P. A. $ 400 00
Unexpended balance   87 83

SUMMIT STREET SIDEWALK W. P. A.

Paid:—
Lester Wyman, sand $ 4 50
Chris Tompkins, gravel   80
A. Wainshilbaum, gas   2 00
A. Culver Co., cement   55 18
Bradford Weston Inc., bit concrete   129 15
Payroll, trucks   96 26

Expended $ 287 89
Trans. from W. P. A. $500 00
Unexpended balance   212 11

SALEM STREET SIDEWALK W. P. A.

Paid:—
Chris Tompkins, gravel $ 1 00
Lester Wyman, sand   4 50
Rockland Coal & Grain, cement   15 00
Payroll, trucks   102 01

Expended $ 122 51
Appropriation $ 700 00
Unexpended balance   577 49

BLOSSOM STREET SIDEWALK W. P. A.

Paid:—
John H. Lamb, supplies $ 2 90
Payroll, trucks   49 00

Expended $ 51 90
Appropriation $ 300 00
Under   248 10

SPRING STREET SIDEWALK W. P. A.

Paid:—

A. Wainshilbaum, supplies	$ 4 07	
Lester Wyman, sand	9 00	
Payroll, trucks	79 89	

Expended	$	92 96
Appropriation	$ 1 000 00	
Unexpended balance	907 04	

RESERVE FUND

Transfer to Reeds Pond improvement	$ 150 00	
Transfer to Nursery School project	150 00	
Transfer to Repairs to steam roller	225 00	
Transfer to Cleaning Union street	100 00	
Transfer to Tree Warden	53 30	
Transfer to Police Dept.	139 16	
Transfer to Catch Basins and Drains	38 25	
Transfer to Miscellaneous Tax Collector	13 96	
Transfer to Elections	51 80	

Expended	$	921 4
Appropriation	$1 000 00	
Under appropriation	78 53	

UNION STREET CONSTRUCTION

App. by Bond issue	$ 35	000	00
Received from U. S. Gov't	28	575	00
App. March 1937, Art. 17		640	87
Acc. Interest		117	89

Expended		$64	333 76
Amt. Trans. 1936	$51	005	33
Bradford Weston final payment	12	253	43
J. R. Worcester Co.		434	13
J. R. Worster Co., App. Art. 17		565	87

		$64 258 76
Under	$	75 00

SUPERVISOR OF BUREAU OLD AGE ASSISTANCE

Appropriation	$ 300 00
No Expenditure	

SOLDIERS' RELIEF 1937

Expended	$12 368 08
Appropriation	$ 8 000 00
Over appropriation	$ 4 368 08

RECAPITULATION OF AMOUNTS AVAILABLE AND EXPENDITURES

(*) Denotes Une... Dec. 31st, but Available for use in 1938

	Raised	Expended	Over	Under	Re... Fund
State Aid	$ 700 00	$ 643 00	$	$ 57 0	$
Military Aid	50 00	10 00		40 0	
Care of Twn	60 00	60 00			
Care of Soldiers Graves	150 00	135 00		15 00	
Burial of ... Soldiers		1 00	100 0		
Clean Up Wk	100 00	70 49		29 51	
Criminal ...es in Court	100 00	95 60		4 40	
Street Lighting	9 234 00	9 200 92		33 08	
Highway Surveyor	1 350 00	1 350 00			
Tarvia and Road Binders	7 000 00	6 977 89		22 11	
Highway Repairs	7 000 0	6 998 38		1 62	
Soldiers' Memorial Library (dog fund) $447.34	4 200 00	4 647 34		*91 55	100 00
Sidewalks	2 500 00	2 408 45			
Rent of American Legion	900 00	900 00			
School Department	104 423 00	104 420 93		2 07	
...g Union Street	1 00 00	1 200 00			
Signs and ...de Boards	1 0 00	100 00			
Spanish War Veterans	288 00	288 00			
Fire Department	10 062 00	10 911 59	849 59		
Forest Fires	700 00	629 75		70 75	

RECAPITULATION OF AMOUNTS AVAILABLE AND EXPENDITURES

(*) Denotes Unexpended Dec. 31st, but Available for use in 1938

	Raised	Expended	Over	Under	Reserve Fund
Police Department	8 800 00	8 929 96		9 20	139 16
Inspector Animals ard Sales	150 00	150 00			
Sealer of Wts and Measures	400 00	400 00			
Board of Health	6 000 00	5 979 62		20 38	
Park Department	3 115 00	3 105 46		9 54	
Moth Department	300 00	300 00			
... uGty Extension Service	50 00	150 00			
Plymouth uGty Hospital	3 633 12	3 633 12			
Fire Dept. Heater app. 1933	500 0	500 00			
Tree Warden	900 00	953 30			53 30
Rent of Tn Offices	1 240 0	1 240 00			
E. Wer St. Land Damage	42 70	35 20		*7 50	
Sealer of Weights and Measures Test Can	70 00	70 00			
Town ...	6 800 00	6 790 00		10 00	
...	850 00	891 80			51 80
Purchase Washington Reed Lot	500 00	29 82		*470 18	
Mass. Hospital School	500 00	500 00		500 0	
Mass. Industrial School	3 000 00	2 264 35		735 65	
Town Report ard Poll Book	1 200 00	1 170 44		29 56	
Tn ... ard Inst	28 500 00	28 229 95		270 05	
Snow	1 000 00	1 083 00	63 00		

RECAPITULATION OF AMOUNTS AVAILABLE AND EXPENDITURES

(*) Denotes Unexpended Dec. 31st, but Available for use in 1938

	Raised	Expended	Over	Under	Reserve Fund
esters	2 500 00	2 500 00			
Miscellaneous Clerk	350 00	349 29		71	
Miscellaneous Selectmen	120 00	104 04		15 96	
Miscellaneous Sealer	105 00	104 92		08	
Miscellaneous Treasurer	800 00	797 68		2 32	
Miscellaneous Assessors	1 100 00	1 079 06		20 94	
Mis Unclassified	1 150 00	1 834 77	684 77		
Beacons	600 00	595 96		4 04	
E. Water St. Cons. app. 1935	224 58	224 58			
Refurnishing Assessors Office, app. of 1934	1 180 00	180 00			
Nurse	1 500 00	1 500 00			
Liberty St. Dam, app. 1936	51 78	41 22		10 56	
Plain St., W. P. A.	1 500 00	1 500 00			
Park W. P. A. 1936 app.	$ 156 50				
Park W. P. A. 1937 app.	3 053 80				
	3 210 30	1 428 40		1 781 90	

W. P. A. Sts

App. 1936	$2 532 36	
App. 1937	3 500 00	
Precast ucb	238 00	
Am unt Available	6 270 36	1 260 83

RECAPITULATION OF AMOUNTS AVAILABLE AND EXPENDITURES

(*) Denotes Unexpended Dec. 31st, but Available for use in 1938

	Raised	Expended	Over	Under	Reserve Fund
Trans. to other projects		4 331 00		*678 53	
W. P. A. Reeds Pond					
Trans. 1936 $411 74					
App. 1937 1 000 00	1 411 74	1 504 58		*57 16	150 00
W. P. A. bal. app. 1936 $301 66					
Part of app. 1937 1 500 00					
App. Sept. 1937 4 000 00					
W. P. A. Division St. trans 1936 $656 12	5 801 66	3 867 94		*1 933 72	
Union St., W. P. A. Labor	656 12	655 40		72	
Bradford Av	900 00	896 20		3 80	
East Water Street Construction	510 00	510 00			
App. 1936 $1 652 53					
Raised 1937 513 60					
Payment from Plymouth County 232 67					
Compensation for Firemen	2 398 80	2 398 60			
Workmen's Compensation	292 50	292 50			
	2 250 00	1 979 93		270 07	
Striping Union St., trans. W. P. A.	106 00	106 00			

RECAPITULATION OF AMOUNTS AVAILABLE AND EXPENDITURES

(*) Denotes Unexpended Dec. 31st, but Available for use in 1938

	Raised	Expended	Over	Under	Re used
Sars Map					
App. 1936	$ 260 02				
App. 1937	500 0				
Seepage Bed High School	760 02	24 97		*735 05	
Striping Streets	2 000 00	168 18		*1 831 82	
Memorial Day	150 00	149 84		16	
Webster Street Sidewalk	400 00	394 00		6 0	
Howard Street drain, trans. W. P. A.	1 00 00	1 00 00			
Salem Street drain, trans. W. P. A.	225 00	221 85		3 15	
Howard Street Sidewalk, trans Sidewalks	275 00	151 29		*123 71	
North Av. Sidewalk, trans. Sidewalks	250 00	250 00		0	
Belmont Street drain, trans. W. P. A.	710 00	699 57		43	
Cleaning Catch Basins and Drains	150 00	148 44		1 56	
E. Wer St., Sidewalk, trans. Sidewalks	500 00	538 25			33 25
Nursery School Project, trans. Reserve Fund	725 00	725 0			
E. Water Street App.		78 50		*71 50	150 00
App.	$5 000 00				
Commonwealth of Mass.	5 489 31				
Fifth County	2 744 65				
	13 233 96	11 570 95		*1 663 01	

RECAPITULATION OF AMOUNTS AVAILABLE AND EXPENDITURES

(*) Denotes Unexpended Dec. 31st, but Able for use in 1938

	Raised	Expended	Over	Under	Reserve Fund
Miscellaneous Tax Collector	1 400 00	*1 413 96			13 96
Material for Sewing Project	1 656 0	828 00		*828 00	
Arlington St., Sidewalk, trans. W. P. A.	425 00	369 49		*55 51	
Plain St. Sidewalk, trans. W. P. A.	350 00	288 23		*61 77	
Prospect St. Sidewalk, trans. W. P. A.	625 00	524 77		*100 23	
Cliff St. Sidewalk trans. W. P. A.	400 00	291 27		*108 73	
Repairs to Sam Roller		225 00			225 0
Hand St. Sidewalk, trans. W. P. A.	400 00	312 17		*87 83	
Summit St. Sidewalk, trans. W. P. A.	500 00	287 89		*212 11	
Salem St. Sidewalk, labor W. P. A.	700 00	122 51		*577 49	
Blossom St. Sidewalk, labor W. P. A.	300 00	51 90		*248 10	
Spring St. Sidewalk, labor W. P. A.	1 000 00	92 96		*907 04	
Reserve Fund	1 000 00	921 47		78 53	
Soldier' Relief	8 000 00	12 368 08	4 368 08		
Old Age Assistance	35 000 00	45 505 61	10 505 61		
Public Welfare	45 000 0	67 013 31	22 013 31		
Mothers Aid	8 000 00	6 003 15	3 15		
Supervisor Old Age Assistance	300 00			300 00	
Miscellaneous Registrars	200 00	177 95		22 05	

Report of Board of Public Welfare

The report of the Board of Public Welfare for the year 1937 is hereby submitted.

BUREAU OF OLD AGE ASSISTANCE

Town Physicians	$ 400	00
Paid Other Towns	661	61
Expended for cases	44 444	00
	$45 505	61
Appropriation	35 000	00
Over Appropriation	$10 505	61

Received from Federal Funds		
Rec. to credit to cases	$39 692	50
Rec. to credit for Admin.	1 308	24
	$41 000	74

Expended on cases	$36 127	14
Balance on hand Dec. 31, 1937	3 565	36
	$39 692	50
Expended for Administration	$ 1 002	41
Balance on hand Dec. 31, 1937	305	83
	$ 1 308	24

Total expended by town and Federal Allowance	$81 632	75

MOTHERS AID

Expended under Chapter 118, General Laws.		
Expended under Town Funds	$ 8 003	15
Appropriation	8 000	00
⸱⸱ Over	$ 3	15
Received from Federal Grant	$ 3 152	65
Expended from Federal Grant	2 993	93
Available for 1938	$ 158	68

INFIRMARY EXPENDITURES

Paid:—

Earl and Blanche Wyatt, salary	$ 1 020	00
Kate Kelly, maid	371	00
Annie Stewart, maid	490	00
New England Telephone, service	51	06
A. Culver Co., feed	432	24
Edison Electric Ill. Co., services	130	12
Rome Bros., supplies	240	81
Rockland Water Dept., service	146	71
Hickey Bros., provisions	169	75
E. L. Murrill, provisions	310	41
Hall & Torrey Co., supplies and rep.	165	33
N. H. Ranney, clothing	123	72
Rockland Coal & Grain, coal	301	50
Fred S. Delay, supplies	295	74
W. F. Barnes, fish	268	80
McIvers Bakery, bread	127	88
Rockland Pharmacy, Med. supplies	167	91
Anthony Fiasschetti, provisions	92	21
A. S. Peterson, tobacco and papers	205	49
Burrell and Delory, shoes	12	85
Hatherly Market, provisions	53	11
Alice L. Holbrook, supplies	13	00
Lillian Hamilton, maid	40	00
John A. Lamb, provisions	194	99

Emil Kelstrand, shoes	2	00
Samuel W. Baker, glasses	21	50
James G. Lamb, provisions	203	85
Rockland Coal and Grain Co., supplies	267	12
Rockland Hardware Co., supplies	60	79
John F. Mahoney, butter	114	48
George W. S. Hyde, shoeing horse	32	65
Dennis L. O'Connor, shoes	29	00
Harold H. Monk, bread	67	84
Lot Phillips Co., slabs and sawdust	47	70
Arthur Wells, papering	37	48
Lelyveld Shoes, shoes	18	35
John E. Campbell, repairs	21	33
David Morse, supplies	2	59
Harry I. Rome, supplies	32	70
Mass. Reformatory, supplies	57	51
J. A. Rice Co., supplies	51	54
I. G. Miller, provisions	197	65
J. S. McCullum, plumbing	29	99
A. Culver Co., coal	346	00
M. Y. Clement, meats	185	00
W. F. Trufant, supplies	31	50
Hickey Bros., provisions	191	32
A. Culver Co., seed and supplies	44	38
McManus Box Co., slabs	35	80
Elbert Chamberlain, supplies	82	87
Chester W. Bandon, plumbing	33	07
William Tracy, provisions	126	71
Warshaw Market, provisions	269	53
Forrest L. Partch, repairs	2	32
Angelo Tedeschi, provisions	212	83
Damon Electric, repairs	9	57
Monument Mills, supplies	28	60
Harold Capen, meats	232	41
John H. Lamb, provisions	240	12
Brockton Wrecking Co., chairs	3	00
C. H. Blanchard, killing hogs	12	00
Rockland Shoe Repair Co., repair shoes	8	25

Howland Insurance Co., insurance	102	47
Handschumaher & Co., curing hams	11	30
Michael Dunn, dental work	4	00
Amos Phelps, insurance	98	26
C. H. Redgate, shoes	6	50
Market Street Grocery, provisions	142	53
Samuel Cannaway, services	3	00
J. Thomas, purchase of horse and cart	155	00
Mass. Whip & Saddlery Co., horse collar	10	50
John S. Chewer, supplies	55	60
George Tyler, cleaning cesspool	30	00
H. I. Stickney, repairing lawn mower	4	65
Walter A. Johnson, burying horse	3	00
Goodco Sanitary Co., supplies	8	75
Harry Wyatt, sawdust	6	00
Everett C. Ford, 40 chicks	6	00
Dr. Ralph C. Briggs, services	9	00
Otis R. Mann, purchase of horse	200	00
Emmons Dairy Co., plowing	30	00
W. H. Clayton, shoeing and repairs	15	50
Lot Phillips and Co., one wagon rocker	1	50
Standard Harness Co., repair harness	2	50
Dr. Benjamin Lelyveld, services	4	00
Herman Petrizza, repair shoes	2	25
James Forgus & Sons, trace chains	7	25
H. F. Gardner, groceries	176	28
John F. Donovan, 3 pigs	15	00
P. T. Manter, provisions	173	03
Arthur G. Batson, repairs	15	75
Herbert J. Hulse, medical	3	00
Genado Lioy, repair shoes	2	50
S. T. Howland, services	3	00
Anthony Fiaschetti, provisions	163	14
Vincent Fitzgibbons, wheels	4	00
Wainshilbaum Bros., repairs	10	65
Elmer Bates, 9 bushel apples	9	00
Emil Kelstrand, repair shoes	4	50
Jenkins & Simmons, express	2	75

Annie Capelis, provisions   157 90
Goodco Sanitary Prod. Co., insectcide   9 50
Ryans Market, provisions   205 17
William Tracey, provisions   48 98

Total $10 739 69

EXPENSES OF OUTSIDE POOR

Hospitals:—
Brockton Hospital $ 716 61
Weymouth Hospital   510 35
Mass. General Hospital   262 89
Goddard Hospital   265 31
Mass Eye & Ear Infirmary   12 95
Pondville Hospital   182 50
Moore Hospital   169 00
New England Hospital for Women   67 50
Children's Hospital   21 20

Total $ 2 208 31

Administration:—
Harriet Anderson, services $ 728 00
A. S. Peterson, supplies   70
Hobbs & Warren, supplies   35 40
Yawman & Erbe, supplies   22 69
Treasury of United States, commodity
    distribution   398 84
Harry S. Torrey, trans. C. C. C. boys   2 50
Becker & Co., supplies   5 00
Douglas Print, printing   13 50
John J. Dwyer, trans. C. C. C. boys 24 00
A. I. Randall, printing   7 80
John J. Dwyer, trans. to hospital   6 00
United States Post Office, envelopes 19 22
Jenkins & Simmons, express   35

Total $ 1 264 00

| Town Physicians | | 450 00 |
| Paid Other Towns | | 4 545 22 |

Cash	$31 701 01	
Other Expenses	16 105 08	
		47 806 09

| Total | | $67 013 31 |

SUMMARY OF BOARD OF PUBLIC WELFARE

Paid for Infirmary	$10 739 69	
Paid for Hospitals	2 208 31	
Paid for Administration	1 264 00	
Paid for Town Physicians	450 00	
Paid Other Towns	4 545 22	
Paid for Outside Poor	47 806 09	

Total		$67 013 31
Expended on Public Welfare	$67 013 31	
Appropriation	45 000 00	

| Over | | $22 013 31 |

CREDITS

Received from State, Old Age Assistance	$16 802 68
Received from Other Towns, Old Age Assistance	1 441 37
Received from Persons, Old Age Assistance	16 72
Received from State, Mothers' Aid	2 718 37
Received from Other Towns, Mothers' Aid	127 55
Received from State, Temporary Aid	18 034 46
Received from Other Towns, Temporary Aid	5 775 50
Received from Persons, Temporary Aid	6 88
Received from Board at Infirmary	1 772 00
Received from Sick State Poor	121 50
Received from State, Dangerous Disease	40 30

Received from Other Towns, Board of
Health   214 37

Total $47 071 70

Due from Other Towns for Board
  at Infirmary $ 1 840 00
Due from State Temporary Aid   5 430 23
Due from Other Towns Temporary Aid   5 007 03
Due from State, Mothers' Aid   4 979 63
Due from Federal Funds Mothers' Aid   416 00
Due from State Old Age Assistance   20 010 80
Due from State, Sick State Poor   472 30
Due from Other Towns Old Age Assistance   1 483 78
Due from Other Towns Board of Health   439 50
Due on Federal Funds, Old Age
  Nov. & Dec.   7 310 25
                                           _____
                                           $47 389 52
             Signed,

             HARRY S. TORREY,
             NORMAN S. WHITING,
             JOHN J. BOWLER,
             Board of Public Welfare and
             Bureau of Old Age Assistance

ESTIMATES OF APPROPRIATIONS FOR THE YEAR
1938 BY HEADS OF DIFFERENT DEPARTMENTS
AND AMOUNTS RAISED IN 1937

	Raised 1937	Est. 1938
School Department	$104 423 00	$108 757 50
State Aid	700 00	700 00
Soldiers' Relief	8 000 00	12 000 00
Military Aid	50 00	50 00
Care of Soldiers' Graves	150 00	150 00
Mem. Library & Dog Fund	4 200 00	4 200 00
Street Lighting	9 234 00	9 134 00

Highway Surveyor	1 350 00	1 350 00
Tarvia & Road Binder	7 000 00	7 500 00
Highway Repairs	7 000 00	8 000 00
Sidewalks	2 500 00	1 000 00
Cleaning Union St.	1 100 00	1 200 00
Clean Up Week	100 00	100 00
Guide Boards and Signs	100 00	200 00
Fire Department	10 062 00	10 725 00
Police Department	8 800 00	9 030 75
Forest Fires	700 00	700 00
Board of Health	6 000 00	6 000 00
Inspecting of Animals	150 00	150 00
Park Department	3 115 00	2 800 00
Old Age Assistance	35 000 00	42 000 00
Moth Department	300 00	600 00
Tree Warden	900 00	1 000 00
Town Officers	6 800 00	6 800 00
Office Rent	1 240 00	1 240 00
Sealer of Weights and Measures	400 00	400 00
Elections	850 00	1 700 00
Compensation Insurance	2 250 00	2 250 00
Mass. Hospital School	500 00	500 00
Mass. Industrial School	3 000 00	2 500 00
Town Report & Poll Book	1 200 00	1 350 00
Support of Poor & Infirm.	45 000 00	60 000 00
Mother's Aid	8 000 00	8 000 00
Town Notes and Interest	25 000 00	28 000 00
Assessors	2 500 00	2 500 00
Snow Removal	1 000 00	12 000 00
Reserve Fund	1 000 00	3 000 00
Misc. Assessors	1 100 00	1 200 00
Misc. Treasurer	800 00	800 00
Misc. Clerk	350 00	350 00
Misc. Selectmen	120 00	120 00
Misc. Registrars	200 00	200 00
Misc. Sealer	105 00	120 00
Misc. Unclassified	1 150 00	1 800 00
Misc. Collector	1 400 00	1 400 00

List of Jurors

As prepared by the Selectmen of the Town of Rockland Under General Laws of Massachusetts, Acts of 1921, Chapter 234, Section 4.

July 1, 1937

Name Street and Number	Occupation
Altsman, Harry J., 849 Union	Poultry Man
Ames, Stanley, 34 Prospect	Engineer
Bacon, Paul, 48 Williams	Salesman
Ball, Percy, 770 Union	Shoe Worker
Baxter, Charles L., 487 Market	Civil Engneer
Beal, George, 739 Market	Weaver
Bell, William, 558 Liberty	Truck Driver
Benham, Carl, 898 Liberty	Salesman
Beverly, George W., 59 Spruce	Laborer
Blakeman, Thomas, 16 Albion	Shoe Worker
Bowler, John J., 99 Hingham	Manager
Brady, Edward F., 89 Green	Foreman
Brassill, Francis J., 99 North Ave.	Barber
Briggs, George E., 139 Exchange	Machinist
Burns, James L., 159 Union	Shoe Operative
Burrell, H. Chester, 340 Liberty	Shoe Operative
Capelice, James H., 108 Howard	Shoe Operative
Chamberlain, Charles, 83 Union	Shoe Worker
Chandler, Russell, 1138 Union	Shoe Operative
Coffey, Dennis F., 134 Liberty	Flagman
Damon, Archer W., 43 Munroe	Shoe Operative
Damon, Frank W., 50 Reed	Electrician
DeLory, Bernard, 54 Stanton	Clerk
Dill, Percy E., 136 North Ave.	Shoe Operative
Dillon, John, 989 Union	Agent

Dondero, Joseph, 412 Webster .... Shoe Operative
Donovan, Daniel H., 117 Liberty .... Machinist
Dyer, Bertrand A., 329 North Ave. .... Shoe Repairer
Easton, Carrol, 858 Union .... Salesman
Ednie, John, 520 Market .... Painter
Estes, Joseph B., 305 Liberty .... Town Assessor
Fass, Carl G., 377 North Ave. .... Draftsman
Fearing, Charles L., 436 East Water .... Mechanic
Fitzgerald, Thomas F., 51 North Ave. ...... Shoe Operative
Ford, Patrick J., 542 Liberty .... Salesman
Gammon, Frank L., 135 Union .... Manager
Garrity, Peter, 162 North Ave. .... Janitor
Gelinas, George O., 99 Exchange .... Asst. Manager
Guilfoyle, Michael, 52 Concord .... Foreman
Harney, Edmund F., 66 Church .... Shoe Operative
Hawes, Fred M., 88 Howard .... Salesman
Hayden, Robert E., 40 Summit .... Laborer
Higgins, Thomas S., 32 Belmont .... Laborer
Hobart, Albert C., 57 School .... Civil Engineer
Holmes, Harry O., 248 Central .... Meter Reader
Howland, Giles W., 181 Webster .... Civil Engineer
Hunt, Lester A., 224 Myrtle .... Shoe Operative
Inglis, Wilbur T., 66 Prospect .... Boxmaker
Jacobs, S. Percy, 137 East Water .... Clerk
Johnson, Clarence B., 266 Plain .... Teamster
Kramer, Charles F., 39 Grove .... Shoe Operative
Lelyveld, Benjamin, 129 Pacific .... Podiatrist
Lewis, Willard A., 69 Hartsuff .... Shoe Operative
Locke, Louis F., 30 Reed .... Webbing
Loud, Fred, 28 Myrtle .... Bookkeeper
Lovell, Jasper, 4 Maple .... Box Cutter
Mahon, Thomas, 31 Summit .... Janitor
Mahoney, Patrick H., 35 Cary Court .... Teamster
Marks, Austin, 477 Webster .... Farmer
Mastrodominico, Joseph, 355 Union .... Shoe Operative
McCarthy, Michael J., 22 School .... Shoe Operative
McKeever, James, 199 Webster .... Clerk
McKim, George, 570 Webster .... Tinsmith

Measures, Ralph, 251A Union .... Painter
Mullen, William, 865 Union .... Shoe Operator
Niles, George R., 137 Pacific .... Carpenter
Phillips, Roland P., 196 East Water .... Manager
O'Grady, Matthew, 108 Belmont .... Laborer
O'Hayre, Bernard F., 278 Reed .... Shoe Operative
Orr, Charles E., 67 Stanton .... Salesman
Partch, Forest L., 57 Taunton Ave. .... Electrician
Patterson, Henry E. L., 889 Union .... Florist
Poole, Norman C., 580 West Water .... Salesman
Ransom, Roger T., 31 Hartsuff .... Engineer
Reardon, Thomas, 101 Summit .... Clerk
Ryan, Patrick C., 122 Myrtle .... Shoe Operative
Scott, Charles N., 91 Pacific .... Clerk
Sheehan, Eugene, 39 Pacific .... Shoe Worker
Sheehan, Maurice, 101 Prospect .... Shoe Operative
Shields, Charles T., 42 Franklin Ave. ...... Shoe Operative
Shurtliff, Alton E., 40 East Water .... Retired
Smith, Bartholomew J., 35 Stanton .... Shoe Operative
Sylvia, John E., 76 Albion .... Cigar Maker
Umbrianna, Michael, 35 Salem .... Shoe Operative
Vargus, Antone J., 215 Crescent .... Auto Supplies
Walls, Magorisk, 663 Liberty .... Inspector
Wallace, Earl, 231 Myrtle .... Truck Driver
Whiting, W. Alton, 455 Webster .... Shoe Operative

HARRY S. TORREY,
NORMAN S. WHITING,
JOHN J. BOWLER,

Selectmen of Rockland

Report of Fire Department

To the Honorable Board of Selectmen:

Gentlemen:

I hereby submit my report as Chief of the Fire Department for the year 1937.

203 calls were answered by the Fire Department during the year 1937, 42 of which were Bell Alarms, 159 telephone or verbal calls, and two A. D. T. calls. We had 12 false alarms. The Chief's car answered twenty-three of the alarms without other apparatus, saving the town a considerable amount of money.

The Triple Combination and the Ladder Truck responded to a call from Abington to help their Department at the Franklin Hall fire. The Lighting outfit was also sent to Hanson and Abington on another call. The Inhalator was sent to Hanover on a call, but was too late to be of any help.

The Department laid 10,750 feet of 2½ inch hose, 2250 feet of 1½ inch, and 5850 feet of Chemical hose. We used 400 gallons of soda and acid, 7½ gallons of foam, 7 quarts of Pyrene, 12 packages of chimney compound, besides the pump tanks. The Light equipment was used about twenty hours.

FIRE ALARM SYSTEM

I wish to bring to your attention the condition of the Fire Alarm system. The present system was installed in

1889 and has been in use since that time. Many of the old boxes have been replaced, but there are at present a number that should be discarded and new ones installed. We will have to begin this year to replace some of our wire and also finish trimming out the trees on account of grounds. About half of our system was trimmed out during 1937.

APPARATUS

The Triple Combination and Ladder Trucks were inspected and placed in condition out of this year's appropriation. The Combination was inspected and overhauled but not in time to be paid for in 1937. All trucks are now in good condition except the paint on the Triple Combination. I recommended that we paint this piece of apparatus in 1937, but the Town voted not to do so and now the paint on the body is cracked and will soon peel off.

RECOMMENDATIONS AND REMARKS

For the year 1938 I recommend an appropriation of $10,725.00, which includes the restoration of pay cuts if approved by the Town.

Many repairs on the Fire Station should be made in 1938. The second floor has dropped about four inches and should be taken care of. The front doors are decayed badly, the north side of the roof needs shingling and the inside and out of the Station should be painted. The north wall of the down stairs needs to be taken out and replaced. The carpenters tell me that the boards under the clapboards are rotted out. Therefore I am asking that an article be placed in the Town Warrant to take care of the repairing of the Station.

CONCLUSION

In concluding this report I wish to thank the Finance

Committee for their co-operation although we did not agree on all articles in my report to them. Also I wish to thank the Board f Selectmen, Board of Water Commissioners and their employees, and the Chief and members of the Police Department for the help and cooperation given the Fire Department. I also wish to express my appreciation to the Officers and Members of the Fire Department and to all others who have assisted me in the performance of my duty as Chief of the Fire Department.

Respectfully submitted,

CLYSON P. INKLEY,
Chief Rockland Fire Department

Report of Forest Fire Warden

To the Honorable Board of Selectmen:

Gentlemen:

I hereby submit my report as Forest Fire Warden for the year 1937.

The Forest Fire Department answered seventy calls for Woods and Grass fires during the year 1937, the largest fire and most expensive occurred November 11th.

For the year 1938 I recommend an appropriation of $700.00.

Respectfully submitted,

CLYSON P. INKLEY,
Forest Fire Warden

Report of Infirmary

To the Honorable Board of Selectmen:
Gentlemen:

I wish to present to you a report of activities and improvements, which have taken place during the year 1937.
We have taken care of thirty-five inmates during the year, four women and thirty-one men, the oldest being eighty-seven and the youngest, four months.

We have had eight in the hospital room.

Two deaths have occurred, both being men. At the present time we have twenty-two inmates, four women and eighteen men.

Raised 10 ton of hay, 125 bushel of potatoes, and other small vegetables, canned 200 quarts of vegetables, produced 225 dozen eggs, produced 7,300 quarts of milk, raised three pigs.

Had the barn shingled which leaked very bad, and other ordinary repairs.

Respectfully submitted,

EARL W. WYATT,

Supt. of Infirmary

Sealer of Weights and Measures

To The Honorable Board of Selectmen:
Gentlemen:

I have with my standards, weights and measures, tested and sealed all weighing and measuring devices which I have jurisdiction over, also several scales for private use.

All gas meters were retested and inspections and weighing of merchandise which is put up for sale and delivery were also made. The inspection and resealing of these measuring devices is an important item after sealing.

Computing scales need attention as in many cases they are found to be incorrect. Inspection of all stores in town that have measuring devices are made frequently. Pedlars increase yearly and I make sure all are properly licensed.

The oil meters on oil trucks are another item which have to be checked more carefully on account of the increasing sale of oil.

The duties of a Sealer of Weights and Measures increase yearly and I am on call at all times. My duties are under State and Town regulations.

Below is an itemized account of the work I have performed for 1937:

	Adjusted	Sealed	Not Sealed	Condemned
Platform over 5,000 lbs.	3	4		
Platform under 100 to 5,000 lbs.	17	37	5	
Counter 100 lbs. or over		2		
Counter under 100 lbs.	3	35	1	
Beam over 100 lbs.				
Beam under 100 lbs.		1	1	
Spring over 100 lbs.	3	9		1
Spring under 100 lbs.	31	65		
Computing under 100 lbs.	16	52	3	1
Personal Weighing	1	8		
Prescription		4		

WEIGHTS

Avoirdupois	19	313		
Apothecary		55		
Metric		49		

CAPACITY MEASURES

Liquid		89	2	2
Dry		5		

AUTOMATIC MEASURING DEVICES

Oil Meters	1	8	3
Gasoline Pumps	7	7	3
Gasoline Meters	13	63	2
Kerosene Pumps	1	13	1

Oil Measuring Pumps   42   16
Quantity Measure on Pump   92
Cloth Measuring devices   1
Yard Sticks   40
Molasses Measure   2

TOTAL UNITS SEALED

Total United Sealed   1000
Weighing and measuring devices
  Adjustted   115
Weighing and measuring devices
  Condemned   4
Weighing and measuring devices
  Not Sealed   37
Sealing fees returned to Town Treasurer $118 74
Over payments   23

REWEIGHING AND REMEASURING

Number Tested   227
Number Correct   191
Over Weight   26
Under Weight   10

Respectfully submitted,

HAROLD J. INKLEY

Highway Surveyor's Report

To the Honorable Board of Selectmen:

I wish to report that all of the work covered by the various appropriations granted to the Highway Department have been completed.

This work included building sidewalks and curbs as follows: South side of East Water Street, west side of Everett Street, north side of Webster Street, west side of Howard Street and the south side of North Avenue.

Various streets were repaired where needed and catch basins and drains were cleaned.

In addition to the above work, another section of East Water Street was completed in co-operation with the State and County.

Respectfully submitted,

RODERICK MacKENZIE

Report of Collector of Taxes

Taxes of 1934

Outstanding January 1, 1937	$	792 81
Collected during year		792 81

1934 Motor Vehicle Excise

Outstanding January 1, 1937	$	70 35
Collected during year		70 35

Taxes 1935

Outstanding January 1, 1937	$	70 666 47
Collected during year		68 539 49
Outstanding January 1, 1938	$	2 126 98

1935 Motor Vehicle Excise

Outstanding January 1, 1937	$	1 804 68
Collected during year		1 319 16
Outstanding January 1, 1938	$	485 52

Taxes of 1936

Outstanding January 1, 1937	$123	928 91
Collected during year		57 161 70
Outstanding January 1, 1938	$ 66	767 21

1936 Motor Vehicle Excise

Outstanding January 1, 1937	$	5 116	54
Collected during year		3 553	70
Outstanding January 1, 1938	$	1 562	84

Taxes of 1937

Amount committed to Collector	$303	730	76
Collected during year	190	102	66
Outstanding January 1, 1938	$113	628	10

1937 Motor Vehicle Excise

Amount committed to Collector	$	13 967	68
Collected during year		10 466	84
Outstanding January 1, 1938	$	3 500	84

1937 Water Liens

Amount committed to Collector	$	1 963	51
Collected during year		315	08
Oustanding January 1, 1938	$	1 648	43

Respectfully submitted

JAMES A. DONOVAN,
Collector of Taxes

Report of Board of Public Welfare

The Board of Public Welfare herewith submits its annual report covering the period from Jan. 1, to December 31, 1937.

Again as in the last several years we are sorry to report that our Welfare problems are still increasing due to the present unemployment depression, which has lasted for the past eight years.

Relief through our Board of Public Welfare has been granted when needed assistance was necessary, using our best judgment in administering to their needs. It has been our aim to provide for those in need and yet restrict expenditures to a minimum.

It is clearly evident that we face a long term problem of increased relief, with a group of relief clients who have become quite conscious of their status as dependents, and who will insist on the relief standards to which they have become accustomed.

Aid to Dependent Children has increased this past year since the acceptance of the Massachusetts plan for Aid to Dependent Children by the Social Security Board, the Federal Government will participate in the program and will make financial grants to the State.

The Civilian Conservation Corp has aided our relief rolls to some extent. Eligible young men who are willing to allot a substantial proportion of their $30.00 monthly allowance to their needy and dependent families have been given healthful outdoor work.

The distribution of food and clothing under the W. P.
A. has continued during the year. The project is under
the supervision of the W. P. A. where needy families receive supplies of food and many articles of clothing.

We wish to thank the Churches, Red Cross, and Fraternal societies and all the workers that have helped in
raising money for the Milk Fund for their helpfulness and
cooperation given us in our Social Service Work.

We also wish to thank the Visiting Nurse who had
charge of the Practical Nurse Project and the Town
Physicians who have given so liberally of their time for
the care of the needy sick.

We have at the present time on Relief Rolls:

    15 Mothers' Aid cases
     4 Child Boarded cases
   161 Families, outside poor
    75 Single Persons, outside poor
    27 Families Soldiers' Relief
    20 Single Persons, Soldiers' Relief
   265 Old Age Assistance cases
    22 Infirmary

                    HARRY S. TORREY,
                    NORMAN S. WHITING,
                    JOHN J. BOWLER,
                    Board of Public Welfare

For financial statement of Board of Public Welfare see
Page 114.

Report of Old Age Assistance

The number of Old Age Assistance cases is steadily increasing each month, due to the new law effective in September 1936, which reduced the age from 70 to 65 years. This has resulted in a large influx of applications. The main parts of the law is as follows: "Adequate assistance to deserving citizens in need of relief, who have reached the age of sixty-five or over, and having resided in the state not less than five years during the nine years preceeding the date of application; and shall have resided in the Commonwealth continuously for one year immediately preceeding date of application."

The main eligibility requirements are as follows:—

(1)   Sixty-five years of age or over
(2)   A Citizen of the United States
(3)   A resident of the State for at least five out of the last nine years.

After the March meeting Miss Mary L. O'Brien was employed as a Supervisor of Old Age Assistance working three days a week. Her work consists in visiting the diffent cases, and making out reports, and clerical work. We feel her work has been efficient and she has taken a real interest in the work, her report is as follows:

The number of people receiving Old Age Assistance has

increased very rapidly since April 1937. At that time there were 235 cases and at the present time we have 265 cases that are active.

After an application for assistance has been made all statements made by applicant must be verified. Questionaires are sent to children of applicant asking them to contribute to their support. Statements made in regard to their salaries are verified. Other questionaires are sent to banks where mortgages are placed, and to insurance companies.

During the past year I found that many recipients of Old Age Assistance were allowing some other person to endorse their checks. This necessitated going over all checks sent out from Oct. 1936 to date, and statements made that all benefits from these checks were received.

Visits are made frequently to all recipients, and wherever sickness occurs plans are made for their care.

I find this work most interesting and I know what a salvation it is to those who are receiving Old Age Assistance.

> HARRY S. TORREY,
> NORMAN S. WHITING
> JOHN J. BOWLER,
> Bureau of Old Age Assistance
> MARY L. O'BRIEN,
> Supervisor

Board of Selectmen,
Town of Rockland:

It is encouraging at this time to find that agriculture is increasing in importance in Plymouth County. The Plymouth County Extension Service has played an important part in making it an annual business of over eight millions of dollars. The Extension service arranges winter meetings for the poultry, dairy, cranberry, orchard and truck crop interests. At these meetings the best practice in production and distribution of agricultural products are discussed with the help of specialists from the State Department of Agriculture.

The Extension service co-operated with the Federal government in bringing $25,000.00 into Plymouth County in payments to farmers who met the requirements of the Federal Conservation Program.

With the recession in our industrial activities it becomes vital to build up a farm population, with some degree of self suufficiency, that will use the country's natural resources to the best possible advantage.

Through boy's and girl's clubs as well as through a great variety of women's clubs the Plymouth County Extension service carries on many projects for the purpose of making the farm more profitable and farm life more attractive. The facilities of the extension service are being used more and more by individuals and organizations in our own town. In addition, Rockland as the trading center for a large part of Plymouth County benefits directly from an increasing farm income of the county.

I recommend that Rockland will continue to co-operate with the other towns in the support of The Plymouth County Extension Service, and will raise and appropriate $150.00 for that purpose.

Respectfully submitted,

JAMES D. MAHONEY,

Town Director

Report of
Inspector of Animals and Stables

To the Honorable Board of Selectmen:

Gentlemen:—

I hereby submit my report for the year ending December 31, 1937:

Number of Stables Inspected	34
Number of Cows Inspected	113
Number of Swine Inspected	342
Number of Goats Inspected	8
Number of visits made in Inspections	113
Number of Dogs Quarantined	10
Number of visits made to premises of quarantined animals	72
Number of animals sent to Division of Livestock Disease Control for Laboratory Test	1

Respectfully submitted,

WILLIAM T. CONDON,
Inspector of Animals and Stables

Assessors Report 1937

The Assessors have assessed the sum of $319,661.95 upon the Polls and Property subject to taxation in the Town of Rockland and have committed said sum to the Collector for collection.

Number of Polls Assessed		2334
Value Real Estate Assessed	$5 665 615 00	
Value Land Assessed	1 538 975 00	

Total Value Real Estate including land $7 204 590 00

VALUE PERSONAL PROPERTY

Value of Stock in Trade	$165 460 00
Value of Live Stock	13 250 00
Value of Machinery	32 205 00
Value of all other Personal	441 096 00

$ 652 011 00

Total valuation real and personal property $7 856 601 00

Town appropriations	$ 369 976 96
State Tax	15 065 00
County Tax	15 459 80
Hospital Tax	60 00
State Parks and Reservation	168 74
Overlay	14 583 34
Water Department	34 200 00
(Used in Est. Receipts)	

$ 449 513 84

ESTIMATED RECEIPTS

Income Tax	$ 26 823	73
Corporation Tax	16 971	64
Motor Vehicle Excise	9 632	39
Licenses	673	00
Fines	126	00
General Government	590	35
Health & Sanitation	787	86
Beverage Licenses	4 310	00
Charities	20 671	72
Old Age Assistance	18 117	98
Soldiers' Benefits	252	76
Schools	1 717	42
Libraries	303	00
Vocational Training	535	02
Water Department	34 200	00
Refund Compensation Policy	516	13
Interest	8 999	36
Tax Costs	137	60
State Aid	676	00
Excess 1936 State Parks	35	05
Excess 1936 County Tax	217	99
Poll Tax	4 668	00

Total Estimated Receipts	$150 963	00
Total Amount to be raised on Property	298 550	84
Tax Rate per Thousand	$ 38	00

Number of Automobiles assessed	2 355
Value of Automobiles	$504 105 00
Number persons, partnerships and Corporations	
assessed for Real Estate	1 907
Number on Personal Estate	301
Number of Dwellings	1 875
Number of Cows	82

Number of Horses   20
Number of swine   34
Number of Fowl   6 370
Value of Fowl $6 640 00
Number of Acres   5 841

AMOUNTS COMMITTED TO COLLECTOR

Real and Personal $298 550 84
Water Liens   2 382 43
Excise Tax   13 967 68
Poll Taxes   4 668 00
December Assessments on Polls   74 00
December Assessments on Property   19 00
                               _____

Total $319 661 95

Respectfully submitted,

DENNIS L. O'CONNOR,
JOSEPH B. ESTES,
NORMAN J. BEALS.

Report of Board of Health

The Board of Health herewith submits its annual report for the year 1937:

Number of cases of reportable diseases as follows:

Scarlet Fever	7
Measles	35
Whooping Cough	50
Lobar Pneumonia	4
Dog Bite	8
Tuberculosis	2
German Measles	10
Chicken Pox	5

The health of the town has been very satisfactory. There has been few cases of serious trouble during the year, if we omit measles and whooping cough.

JOSEPH FRAME,
DR. JOSEPH H. DUNN,
EDWARD CULLINAN,
Board of Health

Report of Tree Warden

To the Honorable Board of Selectmen:

The Elm trees were sprayed this year, for the elm leaf beetle. Spraying is necessary, to keep the beetle under control. Very few trees were taken down this year. Trees that are taken down should be replaced with new ones.

There was a good deal of trimming done in certain sections of the town, much more is needed.

I recommend an appropriation of $1,000.00.

Respectfully submitted,

ALFRED T. METIVIER,
Tree Warden

Report of Gypsy Moth Supt.

To the Honorable Board of Selectmen:

This year much needed work was done in the Cod Pond area, and in the woods north of Salem street, for gypsy moth, spraying was also done in the Cod Pond section with W. P. A. labor.

This section of the town is now getting out of control and is spreading fast to the residential section of the town.

I recommend an appropriation of $600.00.

Respectfully submitted,

ALFRED T. METIVIER,
Gypsy Moth Supt.

Report of
Works Progress Administration

To the Board of Selectmen:

The closing of the year 1937 saw the completion of the articles voted in the annual March Town Meeting that called for W. P. A. Labor with the exception of some side-walks and upon these curbings have been installed. On the Blossom, Salem and Spring Street sidewalks in addition to the installation of the cement curb, gravelling has been placed in preparation for the black top which it is planned to start laying as soon as the temperature permits. On account of the delay in Washington granting approval of funds to pay for Federal labor upon the side-walk projects it was impossible to start work upon them until late in October. The Town's money for the materials was ready, but the government was not.

On Jan. 1, 1937, the number working on W. P. A. Projects was 180. Curtailment on Federal labor started in February and was gradual until June when wholesale slashes were made and in August the number working was reduced to 124. In November, with the advent of cold weather and dearth of private employment, additional men were put to work to relieve the excessive town welfare load and the year closed with 194 on Rockland projects and more additions are to be made in the new year. The largest weekly W. P. A. pay roll was $2,716.45 on the first week in January. The smallest weekly pay roll was in August when the amount was $1,525.05. The year closed with a weekly pay roll of $2,208.88.

The Federal pay roll for year 1937 amounted to $107,800.81, which makes total paid on direct Rockland projects for operation of Federal Emergency Administration from Aug. 1, 1934 to Dec. 31, 1937 $460,248.86.

In addition to the above there has been a number of Rockland W. P. A. employees working upon state supervised projects including the Pre-school Unit, Traffic Research, National Youth Administration, Commodity Distribution, Market Street Sidewalks, Statistical and Engineering projects upon which a fair estimate since the Emergency Act became operative would add at least $65,000 to Federal pay rolls which gives a total of Federal Relief to Rockland families of $525,248.86.

It may be of interest to note that since Jan. 1, 1938, through the intercedence of Mr. Torrey, representing the Board of Welfare, and the Local Co-ordinator, 117 Rockland workers have been added to W. P. A. pay rolls in an endeavor to relieve the Town Welfare load.

Through the hearty co-operation of the W. P. A. field engineers, district supervisors and Mr. MacKenzie, our highway surveyor, Rockland has been able to go through the year with only minor interruption in the operation of projects, a condition only few municipalities in the district can boast. Rockland also closed the year with a 'number of projects having presidential approval and ready to operate when the man quota is available.

It is interesting to note that the Sewing project, under district supervision of Mrs. Godfrey and Miss Helen Purcell have made 12,368 garments for distribution to the needy. Another project that has been of high value is the Housekeeping Aide whose visitors have worked 9,492 hours in families where Miss Williams in cooperation with Miss Dexter, the visiting nurse, have lightened the family load during trying periods.

The many covered drains installed including Belmont, Howard, Liberty and Crescent Streets, have proven their worth in taking care of surplus standing water and made many a wet cellar dry. More drains are contemplated when local funds permit.

During the year a change was made in the assignment of workers on the WPA so that at present all assignments are made by the state headquarters in Boston following investigation of the individual cases by the WPA District Office located in Brockton. The new system does not always work to the advantage of the most worthy cases.

The following table shows projects worked and amount of Federal and Municipal Funds Expended during 1937:

Projects	Amount Paid Federal Labor	Amount Paid by Town for Material, Etc
*Sewing	$ 17 588 29	$ 1 826 63
*Housekeeping Aides	5 048 25	115 40
*Recreation	5 255 60	548 77
Paint High School	1 166 65	569 26
Assessors Index	2 028 58	335 00
*Permanent Sidewalks	21 836 22	4 527 69
Reed Pond Development	5 825 33	399 33
Assessors' Titles	791 51	72 61
Forest St., Water Main	9 857 51	2 315 13
*Mosquito Control	10 336 57	\
Gravel Walks, Memorial Park	3 218 98	239 95
Douglas Street, Gravel	2 561 56	437 19
Division Street	2 994 65	942 48
Moth Control	3 048 47	511 39
Varnish Chairs, School	1 004 01	149 14
Plain Street, Rebuild	5 898 26	2 054 85
*Locate Street Bounds	4 307 18	202 50
Carey Court Water Main	1 870 98	847 23
*Closed Drains	3 784 69	947 31
*Assessors' Deeds	942 28	17 50
*Fire Lanes	760 44	7 19

(*Denotes still in operation.)

Respectfully submitted,

FRED M. RYAN,
W. P. A. Local Coordinator

Report of Trustees of Memorial Library

The Trustees of the Memorial Library submit the following report for 1937:

No extensive repairs on the building were necessary. Minor repairs were made, and as the railings on the front steps had become loosened, new iron rods were put into the posts, and the posts reset in lead in the steps.

In the librarian's report which follows, the attention of the citizens is called to the increase in circulation. This was especially pleasing to the Trustees, as the aim of a library is to supply a community with worthwhile books and magazines. Another gratifying accomplishment was the research work done by students and other adults. In this the librarians gave efficient co-operation. The illustrated lecture on the Diesel engine was in keeping with the trend of the times, for many libraries now include in their work the giving of lectures on various subjects by well-informed people.

The Trustees thank the Rockland Woman's Club for its gift of five dollars, and also those persons who have presented books to the library.

From the Trust Funds, income has been paid out for books as follows:

Hattie Curtis Fund	$ 18 33
Alice L. French Fund	23 02
Zenas M. Lane Fund	19 67
Everett Lane Fund	3 00
Charles Edwin Vinal Fund	30 32
Mary A. Spence Fund	14 82

Sarah J. Spence Fund 9 97
John W. Rice Fund 11 98
John A. Martin Fund 1 88
Mothers Mutual Improvement Society Fund 1 50

$ 134 49

These withdrawals left on deposit in the Rockland Savings Bank on December 31, 1937:

Hattie Curtis Fund $ 497 02
Alice F. French Fund 500 53
Zenas M. Lane Fund 496 23
Everett Lane Fund 100 02
Charles Edwin Vinal Fund 1 000 14
Mary A. Spence Fund 500 27
Sarah J. Spence Fund 300 10
John W. Rice Fund 400 13
John A. Martin Fund 100 12
Mothers Mutual Improvement Society Fund 50 20

By terms of the wills, income from the Zenas M. Lane Fund is restricted to the purchase of books of travel; of the Alice L. French Fund, of the Sarah J. Spence Fund, and of the Mothers Mutual Improvement Society Fund, to the purchase of books for children.

The terms of Annie E. McIlvene and Emily F. Crawford expire in 1938.

An appropriation of $4,200 plus the dog refund of $505.94 is recommended by the Trustees for 1938.

FRANCIS J. GEOGAN,
JOHN B. FITZGERALD,
BURTON L. CUSHING,
ANNIE E. McILVENE,
EMILY F. CRAWFORD,
EMMA W. GLEASON,
Trustees

Librarians Report

To the Trustees of the Rockland Memorial Library:
The fifty-ninth report of this library is herewith submitted.

A total of 61,558 books and magazines have been loaned for home use.

The average monthly circulation, 5,130. The average daily circulation, 209. Largest number delivered in one day, 401. Smallest number delivered in one day, 95.

Received for fines, reserved books, sale of cook books, subscriptions from non-residents, old magazines and books, $311.00.

Number of books added by purchase (including replacements), 325. Number of books presented, 108. Number of books worn out and missing, 50. Number of books rebound, 48. Number of books in library on December 31, 1937, 20,661.

Character of books loaned: literature, 4 per cent; history and travel, 3 per cent; biography, 3 per cent; miscellaneous (adult), 6 per cent; fiction (adult), 54 per cent;; fiction (juvenile), 12 per cent; miscellaneous (juvenile), 5 per cent; magazines, 13 per cent.

The library is the agency which brings books and people together. The past year has not been marked by any unusual events, but has been one of steady service to the townspeople.

Quite a substantial increase in circulation is noted, and there would seem to be no limit to our circulation of books for home reading, were the stock adequate in number and scope. Many come for specific titles, but most are satisfied with any good book on the topic of interest at the time.

Changes in the business, art and industrial world immediately react within the walls of the library. The economic depression brought to the library, individuals who had been previously only potential readers, but now have become active users of books.

It is a day when emphasis is being laid particularly upon adult education, yet without an adequate supply of books neither adults nor children will, of course, continue indefinitely as readers. Books they must have, old and new, if the habit is to persist.

The year was not an important one for the quality of fiction, and yet concentration of public attention upon one novel has been more marked than ever before. Requests for "Gone with the Wind" have been overwhelming. Without questioning the excellence of the book one deplores the interest that distracts attention from other good novels. In the non-fiction there is a broader range for the reader pursues a subject more often than a title.

Fewer replacements were bought this year, and fewer books sent away for rebinding, in an effort to supply the best new books. Old books mended and remended have been kept on the shelves and many are in circulation which are absolutely unfit to be handled.

It is believed that the function of the public library, in its relation to schools, is primarily to supplement the school curriculum, but it is also their privilege to offer schools their knowledge of spontaneous reading interests of young people. Instead of too general use of conventional reading lists we wonder if it isn't wiser to fit books boys and girls can read to their interests. Generalizations about reading are always dangerous and every year finds an amazing diversity in reading ability. Almost everybody will read if they are given books they can read and about subjects of interest to them.

It is this mixture of reading interest and ability which makes the work with young people stimulating and satisfactory.

The reading for State Certificates continues active in the grades of the elementary schools, and in many instances is considered a part of their English course.

A new list of books was printed in 1936, combining with new titles the best of all previous lists. Our collection of these books is being slowly built up as funds allow.

In May, of this year, a free illustrated lecture was given at the library on the Diesel engine, by the Diesel Engine Institute. Our north room was filled to capacity and many benefited from knowledge gained on the scientific subject.

Again, this year, books were sent to the Merchant Marine Library Association. Books are always being solicited for this worthy cause, and we forward them as often as possible.

We are deeply grateful for the many gifts made to the library during 1937. Special mention should be made regarding the money from the Rockland Woman's Club, which was so much appreciated.

Prized highly also were the book marks given to us by the Rockland Savings Bank and Mr. George N. Beal. They are in constant demand and hundreds have been given out to adults as well as to children.

An unusual number of books of fiction were contributed by friends of the library and enough cannot be said in appreciation since it has been hard to meet demands for old popular types.

An attractive array of student paintings and drawings was on display from the schools again this year, although most of our exhibits in 1937 were books and other material owned by the library.

If the work of the library is to grow, it must be aided by the building up of the book stock, for reading grows only through reading.

The librarian wishes to acknowledge here all that she owes to Trustees and loyal assistants.

Respectfully submitted,

LIDA A. CLARK,
Librarian.

Report of Chief of Police

Honorable Board of Selectmen,
Town of Rockland,
Gentlemen:

I herewith submit my report for the Police Department of the Town of Rockland for the year ending December 31st, 1937.

NUMBER OF ARRESTS

Year 1937 199

	Male	Female
Assault and Battery	6	0
Capias	4	0
Disturbing the Peace	4	0
Driving so as to endanger etc.	2	0
Driving under the influence etc	8	0
Drunkenness	124	0
Gaming and being present at	6	0
Insane persons	5	4
Illegimate child act	1	0
Larceny	8	0
Lewdness	2	0
Lottery, promoting	8	0
Malicious mischief	1	0
Motor vehicle violations	4	0
Neglecting children	5	0
Non-support	5	0

Trespass 1 0

Vagrant 1 0

Total 195 4

Males 195
Females 4

Total 199

MISCELLANEOUS

Automobile thefts investigated 9
Automobiles recovered 11
Automobile accidents investigated 60
Complaints investigated 612
Miles traveled by Police cruising car 17,006
Persons reported missing 7
Persons located out of town and local 12
Number of arrests for out of town police 11
Red light calls answered 376
Store doors found unlocked 26
Summonses served for out of town police 68
Telegrams (emergencies) persons notified 21
Reported defects to highway 10
Fires reported 3
Electric lights reported out 15
Number of automobiles stopped for license and
  registrations 800
Trespassing 1
Persons put up at station for night 6

Crimes in Rockland for the year 1937 were of minor nature, and most of the complaints were disposed of; unsolved complaints are still under investigation.

During the past year 1937 this department regrets to report that there were three (3) fatal accidents, two of

these accidents were accidental; one was caused by a hit
and run operator. A thorough investigation was made
by the Inspector of Motor Vehicles of this District and
this department; to date no arrest has been made although the investigation is still in progress.

Upon request of parents who have children attending
the Jefferson school for protection of children crossing
Union Street at Crescent Street, the Board of Selectmen
at the suggestion of this department assigned Percy Albee for duty at this point during hours when children go
to and from school, this has been an added measure of
safety this year. The remaining school hours with the
exception of the McKinley school, (which is under police
protection) are ably taken care of by the principals and
teachers of their respective schools and for this service
this department commends them highly; no accidents to
school children having been reported during school hours
for the year 1937.

During coasting season a special police officer (Thomas
Fitzgerald) was assigned to Union and Taunton Avenue,
hours were established under police protection.

Again I take pleasure in giving the thanks of the entire department to the Town and County officials and to
the many other citizens who have given valuable assistance when given the opportunity. As Chief of the
department I am appreciative of the fine work of the
regular and special officers, all of whom have labored to
give the finest service; and to the Finance Committee
who after consideration and investigation approved of
the appropriation asked for by this department.

Respectfully submitted,

GEORGE J. POPP,
Chief of Police

ANNUAL REPORT

OF THE

WATER. COMMISSIONERS

TOWN OF ROCKLAND
MASSACHUSETTS

1937

ELEVATED TANK ERECTED 1937 ON RICE AVENUE

Capacity of Tank 530,000 gallons

Capacity of 6 ft. riser pipe 25,445 gallons.

Weight of tank and structure 490,000 pounds.

Height from cement footing to top 145 ft. 6 inches.

Distance from bottom of tank to concrete footings 120 ft.

Diameter of tank 60 feet.

Height of tank 25 feet.

COST

Government Grant	$ 30 457 96
Appropriation	37 951 00
Total cost	$ 68 408 96

JOINT WATER BOARD OF ABINGTON
AND ROCKLAND

H. C. WITHERELL, Chairman

S. W. BAKER, Secretary

GEORGE GRAY   E. S. DAMON

F. L. MERRILL   R. FUCILLO

LEWIS E. WHEELER, Water Registrar

WATER BOARD OF ROCKLAND

S. W. BAKER, Chairman

E. S. DAMON   R. FUCILLO

JAMES B. STUDLEY, Superintendent

Regular meetings of the Board every Thursday
evening at 7:30

Main and Superintendent's Office 96 East Water Street
Open 8-12 A. M.   1-5 P. M.   Telephone 901

Collection Office, Room 2, Savings Bank Block

Open 9-12 A. M.   2-5 P. M.

Friday Evenings 7-9 P. M.   Saturday 9-12 A. M.

Telephone 940

Water Commissioners' Report

The Water Commissioners herewith submit their fifty-second annual report.

Services in Rockland	1 942
Services in Abington	1 433
Services in Joint Works	127
New Services in Rockland	4
New Services in Abington	5

Water rates received by Abington	$24	150	12
Water rates received by Rockland	24	080	85
Water rates received by Joint Works	3	327	57
	$51	558	54

JOINT ACCOUNT 1937

Edison Electric Ill. Co., service	$ 3	606	33
William Brown, salary and remittances	1	880	22
Louis Wheeler, salary	1	664	00
Town of Pembroke, taxes		185	75
N. E. T. & T. Co., service		183	36
Rockland Water Department, leaks and services		149	49
Merrimac Chemical Co., ammonia and chlorine		138	50
E. L. LeBaron Foundry Co., foot valve		125	00
Charles Higgins, services as treasurer		100	00
Harrison Witherell, services as chairman		100	00
S. W. Baker, services as secretary		100	00
Standard Oil Co., oil and gasoline		80	40
Ira Richards, labor		60	31
Walworth Co., supplies		53	34
Frank Merrill, services as Commissioner		50	00
George Gray, services as Commissioner		50	00

E. S. Damon, services as Commissioner	50 00
Ralph Fucillo, services as Commissioner	50 00
Vincent Geloran, labor	48 66
The Welch Co., Inc., boat and oars	45 00
Peter DeSimone, labor	44 16
A. W. Chesterton Co., supplies	44 09
Crandell Packing Co., supplies	37 27
Tony Sasso, labor	35 16
George Lang & Co., supplies	33 56
Edwin Richardson, labor	33 18
Raymond Eldridge, labor	31 50
Rome Brothers, supplies	30 19
Curry Brothers Oil Co., supplies	29 50
Douglas Print, printing	28 55
Robert Porter, labor	25 88
Taunton Lumber Co., paint and supplies	25 25
Westinghouse Electric Mfg. Co., repairs to motor	25 08
Coleman Connelly, labor	22 50
Felix McGovern, labor	22 50
Leo Hickey, labor	22 50
The Garlock Packing Co., packing	22 13
Lawrence Sheehan, labor	19 97
W. E. Kingsbury, gravel and loam	19 50
Hayes Pump & Machinery Co., repairs and supplies	17 30
Leslie Brown, labor	16 88
John Foster Lumber Co., supplies	16 56
Hub Wire Cloth & Wire Works Co., wire	15 73
John McMaugh, labor	15 19
Albert Doherty, labor	14 63
Ralph Stetson, labor	13 50
Edward Winslow, labor	12 38
G. W. Mann, tile	12 00
Builders Iron Foundry Co., charts and ink	10 57
Herford Damon, labor	10 13
Commissioner of Public Safety, inspection of boiler	10 00
Amos Phelps, bond insurance	10 00
Harry Arena, labor	9 00
William Santry, labor	9 00

Bradford Weston, crushed stone	8	13
Crosby Steam Gage & Valve Co., charts	7	66
Alden Blanchard, labor	7	16
Gorham Fire Equipment Co., hose and fire extinguisher	6	42
A. I. Randall, rebinding record book	5	45
E. F. Benson Inc., pump rental	5	25
Antonio Tetrowski, labor	4	50
William Hurley, labor	4	50
John Pitchen, labor	4	50
S. C. Crosby, repairs to clock	4	00
Dana Pratt, maps	4	00
Mathewson Machine Works, blueprints	3	50
A. Culver Co., grass seed and fertilizer	3	15
Stearn's Express, express	2	25
Forrest Partch, switches	2	10
Benson's Cafe, food for workers	2	10
Clifton Bates, looking up records	1	50
Railway Express Agency, express		92
Pierce Express, express		75
Rockland Transportation Co., express		35
A. J. Vargus, battery		35

Total	$ 9	544	24
Rockland, one half	$ 4	772	12

REPORT OF SUPERINTENDENT

OF THE JOINT WORKS

Joint Board of Water Commissioners of
Abington and Rockland

Gentlemen:

I herewith submit my report as Superintendent for the year ending December 31, 1937.

I would recommend during the coming year that the Iron standpipe be painted.

The hydrants have been tested during the year and one renewal was installed.

Renewal of foot valve at end of suction-pipe in well house, and minor repairs made at Pumping Station.

The two standpipes at Beech Hill were emptied and thoroughly cleaned.

The usual analysis of water from Big Sandy Pond and Little Sandy Pond has been made by the State Board of Health, also samples of water were mailed each month from March to November inclusive to Lawrence Experiment Station for bacterial examinations.

Two new services added during the year and one renewal installed from main to curb, and three service leaks were repaired.

The shores of the pond are in good condition, except around a few cottages which are being remedied.

The financial account of the joint works will be found under the report of the Water Registrar.

Respectfully submitted,

WILLIAM H. BROWN,
Joint Superintendent

Month	Hours h m	Daily Average h m	Pumped	Daily Average gallons	lbs. coal consumed	Daily Average lbs.	Ave. height Reservoir	Gals. pumped per lbs. of coal	Gals. pumped per K. W. H.
January	287 40	9 17	18 099 000	583 839	15 995	516	97.7	350	732.6
February	275 00	9 49	17 321 000	618 670	14 445	516	97.7	351	734
March	318 00	10 15	19 863 000	640 742	15 920	514	97.7	350	733.5
April	287 35	9 35	18 ? 000	602 267	12 870	429	97.7	351	733
May	316 12	10 12	19 965 000	644 032	14 818	478	96.5	351	743.7
June	360 00	12 00	22 452 000	748 400	7 020	234	96.6	350	743.2
July	428 50	13 50	26 480 000	854 193	800	800	97		736.5
August	467 00	15 4	28 743 000	927 193	2 452	1226	97.2	349	729.5
September	347 30	11 35	21 234 000	707 800	8 090	270	97.3	350	730.7
October	358 05	11 33	20 663 000	666 549	11 812	381	96.6	351	711
November	323 00	10 46	19 425 000	647 500	14 160	472	96.9	349	723
December	282 05	9 6	17 233 000	555 903	13 445	435	97.6	350	735
Totals	4050 57		249 546 000		136 327				
Average	337 35		20 795 500		11 402		97.2	350	733

Average Static Head 218. Average Dynamic Head 279.2. Maximum weekly — 1,530,000 gals. Maximum daily 100 gals. Gallons pumped red Saturday — August 7 — red August 5 to August 11 inclusive. Coal on hand Jan. 1, 1938 — 10,372 lbs. Gallons pumped via daily 245,944,000 gallons. Gal. red 1937, None. Coal on hand Jan. 1, 2,907,000 gals. Gallons pumped via the Engine 695,000 gals. Gasoline on hand. 39, 720 gals. Duty done in foot lbs. per 100 lbs. of coal, 36,037,982. lbs. pumped per gal. of she, 1455 gals.

WILLIAM H. BROWN,
Chief Engineer

REPORT OF WATER REGISTRAR

To the Joint Board of Commissioners of
Abington and Rockland

Gentlemen:

I herewith submit my report as Water Registrar for
the year ending December 31, 1937.

Water Rates	$2 468 86	
New Services and Meters	79 24	
Total Amount Collected		$2 548 10
Water Rates Due		$ 227 91

Two new accounts added this year.

Respectfully submitted,

LEWIS E. WHEELER,

Water Registrar

SUPERINTENDENT'S REPORT

To the Board of Water Commissioners:

Gentlemen:—

I herewith submit my report of the Water Department for the year ending December 31, 1937.

Receipts from Water rates	$24 080	85
Receipts from the installation of services	1 465	10
Receipts from small jobs	456	63
Receipts from meter repairs	120	35
Receipts from Water Liens	517	57
	$26 640	50

COLLECTIONS

On January 1, 1937 there was an outstanding indebtedness to the Department of $11,688.84 for Water Rates. This has been reduced to $7,987.06 as of December 31, 1937.

SERVICES

New service installations	6
Renewal of services	42
Renewals to property lines	9
Services lowered	2
Services discontinued	2
Service goosenecks renewed	13

HYDRANTS, GATES, BOXES

Main gates new and replaced	7
Hydrant gates added	10

Hydrants repaired	7
Hydrants relocated inside curb	2
Hydrants replaced	6
Service Boxes adjusted	147
Gates repacked	5
New hydrants added to system	4

LEAKS

11 leaks were repaired during the year.

MAINS

Forest Street Construction

The work started in 1936 of laying an 8 inch main from the corner of Plesaant to Hingham Street, a distance of 3,998 feet was completed, with labor furnished by the W. P. A., material being furnished by the Water Department.

The additional fire protection on Hingham Street and lower Forest Street has been increased over 500%.

A 6 inch Transite main was laid from the corner of Pleasant and Forest Street to the dead end near Loretta Avenue a distance of 1530 feet. This connection will aid in increasing the flow of water on North Union Street and eliminates two dead ends. Labor for this project was furnished by W. P. A.

Carey Court Construction

A new six inch main was laid to replace the one inch service pipe supplying three houses. The extension was carried a distance of 550 feet in from Reed Street. This main will insure an adequate supply for houses now located on the street, and provision has been made for the installation of a fire hydrant.

Labor on this project was furnished by W. P. A. and material by the Water Department.

Smith Lane Construction

Work has been started on the construction of a 6 inch supply to property located on Smith Lane. Trenching was started by the W. P. A. The project will be finished early in 1938.

GENERAL

Fire Flow Tests

Fire flow tests were conducted by engineers from The New England Insurance Exchange on October 22, 1937, with the new 500,000 gallon tank in service.

The reports show an increase in delivery, in sections of the Town tested, of from 100% to 500% increase in the flow of water, for fire protection.

The following tables show the flows in tests, conducted October 22, 1937, with the new tank in service, and tests conducted May 25, 1934, with the supply from Beach Hill only.

	October 22, 1937	May 25, 1934	Increase
Location	Gal. per min	Gals. per min	Gals per min.
Union and School	2500	1300	1200
Union and Pacific	2240	1060	1180
Howard and Park	2470	1310	1160
Union at Weymouth line	300	250	50
Pleasant and Forest	780	290	490
Forest and Loretta Ave.	780	280	500

Hingham and Forest	730	110	620
Liberty near Summit	1450	810	640
Webster and Liberty	2450	1380	1070
Howard and E. Water	2450	1240	1210
·Webster at Hanover Line	360	240	120
Church opposite Franklin	2170	1080	1090
Franklin and E. Water	2340	1230	1110
Vernon and George	2200	1130	1070
Plain and Grove	1450	1200	250
Central and W. Water	970	670	300
Green and North Ave.	1580	1030	550
Division and Belmont	1900	1250	650
Taunton Ave., South of Division	1410	1120	290
Summer and Concord	1860	1100	760
Market and Union	3280	2020	1260

LOCAL REPORT OF EXPENSES

The following expenditures are included in the total expenditures of $23,522,44.

Forest Street Water Main Extension
(From Pleasant to Hingham St.)

Pipe	$ 954	58
Labor	10	13
Lanterns	18	00
Coal	1	50
Kerosene	18	56
Lead	3	60
Jute	2	15
Gates	72	60
Fittings (tee, sleeves, etc.)	157	50
Hydrolite	20	00
Gravel	11	60
Compressor	190	00

Trucking	259	08
Pump	24	00
Freight	34	00
	$ 1 777	**30**

Forest Street Water Main Extension
(Near Loretta Ave. to Pleasant Street)

Pipe	$ 1 011	66
Labor	33	75
Compressor	240	00
Trucking	175	62
Gravel	13	10
Lanterns	18	00
Coal	2	00
Hydrotite	20	00
Lead	7	20
Jute	2	70
Gates	72	20
Fittings	46	50
Kerosene	16	80
Road Patch	18	00
Freight	55	47
	$ 1 733	**00**

Carey Court Water Main Extension

Pipe	$ 467	50
Labor	2	25
Compressor	36	00
Pump	1	50
Trucking	78	72
Tar Coating	3	75
Gates	48	40
Fittings	22	65
Kerosene	11	20

Coal		50
Hydrotite	15	00
Lead	1	80
Jute		60

	689	87

Smith Lane Water Main Construction

Pipe	$ 161	50
Labor	106	88
Compressor	80	00
Pump	7	00
Trucking	2	00
Hydrotite	10	00
Jute	1	50
Kerosene	4	00
Fittings	4	65

	$ 377	53

Respectfully submitted,

JAMES B. STUDLEY,

Superintendent

LOCAL ACCOUNT 1937

Merchants National Bank, Interest and Bonds on standpipe	$ 2 800	00
James Studley, Salary	2 080	00
Johns Mansville Pipe Co., Transite Pipe	1 978	95
Harry Holmes, Salary	1 628	00
Louis Litchfield, Salary	1 628	00
Lawrence Sheehan, Labor	1 042	28
Edwin Richardson, Labor	955	14
Henry Harris, Labor and Remittances	949	40
Tony Sasso, Labor	960	57
Alice Gammon, Office	900	00

Bradford Weston, Renewals and Services
Union Street Construction   819 85
Edward Winslow, Labor   603 86
William Bell, Use of Truck W. P. A.   473 42
Phoenix Meter Corporation, meter parts   354 55
Red Hed Mfg. Co., Fittings and Supplies   305 55
S. W. Baker, Services as Commissioner   300 00
E. S. Damon, Services as Commissioner   300 00
Ralph Fuccillo, Services as Commissioner   300 00
Corcoran Supply Co., Pipe and Fittings   296 23
John B. Washburn, Recording Water Liens   294 75
Mary Twoomy, Titles on Liens   288 50
John R. Parker, P. M., Stamps and Envelopes   214 52
Socony Vacuum Oil Co., Gasoline   210 19
Homelite Corporation, Pump and Parts   206 10
Renssalaer Valve Co., Hydrants   205 64
N. E. T. & T. Co., Service   199 11
Dolby's Filling Station, Gasoline and repairs   182 65
National Meter Co., Meters and parts   148 85
McAuliffe & Burke Co., Brass Pipe   140 56
A. Culver Co., Kerosene and Coal   129 89
Oberg Engineer Corporation, Gates and Fittings   124 88
Amos Phelps, Insurance   109 00
W. J. Dunn Co., Drills and Bits   98 88
N. H., N. H. & H. R. R. Freight   93 60
Warren Woodward, Insurance   89 12
National Foundry Inc., Boxes   80 31
Hydraulic Developement Corp., Hydrotite   80 00
LeBaron Foundry Inc., Cast Iron Tees   77 13
Thompson Durkee Co., Brass Pipe   74 77
Boston Pipe & Fitting Co., Brass Pipe   69 53
E. S. Damon, Insurance   68 70
Merrimac Chemical Co., Merclor and sulpher   66 85
Alphonse Grant, Labor   62 19
Bramon Dow Co., Brass Pipe   61 35
Neponset Valve Co., Valves   55 50
Theodore Collins, Labor   55 14
Sears Roebuk Co., Supplies   49 52

Cambridge Machine & Valve Co., Hydrant	47	43
Globe Newspaper Co., Advertising Standpipe bids	46	40
M. F. Ellis Co., Supplies	44	21
Serafino Gentle, Dynamiting	43	53
Dennis O'Connor, Insurance	41	15
Douglas Print, Printing	41	05
A. J. Vargus, Batteries and Supplies	37	05
Dominic Delprete, Damage to tire, adjustment	36	50
Charles McGonnigle, Labor	36	28
Hall and Torrey Co., Supplies	36	18
Edison Electric Ill. Co., Service	34	80
Chase Parker & Co., Supplies	34	64
A. Wainshalbaum, Parts and labor on trucks	33	95
Banker & Tradesman, Advertising bids on Tank PWA	32	50
Parker Danner & Co., Couplings and Hose	31	86
Rockland Standard, Printing	30	40
The Edson Pump Co., Supplies	30	24
W. F. Beach, Welding	27	62
Christopher Tompkins, Gravel WPA	24	70
Gulf Oil Corp., Oil	23	95
Irving Torrey, Labor	23	34
Harold Rainsford, Labor	23	06
Ingersoll Rand Co., Bits for Compressor	22	65
Hallamore Express Co., Repairing hydrants	21	00
P. I. Perkins Co., Supplies	20	71
Dodge-Haley Co., Steel	20	48
Diamond Union Stamp Works, Time Clock	20	00
Aldo Botto, Labor	19	68
Percy Simmons, Labor	18	84
Oakite Products Co., Dipping compound for meters	18	48
Bernard Fitzgerald, Labor	18	28
American Bitumals Co., Supplies	18	00
Jenkins & Simmons, Express	17	31
Industrial Lock Nut Co., Supplies	17	15
Joseph Sullivan, Labor	16	31

C. A. Baker, Acetylene gas	16	22
Hidalgo Steel Co., Supplies	15	42
Edward Whitmarsh, Labor	13	78
Becker & Co., Supplies	13	39
Old Colony Gas Co., Gas	12	26
The Austin Print, Printing	12	00
Ira Richards, Labor	11	82
West Side Grocery, Wood	10	90
A. I. Randall, Printing	10	40
Neptune Meter Co., Meter	10	25
William Flynn, Labor	10	13
Waldo Brothers, Tile	10	11
Darling Valve Mfg. Co., Valve	10	04
Edward Meara, Lettering door	10	00
The Hallmite Mfg. Co., Pipe Cement	9	98
Cutter Renewal Co., Sharpening bits	9	80
John C. Moore Corp., Supplies	9	75
Manifold Supply Co., Supplies	8	75
Rockland Transportation, Express	8	61
Underwood Elliot Fisher Co., Repairs and Supplies	8	45
Rockland Coal & Grain Co., Soft Coal	7	86
Charles McCarthy Co., Supplies	7	11
Andrew Thibeault, Labor	6	75
Gorham Equipment Co., Lights	6	45
Bettridge Sales & Service, Supplies	6	29
Chase Brass & Copper Co., Copper	6	11
Earl Wallace, Labor	5	63
Burrell & Delorey, Rubber Boots	5	50
H. & B. American Machine Co., Castings	5	50
A. E. Halperin Co., First aid kit	5	08
Minneapolis Honneywell Co., Supplies	4	96
Chandler & Farquhar Co., Wrenches	4	90
Ward's Stationers, Supplies	4	15
The Equipment Co., Parts for Pump	4	10
Walworth Co., Supplies	3	84
Brown Instrument Co., Charts	3	53
A. B. Dick Co., Stencils	3	50
Worthington Gamon Meter Co., Meter Parts	3	50

Kenneth Everett, Labor	3 00
Bernard Carey, Labor	3 00
Indian Head Washer Co., Meter washers	2 92
George Inglis, Labor	2 81
Blake & Rebhan Co., Supplies	2 48
C. W. Briggs, Blacksmith work	2 25
New England Transportation Co., Express	2 23
Raymond Martel, Labor	2 00
Brockton Transportation Co., Express	1 61
Hill & Magound, Gears	1 50
S. H. Stoddard, Carpenter work	1 50
Ralph Belcher, Certifying Standpipe deed	1 50
Crawford's Service Station, Supplies	1 49
A. S. Peterson, Supplies	1 30
John Lamb, Lye	1 10
John Geary & Co., Stamp	1 00
Brockton Gas Light Co., Hose	80
Bridgewater Brick Co., Bricks	75
George N. Beal, Supplies	70
Mathewson Machine Works, Blueprints	63
Bemis Drug Co., Leads	55
Rome Brothers, Supplies	55
Brown Automobile Co., Cover	45
Addressograph Co., Plates	44
Rockland Hardware Co., Supplies	30

Total Expenditures $23 522 44

SAMUEL W. BAKER,
EVERETT S. DAMON,
RALPH FUCILLO,

Water Commissioners of Rockland

Report of Town Treasurer

TREASURER'S REPORT OF THE RECEIPTS AND
DISBURSEMENTS FOR THE YEAR ENDING
DECEMBER 31, 1937

January 1, 1937, Cash on hand $ 92 076 07

RECEIPTS

Anticipation Tax Notes	$275 000 00	
Taxes—Real Estate, Personal		
and Poll	294 646 42	
Taxes, Excise	15 257 01	
Interest on Taxes	8 637 37	
Tax Titles Redeemed	12 279 74	
Tax, Costs	259 54	
Liquor Licenses	4 810 00	
Licenses, Miscellaneous	767 00	
Trust Funds, (Cemetery)	818 95	
Dog Licenses	588 80	
Water Department Receipts	26 640 48	
Joint Water Department	8 099 70	
Memorial Library	311 00	
Sealer of Weights	118 74	
School Department	219 57	
Court Fines	198 95	
City of Boston, Tuition	557 60	
Unearned Comp. Ins. Premium	689 08	
Board of Health	1 743 39	
		$651 643 34
		$743 719 41

Miscellaneous Receipts
Sale Materials   15 90
B'arrett Co.—Refund   33 93
Cancelled Checks   130 57
                                                            ―――――
                                                                            180 40

County Treasurer
Dog Dividend   447 34
E. Water St. Construction   3 373 39
                                                            ―――――
                                                                        3 820 73

Water Tank Construction
Federal Grant   24 500 00
                                                            ―――――
                                                                      24 500 00

Union St. Construction
Federal Grant   12 140 76
                                                            ―――――
                                                                      12 140 76

Welfare and Old Age Assistance Refunds
Other Towns and Cities   9 615 14
                                                            ―――――
                                                                        9 615 14

State Treasurer
Income Tax   21 987 98
Corporation Tax   14 278 33
Gas and Electric   2 702 20
Income Tax Educational   11 330 88
State Aid   650 00
Veterans Exemption   215 75
E. Water St. Construction   6 281 44
Aid to School   618 21
Aid to Dependent Children   2 718 37

Tuition Children	1 351 41
Old Age Assistance	16 802 68
Temporary Aid	18 232 86
U. S. Grant, O. A. Assistance	38 955 69
U. S. Aid to Children	3 152 65

| | 139 278 45 |
| Total | $933 254 89 |

PAYMENTS

Selectmen's Warrants	$183 269 47
Public Welfare Warrants	75 016 46
School Warrants	104 420 93
Old Age Assistance	45 505 61
Old Age Assistance, U. S. Grant	36 127 14
Old Age Administration, U. S. Grant	1 002 41
Water Warrants	23 522 44
Joint Water Warrants	9 544 24
Town of Abington, Joint Rates	1 435 59
U. S. Grant, Aid to Dependent Mothers	2 993 97
Tax Refunds	24 29
McKinley School Appropriation	409 12
Anticipation Tax Notes	300 000 00
Water Tank—Project 1343R	59 445 82
National Shawmut Bank	1 00
Trust Funds, Cemetery	818 95
County Treasurer	

| County Tax | 14 757 40 |
| Dog Licenses | 599 00 |

| | 15 356 40 |

Commonwealth of Massachusetts
State Tax   16 047 50

State Parks and Reservations   245 17
Hospital care Civil War Veterans   45 00

                                     16 337 67
Cash on Hand December 31, 1937   58 023 38

         Total $933 254 89

OUTSTANDING INDEBTEDNESS

Anticipation of Revenue Notes $100 000 00

PERMANENT LOANS

Junior-Senior School Bonds
  3¾% Maturing $100,000 annually   10 000 00
    1938-1943   60 000 00
  3¾% Maturing $6000 annually
    1938-1948   66 000 00

                             126 000 00
Plymouth County Hospital Notes
  5% Maturing $1000 annually
    1938-1940   3 000 00
Union St. Construction
  2% Coupon Notes 1938-1946 31 000 00
Water Tank Construction
  2% Coupon Note 1938-1956   38 000 00

                                         198 000 00

                                        $298 000 00

JOINT WATER DEPARTMENT

Receipts:
  From Joint Rates $ 3 327 57

From Rockland 1-2 Maintenance   4 772 11
From Abington 1-2 Maintenance   4 772 13

$ 12 871 81

Payments:
Warrants $ 9 544 24
Joint Rates to Abington   1 435 59
Joint Rates to Rockland   1 663 78
Due Abington   228 20

$12 871 81

WATER DEPARTMENT

Receipts:
Water Rates, Construction, etc. $26 660 48
1-2 Joint Rates   1 663 78

$28 324 26

Payments:
Warrants $23 522 44
1-2 Cost Joint Maintenance   4 772 11
Receipts Over Payments   29 71

$28 324 26

WATER TANK CONSTRUCTION PROJECT 1343R

Merchants Nat'l Bank Notes (1936) $40 048 89
Federal Grants to Dec. 31, 1937   24 500 00

64 548 89
Payments to Dec. 31, 1937   62 210 82

Unexpended balance Dec. 31, 1937 $ 2 338 07

ASSETS

Cash
Accounts receivable $58 023 38
Taxes
  Levy 1935 $ 2 126 98
  Levy 1936   66 767 21
  Levy 1937   113 628 10
                            _____
                                         $182 522 29

Motor Excise
  1935   485 52
  1936   1 562 84
  1937   3 500 84
                            _____
                                           5 549 20
Tax Titles   18 869 72
                                         _____
                                         $264 964 59

LIABILITIES

Anticipation Tax Notes $100 000 00
Special Accounts   8 411 70
Unexpended Balances   11 850 54
Water Rates   228 20
Water Tank Project   2 338 07
Surplus Revenue   142 136 08
                                         _____
                                         $264 964 59

CEMETERY TRUST FUNDS

Bequest	By	Balance Jan. 1, 1937	Deposited During 1937	Income	Expended	Balance Dec. 31, 1937
Jeremiah ...aby	St. Patricks	$ 01 54		$1 51		$103 05
My ...ace	St. ...cks	406 18		6 09		412 27
...get Smith	St. Patricks	01 54		1 51		103 05
Pick McCaffrey	St. Patricks	108 75		1 62		110 37
...es H. ...nell	St. ...cks	101 54		1 51		103 05
Gallagher-Driscoll	St. ...cks	239 83		3 58		243 41
Chester Ford	St. Patricks	475 51		7 12		482 63
Mary Gallagher	St. Patricks	101 54		1 51		103 05
...he ...re	St. Patricks	203 09		3 04		206 13
...el Sullivan	St. Patricks	101 54		1 51		103 05
Patrick ...he	St. Pat ...cks	76 15		1 14		77 29
George Hatch	St. Patricks	01 54		1 51		103 05
James Crowley	St. Patricks	01 54		1 51		103 05
Margaret D. Quinlan	St. Patricks	203 09		3 04		206 13
Daniel Crowley	St. Patricks	101 54		1 51		103 05
Bridget Conway	St. Patricks	114 42		1 71		116 13
Patrick O'Hearn	St. Patricks	50 76		75		51 51
Daniel H. Lych	St. Patricks	101 54		1 51		103 05
Nicholas ...nell	St. Pat ...cks	101 54		1 51		103 05
...es Maguire	St. Patricks	101 54		1 51		103 05

CEMETERY TRUST FUNDS—Continued

Bequest	Cemetery	Balance Jan. 1. 1937	Deposited During 1937	Ine	Expended	Balance Dec. 31, 1937
Han Sullivan	St. Patricks	50 76		75		51 51
My J. ฺin	St. Patricks	D0 00		1 50		101 50
Katherine E. Crowley	St. Patricks	203 09		3 04		206 13
ฺel Sullivan	St. Patricks	101 54		1 51		D3 05
Wm (M.h	St. Patricks	D2 59		2 56		105 15
ฺrles ฺy	St. Patricks	203 04		3 04		206 08
ฺle E. ฺon	St. Pat ฺks	D1 54		1 51		D3 05
ฺas ฺll	St. ฺks	D1 54		1 51		D3 05
ฺy ฺr	St. Patricks	152 31		2 28		154 59
Mary J. Samuels	St. Patricks	203 09		3 04		206 13
Wm B. Burke	St. Patricks	50 76		75		51 51
Henry Lyns	St. ฺks	D1 54		1 51		103 05
Sarah J. Spence	St. Patricks	406 18		6 09		412 27
William ฺld	St. Patricks	101 54		1 51		103 05
ฺas J. Wm	St. ฺ ฺks	101 54		1 51		D3 05
John ฺy	St. ฺks	203 09		3 04		206 13
Jhn Parker	St. Patricks	86 30		1 29		87 59
ฺas J. Lych	Holy Family	126 92		1 89		128 81
Jeremiah Santry	Holy Family	203 09		3 04		206 13
ฺa B. ฺrs	Holy Family	D1 54		1 51		103 05

CEMETERY TRUST FUNDS—Cont'

Bequest	Cemetery	Balance Jan. 1. 1937	Deposited During 1937	Income	Expended	Balance Dec. 31, 1937
Mary : [illegible]	Holy Family	126 92	$125 0	1 89		125 00
John W. [illegible]n	Holy Family	101 54		1 51		128 81
Mary E. Kelley	Holy Family	107 57				103 05
Frederic Dill	Mt. [illegible]	100 00		3 23	$4 00	106 80
Ernest M. Paine	Mt. Pleasant	100 00		2 00		102 00
Guy L. Keene	Mt. Pleasant	100 00		2 00		102 00
[illegible]ce Damon	Mt. Pleasant	224 23		1 25		101 25
Collins-Branson	Mt. Pleasant	143 89		3 36		227 59
Elvira S. [illegible]	Mt. Pleasant	82 94		4 33	10 00	138 22
C. A. [illegible]	Mt. Pleasa tn	236 14		2 49	2 00	83 43
[illegible]	Mt. Pl [illegible]	61 18		7 12	4 00	239 26
Emma Hutchinson	Mt. Pleasant	249 13		1 84	2 00	61 02
A. Hilton Studley	Mt. Pleasant	116 85		7 45	8 00	248 58
William G. Perry	Mt. Pleasant	100 01		3 51	4 00	116 36
Gardner-Damon	Mt. Pleasant	100 01		3 01	3 00	100 02
[illegible]es H. Poole	Mt. Pleasant	137 21		3 01	3 00	100 02
Howard [illegible]	Mt. [illegible]	119 34		4 13	2 00	139 34
Charles G. [illegible]	Mt. Pleasant	103 90		3 59	2 00	120 93
Frederic Shaw	Mt. Pleasant			3 11	2 00	105 01

MY TRUST FUNDS—Cont'

Bequest	Cemetery	Balance Jan. 1 1937	Deposited During 1937	Inc	Expended	Balance Dec. 31, 19
?e Mann	Mt. Pl?nt	101 19		3 04	3 00	101 23
? ?e	Mt Pl?nt	52 01		1 56	2 00	51 57
A. A. Crooker	Mt. Pl?nt	132 41		3 99	2 00	134 40
?k P. Lewis	Mt. Pl?nt	54 18		1 62	2 00	53 80
?es J. Donaldson	Mt. Pleasant	318 32		9 61	4 00	323 93
Henry G. ?n	Mt. Pl?nt	533 17		16 10	4 00	545 27
Marsena ?l, ?rs	Mt. Pl?nt	128 66		3 67	3 00	129 53
E. W. ?ing	Mt. Pl?nt	156 06		4 71	4 00	156 77
?ia Estes	Mt. Pl?nt	310 10		9 30	8 00	311 40
?a L. Willi ams	Mt. Pl?nt	?0 0		75		?0 75
?e F. ?ll	Mt. Pl?nt	200 00		50		200 50
Eben P. Everett	Mt. Pl?nt	87 22		2 62	2 00	87 84
Frank, ?. Lawrence	Mt. Pl?nt	177 33		2 65	6 00	173 98
?d	Mt. Pl?nt	236 64		7 08	8 00	235 72
Andrew ?he	Mt. Pl?nt	114 01		1 71		115 72
? ?d Crane	Mt. Pleasant	178 70		5 38	4 00	180 08
L. ??n Dill	Mt. Ple ?ant	127 78		1 90		129 68
Reuben Ellis	Mt. Pl ?ant	107 97		3 23	2 00	109 20
H. J. Cushing	Mt. Pl ?ant	105 69		3 17	2 00	106 86
Harold B. Vesper	Mt. Pl ?ant	100 27		3 01	2 00	101 28

ᴇY TRUST FUNDS—Contin ᴇd

Bequest	Cemetery	Balance Jan. 1, 1937	Deposited During 1937	ᴵne	ᴾd	Balance Dec. 31, 1937
ᴇᴇe H. Turner	Mt. ᴇᴀt	314 36		8 21	6 00	316 57
ᴇn Lot No. 249	Mt. ᴇᴀt	105 74		3 17	2 00	106 91
Henry D. ᵣ ᴇth	Mt. Pleasant		100 00			100 00
Francis Soule	Mt. ᴇᴀt		100 00			DO 00
ᴇge T. ᴇe	Mt. ᴇᴀt	314 49		9 49	6 00	317 98
ᴇp	Mt. Pᴀnt	210 04		3 15		213 19
ᴇs A. Burrell	Mt. ᴇᴀt	101 36		3 04	2 00	102 40
ᴊn Sᴀd	Mt. ᴇᴀt	76 68		2 29	2 00	76 97
Emma M. ᴇy	Mt. ᴇᴀt	102 55		3 09	2 00	103 64
L. Wilfred ᴇe	Mt. Pᴀnt	104 08		3 13	3 00	104 21
Mary H. Breck	Mt. ᴇᴀt	104 34		3 13	2 00	105 47
ᴇe Linton	Mt. Pleasant	104 53		3 15	2 00	105 68
Thompson-Whiting	ᵥ ᴘᴀd	120 43		1 80	2 25	119 98
J. W. ᴇᴀC. Hol aᴇt	ᵥ ᴘᴀd	336 06		5 04	4 50	336 60
ᴇᴅd	ᵥ ᴘᴀd	1 00		25		100 25
Adna Burrell	ᵥ ᴘᴀd	127 16		1 90	2 25	126 81
Flora ᴇᴇh	ᵥ ᴘᴀd	50 00		75	75	50 0
ᴇn W. Harris	ᵥ ᴘᴀd	129 92		1 93	2 25	129 60
aᴇer Torrey	ᵥ ᴘᴀd	123 02		1 84	2 25	122 61
N. A. Beal	ᴹew od	101 27		1 51	2 78	DO 0

CEMETERY TRUST FUNDS—Continued

Bequest	Cemetery	Balance Jan. 1 1937	Deposited During 1937	Income	Expended	Balance Dec. 31, 1937
Hopkins-Damon	Maplewood	103 72		1 54	4 25	101 01
David J. Raz	Mpl wd	50 23		75	98	50 00
Henrietta Son	wd	555 48		8 32	14 50	549 30
William T. Mr	Mpl wd	107 29		1 60	4 25	104 64
M Watt	wd		100 00			100 00
Sdd	wd		166 48			166 48
Albert Hns	wd	52 04		78	2 25	50 57
Aah Davis	wd	332 63		4 98	3 00	61
Mrs. Hge Whiting	wd	118 20		1 77	2 25	17 72
D. W. aObs	wd	161 78		2 41	2 25	61 94
Aly Mg	wd	70 99		1 05	2 25	69 79
Nathaniel Phillips	wd	160 45		2 40	3 00	59 85
Isaac Fn	wd	100 46		1 50	1 96	1 0 00
Henry A. Baker	Spring He	100 10		3 01	3 00	1 0 11
Arms A. Reed	Spring He	152 24		4 57	5 50	51 31
Je Doane	Spring Lake	104 48		3 15	4 00	103 63
Zenas Jenkins	Spring Re	112 75		3 39	4 00	112 14
Irving ld	Spring Lake	152 15		4 59	4 00	52 74
ph J. Burgess	Spring Lake	125 00		3 76	3 00	25 76

CEMETERY TRUST FUNDS—Contiued

Bequest	Cemetery	Balance Jan. 1. 1937	Deposited during 1937	Income	Expended	Balance Dec. 31, 1937
Edbridge Payne	Mill Hill	326 20		9 85	5 00	331 05
Betsey Battles	Beal	254 97		3 61	10 0	248 78
William J. Hayden	Ass Mai	101 95		3 05		105 00

Auditor's Report

We have examined the books of the various departments of the Town of Rockland, including the town clerk, treasurer, tax collector, school and water departments, and sealer of weights and measures, and have found them to be correct. The treasurer's balance has been reconciled with the bank statements.

Respectfully submitted,

H. C. SMITH, Chairman
LEO E. DOWNEY,
C. ELMER ASKLUND

Annual Report
of the
SCHOOL DEPARTMENT
of the

Town of Rockland

For the Year Ending December 31, 1937

SCHOOL CALENDAR 1938

WINTER TERM

Begins Monday, January 3, 1938, seven weeks; ends Friday, February 18, 1938.

SPRING TERM

Begins Monday, February 28, 1938, seven weeks; ends Thursday, April 14, 1938.

SUMMER TERM

Begins Monday, April 25, 1938, nine weeks; ends Wednesday, June 22, 1938. Teachers return Thursday and Friday, June 23 and 24 for year-end duties and organization work.

FALL TERM

Begins Wednesday, September 7, 1938, sixteen weeks; ends Friday, December 23, 1938.

HOLIDAYS

April 15, 1938, Good Friday.
May 30, 1938, Memorial Day.
October 12, 1938, Columbus Day.
October 28, 1938, Teachers' Convention.
November 11, 1938, Armistice Day.
November 23, 1938, Schools close at noon for remainder of week, Thanksgiving Recess.

SIGNALS FOR NO SESSIONS OF SCHOOL
Fire Station Siren
A. M.
7:30—22 repeated: No session of High School.
8:15—22 repeated: No forenoon session for first six grades.

P. M.

12:45—22 repeated: No afternoon session for first six
      grades.

The "No School Signal" is used only in extremely
stormy weather. The school bus starts on its first trip
in the morning ten minutes after seven o'clock in order
to collect the children in time for the opening of high
school at 8:30 A. M. and the elementary schools at 9:00
A. M. Unless the signal is used before 7:00 o'clock many
of the children are already on their way by bus. It is very
difficult to determine weather conditions for the day as
early as seven o'clock except in cases of severe storms.

People in the outskirts of our town often cannot hear
the signal, in which case children appearing in school
are disappointed to learn that they must cover the long
distance back to their homes, while they may be chilled
or wet.

We wish each parent to use his or her best judgment
as to whether or not the weather is auspicious for sending their children to school. No penalty is inflicted upon
any child for non-attendance on account of severe
weather.

Since our teachers are in school and many of the
pupils do not hear the signal, it seems wise to use the
time to good advantage in warm buildings, whereas during days when the signal may be used many children are
out of doors, becoming wet and contracting colds.

Is it not wiser to have them in warm school rooms
under supervision, receiving beneficial instruction?

R. STEWART ESTEN,

Superintendent of Schools

January 1, 1938

School Directory 1937-1938

SCHOOL COMMITTEE

E. STUART WOODWARD, Chairman 385 Market Street
    Tel. 115-W. Term expires March, 1938

MISS M. AGNES KELLEHER   297 Howard Street
    Tel. 1484-W Term expires March, 1938

MRS. HELEN M. HAYDEN   429 Liberty Street
    Tel. 454-R. Term expires March, 1939

DR. WILLIAM A. LOUD   327 Salem Street
    Tel. 430. Term expires March, 1940

DR. BENJAMIN LELYVELD   320A Union Street
    Tel. 16-W. Term expires March, 1940

SUPERINTENDENT OF SCHOOLS

R. STEWART ESTEN   111 Payson Avenue
    Office Tel. 1540   Residence Tel. 1250
Office hours every school day from 8:30 to 9:00 A. M. on
Wednesday evenings from 7:00 to 8:00 o'clock.

SCHOOL DEPARTMENT SECRETARY

HARRIET E. GELINAS   241 Myrtle Street
    Office Tel. 1540. Residence Tel. 1244

PRINCIPAL OF HIGH SCHOOL

GEORGE A. J. FROBERGER   28 Exchange Street
    Office Tel. 1540   Residence Tel. 1302-W
Office hours every school day from 8 to 9 A. M., Mondays
and Thursdays from 3 to 4 P. M., and Wednesday evenings from 7 to 8 o'clock.

ATTENDANCE OFFICER AND SCHOOL NURSE

LOUISE A. CONSIDINE   69 Webster Street
                Office Tel. 1540
Office hours at the high school every school day from
8:30 to 9:30 A. M.

SCHOOL PHYSICIANS

JOSEPH H. DUNN, M. D.   319 Union Street
        Office Tel. 836-W   Residence Tel. 836-R
        Office Hours: 2 to 3 and 7 to 8 P. M.

JOSEPH FRAME, M. D.   144 Webster Street
                Office Tel. 38-W
        Office Hours: 12:30 to 2 and 6:30 to 8 P. M.

DENTAL HYGIENIST

EVELYN DELORY   323 Market Street
Office hours at the McKinley School daily when schools
    are in session from 9:00 A. M. to 12 M., and from 1:30
    to 3:30 P. M.

Digest of Laws and Regulations Relating to
School Attendance

Children who are five years and six months of age by
the opening of school in September 1938 shall be admitted
to the first grade.   Those who become five years of age
after March 1, 1938, may be admitted after passing a satisfactory mental examination.

Children, otherwise eligible to enter school in September for the first time, are required by law to present at
time of entrance either a certificate of vaccinaton or a
certificate of unfitness for vaccination. The school committee and board of health have ruled that certificates of
unfitness for vaccination must be renewed each year.

Children coming into the school system from other places, whether at the opening of the year in September or during the school year, will be required to produce satisfactory evidence regarding vaccination.

Pupils desiring to enter the first grade must enroll on or before October 1. Otherwise they will not be admitted.

The school hours for the first grade children, shall be from 9 until 11:30 A. M. The afternoon session shall correspond with other grades, 1:30 P. M. until 3:30 P. M. The ruling, took effect March 6, 1933. An exception is made during the winter months when the afternoon session of the elementary schools concludes at 3:15 P. M.

Pupils who have been absent from school on account of contagious disease must secure a permit from a school physician before re-entering. In cases of doubt, or in cases where there exists a suspicion of contagion, the parents should advise, and the teachers should require that the pupils consult the school nurse, who may refer the case to a school physician for further examination.

Any pupil having a contagious disease or showing symptoms of such a disease may be temporarily excluded from school by the teacher on her own initiative or at the direction of the school nurse or school physician.

Sickness is the only legal excuse for absence from school.

All children between the ages of fourteen and sixteen years must be in school unless they are actually employed under the authority of an employment certificate, a home permit or a special certificate permitting farm or domestic employment.

Any pupil who habitually violates rules of the schools,

or otherwise seriously interferes with the proper and orderly operation of the school which he attends, may be temporarily excluded by the teacher or the superintendent of schools or may be permanently expelled by the school committee.

Pupils under seven years of age or over sixteen who elect to attend school must conform to the same rules and regulations as those pupils who are within the compulsory age—from seven to fourteen.

Teachers may require a written excuse signed by a parent or guardian covering any case of absence, tardiness or dismissal.

Whenever a pupil is suspended by a teacher or principal, for any cause for any length of time, an immediate report must be made to the superintendent's office.

Those pupils attending the first eight grades will be transported to and from school if they live in the town of Rockland and reside more than one mile and a quarter from the school where they are authorized to attend.

Those pupils attending the high school, grades nine to twelve, inclusive, will be transported to and from school if they live in the town of Rockland and reside more than two miles from the high school.

Recent Rulings Pertaining to Our Schools

There shall be a Supervisor of Buildings who shall represent the School Committee in charge of all school buildings when they are used by outside organizations (other than school organizations.)

The Supervisor's duties shall be to prevent any damage to school property and to be responsible for proper conduct in and on school property. (Prevent smoking, drinking and unbecoming conduct in the buildings).

The organization using the building shall be responsible for the expense of such a supervisor.

The supervisor shall receive his instructions from the Superintendent of Schools.

The supervisor shall receive remuneration at the rate of $2.50 until 10:30 P. M., $4.00 if the function continues until 11:30 P. M.; $5.00 after 11:30 P. M.; 75c per hour will be the charge for the building if used before 6:00 P. M. This ruling took effect December 1, 1934.

All work performed by the School Committee shall be awarded to native born citizens, naturalized citizens, or those who have taken out their first naturalization papers.

The tuition for pupils whose parents reside out of town and wishing to attend the Rockland Schools shall be established as follows: Senior High, $100 per year; Junior High $80; elementary grades, $60.

Post-Graduates who are admitted to the Rockland High School September 4, 1935 or thereafter, shall take a minimum of twenty hours of work per week; shall be satisfactory in conduct; shall be regular in full day's attendance and maintain satisfactory averages in all subjects.

Rulings Regarding Payment of Salaries to Teachers

The teachers of the Rockland Schools shall receive their salaries bi-weekly after two weeks of actual class room teaching — except through July and August when payments shall be made not later than the 15th of each month.

That for each day's absence with the exception of death in the immediate family 1/200 of the yearly salary shall be deducted.

That beginning November 16, 1937, all teachers who are absent on account of illness shall receive the difference between the substitute's pay or its equivalent and the teacher's regular pay.

That a teacher shall receive full pay for five calendar days for death in immediate family. "Immediate" family includes parents, wife, husband, brother, sister or children.

That a teacher absent for more than one half (½) of a session shall lose pay for that entire session.

Visiting schools authorized by the Superintendent of Schools or work pertaining to the schools which has been assisgned by the Superintendent may be allowed without loss of salary.

The word "Teacher" in the above ruling applies to Principals, Special Teachers and all class room teachers excepting the Principal of the Junior Senior High school and the Superintendent of Schools.

REPORT OF ROCKLAND SCHOOL COMMITTEE

To the Citizens of Rockland:

The School Committee herewith submits its annual report for the year 1937.

It has been the aim of the committee to administer the schools of Rockland to the best of their knowledge and judgment in matters of education and finance so that the children will receive the best education possible for the money expended.

We believe that the educational opportunities offered and the results accomplished compare favorably with those in other towns of the same size. This is due large-ly to the keen interest and cooperation of the Superinten-dent of Schools, teachers, and other school employees in promoting the welfare and maintaining the efficiency of our schools.

The town to have a completely modernized system should as soon as possible remedy the situation whereby we still have three grades to a teacher. The results of grade tests by the Superintendent every year show that it is utterly impossible to do justice to the pupils un-der such conditions.

The salary schedule needs adjustment upward because of the 10% cut put into operation several years ago, and it is the hope of the committee that our appropriation this year will allow for this.

The committee is extremely grateful to all the organ-izations and citizens who in any way have contributed in time, effort and money that many pupils might benefit from activities which normal appropriations do not al-low.

For a more complete report of our administration we refer you to the reports of the Superintendent of Schools and High School Principal, and the financial statement giving a detailed account of expenditures.

WE CALL YOUR ATTENTION HEREIN PARTIC-ULARLY TO THE FACT THAT WHILE THE TOTAL APPROPRIATION FOR SCHOOLS WAS $104,420.93, REIMBURSEMENTS AMOUNTING TO $14,851.90 MADE THE NET COST TO THE TOWN FOR SCHOOLS $89,569.03.

Respectfully submitted,

E. STUART WOODWARD, Chairman
HELEN M. HAYDEN, Secretary
BENJAMIN LELYVELD,
WILLIAM A. LOUD,
M. AGNES KELLEHER

FINANCIAL STATEMENT
RESOURCES 1937

General Appropriation $104 423 00

EXPENDITURES

General Expenses	$ 5 060 55
Expense of Instruction	76 077 03
Operation and Maintenance	17 439 77
Auxiliary Agencies	5 101 10
New Equipment	742 48

Total Expenditures $104 420 93

TOWN TREASURER'S RECEIPTS ON
ACCOUNT OF SCHOOLS

State Reimbursements:

Teachers' Salaries	12 822 50
Tuition and Transportation of Wards	1 351 41
City of Boston for Tuition and Transportation of Wards	557 92
Car Ticket Refund from Lovell Bus Company	37 45
Tuition, Mrs. C. W. Scott	15 00
Materials sold in high school shop	63 27
Sale of McKinley Tubes, ashes and painting damages	4 35

Total Receipts $ 14 851 90

NET COST OF SCHOOLS TO TOWN $ 89 569 03

RENTAL OF McKINLEY HALL AND SENIOR HIGH
GYMNASIUM

Town Appropriation to offset expenses $ 100 00

Receipts (turned over
   to Town Treasurer) $ 99 50

Expenditures:

J. J. L. DeCosta	$ 30 50	
Charles Metivier	2 00	
Elmer Dunn	2 00	
Edison Electric Illuminating Co.	62 30	
Maurice Mullen	2 00	
Total Expenditures	98 80	
	————$	98 80
Balance	70————	
Unexpended Appropriation	$	1 20

APPROPRIATION TO OFFSET EXPENSE OF W. P. A. PROJECTS HOUSED AT McKINLEY SCHOOL

Appropriation		$ 400 00
Expenditures:		
Old Colony Gas Company	$ 3 33	
Edison Electric Illuminating Company	52 14	
Abington Coal Corporation	254 85	
Total Expenditures	————$	310 32
Unexpended Appropriation	$	89 68

DETAIL OF 1937 EXPENDITURES

Total Resources $104 423 00

GENERAL EXPENSES

Superintendent's Salary	$ 3 600 00
Other Administrative Expense	1 460 55

EXPENSE OF INSTRUCTION

Supervisors' Salaries	3 497 50
Principals' Salaries	7 007 25

Teachers' Salaries	59 516	78
Text Books	1 722	59
Stationery, Supplies and Miscellaneous	4 332	91

OPERATION AND MAINTENANCE

Janitors' Wages	8 044	79
Fuel	3 757	14
Miscellaneous	2 655	67
Repairs	2 982	17

AUXILIARY AGENCIES

Libraries	61	81
Health	1 953	31
Transportation	1 485	00
Sundries	1 600	98

OUTLAY

New Equipment	742	48
Total Expenditures	$104 420	93
Unexpended Balance	$	2 07

FINANCIAL STATEMENT ITEMIZED

SUPERINTENDENT OF SCHOOLS

R. Stewart Esten, Salary	$ 3 600 00

OTHER ADMINISTRATIVE EXPENSES

Bruce Publishing Company, School Board Journal	$	6 00
Louise A. Considine, mileage attendance officer		96 46
The Education Digest, subscription		3 50

The Macmillan Company, book		
for office procedure	1	23
Harriet E. Gelinas, salary	1 109	20
Elizabeth O. Studley, salary		
(substitute)	76	50
N. E. Tel. & Tel. Co., services	105	50
John R. Parker, P. M., stamped		
envelopes, stamps, cards	44	14
George T. Pascoe Company,		
office supplies	11	89
C. F. Williams & Son, Inc.,		
teachers' record cards	1	10
Wright & Potter Printing Co.,		
ledger blanks	4	16
Yawman & Erbe Mfg. Co., file guides	87	

Total	$ 1 460 55

EXPENSE OF INSTRUCTION

Supervisors' Salaries	3 497 50
Principals' Salaries	7 007 25
Teachers' Salaries	59 516 78

TEXT BOOKS

Allyn & Bacon	72 82
American Book Co.	129 43
Arlo Publishing Co.	23 56
E. E. Babb & Co.	48 60
Beckley-Cardy Co.	51 73
The Bobbs-Merrill Co.	49 23
Bureau of Publications	10 85
Burroughs Adding Machine Co.	40
Champion Publishing Co.	1 69
Character Associates, Inc.	2 00
Circle Book Co.	28 06
Clarence C. Dill	4 98
Educational Service Bureau	5 95

Ginn & Co.	342	30
Gregg Publishing Co.	10	30
Harcourt, Brace & Co., Inc.	7	53
D. C. Heath Co.	35	51
Henry Holt & Co.	2	17
Houghton Mifflin Co.	17	24
Inor Publishing Co.	1	44
Laidlaw Brothers		47
Little Brown & Co.	99	69
Longmans Green & Co.	26	78
Lyons & Carnahan	5	65
The Macmillan Co.	29	83
G. & C. Merriam Co.	8	36
Charles E. Merrill Co.	22	58
McGraw-Hill Book Co., Inc.	14	23
Newson & Co.	7	53
Noble & Noble	6	68
A. N. Palmer Co.	17	47
Public School Publishing Co.	2	50
Row, Peterson & Co.	2	57
Benj. H. Sanborn Co.	166	70
Scott, Foresman & Co.	168	11
Charles Scribner's Sons	58	50
Silver, Burdett & Company	19	73
L. W. Singer Co.	63	01
South Western Publishing Co.	37	16
O. H. Toothaker	6	00
R. W. Wagner Co.	11	00
Webster Publishing Co.	2	25
Wilcox & Follett	4	82
The John C. Winston Co.	73	24
World Book Co.	21	94
Total	1 722	59

SUPPLIES

American Education Press, tests	4	50

American Type Founders Sales
  Corp., shop supplies   16 30
Emil Ascher, Inc., orchestra music   96
Automatic Pencil Sharpener Co.,
  pencil sharpeners   3 57
E. E. Babb & Co., Inc., schoolroom
  supplies   380 22
Babson Institute, 2 frames for posters   3 70
Beaudette & Co., multistamp stencils   2 05
Behr-Manning, sandpaper for shop   3 47
The Boston Music Co., music   27 88
B. U. School of Education,
  film service   5 00
B. U. School of Education,
  arithmetic tests   40
Broadhead Garrett Co., lumber for shop 84 66
Bureau of Publications, tests   10 10
Burroughs Adding Machine Co.,
  paper rolls   1 90
Cambosco Scientific Co., science
  supplies   3 08
Central Scientific Co., science supplies 69 21
John S. Cheever Co.,
  Schoolroom supplies   934 83
Denoyer-Geppert Company, maps   22 99
A. B. Dick Co., stencils and ink   5 40
Dowling School Supply Co., paper   39 81
Eagle Ink Co., ink   3 76
Educational Test Bureau, tests   3 77
Emerson and Company, ink   1 35
Erie County Trust Co., enrolment
  to World Letters   20 05
Gledhill Bros., pen points   28 87
Gregg Publishing Co., notebooks
  and tests   22 06
J. L. Hammett Co.,
  schoolroom supplies   507 93
Iroquois Publishing Co., tests   4 54

Kee Lox Mfg. Co., carbon paper	25 00
Keuffel & Esser Co., drawing sets	2 59
Madeline Lannin, Kindergarten materials	29 75
Levison & Blythe Mfg Co., hektograph work books	12 71
John E. Linnehan, special class supplies	4 00
Edward L. Megill Co., shop gauge pins	3 68
Milton Bradley Co., schoolroom supplies	802 22
H. B. McArdle, schoolroom supplies	97 67
Osgood Globe Corp., shop materials	6 77
Horace Partridge Co., balls for physical education	2 53
George T. Pascoe Co., cards, folders	60 08
A. S. Peterson, protractors, tags, gummed labels	3 32
Phillips Paper Co., paper	17 19
A. I. Randall, Inc., stock for printing	6 10
E. P. Reed Lumber Co., dowels for shop work	12 60
Republic Machinery Sales Corp., shop materials	30 30
J. A. Rice Co., sewing supplies	4 97
Rockland Coal & Grain Co., shop materials	32 75
Rockland Hardware & Paint Co., shop supplies	8 72
Rockland High School Cafeteria, food classes	47 48
Rome Brothers, shop supplies	2 59
M. M. Ross Co., paper	27 00
Royal Typewriter Co., Replacing typewriters and ribbons	446 00
Sleight Metallic Ink Co., ink	1 49
L. C. Smith & Corona Typewriter, Inc., Replacing typewriters and ribbons	141 00

South Western Publishing Co.,
accounting material 107 69
Webster Publishing Co., plan books
arithmetic tablets 28 40
Wensell & Company, speedograph roll 6 15
Guy M. Wilson, arithmetic tests 30
Henry J. Winde Co., shop supplies 33 59
Henry S. Wolkins, poster paints
and supplies 35 99
World Book Co., tests 19 62
John H. Wyatt Co., mimeograph
stencils and paper 60 30

Total 4 332 91

JANITORS' WAGES

Elmer Dunn, Junior-Senior High 1 620 00
Charles Metivier,
Junior-Senior High 1 350 00
Joseph DeCosta, McKinley 1 305 00
Mary Davis, McKinley School 360 00
Andrew Leck, Jefferson 950 00
Frank Hammond, Gleason and
Webster 428 00
Mrs. Frank Hammond, Gleason
and Webster 172 00
Frank Curtis, Webster and Lincoln 566 64
Thomas Gallagher, Lincoln 666 72
Ardelle Cushing, Market Street 350 00
Elizabeth Casey, Central Street 180 00
Joseph Thibeault, helper at McKinley 36 00
Maurice Mullen, helper at McKinley 60 43

Total 8 044 79

FUEL

Abington Coal Corporation, coal $3 013 29

Charles T. Leavitt, Inc., coal	64	51
Lot Phillips & Co., Corp., wood	12	00
Roderick MacKenzie, wood	61	75
Rockland Coal & Grain Co., coal	605	59
Total	3 757	14

MISCELLANEOUS OPERATING EXPENSES

Atlantic Wire and Iron Works Inc., wire guards	9	00
Boston Plate & Window Glass Co., janitors' supplies	13	18
Brockton Public Market, cleaning materials	2	60
Commonwealth Lock Co., sweeping compound	64	80
Arthur M. Condon, cleaning powder	22	75
P. & F. Corbin Co., keys		60
Cutter, Wood & Sanderson Co., janitors' supplies	5	45
Dominic DelPrete, removal of garbage at McKinley	2	50
Ralph Derby, keys	2	80
C. B. Dolge Co., janitors' supplies	90	50
H. J. Dowd Co., Inc., sweeping material	7	50
Edison Electric Illuminating Co., service	1 211	50
The Floor Treatment Co., janitors' supplies	48	75
L. M. Glover Co., Inc., janitors' supplies	253	85
Goodco Sanitary Products, janitors' supplies	18	00
Frank Hammond, cleaning high school cesspool	1	00
A. C. Horn Co., floor wax	84	90
William M. Horner, janitors' supplies	63	38

Geo. T. Johnson Co., paper towels   75 85
Edwin P. Kershaw, dust cloths   14 50
John Lamb, rock salt   1 85
Market St. Garage, gas for cleaning
    printing press   73
Masury-Young Company, floor oils,
    wax   115 06
Old Colony Gas Co., service   41 99
Rockland Hardware & Paint Co., shovel   65
Rockland Water Department, service   280 44
Rome Brothers, janitors' supplies   80 50
L. Sonneborn Sons, Inc., janitors'
    supplies   22 50
Sphinx Chair Glide Co., chair glides   4 50
State Prison Colony, janitors' brushes   37 00
Taunton Lumber Co., floor wax   21 60
George V. Tyler, Pumping out
    cesspool   36 00
Yale & Town Mfg. Co., keys   73
Young Broom Co., Inc. janitor's
    supplies   18 71

Total   2 655 67

REPAIRS

Howard K. Alden, engineering
    service high school building $ 70 00
H. H. Arnold Co., nuts, screws,
    etc., for repairs   8 13
Atlantic Flag Pole Co., 40' halyard   1 36
Automatic Pencil Sharpener Co.,
    sharpeners repaired   2 80
E. E. Babb Co., Inc., replacing
    door holders   8 69
Bailey Motor Sales, welding printing
    machine frame   2 00
Chester Banden, McKinley boiler
    and pipe repairs   104 57

The Barrett Co., tarvia for Lincoln
school yard   395 84
The Bates Mfg. Co., stapler repaired   1 64
Thomas Bosotck and Sons, Printing
press repairs   10 00
Boston Plate & Window Glass Co., glass   38 16
Burroughs Adding Machine Co.,
service contract   5 00
John Campbel, Labor at Lincoln yard   4 00
Edward Casey, labor at Lincoln yard   13 50
Arthur Casey, labor at Lincoln yard   12 00
Robert Casey, labor at Lincoln yard   20 25
Frank Cifello, labor at Lincoln yard   6 75
William S. Clemens, H. S.
Piano casters   8 00
William Condon, labor at Lincoln yard   27 75
P. & F. Corbin, door checks repaired   12 72
Leo Cull, labor at Lincoln yard   31 89
The Albert Culver Co., cement   1 30
O. R. Cummings, ceiling repaired   9 25
Damon Electric, electrical repairs   12 76
Burrill Dill, labor at Lincoln yard   4 50
Luther O. Draper Shade Co., cord   7 93
J. P. Eustis Mfg. Co., replacing mirrors
high school toilets   15 81
Charles Fucillo, labor at Lincoln yard   27 00
Melvin Gay, use of roller for
Lincoln yard   9 00
Hall and Torrey, misc. repairs   97 15
Frank Hammond, setting glass   2 00
George W. S. Hyde, repairing tools   40
International Engineering Works, Inc.,
McKinley boilers   104 80
Johnson Service Co., heating system
repairs at H. S.   13 98
J. E. Kemp, sharpening saws   3 60
Locke, Stevens & Sanitas Co.,
12 gaskets   1 85

Mass. Dept. of Ed. Div. of Blind,
repairing and tuning pianos   31 00
J. S. McCallum, Plumbing repairs   193 13
Paul McDonnell, labor at Lincoln yard 20 25
Patrick McKenna, labor at Lincoln
yard   18 00
Roderick MacKenzie, Sand for
Lincoln yard   10 00
National Foundry, Inc., grates repaired   9 92
Osgood Globe Corp., printing
press repairs   7 85
Forrest L. Partch, electrical repairs   17 10
Pettingell-Andrews Co., replacing
light units at McKinley   57 60
Reed Mfg. Co., shop equipment
repaired   8 32
Robinson & Co., Waterproofing work
at High school   300 00
Rockland Coal & Grain Co.,
materials for repairs   48 73
Rockland Hardware & Paint Co.
materials for repairs   29 80
Rockland Welding and Engineering Co.,
repairing floor washer   3 50
Harry L. Rome, replacing window
shades   17 00
Rome Bros., materials for repairs,
paint etc   430 12
Edwin Schutt, misc. repairs in
school buildings   415 11
Sphinx Chair Glide Co.,
chair glides replaced   11 40
Standard Electric Time Co., clock repairs,
replacing batteries and rectifier   160 36
William Thorpe, electrical repairs   86 84
Underwood Elliot Fisher Co.,
repairing typewriters   5 26

John H. Wyatt Co., repairing
typewriters   4 50

Total   2 982 17

LIBRARIES

Frontier Press Co., copy of
Lincoln Library   15 50
J. L. Hammett Co., library books for
elementary schools   3 27
Albert Najarian, magazine subscrip-
tions for high school library   12 70
Noble & Noble, book   1 71
R. W. Wagner, books   8 93
Yawman, Erbe Mfg. Co., files   19 70

Total   61 81

HEALTH

Bemis Drug Co., supplies   39 37
James W. Brine Co., Inc., physical
education supplies   25 39
Louise A. Considine, mileage   96 48
Fred S. Delay, supplies   27 58
National Education Association, charts   1 34
Plymouth Cty. Health Association,
audiometer rental   2 00
Thomas W. Reed, applicators and
tongue depressors   13 49
Rockland New System Laundry, blankets
laundered   41
Rockland Pharmacy, supplies   4 25
Louise A. Considine, salary   1 393 00
Joseph H. Dunn, M. D., salary   175 00
Joseph Frame, M. D., salary   175 00

Total   1 953 31

TRANSPORTATION

John J. Dwyer, transportation of pupils   1 485 00

SUNDRIES

Ames Radio Service, amplifiers installed for graduation	15	00
The Austin Print, printing	3	50
Babson Institute, poster service	19	55
Buck Printing Co., High School reception tickets	6	62
Phillip S. Collins, insurance premium	319	20
Commissioner of Public Safety, boiler inspection	5	00
The Douglas Print, printing school reports	60	00
J. L. Hammett Co., diploma covers and engrossing diplomas	76	39
Howland's Insurance Office, insurance premium	155	68
Jenkins & Simmons Express, expressage	20	39
Edward A. Lincoln, binet examinations for 1st grade entrance	102	00
Lindstrom & Poole Trans. Co., expressage		50
Maurice Mullen, police work	5	00
Murray Bros., rebinding books	153	10
Albert Najarian, census enumeration	68	00
Amos A. Phelps, insurance premiums	428	29
Pro Merito Society, pins	19	50
A. I. Randall, Inc., printing	70	50
Rockland Standard, advertising	4	00
Rockland Transportation Co., Inc., expressage	9	72
Warren Wheeler, printing	22	95
Warren B. Woodward, insurance premium	36	54

Total   1 600 98

NEW EQUIPMENT

The Arrow System, mats for gym	50	00
Atlantic Wire & Iron Works, Inc.,		
wire guards	3	20
E. E. Babb & Co., Inc., 12		
orchestra chairs	31	20
J. L. Hammett Co., desk and chair	21	30
Massachusetts Reformatory, stool	2	00
Milton Bradley Co., 2 work		
benches for shop	102	00
Narragansett Machine Co., gym		
equipment	199	50
Forrest L. Partch, wiring H. S. stage	68	00
Rockland Coal & Grain Co., cabinet		
for McKinley School	15	28
Security Fence Company, Fence at		
Webster Street School	250	00
Total	742	48

REPORT OF SUPERINTENDENT OF SCHOOLS

To the School Committee of Rockland:

The ninth annual report of my work as Superintendent of Schools is submitted herewith:

Realizing the financial stress through which Rockland has been passing the past six years or more, an honest attempt has been made to cut the cost of our education to the minimum without reducing the efficiency below standard. It is gratifying to know that we ranked seventy-first out of eighty-three towns in our group in the cost per pupil for education. This rating is reported by the Massachusetts State Department of Education as of November 1937. The cost per pupil in Rockland is $72.97.

In several specific ways, stated later herein it will be noticed that we definitely are striving to increase the efficiency of our teaching staff and the character and scholarship of the children under our care and instruction.

I am reporting the accomplishments of the year as concisely as is possible in an effort to eliminate unnecessary printing expense.

OMISSION OF REPORTS

We are continuing to follow the suggestion of the Finance Committee to print only the Superintendent's report to the School Committee and the high school principal's report to the Superintendent along with statistical data that is essential. I belive that while a finian-cial statement should be recorded, a detailed account recording all the checks drawn on the School Department is an unnecessary printing expense. Other towns and cities rarely give space to this printing in their reports. This omission is a measure of economy.

COURSES OF STUDY

Our Arithmetic Course in the elementary schools which has been revised by a teachers committee was adopted and became effective September 8, 1937. We have endeavored in this to simplify the arithmetic in the primary grades as the mechanics of reading is the crux of the program in the first three grades. The more difficult operations of division for example are scheduled for the fourth and fifth grades. There has been for some time in educational thought the principle established that we should not overcrowd our pupils with book learning in the primary grades as reading must form the core of the work.

DEVELOPMENT OF PROJECTS

We are holding professional meetings periodically for the teachers and this year we have discussed the "Superior Teacher." I have presented four phases, Personal Equipment, Professional Equipment, Professional Technique, and Outcomes in Terms of Pupil Growth. At our last meeting five of our teachers offered their views on the Superior Teacher. It is hoped a Code will be worked out that each teacher may have one to assist him in his teaching. Following our meetings the Rockland Teachers' Association holds its sessions. The activities of the Club have tended to bring the members together socially through common interests and to develop an esprit de corps which is so desirable in any organization. The sports program has tended to weld a strong unit for co-operation and service.

We are very much interested in promoting Character Training and Safety and to that end I have appointed two committees of elementary teachers to prepare reports which will be used in our teaching at a later date.

It is indeed gratifying to know that our high school is

given an A rating by the Massachusetts State Board of Education and that we have the privilege of sending our graduates to New England Colleges without examination if they have maintained certificate grade of 85% for the four years in high school. The students who are now attending the State and Liberal Arts Colleges are doing a fine grade of work. We, therefore, have reason to approve the training these boys and girls are receiving under the efficient guidance of our prinicipal and teachers. It is highly desirable that our pupils who are planning to attend institutions of higher learning should know as early as possible in their high school careers what colleges they anticipate attending in order to prepare themselves in accordance with the requirements of those institutions. I cannot urge parents too strongly to have their sons and daughters consult the principal early in their high school courses on this most important matter.

Although we have added a few much needed reference books to our library it is imperative that we improve this phase of our high school work. We are grateful to the loyal alumni who have contributed to a fund which will make possible the addition of several books to our library. With additional supervision needed in the high school for an over crowded study hall during certain periods in the day and at recess periods it is hoped that an additional teacher may be added to our staff this year. This will make possible the opening of our library during certain school periods as well as after school and will also give the additional teaching assistance and supervision which is needed.

A few years ago we enclosed a small section of our general shop for our printing department and this year a section was enclosed for a paint room. This has aided us in completing our projects. If we had additional equipment and room, an auto mechanics department would add to the effectiveness of the practical arts work.

This expansion may be warranted later if business conditions improve.

Improvement has been noticeable in our physical education department as has been evidenced by the additional issuance of certificates for good posture. The new gymnasium equipment which is spoken of elsewhere in my report will greatly improve the physical stamina of our high school pupils.

TEACHER REPLACEMENT

In February 1937 on the expiration of Miss Graves' term as substitute teacher in French, Mrs. Blanche LeRoy of Brockton was appointed substitute for the remainder of the school year. Miss Leona W. Sampson of Brockton, Mass., was elected French teacher beginning in September 1937. Miss Sampson is a graduate of Boston University with an A. M. degree in 1924 and studied at the Sorbonne, Paris, receiving a diploma avec mention in 1929. She had taught French in Massachusetts and Connecticut High school for fifteen years. The past eight years she was the French teacher in the Winchendon, Massachusetts high school.

Mr. John B. Haggerty, in charge of the Industrial Arts department of our high school resigned in June to accept a position in the Abington High school. Mr. George W. Wilson of North Adams, Mass,, was elected to fill the vacancy. Mr. Wilson graduated from the Fitchburg State Teachers' College in 1933 with the degree of B. S. in Education. The past two years he had been the director of W. P. A. Adult Education in Adams, Massachusetts.

In January 1937, Miss Evelyn Murphy of our Commercial Department secured a promotion by receiving an appointment to the Everett High school. Mrs. Marian Ray, a graduate of Boston University and a former teacher in the Commercial Department of the Brockton High school substituted for the remainder of the year.

Mr. Earl Komarin, who had substituted for Miss Rose Magadini who was studying at Boston University the past year was appointed to fill the vacancy caused by the resignation of Miss Evelyn Murphy.

During the summer Miss Louise Flannery resigned to be married. Her place was filled by the appointment of Miss Virginia Ford, a four year graduate of Bridgewater State Teachers' College. Miss Ford had previously taught in the Nursery School for several months.

Miss Eleanor Birch, teacher of our Special Class resigned in June to accept a more lucrative position in the Swampscott School System. Her place was filled by the appointment of Miss Isabel Philbrook of Randolph, Mass. She graduated from the Wheelock School in 1936. Miss Philbrook had pursued graduate study at the Boston School of Occupational Therapy, Boston University and at Simmons College in Social Psychology and Social Service. This past summer she took courses in Special Class Technique at the Hyannis State Teachers' College. During the summer of 1934, '35 and '36 Miss Philbrook taught the Special Class at the North Reading Sanatorium.

Miss Margaret Shortall teacher of grade 5 in the McKinley School resigned in October to be married. Mr. John Ryan of Rockland a graduate of Boston College and State Teachers' College at Bridgewater was appointed to fill the vacancy.

Miss Dorothy Ellershaw, teacher of grades 3 and 4 at the Gleason School resigned to be married. Her place was taken by Miss Helen Kovalchuk who was transferred from the Central Street School. The vacancy in that building was filled by the appointment of Miss Alice Murrill of Rockland who had taught for several months in the Nursery School. Miss Murrill graduated from the State Teachers' College at Bridgewater in 1936 with a B. S. degree in Education.

WORKS PROGRESS ADMINISTRATION ACT AS IT AFFECTS SCHOOLS

Our department has continued its plan to cooperate with the town officials in providing suitable quarters for the Sewing and the Recreation projects of the W. P. A. The sewing project is housed on the third floor of the McKinley School and the Recreation work is carried on in the gymnasium.

The sewing project has a regular weekly schedule whereas the Recreation work is carried on during the fall, winter and spring months in the building when weather conditions are not suitable for out door games. The citizens of the town in their March meeting raised and appropriated a sum of money to help defray the additional expense of opening the building, that these projects might continue.

We have availed ourselves of the opportunity of the National Youth Administration as it operates in schools and colleges throughout the U. S. Boys and girls 16 years of age and over whose parents are on low income may apply for this financial help. Our quota in Rockland since the opening of schools in September is set at $66.00 per month. At present we have eleven who are receiving this financial aid of $6.00 per month for which they render twenty hours of services to the schools. The assistance rendered is clerical or janitor service. The money is given the recipients to assist them in paying for school lunches or to purchase necessary clothing in order to continue their attendance in high school.

NURSERY SCHOOL

The unit of the Nursery School authorized by the Works Progress Administration has continued to operate at the McKinley School the past year with two teachers and a cook employed. There have been several changes in the teaching personnel this year. The teachers have been appointed to regular positions. The unit accommodates the children of parents who are on W. P. A. rolls or those with low income. We have had 57 enrolled with an average attendance of 35. The session of the school is from 9:15 A. M. until 2:00 P. M. with a noon luncheon. This systematic training and care of children by efficient instructors serve this community well.

SCHOOL BUILDINGS AND GROUNDS

Junior-Senior High

The redecoration of the walls and ceilings of the building has been completed as a W. P. A. project. It is extremely unfortunate that leaks in the walls of the building have caused damages to both walls and curtains. It will be necessary yearly to replace some of the shades which are badly water stained and in some cases rotten. The School Committee, very much alarmed over the situation, engaged the services of a consulting engineer who submitted a detailed report after careful inspections of the walls of the high school. A portion of his report follows: "The masonry walls of your building were laid up with a cement mortar which apparently contained a relatively large percentage of sand to its content of cement and the joints in consequence present a rather porous surface to the weather. The brick, which was selected for its wide variation in color, shows a corresponding variation in density, the darker brick being dense, hard, and non-porous, while the lighter colored brick are porous, absorbent, and easy to fracture. During the first two or three years after completion of the construction contract, the wall developed many shrinkage cracks and the open joints between the window frames and the brick work permitted considerable moisture to enter the walls. This accounts for the severe soaponification that occurred in the plastered rooms in the first years of occupancy.

"As you probably know, there are two methods of waterproofing masonry walls. One is to examine all joints, cut out and repoint those that may be defective and eliminate all shrinkage cracks by cutting and repointing or by filling with a thin cement grout brushed-over the surface and helped by capillary attraction to enter those troublesome shrinkage cracks. The other method is to cut out and repoint all defective joints and to coat the entire surface with a waterproofing material to make the masonry impervious to water. The effectiveness of this method depends on the liquids used and the care displayed in their application.

"Some contractors use a wax product which slowly evaporates and loses its affinity in two or three years. Others use chemical products which are permanent and which enter the pores of the brick and mortar, sealing up the shrinkage cracks and densifying the whole surface permanently. The first method is usually effective on walls laid up of non-porous brick with reasonably dense mortar joints. Your building does not come under this classification and consequently some seepage is still taking place during the stormy weather with resulting soaponification of your plaster walls in areas where the outside brickwork is most porous. I believe that the second method would have been entirely successful on your building and I would recommend that you try this method out on the southerly wall of the front wing facing the baseball stands where seepage conditions are most serious."

The committee after careful deliberation of this report and realizing the increased damages to the building with delay in action voted to make this trial demonstration. Since this work was completed that southerly end of the building is practically water tight. It seems imperative that other portions of the building should be similarly treated without undue delay in order to save the interior walls and to reduce the damages to the building.

, No work has been done to date to improve the present drainage system for the high school in accordance with the plans as outlined by the Special Committee appointed by the town at its March meeting in 1936. I understand the special committee has prepared a plan but the work has not been started. It is desirable that this work be done to prevent sewage. odors from entering the building and to prevent the hacking of water into our gymnasium. We are fortunate that these conditions have not prevailed the past two years.

The mastic floors in the corridors and toilets are constantly in need of repairs. This type of floor is less expensive to install but more expensive to maintain than other types of flooring. Our janitors have repaired these floors but it will be necessary to have a major job done this year by having several layers of the mastic replaced as the floors are down to the cement in several places. The gravel walks and drives to the building, if covered with a hard surface will prevent tracking our floors with dirt and gravel and thus prolong the life of the mastic corridors as well as the maple floors in classrooms.

It will be necessary this year to replace several of the large exit doors in the building that are beyond further repair. These doors were large, heavy doors apparently not made of seasoned lumber and not in accordance with the best specifications where weathering plays such an important part in the life of the doors.

The acoustic properties of our auditorium are very poor so that until we are able to install absorbent material in the walls and ceilings an amplifier should be added to our equipment.

For the past ten years we have had no equipment in our gymnasium for our physical education classes and this condition has not promoted the efficiency of this department. This year we have secured a horizontal and vaulting bar, climbing appartaus and parallel bars which will be used by all of the boys and girls in the high school.

For several years the reports from the instructor of our manual training classes indicated the inadequacy of our benches for class work and until this year it has been impossible to add to that equipment. We now have two double manual training benches which will accommodate four students. Others should be added as soon as possible. As I previously suggested, our single printing press is very old and not in good repair and should be replaced with another machine in order to continue our class instruction in printing.

It is earnestly hoped that the new track which has been installed in Memorial Park will be made usable so that our track team will have the use of it. I refer you to the principal's report on this matter.

Again I wish to state that our building will be much more effectively heated when oil units or a stoker can be installed in the boilers. The heat will be much more constant. With the installation of oil heat we shall release the services of a janitor at least half time. Since 1931 we have been working with one less janitor in this building and with a school this size an additional man is needed.

McKinley School

The drainage of the school yard continues to be a problem and probably before it is completely solved major expenditure will need to be made. The topography of the land is such that the yard receives the draining of several properties on Belmont Street. It has been necessary the past year to have the liquid pumped out of the cesspools because of an overflow. At present we have the additional W. P. A. projects, Nursery Unit, Sewing and Recreation projects housed in the building, making additional sewage.

As soon as funds are available the cement walks at the north and south ends of the building should be repaired and the cement and brick work of building repointed.

Roof repairs will be necessary to prevent leaks which are appearing from time to time. Corrosion of the water pipe system in the building will necessitate replacement of pipes. Lighting conditions in this building are inadequate so the School Commttee made a sample installation of a modern lighting system in the room most poorly illuminated and much to their satisfaction great improvement has resulted in this installation. The lighting in several rooms of the elementary buildings should be improved as soon as possible. I would suggest that two or three rooms be improved yearly until the work is completed.

Lincoln

The school yard has been greatly improved by having it hard surfaced. The building is much cleaner as a result Minor repairs have been made in the plumbing and heating apparatus of the building. Because of the age of the present boilers it will be a matter of a short time before replacements will be necessary.

The walk on Howard Street adjoining the school property should be constructed as soon as possible and a cement curb on the southeast side of the property would prevent drainage on the land of Franklin Avenue residents.

Badly grooved stairway floors have been replaced to make them safe. Window ventilators and door stops have been installed in some of the rooms.

Jefferson

The basement doors have been re-enforced with metal gratings. Because of the secluded location of the building, many panes of glass have been broken in the doors and windows. Since the installation of the sewage pump in the buildings, the drainage has been greatly improved.

Webster Street

Upon the completion of the new road on Webster Street the safety of the children at the building was endangered. After careful consideration by the Committee it was decided to install a five foot wire fence on the Webster and East Water Street sides. This has given protection to the children at a very dangerous road junction. The heating equipment continues to be a problem as it is very old.

Market Street

The floors have been refinished with a combination varnish and gum filler. Minor repairs have been made in the building with several panes of glass replaced.

Gleason

Repairs to the veranda have been made. Door checks were repaired and other minor repairs made. The lighting of the rooms in this building is far below the standard. As soon as possible additional lighting equipment should be installed.

Central Street

Minor repairs have been made at this building.

SPECIFIC REQUESTS FROM DEPARTMENTS

As soon as possible additional equipment should be added to our general shop. A power driven jig saw will improve the efficiency of this department. The old Golding printing press which was second hand when installed eleven years ago is worn badly and must be soon replaced by another press whenever a desirable second hand one may be located. In a school of our numbers an additional press could be used to good advantage.

One or two electric sewing machines should be added to the equipment of our sewing department in order to modernize and supply the needed machines. The Domestic Science classes are in need of additional spoons, knives, bowls, sifters and cooking pans.

A moving picture projector for use in the elementary schools will add to the efficiency of our visual instruction and will make more interesting to pupils the teaching of subject matter.

The velour shades in the auditorium are badly stained with water marks and have rotted so that within a year or two it will be necessary to replace them.

Whenever the town can afford to have traffic officers stationed at the Lincoln School for the opening and closing of school sessions a safer condition will prevail. The corner of Church and Howard Streets at noon, especially, is a dangerous spot.

We are indeed grateful to all organizations and individuals who have assisted us by contributing to the milk fund, scholarships and gifts to our schools.

CONCLUSION

The children of Rockland are intrusted to our care and instruction for twelve years during the formative period of their lives and although we are responsible for them only six hours of each day during five days of the week we feel that our school work offers a rich opportunity to help in the development of true manhood and womanhood. To that end the teachers and administrators are striving each year for better, unified, lasting results.

I deeply appreciate the constant aid and encouragement of parents, teachers, principals and school committee members.

Respectfully submitted,

R. STEWART ESTEN,

Superintendent of Schools

REPORT OF THE JUNIOR-SENIOR HIGH SCHOOL PRINCIPAL

Mr. R. Stewart Esten
Superintendent of Schools
Rockland, Massachusetts

Mr. dear Mr. Esten:

My annual report as Principal of the Junior-Senior High School is submitted herewith.

Although the total enrollment of the school is about the same as last year, there has been a substantial increase in the number of pupils in the Junior High. All of the rooms are filled to capacity. In the Senior High, some of the study hall are crowded due to a greater enrollment in some courses of study than in others, but classes as a whole are not too large.

The average attendance for the year was again very good. Our record for punctuality was a good one and it showed an improvement over last year. Credit for this should go to the pupils and parents who have cooperated in this matter.

From results of standard achievement tests given in a few subjects, we can feel that our standards of work in those subjects have been of a high grade. Better measurement of achievement in all subjects awaits the further development of a testing program.

Without expense to the town, our teaching has been strengthened by a program of visual education. A fine 16 mm. movie projector was purchased last spring, and a limited program has been carried on this fall and will continue throughout the year. The program is limited to such free films as are obtainable. However I feel that a very good start has been made. Several boys have been trained to operate the machine, and they have been efficiently showing the films during the fall term.

Our school library will soon receive a large number of needed books. A loyal group of alumni, realizing the need of more books in our library, raised a sizable sum of money for the purchase of these books. This fine gift to the school is indeed appreciated and will do much to make the school more efficient. The Rockland Woman's Club again presented the school with a sum of money for this same purpose. New shelves have been built in the library to hold the new books. One section of these will be devoted to the needs of the Junior High. With this added material and equipment, there only remains the obtaining of a teacher-librarian to make our library what it should be for a good secondary school.

For some years it has been difficult to develop a good program of physical education due to a lack of gymnasium equipment. Now that some equipment of this kind has been obtained, a more interesting and worthwhile program can and will be developed in the immediate future. This year's gym exhibition should be even better than the fine one of last spring.

Our athletic program was enlarged to give a greater number of boys a chance to participate by the addition of track as a major sport. Mr. Pratt, a member of the faculty and a former Dartmouth track man, was appointed coach of track. In the first competition of the track team last spring, a very fine showing was made. Cross-country was established this fall and the team won two out of its three runs. Football, baseball and basketball (which includes boys' and girls' varsity, and Junior High varsity and intermurals) all enjoyed fairly successful seasons. However, in my opinion, greater success in our athletic activities is dependent upon the development of a stronger school spirit. The running track needs attention so th'at its surface may be made suitable for all track events. We also need an enclosed athletic field so as to be able to better underwrite our athletic program for no money appropriated by the town is used for this purpose.

Our other extra-curricular activities have made progress during the year. More of these, non-athletic in character are still needed. There is some demand for debating as a school activity, and I hope that a coach may be obtained so that this most worthwhile activity may be established in the immediate future. In public speaking, our school again did very well. One of our girls won first place in extemporaneous speaking at the district meet in Hingham. There is much talent for speaking in this school, and only the problem of coaching keeps Rockland High from a prominent place in prize-speaking among the high schools in this section of the state.

One club, the Commeroff Club, w̶as organized during the year. Upperclassmen of the Commercial course are eligible for membership therein, and its purpose is to consider various phases of the business world. A well functioning club, organized about some common interest, can play a very important part in the educative process. I trust that more clubs will be organized soon.

Our chapter of Pro Merito accomplished much during the past year. Money was raised to obtain complete robes for the society's induction service. These robes were made in our Sewing department. In March, a private induction service was held to which parents, friends, and delegates from other Pro Merito chapters were invited. A public induction service was held in June and a large group of new members was admitted at that time. Pro Merito continues to be an incentive for high scholarship and good character.

The Student Council is slowly making itself felt as a

beneficial factor in the life of the school. One of its out-standing accomplishments was the taking over of some of the lavatory supervision during the recess periods. This has been done very well to date and is a fine beginning in pupil participation in the running of the school.

A special home-room program was recently started in the three lower classes of the Senior High. A home room should be more than a place where attendance is checked —it should be the pupil's school home. From this program it is hoped that there will evolve the conditions necessary for proper pupil guidance—social, moral, personal, educational and vocational.

In the year to come, we will strive to make Rockland High even more worthy of her fine traditions and keep her standards on the high plane of the past.

I wish to express my sincere thanks for the cooperation and help given to me by the School Committee, the Superintendent of Schools, the faculty, and the pupils of the school.

Respectfully submitted,

GEORGE A. J. FROBERGER,
Principal

REPORT OF SCHOOL PHYSICIANS
AND SCHOOL NURSE

Mr. R. Stewart Esten
Superintendent of Schools
Rockland, Massachusetts

My dear Mr, Esten:

We have carried out our usual program making a physical examination of all the pupils of the elementary grades. High school pupils were examined carefully before being allowed to participate in the competitive sports.

Our Diphtheria prevention program was carried out during the month of May. The group immunization outfit purchased by the Board of Health for use in this work was used for the first time with good results.

We sincerely hope that the Kiwanis Club may find it possible to continue the Milk Fund work as it has been a distinct benefit to the school children.

Following is a list of physical defects found in our examinations:

Number of examinations by school physicians	1001
Cases of enlarged tonsils and adenoids	86
Cases of enlarged cervical glands	16
Cases of defective hearing	28
Cases of defective vision	49
Cases of hilum tuberculosis	14
Number of children given toxoid inoculations	98

ACTIVITIES OF SCHOOL NURSE

An office hour is maintained each school day at the

high school between 8:30 and 9:30 A. M. and the parents may reach the nurse by telephoning the school office.

Each of the elementary classrooms is visited twice weekly. Daily inspections are made if pupils have been exposed to contagious disease.

Pupils are inspected by nurse each month and weighed four times during the school year. Classroom weight charts are used so that the pupil may follow his or her individual gain.

Number of visits to classrooms	1954
Number of visits to homes	483
Number of minor wounds dressed	116
Number of emergency treatments	15
Number taken home ill	56
Number sent to school physicians	10
Number referred to family physician	23
Number excluded from school	14
Number x-rayed	77
Number taken to habit clinic	4
Number of classroom inspections	126
Number of individual inspections	3041
Number of pupils weighed and measured	2756

All cases of non-attendance which have been reported to me have been investigated.

Respectfully submitted,

JOSEPH H. DUNN, M. D.
JOSEPH FRAME, M. D.
LOUISE A. CONSIDINE, R. N.

REPORT OF DENTAL HYGIENIST

My dear Mr. Esten:

I hereby submit my annual report as Dental Hygienist in the Rockland schools for 1937.

At the beginning of the school year the annual dental examinations of school children in grades 1 to 6 inclusive were held with the assistance of the local dentists. The following results were obtained:

Number examined	772
Number in need of temporary extractions	191
Number in need of permanent fillings	470
Number in need of permanent extractions	68

During the year 974 oral prophylaxis were performed and 42 children treated for toothache.

The results of the pre-school examinations held in the spring of 1937 were as follows:

Number examined	61
Number with temporary defects	38
Number with permanent defects	0
Number with fistulae	2
Number with no defects	23

Through the sum of money donated by the Rockland Teachers Association, seven children benefited by emergency extractions.

Classroom instructions in Dental Hygiene have been carried on as usual. We have striven to instill knowledge to form proper habits and develop right attitudes.

Respectfully submitted,
EVELYN DELORY
Dental Hygienist

FINANCIAL REPORT FOR THE ROCKLAND HIGH SCHOOL CAFETERIA

January 1, 1937 to December 31, 1937

Balance on Hand, January 1, 1937	$	5 18
Cash Receipts for 1937	$4	758 46
Total cash receipts	$ 4	763 64

Cash payments for 1937:

Barnes, W. F.	$	15 31
Berwick Cake Co.		188 44
Burke's Rockland Wet Wash		1 22
Casey Arthur		12 00
Cushman's Bakery		120 10
Edison Electric Company		80 00
Ellis, H. R.		81 79
Fitts, E. V. Company		262 63
Globe Ticket Company		22 75
Gumpert, S.		18 01
Gurry, Thomas		6 20
Hickey Brothers		783 50
Hostess Cake Company		12 12
Hunt Potato Chip Co.		67 55
Loose-Wiles Biscuit Company		91 48
Mahoney, John		94 10
Nanking Food Products Company		3 30
National Biscuit Company		24 13
Old Colonial Appliance Corp.		5 00
Old Colony Gas Company		71 54
Peterson, A. S.		395 10
Plymouth Rock Ice Cream Company		996 90
Quinn, Margaret		587 00
Rockland New System Laundry		1 32
Ryan, Michael		1 62
Schuler's Foods, Inc.		4 20

Service Charges	1	95
Standard Brands, Inc.	10	65
Stoddard, A. C.	207	76
Traniello, Paul	5	50
Whiting Milk Company	287	46
Williams, R. W., Inc.	22	10
Wonder Bread Bakery	264	88
Total Cash payments	$4 747	61
Balance on Hand	$ 16	03

Respectfully submitted,

ROSE T. MAGADINI,
ELEANOR B. LOUD

SCHOOL ENROLLMENT
As of December 23, 1937

Teacher	School	Grade	Pupils
Marjorie Smith	McKinley	1	36
Mary H. Greenan	McKinley	2	34
Mildred E. Healey	McKinley	3	38
R. Louise Cone	McKinley	4	39
Elva M. Shea	McKinley	5	30
John F. Ryan	McKinley	5	31
Paul Casey	McKinley	6	35
Nellie M. Ford	McKinley	6	35
Isabel Philbrook	McKinley	Special Class	17
Catherine Coen	Lincoln	1	31
Blanche Thacher	Lincoln	2	32
Harriette Cragin	Lincoln	3	28
Miriam Roberts	Lincoln	4	40
Eileen Fitzgibbons	Lincoln	5	31
Margaret McDermott	Lincoln	6	35
Virginia Ford	Jefferson	1 and 2	32
Bertha Campbell	Jefferson	2 and 3	33
Blanche Crowell	Jefferson	4 and 5	36
Annie A. Shirley	Jefferson	5 and 6	33
Madeline Lannin	Gleason	1 and 2	25
Agnes Lioy (substitute)	Gleason	3 and 4	28
Lillian Murdock	Webster St.	1, 2 and 3	39
Josephine Lannin	Webster St.	4 and 5	26
Ethel Wetherbee	Market St.	1, 2 and 3	21
Margaret Blake	Market St.	4, 5 and 6	25
Alice Murrill	Central St.	1, 2 and 3	20

Total   800

Junior-Senior High School Enrollment,
   Dec. 23, 1937   674

Grand Total   1474

AGE GRADE TABLE AS OF OCTOBER 1, 1937

Grade	5	6	7	8	9	10	11	12	13	14	15	16	17	18	19	20	Total
1	59	53	6	2													120
2		50	63	14	1												128
3			45	57	14	5	1										122
4				59	54	14	6	2									135
5					52	64	20	4	2	1							143
6						52	43	22	10	5	1						133
7							47	52	22	4	2	1					128
8								53	61	11	8	1					134
9									32	58	12	5	3				110
10									14	39	56	9	5	1			124
11										1	27	50	19	4			101
12												16	54	10		1	81
Ungraded			1	4	2	2	2	3	3	1	3						21
Total	59	103	115	136	123	137	119	136	144	120	109	82	81	15		1	1480

ROCKLAND HIGH SCHOOL

GRADUATION EXERCISES

Class of 1937

Wednesday Evening, June twenty-third

Rockland High School Auditorium

PROGRAMME

Processional, "Vienna Forever March"　　Schrammel
R. H. S. Orchestra

Invocation　　　　Rev. John Matteson

Honor Essay　"Glimpses of the Life of Horace Mann"
Ralph Grant Crocker

Song:
(a) "Hymn to America"　　　Gulesian
(b) "Danny Boy"　　　Weatherly
(c) "Country Gardens"　　Arr. by Harold Symthe
Girls' Glee Club

Honor Essay　"Horace Mann - The Educator"
Helen May Santry

Chamber of Commerce Prize Essay "Our Community"
Ruth Catherine Giblin

Music, Selection, "Straussiana" (Waltz selection on
Strauss Melodies)　　Arr. by Seredy-Tocacben
R. H. S. Orchestra

Honor Essay "Our Debt to Books"
Elizabeth Anne Sciarappa

Song "Espana"   ' Waldtenfel
            Rockland High Chorus   Arr. by Page

Honor Essay   "Horace Mann Speaks to 1937"
            Evelyn Richmond Winslow

Athletic Scholarship Award
            Mr. Charles Shalgian
        Chairman of A. A. Scholarship Committee

Chamber of Commerce Scholarship Award
            Dr. Joseph Lelyveld
        President of Chamber of Commerce

Woman's Club Scholarship Award
            Mrs. Rocco Murgida
        Chairman of Scholarship Committee

Awarding of otrer prizes and Presentation of Diplomas
            Mr. E. Stuart Woodward
        Chairman Rockland School Committee

Class Song   Words and Music by Ruth Elsie Southard

Song "America"   Chorus and Audience

Benediction   Rev. John Matteson

Director of Chorus   Miss Blanche G. Maguire
Director of Orchestra   Mr. Michael Cassano
Accompanists   Mary Asklund, '38, Ruth Southard, '37

GRADUATES

Jeanette Frances Angelini   Daniel Anthony LeMotte
*John Burrows Arnold   Gilbert Ellis Leighton
Raymond Francis Austin   Stanley John Levings
Kathleen Emma Benner   Lorraine Nina Lowell
*Beatrice Elizabeth Bennett   Owen Mahon
*Katherine Lena Berry   John Joseph Mahoney
Natalie May Blanchard   Patricia Agnes Maloney

Helen Gertrude Cannaway
Weston Grey Capen
Henry Ward Carson
*Daniel Francis Chenevert
William Herbert Crager
*Ralph Grant Crocker
William Edwin Cronin
Marjorie Eileen Cull
Alexander Richard D'Amato
Marie Elizabeth Damon
Frederick Linwood Dill
James Frederick Donovan
Henry Kenneth Farr
Pearl Marguerite Fisher
Dorothy Estelle Forbes
*Robert Alexander Frame
*Edith Louise Fransosa
John Edwin Gammon
Robert Joseph Geogan
*Ruth Catherine Giblin
Arthur James Golemme
Coleman Hiram Grant
Elsie May Greene
Dorothy Harlow
Frances Hollis Hibberd
Chester Walter Hill
Lawrence Sumner Holbrook
*Eleanore May Hunter
George Loring Inglis
Marchi George Jankowski
*Richard Charles Jasper
*Ethelyn Lorraine Johnson
*Gertrude Marie Kelley
Mary Elizabeth Lee

Gerald Joseph Mastrodomenico
Charles William Mileski
Andrew Laurence McCarthy
Norman Eggleson McWilliams, Jr.
Helen Gertrude O'Brien
Elizabeth Christine Peters
George Warren Popp
James Stephen Prescott
*Evelyn Louise Quinlan
Eveleth Richardson
*Helen May Santry
Helen Nathalie Schapelle
Celestine Elizabeth Schleiff
*Elizabeth Anne Sciarappa
*Dorothy Esther Sears
Howard Glover Senecal
*Eleanor Anne Shores
Henry Lawrence Shortall
Fred Freeman Simmons
*Anna Frances Smith
Ruth Elsie Southard
*Sara Battye Studley
Nathalie Whiton Taylor
Robert Francis Troy
Mabel Luella Turner
*Mary Frances Vinton
Frederick Gratten Walls
*Burton Warren Wheeler
Edith May Whiting
*Evelyn Richmond Winslow
Eleanor Nathaleen Woodward
Stanley Wilson Young

* PRO MERITO—Honor Society. Average of 85 per cent or over for 4 years.

CLASS OFFICERS

COLEMAN GRANT	President
BEATRICE BENNETT	Vice-President
GERTRUDE KELLEY	Secretary
RALPH CROCKER	Treasurer

SOCIAL COMMITTEE

Evelyn Winslow   Eleanore Hunter   Richard Jasper

CLASS COLORS

Blue and Silver

CLASS MOTTO

"Labor Omnia Vincit"

CLASS FLOWER

Supreme Rose

TEACHERS UNDER APPOINTMENT DEC. 31, 1937

Teacher	Grade or subject	Educational and Professional Training	Date of First Appointment in Town	Salary
R. Stewart ...en	SUPERINTENDENT OF S...LS	...hy Col, Col ...bia Univ.	Sept. 1929	$3,600.00
	JUNIOR - SENIOR HIGH SCHOOL			
...ge A. J. Froberger, Principal	Uni. of ...ne		Sept. 1935	2,880.00
Robert C. Healey, Sub-Master, Latin	Boston College, B. U.		Sept. 1919	2,430.00
Katherine S. Burke, Geog., Science	Bridgewater Tea. College		Sept. 1906	1,310.00
Joseph Cogan, Sciences	Bates College		Sept. 1929	1,755.0 0
Mary D. Costello, English, ...lip	Quincy Training School		Sept. 1898	1,310.00
Marguerite ...lk, ...al	Boston University		Sept. 1933	1,300.0 0
Ellen M. Hayes, English	Univ. of Wisconsin		Sept. 1927	1, 6...00
Victoria Howarth, English	Radcliffe College		Sept. 1925	1,800.00
Emma S. Jewett, History	Hyannis Tea. College		Sept. 1908	1,310.00
...r Loud, Household Arts	...ns College		Sept. 1935	1,050.00
Rose T. Magadini, Commercial	Bay Path Inst., B. U.		Sept. 1929	1,440.00
...le H. Mayer, English	o...on ...ity		Sept. 1935	1,250.00
Esther ..., Social Sci. Literature	Bridgewater Tea. ...l.		Sept. 1918	1,310.00
Helen Molloy, ...ior Business Training	Keene, N. H., Normal		Sept. 1930	1,220.00
John B. O'Hayre, History	Boston College, B. U.		Jan. 1931	1,485.00
Malcolm Pratt, Mathematics	Dartmouth ...ge		Jan. 1933	1 4...00
...r Poliks, Phys. Ed., Biology	...n. State College		Jan. 1937	1,710.00
Leona W. Sampson, French	Boston Univ. and Sorbonne, Paris		Sept. 1937	1,500.00
Frances L. Squarey, English, ...re	Bridgewater Tea. College		Sept. 1921	1, 3...00
...ert A. Studley, ...ity	...ity of N. H.		Sept. 1927	1, 5...00
...ria L. Tenney, Sci., Mathematics	Farmington Normal		Sept. 1927	1,310.00
...ce Tobey, Sewing, History	...ity of N. H.		Sept. 1936	1,150.00

TEACHERS UNDER ROI MENT DEC. 31, 1937

Ter	...de or ...bject	...al ad ...al Training	Date of First Appointment in Twn	Salary
Erl I. ...Kan, Commercial		Salem ...Ers College ...e	Sept. 1936	1,250.00
George W. Wilson, ...al Tr · ...ing		Fitchburg ...Ers	Sept. 1937	1,200.00
McKINLEY SCHOOL				
Nellie M. Ford, ...Prin, Grade 6		...gh School, Special ...ds	St. 1896	1,440.00
Marjorie Smith, ...de 1		Bridgewater ...Ers College	St. 1937	1,000.00
...ry H. ...an, ...de 2		B. U., ...Hs ...	St. 1920	1 3...00
...nd E. ...ry, ...de 3		...y ...nl	St. 1930	1,050.00
R. Louise Cone, Grade 4		...Mk, B. U.	Spt. 1930	1,265.00
Elva M. ...Sta, ...de 5		Bridgewater Tea. ...e.	Spt. 1928	1,107:50
...ohn ...n, ...de 6		B. C., ...br ...T.	Oct. 1937	1,000.00·
...ul Casey, ...de 6		Bridgewater ...T College ...Ue	Spt. 1937	1,000.0 0
Isabel ...Pwk, Special Class		...Mk, Boston School of ...Hy	Sept. 1937	1,050.00
LINCOLN SCHOOL				
Margaret ...ntt, ...de 6		...ds ...ers' ...Ue	St. 1925	1,310.00
Eileen Fitzgibbons, ...nl, Grade 5		Bridgewater Tea. College	St. 1925	1,310.00
...de ...Gn, ...de 1		Salem ...F College	St. 1930	1,220.00
...he ...Fr, ...de 2		...k Ktg. School	Jan. 1930	1,175.00
...he E. Cragin, ...de 3		...gh School, Special Courses	St. 1910	1,310.00
Miriam E. Roberts, ...de 4		Bridgewater ...Ue	Spt. 1934	1,050.00
JEFFERSON SCHOOL				
...nie A. ...h...y, Grades 5 and 6		...r ...E. College ...Ta. ...Cl.	Sept. 1912	1,400.00
...Ba ...l ..., ...ds 2 and 3		...as. State, Hyannis ...Ta.	Sept. 1923	1,310.00
Blanche Crowell, ...ds 4 and 5		Framingham ...s College	St. 1931	1,220.00
Virginia Ford, ...ds 1 and 2		Bridgewater ...Ta. College	Sept. 1937	1,000.00

GLEASON SCHOOL

Me En, rads 1 and 2	....	H 1935	1,050.00
En Kovalchuk, rads 3 and 4	Bridgewater Coll ge	Sept. 1937	1,000.00

WEBSTER STREET SCHOOL

Lill' an G. Mk, ras 1, 2 and 3	...... g School	Sept. 1922	1,310.00
Jose ie E, ras 4 and 5	......	Sept. 1932	1,050.00

MARKET STREET SCHOOL

Nt H, ras 4, 5 and 6	Is s Coll ge	Sept. 1929	1,050.00
El Wetherbee, Grades 1, 2, and 3	os Kg. cool	Sept. 1928	1,310.00

CE EL STREET SCHOOL

Alice Mrill, ras 1, 2 and 3	r Tea. Coll ge	Sept. 1937	1,000.00

SPEC AL TEACHERS

*Bl he Maguire, usic	At d B. U. ad	March 1929	887.00
Nel Go	Vi no c School	Sept. 1928	1,175.00
ie A. ie	Private y in c School	Sept. 1922	1,400.00
ie ie is, Phys. Ed. for Girls	St. z. Hosp.	Sept. 1929	1,175.00
Mn S. is ah ek. ug,	Posse-Nissen g School	Sept. 1 80	1,440.00
* Two is ah ek.	Ms. School of Art		

APPOINTMENTS 1937

ba W. Sampson, High School —
re W. Wn, r High

RESI NS 1937

J bn B.   y, Junior h
Kn in, y School   yn   h, h School
Paul Gy, ek, y School   Er th, y School
Marjorie h, ol   gt Shortall, y School
Ae Murrill, ntral Street School —   e Fl , Jeff n School
Helen Kovalc , n School —

INDEX

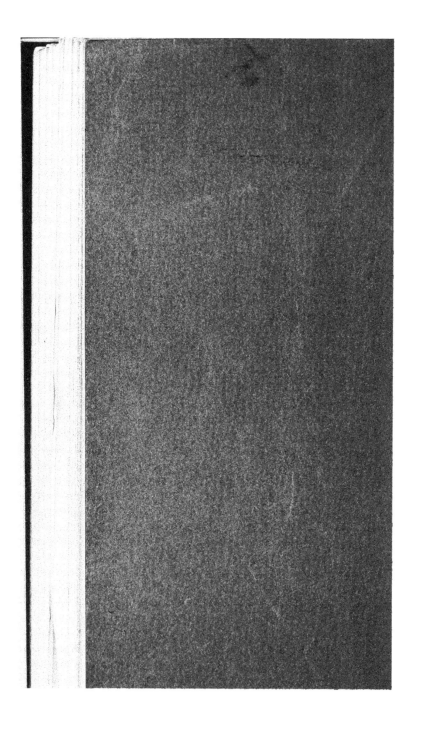

SIXTY · FIFTH

ANNUAL REPORT

OF THE

TOWN OFFICERS

OF THE

Town of Rockland

FOR THE YEAR ENDING DECEMBER 31

1938

A. I. RANDALL, INC.
PRINTERS
ROCKLAND, MASS.

Officers of the Town of Rockland
1938

Town Clerk (elected annually)

RALPH L. BELCHER

Town Treasurer (elected annually)

CHARLES J. HIGGINS

Tax Collector (elected annually)

JAMES A. DONOVAN

Moderator (elected annually)

MAGORISK L. WALLS

Selectmen, Board of Public Welfare and Fence Viewers
(elected annually)

HARRY S. TORREY
JOHN J. BOWLER   NORMAN S. WHITING

Bureau of Old Age Assistance
(appointed by Board of Public Welfare)

HARRY S. TORREY
JOHN J. BOWLER   NORMAN S. WHITING

Supervisor of Old Age Assistance
(appointed by Board of Public Welfare)

MARY L. O'BRIEN

Assessors
(one elected annually for three years)

JOSEPH B. ESTES   Term expires 1941
NORMAN J. BEALS   Term expires 1940
DENNIS L. O'CONNOR   Term expires 1939

School Committee
(for term of three years) .

DANA S. COLLINS   Term expires 1941
M. AGNES KELLEHER   Term expires 1941
WILLIAM A. LOUD   Term expires 1940
BENJAMIN LELYVELD   Term expires 1940
HELEN M. HAYDEN   Term expires 1939

Park Commissioners
(one elected annually for three years)

DANIEL H. BURKE   Term expires 1941
CHARLES T. WALLS   Term expires 1940
PATRICK H. MAHONEY   Term expires 1939

Water Commissioners
(one elected annually for three years)

SAMUEL W. BAKER   Term expires 1941
EVERETT S. DAMON   Term expires 1940
RALPH FUCILLO   Term expires 1939

Board of Health
(one elected annually for three years)

JOSEPH FRAME, M. D.   Term expires 1941
JOSEPH H. DUNN, M. D.   Term expires 1940
EDWARD M. CULLINAN   Term expires 1939

Sewerage Commissioners
(one elected annually for three years)

GILES W. HOWLAND   Term expires 1941
CHARLES M. HINES   Term expires 1940
FREDERIC HALL   Term expires 1939

Trustees of the Memorial Library
(two elected annually for three years)

EMILY CRAWFORD	Term expires 1941
ANNIE McILVENE	Term expires 1941
EMMA W. GLEASON	Term expires 1940
FRANCIS J. GEOGAN	Term expires 1940
BURTON L. CUSHING	Term expires 1939
JOHN B. FITZGERALD	Term expires 1939

Auditors
(elected annually)

HAROLD C. SMITH   GEORGE A. GALLAGHER
LEO E. DOWNEY

Tree Warden
(elected annually)

ALFRED T. METIVIER

Highway Surveyor
(elected annually)

RODERICK MacKENZIE

Constables
(elected annually)

*CORNELIUS J. McHUGH   JOHN H. MURPHY
ADOLPH L. W. JOHNSON   ROBERT J. DRAKE
GEORGE J. POPP

* Deceased, Sept. 27, 1938.

APPOINTMENTS
(by Selectmen)

Chief of Police

GEORGE J. POPP

Police Officers

*CORNELIUS J. McHUGH	JOHN H. MURPHY
ADOLPH L. W. JOHNSON	ROBERT J. DRAKE

* Deceased, Samuel J. Cannaway appointed to fill vacancy.

Special Police Officers

EDWARD J. CULLINAN	EARL WYATT
MAURICE MULLEN	ELMER DUNN
JOHN J. DWYER JR.	CHARLES METIVIER
CHARLES M. HINES	SAMUEL J. CANNAWAY
FORREST L. PARTCH	THOMAS MAHONEY
JAMES McKEEVER	CHARLES BOUDREAU
JOHN DOYLE	JOHN F. HANNON
MICHAEL O'BRIEN	THOMAS FITZGERALD
THOMAS MAHON	FREDERICK J. PERRY
LEE RHODENIZER	GEORGE MANLEY
LEO E. DOWNEY	THOMAS McDONALD
WILLIAM H. ROBERTS	CLIFFORD ROSE
HAROLD ANDERSON	DANIEL C. HINES
FRANCIS W. PATTERSON	BERNARD V. DELOREY

Keeper of the Lock-up

GEORGE J. POPP

Election Officers

Precinct One	Precinct Two

Wardens

WILLIAM J. FLYNN	JOHN A. WINSLOW

Deputy Wardens

ROBERT PARKER	HAROLD C. POOLE

Clerks

IRVIN E. EMERY	FRED RYAN

Deputy Clerks

CARL FASS   J. LOCKE LANNIN

Inspectors

JOHN J. PAULIN   ELLIS BLAKE
MATTHEW O'GRADY   CHARLES F. SHIELDS

Deputy Inspectors

ROBERT D. ESTES   FRANCIS L. GAMMON
TIMOTHY WHITE   E. BURTON RAMSDELL
URSULA M. FRENCH   OLIVE C. WHEELER
HELENA W. HUNT   MARY E. LYNCH

Registrars of Voters
(one appointed annually for three years)

THOMAS MORRISSEY   Term expires 1941
*ANNIE G. GARRITY   Term expires 1940
ESTHER H. RAWSON   Term expires 1939

* Appointed July 12, 1938, to fill vacancy, John D. Carney resigned July 5, 1938.

Sealer of Weights and Measures

HAROLD J. INKLEY

Measurer of Wood and Bark

GILES W. HOWLAND

Weighers of Hay and Coal — Also Public Weighers

RALPH KEENE   EDITH PETRELL
ELIZABETH DONOVAN   ARTHUR PETRELL
PERCY JACOBS   DOMINICK PETRELL

Agent for Burial of Indigent Soldiers and
Care of Soldiers' Graves

LOUIS B. GILBRIDE

Inspector of Animals and Stables

WILLIAM T. CONDON

Town Physicians for Poor and Soldiers' Relief

FREDERICK H. COREY, M. D.
JOSEPH H. DUNN, M. D.

Superintendent Gypsy Moth

ALFRED T. METIVIER

Forest Fire Warden

CLYSON P. INKLEY

APPOINTMENTS
(by School Committee)

Superintendent of Schools

R. STEWART ESTEN

APPOINTMENTS
(by Water Commissioners)

Superintendent of Water Works

JAMES B. STUDLEY

APPOINTMENTS
(by Board of Health)

Inspectors of Plumbing

FREDERIC HALL   J. STUART McCALLUM

Milk Inspectors

BOARD OF HEALTH

APPOINTMENTS
(by Moderator)

Finance Committee

RUSSELL OSGOOD	Term expires 1941
FREDERICK NUGENT	Term expires 1941
RALPH TEDESCHI	Term expires 1941
PATRICK RYAN	Term expires 1941
WILLIAM G. W. HOLLOWAY	Term expires 1941
WILLIAM KANE	Term expires 1940
WESLEY PIERCE	Term expires 1940
EDWARD RYAN	Term expires 1940
MARY CLANCEY	Term expires 1940
JAMES APPLEFORD	Term expires 1940
MARION MANSFIELD DONOVAN	Term expires 1939
FLORENCE DUDLEY	Term expires 1939
JAMES P. KANE	Term expires 1939
BERNARD MONAHAN	Term expires 1939
ARTHUR W. WYMAN	Term expires 1939

Chief of Fire Department

CLYSON P. INKLEY	Tenure of Office

Report of the Town Clerk

MARRIAGES REGISTERED IN THE TOWN OF ROCKLAND FOR THE YEAR 1938

January 21. Orendo Cistaro of Rockland and Irene Fasci of Weymouth.

February 5. Gilbert Chester Strickland and Pearl Marguerite Fisher both of Rockland.

February 12. Charles Dunn and Thelma Ewell both of Rockland.

February 19. Fred Webster of Rockland and Elizabeth A. Gilligan (Donoghue) of Whitman.

February 22. Richard Carney Hayes of Whitman and Anna Elizabeth Reagan of Rockland.

February 22. Fred C. Kelsea and Genevieve B. Bloomer (Thompson) both of Rockland.

February 27. Nick Christos Zigouras of Brockton and and Kleoniki Pantos Demetriadis of Rockland.

February 28. George Maurice Roberts of Rockland and Helen Ann Nichols of So. Braintree.

March 6. John Edward Martell and Christine Dorothy MacPherson both of Quincy.

March 10. Irving George Pennini and Elfrida Maxine Von Beidel both of Rockland.

March 10. Kenneth S. Berryman and Virginia F. Damon, both of Rockland.

March 12. Henry Wallace Brillant of Rockland and Barbara Elisabeth Glastetter of Sharon.

March 12. Delmo Bianchi of Providence, Rhode Island and Bessie Baker of Brockton.

March 14. Charles Clement Carr of Braintree and Mabel Christina McNutt of Rockland.

March 18. Ralph Dennen Berry of Hanover and Meredith Chase of Rockland.

March 26. Irving Willard Gould and Eleanor Shores, both of Rockland.

March 28. Francis Arthur Burbine of Whitman and Mildred Elaine Tibbets of Rockland.

March 31. Edward William Fasci of So. Weymouth and Mildred Leland of Boston.

April 6. George Walter Fisher and Barbara Eliza Smith, both of Rockland.

April 14. E. Guy Carville and Lois M. Clevercey, both of Rockland.

April 17. James Albert Bates of Fall River and Edith Elizabeth Caldwell of Rockland.

April 19. John Thomas Crawford and Francis Elizabeth Costello, both of Rockland.

May 1. George Hale Johnson of Whitman and Ruth Ellen Prior of Rockland.

May 6. Harold Eugene LaBelle of Brockton and Ruth Nelson Wade of Rockland.

May 7. Frederick Leo Condon of Abington and Marie Lillian McHugh of Rockland.

May 14. Harold Alfred Durkee of Stoughton and Tilda Amunda Lincoln of Rockland.

May 17. Harper Allen Estabrook of Rockland and Mary Rita Gilmore of Brockton.

May 28. James Douglas Garfield Bowles and Irene Bates Crehan, both of Rockland.

June 4. Gerald Samuel Shepherd of Hanover and Edith Belle Magoun of Rockland.

June 4. Albert Thomas Ryan of Rockland and Grace Ellen Foley of Randolph.

June 5. Kennth Edward Urquhart of Quincy and Veronica Rita O'Brien of Rockland.

June 12. Bronislaw J. Lukaszewicz of Rockland and Mary Michalowski of W. Hanover.

June 12. Guido Mariani of Rockland and Angie Felaccio, of So. Braintree.

June 15. Leland Collyer Taylor of Rockland and Frances Belle Meserve of Abington.

June 17. Harold Montgomery McKenna of Rockland and Mildred Taylor of Rockland.

June 17. George Aretino and Mary Elizabeth Umbri-anna both of Rockland.

June 24. Ernest Melvin Libby and Phyllis Barbara Tisdale both of Rockland.

June 25. James E. Brigham and Gladys E. Childs (Webster) both of Rockland.

July 2. William Vernon Smith of E. Bridgewater and Geraldine Jennie Damon of Rockland.

July 4. Charles Tedeschi of Rockland and Lillian Ros-enquist of Atlantic.

July 17. David Tucker and Theresa Fucillo, both of Rockland.

July 20. Spencer Percival Joseph of Norwell and Ellen Lincoln Merritt of Scituate.

July 25. Wendell F. Wolfe, Jr., of So. Weymouth and Cordellia M. Cushing of Rockland.

July 26. Stephen Follet and Edrie Sweatt, both of Rockland.

July 29. Henry Francis Anderson and Minnie Flor-ence Shaw, both of Rockland.

July 31. Michael P. Shalgian and Viola B. Osborne, both of Rockland.

August 6. Harry Arthur Davenport and Hazel Mae Fisher, both of Rockland.

August 7. William Hutcheon Lamb of Rockland and Velma Sterling Henderson of Ocean Bluffs.

August 12. Ralph Pringle Hill of Abington and Helena Louise Morrison of Rockland.

August 17. Campbell Carroll Preble and Mary L. Lowell (McLean) both of Randolph.

August 25. Herbert James Jr., of Brockton and Helen Frances Burton of Rockland.

August 28. Joseph Sabina of Brockton and Stanislawa Milewski of Rockland.

August 28. George A. Riley and Mary L. Lamar, both of Rockland.

August 28. Charles Sullivan McDonald of Weymouth and Claire Gertrude O'Brien of Rockland.

September 2. Cedric Ashton Freeman of Abington and Maryna Olive Bennett of Rockland.

September 2. James Francis McParlin of Brockton and Lucille Irma Whiting of Rockland.

September 3. Edward Hart and Rose Frances Lawless, both of Rockland.

September 3. Thomas Henry Ryan of Weymouth and Blanche Arlene Webster of Rockland.

September 4. Irvin Russell Little and Lillian Frances Tilden, both of Rockland.

September 5. George Ernest Lambert of Somerville and Mary Ardelle Fernald of Rockland.

September 11. Warren Howard Dunn and Katherine Ferron, both of Rockland.

September 12. Saaid Eed of Brockton and Dorothy Molander of Rockland.

September 16. John T. Ransom and Helen D. Backus, both of Boston.

September 17. Henry G. Reed of Rockland and Gladys V. Nelson of Roxbury.

September 18. William Henry Pratt, Jr. of Rockland and Kathleen Stimpson of Abington.

September 18. Walter A. Murray of Rockland and Bronislawa Lemiecesz of Hanover.

September 24. Richard Arden Batchelder of Providence, R. I., and Harriet Davies Walker of New York City.

September 24. James B. McCue of Pembroke and Doris E. Ford of Rockland.

September 25. Ernest Napoleon LaCombe and Mary Louise Haggerty, both of Rockland.

September 27. John Francis McKeon of Watertown and Irene Frances Shea of Rockland.

September 28. Philip Lawrence Brown of Rockland and Mary Marguerite Benton of Brockton.

October 2. James Edward Mezzetti of Quincy and Grace Louise Eaniri of Rockland.

October 15. Arthur Aitken and Barbara Louise Damon, both of Rockland.

October 23. Leo Francis Mahoney and Gladys Norman, both of Rockland.

October 27. Lee Franklyn Cary of Rockland and Eleanor Louise Holbrook of Quincy.

October 29. John Vernon Smith of Rockland and Mary Florence Priebis of Norwood.

October 29. Harry C. Barbour of Rockland and Eleanora M. Rose (Matthews) of Roxbury.

November 6. Marcus H. Lowell of Rockland and Màrgaret C. MacRoberts of Whitman.

November 19, Alfred T. Molander and Annie M. Olson, both of Rockland.

November 23. Leon Kendall Rhodes of Rockland and Doris E'. LaPointe of Hanson.

December 11. Robert Arthur Jacob of Abington and Virginia Elvira Batson of Rockland.

December 11. Frank J. Chiminello of Quincy and Rose M. Ingeno of Rockland.

December 27. William O'Shaughnessy of Conn., and Constance Tobey of Rockland.

December 28. John T. Higgins of Rockland and Doris Montgomery of Jericho, Vermont.

December 31. Donald Loring Charlton of Newton and Dorothy Esther Poole of Rockland.

December 31. Kenneth Earle Kendall of Rockland and Phyllis Edna Henshaw of Whitman.

December 31. Norman Everett Little and Virginia Winona Molander, both of Rockland.

BIRTHS REGISTERED IN THE TOWN O ROCKLAND FOR THE YEAR 1938

Date of Birth	Name	Name of Parents with Name of Mother	Residence of Parents	
Jan 1	Donald An Briggs	Fras H. and Barl ana Lewis	Prov, R. I.	M ldn
Jan 6	Josephine Mary	Vincent ard ile Ahi	Boston	Italy
Jan 12	Francis ode Mn	Gis ard E. Esther Glover	N. Weymouth E. Weymouth	
Jan 12	ah Ann Nightingale	Clifton E. and lia M. Ferron	Marshfield	ld
Jan 16	Priscilla Estelle Garl ard	Raymond L. and Ethel A. Morse	Boston	ld
Jan 17	lbert Bruce Lovett	Robert V. and Margaret Bruce	Whitman	ld
Jan 18	rfs Stuart McCallum, Jr.	rfes S. ard Ethel E. Lewis	Hanover	ld
Jan 19	Charles Dwelley M, Jr.	Charles D. and Jennie B. Gtis	Quincy	Boston
Jan 24	William Alfred Morrill	Frank G. ard Ardis C. Hayes	Augusta, M.	Pembroke
Jan 26	Nancy aa Id	Donald S. ard Edna F. Gis	Brockton	Boston
Jan 26	Mm David ant	lae ard Emily T.	Italy	Italy
Jan 30	Robert Anthony Mastro	ae ard Alice A. Mci	Duxbury	Pawtucket, R. I.
Feb 1	Priscilla May Price	Walter H. ard Hilda C. Smith	ld	rh
Feb 2	Vsil An Lee	David V. ard Marion V. Kennedy.	ld	Rockland
Feb 6	Richard Allen Balboni Wn, Jr.	Gn G. and Irene E. Eaniri	rDe	Brockton Manchester, N.H.
Feb 10	Francis Baker	Francis B. and Pansy Mary Finney	Athens, M.	Marshfield
Feb 19	Jane Howard Goodwin ale	Mm C. and Barbara W. Pratt	Ats, Vt.	Gan, Vt.
Feb 21	Rge Simon	Alfred B. ard Etta L. Min	ld	Pbrth
Feb 22	Richard ale Geloran	Vincent A. ard Esther D. Rol bins	ld	S. Boston
Feb 23	(Died ual) Yourell	James F. ard Myrtle G. Courtnell		
Mar 6	Mark Joseph Gilm fm	Peter E. and Ila H. Ke	Boston	ld
Mar 6	Robert Andrew Bedard	Wilfred L. and a M. Saillant	Fall River	Warren, R. I.
Mar 10	Nancy Wa Wyatt	Robert C. and Esther W. Hefler-	Avon	Brockton
Mar 13	John Leo Mahoney	John F. ard Florence M. Bowen	Brighton	ld
Mar 13	Beverly Lynn Stevens	Murray A. ard Ruth F. Ird	E. Burke, Vt.	Everett

BIRTHS REGISTERED IN THE TOWN OF ROCKLAND FOR THE YEAR 1938

Date of Birth	Name	Name of Parents with Name of Mother	Birthplace of Parents
Mar 14	Davis Mark Osborne	Wesley H. and Esther A. Goch	Norwell / Hanover
Mar 17	... Reed	Edward W. and ... A.	Brockton / N.
Mar 21	Jim Freeman Ransom	Roger T. and Florence I.	... Scotia / Rockland
Mar 29	Stuart Bryson	... W. and Mel A. Inglis	... Scotia
Apr 1	Sylvia Arlene Stetson	Harry S. and Lottie W. Torrey	Hanson / Rockland
Apr 8	Leo ... Henry Bourque	J. Henry and Alice Desfosses	Lynn / Lynn
Apr 9	... Smith	Lloyd V. and Evelyn J.	Duxbury / ...
Apr 12	Hiram ... Grant, Jr.	Hiram C. and Dorothy M.	..., Me.
Apr 16	... Louise	Fred R. and Jewelle E.	Fall River Pine Bluff, Ark.
Apr 6	Diane Livingston Statham	Robert C. and Dorothy R. Kennison	Boston / Abington
Apr 17	... Weatherbee	Charles N. and Dorothy E.	... / Boston
Apr 17	Richard Arthur DeYoung	... A. and ... Pinto	Rockland / Brockton
Apr 29	... Louise Felix	... and Edith L. Pike	... / Portugal
May 8	... Louise	Edmund E. and Mary C. Tower	N. Brookfield / Brockton
May 15	Kenneth Lewis Steinl...	... and Jean R.	Boston / Hanover
May 17	...	Sossio and ...	... / Boston
May 21	Ralph E. ...	Ralph E. and ... A. Mann	Abington / ...
May 23	Donald ...	Dominick and Rose Sena	... / Rockland
May 25	...	William A. and Marjorie L. Bonney	P. E. I.
Jun 3	Gail Wilcox	Arthur P. and ... Perry	Saranac ... N.Y. / Rockland
Jun 3	Beverly Ann ...	...	...
Jun 8	Alfred Henry Smith	Alfred and Grace Damon	... / Fitchburg
Jun	Stillborn		Ashby
Jun 9	... Andrew Rose	John A. and Mel E. Fredericksen	Gl...
Jun 11	... McDonnell	Paul J. and ... M.	N. / Rockland

BIRTHS REGISTERED IN THE TOWN OF ROCKLAND FOR THE YEAR 1938

Date of Birth	Name	Name of Parents with Name of Mother	Birthplace of Parents
Jun 16	Jean Patricia Damon	Frederick and Evelyn Henderson	N. Abington — Norwell
Jun 17	Albert Leo Greenwood	Eli O. and Ruth M. Fairy	— Boston
Jun 18	Robert Harmon	Harman B. and Ann T. Nowell	— W. Bridgewater
Jun 20	Andrea	Michele A. and Angelina	Italy — Italy
Jun 20	My Barl ana	Sydney R. and Rose A.	Rd St. — M
Jul 2	Ca Fisher	Ralph S. and Inez M. Warren	Rockland — Duxl ury
Jul 4	ohn Brown	William and Ade Binney	Rockland — Abington
Jul 11	Ann	John W and te E. Git	Pembroke — Hanson
Jul 13	Ann Pike	L. and la Duhamel	Brockton — Abington
Jul 16	Lorraine Harris	William F. and M. Trongeau	Hanover — Lawrence
Jul 17	Shirley	and Irene	th — Concord, N.H.
Jul 25	Aa	Scott W. and R. Wolfe	Maine — Boston
Jul 26	Nancy Louisa Didham	C. and Christine M.	do — Boston
Jul 29	Patricia DelPrete	Albert F. and n	n — E.
Aug 7	Beatrice Ann	Earl W. d Blanche	E. Bridgewater — Abington
Aug 8	William John Hayden	Robert E. and Hermina M.	S. Braintree A t, Vt.
Aug 9	Elizal	es N. and Velma L. Tower	Weymouth — et
Aug 15	My	h and Margaret M.	Boston — Vermont
Aug 15	d Dennis	Leland C. and G. Ledwell	Boston — Rockland
Aug 23	Frank	l E. and C.	— Abington
Aug 26	William	Kenneth E. and Frances L.	Rockland — Somerville
Aug 29	Parker	A. and Victoria M. Bellan	Hyde Park — Boston
Sp 8	Elaine	H. and Verna C. Lovette	— New York
Sp 10	Agnes Maureen Flynn	Ralph S. and Evelyn M.	— o
Sp 14	Steven Herbert		Hanover — Rockland

BIRTHS REGISTERED IN THE [TOW]N OF ROCKLAND FOR THE YEAR 1938

Date of Birth	Name	Name of Parents	Birthplace of
Sep 18			
Sep 20	Kenneth	[Jo]hn E. and [Hel]en L. Barnes	Rhode [Island]
Sep 21	Edward	[Pa]ul J. and Mary L. [Sou]za	Rockland
Sep 21		[Jo]hn A. and Mary G. [Ba]rr	New Brunswick
Sep 22	Estabrook	[Pe]ter A. and Ay R.	
Sep 25	Patrick Brady	[Fre]d S. and Rose M.	
Sep 29	Dorothy	Rob[ert] W. and Ellen C. Peterson	Scituate
Oct 1	Kelly	[Jo]hn E. and Margaret M. Roche	
Oct 10	Gloria Pennini	Irving G. and Elfrida M. VonBeidel	
Oct 10	Joan Paulding	[Fre]d A. Jr. and	
Oct 10		Rob[ert] M. and Ay Louise	
Oct 20	Allen	[Wi]lm F. and [Jo]hn E. Wig	New Brunswick
Oct 21	Marie	Daniel and [M]ay L. Litchfield	Rockport
Oct 25	Bartholomew	[Jo]e F. and Myrtle F. Atwood	Rockland
Oct 29	Ernest George	Ralph E. and Mary E.	New
Oct 31		[Pe]ter C. and [G]eo Helen Earle	N.
Nov 17	Harris	[Ge]o L. and [Ett]a E. Fritz	N.
Nov 28		[Jo]n G.	
Dec 4	Antonio Stella	[Jo]hn and [Jo]hn E.	Brockton
Dec 8	LaBelle	[Har]old E. and Ruth N. Wade	Kingston
Dec 9	Harold Peter	Louis P. and Irene A.	Rockland
Dec 10		[Jo]hn B. and [M]a G. Simmons	New
Dec 11	Herbert [S.] Irwin Treen	Karl F. and [Je]e G. Irwin	Rockland
Dec 23		[Jo]e C. and Margaret E. Skehan	E. Boston
Dec 31	Frances Ann Rubino		

DEATHS REGISTERED IN THE TOWN OF ROCKLAND FOR THE ... 1938

Date	Name	Cause of Death	Age Y	M	D	Place
Jan 3			87	4	18	Falm
Jan 9		sclerosis	70	1	3	Lu
Jan 9			70	11	4	N
Jan 12	Thayer		70	11	21	
Jan 16			38	11	29	
Jan 16	Joseph Stedman		59	2	29	
Jan 18	Joseph E. Condon		65	5	13	
Jan 21			77	9	2	
Jan 28			89	10	27	
Feb 5	Mary Sacks		68		3	
Feb 5			66	11	2	
Feb 11	Ellen		67		3	S.
Feb 13					18	
Feb 16	George	Lymhoblastoma	80	3	17	En,
Feb 21			83	5	3	
Feb 23		Heart disease	71	2	4	Warsaw, N. Y.
Feb 23	Marietta Blake				8	
Mar 3	(Baby Yourell		79	4	2	
Mar 4			79		16	
Mar 7	Wm H.		39	5	22	N.
Apr 19	A.		65	4		
Mar 20			76		25	En,
Apr 1			91	5		Na Scotia
Apr 1						

DEATHS REGISTERED IN THE TOWN OF ROCKLAND FOR THE YEAR 1938

Date	Name	Age Y	M	D	Cause of Death	Birthplace
Apr 3	John ...n	72	2	0	...o sclerosis	Norwell
Apr 4	...ce E. Bell	57	7	7	...y sclerosis	Swanton, Vt.
Apr 4	Emily Adams Ewell	79	8	21	Arterio sclerosis	...ld
Apr 6	...ie L. McCarthy	54	2	5	Cerebral ...hage	Rockland
Apr 6	George C. Clary Jr.	51	11	—	...y sclerosis	Hingham
Apr 16	...as J. Merrill	78	8	29	Coronary sclerosis	Rockland
Apr 19	Louisa C. Shaw	85			...y ...io sclerosis	Hingham
Apr 20	Elmer C. ...b	59	3	5	...er of pancreas	War ...m
Apr 21	Orville Martin	56	8	0	Cardio Vascular Disease	Buffalo, N. Y.
Apr 23	Eliza P. ...er	69	11	8	Arterio ...is	Hingham
May 3	Martha ...ss	73	9	2	Diabetis ...us	Boston
May 4	...ie Canavan	76	2	27	Aortic regurgitation	Nova Scotia
May 6	...ia Benoit	63	6	5	Septicemia Decubitus	Lawrence
May 10	...in O'...	96	3	18	Arterio sclerosis	...nd
May 11	Sadie E. ...ay	67	10	8	...ry ...in	Rockland
May 15	Julia P. Tisdale	48	8	25	...ry sclerosis	Haverhill
May 21	Ada A. ...ll	87	—	25	...y sclerosis	Po...land, Me.
May 22	...is J. Brassill	62	7	12	...y ...osis	Hartford, Conn.
May 24	...e M.	53	9	26	Coronary sclerosis	Denmark
May 29	...na Weston Bryant	71	—	18	...a Pectoris	Rockland
Jun 5	Thomas ...y	79	—	27	...er of esophagus	England
Jun 8	...n					
Jun 15	...el J. ...idine	51	—	—	Lobar ...ia	Rockland
Jun 15	Charles k...rt	50	—	—	Coronary sclerosis	Peru, Mass.

DEATHS REGISTERED IN THE TOWN OF ROCKLAND FOR THE YEAR 1938

Date	Name	Age Y	M	D	Cause of Death	Place
Jun 17	...h S. ...Hps	80	4	13	...cinoma Uterus	...ne, N. H.
Jun 20	...es W. ...	70	3	11	Chr. Nephritis	Rockland
Jun 23	Henry W. ...Md	85	1	11	...al ...mbosis	...
... 26	...ard W. McCarthy	73	2	18	...tis	...
Jun 29	...d P. FitzGerald	81	3	14	...onary s ...osis	...
Jun 30	Sarah ...n ...keman	92	3	13	Chr. Myocarditis	...
Jul 2	Lucy Ellen Ford	81	1	13	...onary ...mbosis	...
Jul 6	John M. Lynch	80	—	18	...o ...tis	...
Jul 10	Mary E. ...n	66	2	—	Me P ...tis Stomach	Rockland
Jul 12	Dorothy Porter ...eff	44	11	29	...na breast	Rockland
Jul 13	...et D. Healey	73	2	—	Broncho p... ...ia	...
Jul 16	Peter L. ...e	78	6	16	...inoma ...n	...
Jul 18	...nes ...h ...	75	—	—	...r. ...arditis	...
Jul 18	Margaret E. ...My	68	5	—	Chr ...itis	...
Jul 29	...ie ...n ...Wg	64	3	1	...onary ...sion ... M	...
Jul 31	...r E. Hayward	59	8	12	...onary ...sis ... C	...
Aug 1	...l ...o	63	—	28	...h shot abdomen	Portugal
Aug 1	...e Me Ferron	16	5	2	...is lungs	Rockland
Aug 3	...	26	10	30	Pulmonary Tuberculosis	Rockland
Aug 6	Rosella K. Callahan	2	5	13	Peritonitis	Brockton
Aug 13	...h ...as Barry	45	2	12	...e ...tis	Rockland
Aug 16	...h F. ...h	86	7	15	...y sclerosis	Boston
Aug 18	Katharine ...n Gilbride	69	—	—	...al ...rrhage	Rockland
Aug 20	...n Kemp	7	5	27	...a	Rockland

DEATHS REGISTERED IN THE TOWN OF ROCKLAND FOR THE YEAR 1938

Date	Name	Y	M	D	Cause of Death	Birthplace
Aug 23	Thomas F. …	63	8	4	…	…
Aug 25	… H. …	80	—	10	…	Me.
Aug 27	Wm L. …	82	1	20	… Po …	…
Aug 28	… My Osborne	59	10	24	…	…
Aug 31	… A. …	4	5	6	…	…
Sept 4	…	60	11	10	… Mapl …	Me.
Sept 5	… Flynn	83	—	2	…	…
Sept 6	… Kelsea	68	5	28	…	…
Sept 15	… O'Connor	69	—	—	…	…
Sept 18	Stillborn					
Sept 22	…	57	—	25	… M …	…
Sept 26	…	81	11	24	… sclerosis Sandwich	
Sept 27	… J. McHugh	67	6	23	… New York City	
Sept 29	…	75	10	13	… Sw …	
Sept 29	… Studley	81	6	3	… Ireland	
Oct 1	…	83	3	3	… R …	
Oct 8	… J. Smith	65	9	9	…	…
Oct 9	Bethia …	86	5	27	Cerebral hemorrhage Bos …	
Oct 10	…	69	9	19	… Hanover	
Oct 14	…	69	6	1	Arterio sclerosis … Be …	
Oct 20	… Miller	71	2	19	…	…
Oct 31	… F. …	44	11	5	… Sweden	
Nov 11	… Ellen Ham	64	5	12	… So …	…

DEATHS REGISTERED IN THE TOWN OF ROCKLAND FOR THE YEAR 1938

Date	Name	Age Y	M	D	Cause of Death	Birthplace
Nov 11	Mia Van Pelt Rainsford	63	9	1	Mat... hemorrhage	Mat... R. I.
Nov 25	William F. Lonergan	56	11	28	Cerebral hemorrhage	Weymouth
Nov 28	Daniel Francis Hamilton	88	1	—	Broncho pneumonia	Na Scotia
Nov 28	Lucinda Webb Charles	82	7	29	Myocarditis	Chatham, N. H.
Dec 4	Elizabeth Jane Mellefont	68	2	26	Cerebral hemorrhage	Rockland
Dec 8	Charles E. Bowler	68	11	19	Coronary thosis	Rockland
Dec 16	Mary E. Gallagher	80	3	2	Nephritis	Weymouth
Dec 25	Nils A. Johnson	75	5	—	Arterio sclerosis	Sweden
Dec 26	Louisa C. Farnham	70	3	21	Carcinoma of Intestine	Lowell
Dec 27	Charles H. Josselyn	57	10	15	...ry sclerosis	Rockland
Dec 31	George A. Hurley	60	9	19	Carcinoma of stomach	Hanover

Report of the Records for the Year 1938

ANNUAL TOWN MEETING, MARCH 7, 1938

Pursuant to the warrant a meeting was held in the Rockland Opera House, beginning at 7:30 o'clock P. M. and the following votes were passed and action taken.

The meeting was called to order at 7:30 P. M. by the Moderator, Magorisk L. Walls.

The warrant and Constable's return of service thereof was read by the Town Clerk.

The Moderator apponted the following tellers for the meeting: Dora Fihelly, Elizabeth Walsh, Marjorie Allison, Esther Rawson, Abraham Lelyveld, William G. W. Holloway, Alonzo W. Ford and Mildred Harney.

Article 1. Voted to accept the reports of the various Town Officers and Committees as published in the Town Report.

Article 2. Voted to raise and appropriate the following amounts for the purposes named:

School Department	$104 373 00
State Aid	650 00
Soldiers' Relief	8 000 00
Care of Soldiers' Graves	125 00
Memorial Library and Dog Fund	4 200 00
Street Lighting	9 134 00

Highway Surveyor	1	350	00
Tarvia and Road Binder	3	500	00
Highway Repairs	3	500	00
Sidewalks	1	000	00
Cleaning Union Street	1	200	00
Clean-up Week		75	00
Fire Department	10	126	68
Police Department	8	956	20
Forest Fires		500	00
Board of Health	5	000	00
Inspection of Animals		150	00
Park Department	2	800	00
Old Age Assistance	35	000	00
Moth Department		300	00
Tree Warden		900	00
Town Officers	6	800	00
Office Rent	1	240	00
Sealer of weights and measures		400	00
Elections	1	700	00
Compensation Insurance	2	250	00
Massachusetts Industrial School	2	000	00
Town Report and Poll Book	1	200	00
Support of Poor and Infirmary	45	000	00
Mothers' Aid	8	000	00
Town Notes and Interest	28	000	00
Assessors	2	500	00
Snow Removal	12	217	68
Miscellaneous Assessors	1	100	00
Miscellaneous Treasurer		800	00
Miscellaneous Clerk		350	00
Miscellaneous Selectmen		120	00
Miscellaneous Registrars		200	00
Miscellaneous Sealer		120	00
Miscellaneous Unclassified	1	150	00
Miscellaneous Collector	1	400	00

Total amount raised under this article $317 387 56

Under Article No. 2. Meeting of March 7, 1938.

Voted to pass over appropriations for the following: Military Aid; Guide Boards and Signs; Massachusetts Hospital School; Reserve Fund.

Under Article No. 2. Adjourned meeting March 14, 1938
Voted to reconsider Article No. 2, pertaining to Cleaning Union Street.

Voted to raise and appropriate the sum of $1,200.00 for the Cleaning of Union Street, which amended the amount of $1,100.00 raised and appropriated at the meeting of March 7.

Article 3. Voted to authorize the Town Treasurer, with the approval of the Selectmen, to borrow money from time to time in anticipation of the revenue of the financial year beginning January 1, 1939, and to issue a note or notes therefore, payable within one year, and to renew such note or notes as may be given for a period of less than one year in accordance with Section 17, Chapter 44, General Laws.

Article 4. Voted to raise and appropriate the sum of fifteen hundred dollars ($1,500.00) to be spent under the direction of the Selectmen for the part payment of a Visiting Nurse.

Article 5. Voted to appropriate the sum of twenty-six thousand dollars ($26,000.00) for the use of the Water Department from which shall be paid the salaries of the Water Commissioners and other expenses of the Water Department the same to be taken from the Water Revenue.

Article 6. Voted to raise and appropriate the sum of two hundred eighty-eight dollars ($288.00) to be spent under the direction of the Selectmen for the purpose of renting quarters for the use of the Veterans of the Spanish-American War.

Article 7. Voted to raise and appropriate the sum of four hundred dollars ($400.00) to be spent under the direction of the Selectmen for the observance of Memorial Day.

Article 8., Voted to raise and appropriate the sum of sixty dollars ($60.00) for the care of the Town Cemetery.

Article 9. Voted to raise and appropriate the sum of nine hundred dollars ($900.00) to be spent under the direction of the Selectmen for the purpose of renting quarters for the use of the Rockland Post No. 147 of the American Legion.

Article 10. Voted to raise and appropriate the sum of one hundred and fifty dollars ($150.00) for the use of the Plymouth County Trustees for County Aid to Agriculture and to choose James D. Mahoney as Town Director as provided in Sections 41 and 45 of Chapter 128, General Laws.

Article 11. Voted to raise and appropriate one hundred fifty dollars ($150.00) to be used by the School Committee to pay for the expense of heating, lighting and for Casualty Insurance of Junior-Senior High and McKinley School Buildings as well as additional expense for janitors when the buildings are used for individuals and associations for educational, recreational, and like purposes under the provision of Chapter 71, Section 71, or the General Laws.

Article 12. Voted to accept Chapter 77, Section 1, of the Acts of 1937, "An act providing for absentee voting" at the regular town elections.

Affirmative 349   Negative 6

Voted to take up article 97 in conjunction with Article 13.

Article 97. Voted to create a Board to be designated as the Supervisory Real Estate Board to consist of the Assessors, Chairman of the Board of Selectmen and the Town Treasurer. Said Board shall have charge and custody of all Real Estate acquired by the town by foreclosure of Tax Liens or without foreclosure under the provisions of Chapter 60, Sections 79 and 80 of the General Laws (Ter. Ed.) and amendments thereof. The Selectmen with the written approval of said Board and on terms satisfactory to it, may sell or convey all lands held by the Town under foreclosure of tax liens or without foreclosure as above set forth.

Article 13. Voted to pass over the authorizing of the selectmen to sell and convey by proper deed or deeds and on terms satisfactory to them any lands now or hereafter owned by the town by virtue of foreclosure of tax titles or deeds to the town without foreclosure under the provisions of Chapter 60, sections 79 and 80 of the General Laws (Ter. Ed.) and amendments thereof.

Article 14. Voted to pass over the raising and appropriating of the sum of one hundred fifty dollars ($150.00) for striping streets where needed.

Article 15. voted to raise and appropriate the sum of One hundred dollars $(100.00) for Criminal Cases in Court.

Article 16. Voted to raise and appropriate the sum of thirty-eight thousand six hundred seven dollars and fifty-one cents ($38,607.51) to be paid into the Town Treasury on account of overlays in the following departments:

Burial of Indigent Soldiers	$	100 00
Fire Department		849 59

Snow	83	00
Miscellaneous Unclassified	684	77
Soldier's Relief	4 368	08
Old Age Assistance	10 505	61
Public Welfare	22 013	31
Mother's Aid	3	15

$38 607 51

Article 17. Voted to raise and appropriate the sum of two hundred ninety-two dollars and fifty cents ($292.50) to insure the Firemen of the Town of Rockland that they might receive compensation in case of accident when on duty.

Article 18. Voted to raise and appropriate the sum of thirty-five hundred dollars to be spent in conjunction with the State and County to rebuild East Water Street from where the rebuilding ended in 1937 to Webster Street.

Article 19. Voted to raise and appropriate the sum of twelve hundred fifty-seven dollars and seventy cents ($1257.70) to be paid as land damage to various persons for the taking of land in East Water Street as laid out by the County Commissioners.

Article 20. Voted to pass over the raising and appropriating of a sum of money to build a cement curb and asphalt sidewalk on the easterly side of Liberty Street from Vernon Street to East Water Street.

Article 21. Voted to pass over the raising and appropriating of one thousand dollars ($1000.00) to build an asphalt sidewalk and curb on the northerly side of Exchange Street from Union Street to Myrtle Street a distance of 845 feet.

Article 22. Voted to raise and appropriate the sum of

five hundred fifty dollars ($550.00) for materials to build an asphalt sidewalk with curb on the east side of Union Street from residence of Dr. Frederic Corey to Bigelow Avenue, approximately 878 feet, the labor to be furnished by the W.P.A.

Article 23. Voted to raise and appropriate the sum of five hundred ten dollars ($510.00) to be used for materials to build an asphalt sidewalk with curb where necessary on the north side of East Water Street, from Howard Street to Sunnybank Avenue, a distance of 1265 feet, the labor to be furnished by the W.P.A.

Article 24. Voted to pass over the raising and appropriating of the sum of eighteen hundred dollars ($1800.00) to build a sidewalk and curb on the east side of Liberty Street from Webster Street to the Arnold factory a distance of 1500 feet.

Article 25. Voted to construct a sidewalk and curb on the easterly side of Myrtle Street commencing at the junction of Myrtle and Summit Streets and continuing to the residence of Dr. Joseph H. Dunn, a distance of 550 feet, and raise and appropriate the sum of three hundred fifty dollars ($350.00) for materials, the labor to be furnished by the W.P.A.

Article 26. Voted to pass over the raising and appropriating of twelve hundred seventy-five dollars ($1275.00) to build a sidewalk and curb on the north side of Custer Street from Howard Street to Liberty Street, a distance of approximately 1050 feet.

Article 27. Voted to pass over the installing of a sidewalk on the south side of Webster Street from East Water Street to the Hanover line where the curb has already been installed and raising and appropriating a sum of money necessary for the same.

Article 28. Voted to pass over the raising and appropriating of the sum of seven hundred eighty dollars ($780.00) to build a sidewalk and curb on the west side of Liberty Street between Stanton Street and East Water Street, a distance of Approximately 650 feet.

Article 29. Voted to raise and appropriate the sum of three hundred fifty dollars ($350.00) to be used for materials to rebuild with asphalt top with cement curb the sidewalk on the south side of School Street from Union Street to Franklin Avenue, the labor to be furnished by the W.P.A.

Article 30. Voted to accept a Town Way known as Dexter Road a distance of seventy-five feet (75 feet) as laid out by the Selectmen and filed with the Town Clerk from the present road southerly.

Article 31. Voted to pass over the raising and appropriating of a sum of money to be used to employ a Supervisor of Bureau of Old age assistance.

Article 32. Voted to raise and appropriate the sum of seven thousand dollars $7,000.00) to be spent for the cost of material and general expenses under the W.P.A.

Article 33. Voted to raise and appropriate the sum of four hundred dollars ($400.00) to pay for the expense of heating, lighting, gas and removal of garbage in the McKinley School Building when the building is used by the Nursery, Sewing and Recreational projects of the Works Progress Administration.

Article 34. Voted to raise and appropriate the sum of four thousand thirteen dollars and seventy-three cents ($4,013.73) for the maintenance of the Plymouth County Hospital.

Article 35. Voted to raise and appropriate the sum of

six hundred dollars ($600.00) for the maintenance of traffic beacons and signals.

Article 36. Voted to clean catch basins and gutters and that the amount of six hundred dollars ($600.00) be appropriated from the amount raised under Article No. 2 for Highway Repairs to pay for the cost of same.

Article 37. Voted to raise and appropriate the sum of one thousand two hundred fifty dollars ($1,250.00) for materials to build a sidewalk and curb on the west side of Union Street from Oregon Avenue to the Weymouth line, a distance of 2600 feet, the labor to be furnished by the W.P.A.

Article 38. Voted to pass over the raising and appropriating of the sum of twelve hundred and fifty dollars ($1,250.00) to build a sidewalk and curb on the north side of Pacific Street a distance of 1100 feet.

Article 39. Voted to raise and appropriate the sum of two hundred twenty-five dollars ($225.00) for materials to build a sidewalk and curb on the south side of Belmont Street from Union Street a distance of 550 feet, the labor to be furnished by the W.P.A.

Article 40. Voted to pass over the raising and appropriating of the sum of twelve hundred dollars ($1,200.00) to build a sidewalk and curb on the south side of Vernon Street a distance of 1000 feet.

Article 41. Voted to raise and appropriate the sum of three hundred sixty dollars ($360.00) for materials to build a sidewalk and curb on the east side of George Street from Vernon Street a distance of 600 feet, the labor to be furnished by the W.P.A.

Article 42. Voted to pass over the raising and appropriating of the sum of three hundred seventy-five dollars ($375.00) to build a sidewalk and curb on the west side of Concord Street from Market Street, a distance of 300 feet.

Article 43.   Voted to pass over the raising and appropriating of the sum of nine hundred seventy-five dollars ($975.00) to build a sidewalk and curb on the south side of William Street from Plain Street a distance of 800 feet.

Article 44.   Voted to raise and appropriate the sum of seven hundred twenty-five dollars ($725.00) for materials to build a sidewalk and curb on the north side of Central Street from Centre Avenue a distance of 2500 feet, the labor to be furnished by the W.P.A.

Article 45.   Voted to pass over the raising and appropriating of the sum of twelve hundred dollars ($1,200.00) to build a sidewalk and curb on the south side of Albion Street from Concord Street a distance of 1000 feet.

Article 46.   Voted to raise and appropriate the sum of six hundred dollars ($600.00) for materials to build a sidewalk and curb on the west side of Liberty Street southerly from East Water Street a distance of 1000 feet, the labor to be furnished by the W.P.A.

Article 47.   Voted to pass over the raising and appropriating of the sum of three hundred sixty dollars ($360.00) to build a sidewalk and curb on the east side of Wall Street a distance of 300 feet.

Article 48.   Voted to pass over the raising and appropriating of the sum of eleven hundred dollars ($1,100.00) to build a sidewalk and curb on the south side of Webster Street between Union and Howard Streets a distance of 900 feet.

Article 49. Voted to adopt the following By-Law:-No person except the Superintendent of Streets, or Highway Surveyor, and those acting under his order in the lawful performance of their duties, shall break up or dig up the ground or stones in any street or way which the town is bound to keep in repair, without first obtaining a written permit from the Selectmen therefor, and the person so licensed shall erect and maintain a suitable railing or fence around the section or parts of any street or way so dug up or broken as long as the same shall remain unsafe or inconvenient for travellers, and also during the whole of every night, from twilight in the evening to sunrise in the morning, lighted lanterns shall be so placed as to be a warning to travellers on such street or way.

Violation of this By-Law shall be punished by a fine not to exceed twenty dollars for each offence.

Article 50. Voted to pass over the raising and appropriating of the sum of one thousand dollars ($1,000.00) to purchase a sand pit, comprising of approximately 40 acres, off Beech Street, owned by John Nelson of Hanover.

Article 51. Voted to raise and appropriate the sum of four hundred dollars ($400.00) for materials to rebuild a sidewalk and curb on the north side of Payson Avenue from Union Street to Arlington Street, the labor to be furnished by the W.P.A.

Article 52. Voted to pass over the raising and appropriating of the sum of four hundred fifty-six dollars and fifty cents ($456.50) to reimburse Louis Kramer in part for the rebuilding of cement sidewalk on Union and School Streets.

Article 53. Voted to raise and appropriate the sum of fifteen dollars ($15.00) to place a street light on Spring Street near the residence of Elmer Bates at 134 Spring Street.

Article 54. Voted to raise and appropriate the sum of six hundred dollars ($600.00) for materials for the installation of a curb and sidewalk on the westerly side of Plain Street, from Emerson Street to North Avenue, the labor to be furnished by the W.P.A.

Article 55. Voted to pass over the raising and appropriating of a sum of money to install a sidewalk and curb on the southerly side of Reed Street, from the residence of Patrick Mahoney to Plain Street

Article 56. Voted to raise and appropriate the sum of sixty-three dollars and eighty-three cents ($63.83) to pay the bill of Giles W. Howland for surveying and establishing street bounds on Liberty Street, required for Land Court Survey. (See Chapter 86 Section 1 (Ter. Ed) General Laws of Massachusetts).

Article 57. Voted to accept a Town way, known as Curry Street, as laid out by the Selectmen and filed with the Town Clerk, from Pond Street westerly, a distance of two hundred seventy-one 9/10 (271.9) feet.

Article 58. Voted to raise and appropriate the sum of six hundred fifty dollars ($650.00) for materials to build a sidewalk with curb on the westerly side of Division Street, northerly from Reed Street, the labor to be furnished by the W.P.A.

Article 59. A motion to raise and appropriate $600.00 for materials the labor to be furnished by the W.P.A. for the purposes of carrying out this article not agreed to:
Affirmative 144   Negative 157

Voted to pass over the raising and appropriating of a sum of money to purchase material for building a sidewalk and curb on the westerly side of Union Street from the residence of Michael Cullinan to Salem Street, the labor to be furnished by the W.P.A.

Article 60. Voted to pass over the raising and appropriating of a sum of money to build a sidewalk and curb on the north side of Webster Street from Wright's Brook to Hartsuff Street a distance of approximately 1000 feet.

Article 61. Voted to raise and appropriate the sum of two thousand nine hundred fifteen dollars ($2,915.00) for repairs at Infirmary.

At 10:15 P. M.
Voted to adjourn until March 14, 1938 at 7:30 P. M.

Article 62. Voted to raise and appropriate the sum of two hundred fifty dollars $250.00) to reimburse Thomas Murrill for damage to truck on Spring Street.

Article 63. Voted to raise and appropriate the sum of four hundred dollars ($400.00) for materials to build a sidewalk and curb on the easterly side of Howard Street from 71 Howard Street to Market Street a distance of approximately 671 feet, the labor to be furnished by the W.P.A.

Article 64. Voted to pass over the raising and appropriating of the sum of fifteen hundred dollars ($1,500.00) to build a sidewalk and curb on the north side of Belmont Street from the residence of Charles McGonagle to Division Street, a distance of 522 feet.

Article 65. Motion to raise and appropriate the sum of $700.00 for materials the labor to be furnished by the W.P.A. not agreed to.

Voted to pass over the raising and appropriating of a sum of money to rebuild the sidewalk with curb on the west side of Spring Street from the end of the present rebuilt sidewalk to Summer Street.

Article 66. Motion to pass over this article not agreed to.

Affirmative 338 Negative 339

It was voted not to accept the provisions of Chapter 31, Section 48, of the General Laws relative to placing members of the Police Department under Civil Service Laws.

Affirmative 365 Negative 431

Article 67. Voted to raise and appropriate the sum of four hundred dollars ($400.00) to clean, grade, and tarvia both gutters of Hartsuff Street a distance of 700 feet and to Tarvia the whole length of Hartsuff Street.

Article 68. Voted to finish with asphalt top the end of sidewalk at Webster and Beal Streets a distance of 12 feet, and the corner of Webster and Hartsuff Streets on east side to end of curbing, a distance of 20 feet, and that the amount of fifty dollars ($50.00) be appropriated from the amount raised under Article No. 2 for Sidewalks to pay for the cost of same.

Article 69. Voted to raise and appropriate the sum of eighty-five dollars ($85.00) to build a catch basin and drain at the east corner of Webster and Beal Streets (to connect catch basin on Beal Street).

Article 70. Voted to raise and appropriate the sum of four hundred fifty dollars ($450.00) for materials to build a cement curb and black top sidewalk a distance of 719 feet on the easterly side of Concord Street, beginning at the end of the Winthrop Perry estate and continuing to Norman Street, the labor to be furnished by the W.P.A.

Article 71. Voted to pass over the raising and appropriating of the sum of four thousand dollars ($4,000.00) to pay for the cost of material for the rebuilding of Liberty Street, from Market Street to East Water Street, the labor to be done under the W.P.A., a distance of approximately 2600 feet.

Article 72. Voted to pass over the raising and appropriating of a sum of money to build a sidewalk on the north side of West Water Street, extending from Plain Street to a point opposite Prospect Street, a distance of approximately 625 feet.

Article 73. Voted to raise and appropriate the sum of five hundred dollars ($500.00) for the purchase of new hose for the Fire Department.

Article 74. Voted to pass over the raising and appropriating of a sum of money for the painting and repairing of the Fire Station, but voted that the Moderator appoint a committee of five to report at a future town meeting on the same.

Committee appointed: Clyson P. Inkley, Roland T. Phillips, James W. Spence, Daniel DeC. Donovan, Norman J. Beals.

Article 75. Voted to pass over the installing of a Street Light on Arlington Street opposite the residence of Edward Holbrook.

Article 76. Voted to raise and appropriate the sum of twenty-four hundred dollars ($2400.00) as part payment for the Sewing Material used in the Sewing Unit of the W.P.A.

Article 77. Voted that the Moderator appoint a World War Memorial Committee consisting of five members of the Veterans of Foreign Wars, five members of the American Legion and five citizens not affiliated with either to draw up and present to the town at a special or next annual meeting plans for a suitable World War Memorial. The surplus poll tax fund amounting to $4,021.70 now in the treasury of the town of Rockland, accumulated by the General Acts of 1919, Chapter 238 Acts of the Commonwealth whereby a poll tax of $5.00 was levied in 1920-21-22 and 1923, to be used for the purpose of constructing and erecting a suitable World War Memorial.

Committee appointed: Harry Holmes, Frank Dixon, William Watson, Harold Morse, Augustine Ledwell, Charles T. Walls, Ralph Bingham, Harold Anderson, Arthur O'Neil, William Christie, John Troy Jr., Joseph B. Estes, Bernard DeLorey, Abram Lelyveld, Russell Hawes.

Article 78. Voted to pass over the raising and appropriating of a sum of money to reopen the former drain pipes at Wright's Brook on Webster Street near Liberty Square, with the curb recessed opening type of catch basin tops.

Article 79. Voted to raise and appropriate the sum of seventy-five dollars ($75.00) to install an electric light in the vicinity of the McKinley School on Union Street on pole 49/43.

Article 80. Voted to cover the rough serface with a fine mixture of asphalt on the sidewalk on Webster Street near E. T. Wright Co., shop a distance of 100 feet and that the amount of seventy-five dollars ($75.00) be appropriated from the amount raised under Article No. 2 for sidewalks to pay for the cost of same.

Article 81. Voted to raise and appropriate the sum of one hundred fifteen dollars ($115.00) for materials to cover the rough surface with fine mixture of asphalt on the sidewalk on East Water Street, from Wainshilbaum's Store to a point near Franklin Avenue, the labor to be furnished by the W.P.A.

Article 82. Voted to raise and appropriate the sum of eighty dollars ($80.00) for materials to install a catch basin on the north side of Vernon Street near number 226, and the labor to be furnished by the W.P.A.

Article 83. Voted to raise and appropriate the sum of two hundred fifty-two dollars ($252.00) for materials to build an asphalt sidewalk with curb on the east side of Glen Street from Exchange Street, northerly, a distance of 360 feet, the labor to be furnished by the W.P.A.

Article 84. Voted to authorize the Moderator and the Board of Selectmen jointly to appoint a committee of five to investigate the matter of a Zone Planning Board for the town, said committee to report with recommendations at a subsequent meeting.

Committee appointed: Arthur P. Wilcox, James A. Cody, Francis L. Gammon, Joseph Lelyveld, Carl G. Fass.

Article 85. Voted to pass over the raising and appropriating of the sum of three hundred dollars ($300.00) for materials for a drain and two catch basins on the easterly side of Concord Street starting at the end of the present drain near the residence of Domenic DelPrete and running a distance of 300 feet southerly, the labor to be furnished by the W.P.A.

Article 86. Voted to install covered drains on Maple and Munroe Streets to consist of 600 feet of pipe and 3 catch basins on Myrtle and Exchange Streets to consist of 575 feet of pipe and 4 catch basins; and on Crescent Street to consist of 300 feet of pipe and 2 catch basins, and raise and appropriate the sum of six hundred fifty dollars ($650.00) for materials, the labor to be furnished by the W.P.A.

Article 87. Voted to pass over the raising and appropriating of a sum of money to relevel the cement sidewalk and curb and to cement in the grass plot on the north side of Webster Street, at Lannin's Garage.

Article 88. Voted to raise and appropriate the sum of five hundred dollars ($500.00) for materials for a sidewalk and curb on the northerly side of Williams Street, from Plain Street to Prospect Street a distance of approximately 815 feet, the labor to be furnished by the W.P.A.

Article 89. Voted to pass over the raising and appropriating of a sum of money to rebuild road and install proper drains on Deering Square.

Article 90. Voted to raise and appropriate the sum of eighty-five dollars ($85.00) for materials for a drain and catch basin on the easterly side of Howard Street starting at the Railroad Track and running north to Custer Street a distance of 186 feet, the labor to be furnished by the W.P.A.

Article 91. Voted to raise and appropriate the sum of two hundred seventy-five dollars ($275.00) for materials for a drain and three catch basins on the Westerly side of Hartsuff Street, starting at Webster Street and running a distance of 660 feet northerly and to repair the gutter an additional 50 feet, the labor to be furnished by the W.P.A.

Article 92. Voted to raise and appropriate the sum of three hundred dollars ($300.00) to pay the expense of foreclosing tax titles in the Land Court.

Article 93. Voted to pass over the raising and appropriating of the sum of one thousand dollars ($1,000.00) for a Fourth of July Celebration. The money to be spent under a Committee appointed by the Moderator.

Article 94. Voted to pass over the raising and appropriating of the sum of one thousand dollars ($1,000.00) for expenses in connection with cases before the Appellate Tax Board.

Article 95. Voted to raise and appropriate the sum of two hundred dollars ($200.00) for materials for improvements of the grounds at Reed's Pond, the labor to be furnished by the W.P.A.

Article 96. Voted to pass over the installing of a sidewalk on the west side of Franklin Avenue from Church to School Streets, a distance of 525 lineal feet; sidewalk to consist of cement curb and bituminous top and raising and appropriating of the sum of nine hundred seventy-five dollars ($975.00) for the same.

Article 97. Taken up with Article 13.

Article 98. Voted to install a street light on Goddard Avenue near the entrance to the Episcopal church and raise and appropriate the sum of fifteen dollars ($15.00) for the same.

Article 99. Voted to raise and appropriate the sum of five hundred seventy-five dollars ($575.00) for materials to build an asphalt sidewalk with curb on the northerly side of Emerson Street from Plain Street, westerly a distance of 900 feet, the labor to be furnished by the W.P.A.

Article 100. Voted to appropriate from the amount raised under Article No. 32, the sum of three hundred twenty-one dollars and eighty-eight cents ($321.88) to pay in part for administrative expenses for Federal Commodity Distribution.

A Subsequent meeting for the election of Town Officers was held in the Rockland Opera House, Savings Bank Building, Monday, March 14th, 1938. The polls opened at 5:45 in the forenoon and closed at 4:00 in the afternoon.

The following Election Officers, appointed by the Selectmen, were sworn to the faithful performance of their duties by the Town Clerk.

Ballot Clerks

URSULA FRENCH	MARY LYNCH
EVELYN WHITING	OLIVE WHEELER

Checkers

ELIZABETH CRANE	E. BURTON RAMSDELL
JEREMIAH SHEA	CHARLES CALLANAN

Ballot Boxes

ROBERT PARKER	RALPH MEASURES

Tellers

MATTHEW O'GRADY	JAMES McPARTLAND
JOANNA SUTHERLAND	ALBERT RYAN
TIMOTHY WHITE	ELLIS BLAKE
LAVINIA CONDON	HELEN MORRISSEY
JOHN HUNT	JOHN WINSLOW
ANGELINA BALL	JOHN DILLON
JOHN PAULIN	RALPH McVEIN
LILLIAN RAINSFORD	ANNA ANDERSON
KATHRYN TOBIN	PHILLIP MURPHY

Tabulators

ANNIE GARRITY	JOSEPHINE GAMMON
HELENA HUNT	CARL FASS

Before the opening of the polls, cards of instructions and cards containing abstracts of the laws imposing pen-alties upon voters and specimen ballots were posted as re-- quired by the laws of the Commonwealth relating to the "Conduct of Elections" and all other provisions thereof complied with.

Two packages said to contain 4500 ballots were de- livered to the Presiding Election Officer by the Town Clerk and receipt taken from the ballot clerks therefor by the Town Clerk.

At the opening of the polls ballot boxes wre publicly opened and shown to be empty; and they registered 0000. The keys to the ballot boxes were then placed in the cus- tody of the Police Officers on duty at the polls.

The ballot boxes were opened and ballots taken there- from for counting before the close of the polls upon the order of the Moderator and Town Clerk.

Upon the closing of the polls the ballot boxes registered as follows:

Ballot Box No. 1, Eighteen hundred thirty-three   (1833)
     (three more than there was ballots cast)
Ballot Box. No. 2 Nineteen hundred sixty-six   (1966)
     (one more than there was ballots cast)

The total number of names of voters checked on the voting lists as having voted was
Thirty seven hundred ninety-five   (3795
    Men 1944   Women 1851

The total number of ballots cast was
   Thirty seven hundred and ninety-five   (3795)
     Ballot Box No. 1   1830
     Ballot Box No. 2   1965
                                3795

The result of the balloting was declared to the meeting at 10:15 o'clock P. M. and was as follows:

MODERATOR—One Year

Magorisk L. Walls, Twenty nine hundred and seven 2907
Blanks, Eight hundred eighty-eight •   888

TOWN CLERK—One Year

Ralph L. Belcher, Thirty one hundred fifty-five   3155
Blanks,. Six hundred forty   640

TOWN TREASURER—One Year

Nathaniel S. Groce, Four hundred sixty-four   464
Charles J. Higgins, Three thousand eighty   3080
Blanks, Two hundred fifty-one   251

TAX COLLECTOR—One Year

James A. Donovan, Three thousand seventy-seven   3077
Blanks, Seven hundred eighteen   718

-SELECTMEN, BOARD OF PUBLIC WELFARE AND FENCE VIEWERS—One Year

Joseph Belanger, Four hundred ninety-five   495
John J. Bowler, Eighteen hundred   1800
Elmer C. Cobb, Sixteen hundred forty-five   1645
Matthew D. Gay, Eleven hundred seventy-four   1174
Harry S. Torrey, Eighteen hundred fifty-nine   1859
Norman S. Whiting, Two thousand twenty-two   2022
Blanks, Twenty three hundred ninety   2390

HIGHWAY SURVEYOR—One Year

William Bell, Five hundred forty-seven   547
William H. Friary, Twelve hundred ninety   1290

Toiva M. Jarvinen, One hundred seventy-one   171
Roderick MacKenzie, Seventeen hundred forty-three 1743
Blanks, Forty-four   44

ASSESSOR—Three Years

Joseph B. Estes, Twenty eight hundred seventeen   2817
William P. O'Neil, Six hundred fifty   650
Blanks, Three hundred twenty-eight   328

AUDITORS—One Year

Leo E. Downey, Eighteen hundred and seven   1807
George A. Gallagher, Two thousand and five   2005
Noel F. Menard, Eight hundred ninety-one   891
Harold B. Monahan, One thousand seventy-one   1071
Edward M. Reardon, Six hundred twenty-seven   627
Harold C. Smith, Sixteen hundred thirty-five   1635
Blanks, Thirty three hundred forty-nine   3349

SCHOOL COMMITTEE—Three Years

Florence G. Cantelmo, Three hundred thirty-four   334
William B. Carey, Fourteen hundred eighty-nine   1489
Dana S. Collins, Two thousand twenty-two   2022
M. Agnes Kelleher, Two thousand twelve   2012
Blanks, Seventeen hundred thirty-three   1733

WATER COMMISSIONER—Three Years

Samuel W. Baker, Two thousand fifty-eight   2058
Fred Stevenson, Fifteen hundred forty-one   1541
Blanks, One hundred ninety-six   196

BOARD OF HEALTH—Three Years

Joseph Frame, Twenty six hundred thirty-six   2636
Blanks, Eleven hundred fifty-nine ·   1159

BOARD OF HEALTH—One Year

Arthur W. Casey, Four hundred twenty-five	425
Edward M. Cullinan, One thousand ninety-six	1096
Domenico DelPrete, Two hundred seventy-two	272
Thomas Fox, Six hundred seventeen	617
John V. Hoadley, Three hundred twenty-two	322
Wesley B. Sears, Two hundred twenty-nine	229
Daniel H. Shoughrow, Four hundred seventy-one	471
Blanks, Three hundred sixty-three	363

LIBRARY TRUSTEES—Three Years

Emily F. Crawford, Twenty seven hundred forty two	2742
Annie E. McIlvene, Twenty four hundred fifty-nine	2459
Blanks, Twenty three hundred eighty-nine	2389

PARK COMMISSIONER—Three Years

Daniel H. Burke, Twenty one hundred nine-two	2192
Elwin E. Gould, Eleven hundred fifty-one	1151
Blanks, Four hundred fifty-two	452

SEWER COMMISSIONER—Three Years

Giles W. Howland, Twenty five hundred seventy-three	2573
Blanks, Twelve hundred twenty-two	1222

TREE WARDEN—One Year

Charles L. Hunt, Eleven hundred sixty-four	1164
Alfred T. Metivier, Sixteen hundred nine-five	1695
Daniel J. Reilly, Two hundred fifty-five	255
John T. Ricca, Three hundred seventy-five	375
Blanks, Three hundred six	306

CONSTABLES—One Year

Ralph H. Badger, Four hundred ninety-two	492

Norman S. Crosby, Eight hundred thirty-eight	838
Clarence S. Damon, Seven hundred forty-two	742
Robert J. Drake, Twenty five hundred eighty-five	2585
Adolph L. W. Johnson, Twenty nine hundred four	2904
Cornelius J. McHugh, Twenty four hundred eighty-five	2485
John H. Murphy, Twenty five hundred forty-seven	2547
George J. Popp, Twenty three hundred fifty-nine	2359
Joseph Rushwick, One hundred sixty-two	162
Blanks, Thirty eight hundred sixty-one	3861

The Moderator declared the following persons duly elected to the offices named and the terms specified: Moderator, one year, Magorisk L. Walls; Town Clerk, one year, Ralph L. Belcher; Town Treasurer, one year, Charles J. Higgins; Tax Collector, one year, James A. Donovan; Selectmen, Board of Public Welfare and Fence Viewers, one year, John J. Bowler, Harry S. Torrey and Norman S. Whiting; Highway Surveyor, one year, Roderick Mac-Kenzie; Assessor, three years, Joseph B. Estes; Auditors, one year, Leo E. Downey, George A. Gallagher, and Harold C. Smith; School Committee, three years, Dana S. Collins, M. Agnes Kelleher; Water Commissioner, three years, Samuel W. Baker; Board of Health, three years, Joseph Frame; Board of Health, one year, Edward M. Cullinan; Library Trustees, three years, Emily F. Crawford, Annie E. McIlvene; Park Commissioner, three years, Daniel H. Burke; Sewer Commissioner, three years; Giles W. Howland; Tree Warden, one year, Alfred T. Metivier; Constables, one year, Robert J. Drake, Adolph L. W. Johnson, Cornelius J. McHugh, John H. Murphy, George J. Popp.

At 10:30 P. M. Voted to adjourn.

A true copy, ATTEST:

RALPH L. BELCHER,
Town Clerk

AMOUNTS RAISED AND APPROPRIATED

ANNUAL TOWN MEETING, MARCH 7, 1938

School Department	$104 373 00·
State Aid	650 00
Soldiers Relief	8 000 00
Care of Soldiers Graves	125 00
Memorial Library and the Dog Fund	4 200 00
Street Lighting	9 134 00
Highway Surveyor	1 350 00
Tarvia and Road Binder	3 500 00
Highway Repairs	3 500 00
Sidewalks	1 000 00
Cleaning Union Street	1 200 00
Clean-Up Week	75 00
Fire Department	10 126 68
Police Department	8 956 20
Forest Fires	500 00
Board of Health	5 000 00
Inspection of Animals	150 00
Park Department	2 800 00
Old Age Assistance	35 000 00
Moth Department	300 00
Tree Warden	900 00
Town Officers	6 800 00
Office Rent	1 240 00
Sealer of Weights and Measures	400 00
Elections	1 700 00
Compensation Insurance	2 250 00
Massachusetts Industrial School	2 000 00
Town Report and Poll Book	1 200 00
Support of Poor and Infirmary	45 000 00
Mother's Aid	8 000 00
Town Notes and Interest	28 000 00
Assessors	2 500 00
Snow Removal	12 217 68

Miscellaneous Assessors	1 100	00
Miscellaneous Treasurer	800	00
Miscellaneous Clerk	350	00
Miscellaneous Selectmen	120	00
Miscellaneous Registrars	200	00
Miscellaneous Sealer	120	00
Miscellaneous Unclassified	1 150	00
Miscellaneous Collector	1 400	00
Part Payment Visiting Nurse	1 500	00
Quarters Spanish-American War Veterans	288	00
Observance Memorial Day	400	00
Care Town Cemetery	60	00
Quarters American Legion	900	00
County Aid to Agriculture	150	00

Expenses & Casualty Insurance, McKinley
and Junior-Senior High when used under
provisions Chap. 71, Sec. 71 Gen. Laws 150 00

Criminal Cases in Court 100 00

Overlays

Burial Indigent Soldiers	$	100	00	
Fire Department		849	59	
Snow		83	00	
Misc. Unclassified		684	77	
Soldiers Relief	4	368	08	
Old Age Assistance	10	505	61	
Public Welfare	22	013	31	
Mother's Aid		3	15	38 607 51

Insure Firemen 292 50

Rebuild E. Water St. in conjunction State
& County 3 500 00

Land Damages E. Water St. 1 257 70

Asphalt sidewalk and curb East side
Union St. Corey's to Bigelow Ave. 550 00

Asphalt sidewalk and curb North side
E. Water St. Howard to Sunnybank Ave. 510 00

Sidewalk and curb East side Myrtle St.,
Summit St. to residence Dr. Jos. H.
Dunn   350 00
Asphalt sidewalk with curb South side
. School St., Union St. to Franklin Ave.   350 00
Cost of Material and General Expense
W.P.A.   7 000 00
Expense at McKinley School account W.P.A.
projects   400 00
Maintenance Plymouth County Hospital   4 013 73
Traffic Beacons and Signals   600 00
Sidewalk and curb West side Union St.
Oregon Ave. to Weymouth line   1 250 00
Sidewalk and curb South side Belmont St.
From Union St. 550 feet   225 00
Sidewalk and curb East side George St.
. Vernon St. to a distance of 600 feet   360 00
Sidewalk and curb North side Central St.
. from Centre Ave. a distance 2500 feet   725 00
Sidewalk and curb West side Liberty St.
Southerly from E. Water St.   600 00
Rebuild sidewalk and curb North side Pay-
son Ave., Union St. to Arlington St.   400 00
Install Elec. light near 134 Spring St.   15 00
Sidewalk and curb West side Plain St.
Emerson St. to North Ave.   600 00
Pay Giles W. Howland establishing bounds
on Liberty Street for Land Court survey   63 83
Sidewalk with curb West side Division St.
Northerly from Reed St.   650 00
Repairs at Infirmary   2 915 00
Reimburse Thomas Murrill damage to truck   250 00
Sidewalk and curb East side Howard St.
from 71 Howard St. to Market St.   400 00
Clean, grade and Tarvia Hartsuff St.   400 00
Build catch basin and drain at East Corner
. Webster and Beal St.   85 00
Sidewalk and curb East side Concord St.

Beginning end of Winthrop Perry Estate to Norman St.	450	00
New Hose Fire Department	500	00
Part payment material W.P.A. Sewing Project	2 400	00
Install Elec. light pole 49/43 near McKinley School on Union Street	75	00
Asphalt top on sidewalk North side E. Water St. from Wainshilbaums Store to Franklin Ave.	115	00
Catch basin North side Vernon St. near No. 226	80	00
Asphalt sidewalk and curb East side Glen St. from Exchange St. northerly	252	00
Catch basins and drains, Maple and Monroe Sts., Myrtle and Exchange, Crescent Sts.	650	00
Sidewalk and curb North side of Williams St. from Plain St. to Prospect St.	500	00
Catch basin and drain easterly side of Howard St. from Railroad track north to Custer St.	85	00
Drain and three catch basins West side Hartsuff St. running northerly from Webster St. 660 feet and repair gutter an additional 50 feet	275	00
Expense foreclosing tax titles in Land Court	300	00
Materials for improvements to grounds Reed's Pond	200	00
Install Elec. light on Goddard Ave. near Episcopal Church	15	00
Asphalt sidewalk with curb North side Emerson St. from Plain St. westerly 900 ft.	575	00

$393 777 83

Appropriations from Water Revenue
Water Commissioners Salaries and other

expenses of the Water Dept.   26 000 00

$419 777 83

A true copy ATTEST:

RALPH L. BELCHER,

Clerk

<hr />

SPECIAL TOWN MEETING
AUGUST 8, 1938

<hr />

Pursuant to the foregoing warrant a meeting was held in the Rockland Opera House, Savings Bank Building on Monday, August 8, 1938, beginning at 7:30 P. M. and the following votes were passed and action taken:

The meeting was called to order by the moderator, Mr. Magorisk L. Walls, at seven thirty o'clock.

The Clerk read the call for the meeting.

The Moderator stated that if there were no objections the articles in the warrant would be read as they were acted upon, there being no objections this proceedure was observed.

Article 1.   Voted to accept the report of the committee appointed at the last annual town meeting to investigate the question of painting and repairing the Fire Station.

The Moderator appointed the following Tellers for the meeting who were sworn by the Clerk.

Abram Lelyveld, Roland Phillips, Dennis O'Connor, Herbert Hunt, Benjamin Lelyveld.

At 7:45 o'clock a count of the voters present was order-
ed by the Moderator and 260 voters were reported as present by the Tellers.

Voted to adjourn until 8:00 o'clock.

At 8:00 o'clock a count of the voters present was made
and 324 voters were reported as present by the Tellers
and the Moderator ruled a quorum was present for action
on the aticles in the warrant.

Article 2. An amendment to insert "Municipal Building to house Town Offices, Police and Fire Stations" in
place of "Fire Station" in motion under this article was
ruled out of order by Moderator upon question of point of
order.

Voted: That for the purpose of financing and constructing a Fire Station on a site to be chosen by the
town and to enable the town to secure the benefits of
funds granted by the Federal Government under the Public Works Administration Appropriation Act of 1938,
there be raised and appropriated the sum of $67,000.00
and the treasurer, with the approval of the selectmen,
be and hereby is authorized to borrow the sum of
$40,000.00 and to issue bonds or notes of the town there-
for, under authority of and in accordance with the provisions of Chapter 50 of the Acts of 1938, said bonds or notes
to be payable in not more than twenty (20) years at such
term and maximum rate of interest as may be fixed by
the Emergency Finance Board.

All moneys received by way of grant from the Federal
Government on account of this project shall be applied
first to meet the cost of construction thereof and any balance shall be applied to the payment of the loan herein
authorized.

The Selectmen are hereby authorized and directed to

accept on behalf of the town, for use in carrying out such project, a Federal grant of money, pursuant to the Public Works Administration Appropriation Act of 1938: and a building committee of five citizens, to be chosen by the Moderator, is authorized to proceed with the construction of said project and enter into all necessary and proper contracts and agreements in respect thereto, all subject to applicable Federal regulations; and the Selectmen and the Building Committee are authorized to do all other acts and things necessary or convenient for obtaining said grant, making said loan, and constructing said project.

Affirmative votes   208   Negative votes 54

Necessary two thirds vote required for adoption of the article being 175 votes.

(See further action under article No. 2 after article No. 5.)

Article 3.   Voted to pass over the erecting of a new Fire Station on the site of the present Fire Station and the raising and appropriating of a sum of money for a temporary station while the new building is being erected.

Article 4.   Voted to appropriate the sum of $5,000 now held by the town and known as the "Real Estate Fund" towards payment of the purchase price of land to be used as a site for a new Fire Station.

Article 5.   A motion to pass over the article not agreed to.
Affirmative votes 60   Negative votes 162.

Voted to purchase from Alice M. Greeley her land on the corner of Union and Exchange Streets as a site for a new Fire Station (affirmative votes 187, negative votes 30, the necessary two thirds vote required for the purchasing of the land being 145 votes) then it was further

voted that the sum of $5,000 appropriated under Article
No. 4 plus $1,500 from the amount raised and appropriat-
ed under Article No. 2 be appropriated for the purchase
of said land.

Voted to return to Article 2.

Under article 2.   Voted for the purpose of financing and
constructing a Fire Station on a site to be chosen by the
town and to enable the town to secure the benefits of funds
granted by the Federal Government under   the   Public
Works Administration Appropriation Act of 1938, there
be raised and appropriated the sum of $61,500 and the
treasurer, with the approval of the selectmen be and hereby is authorized to borrow the sum of $40,000 and to is-
sue bonds or notes of the town therefor, under authority
of and in accordance with the provisions of Chapter 50
of the Acts of 1938, said bonds or notes to be payable in
not more than twenty (20) years at such term and maximum rate of interest as may be fixed by the Emergency
Finance Board.

All moneys received by way of grant from the Federal
Government on account of this project shall be applied
first to meet the cost of construction thereof and any balance shall be applied to the payment of the loan herein
authorized.

The selectmen are hereby authorized and directed to
accept on behalf of the town, for use in carrying out such
project, a Federal grant of money, pursuant to the Public
Works Administration Appropriation Act of 1938; and a
building committee of five citizens, to be chosen by the
Moderator, is authorized to proceed with the construction
of said project and enter into all necessary and   proper
contracts and agreements in respect thereto all subject to
applicable Federal regulations; and the selectmen and the
building committee are authorized to do all other acts and

things necessary or convenient for obtaining said grant, making said loan, and constructing said project.

Affirmative votes 201 Negative votes 14

Necessary two thirds vote required for adoption of motion being 144 votes.

Voted to again return to Article No. 2.

Under Article 2. (This is the final vote.)

Voted: That for the purpose of financing and constructing a Fire Station on a site to be chosen by the town and to enable the town to secure the benefits of funds granted by the Federal Government under the Public Works Administration Appropriation Act of 1938, there be raised and appropriated the sum of $61,500 and the treasurer, with the approval of the selectmen, be and hereby is authorized to borrow the sum of $34,500 and to issue bonds or notes of the town therefor, under authority of and in accordance with the provisions of Chapter 50 of the Acts of 1938, said bonds or notes to be payable in not more than twenty (20) years at such term and maximum rate of interest as may be fixed by the Emergency Finance Board.

All moneys received by way of grant from the Federal Government on account of this project shall be applied first to meet the cost of construction thereof and any balance shall be applied to the payment of the loan herein authorized.

The selectmen are hereby authorized and directed to accept on behalf of the town, for use in carrying out such project, a Federal grant of money, pursuant to the Public Works Administration Appropriation Act of 1938; and a building committee of five citizens, to be chosen by the Moderator, is authorized to proceed with the construction of said project and enter into all necessary and proper contracts and agreements in respect thereto, all subject to applicable Federal regulations; and the selectmen and the building committee are authorized to do all other acts and things necessary or convenient for obtaining said grant, making said loan, and constructing said project.

Affirmative votes 191   Negative votes 6

Necessary two thirds vote required for the adoption of the article being 131 votes.

Committee appointed: James Spence Chairman, Roland Phillips, Clyson Inkley, Norman Beals, Daniel DeC. Donovan.

Article 6.   Voted to pass over the purchasing from the Rockland Trust Company its land on the corner of Union Street and North Avenue as a site for a new Fire Station.

Article 7.   Voted that the sum of fifteen hundred dollars ($1,500.00) be appropriated for Highway Repairs, said appropriation to be provided for by transfer from Surplus Revenue fund now available in the Treasury.

Article 8.   Voted to appropriate the sum of Five hundred dollars ($500.00) from the Overlay Surplus Fund for the Forest Fire Department, for extinguishing and prevention of Forest Fires.

Article 9.   Voted to appropriate the sum of Seventeen thousand dollars ($17,000.00) to defray the cost of Old Age Assistance, said appropriation to be provided for by transfer from Surplus Revenue Fund now available in the Treasury.

Article 10.   Voted to appropriate the sum of Fifteen thousand dollars ($15,000.00) to defray expenses of Public Welfare, said appropriation to be provided for by transfer from Surplus Revenue Fund now available in the Treasury.

Article 11. Voted to appropriate the sum of Three thousand dollars ($3,000.00) to defray expenses of Soldiers' Relief said appropriation to be provided for by transfer from Surplus Revenue Fund now available in the Treasury.

Article 12. Voted to appropriate the sum of Four hundred eighty dollars and ninety-one cents ($480.91) for the Removal of Snow, said appropriation to be provided for by transfer from Surplus Revenue Fund now available in the Treasury.

Article 13. Voted to raise and appropriate the sum of Twenty-nine thousand dollars ($29,000.00) for the cost of materials for the construction of sidewalks and curbings on the various streets of the town, the labor to be furnished by the W. P. A. and that to meet said appropriation the treasurer, with the approval of the selectmen, be and hereby is authorized to borrow, under authority of and in accordance with the povisions of Chapter 58 of the Acts of 1938, the sum of $29,000.00 and to issue bonds or notes of the town therefor, said bonds or notes to be paid in not more than ten (10) years or at such times as may be directed by the Emergency Finance Board named in Chapter 49 of the Acts of 1933.

Affirmative votes 197   Negative votes 40

Necessary two thirds vote required for adoption of the article being 158 votes.

Article 14. Voted to pass over the raising and appropriating of the sum of Three thousand two hundred dollars ($3,200.00) for the cost of material to rebuild Exchange Street from Union Street to Liberty Street, the labor to be furnished by the W. P. A. the appropriation to be provided for by bond issue under Chapter 58, Acts of 1938.

Article 15. Voted to raise and appropriate the sum of Four thousand two hundred dollars ($4,200.00) for the cost of material to rebuild Liberty Street from Market Street to East Water Street a distance of 2600 feet, the labor to be furnished by the W. P. A., and that to meet said appropriation the treasurer, with the approval of the selectmen be and hereby is authorized to borrow under authority of and in accordance with the provisions of Chapter 58 of the Acts of 1938, the sum of $4,200.00 and to issue bonds or notes, of the town therefor, said bonds or notes to be paid in not more than five (5) years or at such times as may be directed by the Emergency Finance Board named in Chapter 49 of the Acts of 1933.

Affirmative votes 134   Negative votes 7

Necessary two thirds vote required for adoption of the article being 94 votes.   .

Article 16. Voted to raise and appropriate the sum of Six hundred dollars ($600.00) for the cost of material and other expenses for an Engineering Project, the labor to be furnished by the W. P. A. and that to meet said appropriation the treasurer, with the approval of the Selectmen, be and hereby is authorized to borrow under authority of and in accordance with the provisions of Chapter 58 of the Acts of 1938, the sum of $600.00 and to issue bonds or notes of the town therefor, said bonds or notes to be paid in not more than ten years or at such times as may be directed by the Emergency Finance Board named in Chapter 49 of the Acts of 1933.

Affirmative votes 134   Negative votes 3

Necessary two thirds vote required for adoption of the article being 92 votes.

Article 17. Voted that the sum of Two thousand dollars ($2,000.00) be appropriated for the cost of materials for improvements of grounds at Reed's Pond, the labor to be furnished by the W. P. A., said appropriation to be provided for by transfer from Surplus Revenue Fund now available in the Treasury.

Article 18. Voted to raise and appropriate the sum of One thousand dollars ($1,000.00) for the cost of materials and supplies to be used in the construction of a sewerage bed at the McKinley School, the labor to be furnished by the W. P. A., and that to meet said appropriation the treasurer, with the approval of the selectmen, be and hereby is authorized to borrow under authority of and in accordance with the provisions of Chapter 58 of the Acts of 1938, the sum of $1,000.00 and to issue bonds or notes of the town therefor, said bonds or notes to be paid in not more than ten years or at such time as may be directed by the Emergency Finance Board named in Chapter 49 of the Acts of 1933.

Affirmative votes 127   Negative votes 0
            Unanimous vote.

Necessary two thirds vote required for adoption of the article being 86 votes.

Article 19. Voted to appropriate the sum of Two Hundred Dollars ($200.00) for the Burial of Indigent Soldiers, said appropriation to be provided for by transfer from Surplus Revenue Fund now available in the Treasury.

Article 20. Voted to appropriate the sum of Fifteen hundred dollars ($1,500.00) to defray the expenses of the Board of Health, said appropriation to be provided for by transfer from the Surplus Revenue Fund the amount of $819.09 and from the Overlay Surplus Fund the amount of $680.91, said funds being now available in the Treasury.

Article 21.   Voted to appropriate the sum of Three hundred dollars ($300.00) for Miscellaneous Assessors, said appropriation to be provided for by transfer from Overlay Surplus Fund now available in the Treasury.

Meeting adjourned at 10:15 P. M.

A true copy, Attest:

RALPH L. BELCHER,
Town Clerk

AMOUNTS RAISED AND APPROPRIATED

SPECIAL TOWN MEETING, AUGUST 8, 1938

*Financing and construction of Fire Station $61 500 00
**Construction of Sidewalks and Curbs
  various street (Cost of materials)
  W. P. A. Project   29 000 00
**Rebuild Liberty St. from Market St. to
  E. Water St. (Cost of Materials)
  W. P. A. Project   4 200 00
**Engineering Project (W. P. A.)
  (Cost of materials and other expenses   600 00
**Construction of sewerage bed at McKinley
  School (Cost of materials and supplies)
  W. P. A. Project   1 000 00
 * This appropriation provided
   for by Bond or note issue,
   provisions Chap. 50, Acts
   1938 $34 500 00
   Federal grant of money   27 000 00

                                   $61 500 00

** These appropriations provided for by Bond or note issue,
provisions Chap. 58, Acts
1938 $34 800 00

Amounts Appropriated, Special Town Meeting
August 8, 1938

From "Real Estate Fund"
   Toward purchase of Alice M. Greeley land $5 000 00
From Bond or note issue under Chap. 50, Acts 1938
   Toward purchase Alice M. Greeley land $1 500 00
   (Note that this item is included in $61,500.00 in first
item on this sheet)
From Surplus Revenue Fund

For Highway Repairs	$ 1 500 00
For Old Age Assistance	17 000 00
For Public Welfare	15 000 00
For Soldiers' Relief	3 000 00
For Removal of Snow	480 91
For Improvements Reed's Pond (Cost of materials) W. P. A. Project	2 000 00
For Burial Indigent Soldiers	200 00
For Board of Health	819 09
Total from Surplus Revenue	$ 40 000 00

From Overlay Surplus Fund

For Forest Fire Dept.	$ 500 00
For Board of Health	680 91
For Miscellaneous Assessors	300 00
Total from Overlay Surplus	$ 1 480 91

Total amount raised and appropriated and
   provided for by Federal grant and bond
   or note issue $ 96 300 00

Total amount appropriated from available
    funds   46 480 91

                                           $142 708 91

A true copy.

                    RALPH L. BELCHER
                            Town Clerk

SPECIAL TOWN MEETING
AUGUST 31, 1938

Pursuant to the foregoing warrant a meeting was held
at the Rockland Opera House, Savings Bank Building, on
August 31, 1938, beginning at 7:30 o'clock P. M.

The meeting was called to order by the Moderator, Magorisk L. Walls.

The warrant with Constables return of service thereof
was read by the Town Clerk.

The Moderator ruled that it would require a two thirds
vote of those present and voting to adopt Article No. 1 and
that a quorum of 300 voters must be present for action
under Article No. 2.

The following tellers were appointed by the Moderator
for the meeting and were sworn to the faithful discharge
of their duties, by the Town Clerk.

Emil Kellestrand, Charles Callanan, Charles Howland
and Nellie K. Lonergan.

Article 1.   Voted to rescind action taken under Article

No. 5 of the Special Town Meeting of August 8, 1938, whereby the town voted to purchase from Alice M. Greeley, her land situated on the corner of Union and Exchange Streets as a site for a new Fire Station, and appropriated the sum of $5000 from the "Real Estate Fund," so called, plus $1500 from amount raised and appropriated under Article 2 of said Special Town Meeting for the purchase of the land.

Affirmative votes 240   Negative votes 26

Necessary two thirds vote required for adoption of the article being 177 votes.

Article 2. An amendment to Article No. 2 that the Fire Station Building Committee, as now constituted, be authorized to look into the possiblity of obtaining a strip of land 12 feet wide on the south side of the present fire station lot and report back to an adjourned meeting in two weeks time was not agreed to.

Voted: To erect a new Fire Station on the site of the present Fire Station (using a strip of land 12 feet wide northerly from the present Fire Station on the Memorial Library lot and such land on the westerly side of the Library as may be necessary for septic tanks) and to appropriate the sum of $1500 to provide for a temporary station while the new one is being erected, said sum to be taken from the appropriation under Article No. 2 which was adopted at the meeting held on August 8th, 1938.

Voted that there be paid from the appropriation for Elections the amount of $35.00 for the rent of the hall and the amount of $10.00 for the services of the Moderator for this meeting.

Meeting adjourned at 8:45 P. M.

A true copy ATTEST:

RALPH L. BELCHER,
Town Clerk

SPECIAL TOWN MEETING
SEPTEMBER 19, 1938

Pursuant to the foregong warrant a meeting was held at the Rockland Opera House, Savings Bank Building, on Sept. 19, 1938, beginning at 7:30 o'clock P. M.

The meeting was called to order by the Moderator, Magorisk L. Walls.

The warrant with the Constable return of service thereof was read by the Town Clerk.

Article No. 1. The following motion was voted in the negative by the meeting:

M$_{ov}$ed: That for the purpose of financing and constructing a sewage system and disposal plant and to enable the Town to secure the benefit of funds granted by the Federal Government under the Public Works Administration Appropriation Act of 1938, there be raised and appropriated the sum of Three Hundred and sixty thousand dollars ($360 000 00) (total estimated cost) and the treasurer, with the approval of the selectmen, be and hereby is authorized to borrow the sum of One Hundred Ninety-eight thousand dollars ($198,000.00) (outside the debt limit) and to issue bonds or notes of the town therefor, under authority of and in accordance with the provisions of Chapter 338 of the Acts of 1913 and of Chapter 50 of the Acts of 1938. Said bonds or notes are to be payable in not more than thirty years, at such terms and maximum rate of interest as may be fixed by the Emergency Finance Board.

All monies received by way of grant from the Federal Government on account of this project shall be applied first to meet the cost of construction thereof and any balance shall be applied to the payment of the loan herein authorized.

The Selectmen are hereby authorized and directed to accept on behalf of the town, for use in carrying out such project, a Federal grant of money pursuant to the Public Works Administration Appropriation Act of 1938 and the sewer commissioners, with the approval of the selectmen, are outhorized to proceed with the construction of said project and to enter into all necessary and proper contracts and agreements in respect thereto, all subject to applicable Federal regulations, and the selectmen and the sewer commissioners are authorized to do all other acts and things necessary or convenient for obtaining said grant, making said loan and constructing said project.

Article 2. Voted to instruct the Building Committee to specify preference for the employment of Rockland men in the contracts issued for the construction of the Fire Station.

Article 3. Voted to pass over the appropriating of a sum of money for the purchase or taking of a strip of land south of the present Fire Station lot to be used as part of the site for the new Fire Station, this strip not to exceed twelve feet fronting on Union Street and one hundred two feet deep (102) said sum to be taken from the Real Estate Fund.

Voted that there be paid from the appropriation for Elections the amount of $35.00 for the rent of the hall and the amount of $10.00 for the services of the Moderator for this meeting.

Meeting adjourned at 8:10 P. M.

A true copy ATTEST:

RALPH L. BELCHER,
Town Clerk

TOTAL VOTE   ROCKLAND

STATE PRIMARY
SEPT. 20, 1938

	Pre 1	Pre. 2	Total
Republican ballots cast	479	533	1012
Democratic ballots cast	277	228	505
Union Party ballots cast	2	1	3
	758	762	1520
Total number of ballots cast			1520

REPUBLICAN PARTY

	Pre 1	Pre. 2	Total
Governor			
Frederick Butler	28	18	46
William H. McMasters	53	67	120
Leverett Saltonstall	310	349	659
Richard Whitcomb	29	29	58
Joseph Heffernan	1	2	3
Blanks	58	68	126
Lieutenant Governor			
Dewey G. Archambault	27	17	44
Horace T. Cahill	143	175	318
J. Watson Flett	13	15	28
Charles P. Howard	59	72	131
Kenneth D. Johnson	89	97	186
Robert Gardiner Wilson, Jr.	20	27	47
F. Joseph Harney	1	2	3
Blanks	127	128	255
Secretary			
Frederic W. Cook	334	374	708

John E. Spillane	1	2	3
Blanks,	144	157	301
Treasurer			
William E. Hurley	213	216	429
Alonzo B. Cook	140	170	310
John J. Hurley	22	22	44
Ralph Jackson		2	2
Blanks	104 ✳	123	227
Auditor			
Carl D. Goodwin	130	119	249
Russell A. Wood	167	211	378
Ralph Williams	1	2	3
Blanks	181	201	382
Attorney General			
Howe Coolidge Amee	70	63	133
Clarence A. Barnes	149	171	320
Frank F. Walters	45	50	95
John Joseph Murphy	1	2	3
Blanks	214	247	461
Congressman, Fifteenth District			
Charles L. Gifford	273	309	582
Harry L. Avery	29	38	67
William B. Taylor	62	59	121
Blanks	115	127	242
Councillor, Second District			
Christian A. Burkard	69	69	138
Clayton L. Havey	114	131	245
William J. MacHale	18	21	39
David S. McIntosh	58	72	130
Sidney Rosenberg	10	5	15
Thomas Walter Taylor	44	49	93
Blanks	166	186	352

Senator, Norfolk and Plymouth District
Newland H. Holmes	217	257	474
Richard F. Paul	146	138	284
Blanks	116	138	254

Representative in General Court,
    4th Plymouth District
Frederick M. Barnicoat	224	294	518
Norman S. Whiting	241	225	466
Blanks	14	14	28

District Attorney, Southeastern District
Edmund R. Dewing	294	333	627
Joseph G. Schumb	35	48	83
Blanks	150	152	302

County Commissioner, Plymouth County
George M. Webber	73	97	170
Joseph B. Estes	343	369	712
Oscar H. Tracy	6	10	16
Blanks	57	57	114

County Commissioner, Plymouth County
    (to fill vacancy)
Horace C. Baker	83	81	164
Elva M. Bent	213	235	448
Elroy S. Thompson	31	19	50
James A. White	26	36	62
LeRoy A. Whitten	10	12	22
Oscar E. Young	4	11	15
Blanks	112	139	251

Sheriff, Plymouth County
Charles H. Robbins	282	314	596
Blanks	197	219	416

Delegate to State Convention
Charles P. Howland	274	306	580

Joseph B, Estes	327	356	683
Norman S. Whiting	324	319	643
Esther H. Rawson	259	306	565
Dana S. Collins	297	344	641
Ruth Torrey	258	291	549
Geraldine Gardner	263	306	569
Emil Kelstrand	1		1
Charles Orr		1	1
Blanks	1350	1502	2852

DEMOCRATIC PARTY

	Pre 1	Pre. 2	Total
Governor			
Charles F. Hurley	145	117	262
James M. Curley	80	71	151
Francis E. Kelly	46	25	71
Richard M. Russell	3	13	16
Joseph M. Heffernan		1	1
Blanks	3	1	4
Lieutenant Governor			
James Henry Brennan	77	66	143
Edward T. Collins	34	18	52
Alexander F. Sullivan	30	24	54
Joseph C. White	91	87	178
William P. Yoerg	5	2	7
F. Joseph Harney		1	1
Blanks	40	30	70
Secretary			
William J. Ahearne	40	21	61
John M. Bresnahan	39	34	73
Henry Clay	9	2	11
Katherine A. Foley	69	77	146
William F. Sullivan	25	23	48
John H. Wallace	28	21	49
John E. Spillane		1	1
Blanks	67	49	116

Treasurer

William F. Barrett	32	11	43
Ernest Joseph Brown	6	10	16
William H. Burke, Jr.	18	14	32
Joseph W. Doherty	33	22	55
Owen Gallagher	76	65	141
John Frederick Harkins	3	11	14
Daniel J. Honan	12	14	26
John J. McGrath	34	26	60
Ralph D. Jackson		1	1
Blanks	63	54	117

Auditor

Thomas H. Buckley	228	179	407
John J. Barry	21	21	42
Leo D. Walsh	15	10	25
Blanks	13	18	31

Attorney General

Paul A. Dever	221	183	404
John Joseph Heffernan		1	1
Blanks	56	44	100

Congressman, Fifteenth District

John D. W. Bodfish	88	89	177
Henry L. Murphy	126	96	222
Blanks	63	43	106

Councillor, Second District

John Joseph Cheever	25	18	43
James A. Cresswell	39	13	52
Francis M. Kelly	59	36	95
Timothy Lyons, Jr.	36	41	77
Thomas C. McGrath	24	19	43
Clement A. Riley	6	10	16
John J. Sawtelle	23	35	58
Louis Shindler	1	0	1
Blanks	64	56	120

Senator, Norfolk and Plymouth District

Noel C. King	174	145	319
Blanks	103	83	186

Representative in General Court,
4th Plymouth District

Arthur H. Marks	219	185	404
Blanks	58	43	101

District Attorney, Southeastern District

Alonzo Bartlett Greene	29	26	55
Daniel L. Kelleher Jr.	183	156	339
Blanks	65	46	111

County Commissioner, Plymouth County

Louis A. Reardon	225	173	398
Blanks	52	55	107

County Commissioner, Plymouth County
(to fill vacancy)

William Leslie Ross	163	130	293
Blanks	114	98	212

Sheriff, Plymouth County

Albert M. Heath	186	137	323
Blanks	91	91	182

Delegate to State Convention

Magorisk L .Walls	215	178	393
George Hart	1		1
Arthur Wyman		1	1
Blanks	61	49	110

UNION PARTY

	Pre 1	Pre. 2	Total
Governor			
John M. Heffernan	2		2
Blanks			1

Lieutenant Governor
F. Joseph Harney   2   2
Blanks   1   1

Secretary
John Spillane   2   2
Blanks   1   . 1

Treasurer
Ralph Jackson   2   2
Blanks   1 ·   1

Auditor
Ralph S. Williams   2   2
Blanks   1

Attorney General
John Joseph Murphy   2   2
Blanks   1

Congressman, Fifteenth District
Blanks   2   1   3

Councillor, Second District
Blanks   2   · 1   3

Senator, Norfolk and Plymouth District
Blanks   2   1   3

Representative in General Court,
4th Plymouth District
Blanks   2   1   3

District Attorney, Southeastern District
Blanks   2   1   3

County Commissioner, Plymouth County
Blanks   2   1   3

County Commissioner, Plymouth County
(to fill vacancy)
Blanks   2   1   3

Sheriff, Plymouth County
Blanks   2   1   3

Delegate to State Convention
Blanks   2   1   3

A true copy ATTEST:

RALPH L. BELCHER,
Town Clerk

STATE ELECTION
NOVEMBER 8, 1938

Whole Number of ballots cast.
Precinct One   1949
Prescinct Two   2127
                                      ————
                                      4076

	Pre 1	Pre. 2	Total
Governor			
Henning A. Blomen, Socialist			
Labor Party	4	3	7
Roland S. Bruneau, Independent	3	2	5
Jeffrey W. Campell, Socialist	4	9	13
James M. Curley, Democrat	969	902	1871
William A. Davenport, Ind. Tax Refor	1	3	4
Otis Archer Hood, Communist Party	2	1	3
Charles L. Manser, Sound, Sensible			
Government	1		2
William H. McMasters, Townsend			
Recovery Plan	7	12	19

Leverett Saltonstall, Republican	927	1166	2093
George L. Thompson, Prohibition	0	0	0
Blanks	31	28	59

Lieutenant Governor

Manuel Blank, Communist Party	8	3	11
James Henry Brennan, Democrat	933	887	1820
Horace T. Cahill, Republican	911	1149	2060
Freeman W. Follett, Prohibition	13	7	20
Joseph F. Massidda, Socialist	9	8	17
George L. McGlynn, Socialist Labor Party	9	9	18
Blanks	66	64	130

Secretary

Frederic W. Cook, Republican	963	1189	2152
Hugo DeGregory, Communist Party	8	8	16
Katherine A. Foley, Democrat	863	820	1683
Eileen O'Connor Lane, Socialist	21	14	35
Malcolm T. Rowe, Socialist Labor Party	4	10	14
Blanks	90	86	176

Treasurer

Frank L. Asher, Communist Party	5	5	10
Albert Sprague Coolidge, Socialist	16	24	40
Owen Gallagher, Democrat	847	788	1635
John J. Hurley, Independent	32	37	69
William E. Hurley, Republican	954	1172	2126
Ralph Pirone, Socialist Labor Party	8	9	17
Blanks	87	92	179

Auditor

Thomas H. Buckley, Democrat	1099	995	2094
Michael C. Flaherty, Socialist	13	16	29
Horace I. Hillis, Socialist Labor Party	3	6	9
Michael Tuysuzian, Communist Party	4	3	7
Guy S. Williams, Prohibition	11	59	70

| Russell A. Wood, Republican | 768 | 973 | 1741 |
| Blanks | 51 | 75 | 126 |

Attorney General

Clarence A. Barnes, Republican	785	996	1781
Paul A. Dever, Democrat	1047	1033	2080
Joseph C. Figueiredo, Communist Party	9	1	10
George F. Hogan, Prohibition	8	4	12
Alfred Baker Lewis, Socialist	18	16	34
Fred E. Oelcher, Socialist Labor			
Party	2	6	8
Blanks	80	71	151

Congressman, Fifteenth District

John D. W. Bodfish, Democrat	951	935	1886
Charles L. Gifford, Republican	874	1079	1953
Blanks	124	113	237

Councillor, Second District

Saul Friedman, Socialist	27	57	84
Clayton L. Havey, Republican	842	1037	1879
John J. Sawtelle, Democrat	917	863	1780
Blanks	163	170	333

Senator, Norfolk and Plymouth District

Newland H. Holmes, Republican	886	1091	1977
Noel C. King, Democrat	905	869	1774
Blanks	158	167	325

Representative in General Court,
4th Plymouth District

Frederick M. Barnicoat, Republican	710	903	1613
Arthur H. Marks, Democrat	1034	998	2032
Norman S. Whiting, Ind. Progressive	172	186	358
Blanks	33	40	73

District Attorney, Southeastern District

| Edmund R. Dewing, Republican | 894 | 1108 | 2002 |

| Daniel L. Kelleher, Jr., Democrat | 937 | 892 | 1829 |
| Blanks | 118 | 127 | 245 |

County Commissioner, Plymouth County

Louis A. Reardon, Democrat	1057	1004	2061
George M. Webber, Republican	781	1004	1785
Blanks	111	119	230

County Commissioner, Plymouth County
  (to fill vacancy)

Elva M. Bent, Republican	945	1181	2126
William Leslie Ross, Democrat	860	777	1637
Blanks	144	169	313

Sheriff, Plymouth County

Albert M. Heath, Democrat	885	846	1731
Charles H. Robbins, Republican	910	1113	2023
Blanks	154	168	322

Question No. 1.

Proposed Amendment to Constitu-
tion Providing Biennial Session Leg-
lature and Biennial Budget

Yes	706	763	1469
No	363	446	809
Blanks	880	918	1798

Question No. 2.

Law Proposed by Initiative Petition
Relative to Free Public Taxicab Stands

Yes	730	762	1492
No	480	573	1053
Blanks	739	792	1531

Shall licenses be granted in this
town for the sale therein of all alcoholic beverages?

| Yes | 1076 | 1101 | 2177 |

No	457	583	1040
Blanks	416	443	859

Shall licenses be granted in this town for the sale therein of wines and malt beverages?

Yes	1054	1092	2146
No	413	539	952
Blanks	482	496	978

Shall licenses be granted in this town for the sale therein of all alcoholic beverages in packages, so called, not to be drunk on the premises?

Yes	1101	1159	2260
No	383	480	863
Blanks	·465	488	953

Shall the pari-mutuel system of betting on licensed horse races be permitted in this county?

Yes	982	1000	1982
No	476	608	1084
Blanks	491	519	1010

Shall the pari-mutuel system of betting on licensed dog races be permitted in this county?

Yes	876	875	1751
No	544	693	1237
Blanks	529	559	1088

A true copy ATTEST:

RALPH L. BELCHER,
Town Clerk

FOURTH PLYMOUTH REPRESENTATIVE DISTRICT

At a meeting of the Town Clerks of the Fourth Plymouth Representative District held in the Town Clerk's Office, Rockland, Mass., on Friday, November 18, 1938 at 12:00 o'clock noon, the records of votes cast in each precinct and town for Representative in General Court, Fourth Plymouth District, were duly examined and Frederick M. Barnicoat, of Hanover, appeared to be elected.

The following is a schedule of the votes cast in said district.

Frederick M. Barnicoat, of Hanover, (R) three thousand three hundred and fourteen (3314).

Arthur H. Marks, of Rockland, (D) two thousand four hundred and thirty-eight (2438).

Norman S. Whiting, of Rockland, (Ind.) four hundred and twelve (412).

Blanks, one hundred and twenty five (125).

Whole number of ballots cast, six thousand two hundred and eighty-nine (6289).

BERNARD STETSON,
Town Clerk, Hanover

WARREN T. HOWARD,
Town Clerk, Hanson

RALPH L. BELCHER,
Town Clerk, Rockland

Detail of vote by towns

	Rockland	Hanover	Hanson	Total
Frederick M. Barnicoat	1613	989	712	3314
Arthur H. Marks	2032	161	245	2438
Norman S. Whiting	358	36	18	412
Blanks	73	15	37	125
	4076	1201	1012	6289

REPORT OF AN AUDIT

OF

THE ACCOUNTS OF

THE TOWN OF ROCKLAND

For the Period from May 18, 1933 to November 6, 1937
Made in Accordance with the Provisions of Chapter 44,
General Laws

May 9, 1938

AUDITOR'S REPORT

The Commonwealth of Massachusetts
Department of Corporations and Taxation
Division of Accounts
State House, Boston

May 9, 1938

To the Board of Selectmen
Mr. Harry S. Torrey, Chairman
Rockland, Massachusetts.

Gentlemen:

I submit herewith my report of an audit of the books
and accounts of the town of Rockland for the period from
May 18, 1933 to November 6, 1937, made in accordance
with the provisions of Chapter 44, General Laws. This is
in the form of a report made to me by Mr. Herman B.
Dine, Assistant Director of Accounts.

Very truly yours,
THEODORE N. WADDELL,
Director of Accounts

TNW:O

Mr. Theodore N. Waddell
Director of Accounts
Department of Corporations and Taxation
State House, Boston

Sir:

In accordance with your instructions, I have made an

audit of the books and accounts of the town of Rockland for the period from May 18, 1933, the date of the previous examination, to November 6, 1937, the following report being submitted thereon:

The financial transactions, as recorded on the books of the several departments receiving or disbursing money for the town or committing bills for collection, were examined and checked.

The charges against appropriations were checked, general ledger accounts were compiled, and a balance sheet, showing the financial condition of the town on November 6, 1937, was prepared and is appended to this report.

An examination of the appended balance sheet indicates that several appropriations were overdrawn on November 6, 1937. To incur liabilities in excess of the appropriations voted by the town is contrary to the provisions of Section 31, Chapter 44, General Laws, which reads as follows:

"No department of any city or town, except Boston, shall incur liability in excess of the appropriation made for the use of such department, except in cases of extreme emergency involving the health and safety of persons or property, and then only by a vote in a city of two thirds of the members of the city council, and in a town by a vote of two thirds of the selectmen."

Attention is also called to Section 62, Chapter 44, General Laws, which reads as follows:

"Any city, town or district officer who knowingly violates, or authorizes or directs any official or employee to violate, any provision of this chapter, or any other provision of general law relating to the incurring of liability or expenditure of public funds on account of any city, town or district, or any provision of special law relating to the incurring of liability or expenditure of public funds as aforesaid, shall, except as otherwise provided, be punished by a fine of not more than one thousand dollars or by imprisonment for not more than one year, or both; and the mayor, selectmen, prudential committee, or commissioners, shall, and five taxpayers may, report such violation to the district attorney who shall investigate and prosecute the same."

It is recommended that steps be taken toward the establishment of a proper system of accounting, so that complete records may be available in a single town office and so that the true financial condition of the town may be determined at any time.

In checking the paid vouchers on file it was noted that, in addition to their salaries fixed by vote of the town, compensation has been paid to elected officials of the town and charged to the federal grant on account of old age assistance. Attention in this connection is called to the provisions of Sections 4A and 108, Chapter 41, General Laws.

The books and accounts of the town treasurer were examined and checked in detail. The recorded receipts were analyzed and compared with the collectors' records of payments to the treasurer, with the records in the several departments collecting money for the town, and with other sources from which money was paid into the town treasury, while the payments were checked with the selectmen's warrants to the treasurer. The cash balance on November 6, 1937, was proved by actual count of the cash in the office and by a reconciliation of the bank balances with statements furnished by the banks in which the town funds are deposited.

The payments of debt and interest were checked with

the amounts falling due and with the cancelled securities on file.   •

The savings bank books representing the investment of the trust funds in the custody of the library trustees and the town treasurer, were examined and listed, the income being proved and the withdrawals verified.

The tax title deeds on hand were examined and listed. The amounts transferred from the several tax levies to the tax title account were verified, and the tax title deeds as listed were checked with the records in the Registry of Deeds.

Considerable difficulty was experienced in reconciling the tax title records kept by the town treasurer with the collector's accounts, due to the fact that the clerical work was incomplete and a number of accounts were missing from the files.   It is recommended that more care be taken in recording the various transactions affecting the tax titles and that a proper and complete record of all tax titles be kept as required by Section 50, Chapter 60 General Laws.   It was also noted that the treasurer has accepted partial payments on the redemption of tax titles which are less than the minimum prescribed by the statutes.

The records of licenses and permits issued by the selectmen, town clerk and the health department were examined and checked, and the payments to the State and the town were verified.

The books and accounts of the collector of taxes were examined and checked.   The levies outstanding at the time of the previous examination were audited, and all subsequent commitment lists were added and reconciled with the warrants of the assessors committing the taxes for collection.

The collector's cash books were footed, the payments to the treasurer by the collector were checked to the treasurer's books, the abatements were compared with the assessors' records of abatements granted, and the outstanding accounts were listed and proved.

It is recommended that the collector make weekly payments to the treasurer of all collections as required by Section 2, Chapter 60, General Laws.

It is also recommended that prompt settlement of all prior years' taxes be secured.

The surety bonds of the financial officials bonded for the faithful performance of their duties were examined and found to be in proper form.

The records of departmental and water accounts receivable committed for collection were examined and checked. The commitment lists were proved, the recorded collections were compared with the payments to the treasurer, the abatements were checked with the records in the departments authorized to grant abatements, and the outstanding accounts were listed and proved.

Verification of the outstanding tax, departmental, and water accounts were made by mailing notices to many persons whose names appeared on the books as owing money to the town, the replies received thereto indicating that the accounts, as listed, are correct.

A considerable amount of detailed checking was necessary to balance the tax and tax title accounts, which increased the length of the audit and consequently its cost.

It is important that the provisions of Sections 42A to 42D, inclusive, Chapter 40, General Laws, be followed in recording water liens and adding unpaid accounts to the next annual tax.

The accounts of the sealer of weights and measures
and the library department, as well as of all other departments collecting money for the town or committing bills
for collection, were examined and checked with the treasurer's books.

In addition to the balance sheet referred to, there are
appended to this report tables showing a reconciliation of
the treasurer's and the collector's cash, summaries of the
tax, tax title, departmental, and water accounts, as well
as tables showing the condition and transactions of the
trust funds.

While engaged in making the audit, cooperation was
received from the officials of the town, for wish, on behalf of my assistants and for myself, I wish to express
appreciation.

Respectfully submitted,
HERMAN B. DINE,
Assistant Director of Accounts

HBD:O

RECONCILIATION OF TREASURER'S CASH

Balance May 18, 1933			$ 48 171, 42
Receipts			
May 18 to Decem-			
ber 31, 1933	$506 478 29		
1934	728 917 49		
1935	778 201 24		
1936	783 435 30		
		2 797 032 32	
			$2 845 203 74
Payments:			
May 18 to			
December 31,			
1933,	$521 669 43		

1934	715 325 09	
1935	777 567 90	
1936	738 588 36	
	2 753 150 78	
Balance December 31, 1936,	92 052 96	
		$2 845 203 74

Balance January 1, 1937,		$ 92 052 96
Receipts January 1 to		
November 6, 1937		698 366 03
Overdeposit in 1934,		
to be adjusted	23 11	
Excess cash November 6, 1937,	57	
		$790 442 67

Payments January 1 to		
November 6, 1937,	$662 459 37	
Balance November 6, 1937:		
Cash in office verified $1 502 11		
Rockland Trust		
Company 82 456 02		
Merchants National Bank, Boston:		
General $41 472 41		
P.W.A. Docket No. 1143,		
Union St. Con-		
struction 45 00		
P.W.A. Docket No. 1343		
Water		
Tank 2 338 07		
	43 855 48	
National Shawmut Bank,		
Boston 169 69		
	127 983 30	
		$790 442 67

Rockland Trust Company

Balance November 6, 1937,	
per statement	$84 469 30

Deposit in transit November
6, 1937, verified   4 356 18
                                                      $ 88 825 48
Balance November 6, 1937,
per check register $82 456 02
Outstanding checks November 6,
1937, per list,   6 369 46
                                                      $ 88 825 48

Merchants National Bank of Boston
General Account

Balance November 6, 1937, per statement $41 837 18
Balance November 6, 1937,
per check book, $41 472 41
Outstanding checks November 6,
1937, per list,   364 77
                                                      $41 837 18

Merchants National Bank of Boston
P. W. A. Docket No. 1143, Union Street Construction

Balance November 6, 1937, per statement, $45 00
Balance November 6, 1937, per check book, $45 00

Merchants National Bank of Boston
P. W. A. Docket No. 1343, Water Tank Construction

Balance November 6, 1937, per statement, $2 338 07
Balance November 6, 1937, per check book, $2 338 07

The National Shawmut Bank

Balance November 6, 1937, per statement, $169 69
Balance November 6, 1937, per check book, $169 69

RECONCILIATION OF COLLECTOR'S CASH

Balances November 6, 1937, per tables:

Taxes 1931	10		
Taxes 1934,	7 88		
Taxes 1935	118 00		
Taxes 1936	389 57		
Taxes 1937	338 05		
Motor vehicle excise taxes 1934	1 88		
Motor vehicle excise taxes 1935,	31 90		
Motor vehicle excise taxes 1936	92 76		
Motor vehicle excise taxes 1937	205 48		
Interest and costs on taxes	189 79		
Water liens added to taxes 1937	2 75		
		1 378 16	
Excess cash November 6, 1937,		179 67	
			$1 557 83
Overpayment to treasurer, per table:			
Taxes 1933,		40 00	
Cash on hand November 6, 1937, verified,		1 517 83	
			$1 557 83

TAXES - 1929

Outstanding May 18, 1933,	$17 50
Payments to treasurer May 18 to December 31, 1933,	$17 50

TAXES - 1930

Outstanding May 18, 1933,	$71 28

Payments to treasurer May 18 to
  December 31, 1933, $71 28

TAXES - 1931

Outstanding May 18, 1933, $52 717 97
Payments to treasurer:
May 18, to December
  31, 1933, $45 277 58
  1934   726 34
  1935,   103 13
                                            $46 107 05
Abatements:
May 18 to December
  31, 1933, $1 409 48
  1934,   588 09
  1935,   6 51
                                 2 004 08
Tax titles taken May 18 to
  December 31, 1933,   2 666 17
Added to tax titles May 18 to
  December 31, 1933,   1 927 52
Outstanding December 31, 1936   13 15
                                            $52 717 97.

Outstanding January 1, 1937, $13 15
Outstanding November 6, 1937, per list $13 05
Cash balance November 6, 1937,   10
                                                     $13 15

TAXES - 1932

Outstanding May 18, 1933, $95 238 41
Payments to treasurer:
May 18 to December
  31, 1933, $34 791 24

1934,	51 093 58	
1935,	703 40	
1936,	4 29	
	$86 592 51	

Abatements:

May 18 to December 31, 1933,	$1 285 57	
1934,	1 711 98	
1935,	520 72	
	3 518 27	
Tax titles taken 1934,	2 416 80	
Added to tax titles May 18 to December 31, 1933,	2 689 20	
Outstanding December 31, 1936	21 63	
		$95 238 41

Outstanding January 1, 1938,		$21 63
Unlocated different November 6, 1937, adjusted		4 29
		$25 92
Outstanding November 6, 1937, per list,		$25 92

TAXES - 1933

Commitment per warrant	$278 350 05	
Additional commitment	506 65	
Abatements and payments refunded 1934,	17 00	
Overpayment to collector refunded 1933,	49 71	
Collection not committed 1935,	86 02	
Tax title disclaimed 1935,	7 65	
		$279 017 08

Payments to treasurer:

1933,	$149 703 95	
1934,	60 876 80	
1935,	53 415 95	
1936,	1 859 03	
	$265 855 73	

Abatements:
1933,	$4 579 76	
1934,	1 972 27	
1935,	1 922 67	
1936,	667 26	
	9 141 96	
Tax titles taken 1935,	845 91	
Added to tax titles 1934,	3 103 52	
Outstanding December 31, 1936,	69 96	
		$279 017 08

Outstanding January 1, 1937,	$69 96	
Interest on taxes 1933 reported as taxes 1933,	1 87	
Overpayment to collector, adjusted,	09	
Unlocated difference November 6, 1937, adjusted,	63	
Overpayment to treasurer, to be refunded,	40 00	
		$112 55
Payments to treasurer January 1 to November 6, 1937	$25 60	
Abatements January 1 to November 6, 1937,	7 60	
Outstanding November 6, 1937, per list,	79 35	
		$112 55

TAXES - 1934

Commitment per warrant,	$310 739 75	
Additional commitment,	95 34	
Abatement and payment refunded 1935,	7 56	
Tax title disclaimed 1935,	8 51	
		$310 851 16
Payments to treasurer:		
1934,	$164 507 38	
1935,	71 373 84	
1936,	54 401 24	
	$290 282 46	

Abatements:

1934,	5 934 03	
1935,	1 628 80	
1936,	2 649 82	
		10 212 65
Tax titles taken 1936,		3 289 68
Added to tax titles 1935,		4 094 62
Outstanding December 31, 1936,		2 971 75
		$310 851 **16**

Outstanding January 1, 1937,		$2 971 75
Overpayments to collector:		
Adjusted,	07	
To be refunded,	22 85	
		22 92
		$2 994 **67**
Payments to treasurer January 1 to		
November 6, 1937,		$2 136 91
Abatements January 1 to		
November 6, 1937,		770 04
Unlocated difference November		
6, 1937, adjusted,		2 00
Outstanding November 6, 1937, per list		77 84
Cash balance November 6, 1937,		7 88
		$2 994 **67**

TAXES - 1935

Commitment per warrant		$312 221 61
Additional commitment,		22 00
		$312 243 **61**
Payments to treasurer:		
1935,	$174 301 89	
1936,	61 667 06	
		$235 968 95
Abatements:		
1935,	$7 422 96	

1936,   1 034 26
                                            8 457 22
Added to tax titles 1936,   6 707 05
Outstanding December 31, 1936, 61 110 39 —
                                                      $312 243 61

Outstanding January 1, 1937 $61 110 39
Interest on taxes 1935 reported as
    taxes 1935,   87 57
                                                      $61 197 96
Payments to treasurer January 1 to
    November 6, 1937, $51 588 19
Abatements January 1 to November
    6, 1937,   2 377 42
Tax titles taken January 1 to
    November 6, 1937,   1 721 82
Outstanding November 6, 1937,
    per list,   5 392 53
Cash balance November 6, 1937,   118 00
                                                      $61 197 96

TAXES - 1936

Commitment per warrant $326 370 60
Additional commitment,   91 79
Collections not committed,   4 00
Abatements and payments refunded, 218 35
                                                      $326 684 74
Payments to treasurer, $188 170 60
Abatements:
    Polls and property, $7 684 63
    Machinery,   6 874 78
                                     14 559 41
Outstanding December 31, 1936, 123 954 73
                                                      $326 684 74

Outstanding January 1, 1937, $123 954 73

Abatements and payments refunded
  January 1 to November 6, 1937,   4 96
Overpayment to collector,
  to be refunded,   90
Unlocated difference November 6,
  1937,   . 1 00
                  $123 961 59

Payments to treasurer January 1 to
  November 6, 1937, $49 469 96
Abatements January 1 to
  November 6, 1937,   538 02
Added to tax titles January 1 to
  November 6, 1937,   7 986 56
Oustanding November 6, 1937,
  per list,   65 577 48
Cash balance November 6, 1937,   389 57
                  $123 961 59

TAXES - 1937

Commitment January 1 to November
  6, 1937, per warrant $303 218 84
Collections not committed   12 00
Abatements and payments refunded
  January 1, to November 6, 1937,   2 00
                  $303 232 84

Payments to treasurer January 1 to
  November 6, 1937, $171 073 83
Abatements January 1, to
  November 6, 1937,   5 182 53
Outstanding November 6, 1937,
  per list,   126 638 43
Cash balance November 6, 1937,   338 05
                  $303 232 84

OLD AGE ASSISTANCE TAXES - 1931

Outstanding May 18, 1933, $252 00

Payments and refunds by State   13 00
Abatements and refunds by State,   20 00
Duplicate refund by State,   1 00
                                                        $286 00
Payments to treasurer:
 May 18 to December 31,
    1933, $121 00
    1934,   26 00
    1935,   5 00
                               $152 00
Refunds by State, May 18, to
   December 31, 1933,   63 00
Abatements, 1934,   71 00
                                                        $286 00

OLD AGE ASSISTANCE TAXES - 1932

Outstanding May 18, 1933, $958 00
Payments and refunds by State,   28 00
Abatements and payments adjusted,   2 00
                                                        $988 00
Payments to treasurer:
 May 18 to December 31, 1933, $472 00
    1934 ,   333 00
    1935,   16 00
    1936,   1 00
                               $822 00
Abatements 1935,   166 00
                                                        $988 00

OLD AGE ASSISTANCE TAXES - 1933

Commitment per warrant, $2 500 00
Additional commitment,   20 00
                                                    $2 520 00

Payments to treasurer:
  May 18 to December

31, 1933,	$1 231 00	
1934,	579 00	
1935,	233 00	
1936,	163 00	
	$2 206 00	
Abatements 1936,	310 00	
Outstanding December 31, 1936	4 00	
		$2 520 00

Outstanding January 1, 1937,	$4 00
Unlocated difference November 6, 1937, adjusted	1 00
	$5 00
Payments to treasurer January 1 to November 6, 1937,	$1 00
Oustanding November 6, 1937, per list,	4 00
	$5 00

MOTOR VEHICLE EXCISE TAXES - 1930

Outstanding May 18, 1933, $ .20
Payments to treasurer May 18 to December 31, 1933, $ .20

MOTOR VEHICLE EXCISE TAXES - 1931

Outstanding May 18, 1933,		$1 110 82
Payments to treasurer:		
May 18, to December		
31, 1933,	$420 20	
1934,	168 74	
1935,	70 68	
	$659 62	
Abatements:		
May 18, to December		
31, 1933,	$265 84	

1934,   139 04
1935,   2 00
                                                  406 88
Motor vehicle excise taxes 1931 reported
    as motor vehicle excise taxes 1932
    in 1934,   42 66
Unlocated difference December 31, 1935,
    adjusted   1 66
                                             $1 110 82

MOTOR VEHICLE EXCISE TAXES - 1932

Outstanding May 18, 1933, $3 324 23
Abatements and payments refunded,
    May 18 to December 31, 1933,   2 00
Motor vehicle excise taxes 1931
    reported as motor vehicle excise
    taxes 1932, in 1934,   42 66
                                            $3 368 89
Payments to treasurer:
  May 18, to December
    31, 1933, $1 355 95
    1934,   1 086 19
    1935,   255 34
    1936,   4 49
                          $2 701 97
Abatements:
  May 18, to December
    31, 1933, $ 42 34
    1934,   334 25
    1935,   289 54
                                      666 13
Outstanding December 31, 1936,   79
                                            $3 368 89

Outstanding January 1, 1937, $ .79

Unlocated difference November 6,
 1937, adjusted,   2 50
                                                  $3 29
Outstanding November 6, 1937, per list, $3 29

MOTOR VEHICLE EXCISE TAXES - 1933

Outstanding May 18, 1933, $4 171 94
Additional committments May 18 to
 December 31, 1933,   3 701 39
Abatements and payment refund, 1934,   3 78
                                              $7 877 11
Payments to treasurer:
 May 18 to December
 31, 1933, $3 715 53
 1934,   1 991 34
 1935,   613 06
 1936,   610 30
                                 $6 930 23
Abatements:
 May 18 to December
 31, 1933, $291 49
 1934,   100 74
 1935,   26 69
 1936,   515 03
                                   933 95
Outstanding December 31, 1936,   12 93
                                              $7 877 11

Outstanding January 1, 1937, $12 93
Unlocated difference November
 6, 1937, adjusted,   3 89
                                              $16 82
Abatements January 1 to
 November 6, 1937, $7 30
Oustanding November 6, 1937, per list, 9 52
                                              $16 82

MOTOR VEHICLE EXCISE TAXES - 1934

Commitment per warrants,		$10 039 56
Abatements and payments refunded:		
1934,	$13 35	
1935,	16 19	
	29 54	
		$10 069 10
Payments to treasurer:		
1934,	$5 688 68	
1935,	1 814 27	
1936,	908 98	
	$8 411 93	
Abatements:		
1934,	$374 51	
1935,	118 18	
1936,	12 95	
	505 64	
Outstanding December 31, 1936,	1 151 53	
		$10 069 10

Outstanding January 1, 1937,		$ 1 151 53
Payments to treasurer January 1 to		
November 6, 1937,	$627 62	
Abatements January 1 to		
November 6, 1937 ,	451 76	
Unlocated difference November		
6, 1937, adjusted	37	
Outstanding November 6, 1937, per list,	69 90	
Cash balance November 6, 1937,	1 88	
		$ 1 151 53

MOTOR VEHICLE EXCISE TAXES - 1935

Commitment per warrants,	$10 765 87	
Abatements and payments		
refunded 1936,	17 26	
		$10 783 13

Payments to treasurer:
   1935, $6 171 74
   1936,   2 212 56
                             $8 384 30
Abatements:
   1935, $451 20
   1936,   90 93
                        542 13
Outstanding December 31, 1936,   1 856 70
                                  $10 783 13

Oustanding January 1, 1937, $ 1 856 70
Payments to treasurer January 1 to
   November 6, 1937, $ 972 11
Abatement January 1 to
   November 6, 1937,   196 66
Unlocated difference November
   6, 1937,   61
Oustanding November 6. 1937
   per list,   655 42
Cash balance November 6, 1937   31 90
                                $ 1 856 70

MOTOR VEHICLE EXCISE TAXES - 1936

Commitment per warrants, $12 513 36
Abatement and payment refunded,   34
                               $12 513 70
Payments to treasurer, $5 896 06
Abatements,   556 41
Outstanding December 31, 1936,   6 061 23
                               $12 513 70

Outstanding January 1, 1937, $6 061 23
Abatements and payments January 1 to
   November 6, 1937:
      Refunded, $1 08

To be refunded   34
                                      1 42
                                         $ 6 062 65

Payments to treasurer January 1 to
  November 6, 1937, $4 104 99
Abatements January 1 to
  November 6, 1937   174 26
Outstanding November 6, 1937,
  per list,   1 690 64
Cash balance November 6, 1937,   92 76
                                         $ 6 062 65

MOTOR VEHICLE EXCISE TAXES - 1937

Commitment January 1 to November 6, 1937,
  per warrants $13 545 76
Abatements and payments January 1 to
  November 6, 1937:
    Refunded, $16 25
    To be refunded   13 10
                                  29 35
                                         $13 575 11
Payments to treasurer January 1 to
  November 6, 1937, $7 899 77
Abatements January 1 to
  November 6, 1937,   689 92
Outstanding November 6, 1937,
  per list,   4 779 94
Cash balance November 6, 1937,   205 48
                                         $13 575 11

INTEREST AND COSTS ON TAXES

Cash balance May 18, 1933, $ 121 65
Interest and costs collections:
  May 18 to December 31, 1933,
    Taxes 1931, $5 279 95

Taxes 1932,	1 749 57	
Taxes 1933,	130 03	
Motor vehicle excise taxes 1931,	52 69	
Motor vehicle excise taxes 1932,	91 07	
Motor vehicle excise taxes 1933,	19 82	
		7 323 13

1934:

Taxes 1931,	$ 223 48	
Taxes 1932,	5 307 26	
Taxes 1933,	2 343 16	
Taxes 1934,	119 80	
Motor vehicle excise taxes 1931,	20 98	
Motor vehicle excise taxes 1932,	135 14	
Motor vehicle excise taxes 1933,	76 79	
Motor vehicle excise taxes 1934,	12 56	
		8 239 17

1935:

Taxes 1931,	$ 25 04	
Taxes 1932,	469 14	
Taxes 1933,	5 797 79	
Taxes 1934,	2 516 19	
Taxes 1935,	91 60	
Motor vehicle excise taxes 1931,	12 23	
Motor vehicle excise taxes 1932,	31 15	
Motor vehicle excise taxes 1933,	67 78	
Motor vehicle excise taxes 1934,	64 81	

Motor vehicle excise
  taxes 1935,   14 45
                         9 090 18
1936:
  Taxes 1932,   1 50
  Taxes 1933,   388 55
  Taxes 1934,   5 609 67
  Taxes 1935,   1 770 42
  Taxes 1936,   84 90
  Motor vehicle excise
    taxes 1932,   30
  Motor vehicle excise
    taxes 1933,   90 96
  Motor vehicle excise
    taxes 1934,   101 35
  Motor vehicle excise
    taxes 1935,   80 75
  Motor vehicle excise
    taxes 1936,   26 77
                    8 155 17
                            $32 929 30

Payments to treasurer:
  May 18 to December
    31, 1933, $7 322 13
  1934,   8 244 71
  1935,   9 090 18
  1936,   8 155 17
                  32 812 19
Cash balance December 31, 1936,   117 11
                            $32 929 30

Cash balance January 1, 1937,   117 11
Interest and costs collections January 1
  to November 6, 1937,
  Taxes 1933,   43 29
  Taxes 1934,   496 08
  Taxes 1935,   4 611 90
  Taxes 1936,   1 509 95

Taxes 1937,	4 11	
Motor vehicle excise		
taxes 1934,	85 52	
Motor vehicle excise		
- taxes 1935,	128 47	
Motor vehicle excise		
taxes 1936,	127 19	
Motor vehicle excise		
taxes 1937,	19 33	
	7 025 84	
		$ 7 142 95

Payments to treasurer January 1 to		
November 6, 1937	$6 863 72	
Interest on taxes 1933		
reported as taxes 1933,	1 87	
Interest on taxes 1935		
reported as taxes 1935,	87 57	

Cash balance November 6, 1937:		
Taxes 1930,	$116 68	
Taxes 1931,	40	
Taxes 1934,	21 00	
Taxes 1935,	26 99	
Taxes 1936,	9 69	
Taxes 1937,	92	
Motor vehicle excise		
taxes 1930,	03	
Motor vehicle excise		
taxes 1934,	25	
Motor vehicle excise		
taxes 1935,	3 99	
Motor vehicle excise		
taxes 1936,	8 56	
Motor vehicle excise		
taxes 1937,	1 28	
	189 79	
		$ 7 142 95

TAX TITLES

Balance May 18, 1933, $6 416-87
Tax titles taken:
May 18, to December 31, 1933:
   Taxes 1931, $2 666 17
   Interest and costs,   502 19
                               $3 168 36
1934:
   Taxes 1932, $2 416 80
   Interest and costs,   556 02
                                2 972 82
1935:
   Taxes 1933,   845 91
   Interest and costs,   286 66
                                1 132 57
1936:
   Taxes 1934,   3 289 68
   Interest and costs   517 72
                                3 807 40
                                       11 081 15
Added to tax titles:
May 18 to December 31, 1933:
   Taxes 1931, $1 927 52
   Taxes 1932,   2 689 20
                                4 616 72
1934:
   Taxes 1933,   3 103 52
   Interest,   33 38
                                3 136 90
1935:   ·
   Taxes 1934,   4 094 62
   Interest   31 05
                                4 125 67
1936:
   Taxes 1935,   6 707 05
   Interest,   75 26
                                6 782 31
                                       18 661 60
                                            $36 159 62
Tax titles redeemed:
May 18 to December 31, 1933 $2 805 23
  1934,   4 810 81
  1935,   5 495 03
  1936,   6 321 71
                                  $19 432 78

Tax titles disclaimed:
1935:
  Taxes 1933, $7 65
  Taxes 1934,   8 51
  Interest and costs,   7 98
                            24 14
Balance December 31, 1936,   16 702 70
                         • $36 159 62

Balance January 1, 1937, $16 702 70
Tax titles taken January 1 to November 6, 1937:
  Taxes 1935, $1 721 82
  Interest and costs,   305 61
                           2 027 43
Added to tax titles January 1 to
  November 6, 1937:
  Taxes 1936, $7 986 56
  Interest,   98 84
                           8 085 40
                            $26 815 53
Tax titles redeemed January 1 to
  November 6, 1937, $10 331 56
Tax title released in 1927 not previously
  reported   14 11
Balance November 6, 1937, per list,   16 469 86
                            $26 815 53

TOWN CLERK

DOG LICENSES

Licenses issued January 1 to November 6, 1937:
  Males, 170 @ $2.00 $340 00
  Spayed females, 72 @ $2.00   144 00
  Females, 23 @ $5.00   115 00
  Kennel, 1 @ $25.00   25 00
                            $624 00
Payments to treasurer January 1 to
  November 6, 1937, $567 20
Fees retained January 1 to
  November 6, 1937,   53 20

Cash on hand November 6, 1937,
    verified,   3 60
                                      ― $624 00

SPORTING AND TRAPPING LICENSES

Licenses issued January 1
    to November 6, 1937, $548 00
Payments to Division of Fisheries and
    Game, January 1 to
    November 6, 1937, $465 50
Fees retained January 1
    to November 6, 1937,   62 25
Cash on hand November 6,
    1937, verified,   20 25
                                      $548 00

LICENSES AND PERMITS

Licenses and permits issued:
    June 30 to December 1, 1933, $770 00
    1934,   4 553 50
    1935,   5 170 58
    1936,   4 980 00
                                  $15 474 08
Payments to treasurer:
    June 30 to December 31, 1933, $ 770 00
    1934,   4 553 50
    1935,   5 170 58
    1936,   4 980 00
                                  $15 474 08

Licenses and permits issued January 1 to
    November 6, 1937 $ 5 424 00
Payments to treasurer January 1 to
    November 6, 1937 $ 5 424 00

SEALER OF WEIGHTS AND MEASURES

Charges:
  July 3 to December
  ˙ 31, 1933, $ 77 70
  1934,   128 68
  1935,   122 43
  1936,   108 55
                                          $437 36
Overpayments to treasurer:
  July 3 to December
    31, 1933, $9 19
  1935,   14
  1936,   80
                                   10 13
                                          $447 49

Payments to treasurer:
  July 3 to December 31, 1933, $ 86 89
  1934,   128 68
  1935,   122 57
  1936,   109 35
                                          $447 49

Charges 1937, $118 51
Overpayments to treasurer July 3, 1933
  to December 31, 1937,   10 36
                                          $128 87

Payments to treasurer:
  January 1 to November
    6, 1937, $50 31
  November 7 to December
    31, 1937,   68 43
                                  $118 74
Overpayments to treasurer July 3, 1933 to
    December 31, 1937,   10 13
                                          $128 87

HEALTH DEPARTMENT
Accounts Receivable

Outstanding May 18, 1933,	$196 80	
Charges:		
May 18 to December		
31, 1933	$1 996 42	
1934	1 343 06	
1935	1 300 16	
1936	1 612 70	
	6 252 34	
		$6 449 14
Payments to treasurer:		
May 18 to December		
31, 1933,	$ 522 93	
1934	1 316 50	
1935	1 293 07	
1936	1 021 86	
	$4 154 36	
Abatements:		
May 18 to December		
31, 1933	114 30	
Outstanding December		
31, 1936	2 180 48	
		$6 449 14
Outstanding January		
1, 1937		$2 180 48
Payments to treasurer		
January 1 to November		
6, 1937	$1 488 72	
Outstanding November 6,		
1937, per list	691 76	
		$2 180 48

Licenses

Licenses issued:	
July 13 to December	
31, 1933	$17 50

1934	40 00	
1935	33 50	
1936	29 00	
		$120 00

Payments to treasurer:
July 13 to December

31, 1933	$ 4 50	
1934	51 00	
1935	35 50	
1936	27 00	
	$118 00	

Cash balance December

31, 1936	2 00	
		$120 00

Cash balance January

1, 1937	$2 00	
Licenses issued	44 00	
		$46 00
Payments to treasurer	$39 00	

Cash balance December

31, 1937	7 00	
		$46 00

HIGHWAY DEPARTMENT
Accounts Receivable

Outstanding May 18, 1933	$88 61	
Charges:		
May 18 to December		
31, 1933	$67 50	
1935	16 50	
1936	119 95	
	203 95	
		$292 56

Payments to treasurer:
May 18 to December

31, 1933	$67 50	

1935	16 50	♦
1936	119 95	
		$203 95

Abatements:

May 18 to December 31,		
1933	52 86	
Outstanding December 31, 1936		
and November 6, 1937, per list	35 75	
		$292 56

PUBLIC WELFARE DEPARTMENT
Infirmary - Accounts Receivable

Outstanding May 18, 1933	$1,444 39	

Charges:

May 18 to December 31,		
1933	$1 436 54	
1934	1 387 10	
1935	1 139 40	
1936	1 664 00	
	5 627 04	
		$7 071 43

Payments to treasurer:

1934	$1 444 39	
1935	1 436 54	
1936	2 526 50	
	$5 407 43	
Outstanding December		
• 31, 1936	1 664 00	
		$7 071 43

Outstanding January 1, 1937	$1,664 00	
Charges January 1 to		
November 6, 1937	832 00	
		$2 496 00
Payments to treasurer		
January 1 to November		
6, 1937	$1 664 00	

Outstanding November 6,
  1937, per list   832 00
                                       $2 496 00

PUBLIC WELFARE DEPARTMENT

Aid to Dependent Children - Accounts Receivable

Outstanding May 18, 1933		$21 02
Charges:		
May 18 to December		
31, 1933	$2 709 29	
1934	2 946 50	
1935	2 922 14	
1936	4 461 87	
		13 039 80
		$13 060 82
Payments to treasurer:		
1934	$2 730 31	
1935	2 946 50	
1936	3 052 72	
	$8 729 53	
Outstanding December		
31, 1936		4 331 29
		$13 060 82

Outstanding January 1, 1937		$4 331 29
Charges January 1 to		
November 6, 1937		1 922 09
		$6 253 38
Payments to treasurer January		
1 to November 6, 1937		$2 845 92
Disallowances January		
1 to November 6, 1937		172 00
Outstanding November 6,		
1937, per list		3 235 46
		6 253 38

Temporary Aid - Accounts Receivable

Outstanding May 18, 1933		$4 929 55	
Charges:			
May 18 to December			
31, 1933	$17 447 79		
1934	10 576 41		
1935	14 027 29		
1936	13 270 59		
		$55 322 08	
			$60 251 63
Payments to treasurer:			
May 18 to December			
31, 1933	$9 880 34		
1934	14 634 27		
1935	13 601 33		
1936	5 081 80		
		$43 197 74	
Abatements:			
May 18 to December			
31, 1933	$264 35		
1935	37 00		
		301 35	
Outstanding December			
31, 1936		16 752 54	
			$60 251 63
Outstanding January			
1, 1937		$16 752 54	
Charges January 1 to			
November 6, 1937		11 340 62	
			$28 093 16
Payments to treasurer January			
1 to November 6, 1937		$15 935 57	
Abatements January 1 to			
November 6, 1937		9 14	
Outstanding November 6,			
1937, per list		12 148 45	
			$28 093 16

BUREAU OF OLD AGE ASSISTANCE

Accounts Receivable

Outstanding May 18, 1933		$4 386 07
Charges		
May 18 to December		
31, 1933	$1 000 00	
1934	6 414 89	
1935	8 801 88	
1936	13 338 21	
	29 554 98	
		$33 941 05
Payments to treasurer:		
May 18 to December		
31, 1933	$4 338 84	
1934	6 774 22	
1935	8 513 20	
1936	11 781 23	
	$31 407 49	
Abatements:		
May 18 to December		
31, 1933	$108 75	
1934	116 00	
1935	64 50	
	289 25	
Outstanding December		
31, 1936		2 244 31
		$33 941 05
Outstanding January		
1, 1937		$2 244 31
Charges January 1 to		
November 6, 1937		17 148 51
		$19 392 82
Payments to treasurer		
January 1 to November		
6, 1937		$14 654 22

Outstanding November 6, 1937, per list	4 738 60	
		$19 392 82

STATE AID
Accounts Receivable

Charges:

May 18 to December 31, 1933	$1 047 00	
1934	920 00	
1935	676 00	
1936	650 00	
		$3 293 00

Payments to treasurer:

1934	$1 047 00	
1935	920 00	
1936	676 00	
	$2 643 00	
Outstanding December 31, 1936	650 00	
		$3 293 00

Outstanding January 1, 1937	$650 00	
Charges January 1 to November 6, 1937	556 00	
		$1 206 00
Outstanding November 6, 1937		$1 206 00

MILITARY AID
Accounts Receivable

Charges:

May 18 to December 31, 1933	$20 00	
1934	10 00	
		$30 00

Payments to treasurer:

1934		$20 00
1935		10 00
		$30 00

Charges January 1 to
November 6, 1937 $5 00
Outstanding November 6, 1937 $5 00

SCHOOL DEPARTMENT
Accounts Receivable

Outstanding May 18, 1933		$7 50	
Charges:			
May 18 to December			
31, 1933	$1 437 11		
1934	1 048 42		
1935	1 196 80		
1936	1 618 02		
		5 300 35	
			$5 307 85
Payments to treasurer:			
May 18 to December			
31, 1933	$1 437 11		
1934	1 048 42		
1935	1 196 80		
1936	1 618 02		
		$5 300 35	
Abatements:			
May 18 to December			
31, 1933		7 50	
			$5 307 85

Charges January 1 to
November 6, 1937 $1 909 33
Payments to treasurer
January 1 to November
6, 1937 $1 909 01

Abatements January 1 to
    November 6, 1937   32
                                                  $1 909 33

TOWN OFFICIALS' TELEPHONES

Outstanding May 18, 1933 $133 65
Abatements May 18 to December 31, 1933 $133 65

LIBRARY DEPARTMENT

Cash on hand July 13, 1933 $31 28
Receipts:
  July 13 to December
    31, 1933 $116 67
    1934   309 43
    1935   295 25
    1936   307 25
                                     1 028 60
                                                  $1 059 88
Payments to treasurer:
  July 13 to December
    31, 1933 $142 00
    1934   307 00
    1935   298 00
    1936   303 00
                                     $1 050 00
Cash balance December
    31, 1936   9 88
                                                  $1 059 88

Cash balance January 1, 1937   9 88
Receipts 1937   318 89
                                                  $328 77
Payments to treasurer:
  January 1 to November
    6, 1937 $250 50

November 7 to December
  31, 1937   60 50
                           $311 00
Cash on hand December
  31, 1937, verified   17 77
                               $328 77

WATER DEPARTMENT

Rates

Outstanding January 1, 1936	$19 448 68	
Charges	23 904 98	
Overpayments adjusted	33 69	
		$43 387 35
Payments to treasurer	$25 804 26	
Abatements	96 86	
Outstanding December 31, 1936	17 486 23	
		$43 387 35

Outstanding January 1, 1937	17 486 23	
Charges January 1 to November 6, 1937	17 937 71	
Overpayments:		
Adjusted	$20 90	
To be refunded	78	
	21 68	
		$35 445 62
Payments to treasurer January 1 to November 6, 1937	$20 622 25	
Abatements January 1 to November 6, 1937	1 392 90	
Transferred to water liens January 1 to November 6, 1937	1 564 11	
Added to tax bills 1937 January 1 to November 6, 1937	289 92	
Outstanding November 6, 1937, per list	11 219 76	

Cash on hand November 6, 1937,
verified   356 68
                                                          $35 445 62

Miscellaneous Charges

Outstanding January 1, 1936	$1 435 01	
Charges	2 259 13	
		$3 694 14
Payments to treasurer	2 342 72	
Abatements	25 57	
Outstanding December 31, 1936	1 325 85	
		$3 694 14

Outstanding January 1, 1937	$1 325 85	
Charges January 1 to November 6, 1937	1 630 10	
		$2 955 95
Payments to treasurer January 1 to November 6, 1937	$1 332 31	
Abatements January 1 to November 6, 1937	90 08	
Transferred to water liens January 1 to November 6, 1937	4 90	
Outstanding November 6, 1937, per list	1 449 48	
Cash on hand November 6, 1937, verified	79 18	
		$2 955 95

WATER LIENS

Water liens taken January 1 to
November 6, 1937:

Water rates	$1 564 11	
Miscellaneous	4 90	
Costs	394 50	
		$1 963 51

Payments to treasurer January 1
  to November 6, 1937 $178 36
Outstanding November 6, 1937
  per list   1 785 15
                                                    $1 963 51

WATER LIENS ADDED TO TAXES - 1937

Commitment per warrant $418 92
Payments to treasurer January 1
  to November 6, 1937 $175 16
Outstanding November 6, 1937,
  per list   241 01
Cash balance November 6, 1937   2 75
                                                    $418 92

ABINGTON-ROCKLAND JOINT WATER RATES

Outstanding October 24, 1936 $1 055 55
Charges October 24 to December
  31, 1936   545 99
                                                    $1 601 54
Payments to treasurer October 24
  to December 31, 1936   372 21
Abatements October 24 to December
  31, 1936   383 40
Outstanding December 31, 1936   845 93
                                                    $1 601 54

Outstanding January 1, 1937 $845 93
Charges January 1 to November
  7, 1937   2 502 19
                                                    $3 348 12
Payments to treasurer January
  1 to November 7, 1937 $2 955 32
Abatements January 1 to
  November 7, 1937   36 63

Outstanding November 7, 1937,
  per list   314 97
Cash on hand November 7, 1937, •
  verified   41 20
                                        $3 348 12

TOWN OF ROCKLAND IN ACCOUNT WITH TOWN OF ABINGTON

Joint Water Rates

Due town of Abington October 24,
  1936 $632 46
Due town of Abington - one half of
  joint rates received by the town
  of Rockland, October 24 to
  December 31, 1936   186 10
                                          $818 56
Payments to town of Abington
  October 24 to December 31, 1936   722 82
Due town of Abington December
  31, 1936   95 74
                                          818 56
Due town of Abington January 1,
  1937   95 74
Due town of Abington - one half of
  joint rates received by the town of
  Rockland January 1 to November 7,
  1937   1 477 66
                                      $1 573 40
Payments to town of Abington January
  1 to November 7, 1937   1 435 59
Due town of Abington November 7,
  1937   137 81
                                        $1 573 40

LIBRARY TRUST FUNDS
In Custody of Library Trustees

	Savings Deposits	Total
On hand My 18, 1933, 39,	$3 590 58	$3 590 58
On hand December 31, 1933,	$3 547 08	$3 547 08
On hand December 31, 1934,	$3 963 72	$3 963 72
On hand December 31, 1935,	$3 842 98	$3 842 98
On hand December 31, 1936,	$3 961 57	$3 961 57
On hand er 6, 1937,	$3 944 76	$3 944 76

Receipts

May 18, 1933 to December 31, 1936

Withdrawn from savings deposits:
May 18 to December 31,

1933, $ 43 50
1934, 83 36
1935, 120 74
$ 247 60

I me:
May 18 to December 31, 1933, $ 10 71
1934, 170 58

Payments

Added to savings deposits:

1934, $ 500 00
1936, 118 59
$ 618 59

Expenditures:
My 18 to December 31, 1933, $ 54 21
1934, 253 94
1935, 247 39
1936, 96 73

1935,   126 65
1936,   115 32   423 26   652 27

Bequests:
1934,   500 00
1936,   100 00   600 00

     $ 1 270 86 $ 1 270 86

July 1 to November 6, 1937   Expenditures,

Withdraw from savings deposits, $ 16 81
I one,   117 68

     $ 134 49 $ 134 49

     $ 134 49

CEMETERY PERPETUAL CARE FUNDS
In Custody of Town Treasurer

	Cash	Savings Deposits	Total
On hand May 18, 1933,	$100 00	$15 068 61	$15 068 61
On hand December 31, 1933,		$14 978 82	$15 078 82
On hand December 31, 1934,		$15 761 98	$15 761 98
On hand December 31, 1935,		$16 225 59	$16 225 59
On hand December 31, 1936,		$17 298 43	$17 298 43
On hand ..ber 6, 1937,		$17 930 24	$17 930 24

Receipts

May 18, 1933 to December 31, 1936

Withdrawn from savings deposits:

May 18 to December 31, 1933,		$ 289 79
Interest:		
May 18 to December 31, 1933,	$ 259 39	
1934,	515 26	
1935,	510 27	
1936,	502 17	1 787 09

Payments

May 18, 1933 to December 31, 1936

Added to savings deposits:

May 18 to December 31, 1933,	$ 200 00	
1934,	783 16	
1935,	463 61	
1936,	1 072 84	
Paid to town for care:		
May 18 to December 31, 1933,	449 23	
1934,	517 10	$2 519 61

Bequests:
May 18 to December

31, 1933, $ 200 00
1934, 685 00
1935, 375 00
1936, 1 025 00

Transferred from town, 1933, 2 285 00
05

$4 361 93

1935, 421 66
1936, 454 33
1 842 32

$4 361 93

ary 1 to November 6, 1937

Income, $ 352 80 ...d to savings deposits, $ 631 81
Bequests, 491 48 Transferred to town for care, 212 47

$ 844 28 $ 844 28

TOWN OF ROCKLAND
Balance Sheet, N⟍ ᵐber 6, 1937

GENERAL ACCOUNTS

ASSETS

Cash:

General,	$127 959 62		
Water Department, Petty,	25 00		
		$127 984 62	

udⁱts Receivable:

Taxes:

Levy of 1931,	13 15	
Levy of 1932,	25 92	
Levy of 1933,	79 35	
Levy of 1934,	62 87	
Levy of 1935,	5 510 53	
Levy of 1936,	65 965 15	
Levy of 1937,	126 976 48	
		198 633 45

Old Age Assistance Taxes:

Levy of 1933,		4 00

Motor Vehicle Excise Taxes:

Levy of 1932,	3 29
Levy of 1933,	9 52
Levy of 1934,	71 78
Levy of 1935,	687 93

LIABILITIES AND RESERVES

Temporary Loans:

In Anticipation of Revenue,		$175 000 00
Reserve for Petty Cash, Due:		25 00
Water Department,		

Collector's Overpayment to Treasurer:

Taxes 1933,		40 00
Dog Licenses, Due County,		322 20
Sale of Real Estate Fund,	5 190 00	
State Tax and Assessments,	15 293 74	
Overestimate, County Tax,		702 40
Abington and Rockland Joint Water		
Rates, Due Town of Abington		137 81

Federal Grants:

Old Age Assistance, Administration,	212 99	
Old Age Assistance, Assistance,	490 26	
Aid to Dependent Children	77 02	
Unexpended Balances,	780 27	
	65 619 97	

Levy of 1936, 1 783 06
Levy of 1937, 4 972 32

Tax Titles,   7 527 90
   16 469 86

Departmental:
Health, 691 76
Highway, 35 75
Public Welfare:
Infirmary, $832 00
Mothers' Aid 3 235 46
Temporary
Aid, 12 148 45   16 215 91

Old Age Assistance, 4 738 60
State Aid, 1 206 00
Military Aid, 5 00   22 893 02

Aid:
Rates, 11 575 66
Miscell. Aid, 1 528 66
Liens, 1 785 15
Aid to Aids
1937, 243 76
Abington and Rockland
Joint Rates, 356 17   15 489 40

Reserve Fund, Only Surplus 2 239 59
Overlays, Reserved for ment of
Taxes:
Levy of 1932, 25 92
Levy of 1933, 79 35
Levy of 1937, 342 57   447 84

Revenue, Reserved until Collected:
Motor Vehicle
Excise Tax, $ 7 527 90
Tax Title, 16 469 86
Departmental, 22 893 02
Aid, 15 489 40   62 380 18

Surplus Revenue, 133 416 50

Overlay Deficits:
Levy of 1931, 90 93
Levy of 1934, 275 97
Levy of 1935, 2 358 28
Levy of 1936, 504 03
                        3 229 21

Own accounts:
Election Salaries, 32 55
Public Welfare, 11 813 57
Old Age Assistance, 6 362 81
Soldiers' Relief, 1 930 05
Unclassified, 194 12

Estimated Receipts to be Collected, 20 333 10
                                    39 874 94
Revenue 1938, To be Provided for, 9 156 00

                        $461 595 50 $461 595 50

DEBT ACCOUNTS

Inside Debt Limit:
Schoolhouse Loan, $66 000 00
Outside Debt Limit:
County Hospital Loan, $ 3 000 00
Schoolhouse Loan,   60 000 00

Net Funded or Fixed Dept:
Inside Debt Limit, $ 66 000 00
Outside Debt Limit, 134 000 00

Union Street Construction
Loan, 31 000 00
Water Tank Construction
Loan, 40 000 00
134 000 00

$200 000 00

$200 000 00

TRUST ACCOUNTS

Trust Funds, Cash and Securities:
In Custody of Library Trustees $ 3 944 76
In Custody of Town Treasurer, · 17 930 24

Hattie Curtis Library Fund, 497 02
Zenas M Lane Library Fund, 496 23
Everett Jane Library Fund, 100 02
Alice Linwood French
Library Fund, 500 53
Mary A. Spence Library
Fund, 500 27
Sarah J. Spence Library
Fund, 300 10
Charles Edwin Vinal
Library Fund, 1 000 14
John W. Rice Library Fund, 400 13
John A. Martin Library
Fund, 100 12

Mothers' Mutual Improvement
Society Library Fund,   50 20
Cemetery Perpetual Care Funds,   17 930 24

3 944 76

$21 875 00

$21 875 00

Sixty-Fifth Annual Report
Of the Selectmen

STATE AID 1938

Paid under Chapter 19, Revised Laws and Amendments thereto.

Total Amount of State Aid Paid		$ 514 00
Appropriation	$ 650 00	
Under appropriation	$ 136 00	

CARE OF TOWN CEMETERY

Paid:—

William E. Vining, services		$ 60 00
Appropriation	$ 60 00	

SOLDIERS' RELIEF

Appropriation, March		$8 000 00
August		3 000 00
		$11 000 00

Paid:—

Town Physicians	$ 200 00	
Other Towns	5 00	
To cases	$9 991 99	
Expended	$10 196 99	
Under	$ 803 01	

CARE OF SOLDIERS' GRAVES

Paid:—

W. R. Hunt, labor	$ 12 50

C. S. Tilden, labor	47 50	
W. A. Whiting, labor	12 50	
James Maguire	4 00	
'Louis B. Gilbride	48 50	

Expended		$ 125 00
Appropriation	$ 125 00	

BURIAL OF INDIGENT SOLDIERS

Paid:—

C. L. Rice & Son, burial		$ 100 00
Appropriation $200 00		
Appropriation from August 8 meeting		
from Surplus Rev. Fund		$ 200 00
Under appropriation		$ 100 00

CLEAN-UP WEEK

Paid:—

Lester W. Strang, removing rubbish $	60 00	
Rockland Standard, advertising	4 00	
Expended		$ 64 00
Appropriation	$ 75 00	
Under appropriation	11 00	

CRIMINAL CASES IN COURT

Paid:—

Robert Jackson	$ 28 50	
Leroy Phinney	13 50	
John J. Dwyer	6 00	
Delia M. Phinney	6 85	
George J. Popp	44 00	

Expended		$ 98 85
Appropriation	$ 100 00	
Under appropriation	1 15	

THOMAS MURRILL DAMAGE TO TRUCK

Appropriation	$ 250 00
Nothing expended	
Under appropriation	$ 250 00

STREET LIGHTING 1938

Appropriation, street lighting	$9 134 00
Appropriation, install light Union street	75 00
Appropriation, install light Goddard Avenue	15 00
Appropriation, install light Spring street	15 00
Expended Edison Electric Ill. Co.	$9 279 00

Overpaid $40.00 to be deducted from January account 1939.

HIGHWAY SURVEYOR

Paid:—

Roderick MacKenzie, salary		$1 350 00
Appropriation	$1 350 00	

TARVIA AND ROAD BINDER

Paid:—

Payroll, labor	$ 1 777 15
M. F. Ellis Co., lanterns	12 50
Rockland Coal & Grain, supplies	4 60
Bradford Weston, bit. concrete	361 71
Market Street Garage, supplies and storage	33 00
J. Thomas Condon, surveying	15 00
Rockland Welding, repairs	12 00
E. L. LeBarron Foundary, supplies	10 40
N. E. Concrete Pipe Co.	16 20
The Barrett Corp., tarvia B.	1 183 84
Southeastern Cons. Co., supplies	22 05

Gordon Mann, rent of pit	37 50	
P. J. Perkins, supplies	8 70	
Buffalo-Springfield Co., supplies	5 35	

| Expended | | $ 3 500 00 |
| Appropriation | $ 3 500 00 | |

List of Payroll Tarvia and Road Binder

Paul McDonald	$ 6 75
George Ingalls	1 13
William Cannaway	118 12
Ralph Tedeschi	15 75
Raymond LaCombe	25 88
George Taylor	281 37
George Beverly	49 60
Patrick Mahoney	91 50
Melvin Gay	34 50
Thomas Murrill	7 50
Leo Cull	58 50
John Ricca	42 75
Michael Murphy	72 00
Thomas Bailey	117 00
Leon Ignatawicz	29 25
George Auteno	9 56
Domenic DelPrete	265 50
Peter Hussey	43 31
Austin Marks	56 81
Joseph Arena	76 50
Arthur Deacon	38 81
Abe Wainshilbaum	19 50
Domenic DelPrete, Jr.	25 31
John J. Dwyer	76 50
Arthur Smith	42 75
Joseph Daley	23 63
William Condon	18 00
Felix Carreaux	22 50
Paul Nolan	13 50
Edward Tobin	11 25
Ray Martel	2 25
John White	15 75

Russell Hawes	15 75
Joseph Costello	11 25
Charles Fucillo	2 25
Donald Baker	7 31
John Peabody	5 06
Edward Lynch	2 25
Meyer Marcus	2 25
John Butler	2 25
Lyle Tibbetts	2 25
Charles Clark	2 25
Joseph DelPrete	2 25
Harold Dill	2 25
J. Sullivan	2 25
R. Brown	2 25
Phillip Brown	2 25

Total $1 777 15

HIGHWAY REPAIRS

Paid:—

Gordon Mann, rent of pit	$ 75	00
Bradford Weston Inc., supplies	1 431	06
C. H. Swift, oil	1	00
George N. Beal, supplies	11	75
Rockland Coal & Grain Co., supplies	139	56
Bay State Nurseries, grass seed	19	75
Rockland Water Dept., service	52	93
Payroll, labor	1 417	75
Roderick MacKenzie, use of car	312	45
George W. S. Hyde, repairs	63	30
Rome Bros., supplies	138	15
M. F. Ellis Co., supplies	85	87
E. L. LeBarron Foundry, catch basin	117	68
N. E. Concrete Pipe Co., pipe	127	80
Brockton Welding Co, repairs	70	90
Hall & Torrey Co., supplies	6	67
Comm. of Public Safety, ins of boiler	10	00
H. H. Arnold Co., supplies	4	12

Rockland Disposal Service, removal
of rubbish   51 00
Market St. Garage, storage   93 40
A. Culver Co., cement   4 20
Southeastern Cons. Co., cement blocks 101 48
Atlantic Coast Rulf. Co., supplies   15 68
Herbert F. Gardner, supplies   10 90
Reed Lumber Inc., supplies   75
Buffalo-Springfield Co., repairs   5 71
Crawford Service Station, supplies   13 20

Expended $4 382 06
Appropriation $ 3 500 00
Deduct under Article No. 36   600 00

                                       $ 2 900 00
Appropriate August 8 from
Surplus Rev.   1 500 00

Total Appropriation $ 4 400 00
Under Appropriation $ 17 94

LIST OF PAYROLL HIGHWAY REPAIRS

Paid:—
George Tyler $ 438 63
William Condon   104 25
Raymond LaCombe   15 85
George Arteno   13 50
Roderick MacKenzie   74 25
Joseph Daley   9 00
Joseph Arena   12 10
Patrick Mahoney   34 50
'A. Wainshilbaum   51 00
Leo Cull   48 94
Fred Tibbetts   9 00
Lyle Tibbetts   4 50
Melvin Gay   43 20
Lawrence Cull   25 05

Ralph Tedeschi	20 55
Earl Wallace	9 00
Domenic DelPrete	69 00
Herbert Nolan	25 50
Arthur Casey	22 50
John J. Dwyer	59 25
George Beverly	20 25
John Ricca	22 50
Thomas Bailey	64 41
William Cannaway	69 75
Michael Mahoney	20 25
Weston Capon	22 50
James Smith	4 50
Joseph Sullivan	13 50
Kenneth Kemp	15 75
Arthur Smith	28 68
Joseph Shoughrow	2 25
Charles O'Kelley	2 81
Austin Marks	9 00
Charles Clark	1 69
Charles Fucillo	2 81
Felix Carreaux	2 53
Charles S. Tilden	25 00

Total $ 1 417 75

DIVISION STREET SIDEWALK

(W. P. A. Labor)

Paid:—

Payroll, truck	$ 215 72
Rockland Coal & Grain Co., cement	63 09
A. Wainshilbaum, gas and oil	9 81
William Condon, gravel	7 75
A. Culver Co., cement	34 00
Bradford Weston Inc., bit. concrete	81 64

Expended $ 412 01

Appropriation under Article
    No. 20 $ 650 00
Unexpended balance   237 99

CATCH BASINS AND DRAINS

Paid:—
Lawrence Cull, labor	$ 4 50
John Ricca, labor	19 68
William Cannaway, labor	29 27
Charles Heath	4 50
Fred Tibbetts	25 89
Howard Callahan	25 89
Clarence Damon	18 00
Thomas O'Connor	4 50
Wilbur Adams	18 00
Maurice Mahoney	17 17
Burrell Dill	24 48
Michael Murphy	24 20
Frank Webster	25 05
Vincent Martin	18 00
Myron Bacon	9 00
Raymond LaCombe	25 60
Dominic DelPrete	23 17
George Blake	23 08
Leo Cull	15 19
Paul Nolan	8 72
Arthur Casey	6 00
Gene Greene	17 17
Frank Green	12 67
Arthur Smith	18 58
Daniel Costello	3 66
Anthony Gudalowicz	8 16
Raymond Arkel	8 16
John Arkel	8 16
Joseph Murphy	12 67
Joseph Kelliher	12 39
Alfred DelPrete	3 38
James Mahoney	7 88

Joseph Costello	21 39	
Timothy White	4 50	
Thomas Bailey	7 88	
George Ingalls	3 66	
Patrick Mahoney	33 00	
William Condon	18 75	

Expended		$ 580 95
Appropriation taken from Article 2	$ 600 00	
Under appropriation	19 05	

CLIFF STREET SIDEWALK

Paid:—		
Payroll on truck	$ 21 00	
Bradford Weston bit. concrete	87 73	

Expended		$ 108 73
Transfer from 1937	$ 108 73	
Expended	108 73	

SOLDIERS' MEMORIAL LIBRARY

Paid:—	
Edison Electric Ill. Co., service	$ 103 76
N. E. Tel. & Tel. Co., service	39 96
Rockland Water Dept., service	4 90
Union Market Co., supplies	80
A. S. Peterson, supplies	24 70
Junior Literary Guild, books	62 53
Library Book House, books	113 06
Lida A. Clark, salary	1 200 00
Lida A. Clark, supplies	11 59
Elida Butler, salary	600 00
Natalie F. Holbrook, salary	600 00
Winifred G. Holbrook, salary	900 00
Library of Congress, books	2 56
Howland's Ins. Office, insurance	78 40
Amos A. Phelps, insurance	111 90

Little Brown & Co., books	1	46
Ginn & Co., books	10	29
Noble & Noble Pub. Co., books	2	82
O. H. Toothaker, books		63
N. England News Co., books	311	33
Hall & Torrey Co., supplies	11	36
Rockland Coal & Grain Co., coal	46	31
James Thibeault, repairs	1	50
W. A. Wilson Co., subscriptions	22	10
W. H. Wilder Co., subscription	7	20
Rockland Hardware & Paint Co., supplies	4	64
Jenkins & Simmons, express	1	79
Gaylord Bros., Inc., supplies	29	40
American Book Co., books	4	04
Filing Equip. Bureau, supplies	1	60
A. Culver Co., coal	127	39
America Coop. encyclopedia	119	50
The American News Co., subscriptions	90	15
L. A. Wells, binding	23	06
R. R. Bowker Co., book		45
Douglas Print, printing	21	00
O. R. Hunting Co., supplies	3	03
Ellis Smith, stamp pad	2	00
Animal Rescue League, subscription		60
Christian Science Pub. Co, subscription	3	00
American Library Asso., books	5	00

Expended		$ 4 705 81
Appropriation	$ 4 200 00	
Dog Fund	505 94	
Total available	$ 4 705 94	
Under appropriation	13	

SIDEWALKS 1938

Paid:—

Payroll, labor	$ 492 57

Rockland Coal & Grain, supplies	34 64	
Bradford Weston Inc, bit. concrete	313 06	
Crawford Service Station, gas	1 35	
W. Condon, sand	32 00	

Expended		$ 873 62
Appropriation	$ 1 000 00	
Trans. Webster & Beal St., Article 66	50 00	
Trans. Webster St. Article 80	75 00	
Total Available	875 00	
Under appropriation	1 38	
List of payroll:		
George Beverly	$ 52 31	
Raymond LaComb	37 13	
Ralph Tedeschi	49 50	
George Tyler	191 25	
William Condon	12 00	
Charles Conlon	12 00	
Joseph Costello	9 00	
H. Cushing	2 25	
Leo Cull	47 25	
Edward Lynch	27 00	
Burrell Dill	23 63	
John Ricca	4 50	
Joseph Arena	6 75	
Michael Murphy	11 25	
Joseph Daley	4 50	
Lyle Tibbetts	2 25	

Total		$ 492 57

WEBSTER AND BEAL STREET

Paid:—		
Payroll, Labor	$ 43 50	
E. L. LeBaron Foundry, Basin	6 50	

Expended		$ 50 00
Appropriation Article No. 66		$ 50 00

LIST OF PAYROLL

George Beverly	$	9 00
Thomas Bailey		4 50
John Ricca		2 25
Leo Cull		4 50
William Cannaway		2 25
Michael Murphy		4 50
George Areteno		4 50
George Tyler		12 00
Total		$ 43 50

WEBSTER STREET SIDEWALK
Near E. T. Wright Factory, Article No. 80

Paid:—

Payroll, Truck	$	36 00
W. H. Clayton, Supplies		5 52
Bradford Weston Inc., Bit. Concrete		17 06
Rockland Coal & Grain Co., supplies		1 00
Expended		$ 59 58
Appropriation	$75 00	
Under Appropriation	$15 42	

AMERICAN LEGION POST No. 147

Paid:—

American Legion Building Association		$900 00
Appropriation	$900 00	

CLEANING UNION STREET

Paid:—

Thomas J. Higgins, Labor	$1 092 77	
William Cannaway, Labor	4 50	
Expended		$1 097 27

Appropriation	$1 200 00
Under Appropriation	102 73

PETER A. BOWLER CAMP, No. 63
SPANISH WAR VETERANS

Paid:—

Old Colony Post Building Association, rent		$ 288 00
Appropriation	$ 288 00	

FIRE DEPARTMENT MAINTENANCE

Payrolls:

C. P. Inkley, Chief	$1 356 00
G. W. Clark, Supt. Fire Alarm	366 63
J. P. Barry, Dep. Chief	100 00
James Fitzgibbons	1 764 90
William Parker	1 669 50
J. Mulready, Sub.	120 00
Engine Co. No. 1, Payroll	1 369 00
Ladder Company Payroll	1 172 00

$ 7 918 03

Department Expense:

A. Culver Co., Fuel	$ 115 60
Rockland Coal & Grain, Fuel	101 99
Telephone Co.	69 25
Edison Light Co.	180 78
Old Colony Gas Co.	38 30
Water Department	23 99
A. J. Vargus	58 97
Hall & Torrey, supplies	21 37
Rome Bros., supplies	8 60
Gorham Fire Equipment Co.	69 55
Gamewell Fire Alarm Co.	28 54
American LeFrance Co. (Labor and materials)	264 27
W. W. Fyffe & Co., material	101 59

A. A. Phelps, Insurance	225	92
Kohler Mfg. Co., supplies	23	26
Bailey Motor Co.	41	02
Columbia Electric Co., wire	73	58
M. E. Ellis & Co., supplies	11	84
F. Metivier, labor on fire alarm	18	00
A. Clark, labor on fire alarm	18	00
H. Cook, labor on fire alarm	6	00
N. H. Ranney, supplies	24	00
A. H. Blanchard Co., supplies	17	00
C. P. Inkley, telephone and expense	98	25
M. Mastrodomenico	2	60
Woodward Spring Co.,	10	13
G. Tyler	5	00
Rockland Hardware Co.		35
Jenkins & Simmon's Express		85
Stanley Ames		75
Boston Coupling Co.		50
N. J. Whalen Co.	18	29
Hallamore Machine Co., labor	8	50
Bemis Drug Co., supplies	7	60
Beacon Cloth Co., Wiping Cloths	9	76
Union Market, supplies	2	10
Mat's Radio, Bulbs	1	00
Douglas Print	3	50
Rockland Transportation Co.	1	75
F. L. Moore, Motor oil	41	25
W. Eamon, labor	8	00
Snap-on Tools Co., supplies	1	45
Weymouth Hospital	5	00
J. A. Rice Co., supplies	4	60
Joseph Riordon, supplies	3	00
George Beals, truck hire	10	00
G. Crawford, labor on fire alarm	12	00
N. Bryant, labor on fire alarm	20	00
R. Measures, labor	10	35
Homelite Co., supplies		50
J. J. Dwyer, truck hire	7	00
P. Ouelette, labor	12	00

G. W. Hyde, labor and material	1	95
Rockland Flower Shop	5	00
C. P. Inkley, use of auto	250	00

$ 2 206 45

Total Expense	$10	124 48
Appropriation	10	126 68

Under Appropriation $ 2 20

FOREST FIRE DEPARTMENT

Payrolls		$ 979 00
Appropriation	$500 00	
Appropriation from Overlay	500 00	

$ 1 000 00

Under Appropriation $ 21 00

POLICE DEPARTMENT 1938

Paid:—

Cornelius J. McHugh, patrol service	$	096 00
Robert J. Drake, patrol service		452 20
John H. Murphy, patrol service		461 80
Adoph Johnson, patrol service		452 20
George J. Popp, service as Chief	1	961 00
Samuel Cannaway, patrol service		345 48
George J. Popp, use of car		265 00
John J. Dwyer, police service		106 84
Micheal O'Brien, police service		15 00
Thomas Fitzgerald, police service		26 00
Maurice J. Mullen, police service		96 88
John F. Hannon, police service		4 00
Charles Hines, police service		4 00
N. E. Tel. & Tel. Co., service		77 51

Edison Electric Ill. Co., service	73	24
Bailey Motor Sales Co.,		
Gas and supplies	210	43
Rockland Coal & Grain Co., coal	88	30
Rockland Standard Pub. Co., printing	13	50
George N. Beals, Repairs	32	55
Edward Beary, labor	6	00
Wallace Vogel, labor	4	50
Edward Meara, sign	1	50
Ralph Measures, labor	27	00
Lake Erie Sales Co., spot light	15	00
Amòs A. Phelps & Son., Insurance	5	00
U. S. Post Office, postage	3	00
A. S. Peterson, supplies	3	10
Market St., Garage, supplies	1	80
Fred Yelland, supplies	3	00
Iver-Johnson, Pistol	27	64
George Fourlas, food for prisoners	18	05
Rome Bros., Supplies	11	72
Hancock Paint & Varnish Co., paint	1	85
A. Wainshilbaum supplies	32	85
Lannin's Lunch, food for prisoners	4	30
Estes Auto Supply, supplies	7	19

Expended		$ 8 955 43
Appropriation	$ 8 956 20	
Under Appropriation	77	

INSPECTION OF ANIMALS AND STABLES

Paid:—

William T. Condon, Inspector	$ 150	00
Appropriation	$ 150	00

SEALER OF WEIGHTS AND MEASURES

Paid:—

Harold J. Iinkley, Services	$ 400	00
Appropriation	$ 400	00

BOARD OF HEALTH

Paid:—

Plymouth County Hospital, Care of Patients	$1 877	70
Dr. J. H. Dunn, services on contagious cases	291	50
Burying cats and dogs	28	00
Evelyn Delorey, salary	1 266	64
Payroll, labor	776	82
J. A. Carrols, M. D., special service	9	00
N. E. Concrete Pipe Co., pipe	171	42
Dr. Joseph Frame, visits and fumigation	459	00
Dr. Joseph Frame, salary	100	00
Dr. Norbert Lough, services	3	00
Rome Bros., supplies	134	60
Hall & Torrey Co., supplies	101	46
Nellie Mileski, nursing	60	00
Rockland Coal & Grain Co., supplies	22	47
George E. Bolling, services	1	00
Bemis Drug Co., supplies	32	50
M. F. Ellis Co., supplies	1	92
Rockland Standard Pub. Co., cards	17	50
Fred S. Delay, supplies	12	46
Mass. Memorial Hospital, Care of patients	806	00
Charles E. Meara, painting sign	5	00
Everready Supply Co., towels	20	05
Rockland Paint & Hardware Co., Supplies	5	73
Sears & Roebuck Co., supplies	5	11
George W. S. Hyde, repairs		75
Thomas Welsh, repairs	2	05
Edward Cullinan, salary	50	00
Dr. J. H. Dunn, salary	50	00
Dr. M. J. Dunn, dental work	10	00
Dr. James B. Gallagher, dental work	10	00
Dr. Daniel Burke, Dental work	10	00

Dr. Frederick Billings, Dental work
   1937 - 1938   20 00
Henry T. Roche Sr., Care of town
   dump   150 00
Dr. F. H. Corey, service   2 00
Woodman Dental Co., supplies   12 60
Market St., Garage, supplies   1 75
John J. Gallagher, tile   2 64

Expended		$ 6 481 17
Appropriation	$5 000 00	
Aug. 8, 1938, Article No. 20	1 500 00	
Total Appropriation		$6 500 00
Under Appropriation		18 83

LIST OF PAYROLL, BOARD OF HEALTH

Paid:—

Harold Corcoran	$ 69 75
Thomas Bailey	67 51
Edward Cullinan	303 32
Paul Golemme	18 69
Philip Murphy	10 69
George Umbrianna	18 00
Albee Richards	4 50
William Santry	2 25
Calvin Bryant	4 50
John J. Dwyer	102 94
Paul MacDonald	6 75
Joseph Arena	3 10
Edward Vegina	1 69
Joseph Shoughrow	1 69
Henry Roche, Sr.	18 00
Samuel Cannaway	4 50
Warren Corcoran	4 50
Charles McGonagle	18 00
Joseph Meade	21 38
Louis Roche	21 38
Joseph Melenski	9 56

John Kelley	8 44	
Joseph Sullivan	14 06	
Michael Haggerty	9 56	
Matthew O'Grady	9 56	
Joseph Cistero	9 56	
Felix Carreaux	7 31	
Dennis Murray	4 50	
William Emerson	1 13	
Total		$ 776 82

PARK DEPT. 1938

Paid:—

Payroll, labor	$2 625 75	
D. H. Burke, expenses	6 40	
Rockland Standard, supplies	4 50	
A. Wainshilbaum, supplies	18 91	
Patrick Mahoney, truck	46 00	
A. Culver Co., Lime	2 40	
James D. Mahoney, repairs	46 50	
Rockland Hardware & Paint Co.		
Supplies	10 75	
Rockland Coal & Grain Co., supplies	6 40	
M. Vincent Fitzgibbons, Insurance	17 40	
J. S. McCallum, supplies	75	
Rome Bros., supplies	1 96	.
Rockland Water Dept., service	50	
James E. Kemp, sharpening mower	7 50	
Expended		$ 2 797 72
Appropriation	$2 800 00	
Under Appropriation	2 28	

LIST OF PAYROLL

Peter Hickey	$ 672 75
Joseph Meade	668 75
James Mahoney	672 75

John Burke   612 00

Total $2 625 75

MEMORIAL DAY OBSERVANCE

Paid:—

S. P. Bruinsma, 500 wreaths	$	60 00
C. F. Staples, 7 gross flags		56 00
E. L. Chamberlin, flowers		9 00
American Legion, band		100 00
Rockland High School Band		35 00
Old Colony Post Junior Drum Corps		35 00
Reed St. Lunch, 300 dinners		105 00

Expended	$	400 00
Appropriation	$	400 00

PURCHASE WASHINGTON REED LOT

Paid:—

Trustees of Washington Reed Est.	$	470 18
Unexpended Balance of 1937	$	470 18

MOTH DEPT. 1938

Paid:—

Payroll, labor	$	160 41
Sherwin & Williams, Creosote and		
Arsenate of Lead		139 50

Expended	$	299 91
Appropriation	$ 300 00	
Under Appropriation		09

LIST OF PAYROLL MOTH DEPT.

Paid:—

Alfred Metivier	$	123 03
Russell Shea		18 00

John White	18 00	
Joseph Kelliher	1 38	
Total		$ 160 41

PLYMOUTH COUNTY EXTENSION SERVICE

Paid:—

| Plymouth County Extension Service | $ 150 00 |
| Appropriation | $ 150 00 |

PLYMOUTH COUNTY HOSPITAL

Paid:—

| Treasurer Plymouth County, Maintenance | $4 013 73 |
| Appropriation | $4 013 73 |

COMPENSATION INSURANCE FOR FIREMEN

Paid:—

| Torrey Bros., Insurance | $ 292 50 |
| Appropriation | $ 292 50 |

TREE WARDEN 1938

Paid:—

Rome Bros., supplies	$ 34 86	
Acme Rubber Mfg. Co., rubber hose	111 40	
Jenkins & Simmons, express	3 75	
Rockland Hardware & Paint Co.		
Supplies	5 90	
Payroll, labor	744 09	
Expended		$ 900 00
Appropriation		$ 900 00

LIST OF PAYROLL, TREE WARDEN

| Arthur Casey | $ 12 00 |
| Russell Shea | 29 25 |

Alfred Metivier	477	72
John White	51	75
Herbert Brown	6	75
John Dill	6	75
Ed. Metivier	2	25
William Green	21	00
Joseph Kelleher	133	62
William Bell	3	00

Total	$ 744	09

TOWN OFFICERS

Harry S. Torrey, Selectman, Board of Public Welfare, Fence Viewer and Old Age Assistance	$ 1 980	00
Norman S. Whiting, Selectman, Board of Public Welfare, Fence Viewer and Old Age Assistance	300	00
John J. Bowler, Selectman, Board of Public Welfare, Fence Viewer and Old Age Assistance	300	00
Charles J. Higgins, Treasurer	1 350	00
James A. Donovan, Tax Collector	1 500	00
Ralph L. Belcher, Town Clerk	699	96
Ralph L. Belcher, Registrar of voters	75	00
Esther Rawson, Registrar of voters	75	00
Thomas Morrissey, Registrar of voters	75	00
John Carney, Registrar of voters 6 months	37	50
Annie Garrity, Registrar of voters 6 months	37	50
C. Elmer Asklund, Auditor	8	33
Leo Downey, Auditor	100	00
Harold Smith, Auditor	110	00
George Gallagher, Auditor	80	00

Magorisk L. Walls, moderator   60 00

Expended		$ 6 788 29
Appropriation	$6 800 00	
Under Appropriation	11 71	

RENT OF TOWN OFFICE

Paid:—

Rockland Savings Bank, Rent		$ 1 239 99
Appropriation	$1 240 00	
Under Appropriation	01	

ELECTIONS 1938

Paid:—

Rockland Standard Pub. Co., Printing	394 80
Becker & Co., pencils	3 00
Payroll, Tellers	815 00
Reed St. Lunch, dinners	13 20
Rockland Lunch, dinners	1 05
Mrs. H. M. Green, dinners	2 75
Mrs. Fred Hall, dinners	3 00
Bemis Drug Co., dinners	22 65
George Fourlas, dinners	28 20
John L. Bemis, dinners	1 25
John J. Bowler, rent of Opera House	320 00
Magorisk Walls, services as Moderator	
Special Meeting	20 00

Expended		$ 1 624 90
Appropriation	$1 700 00	
Under Appropriation	75 10	

TOWN REPORT AND POLL BOOK

Paid:—

Ralph Measures, Delivery	
Town Reports	9 00

Earl Wallace, Delivering
  Town Reports   9 00
Russell Chandler, Delivering
  Town Reports and Car   29 00
Rockland Standard Pub. Co.
  Printing Reports   836 57
A. I. Randall Inc. Printing Poll Book   316 43
                                            _____
Expended $ 1 200 00
Appropriation $ 1 200 00

WORKMEN'S COMPENSATION INSURANCE

Paid:—
Amos A. Phelps, Insurance $ 1 869 59
  Appropriation $2 250 00
  Under Appropriation   380 41

TOWN NOTES AND INTEREST

Paid:—
Director of Accounts, Certifying
  Notes $ 96 00
Payment School Bonds   16 000 00
Interest, School Bonds   5 425 00
Plymouth County Hospital, Notes   1 000 00
Plymouth County Hospital, Interest   125 00
Discount on Notes   918 68
Interest on Notes   28 04
Payment Union Street, Note   4 000 00
Interest Union Street Note   580 00
                                       _____
Expended $27 172 72
Appropriation $28 000 00
Under Appropriation   827 28

REPAIRS AT TOWN INFIRMARY

Paid:—
Norman J. Beal, Contract $2 456 50

Joseph Burton, repairing plaster   319 00
Rockland Coal & Grain Co.,
  Lumber and supplies   43 22

Expended $ 2 818 72
Appropriation $2 915 00
Unexpended Balance   96 28

MASS. INDUSTRIAL SCHOOLS

Paid:—
Town of Weymouth, Mass. $1 295 46
City of Quincy, Mass.   188 84
Norfolk County Agri. School   98 00
City of Boston, Mass.   256 35
City of Brockton, Mass.   35 85

Expended $ 1 874 50
Appropriation $2 000 00
Under Appropriation   125 50

SNOW REMOVAL 1938

Paid:—
Payroll, labor and trucks $12 158 39
Market St. Garage, Storage and
  Repairs   340 85
Rockland Welding Co., repairs   154 00
John Nelson, sand   11 20
Austin Print, printing   1 00
Rome, Bros., supplies   3 40
Reed Lumber Co., supplies   4 75
The Heil Co., parts for plow   8 80
Thomas Murrell, sand   5 50
George W. S. Hyde, repairs   4 30
H. H. Arnold Co., Inc., repairs   6 40

Expended $12 698 59
Appropriation $12 217 68 /

Appropriation, Aug. 8   480 91

Total Appropriation $12 698 59

ASSESSORS

Paid as Salary:

Joseph B. Estes	$1 440 00
Dennis L. O'Connor	530 00
Norman J. Beal	530 00

Expended	$ 2 500 00
Appropriation	$ 2 500 00

MISCELLANEOUS, CLERK

Paid:—

Ralph L. Belcher, vital statistics	$ 254 00
J. Emmet Sullivan & Son, 26 Death Returns	5 75
Murray Bros., Binding Rockland Standard	3 25
H. C. Metcalf, Replace and Repair Typewriter	17 00
Becker & Co., supplies	26 25
C. L. Rice & Son, 25 death returns	6 50
H. H. Hulse, M. D., 3 birth returns	75
J. F. Curtin, M. D., 2 birth returns	50
A. H. Barron, M. D., 2 birth returns	50
H· P. Russell, M. D., 2 birth returns	50
Norbert F. Lough, M. D., 7 birth returns	1 75
F. H. Corey, M. D., 7 birth returns	1 75
Joseph Frame, M. D., 2 birth returns	50
Ralph L. Belcher, postage	2 49
Warren B. Woodward, bond	7 50
Rockland Standard Pub. Co., Adv.	7 50
A. S. Peterson, supplies	1 00
W. H. Sperry, 1 gross pencils	4 50

Ralph L. Belcher, expense Town
   Clerk Meeting   5 50

Expended		$ 347 49
Appropriation	$ 350 00	
Under Appropriation	2 51	

MISCELLANEOUS, SELECTMEN

Paid:—

A. S. Peterson, supplies	$ 1 85
Hobbs & Warren Inc., supplies	1 75
Plymouth County Selectmen's Association Dues	6 00
John O. Donovan, repair typewriter	1 00
Becker & Co., supplies	11 25
Expense Selectmen's meeting	2 25
William H. Sperry, desk pad	3 00
Francis J. Geogan, legal service	87 21

Expended		$ 114 31
Appropriation	$ 120 00	
Under Appropriation	5 69	

MISCELLANEOUS, SEALER WEIGHTS
AND MEASURES

Paid:—

Robinson Seal Co., Record Book	$ 15 18
Amos A. Phelps & Son, Insurance	16 38
W. & L. Gurley, Seals and supplies	12 68
Harold J. Inkley, expense State meeting	7 00
Harold J. Inkley, use of auto	65 00

Expended		$ 116 24
Appropriation	$ 120 00	
Under Appropriation	3 76	

MISCELLANEOUS, REGISTRARS

Paid:—

Rockland Standard Pub. Co.,
Adv., Check lists and Poll Lists 132 45
Ralph L. Belcher, mailing ballots 3 88
Thomas Grow & Co., Inc., 6000 cards 62 00

Expended		$ 198 33
Appropriation	$ 200 00	
Under Appropriation	1 67	

MISCELLANEOUS, TREASURER

Paid:—

L. E. Moran, Filing cases	$ 6 30
The Todd Co., checks	133 40
A. S. Peterson, supplies	1 15
Charles J. Higgins, expense to Boston	39 61
Ward's Stationer, supplies	2 25
Hobbs & Warren Co., supplies	9 47
Annette White, service	200 00
C. J. Higgins, postage and mailing	22 88
U. S. Post Office, envelopes	154 72
Amos A. Phelps & Son, Insurance	17 78
Amos A. Phelps & Son, Bond	200 00
Douglas Print, printing	3 00
Emerson & Co., stamps	1 98
Becker and Co., supplies	4 00
Rockland Standard Pub. Co., Adv.	2 50

Expended		$ 799 04
Appropriation	$ 800 00	
Under Appropriation	96	

MISCELLANEOUS, TAX COLLECTOR

Paid:—

A. S. Peterson, supplies $ 6 50

A. I. Randall, Inc., Printing and		
books	46	70
J. A. Donovan, expense to Boston	12	00
Emerson & Co., Stamps	3	50
Hobbs & Warren Inc., supplies	42	50
Austin Print, letterheads and printing	28	13
James A. Donovan, postage and mis.	23	61
Douglas Print, excise and tax bills	33	00
Amos A. Phelps & Son, insurance	17	76
Amos A. Phelps & Son, bond	410	00
Ralph L. Belcher, service	200	00
U. S. Post Office, envelopes	298	86
Brockton Enterprise, Adv.	12	00
Rockland Standard Pub. Co., Adv.		
Tax Sale	79	25
Francis J. Geogan, legal service		
on tax sale	159	00
Robinson Seal Co., notices	8	64
Commercial Supply Co., supplies	17	26

Expended			$ 1 398 71
Appropriation	$1 400	00	
Under Appropriation	1	29	

MISCELLANEOUS, ASSESSORS

Paid:—

N. E. Tel. & Tel. Co., service	71	96
Brockton Trans. Co., express	1	40
L. E. Muran, loose binders	47	50
A. S. Peterson, supplies	9	75
Fred S. Delay, supplies	6	92
Hobbs & Warren Inc., supplies	2	39
Geo. A. Barnstead & Son, printing cards	1	00
Amos A. Phelps & Son, Insurance	10	00
Mary E. Dotton, service	645	00
I. E. Muran, cards and poll sheets	45	00
H. C. Metcalf, repairs on machines	11	00
Dennis L. O'Connor, auto expense	62	10

Edison Electric Ill. Co., lamps	1	85
Alton F. Lyons, transfer cards and		
services	123	25
Banker and Tradesman, subscription	10	00
Spaulding Mass., supplies	4	65
Joseph B. Estes, auto expense	112	85
L. E. Muran, supplies	30	94
Norman J. Beal, repairs on chair	1	00
N. E. Iron and Steel Co., supplies	1	25
Norman J. Beal, auto expense	76	85
Douglas Print, printing	20	50
U. S. Post Office, envelopes	30	00
Joseph B. Estes, School of Instruction	12	00
Dennis L. O'Connor, School of		
Instruction	12	00
Norman J. Beal, School of Instruction	12	00
Warren B. Woodward, Insurance	9	44
A. I. Randall Inc., printing	17	95
James F. O'Connor, Insurance	9	18

Expended		$ 1 399 73
Appropriation	$1 100 00	
Appropriation Article No. 21		
Aug. 8	300 00	

Total Appropriation		$ 1 400 00
Under Appropriation		27

MISCELLANEOUS, UNCLASSIFIED

Paid:—

Edison Electric Ill. Co., service	$ 127	99
Edison Electric Ill. Co., Lamps Town		
Clock	17	86
L. E. Muran, Filing Cases	6	30
Charles Hines, Cleaning town office	260	00
N. E. Tel. & Tel. Co., service	125	77
Roland S. Poole, care of town clock	52	00
Howland & Howland, survey,		
Dexter Rd.	10	00

C. L. Baxter, survey Curry St.	19	40
Bostitch Boston Inc., machine	3	50
Comm. of Public Safety, License		
Blanks	1	90
John T. Renaghan, repairs adding		
machine	22	15
Becker & Co., supplies	3	60
Charles E. Meara, lettering door	8	00
Rockland Standard Pub. Co., Adv.		
By-Laws	18	00
Frederick Verdone, accident case	20	00
Hall & Torrey Co., supplies	7	55
The Austin Print, 200 Street permits	6	00
Ralph Measures, striping St., and		
repairs	8	70
Douglas Print, payroll sheets	31	00
Hobbs & Warren Inc., supplies	7	30
American Writing Ink Co., record ink	1	91
John J. Dwyer, putting out flags	37	50
Harry S. Torrey, expenses to Boston		
and postage	13	49
A. J. Vargus, supplies		80
Franklin & Perkins, paper towels	4	50
N. S. Whiting, services	95	75
A. I. Randall Inc., warrants	14	75
Chas. A. Vaughan, 2 railroad signs		
and repairs	10	50
John J. Dwyer, car patient to	1	
hospital	5	00
Eleanor Leslie, attendant to hospital	3	00
Marion Lee, attendant to hospital	3	00
H. C. Metcalf, repairs	1	00
Jared Gardner, photo lost person	2	00
Leo M. Cushing, damage auto	6	00
J. H. Dunn, M. D., accident case	7	00
Mrs. Nettie Wade, accident case	62	00
Amos A. Phelps & Son, Insurance		
Tax Title property		00
Postage for sale of land of low value	4	42

James F. Shannahan, sale of property 5 00
Damon Electric, wiring 5 00
Emma W. Gleason, storage of flags 24 00
Francis J. Geogan, legal services 48 99

Expended $ 1 127 63
   Appropriation $1 150 00
   Under Appropriation 22 37

BEACONS - 1938

Paid:—
Edison Electric Ill. Co., service $ 140 63
Damon Electric, care of stop and go
   Lights 75 00
Traffic Equipment Co., care of beacons 384 37
   Expended $ 600 00
   Appropriation $ 600 00

VISITING NURSE

Paid:—
Mrs. Harry W. Burrill, Treasurer $ 1 500 00
   Appropriation $ 1 500 00

SEWING PROJECT W. P. A.

Paid:—
Treasurer of the United States, part
   payment on material $ 2 868 00
   Transfer from 1937 appropriation 828 00
   Transfer 1938 appropriation 2 400 00

   Total appropriation $ 3 228 00
   Unexpended balance 360 00

PURCHASE OF FIRE HOSE

Paid:—
Crandall Packing Co., 500 feet of hose $ 500 00

Appropriation $ 500 00

SUMMIT STREET SIDEWALK

Paid:—
Spurr & Tedeschi, range oil $ 1 50
Payroll, truck   48 13
Rockland Coal & Grain Co., cement   7 70
A. Culver Co., cement   9 00
Bradford Weston Inc., Bit. concrete   131 39

Expended · $ 197 72
Transfer from 1937   212 11
Unexpended Balance   14 39

SALEM STREET SIDEWALK

Paid:—
Spurr & Tedeschi, oil $ 7 45
Payroll, truck   182 47
Thomas Mahoney, rent of mixer   44 50
Rockland Coal & Grain Co., supplies   152 75
A. Culver Co., supplies   20 66
Hall & Torrey Co., supplies   8 14
Bradford Weston, Inc., Bit. concrete   161 52

Expended $ 577 49
Transfer from 1937 $ 577 49

BLOSSOM STREET SIDEWALK

Paid:—
Payroll, truck $ 62 55
Rockland Coal & Grain Co., supplies   35 35
A. Culver Co., cement   25 35
Bradford Weston Inc., Bit. Concrete   97 46

Expended · $ 220 71
Transfer from 1937   248 10
Unexpended balance   27 39

HIGHLAND STREET SIDEWALK

Paid:—

Rockland Coal & Grain Co., supplies	$ 8	70
Payroll, truck	20	13
Bradford Weston Inc., bit. concrete	35	09

Expended			$ 63 92
Transfer from 1937	87	83	
Unexpended balance	23	91	

ARLINGTON STREET SIDEWALK

Paid:—

C. H. Swift, supplies	$ 3	78
Rome Bros., supplies	38	74
Hall & Torrey, tools	8	38

Expended			$ 50 90
Transfer from 1937	55	51	
Unexpended balance	4	61	

SPRING STREET SIDEWALK

Paid:—

Payroll, trucks	$ 431	51
Rockland Coal & Grain Co., supplies	177	20
Lester Wyman, sand	17	00
A. Culver Co., cement	10	46
James G. Lamb, oil	5	25
C. A. Paulding, supplies	8	95
Chris Tompkins, gravel	29	60
Rome Bros., supplies	4	25
Bradford Weston Inc., Bit. concrete	222	82

Expended	$	907 04
Transfer from 1937	$	907 04

W. P. A. ADMINISTRATION 1938

Paid:—

Fred M. Ryan, services	$1 248	00
Fred M. Ryan, use of car	121	15
M. Warren Wright, services	1 150	00
Stall & Dean, supplies recreational project	60	59
John J. Bowler, use of car	326	00
John J. Dwyer, trucking commodity supplies	306	50
John J. Bowler, rent of offices	380	00
Joseph H. Dunn, M. D., accident case	4	00
H. C. Metcalf, repairs	8	25
N. E. Tel. & Tel. Co., service	121	80
Rockland Pharmacy, Medical supplies	25	90
Singer Sewing Machine Co., repairs	3	25
John S. Chever Co., drinking Cups	31	15
J. A. Rice Co., sewing supplies	9	69
Franklin-Perkins Co., bags	161	32
A. S. Peterson, supplies	34	30
Treasurer of the United States, Local contribution on commodity distribution	321	88
Rockland Hardware & Paint Co., supplies		20
Peters Grocery, supplies sewing project	9	19
Rockland Standard Pub. Co., printing	7	25
Chas. N. Weatherbee, milk nursing project	52	11
Norman S. Crosby, expenses	11	08
James G. Lamb, groceries nursery project	126	62
Roderick Mackenzie, ice for nursery project	12	90
Helen Purcell, expenses	5	00
Lois Williams, expenses	5	00
Damon Electric, change of wiring	15	00

Harry S. Torrey, expense and mis.	7	60
The Sport Shop, supplies for Recreational project	40	50
Elmer A. Gould, drinking cups		50
Rockland Coal & Grain Co., supplies	1	55
Edison Electric Ill. Co., lamps	4	40
Hancock Paint & Varnish Co., paint	1	85
Works Progress Adm., Federal Music project	18	00
Hall & Torrey Co., supplies	16	67
Carey's Motor Trans. Co., trans. workers on project	40	00
Douglas Print, cards	31	30
M. Warren Wright, expenses to Boston	1	75

Expended		$ 4 722	25
Balance 1937 appropriation	$1 933 72		
Part 1938 appropriation	4 000 00		

Total Appropriation	5 933	72
Unexpended balance	1 211	47

W. P. A. STREETS - 1938

Paid:—

Payroll, trucks	$ 690	01
Hall & Torrey Co., tools and supplies	157	02
Badford Weston Inc., Bit. concrete	99	82
John H. Lamb, supplies	1	43
N. E. Concrete Pipe Corp., tile	242	88
Rockland Coal & Grain Co., cement and supplies	121	03
Rome Bros., tools and supplies	87	91
Southeastern Cons. Co., catch basin	143	85
Chris Tompkins, gravel	33	20
A. Culver Co., cement	76	85
Rockland Paint & Hardware Co., Supplies	17	89
A. Wainshilbaum, use of truck and crane	48	10

Spurr & Tedeschi, oil	8	80
Warren A. Vinton, oil	1	35
C. A. Paulding, oil ·	1	67
E. L. LeBaron Foundry, catch basin	72	00
Rockland Water Dept., flares	9	72
Henry Roche Jr., gravel·	4	80 .
Esther Tuttle, gravel	17	25
Lester Wyman, sand	34	00
John S. Cheever Co., drinking Cups	7	00
Miller Store, oil	1	00
H. F. Gardner, supplies	14	21
Rockland Pharmacy, Medical supplies	15	43
Fred S. Delay, medical supplies	7	95
Carey Motor Trans. Co., transporting		
men to Hingham	560	00
A. M. Eaton Paper Co., supplies	3	00
Bemis Drug Co., medical supplies	2	25
Rockland Welding Co., repairs	9	50
Thomas Fox, tools	10	00
Market St., Garage, repairs	13	43
Norman J. Beal, use of mixer	13	00
M. F. Ellis Co., twine · ·	3	70

Expended		$ 2 530 04
Balance 1937 appropriation	678 53	
Part 1938 appropriation	3 000 00	

Total appropriation	$ 3 678 53
Unexpended balance	$ 1 148 49

EAST WATER STREET CONSTRUCTION 1938

Paid:—

Payroll, trucks and labor	$9 066	05
Christ. Thompkins, gravel	147	75
Southeastern Cons. Co., catch basin		
blocks	211	86
Bradford Weston Inc., stone	1 838	02
Corcoran Supply Co., pipe	163	20

Edward T. Dwyer, use of Steam shovel 953 50
Brockton Welding Co., repairs roller 24 00
N..E. Cons. Pipe Corp, tile pipe 777 17
Hall & Torrey Co., supplies 87 68
Crawford Service Station, supplies 62 01
Trimount Bit. Products Co., asphalt 424 85
W. H. Claton, stakes 5 52
Rockland Water Dept.
 use of compressor 211 50
Crystal Concrete Corp., cement 102 00
E. L.LeBarron Foundry, manhole
 covers 276 50
Rome Bros., supplies 18 92
George N. Beal, repairs on mixer 5 25
Lot Phillips Corp., lumber 4 60
Reed Lumber Co., supplies 8 86
Rockland Coal & Grain Co., supplies 253 75
A. Culver Co., Coal 78 16
J. S. McCallum, oakum 6 30
Roderick Mackenzie, gravel 35 85
State Prison Colony, pipe 74 55

Expended		$14 837 85
Balance 1937 appropriation	$1 663 01	
Received Comm. of Mass	7 655 30	
Received from County of Plymouth	3 827 65	
Appropriation 1938	3 500 00	
Total available		16 645 96
Unexpended balance		1 808 11

LIST OF PAYROLL — EAST WATER STREET CONSTRUCTION - 1938

Leo Cull 626 48
George Beverly 661 41
Paul MacDonnell 316 19
Lawrence Cull 299 34

Michael Murphy	72 54
John Ricca	362 24
Carl Nelson	312 93
Chas. Fucillo	316 88
Thomas Bailey	67 35
George Tyler	639 75
Wm. Condon,	276 19
Louis Roche	184 13
George Aretino	226 55
George Ingalls	308 17
Edward Lynch	83 80
John McQuaide	133 02
Chas. Brennick	122 61
Henry Roche	30 36
Wm. Santry	70 61
Richard Mann	312 44
Joseph Costello	417 66
Chas. Lonergan	9 00
John J. Dwyer	297 39
Joseph Arena	37 52
Joseph DelPrete	25 30
Joseph Casey	228 73
Fred Cormier	248 88
Clarence Damon	210 20
Daniel Smith	120 63
James Smith	5 06
Kenneth Kemp	37 68
John Arkell	47 24
Thomas Fitzgerald	61 25
James Reardon	41 75
Peter Hussey	32 62
Harold Rainsford	58 49
George Umbrianna	27 56
John Lonergan	39 75
Ab Wainshilbaum	106 50
Dominic DelPrete	167 25
Percy Simmons	12 93
Ralph Tedeschi	31 96
Edward Casey	38 17

Russell Chandler	20 24
Donald Baker	30 37
Ernest McNutt	20 24
Fred Chute	17 44
Frank Webster	12 38
Samuel Cannaway	23 50
Wm. Morrison	52 58
Thomas DeSimione	24 75
Arthur Hammond	35 84
Arthur Casey	119 25
Foster Chute	55 39
Francis Hamilton	63 28
Melvin Gay	243 75
Tovia Jarvinen	27 75
Micheal Bowen	28 88
Roy Blanchard	66 00
Patrick Mahoney	66 00
Waldo McPhee	5 06
Thomas Reardon	6 00
Wm. J. Hall	6 00
Paul Nolan	34 87
Robert Yourell	14 90
Raymond LaComb	217 64
Alfred Durant	14 90
Joseph Golemme	21 00
Wm. Green	27 00
Roderick Mackenzie	6 75
Wilbur Adams	35 75
Fred Stevenson	9 00
Oscar Lincoln	2 53
George Popp Jr.	4 00
Lucius Burgess	6 88
Arthur Deacon	11 81
Russell Hawes	11 81
Total	$ 9 066 05

SEEPAGE BED JUNIOR-SENIOR HIGH SCHOOL

Paid:—

Howland & Howland, Plans	$ 9	56
Spaulding Mass., blue prints	2	74
Payroll, trucks	744	40
P. Lanzellotta & Son, use of bulldozer	30	00
Rockland Coal & Grain Co., supplies	202	38
Hall & Torrey Co., tile pipe	388	10
Rome Bros., supplies	17	29
Crystal Concrete Corp., cement	177	00
Thomas Murrell, sand	197	00
Alice Hannigan, gravel	44	75
Henry Cole, supervisor	10	00
A. Culver Co., cement	5	60

Expended		$ 1 828	82
Unexpended balance of 1937	1 831	82	
Unexpended balance	3	00	

NURSERY SCHOOL PROJECT W. P. A.

Paid:—

James G. Lamb, supplies	$ 54	55
Roderick Mackenzie, ice	4	80
Chas. N. Weatherbee, milk	11	73

Expended		$ 71	08
Unexpended balance 1937	71	50	
Unexpended balance		42	

W. P. A. REEDS POND IMPROVEMENT 1938

Paid:—

Edison Electric Ill. Co., service	4	88
A. J. Vargus, supplies	2	75
Elbert Chamberlin, supplies	4	08
Payroll, trucks	662	00
H. H. Arnold Inc., repairs	1	75

Rockland Coal & Grain Co., supplies   114 27
Rome Bros., supplies   18 13
C. W. Briggs, repairs   8 50
Hall & Torrey Co., supplies   62 01
A. Wainshilbaum, stone   1 00
Norman J. Beal, repairs   66 33
Rockland Paint & Hardware Co.,
    Supplies   2 74
George W. S. Hyde, repairs   5 80
J. S. McCallum, labor   13 98
Rockland Water Dept., 1-6″ gate and
    use of compressor   27 40
F. H. Carey, blasting   30
George Tyler, use of pump   00
Forest L. Partch, electric, switch   00
A. Culver Co., cement   4 20
Wm. Condon, gravel   5 75
C. A. Paulding, supplies   50

Expended $ 1 059 37
Unexpended balance 1937
    Appropriation   57 16
1938 Appropriation   200 00
    Article No. 17, appropriation
      Aug. 8, 1938   2 000 00

Total available $ 2 257 16
Unexpended balance   1 197 79

PLAIN STREET SIDEWALK

Paid:—
Payroll, trucks $ 122 52
Hall & Torrey Co., supplies   7 15
A. Culver Co., cement   81 02
James G. Lamb, oil and gas   1 50
Rockland Coal & Grain Co., lumber   6 75
Depot Service Station, gas   5 23

Thomas Mahoney, use of mixer and
   sand   34 00

Expended		$ 258 17
Transfer 1937 appropriation	$ 61 77	
1938 appropriation	600 00	

Total available	$ 661 77
Unexpended balance	403 60

LAND COURT TAX TITLES

Paid:—

Plymouth County Land Court,		
expenses on Tax titles	$180 00	
Francis J. Geogan, legal services	120 00	

Expended	$ 300 00
Appropriation	$ 300 00

GILES W. HOWLAND

Paid:—

Giles W. Howland, Land Court	
Survey	$ 63 83
Appropriation	$ 63 83

MAPLE, MUNROE, EXCHANGE AND CRESCENT STREET DRAINS

Paid:—

Rockland Coal & Grain Co., supplies	8 28
Southeastern Cons. Co., catch basin tile	76 05
N. E. Concrete Pipe Corp., tile pipe	350 62
E. L. LeBarron Foundry, catch basin	
covers	52 00
Market Street Grocery, oil	1 55
Payroll, trucks	150 30
Rome Bros., supplies	7 47

C. A. Paulding, supplies   2 83

Expended $ 649 10
Appropriation $ 650 00
Unexpended balance   90

UNION STREET SIDEWALK TO WEYMOUTH LINE

Paid:—

Payroll, trucks	$ 395 33
Rockland Coal & Grain Co., cement and supplies	232 35
Bemis Drug Co., medical supples	2 00
A. Culver Co., supplies	55 65
Spurr & Tedeschi, gas and oil	7 55
Chris Thompkins, gravel	13 00
Lester Wyman, sand	16 00
Pete Hart, oil	4 65
Rockland Paint & Hardware Co., Tools	1 97
W. A. Vinton, oil	1 80
Old Colony Asphalt Co., Bit. concrete	422 20
Bradford Weston Inc., Bit. concrete	89 25
E. E. Tuttle, gravel	8 25

Expended $ 1 250 00
Appropriation Article 47 $ 1 250 00

PARK DEPT. W. P. A., 1938

Paid:—

Quincy Sand & Gravel Co., filling	$ 130 00
Hall & Torrey, tools	66 89
Payroll, trucks	453 91
Rockland Coal & Grain Co., cement	7 30
Edmund Vazinia, gravel	20 25
Alice Hennigan, gravel	128 00
Rome Bros., supplies	18 21

Rockland Paint & Hardware Co.,
  Supplies   22 10
A. Wainshilbaum, gas   7 05
Hickey Bros., gas   12 90
Patrick Mahoney, dynamite   10 18
Roderick Mackenzie, gravel   22 70
Rockland Water Dept., use of
  compressor   6 60
Melvin Gay, labor   12 00
George W. S. Hyde, repairs   1 35

Expended $ 919 50
Unexpended balance
  1937 appropriation $1 781 90
Unexpended balance   862 40

CENTRAL STREET SIDEWALK W. P. A.

Paid:—
Payroll, trucks $ 311 57
A. Culver Co., cement   108 00
Rockland Coal & Grain Co., forms   68 44
Rome Bros., supplies   1 26
George Fairbane, use of mixer   37 00
Wm. Condon, gravel   39 25
James G. Lamb, gas and oil   3 37
Quincy Service Station, gas and oil 6 34
Bradford Weston Inc., Bit. concrete 149 77

Expended $ 725 00
Appropriation $ 725 00

BELMONT STREET SIDEWALK, W. P. A.

Paid:—
Bradford Weston Inc., Bit. concrete 211 00
Norman J. Beal, use of mixer   14 00

Expended $ 225 00
Appropriation $ 225 00

ASSESSORS MAP, W. P. A. 1938

Paid:—

L. E. Muran Co., tracing paper	$ 4 65	
Rome Bros., supplies	7 70	
Mary Dotton, services	90 00	
Hall & Torrey Co., supplies	8 89	
Expended		$ 111 24
Transfer 1937 appropriation	735 05	
Unexpended balance	623 81	

GLENN STREET SIDEWALK, W. P. A.

Paid:—

Rockland Coal & Grain Co.,		
Cement and forms	$ 51 58	
Thomas Mahoney, use of mixer	18 00	
Payroll, trucks	13 13	
Rockland Motors Inc., oil	60	
Preston T. Manter, oil	1 43	
Old Colony Asphalt Co.,		
Bit. concrete	29 96	
Bradford Weston Inc., bit. concrete	48 04	
Expended		$ 162 74
Appropriation	252 00	
Unexpended balance	89 26	

GEORGE STREET SIDEWALK, W. P. A.

Paid:—

Rockland Coal & Grain Co., cement	$ 49 20	
Thomas Mahoney, use of mixer	18 00	
Payroll, trucks	70 65	
Lester Wyman, gravel	14 50	
Wainshilbaum Bros., gas and oil	2 94	
Bradford Weston Inc., Bit. concrete	153 83	
Expended		$ 309 12

| Appropriation | $ 360 00 |
| Unexpended balance | 50 88 |

LIBERTY STREET SIDEWALK, W. P. A.

Paid:—

Payroll, trucks	$ 136 08	
John H. Lamb, gas and oil	5 77	
Rockland Coal & Grain Co., cement and forms	135 22	
George Fairbane, use of mixer	23 50	
Thomas Mahoney, use of mixer	23 25	
Wm. Condon, gravel	20 75	
Cora Johnson, stone	1 00	
Chris. Thompkins, gravel	17 25	
Henry Roche, gravel	2 60	
Expended		$ 365 42
Appropriation	$ 600 00	
Unexpended balance	234 58	

MYRTLE STREET SIDEWALK, W. P. A.

Paid:—

Payroll, trucks	$ 70 01	
Norman J. Beal, use of mixer	12 00	
A. Culver Co., cement	28 20	
Bradford Weston Inc., Bit. concrete	164 04	
Rockland Coal & Grain Co., cement	6 30	
Expended		$ 280 55
Appropriation	$ 350 00	
Unexpended balance	69 45	

EAST WATER STREET SIDEWALK, W. P. A.

Paid:—

| Payroll, trucks | $ 140 90 |
| Rockland Coal & Grain Co., cement | 41 80 |

Bradford Weston Inc., bit. concrete   267 23
Henry Roche Jr., gravel   5 00
Wm. Condon, gravel   6 50

Expended $ 461 43
Appropriation $ 510 00
Unexpended balance   48 57

. UNION STREET SIDEWALK
Dr. Corey's to Bigelow Ave. W. P. A.

Paid:—
Payroll, trucks $ 99 77
Norman J. Beal, use of mixer   11 00
A. Culver Co., cement   55 20
Rome Bros., supplies   8 65
Spurr & Tedeschi, gas and oil   3 25
Crawford's Service Station, gas and
oil   2 50
Bradford Weston Inc., bit. concrete   265 12

Expended $ 445 49
Appropriation $ 550 00
Unexpended balance   104 51

WILLIAM STREET SIDEWALK, W. P. A.

Paid:—
Thomas Mahoney, use of mixer $ 18 00
Payroll, trucks   182 91
Rockland Coal & Grain Co., cement   72 67
Wm. Condon, gravel   14 00
James G. Lamb, oil and gas   4 53
Thomas Welsh, sharpening tools   5 40
Rome Bros., supplies   1 05
Bradford Weston Inc., Bit. concrete   178 50

Expended $ 477 06
Apropriation $500 00
Unexpended balance   22 94

HARTSUFF STREET DRAIN
W. P. A. Labor Article 91

Paid:—

Payroll, trucks	$ 78	67
E. L. LeBaron Foundry, catch basin	20	80
Rome Bros., supplies	7	65
Southeastern Cons. Co, cement blocks	31	90
N. E. Concrete Pipe Corp, tile pipe	132	00
H. Robichaud, oil		50

Expended			$ 271	52
Appropriation	$ 275	00		
Unexpended Balance	3	48		

PROSPECT STREET SIDEWALK

Paid:—

Bradford Weston Inc, bit concrete	$ 47	85
Quincy Oil Co., gas and oil	4	13
Rockland Paint & Hardware Co., tools	9	29

Expended			$ 61	27
Unexpended 1937 appropriation	$ 100	23		
Unexpended balance	38	96		

HARTSUFF STREET ARTICLE 67

Paid:—

Payroll, labor	$ 258	88
The Barret Co., tarvia	117	42

Expended			$ 376	30
Appropriation	$ 400	00		
Under appropriation	23	70		
List of Payroll Hartsuff Street:				
Thomas Bailey	$ 22	50		
Leo Cull	22	50		
Michael Murphy	22	50		

George Beverly	30 13	
John Ricca	24 75	
William Cannaway	20 25	
Louis Roche	11 25	
William Condon	16 50	
Joseph Arena	4 50	
George Tyler	66 00	
John J. Dwyer	18 00	
Total		$ 258 88

PAYSON AVENUE SIDEWALK W. P. A.

Paid:—

Payroll, trucks	$ 121 65	
A. Culver, cement	45 00	
Rockland Coal & Grain Co., lumber	38 80	
William Condon, gravel	2 00	
Bradford Weston Inc., bit. concrete	126 00	
C. A. Paulding, gas and oil	1 18	
Expended		$ 334 63
Appropriation	$ 400 00	
Unexpended balance	65 37	

ENGINEERING PROJECT W. P. A.
UNDER CHAPTER 58

Paid:—

Spaulding Moss Co., instruments and supplies	$ 89 45	
Expended		$ 89 45
Appropriation August 8, 1938	$ 600 00	
Unexpended balance	510 55	

McKINLEY SCHOOL SEWAGE 1938

Paid:—

Payroll, trucks	$ 391 20	

Rockland Coal ,& Grain Co., supplies   31 16
Hall & Torrey Co., tile   109 41
Bradford Weston Inc., gravel   12 15
Pacific Flush Tank Co., sewage siphon   33 33
Alice Hannigan, gravel   69 00
Thomas Murrill, sand   113 50
Crystal Concrete Corp, concrete   30 75
Howard E. Bailey, engineering service   94 10
George Tyler, use of pump   7 00
A. Culver Co., cement   9 70
Rome Bros. supplies   4 00
C. A. Paulding, oil   40

Expended		$ 905 70
Appropriation	$1 000 00	
Unexpended balance	94 30	

CONCORD STREET SIDEWALK W. P. A.

Paid:—

Payroll, trucks	$ 202 28	
A. Culver Co., cement	45 60	
Rockland Coal & Grain Co., supplies	6 00	
Norman J. Beal, use of mixer	17 50	
William Condon, gravel	15 00	
Bradford Weston Inc., bit concrete	136 76	

Expended		$ 423 14
Appropriation	$ 450 00	
Unexpended balance	26 86	

HOWARD STREET SIDEWALK W. P. A.

Paid:—

Payroll, trucks	$ 120 77
William Condon, gravel	6 25
A. Culver Co., cement	27 00
Rockland Coal & Grain Co., supplies	9 00
Thomas MacDonald, supplies	2 00

Henry Roche, Jr., gravel	3 00	
Agnes Kelliher, gravel	5 00	
Expended		$ 173 02
Appropriation	$ 400 00	
Unexpended balance	226 98	

EAST WATER STREET LAND DAMAGE

Paid:—

Rockland Trust Co., land damage	$ 79 50	
George L. Peabody, land damage	32 60	
Lena M. Pratt, land damage	7 00	
Charles L. Fearing, land damage	78 00	
Annie G. Whiting, land damage	66 00	
Heirs Sumner Turner, land damage	90 00	
Rockland Savings Bank, land damage	26 00	
Francis A. Poole, land damage	54 50	
Daniel H. Beal et al, land damage	6 00	
George K. Peabody, land damage	13 60	
Francis J. Dowd, land damage	13 00	
William V. Loud, land damage	26 10	
Grace Vining, land damage	9 70	
Racheal Lioy, land damage	75 00	
Home Owners' Loan Corp, land damage	61 00	
Joseph Oliker, land damage	30 50	
James Yourell, land damage	33 00	
Ralph Llewellyn, land damage	75 50	
Stephen Sayian, land damage	122 10	
Rena M. Gallagher, land damage	40 10	
William P. & Bina Santry, land damage	182 75	
Reah B. Ellis, land damage	17 70	
Expended		$ 1 139 65
Appropriation	$ 1 257 70	
Left to be paid on damage	118 05	

SCHOOL STREET SIDEWALK W. P. A.

Paid:—

Payroll, trucks	$ 68 52	
Rockland Coal & Grain Co., lumber	6 31	
A. Culver Co., cement	34 80	
William Condon, gravel	4 00	
Bradford Weston Inc., bit. concrete	194 52	
George B. Campbell, gas	1 89	
Expended		$ 320 04
Appropriation	$ 350 00	
Unexpended balance	29 96	

EAST WATER STREET SIDEWALK TO FRANKLIN AVENUE

Paid:—

Wainshilbaum Bros., gas and oil	$ 4 26	
Payroll, trucks	28 00	
Bradford Weston Inc., bit. concrete	74 82	
Expended		$ 107 08
Appropriation	$ 115 00	
Unexpended balance	7 92	

VERNON STREET DRAIN

Paid:—

Payroll, truck	$ 44 64	
A. Culver Co., cement	3 90	
Rome Bros., tile	13 44	
Expended		$ 61 98
Appropriation	$ 80 00	
Unexpended balance	18 02	

FIRE STATION HOUSING

Paid:—

Percy Dwelley, building for equipment	$	85 00
Damon Electric, repairs		36 21
George W. N. Clark, install fire system		325 00
Bailey Motor Sales, rent for storage		35 00
Rockland Coal & Grain Co., lumber		14 68
Jenkins & Simmons, express		17 00

Expended			$ 512 89
Appropriations by committee for Housing equipment	$	1 500 00	
Unexpended balance		987 11	

ERECTION OF FIRE STATION P. W. A.

Paid:—

American Bank Note Co., coupons	$	37 74
J. William Beal, part payment for services		1 440 00
Charles L. Callahan, Advertising Boston Globe		62 40
Rockland Coal & Grain Co., supplies		16 29
Banker & Tradesman, advertising		21 50
Norman J. Beal, clerk of works		388 75
Rockland Standard Pub. Co., advertising		14 00
Ernest W. Branch Inc., surveying		75 00
Francis J. Geogan, legal services		50 00
Edison Electric Ill. Co., services		24 54

Expended			$ 2 130 22
Appropriation August 8, 1938	$33	000 00	
Unexpended balance	30	869 78	

EMERSON STREET SIDEWALK W. P. A.

Paid:—

Payroll, trucks	$ 100	65
Appropriation	$ 575	00
Unexpended balance	474	35

HOWARD STREET DRAIN NEAR CUSTER STREET

Appropriation	$ 85	00

Nothing expended

W. P. A. SIDEWALKS

Paid:—

Hall & Torrey Co., supplies	$ 116	84
Rome Bros., supplies	154	50
Rockland Paint & Hardware Co., supplies	34	78
A. M. Eaton Paper Co., cord line	3	00
Rockland Coal & Grain Co., lumber and supplies	90	30
Bradford Weston Inc., bit. concrete	875	08
A. Wainshilbaum, repairs	7	00
Payroll, trucks	256	87
Hedge & Matthis, supplies	8	95
Quincy Oil Co., oil	1	54
Chase & Parker Co., repairs	9	64
H. H. Arnold Inc., repairs	1	95
Expended	$ 1 560	45

UNION STREET SIDEWALK NEAR SALEM STREET
Part of Article 13 - August 8, 1938 Meeting

Paid:—

Payroll, trucks	$ 161	91
Norman J. Beal, use of mixer	17	00
A. Culver Co., cement	34	16

Rome Bros., supplies   18 72
Rockland Coal & Grain Co., supplies   5 00
Agnes Kelliher, gravel   9 75
Pete Hart, gas and oil   12 82

Expended $ 259 36

LIBERTY STREET SIDEWALK W. P. A.
Part of Article 13, August 8, 1938 Meeting

Paid:—
Payroll, truck $ 152 27
William Condon, gravel   6 00
Rockland Coal & Grain, cement and
  supplies   193 26
Carmine Ingeno, supplies   9 00
John S. Cheever, drinking cups   7 00
George L. Fairbain, use of mixer   17 00
Norman J. Beal, use of mixer   20 00
Charles W. Briggs, supplies   1 10
Bradford Weston·Inc., bit. concrete   218 14
Chase & Parker, repairs   98

Expended $ 624 75
Expended Liberty Street $ 624 75
Expended Union near Salem   259 36
Expended gen. sidewalks   1 560 45

Total $2 444 56
Appropriation August 8, 1938 $29 000 00
Expended on program   2 444 56

Unexpended balance $26 555 44

LIBERTY STREET W. P. A.

Paid:—
Payroll, trucks   280 05
Rockland Coal & Grain Co., supplies   2 70

Alice Hannigan, gravel	2	25
William Condon, gravel	42	00
John H. Lamb, oil and gas	16	06
Southeastern Cons. Co, rings and		
blocks .	18	63
Melvin Gay, op. steam roller	46	50
Wainshilbaum Bros., oil	4	08
Bradford Weston Inc., bit. concrete	3 496	55
Roderick Mackenzie, gravel	4	00

Expended		$3 912 82
Appropriation	$ 4 200 00	
Unexpended balance	287 18	

REFUND FROM GAS TAX CHAPTER 500

(Memo. Warrant) Used for Storm Damage
September 23, 1938

Received from Comm. of Mass.	$6 850 00
Expended	6 849 60

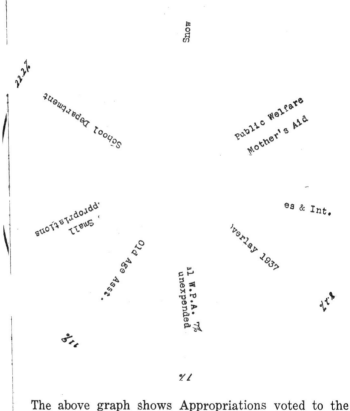

The above graph shows Appropriations voted to the different Departments in 1938. Except Water Department and Erecting of Fire Station.

Amount of Appropriations $469,986.74

RECAPITULATION OF AMOUNTS AVAILABLE AND EXPENDITURES

* Denotes Unexpended Balance December 31, but available for use in 1939

	Raised previous year	Raised Mch 1938	Raised August 1938	Expended	Spent Under
State Aid		650 00		514 00	136 0
Care of Town Cemetery		60 00		60 00	0
Soldiers' Relief		8 000 00	3 000 0	10 196 99	803 01
Fire of Soldiers' Fires		125 00		125 00	0
Burial of Indigent Soldiers			200 00	100 00	100 0
Clean Up Week		75 00		64 00	11 0
Tal ages in tG		100 0		98 85	1 15
Thos Murrill, damage to truck		250 00			250 00
Street Light App. $9,134.00		9 239 00		9 279 00	over 40 0
Union St. $75; Goddard Ave $15; Spring St. $15.					thru error paid Jan. 3, 1939
Highway Surveyor		1 350 00		1 350 00	
Tarvia and Road		3 500 00		3 500 00	
Highway Repair (less $600 trans. to catch Basins and drains,		2 900 00	1 500 00	4 382 06	17 94
Division Street Sidewalk		650 00		412 01	*237 99
Cth Basins and Drains, (trans. highway)		600 00		580 95	19 05
Cliff Street Sidewalk	108 73			D8 73	
Soldiers' Memorial Library and Dog Fund		4 705 94		4 705 81	13
Sidewalks (less 2 Webster St. app. $125.)		875 00		873 62	1 38

...r, Beal and Hartsuff Sts., (trans. sidewalks)		50 00		50 0 0	
...r Street Rep., (trans. sidewalks)		75 00		59 58	15 42
Rent ... Legion		900 00		900 00	
School Department		104 373 00		104 372 33	67
...g Union Street		1 200 00		1 097 27	102 73
Spanish War Veterans		288 00		288 00	
Fire Department		10 126 68	500 00	10 124 48	2 20
orest Fires		500 00		979 00	21 00
Police Department		8 956 20		8 955 43	77
Inspector of Animals and Stables		150 00		150 0	
Sealer of Weights and Measures		400 00		400 00	
Board of Health		5 000 00	1 500 00	6 481 17	18 83
Park Department		2 800 00		2 797 72	2 28
Observance of ...morial Day		400 00		400 00	
Purchase of Washington Reed ...t	470 18			470 18	
...th Department		300 00		299 91	09
Plymouth ...ty Extension Service		150 00		150 00	
Plymouth ...ty Hospital Maintenance		4 013 73		4 013 73	
Compensation to Firemen		292 50		292 50	
Tree Warden		900 00		900 00	
Town ...rs		6 800 00		6 788 29	11 71
Rent of Tn ...		1 240 00		1 239 99	01
Elections		1 700 00		1 624 90	75 10
...n Report and Poll Book		1 200 00		1 200 00	
...h Insurance		2 250 00		1 869 59	380 41
Town ...es and ...		28 000 00		27 172 72	827 28

RECAPITULATION OF AMOUNTS AVAILABLE AND EXPENDITURES

* Denotes Unexpended Balance December 31, but available for use in 1939

	Raised previous year	Raised Mrh 1938	Raised August 1938	Expended	Amount Under
Repairs Town Infirmary		2 915 00		2 818 72	*96 28
Mass. Industrial School		2 000 00		1 874 50	125 50
Snow		12 217 68	480 91	12 698 59	
Assessors		2 500 00		2 500 00	
Miscellaneous Clerk		350 0		347 49	2 50
Miscellaneous Selectmen		120 00		114 31	5 69
Miscell aus Sealer		120 0		116 24	3 76
Miscellaneous Registrars		200 00		198 33	1 67
Miscellaneous Treasurer		800 0		799 04	96
Miscell aus for		1 400 00		1 398 71	I 29
Miscellaneous Assessors		1 100 00		1 399 73	27
Miscellaneous Unclassified		1 150 00	300 0	1 127 63	22 37
Beacons		600 00		600 0	
Visiting Nurse		1 500 00		1 500 00	
Sewing Project W. P. A.	828 00	2 400 00		2 868 00	*360 00
Purchase of Fire Hose		500 00		500 00	
Summit Street Sidewalk	212 11			197 72	*14 39
Salem Street Sidewalk	577 49			577 49	
Blossom Street Sidewalk	248 10			220 71	*27 39
Highland Street walk	87 83			63 92	*23 91
n Street walk	55 51			50 90	*4 61

Spring Street Sidewalk	907 04		907 04	
W. P. A. ard (part of 1938 App.)	1 933 72	4 000 00	4 722,'25	*1 211 47
W. P. A. Sts (part of 1938 App.)	678 53	3 000 00	2 530 04	*1 148 49
East Water Street Construction				
Bal. Jan. 1, '38 - $1663.01; St. State and uity 072	2 563 73	3 500 00	14 837 85	*1 808 11
Received State and uity	1 831 82	10 582 23	1 828 82	3 00
Seepage Bed Junior-Senior School	71 50		71 08	42
My School Project W. P. A.	57 16	200 00	1 059 37	*1 197 79
Reed's Pond W. P. A.	61 77	600 00	258 17	*403 60
Plain St Sidewalk		300 00 / 2 000 00	300 0	
Land Court Tax Titles		63 83	63 83	
Ges W. Howland		650 00	649 10	90
Maple, Munroe Street Drains				
Union St, Sidewalk to Weymouth Line		1 250 00	1 250 00	
Park Department W. P. A.	1 781 90		919 50	*862 40
Central Street Sidewalk		725 00	725 0	
Belmont Street Sidewalk		225 00	225 00	
Assessors Map W. P. A.	735 05		111 24	*623 81
Glen Street Sidewalk		252 00	162 74	*89 26
George Street Sidewalk		360 00	309 12	*50 88
Liberty Street Sidewalk		600 00	365 42	*234 58
Myrtle Street Sidewalk		350 00	280 55	*69 45
East Wer Street Sidewalk		510 00	461 43	*48 57
Union Street Sidewalk		550 00	445 49	*104 51
Williams Street Sidewalk		500 00	477 06	*22 94

RECAPITULATION OF AMOUNTS AVAILABLE AND EXPENDITURES

* Denotes Unexpended Balance December 31, but available for use in 1939

	Raised previous year	Raised March 1938	Raised August 1938	Expended	Amount Under
Hartsuff Street Drain		275 00		271 52	3 48
Prospect St. Sidewalk	100 23			61 27	*38 96
Hartsuff Street		400 00		376 30	23 70
Payson / Ave Sidewalk		400 00		334 63	*65 37
Engineering Project			600 00	89 45	*510 55
1 ...ey School Sewage		1 000 00		905 70	*94 30
Liberty Street			4 200 00	3 912.82	*287 18
Concord St. Sidewalk		450 00		423 14	*26 86
Howard Street Sidewalk		400 00		173 02	*226 98
East Water Street Land Damage		1 257 70		1 139 65	*118 05
School Street Sidewalk		350 00		320 04	*29 96
East ... St. Sidewalk		115 00		107 08	7 92
Ver... Street Drain		80 00		61 98	18 02
Fire Station Housing			1 500 00	512 89	*987 11
Erection of Fire Station			33 000 00	2 B0 22	*30 869 78
Emerson Street Sidewalk		575 00		100 65	*474 35
Howard St. Drain		85 00			*85 00
General Sidewalks W. P. A.			29 000 00	2 444 56	*26 555 44
Refund from Gas Tax a$ 500 Mem.					
Received $6,850.00				6 849 60	40

Bureau Old Age Assistance	35 000 00	17 000 00	51 995 26	
Public Welfare	45 000 00	15 000 00	59 701 87	4 74
Mothers' Aid (trans. Public Welf. $365.71)	8 000 00		8 365 71	298 13

Financial Report of Public Welfare

The report of the Board of Public Welfare for the year
1938 is hereby submitted.

BUREAU OF OLD AGE ASSISTANCE

Town Physicians, services	$ 400 00	
Paid Other Towns	852 95	
Expended for cases	50 742 31	
Total		$51 995 26
Appropriation	$52 000 00	
Expended	51 995 26	
Under appropriation		$4 74

Received from Federal Funds		
Balance on hand Jan. 1, 1938	$ 3 565 00	
Credited to cases	45 378 25	
	$48 943 25	
Expended	$44 249 85	
Balance		$1 693 76

Received from Federal Funds for Administration		
Balance January 1, 1938	$ 305 83	
Credited for Administration	1 512 58	
Total	$1 818 41	
Expended	1 193 36	
Balance		$625 05

List of Expenditures Spent Under Bureau of Old Age
Assistance Administration

Yawman & Erbe, 1 office chair	$ 14	25
Harry S. Torrey, cash paid exp. to Boston	2	50
A. S. Peterson, supplies	2	90
Arthur Sullivan, fees		50
Yawman & Erbe Mfg. Co., visible cards	20	84
Yawman & Erbe Mfg. Co., visible hinges	2	00
John O. Donovan, supplies	1	00
Harry S. Torrey, cash paid for postage	8	00
Katherine McGee, clerical	10	00
Yawman & Erbe Mfg. Co., cabinet and guides	23	80
U. S. Post Office, 3,000 envelopes	69	12
H. C. Metcalf, rep. typewriter	1	00
Mary L. O'Brien, trips to Pondville	15	00
Ralph L. Belcher, copies of records	6	25
Becker & Co., supplies	24	65
Hobbs & Warren, supplies	23	55
Mary L. O'Brien, services	754	00
Harriet Anderson, services	170	00
Annette White, services	44	00

$1 193 36

Amount expended by town from Local
and Federal Funds $96 245 11

MOTHER'S AID

Expended under Chapter 118, General Laws.

Expended from Town Funds		$8 365 71
Appropriation	$8 000 00	
Trans. from Public Welfare	365 71	

$8 365 71

Received from Federal Grant $2 669 35
Expended from Federal Grant   2 669 99

Amount due on Fed. Funds $ 64
Total Expenditures by Federal and
    Local Funds $11 035 70

INFIRMARY

Paid:—
Kate Kelly, services $ 402 00
Annie Stewart, services   524 00
Earl and Blanche Wyatt, salary   1 020 00
N. E. Tel. & Tel. Co., service   48 96
Edison Electric Light Co., service   113 16
Fred S. Delay, medical supplies   204 70
Market Street Grocery, provisions   202 87
E. L. Murrill, provisions   204 23
W. F. Barnes, fish   215 28
M. Y. Clements, provisions   236 51
Rockland Laundry, washings   16 82
A. Culver Co., feed   391 89
Rome Bros., supplies   71 26
Ranney's, clothing   90 90
Rockland Pharmacy, med. supplies   83 68
S. W. Baker, glasses   14 50
Handchumacher Co., curing hams   38 83
Charles Blanchard, butchering   15 00
W. E. Trufant, blanket   4 50
Rockland Water Dept., water service   119 48
Roland Poole, glasses   29 50
W. H. Clayton, shoeing horse etc.   60 30
Com. of Mass., supplies   69 79
Elbert Chamberlain, supplies   71 67
Alice Holbrook, extracts   11 00
John H. Lamb, provisions   175 42
Chester Banden, repairs   17 84
McManus, sawdust   32 00
Elmer Bates, apples   7 00

Dennis L. O'Connor, shoes	8	50
Ferbers Shoppe, clothing	32	51
Jerry Lioy, repair shoes	4	25
Rockland Coal & Grain Co., supplies	62	82
Harold N. Capen, meats	188	78
J. S. McCallum, repairs	72	96
Burrell & Delory, shoes	15	88
Angelo Tedeschi, provisions	161	94
Tracey's Store, provisions	176	23
Lelyveld's Store, shoes	38	70
Monument Mills Co., supplies	28	60
S. T. Howland, medical	10	00
J. A. Rice Co., supplies	19	65
Rockland Shoe Rep. Co., shoes	3	30
Harry L. Rome, shades	8	75
Samuel Morse, supplies	4	32
Rockland Coal & Grain Co., coal	638	40
A. S. Peterson, papers and supplies	50	83
Emmons Dairy, service	2	00
Hall & Torrey Co., supplies	57	74
Dr. Benjamin Lelyveld, shoes	2	00
William Sanborn, supplies	6	50
Daniel Reilly, wood	10	00
Goodco Products Co., supplies	45	00
Lot Phillips & Co., slabs and lumber	22	65
A. J. Vargus, supplies	1	25
Hatherly Market, provisions	164	74
Wainshilbaum Bros., repairs	13	90
O. R. Cummings, repairs	24	80
Leslie R. Lewis, repairs	8	25
Dr. John Young, dental work	3	00
Howard Street Grocery, provisions	95	00
The Leonard Co., supplies	2	20
Rockland Hardware & Paint Co. Supplies	49	08
Edith Estes, services	33	00
Annie Capelis, provisions	68	25
Michael Ryan, provisions	138	65
Harold Mock, bread	163	51

Henry Manoli, provisions	71	72
Dr. Phillip Briggs, services	6	00
Edison Electric Light Co., supplies	2	95
H. O. Ford, 50 chicks	7	50
J. & S. Express Co., express	2	50
James Bowser, repairs	8	45
Maurice Cunningham, repairs	1	00
Herbert F. Gardner, provisions	118	16
Wesley H. McPhee, repairs	16	75
John S. Cheever, supplies	4	60
J. H. Baker, clock	7	00
A. Culver Co., supplies	4	20
Michael Bowen, truck	2	00
Thomas MacDonald, stone	2	00
Hickey Bros., provisions	173	70
A. Culver Co., coal	55	08
Brockton Hospital, service	1	50
Theodore Collins, shoes	2	75
H. I. Stickney, repair lawn mower	4	50
Raymond LaCombe, plowing	9	38
John A. Lamb, provisions	3	00
P. T. Manter, provisions	121	90
Comm. of Mass., inspecting boiler	5	00
A. S. Peterson, tobacco	81	97
John Donovan, 4 pigs	20	00
James G. Lamb, provisions	157	80
Ivar G. Miller, groceries	104	52
Frank H. Shaw, services	1	40
Chester S. Clark, painting	13	95
Rockland Pharmacy, medical supplies	7	25
Anthony Fiaschetti, medical supplies	64	32
Rockland Pioneer Store, provisions	86	12

Total $ 8 100 00

EXPENSES OF OUTSIDE POOR

Hospitals:
Goddard Hospital $ 5 00

Brockton Hospital	836 97	
Weymouth Hospital	257 48	
Mass. General Hospital	286 29	
Children's Hospital	331 90	
Mass. Eye and Ear Infirmary	18 08	
Pondville Hospital	160 00	
City of Quincy Hospital	351 00	
Total		$ 2 246 72

Administration:

Hobbs and Warren Inc., supplies	26 38	
John J. Dwyer, trans. CCC. boys	24 00	
Becker & Co., Fibertax Wallets	4 80	
John J. Dwyer, ambulance to hospitals	22 00	
H. C. Metcalf, repair typewriter	7 50	
Austin Print, work slips	3 00	
Harry S. Torrey, cash paid trans. CCC boys	7 36	
Douglas Print, order blanks	13 00	
U. S. Gov't. local contribution on butter	126 70	
Harriet Anderson, services	706 00	
		$ 940 74

Town Physicians		$ 500 00
Paid Other Towns		3 980 18
Cash		25 939 42
Other expenses including fuel, rent, and medical		17 629 10
Transfer from Mother's Aid		365 71
Total		$59 701 87

Appropriation		$60 000 00
Expended		59 701 87
Under appropriation		$ 298 13

SUMMARY OF BOARD OF PUBLIC WELFARE

Paid for Infirmary	$8 100 00	
Paid for Hospitals	2 246 72	
Paid for Administration	940 74	
Paid for Town Physicians	500 00	
Paid for Other Towns	3 980 18	
Paid for Outside Poor	43 568 52	
Transfer to Mother's Aid	365 71	
		$59 701 87

CREDITS

Received From—

State, Sick State Poor	$ 163 45	
State, Mothers' Aid	5 154 29	
State, Old Age Assistance	29 833 40	
State, Temporary Aid	11 537 42	
Other Towns, Old Age Assistance	1 435 70	
Other Towns, Board of Health	225 71	
Other Towns, Temporary Aid	3 686 75	
Other Towns, Soldiers' Relief	199 58	
Other Towns, Infirmary	1 040 00	
Federal Emergency Relief	170 56	
Personal Refund Old Age	30 00	
		53 476 86

Due from—

Other Towns, for board at infirmary	$1 566 54	
State, Temporary Aid	4 575 57	
Other Towns, Temporary Aid	4 673 81	
State, Mothers' Aid	3 469 92	
Federal Funds, Mother's Aid, Nov. & Dec.	502 57	
State, Old Age Assistance	24 300 31	
State, Sick State Poor	303 81	

Other Towns, Old Age Assistance	1 564	47
Other Towns, Board of Health	267	00
Federal Funds, Old Age, Nov. & Dec.	8 010	25
State, Dangerous Diseases	120	00
∴ Total	$49 354	19

ESTIMATES OF APPROPRIATIONS FOR THE YEAR 1939 BY HEADS OF DIFFERENT DEPARTMENTS AND AMOUNTS RAISED IN 1938

	Raised 1938		Estimated 1939	
School Dept.	$104 373	00	$107 167	23
State Aid	650	00	650	00
Soldiers' Relief	11 000	00	11 000	00
Care of Soldiers' Graves	125	00	125	00
Memorial Library and Dog Fund ($415.50)	4 200	00	4 400	00
Street Lighting	9 239	00	9 000	00
Highway Surveyor	1 350	00	1 350	00
Tarvia and Road Binder	3 500	00	5 000	00
Highway Repairs	5 000	00	6 000	00
Sidewalks	1 000	00	1 000	00
Cleaning Union Street	1 200	00	1 100	00
Clean-up Week	75	00	75	00
Fire Department	10 126	68	11 830	00
Police Department	8 956	20	9 150	00
Forest Fires	1 000	00	1 000	00
Board of Health	6 500	00	6 000	00
Inspection of Animals	150	00	150	00
Park Department	2 800	00	3 420	00
Old Age Assistance	52 000	00	57 000	00
Moth Department	300	00	300	00
Tree Warden	900	00	900	00

Town Officers	6 800 00	8 500 00
Office Rent	1 240 00	1 240 00
Sealer of Weight and Measures	400 00	400 00
Elections	1 700 00	1 000 00
Compensation Insurance	2 250 00	2 250 00
Mass. Industrial School	2 000 00	1 800 00
Town Report and Poll Book	1 200 00	1 400 00
Support of Public Welfare and		
Infirmary	60 000 00	60 000 00
Mothers' Aid	8 000 00	9 500 00
Town Notes and Interest	28 000 00	36 000 00
Assessors	2 500 00	2 500 00
Snow Removal	12 698 59	12 000 00
Miscellaneous Assessors	1 400 00	1 550 00
Miscellaneous Treasurer	800 00	800 00
Miscellaneous Clerk	350 00	350 00
Miscellaneous Selectmen	120 00	120 00
Miscellaneous Registrars	200 00	1 500 00
Miscellaneous Sealer	120 00	190 00
Miscellaneous Collector	1 400 00	1 550 00
Miscellaneous Unclassified	1 150 00	1 500 00
Part Payment Visiting Nurse	1 500 00	1 500 00
Quarters, Spanish Am. War Vets.	288 00	288 00
Observance Memorial Day	400 00	500 00
Care of Town Cemetery	60 00	60 00
Traffic Beacon and Signals	600 00	1 000 00
Quarters for American Legion	900 00	900 00
County Aid to Agriculture	150 00	150 00
Criminal Cases in Court	100 00	100 00
Care of Guide Board and Signs		200 00
Burial of Indigent Soldiers	200 00	100 00
Reserve Fund		2 000 00
Military Aid		100 00
Massachusetts Hospital School		100 00

Report of Board of Public Welfare

The Board of Public Welfare herewith submits its annual report covering the period from January 1 to December 31, 1938.

The Board is pleased to report the cost of Public Welfare and Infirmary is $7,311.44 less than in 1937, due largely to the increase of enrollment in W. P. A. and increase in Bureau of Old Age Assistance benefits. This decrease may be only temporary dependent mostly on the number kept on the W. P. A. rolls.

We have compiled for comparison Welfare costs from 1928 to 1938 to show the magnitude of increased amounts in the past 10 years.

Comparison of Expenditures of Public Welfare
1928 to 1938

	Outside Poor	Mothers Aid	Infirmary	Old Age Assistance	Reimbursements
1928 -	$20,131.24	$ 4,313.85	$ 6,532.40		$10,176.35
1930 -	23,569 07	3,498.56	6,464.48		12,694.20
1933 -	53,942.35	4,700.15	7,274.56	4,621.01	41,606.56
1935 -	50,759.61	4,004.68	8,976.76	24,307.61	27,031.24
1937 -	56,273.62	10,997.08	10,739.68	81,632.75	47,071.70
1938 -	51,601.87	11,035.70	8,100.00	96,245.11	53,476.86

There are other agencies that have greatly helped needy families this past year. Many young men have enrolled in the Civilian Conservation Corps and are helping their families to the amount of $22.00 per month learning a useful trade while doing healthful outdoor work.

There is also a youth program connected with the W. P. A. that allows a limited number of young people to earn $15 to $20 a month to supplement the earnings of their parents.

The distribution of Food Commodities and clothing to needy families has continued and increased during the year. The cost of these commodities in Rockland during 1938 was $22,902.00 and the cost of clothing distributed was $15,486.22. By contributing $126.70 we are to receive 12670 lbs. of butter during the next few months to be distributed through the same agency.

The Recreational Project, the Practical Nurse and Nursing Projects are adding sources of value to our community that cannot be expressed in dollars, but very helpful in our Social Service Work.

The Churches, Red Cross, Fraternal and Patriotic Societies have always co-operated with our Department and we wish to take this opportunity to thank them for their assistance.

We wish to highly commend the services of Drs. Joseph H. Dunn and Frederick H. Corey our town physicians and Miss Miriam Dexter our Visiting Nurse, who have given so unsparingly of their time in caring for our needy sick.

We have at the present time on Relief Rolls:
   . 18 Mothers' Aid cases.
     2 Child Boarded cases

87 Families on Outside Poor
67 Single persons on Outside Poor
11 Families on Soldiers' Relief
14 Single Persons, on Soldiers' Relief
293 Old Age Assistance cases
 9 At Infirmary

Signed,

> HARRY S. TORREY
> JOHN J. BOWLER
> NORMAN S. WHITING
>
> Board of Public Welfare

Report of Supervisor of Old Age Assistance

At the present time there are 293 persons receiving Old Age Assistance. Some of these are living in Rest Homes, but the majority are in their own homes.

Many persons are finding it difficult to obtain certified copies of their birth. The State however insists that these records must be definitely established, and in cases where only a Bible record can be found, a certified copy from the Notary who has seen this record must accompany the application.

On September 28, 1938, the law in regard to property equity was changed. Hereafter applicant is allowed an equity of $3000 in property, provided that such equity computed on assessed valuation does not exceed $3000. If property is in excess of this amount, a bond may be given to the Town, without interest, on condition that repayment be made to the Town, by mortgage of the applicants real estate.

The State law that says children must support their parents is being strictly enforced, and when there is sufficient income, a parent is denied Old Age Assistance.

Our local Board gives many cases the benefit of a doubt, but many times either the State or Federal investigator will refuse to accept these cases.

Altho the amount allowed for each recipient is only enough for their needs, at the same time I find that it makes many independent, who would otherwise be a burden to their children, or relatives.

Respectfully submitted,

MARY L. O'BRIEN

List of Jurors

As prepared by the Selectmen of the Town of Rockland under General Laws of Massachusetts, Acts of 1921, Chapter 234, Section 4.

July 1, 1938

Name Street and Number	Occupation
Altsman, Harry J., 849 Unnion	Poultry Man
Ames, Stanley, 34 Prospect	Engineer
Bacon, Paul, 48 Williams	Salesman
Ball, Percy, 770 Union	Shoe Worker
Bates, Kelton F., Union	Shoe Operative
Beal, George, 739 Market	Weaver
Bell, William, 558 Liberty	Truck Driver
Blakeman, Thomas, 16 Albion	Shoe Worker
Bray, Charles A., Jr., 95 Reed	Shoe Operative
Brady, Edward F., 89 Green	Foreman
Briggs, George E., 139 Exchange	Machinist
Burrell, H. Chester, 340 Liberty	Shoe Operative
Burbank, Edward, 25 Hartsuff	Shoe Operative
Callanan, Charles, 7 West Water	Reporter
Capelice, James H., 108 Howard	Shoe Operative
Coffey, Dennis F., 134 Liberty	Flagman
Damon, Archer W., 43 Munroe	Shoe Operative
Damon, Frank W., 50 Reed	Electrician
DeLory, Bernard, 54 Stanton	Clerk
Dill, Percy E., 136 North Ave.	Shoe Operative
Dolan, Edward, Union	Shoe Operative
Dondero, Joseph, 412 Webster	Shoe Operative
Donovan, Daniel H., 117 Liberty	Machinist
Easton, Carrol, 858 Union	Salesman
Ednie, John, 520 Market	Painter

Estes, Joseph B., 305 Liberty	Town Assessor
Fass, Carl G., 377 North Ave.	Draftsman
Fearing, Charles L., 436 East Water	Mechanic
Feeney, James, 171 North Ave.	Chef
Fitzgerald, Thomas F., 51 North Ave.	Shoe Operative
Ford, Patrick J., 542 Liberty	Salesman
Gammon, Frank L., 135 Union	Manager
Garrity, Peter, 162 North Ave.	Janitor
Greenan, James, 39 East Water	Retired
Guilfoyle, Michael, 52 Concord	Foreman
Harney, Edmund F., 66 Church	Shoe Operative
Hawes, Fred M., 88 Howard	Salesman
Hayden, Robert E., 40 Summit	Laborer
Higgins, Thomas S., 32 Belmont	Laborer
Hobart, Albert C., 57 School	Civil Engineer
Holmes, Harry O., 248 Central	Meter Reader
Howland, Giles W., 181 Webster	Civil Engineer
Hunt, Charles L., Belmont	Chauffeur
Hunt, Lester A., 224 Myrtle	Shoe Operative
Inkley, Harold J., 230 Greenwood	Shoe Operative
Johnson, Clarence B., 266 Plain	Teamster
Kramer, Charles F., 39 Grove	Shoe Operative
Leighton, Ellis, 233 Liberty	Electrician
Lelyveld, Benjamin, 129 Pacific	Podiatrist
Lewis, Willard A., 69 Hartsuff	Shoe Operative
Locke, Louis F., 30 Reed	Webbing
Loud, Fred, 28 Myrtle	Bookkeeper
Lovell, Jasper, 4 Maple	Box Cutter
Mahoney, John F., 838 Union	Chauffeur
Mahoney, Patrick H., 35 Carey Court	Teamster
Mahon, Thomas, 31 Summit	Janitor
Mastrodominico, Joseph, 355 Union	Shoe Operative
McCarthy, Michael J., 22 School	Shoe Operative
McKeever, James, 199 Webster	Clerk
Measures, Ralph, 251A Union	Painter
Mullen, William, 865 Union	Shoe Operator
Najarian, Arthur, 112 Webster	Laborer
Newhall, Otis A., 186 Howard	Shoe Operative
Niles, George R., 137 Pacific	Carpenter

Phillips, Roland P., 196 East Water	Manager
O'Grady, Matthew, 108 Belmont	Laborer
O'Hayre, Bernard F., 278 Reed	Shoe Operative
Orr, Charles E., 67 Stanton	Salesman
Partch, Forest L., 57 Taunton Ave.	Electrician
Patterson, Henry E. L., 889 Union	Florist
Poole, Norman C., 580 W. Water	Salesman
Ransom, Roger T., 31 Hartsuff	Engineer
Reardon, Thomas, 101 Summit	Clerk
Rose, Lester E., 348 Liberty	Laborer
Ryan, Patrick C., 122 Myrtle	Shoe Operative
Scott, Charles N., 91 Pacific	Clerk
Sears, Clifford H., 22 Blanchard	Shoe Operative
Sheehan, Eugene, 39 Pacific	Shoe Worker
Sheehan, Maurice, 101 Prospect	Shoe Operative
Shields, Charles T., 42 Franklin Ave.	Shoe Operative
Smith, Bartholomew J., 35 Stanton	Shoe Operative
Smith, Leslie G., 30 Everett	Bus Driver
Sylvia, John E., 76 Albion	Cigar Maker
Umbrianna, Michael, 35 Salem	Shoe Operative
Vargus, Antone J., 215 Crescent	Auto Supplies
Walls, Magorisk, 663 Liberty	Inspector
Wallace, Earl, 231 Myrtle	Truck Driver
Whiting, W. Alton, 455 Webster	Shoe Operative

HARRY S. TORREY,
NORMAN S. WHITING,
JOHN J. BOWLER,
Selectmen of Rockland

Report of Fire Department

To the Honorable Board of Selectmen:

Gentlemen:

I hereby submit my report as Chief of the Fire Department for the year 1938.

The number of fire alarms is increasing each year and with the amount of money which is available for the call men's payroll remaining the same year after year it is impossible to remain within the appropriation.

215 calls were answered by the Fire Department during the year 1938, an increase of 12 over 1937, and about 130 more than the year 1928. 66 of the alarms were box alarms, 147 were still or verbal alarms, and two A. D. T. calls. Of the 66 bell alarms 25 were false. The Chief's car answered 28 calls without other apparatus. The nights of July 3rd and 4th it was necessary to hire other trucks to take care of the alarms.

The Department laid 11, 900 feet of 2½ inch hose, 4,100 feet of 1½ inch and 8,100 feet of chemical hose. We also used 585 gallons of soda and acid, 2½ gallons of foam, besides chimney compound and pump tank. The Light equipment was used about twenty-five hours besides being used to charge our fire alarm batteries after the hurricane.

Fire Alarm System

Owing to the hurricane of September 21, 1938, the fire

alarm wire and cross arms on a number of the streets are in a make-shift condition due to lack of money to repair them.   Market, Vernon, Summit and Union Streets should be rebuilt at once.

Although our present whistle is giving us results, there has been a move for a number of years to replace it, and if this is going to be done, now is the time before the finish of the new station.

APPARATUS

Believing a year ago that no repairs would have to be made on the apparatus I asked for only a small amount for repairs.   In order to keep the Combination running it will be necessary to install a new clutch and a new rear end as well as new tires during the year 1939.   I believe it would be more practical and economical to buy a new truck rather than to keep repairing the present one which is about 27 years old.

As far as I know now, the other two pieces of fire apparatus are in good condition, except that the paint on Engine No. 1 is in bad condition.

Recommendations

For the year 1939 I recommend an appropriation of $11,830.00 for Fire Department Maintenance.

Conclusion

In concluding this report I wish to thank the Finance Committee for their co-operation, Board of Selectmen, Board of Water Commissioners and their employees, and the Chief and members of the Police Department for the help and co-operation given the Fire Department.   I also wish to express my appreciation to the officers and members of the Fire Department and to all others who have assisted me in the performance of my duty as Chief of the Fire Department.

Respectfully submitted,

CLYSON P. INKLEY,
Chief Rockland Fire Department

Report of Forest Fire Warden

To the Honorable Board of Selectmen:

Gentlemen:—

I hereby submit my report as Forest Fire Warden for the year 1938.

The Forest Fire Department answered 76 calls for wood and grass fires during the year 1938.

Due to the fact that people are burning their grass rather than mowing it, has resulted in an increased number of grass fires the past year.

For the year 1939 I recommend an appropriation of $1,000.00.

Respectfully submitted,

CLYSON P. INKLEY,
Forest Fire Warden

Report of Infirmary

To the Honorable Board of Selectmen:

Gentlemen:—

I wish to present to you a report of activities and improvement which have taken place during the year 1938.

We have taken care of twenty-nine inmates during the year. The youngest being one year and a half and the oldest being eighty-eight.

Six have died, three men and three women.

At present we have nine, two women and seven men.

New sills were placed in the basement where needed, also new lally columns replaced the old rotted wooden one.

The home roof was completely shingled.
All walls that were cracked caused by raising of the house were replaced.

Respectfully submitted,

EARL W. WYATT,
Supt. of Infirmary

Report of
Sealer of Weights and Measures

To the Honorable Board of Selectmen:

Gentlemen:—

` I have with my standard weights and measures, tested and sealed all weighing and measuring devises which I have jurisdiction over, also several scales for home use.

I make frequent inspections of all stores in town, which have measuring devises. These inspections benefit the buying public. Computing and spring scales need the most attention, as in many cases I have found them to be incorrect.

All peddlars must have a license. The fee received from them reverts back to State and Town. I keep a careful check on all peddlars and hawkers.

Another item which has to be checked more carefully, on account of the increasing sale of oil, is oil meters on oil trucks.

The reweighing of goods put up for sale is another item to which I give special attention.

The duties of a Sealer of Weights and Measures increase yearly and I am on call at all times. My duties are under State and Town regulations.

Following is an itemized account of the work I have performed for the year 1938:

	Adjusted	Sealed	Not Sealed	Condemned
SCALES				
Platform over 10,000 lbs.	2	4		
Platform over 5,000 lbs.	1	1		
Platform 100 to 5,000 lbs.	8	33	1	
Counter 100 or over	1	4		
Counter under 100 lbs.	2	31	1	
Beam over 100 lbs.		1		
Beam under 100 lbs.	1	2		
Spring 100 lbs. or over	2	9		
Spring under 100 lbs.	23	57	3	
Computing under 100 lbs.	14	62		
Personal Weighing	1	9		
Prescription		4		
WEIGHTS				
Avoirdupois	14	284		
Apothecary		48		
Metric		42		
CAPACITY MEASURES				
Liquid over 1 gal.		8		
Liquid under 1 gal.		51		4
Dry		5		
AUTOMATIC DEVICES				
Oil Meters	3	7		
Gasoline Pumps		5	3	
Gasoline Meter	13	60		4
Kerosene Pumps		12		
Molasses Measuring Devices		2		
Oil Measuring Pumps		31		
Quantity Measure on Pumps	3	73		
Cloth Measuring Devices		2		

LINEAR MEASURE
Yard Sticks   46   2

Totals units sealed   893
Weighing .and measuring devices adjusted   88
Weighing and measuring devices condemned   ·   10
Weighing and measuring devices not sealed   8

REWEIGHING AND MEASURING

Number tested   430
Number correct   396
Overweight   20
Underweight   14

Total sealing fees for year 1938 $112 51
Paid to Town Treasurer $102 15
Cash credit, H. J. Inkley, for over payments
   as per order of State Auditor   10 36

Respectfully submitted,

HAROLD J. INKLEY

Report of Highway Surveyor

To the Honorable Board of Selectmen:

I wish to report that all of the work covered by the various appropriations granted to the Highway Department has been completed.

This work included making necessary repairs to various streets, putting on tarvia, and cleaning out catch basins and drains.

During the past year a number of sidewalks were constructed in different sections of the town as W. P. A. projects.

Another section of East Water Street was completed by the Highway Dept. in co-operation with the State and County.

Respectfully submitted,

RODERICK MACKENZIE,
Highway Surveyor

Report of
Plymouth County Aid to Agriculture

Honorable Board of Selectmen
Town of Rockland:—

The work of the Plymouth County Extension Service followed the usual lines during the past year. The best information on soil and crop practice, pest control, dairy, poultry, orchard and small fruit activities, have been available to those needing this service. 4-H club work and domestic science projects have been carried on under experts from the County Extension service and from the State College. Advice has been available on the care of public parks, and private estates.

Unfortunately the work of the Plymouth County Extension Service has been marred by dissensions amongst those entrusted with the duty of carrying on its work, during 1938. Whether harmony has been restored or not I am unable to state at this time. Therefore I am recommending that the voters at the annual meeting consider the advisability of appropriating the usual sum of $150.00 for the use of the Plymouth County Extension Service and Aid to Agriculture.

Sincerely yours,

JAMES D. MAHONEY,
Town Director

Report of
Inspector of Animals and Stables

To the Honorable Board of Selectmen:

Gentlemen:—

I herewith submit my report as Inspector of Animals and Stables, for the year ending Dec. 31, 1938.

Number of Stables inspected	36
Number of Cows inspected	136
Number of Swine inspected	282
Number of Goats inspected	5
Number of visits made in inspections	99
Number of Dogs quarantined	10
Number of Swine quarantined	13
Number of visits made to premises of quarantined animals	78

Respectfully submitted

WILLIAM T. CONDON,
Inspector of Animals and Stables

Assessors' Report 1938

The Assessors have assessed the sum of $327,802.15 upon the Polls and Property subject to taxation in the Town of Rockland and have committed said sum to the Collector for collection.

Number of Polls Assessed		2406
Value of Real Estate Assessed	$5 681 360 00	
Value Land Assessed	1 538 965 00	

Total Value Real Estate Including Land $7 220 325 00

VALUE PERSONAL PROPERTY

Value of Stock in Trade	$170 215 00
Value of Live Stock	12 515 00
Value of Machinery	35 340 00
Value of all other Personal	448 677 00

Total Value Personal Property $666 747 00

Total valuation Real and personal property $7,887 072 00

Town Appropriations	$402 933 83
State Tax	10 960 00
County Tax	15 899 06
Hospital Tax	60 00
State Parks and Reservations	266 54
Overlays	13 787 36
Water Department	26 000 00
(Used in Est. Receipts)	
Auditing Municipal Accounts	1 749 98
State Tax Underestimate 1937	982 50

State Parks and Reservations
Underestimate 1937   76 43

$472 715 70

ESTIMATED RECEIPTS

Income Tax	$34 046	17
Corporation Taxes	12 334	42
Motor Vehicle Excise	15 257	01
Licenses	5 577	00
Fines	198	95
General Government	134	64
Health & Sanitation	1 743	39
Charities	31 216	37
Old Age Assistance	21 802	68
Schools	2 746	79
Libraries	311	00
Water Department	26 000	00
Tax Costs	259	54
Interest	8 637	37
Veterans Exemptions	213	48
Refund Compensation Policy	689	08
Overestimate County Tax 1937	702	40
Overestimate Hospital Tax 1937	15	00
Poll Taxes	4 812	00

Total Estimated Receipts $166 697 29

Total amount to be raised on Property   306 018 41

Tax Rate Per Thousand $38.80

Number of Motor Vehicles and Trailers assessed   2265
Value of Motor Vehicles and Trailers $462 930 00

Number Persons assessed on Personal
   Estate only   194
On Real Estate only   1799
On both Personal and Real Estate   109

Total Number of Persons assessed   2102

Number of Dwellings   1880
Number of Cows   75
Number of Horses   17
Number of Yearlings, Bulls etc.   9
Number of Swine   215
Number of Fowl   5269
Number of Acres   5780

AMOUNTS COMMITTED TO COLLECTOR

Real and Personal	$306	018	41
Water Liens	2	758	89
Poll Tax	4	812	00
December Assessment on Polls		78	00
December Assessment on Property		333	68
Excise Tax	13	801	17
Total	$327	802	15

Respectfully submitted,

JOSEPH B. ESTES,
NORMAN J. BEALS,
DENNIS L. O'CONNOR,
Board of Assessors

Report of Collector of Taxes

Taxes of 1935

Outstanding January 1, 1938	$ 2 126 98
Collected during year	$ 2 126 98

1935 Motor Vehicle Excise Tax

Outstanding January 1, 1938	$ 485 52
Collected during year	$ 485 52

Taxes of 1936

Outstanding January 1, 1938	$66 767 21
Collected during year	65 956 30
Outstanding, January 1, 1938	$ 810 91

1936 Motor Vehicle Excise Tax

Outstanding January 1, 1938	$ 1 562 84
Collected during year	1 341 19
Outstanding January 1, 1939	$ 221 65

Taxes of 1937

Outstanding January 1, 1938	$113 628 10
Collected during year	46 557 92
Outstanding January 1, 1939	$ 67 070 18

1937 Motor Vehicle Excise Tax

Outstanding January 1, 1938	$ 3 500 84

Collected during year	1 892 18

Outstanding January 1, 1939	$ 1 608 66

Taxes of 1938

Amount committed to Collector	$311 242 09
Collected during year	197 771 47

Outstanding January 1, 1939	$113 470 62

Water Liens added to 1938	
Real Estate Taxes	$ 1 744 34
Collected during year	342 94

Outstanding January 1, 1939	$ 1 401 40

1938 Motor Vehicle Excise Tax

Amount committed to Collector	$13 801 17
Collected during year	13 141 50

Outstanding January 1, 1939	$ 659 67

Water Liens

Outstanding January 1, 1938	$ 1 648 43
Amounts committed during year	1 014 55

Total	$ 2 662 98
Amount re-committed with 1938 Real Estate Taxes	1 744 34
Total of water liens not yet added to taxes	$ 918 64
Collected during year	161 69

Outstanding January 1, 1939	$ 756 95

Respectfully submitted,

JAMES A. DONOVAN,
Collector of Taxes

Report of
Works Progress Administration

To the Board of Selectmen:

The operation of the Works Progress Administration-in Rockland for the year of 1938 has proven more active than in the past. Continuity of work on projects has improved to a great extent under the set program adopted by the Town. Particularly by the installation of sidewalks whereby all streets would have a concrete curb and bituminous walk on one side and that streets leading from Union Street in the business section on both sides. The blanket sidewalks approved by the town in the August special town meeting obviated the delays previously encountered where Federal approved projects lacked allocated sponsors funds.

The number of Rockland persons working on W. P. A. projects in January 1, 1938 was 194. This number was gradually increased so that on March 30th there were 314 on payrolls and in August the all time high was reached with one person from 383 different families working. To this figure should be added Rockland persons working on Federal and State projects to the number of 52. Making a total top figure of 435 persons receiving Federal Emergency Relief checks weekly. The effect of these checks locally is reflected in reduction of expenditure in the Town Welfare Department.

The W. P. A. started off on direct Rockland projects with the lowest weekly payroll of the year at $2,208.88. the largest payroll was $4,872.15 to which should be added approximately $660.50 on account of other than direct Rockland projects upon which local persons worked, making a weekly payroll of $5,532.65 for which Federal checks arrived in Rockland. The year closed with total weekly payroll of $5,281.37. How long the weekly pay checks will aggregate over $5,000 depends upon the results of Congressional action on the deficiency appropriation now before Congress to cover expenditures to June 30, 1939, which is the end of the Government fiscal year.

The total federal payrolls for the year 1938 on direct Rockland projects was $226,700.14 which is more than double the amount for the year of 1937 when the total was $107,800.81. The total amount expended for Federal labor on direct Rockland projects since operation of the Federal Emergency Relief Act on August 1, 1934, to December 1, 1938 is $686,962.76. To this later figure may be added money received by Rockland employees on Federal and State projects for similar period of $92,888 making a total of $779,850.76. Truly a sizeable figure in dollars and cents equivalent to a large working private industry. The Town's expenditures for materials in connection with W. P. A. projects during 1938 was $19,243.12.

The Sewing, Housekeeping Aides, and Recreational projects have successfully operated throughout the entire year. The Sewing project under supervision of Miss Helen Purcell, located in the McKinley school building, has made 15,312 pieces of wearing articles. The Housekeeping Aides project under the able supervision of Miss Lois Williams has rendered 13,560 hours assistance to families requested through the various relief agencies and doctors. The Recreational project directed by Mr. Norman S. Crosby, has become recognized as one of the best in Southeastern Massachusetts; and its boxing and fun band have made public appearances before many of the local organizations in Rockland and the surrounding district. The Commodities Division dispenses food and wearing apparel to the needy under the direction of Mr.

John J. Bowler assisted by Mrs. Lillian Rainsford. During the year 1938 it has issued 20,646 pieces of clothing; 24,312 cans of goods; 3,874 pounds of butter; and 443,092 pounds of flour, vegetables, fruit etc.

During 1938 two sewage disposal beds have been built, one 34x60 foot to serve the McKinley School Building and a much larger one 80 x 160 feet at the junction of Grove and Plain street to care for the Senior-Junior high school.   Both beds are functioning perfectly eradicating bad conditions that have existed for years.   Another project that disposed of a contaminating condition was the clearing of Cushing's pond, which had been a breeding place for mosquitos and bad odors.

Work has been started upon tennis courts at Memorial Park, which should be completed next year, widening the scope of activities at this beautiful recreational center.   A project has also been completed for beautifcation of the grounds surrounding the new standpipe on Rice avenue by the installation of cement curbs, grading and seeding.

The rebuilding of Liberty street from Market to East Water street, a distance of one-half mile, is one of the outstanding projects of the year and the town has a W. P. A. project for similiar rebuilding of Exchange street, but has no local funds to operate.

Covered drains with catch basins have been installed by the W. P. A. on Salem, Hartsuff, Maple and Monroe, Crescent, Exchange and Myrtle, Park and Vernon streets and Taunton Avenue using 3, 533 feet of pipe and eleven catch basins.

All W. P. A. sidewalks voted in town meetings in 1938 have had cement curbs installed and, with the exception of a few cases, all the bituminous mixture has been placed.   The few walks not completed will be finished with warm weather in the spring.

With the adoption of a specific program at the special town meeting, August 8, of a curb and bituminous walk on at least one side of practically each street in-town, a solution has been found for this annual controversy.

Over five and a half miles of cement curb, to be exact 30,253 feet, have been installed for side walks during the year. The program is proving exceptionally valuable, not only in the control of storm drainage but by taking pedestrians off the street and, particularly in outlying sections, should prove a safeguard for auto fatalities and injuries. A total of thirty-three sidewalk locations have received curbs and bituminous top the past year.

A valuable project started late in the year is the indexing, revising, typing and binding of the vital statistics in the office of the town clerk to conform to federal requirements. Another white collar project in operation is the bringing of the street and property boundaries in accord with governmental specifications through surveying and mapping.

Reed's pond as a recreation center has had further improvement made by the W. P. A. through the building of a wharf and development of the east side of Market street. This work is still under way with the close of the year.

In closing, I wish to extend my sincere thanks for the whole hearted co-operation I have received from our highway surveyor, Mr. Roderick Mackenzie, who has given so much of his time and experience the past year, and the advice and assistance from the various federal W. P. A. district engineers and supervisors.

Respectfully submitted,

FRED M. RYAN,
Sponsor Agent

Report of World War Memorial Committee

Your committee have endeavored to prepare and present plans for a suitable memorial, having met on numerous occasions and considering various types of memorials, also, suitable locations. The vote of the Town did not provide an appropriation of money for the preparation of architectural plans. The committee felt it was necessary to seek the assistance of an architect, so Mr. John Beal of the J. Williams Beal, Sons concern of architects was asked to assist the committee and he most graciously accepted with no expense to the Town.

Mr. Beal offered several suggestions which were all given due consideration, one, which the committee were unanimous in, that was to provide a memorial entrance to Memorial Park from Union street at Goddard avenue.

Before plans of the memorial could be placed before the committee it was learned that a gasoline station and parking space was to occupy one corner. The committee have taken this into consideration and now feel that it would not be a desirable location because of traffic conditions.

Your committee have been very co-operative and faithful to the duties assigned them and would recommend that the surplus poll tax fund from a tax levied in 1920-

21-22 and 1923 amounting to $4,021.70 be placed on deposit so that it will draw interest and that it be known as a World War Memorial Fund, and further recommend the report be accepted as progressive.

V. F. W.

American Legion

Harry O. Holmes, Chairman
Frank Dixon
Frank Watson
Augustus Ledwell
Harold Morse

Charles T. Walls,
Ralph Bingham
Harold Anderson, vice chairman'
Arthur O'Neill
William Christie

Citizens
John Troy Jr.
Joseph Estes
Bernard Delory
Abram Lelyveld
Russell Hawes, Secretary

Report of Trustees
Memorial Library

The trustees of the Memorial Library submit the following report for 1938:

An account of the circulation, reference work, and special activities of the library is given by the librarian in her report which follows this report and to which the trustees call the attention of the citizens.

The library property was somewhat damaged by the hurricane in September. A tree on the lawn was destroyed, and the glass in the dome of the building was shattered. The cost of repairing the latter was $80.02, a sum which must be taken from the appropriation of 1939.

The trustees are grateful to the two clubs which have made donations to the library: the Rockland Woman's club for a gift of five dollars, and the Rockland Garden Club for four books helpful to garden·lovers. Thanks are also due those who have contributed other books, magazines, and book marks.

Income from the trust funds was expended as follows:

Hattie Curtis Fund	$ 8 13
Zenas M. Lane Fund	5 73
Everett Lane Fund	2 46
Alice L. French Fund	12 95
Mary A. Spence Fund	12 33
Sarah J. Spence Fund	6 90
Charles Edwin Vinal Fund	24 83

John W. Rice Fund	9 89
John A. Martin Fund	1 83
Mothers' Mutual Improvement Society Fund	1 24

$86 29

These withdrawals left on deposit in the Rockland Savings Bank on December 31, 1938:

Hattie Curtis Fund	$ 501 35
Zenas M. Lane Fund	502 96
Everett Lane Fund	100 06
Alice L. French Fund	500 08
Mary A. Spence Fund	500 44
Sarah J. Spence Fund	300 70
Charles Edwin Vinal Fund	1 000 31
John W. Rice Fund	400 24
John A. Martin Fund	100 79
Mother's Mutual Improvement Society Fund	50 20

The terms of John B. FitzGerald and Burton L. Cushing expire in 1939.

An appropriation of $4,400. plus the dog refund of $415.50 is recommended for 1939. This amount will care for the usual expenses, meet the repair bill of $80.02, and offset the decrease in the dog refund.

FRANCIS J. GEOGAN,
JOHN B. FITZGERALD,
BURTON L. CUSHING,
ANNIE E. McILVENE,
EMILY F. CRAWFORD,
EMMA W. GLEASON,
Trustees

Librarians Report

To the Trustees of the Rockland Memorial Library:

The sixtieth report of this library is herewith submitted.

A total of 62,911 books and magazines have been loaned for home use.

The average monthly circulation, 5,242. The average daily circulation, 214. Largest number delivered in one day 368. Smallest number delivered in one day, 95.

Received for fines, reserved books, sale of cook books, subscriptions from non-residents, old magazines and books, $340.

Number of books added by purchase (including replacements, 448. Number of books presented, 51. Number of books worn out and missing 60. Number of books rebound 56. Number of books in library on December 31, 1938, 21,100.

Character of books loaned: Literature, 4 per cent; history and travel, 4 per cent; biography, 3 per cent; miscellaneous (adult), 5 per cent; fiction (adult), 56 per cent; fiction (juvenile) 12 per cent; miscellaneous (juvenile), 5 per cent; magazines, 11 per cent.

The year just over, was one in all ways most satisfactory. Our circulation, which is the chief measure of our activity, has increased once again. Although figures serve as a barometer to economic conditions, we must remem-

ber that requests for library service are more thought-
fully directed than when the "latest fiction" was the chief
consideration. Too, as the staff becomes better acquainted with an increasing number of books, activitiy is reflected. Never have the books for so-called library use
only been used as during the past year.

Today libraries need to provide information on all questions, to all men.

Contrary to the idea that people would cease reading
books because they were going to the movies or listening
to the radio for entertainment, they have actually turned
to the library for book information about new interests in
hobbies, photography, history, and even travel. And
no substitute has been found for the fiction so abiding in
its appeal as to become standard.

Civil service material of every kind has been used to
its full capacity. These include secretarial handbooks,
books on civics, science, useful arts, as well as mathematics, geography and English.

The latest edition of the Americana Encycloyedia brings
to the library patrons up-to-the-minute information on
new subjects. It is a reference set of great usefulness.

The clamor for new books must be satisfied as far as
we are able, and in selecting an effort is made to add
books which give evidence of being worthwhile and to
strike a balance between books for pure entertainment
and the heavier reading. Each group has its place in the
library.

Gifts received were greatly appreciated, especially the
books on gardening by the Rockland Garden Club and
the substantial check from the Rockland Woman's Club.

Again we express consideration for the book marks

given by local merchants and the Rockland Savings Bank. The idea is a big factor in advertising the library, as well as a commercial interest.

Many old books were given by friends and those which were duplicates were forwarded to the Merchant Marine Library Association. Also, over two hundred National Geographic magazines were given for this special request.

Helpful suggestions received in the spirit of co-operation are likewise acknowledged.

Those who visited the library during the fall months probably noticed the exhibit by the Girl Scouts. This was of great value to those who studied it carefully.

As a matter of economy many books have been recased and rebacked at the library this year. While we have not the facilities nor skill to do work of professional standard, they are neat, and strong, and we are retaining in circulation many books which otherwise would have had to be thrown away.

To encourage children to read books, to love and appreciate literature, and to gain cultural advantages and tastes is still the purpose of the Children's room.

Where can we find such values as in the public library? May we not only live up to the past standards, but may we set new and better ones in the future.

Respectfully submitted,

LIDA A. CLARK,
Librarian

Auditor's Report

We have audited and verified the books of the various departments of the town, including those of the treasurer, tax collector, town clerk and sealer of weights and measures. Also the books of the water department and the school departments.

All balances have been reconciled with statements furnished by the banks.

Respectfully submitted,

HAROLD C. SMITH
GEORGE A. GALLAGHER
LEO E. DOWNEY

Report of Sewerage Commissioners

To the Citizens of Rockland:—

The Board of Sewer Commissioners herewith submit its annual report for the year 1938.

The year of 1938 has been a busy one for the Sewer Commissioners, since early in the year the State Board of Health has been much interested in the health condition of the Town.

In the first part of June 1938 it was suggested by the Federal Emergency Administration of Public Works at Boston that the Town make an application for a grant towards installing a Sewerage System. This came to our Board through the Selectmen's office and from that time on until the award of $162,000.00 was alloted to the town, we have worked together with the Chairman of the Board of Selectmen. With the assistance of Mr. C. A. Williams, Engineer of the P. W. A. regional office, Mr. Wright of the State Board of Health, Senator Walsh, Senator Lodge and Congressman Gifford, who all assisted us by their personal attention and efforts, the application was completed and after receiving the approval of the State and Federal Officials was forwarded to National Headquarters at Washington.

On September 9th, 1938 telegrams from Washington notified us of the approval of our application and the grant of funds to the town, subject to approval by the town and vote of same to raise the sum of $198,000.00 to be used with the Federal Grant for the building of a sewerage system.

The matter was brought before the Town as a special town meeting held September 19th, 1938 and after a presentation of the subject to the meeting by the Board and some discussion it was voted not to accept the offer of the Federal Grant.

While the entire Board felt that the Town very much needed a sewerage system from the viewpoint of health, convenience and industrial development it also felt that a presentation to the citizens of the town of facts and figures in connection with the Federal Grant was all it was suitable and proper for us to present to the meeting.

Mr. Worthington, Sanitary Engineer who made the original survey of the proposed system in 1912, made up the figures and computation which were required in much detail and also made a survey of a few minor alterations as required to fill out the necessary application blanks. Mr. Worthington at the same time was in charge of applications of several other towns.

On August 25th, 1938, the whole Board being in session it was voted as follows:—"All proposed construction in Rockland of Sewerage projects or changes shall be submitted to this Board for its consideration and approval or disapproval." This vote of the Board was submitted to the Town Counsel for his consideration and upon his suggestion a notice of the vote was published in the Rockland Standard.

The Federal Project to care for the Sewerage disposal of the Junior-Senior High school building was completed this year, but not in accordance with plans approved by the Federal and State Sanitary Engineers.

A sewerage disposal system for the McKinley school

building under a Federal Grant has been completed and is giving satisfactory service.

Respectfully submitted,

FREDERIC HALL,
CHARLES M. HINES,
GILES W. HOWLAND,
            Sewerage Commissioners

Report of Zoning Committee

To the Honorable Board of Selectmen:

We wish to report to you under Article 84 of the 1938 Town Warrant whereby the voters directed the Moderator and the Board of Selectmen to select a committee to investigate the matter of a Zone Planning Board for the town.

The undersigned committee organized with Arthur Wilcox, chairman, and Carl Fass, secretary, and have held several meetings throughout the year. It was the unanimous opinion of the committee that the town should establish a Planning Board to become effective January 1, 1941, under the provision of General Laws, Chapter 41, Section 81A as added by Chapter 211 of 1936, the Board to consist of five members to be appointed by the Moderator and Selectmen.

To instruct said committee to prepare a map showing proposed zoning and cause same to be posted six weeks before the next annual Town meeting for approval of the -voters.

We have inserted an article in the 1939 Town Warrant.

Respectfully submitted,

ARTHUR P. WILCOX,
CARL G. FASS
DR. JOSEPH LELYVELD
JAMES A. CODY
FRANCIS L. GAMMON

In Memoriam

CORNELIUS J. McHUGH
1871 - 1938

A police officer of Rockland for 23 years. Steadfast, Dependable, Trustworthy, fulfilling his duties with high courage as he protected human life and public and private property.

We regret the passing of a splendid police officer and a real friend.

ROCKLAND POLICE DEPARTMENT

Report of Chief of Police

To the Honorable Board of Selectmen:

Gentlemen.

I herewith submit my report for the Police Department of the Town of Rockland for the year ending December 31st, 1938.

NUMBER OF ARRESTS

Year 1938   206

Subdivision

	Male	Female
Assault and Battery	3	
Breaking and Entering	3	
Disturbance	2	
Delinquent children	4	
Drunkeness	143	3
Illegitimate child act	1	
Insane persons	4	2
Larceny	6	
Lottery (promoting)	1	
Motor Vehicle violations	18	
(a) operating under etc.	11	
(b) minor infractions	7	
Non-support	7	
Practicing medicine without license	2	
Receiving stolen goods	1	
Stubborn child	2	
Violation milk laws	2	
Violation Painting laws	2	
Total	201	5

Males	201
Females	5
Total	206

MISCELLANEOUS

Automobiles thefts investigated	3
Automobiles recovered	7
Automobile accidents investigated	81
Complaints investigated	789
Miles traveled by Police cruiser	16 094
Persons reported missing	4
Persons located out-of-town and local	7
Number of arrests for out-of-town police Departments	15
Red light calls answered	409
Stores found unlocked	31
Summons served for out-of-town police	76
Telegrams (emergencies) persons notified	16
Reported defects in highway	9
Fires reported	2
Electric light reported out	18
Number of autos stopped for license and registrations	920
Persons put up for the night	12

Rockland was most fortunate the past year 1938 that crime was of a minor nature; persons convicted of operating a motor vehicle under the influence of intoxicating liquor increased from eight (8) in 1937 to eleven (11) in 1938.

In the annual report as compiled by the Massachusetts Safety Council, Rockland's standing is seventh on the list of 47 towns of approximately the same population of our town. During the past year of the 47 towns, ten had "No fatal" accidents Rockland being included in the ten towns. The average improvement during the past three years, Rockland is in ninth place with a total percent change for the better of 37.0 average over a period of three years.

This department feels gratified in making mention of this report showing a vast improvement over 1937 when three fatal accidents occured. I am informed that an article will be inserted in the town warrant requesting a sum of money for painting parking spaces on Union St., and also "Warning signs" on the streets which are danger points; I highly recommend this precautionary measure as I firmly believe that this is added assistance for "Safety."

The police cruiser which was purchased in 1936 is nearing three years of service and has traveled approximately 50,000 miles. An article has been inserted in the town warrant requesting purchase of a new police car and to trade in the present car.

Again I take pleasure in giving the thanks of the entire department to the town and county officials and to the many other citizens who have given valuable assistance when at an opportune time. As chief of the department I am appreciative of the excellent work of the regular and special officers, all of whom have labored to give the finest service; and to the Finance committee who after consideration and investigation approved of the appropriation asked for by this department.

Respectfully submitted,

GEORGE J. POPP,
Chief of Police

Committee On Parking

The growth of business in the Rockland business district and the social activities bringing visitors to Rockland by automobile have overcrowded the parking spaces on Union Street and the nearby side streets, It has, therefore, become necessary to take action to protect the business interests on Union Street, essential as they are to the prosperity of the town, by making provision for additional parking space.

We have met with the committees of the Rockland Retail Merchants Association and the Rockland Chamber of Commerce, and after a careful study of the situation the following areas are offered for the consideration of the townspeople:

The land east of the Rockland High School between Taunton Avenue and Goddard Avenue.

The land in the rear of buildings on Union Street, between Reed Street and Taunton Avenue.

The town lot on School Street.

Plans for these spaces will be duly presented with complete details in the annual Town Warrant, and we earnestly request your most serious consideration.

COMMITTEE ON PARKING,

LAWRENCE E. BLANCHARD,
GEORGE POPP
JOSEPH LELYVELD, Chairman

Report of Board of Health

The Board of Health herewith submits its report for 1938.

The number of reportable diseases is as follows:

Scarlet Fever	74
Lobar Pneumonia	4
Pulmonary Tuberculosis	3
Measles	5
Whooping Cough	6
Dog Bite	6

The cases of Scarlet Fever were as a rule light. The disease was quite general in all the surrounding towns.

Respectfully submitted,

JOSEPH H. DUNN, M. D.,
JOSEPH FRAME, M. D.,
EDWARD CULLINAN,
Board of Health

Report of Town Treasurer

TREASURER'S REPORT OF THE RECEIPTS AND
DISBURSEMENTS FOR THE YEAR 1938

January 1, 1938 Cash on hand $58 023 38

RECEIPTS

Anticipation Tax Notes	$325 000	00
Taxes—Real Estate, Personal,		
and Poll	286 968	72
Taxes, Excise	15 872	33
Taxes, Interest	6 940	36
Taxes, Costs	284	83
Tax Titles Redeemed	5 450	53
Licenses, Liquor etc	4 593	00
License, Miscellaneous	597	00
Trust Funds (Cemetery)	804	69
Dog Licenses	518	60
Water Department	23 502	91
Joint Water Department	7 533	41
Memorial Library	340	00
Sealer of Weights	102	15
School Department	167	65
Court Fines	124	80
City of Boston, Tuition	561	18
Unearned Comp. Ins., Premium	527	90
Board of Health	225	71
Miscellaneous, Infirmary, Highway	62	79
Sales, Tax Title Property	1 396	34

County Treasurer
Dog Dividend   505 94

E. Water St., Cons.   3 827 65
                              ————$4 333 59
                                              ————————

                                                      $685 908 49
                                                      ————————

                                                      $743 931 87

Water Tank Construction
  Federal Grant, Bal. $5 957 96
  Contractors Refund   43 33
                                   ————————

                                                      $ 6 001 29

Fire Station Project 1440F
Issue Notes   34 500 00
Premium   362 60
Accrued Interest   34 50
                                   ————————

                                                      $34 897 10

Emergency Relief Loan
  Issue Notes   34 800 00
  Premium   19 84
  Accrued Interest   18 85
                                   ————————

                                                      34 838 69

Welfare and Old Age Assistance
  Towns and Cities   6 468 33

State Treasurer
  Old Age Assistance   30 898 08
  Temporary Aid   11 700 87
  Soldiers' Burial   100 00
  Aid to Schools   730 83
  Tuition of Children   1 143 22
  Federal Emergency Relief Fund   170 56
  Public Health   419 29
  Aid to Dependent Mothers'   5 154 29
  State Aid   643 00
  Military Aid   5 00

Income Tax	31	345	46
Corporation Tax	10	747	31
Gas & Elec. Tax	2	871	13
Veterans Exemption		241	78
U. S. Grant Old Age Assistance	46	890	83
U. S. Grant Aid Children	2	510	67
Chap. 500 Highway Fund	6	850	00
East Water St. Construction	7	655	30

Total	$160	077	62
Total	$986	214	90

PAYMENTS

Selectmen's Warrants	$190	710	72
Public Welfare	67	701	87
School Department	104	372	33
Old Age Assistance	51	995	26
Old Age Assistance, U. S. Grant	44	249	85
Old Age Administration U. S. Grant	1	193	36
Water Department Warrants	19	438	78
Joint Water Warrants	10	417	26
Town of Abington, Joint Rates	1	390	59
Tax Refunds		465	16
Aid to Dependent Mothers, U. S. Grant	2	669	99
Cemetery Trust Funds		804	69
Anticipation Tax Notes	300	000	00
McKinley School Appropriations		497	20
Water Tank Project, 1343R	8	198	14
Fire Station Project 1440F	2	643	11
Chapter 500, Hurricane Repairs	6	849	60
Miscellaeous Refunds		24	96

County Treasurer

County Tax	15	929	96
Dog Licenses		518	60

16 448 56

Commonwealth of Massachusetts

State Tax	23 290 00	
Care C. W. Veterans	60 00	
Auditing of Accounts	1 749 98	
State Parks etc	293 86	

	25 393 84
Cash on hand December 31, 1938	130 749 63

Total	$986 214 90

OUTSTANDING INDEBTEDNESS

Anticipation of Revenue Notes	$125 000 00

PERMANENT LOANS

Junior-Senior School Bonds

3¾% maturing $10,000 annually 1939-1943	$50 000 00	
3¾% maturing $6,000 annually 1939-1948	60 000 00	

	$110 000 00

Plymouth County Hospital Notes

5% maturing $1,000 annually 1939-1940	2 000 00	

	$ 2 000 00

Union Street Construction Notes 2% maturing 1939-1946	27 000 00

Water Tank Construction 2% maturing 1939-1956	36 000 00

Municipal Relief Loan, Chapter 58 1½% maturing 1939-1948	34 800 00

Fire Station Notes
2¼% maturing 1939-1958   34 500 00

JOINT WATER DEPARTMENT

Receipts:
From Joint Rates, etc	2 324 77
From Rockland ½ Maintenance	5 208 62
From Abington ½ Maintenance	5 208 64
Due Abington from 1937	228 20
	$12 970 23

Payments:
Warrants	$10 417 26
Joint Rates to Abington	1 162 39
Joint Rates to Rockland	1 162 38
Abington Balance 1937	228 20
	$12 970 23

WATER DEPARTMENT

Receipts:
Water Rates, Construction etc	$23 502 91
½ Joint Rates	1 162 38
	$24 665 29

Payments:
Warrants	19 438 78
½ Cost Joint Maintenance	5 208 62
Receipts over Payments	17 89
	$24 665 29

WATER TANK PROJECT 1343R

January 1, 1938 Balance	2 338 07
Receipts	6 001 29
	8 339 36

Payments   8 198 14

Unexpended balance, Dec. 31, 1938   141 22

FIRE STATION PROJECT 1440F
Sale of Notes $34 897 10
Payments   2 643 11

Unexpended balance, Dec. 31, 1938 $32 253 99

ASSETS
Cash $130 749 63
Accounts Receivable
  Taxes 1936   810 91
  Taxes 1937   67 070 18
  Taxes 1938   113 470 62

                                           181 351 71

  Motor Excise 1936   221 65
  Motor Excise 1937   1 608 66
  Motor Excise 1938   659 67

                                             2 489 98

Tax Titles   12 104 25

                                          $326 695 57

LIABILITIES
Anticipation Tax Notes $125 000 00
Unexpended Balances   67 851 96
Real Estate Fund   5 190 00
Special Fund (War Taxes)   4 021 70
Water Tank Project   141 22
Tax Titles Foreclosed   1 396 34
Surplus Revenue   123 094 35

                                          $326 695 57

CEMETERY TRUST FUNDS

Bequest	Cemetery	Balance Jan. 1, 1938	Deposited During 1938	Income	Expended	Balance Dec. 31, 1938
Jeremiah Leahy	St. Patricks	$103 05		$4 11	$7 16	$100 00
Mary Spence	St. Patricks	412 27		16 53	24 52	404 28
Margaret Smith	St. Patricks	103 05		4 11	7 16	100 00
Patrick McCaffrey	St. Patricks	110 37		4 42	7 27	107 52
James H. ' Hill	St. Patricks	103 05		4 11	6 05	101 11
Gallagher-Driscoll	St. Patricks	243 41		9 72	20 00	233 13
Peter Ford	St. Patricks	482 63		19 30	28 00	473 93
Mary Gallagher	St. Patricks	103 05		4 11	6 05	101 11
Catherine Moore	St. Patricks	206 13		8 26	12 13	202 26
Daniel Sullivan	St. Patricks	103 05		4 11	6 05	101 11
Patrick Cullinane	St. Patricks	77 29		3 08	5 29	75 08
George Hatch	St. Patricks	103 05		4 11	6 05	101 11
James Crowley	St. Patricks	103 05		4 11	6 05	101 11
Margaret D .Quinlan	St. Patricks	206 13		6 26	12 13	202 26
Daniel Foy	St. Patricks	103 05		4 11	6 05	101 11
Pridget Foy	St. Patricks	116 13		4 62	10 00	110 75
Patrick O'Hern	St. Patricks	51 51		2 04	3 51	50 04
Daniel H. Lynch	St. Patricks	103 05		4 11	6 05	101 11
Nicholas O'Donnell	St. Patricks	103 05		4 11	6 05	101 11
James Maguire	St. Patricks	103 05		4 11	6 05	101 11

CEMETERY TRUST FUNDS - Continued

Bequest	Cemetery	Balance Jan. 1. 1938	Deposited During 1938	Income	Expended	Balance Dec. 31, 1938
Ellen Sian	St. Patricks	51 51		2 04	3 51	50 04
Mary J. Coughlin	St. Patricks	101 50		4 06	4 50	101 06
Katherine E. Klley	St. Patricks	206 13		8 26	12 13	202 26
Mel Sullivan	St. Parks	103 05		4 11	6 05	101 11
William McGrath	St. Patricks	105 15		2 53	6 86	100 82
James Tangney	St. Patricks	206 08		8 26	12 08	202 26
Catherine E. Brien	St. Patricks	103 05		4 11	6 05	101 11
Thas Russell	St. Parks	103 05		4 11	6 05	101 11
Timothy Kelliher	St. Parks	154 59		6 18	9 59	151 18
Mry J. Siels	St. Patricks	206 13		8 26	12 13	202 26
William B. Brke	St. Patricks	51 51		2 04	3 01	50 54
Henry Lyns	St. Parks	103 05		4 11	6 05	101 11
Srah J. Spence	St. Parks	412 27		16 53	24 27	404 53
William Fitzgerald	St. Parks	103 05		4 11	6 05	101 11
Mas J. Flynn	St. Patricks	103 05		4 11	6 05	101 11
John Leahy	St. Patricks	206 13		8 26	12 13	202 26
John Parker	St. Patricks	87 59		3 48	5 09	85 98
Thomas J. Lych	Holy Family	128 81		5 14	8 81	125 14
Jeremiah Santry	Holy Family	206 13		8 26	12 13	202 26
Antonia B. Rogers	Holy Family	103 05		4 11	7 05	100 11

CEMETERY TRUST FUNDS - Continued

Bequest	Cemetery	Balance Jan. 1, 1938	Added During 1938	Income	Expended	Balance Dec. 31, 1938
Mary Clancey	Holy Family	125 00		2 08	2 00	125 08
John W. Cullinan	Holy Family	128 81		5 14	8 81	125 14
Mary E. Kelley	Holy Family	103 05		4 11	6 05	101 11
Frederic Dill	Mt. Pleasant	106 80		2 67		109 47
Ernest M. Paine	Mt. Pleasant	102 00		4 11		106 11
Guy L. Keene	Mt. Pleasant	102 00		4 11	2 00	104 11
Wallace Damon	Mt. Pleasant	101 25		4 08		105 33
Collins, Branson	Mt. Pleasant	227 59		9 18	4 00	232 77
Elvira S. Holmes	Mt. Pleasant	138 22		3 45		141 67
C. A. Johnston	Mt. Pleasant	83 43		2 08	2 00	83 51
Henry Chase	Mt. Pleasant	239 26		6 00	4 00	241 26
Emma Hutchinson	Mt. Pleasant	61 02		1 52	2 00	60 54
A. Hilton Studley	Mt. Pleasant	248 58		6 18	8 50	246 26
William G. Perry	Mt. Pleasant	116 36		2 91	4 00	115 27
Gardner-Damon	Mt. Pleasant	100 02		2 51	2 53	100 00
Charles H. Poole	Mt. Pleasant	100 02		2 51	2 53	100 00
Howard Wheeler	Mt. Pleasant	139 34		3 49	4 00	138 83
... G. ...ller	Mt. Pleasant	120 93		3 02	4 00	119 95
Frederic Shw	Mt. Pleasant	105 01		2 63	4 00	103 64
Lottie Mn	Mt. Pleasant	101 23		2 53	3 00	100 76

CEMETERY TRUST FUNDS - Continued

Bequest	Cemetery	Balance Jan. 1, 1938	Deposited During 1938	Income	Expended	Balance Dec. 31, 1938
McManus-Horne	Mt. Pleasant	51 57		1 28	1 00	51 85
A. A. Crooker	Mt. Pleasant	134 40		3 37	2 00	135 77
Frank P. Lewis	Mt. Pleasant	53 80		1 33	2 00	53 13
James J. Donaldson	Mt. Pleasant	323 93		8 11	4 00	328 04
Henry G. Moulton	Mt. Pleasant	545 27		13 71	4 00	554 98
Marsena Lovell, Heirs	Mt. Pleasant	129 53		3 24	4 00	128 77
E. W. Whiting	Mt. Pleasant	156 77		3 92	4 00	156 69
Fidelia Estes	Mt. Pleasant	311 40		7 75	9 00	310 15
Emma L. Williams	Mt. Pleasant	100 75		4 05		104 80
Aie F. Merrill	Mt. Pleasant	200 50		8 10	2 00	206 60
Eben P. Everett	Mt. Pleasant	87 84		2 18	2 00	88 02
Frank, Geo. Lawrence	Mt. Pleasant	173 98		6 96	4 00	176 94
Thomas-Litchfield	Mt. Pleasant	235 72		5 84	9 00	232 56
Andrew McIlvene	Mt. Pleasant	115 72		4 61	5 00	115 33
Edward Crane	Mt. Pleasant	180 08		4 52	3 00	181 60
L. Evelyn Dill	Mt. Pleasant	129 68		5 22	4 00	130 90
Reuben Ellis	Mt. Pleasant	109 20		2 73	2 00	109 93
H. J. Cushing	Mt. Pleasant	106 86		2 67	2 00	107 53
Harold B. Vesper	Mt. Pleasant	101 28		2 53	3 00	100 81
Avin G. Bates	Mt. Pleasant		100 00			100 00

CEMETERY TRUST FUNDS - Continued

Bequest	Cemetery	Balance Jan. 1. 1938	Deposited During 1938	Income	Expended	Balance Dec. 31, 1938
Fannie H. Turner	Mt. Paint	316 57		7 95	6 00	318 52
Easton Lot No. 249	Mt. Pleasant	106 91		2 67	2 00	107 58
Henry D. Smith	Mt. Pleasant	100 00		2 30	2 30	100 00
Francis Soule	Mt. Pleasant	100 00		1 66	1 66	100 00
George T. Poole	Mt Pleasant	317 98		7 97	8 00	317 95
Dill-Lothrop	Mt. Pleasant	213 19		8 59	6 00	215 78
Elias A. Burrell	Mt. Pleasant	102 40		2 55	2 00	102 95
John Stoddard	Mt. Pleasant	76 97		1 91	2 00	76 88
Emma M. Coy	Mt. Pleasant	103 64		2 58	2 00	104 22
L Wilfred Poole	Mt. Pleasant	104 21		2 61	3 00	103 82
Mary H. Breck	Mt. Pleasant	105 47		2 63	2 00	106 10
Lucie Linton	Mt. Pleasant	105 68		2 63	2 00	106 31
Thompson-Whiting	Maplewood	119 98		4 80	2 25	122 53
J. W. Poole-C. Hobart	Maplewood	336 60		13 56	4 50	345 66
Phillips-Goodspeed	Maplewood	100 25		4 01	3 00	101 26
Adna Burrell	Maplewood	126 81		5 09	2 25	129 65
Flora Thurlough	Maplewood	50 00		2 00	2 00	50 00
John W. Harris	Maplewood	129 60		5 16	4 25	130 51
Later Torrey	Maplewood	122 61		4 91	2 25	125 27
N. A. Beal	Maplewood	100 00		4 03	4 00	100 03

CEMETERY TRUST FUNDS - Continued

Bequest	Cemetery	Balance Jan. 1, 1938	Deposited During 1938	Income	Expended	Balance Dec. 31, 1938
Hopkins-Damon	Maplewood	101 01		4 06	4 25	100 82
aDid J. Lantz	Maplewood	50 00	60 00	2 38	2 25	110 13
Henrietta Stetson	Maplewood	549 30		23 17	14 50	556 97
William T. Walker	Maplewood	104 64		4 16	4 25	104 55
Nahum Leavitt	Maplewood	100 00		1 25		101 25
Stoddard-Loud	Maplewood	166 48		4 17	4 00	166 65
Albert Phillips	Maplewood	50 57		2 01	2 25	50 33
Adah Davis	Maplewood	334 61		13 49	3 00	345 10
Mrs. Elbridge Whiting	Maplewood	117 72		4 70	2 25	120 17
D. W. Jabs	Maplewood	161 94		6 51	2 25	166 20
Nancy Whiting	Maplewood	69 79		2 76	2 25	70 30
Nathaniel Phillips	Maplewood	159 85		6 41	3 00	163 26
Isaac Everson	Maplewood	100 00		4 01	2 76	101 25
Henry A. Baker	Spring Lake	100 11		2 51	2 62	100 00
Amos A. Reed	Spring Lake	151 31		3 76	5 07	150 00
Jessie Doane	Spring Lake	103 63		2 58	4 00	102 21
Zenas Jenkins	Spring Lake	112 14		2 81	4 00	110 95
Irving Arnold	Spring Lake	152 74		3 82	4 00	152 56
Joseph J. Burgess	Spring Lake	125 76		3 14	3 90	125 00
Edbridge Payne	Mill Hill	331 05		6 31	8 00	331 36

CEMETERY TRUST FUNDS - Continued

Bequest	Cemetery	Balance Jan. 1. 1938	Deposited During 1938	Income	Expended	Balance Dec. 31, 1938
Betsey Battles	Beal	248 78		9 90	12 00	246 68
William J Hayden	Assinippi	105 00		4 22		109 22

CHARLES J. HIGGINS,
Town Treasurer

ANNUAL REPORT

OF THE

WATER COMMISSIONERS

TOWN OF ROCKLAND

MASSACHUSETTS

1938

JOINT WATER BOARD OF ABINGTON
AND ROCKLAND

H. C. WITHERELL, Chairman

S. W. BAKER, Secretary

GEORGE GRAY   E. S. DAMON

F. L. MERRILL   R. FUCILLO

LEWIS E. WHEELER, Water Registrar

WATER BOARD OF ROCKLAND

S. W. BAKER, Chairman

E. S. DAMON   R. FUCILLO

JAMES B. STUDLEY, Superintendent

Regular meetings of the Board every Thursday
evening at 7:30

Main and Superintendent's Office 96 East Water Street
Open 8-12 A. M.   1-5 P. M.   Telephone 901

Collection Office, Room 2, Savings Bank Block

Open 9-12 A. M.   2-5 P. M.

Friday Evenings 7-9 P. M.   Saturday 9-12 A. M.

Telephone 940

Water Commissioners Report

The Water Commissioners herewith submit their fifty-third annual report.

Services in Rockland	1953
Services in Abington	1534
Services in Joint Works	126
New Services in Rockland	11
New Services in Abington	10

Water rates received by Abington	$	25 178	68
Water rates received by Rockland		21 003	63
Water rates received by Joint Works		2 324	76
	$48	507	07

JOINT ACCOUNT 1938

Brockton Edison Ill. Co., service	$	3 387	54
William Brown, salary		2 076	11
Louis Wheeler, salary		1 664	00
A. Culver Co., coal and paint		318	94
P. J. Corbett, painting and installing ladder		303	00
Abington Coal Corp., coal		281	67
N. E. T. & T. Co., service		183	43
Town of Pembroke, taxes		177	21
Monsanto Chemical Co., chlorine		147	42
Keith, Reed & Wheatley, legal services		113	30
C. J. Higgins, services as treasurer		100	00
Harrison Witherell, services as chairman		100	00
S. W. Baker, services as secretary		100	00

E. A. Masefield Co., repairs at station	93	08
Howland and Howland, surveying	83	50
Curry Brothers Oil Co., motor oil and supplies	61	97
Franklin Print, printing	61	25
Matthew O'Grady, labor	57	67
Crandall Packing Co., supplies	54	09
George Gray, services as Commissioner	50	00
Frank Merrill, services as Commissioner	50	00
E. S. Damon, services as Commissioner	50	00
Ralph Fucillo, services as Commissioner	50	00
Robert Wheeler, labor	41	62
Lawrence Griffin, labor	40	50
Howland, Nash, & Cole Inc., insurance	36	80
Anthony Balchunas, labor	36	00
The Douglas Print, printing	27	51
Lawrence Sheehan, labor	27	28
Crawford's Service Station, removing stumps after hurricane	25	00
Hallamore Machine Co., valve and repair outfit	25	00
Sanderson Brothers, printing and envelopes	24	45
George Bolling, consultation and analysis	23	00
Daniel Hines, labor	22	22
Herbert Hunter, labor	19	75
George Lang & Co., supplies	19	33
A. W. Chesterton Co., supplies	19	00
Reed Lumber & Coal Co., cement, supplies	18	97
Edgar E. Pillson, labor	18	00
Parker Tisdale, labor	18	00
Malcolm Nash, labor	18	00
Williard Nickerson, labor	16	31
Leslie Brown, labor	15	75
Edwin Richardson, labor	14	33
Abington Water Dept., material for leaks	14	90
Francis Shea, labor	13	50
John McMaugh, labor	12	94
Sears, Roebuck Co., chairs for station	11	85
W. E. Kingsbury, gravel and ashes	11	50
Rockland Water Dept., repairs Joint Works	11	46
Peter DeSimone, labor	10	69

Commissioner of Public Safety, inspection of boiler	10 00
A. A. Phelps and Son, Wheeler Bond	10 00
The Welsh Co., paint and brushes	9 70
Builders Iron Foundry, ink and charts	9 56
Tony Sasso, labor	9 56
William Brown, remittances	9 28
S. E. Whitmarsh, labor	9 00
Felix McGovern, labor	9 00
Francis Benoit, labor	9 00
Walter Melewski, labor	9 00
Harvey Hemmings, labor	9 00
Coleman Connelly, labor	9 00
General Electric Co., brushes	8 85
Socony Vacuum Oil Co., oil	8 40
Rockland Transportation Co., express	8 37
Albert Doherty, labor	7 31
Donald Robertson, labor	7 31
Robert Porter, labor	6 75
Atwood & Morrill Co., weights	6 00
Dana Pratt, line at station	6 00
Crosby Steam Guage & Valve Co., charts	5 77
Hohman Flower Shop, loma and grass seed	5 65
Frank H. Hovey, wedges and hoes	5 65
A. S. Peterson, supplies	5 55
Dodge Haley & Co., pressure snubber	5 00
John Foster Lumber Co., supplies	4 96
Edward Winslow, labor	4 50
Harold West, labor	4 50
Vernon Pierce, labor	4 50
Stanley Ransom, labor	4 50
Hayes Pump & Machinery Co., supplies	4 43
Raymond Martel, labor	4 20
William B. Carey, labor	4 20
Stearns Express, express	3 75
Ira Richards, labor	3 38
Walworth Co., pressure valve	2 95
George O'Donnell, labor	2 81
Henry Nickerson, labor	2 25

Rockland Hardware & Paint Co., batteries	2	00
Corcoran Supply Co., curb cock	2	00
A. J. Vargus, batteries	1	85
Hosea Benson, food for laborers	1	60
Vincent Geloran, labor	1	13
Nemasket Transportation Co., express	·	70
Bryantville Motor Sales, grinding compound		50

$10 417 26

Rockland, one-half $ 5 208 63

REPORT OF SUPERINTENDENT
OF THE JOINT WORKS

Joint Board of Water Commissioners of
Abington and Rockland

Gentlemen:

I hereby submit my report as Superintendent for the year ending December 31, 1938.

The usual analysis of water from Big Sandy and Little Sandy Pond has been made by the State Board of Health. Also, samples of water from Big Sandy Pond were mailed each month from March to October, inclusive, to Lawrence Experiment Station for bacterial examinations.

Mr. Bolling of Brockton made analysis twice during the summer.

The residence was partly painted last fall and will be finished this year.

Due to the heavy rain in July and the hurricane in September extra labor was required to repair damage.

The hydrants were painted and tested during the year.

Two services were renewed and one service leak repaired.

I would recommend during the coming year that some repairs in masonry be done at the Pumping Station.

The cottage owners' property has been inspected three times during the past year and it is in good condition.

The financial report of the Joint Works will be found under the report of the Water Registrar.

Respectfully submitted,

WILLIAM H. BROWN,
Joint Superintendent

Month	Hours Pumping h m	Daily Average h m	Gallons Pumped	Daily Average	Lbs. Coal Consumed	Daily Ave.	Ave. Height in Reservoir	Gals. pumped per lb. coal	Gals. pumped per K. W. H.
January	286 15	9 14	17 474 000	563 677	18 569	599	97.5	352	733.0
February	260 40	9 19	15 939 000	569 249	18 458	659	97.5	353	734.7
Mch	286 45	9 15	17 545 000	565 968	15 490	500	97.4	354	732.0
April	281 30	9 23	17 099 000	569 967	12 268	409	97.5	352	733.0
May	332 40	10 44	19 030 000	613 871	11 470	370	96.5	352	713.7
June	342 30	11 25	19 642 000	654 733	6 065	269	96.6	353	718.2
July	355 20	11 28	20 475 000	660 484	none		96.0		720.0
August	403 00	13 00	22 873 000	737 839	702	702	96.9		710.4
Sept	336 00	11 12	19 818 000	660 600	23 032	768	97.4	353	708.2
Oct	346 40	11 11	19 869 000	640 935	9 920	320	97.5	352	709.5
November	311 00	10 22	17 785 000	592 834	9 720	324	97.2	352	708.6
December	335 10	10 49	19 317 000	623 129	18 850	603	97.3	354	703
Tals	3877 30		226 866 000		146 544				
vage	323 08		18 905 500		12 212		97.1		719.3

Average Static Head 218.5. Average Dynamic Head 281. Maximum daily record August 2 to August 8 in-
... daily record Friday, August 5 - 881,000 gals. Coal used 1938 - ...
lbs. Coal on hand Jan. 1, 1939 - 22,760 lbs. Gals. pumped via electricity, 220,794,000 gals. Gals. pumped via
... 5,217,000 gals. Gals. pumped via gasoline ... gage, 36,000 gals. Gasoline on hand Jan. 1, 1939 - 460 gals.
Duty done in foot lbs. per 100 lbs. of coal - 85,583,593. Gals. ... per gal. of gasoline - 4450.

WILLIAM H. BROWN, Chief Engineer

REPORT OF WATER REGISTRAR

To the Joint Board of Commissioners
of Abington and Rockland

Gentlemen:

I herewith submit my report as Water Registrar for
the year ending December 31, 1938.

Water Rates	$2 291 14
New Services	15 91
Total Amount Collected	$ 2 307 05
Water Rates Due	$ 312 52

One account changed over to Hanson.

Respectfully submitted,

LEWIS E. WHEELER,

Water Registrar

SUPERINTENDENT'S REPORT

To the Board of Water Commissioners:

Gentlemen:

I herebwith submit my report of the Water Department for the year ending Dec. 31, 1938.

Receipts from Water Rates	$21 003 63
Receipts from Installation of services	1 013 80
Receipts from Small Jobs	815 52
Receipts from Meter repairs	144 59
Receipts from Water Liens	510 87
Receipts from ½ Joint Works	1 162 38
	$24 650 79

COLLECTIONS

On January 1, 1938 there was an outstanding indebtedness to the Department of $13,700.79 for Water Rates. This has been reduced to $9,621.62 as of December 31, 1938.

SERVICES

New service installations	11
Renewal of services	22
Renewals to Property lines	9
Services lowered	1
Services discontinued	1
Services cleaned	3
Meter pit installations	5
Hydrant bleeders	4

HYDRANTS, GATES, BOXES

Main gates (new)	1
Hydrant gates added	6
Hydrants repaired	4
Hydrants relocated inside surb	7
Hydrants replaced	4
Service boxes adjusted	65
Gates repacked	4
New hydrants added to system	1

LEAKS

20 Leaks were repaired during the year.

MAINS

Smith Lane Construction

This project was started in 1937, but due to insufficient funds, was held over until 1938 for completion. The project has now been finished and gives water service and fire protection to three houses.

Dexter Road Construction

24 feet of 6" main was added to the present main on Dexter Road to supply water service to one new house.

General

During the year, the lot on which the elevated tank is located was graded and seeded and a cement curbing put around it. The labor was furnished under a WPA Project with the Water Department furnishing all material necessary.

LOCAL REPORT OF EXPENSES

The following expenditures are included in the total expenditures of $19,438.78.

Smith Lane Extension

Pipe, 160 ft.	$ 118	40
Labor	118	30
Lanterns	9	00
Merchlor	1	00
Wood	2	00
Gate Boxes	11	00
Kerosene	4	00
Lead	8	00
Jute	1	00
6" Gate	18	50
Hydrant	60	88
Tapping Sleeve and Gate	46	25
Hydrotite	5	00
Truck	16	00
Compressor	32	00
	$ 451	33

Dexter Road Extension

Labor	$ 22	50
Pipe	24	00
Lead	3	00
Jute		30
Kerosene		40
Wood	1	00
	$ 51	20

Tank Lot Grading

Hardware	14	12
Oil and Kerosene	1	55
Lumber and Coal	4	13
Cement	101	40
Truck Hire	286	62
Sand and Gravel	63	30

Loam		108 00
Seed and fertilizer		49 50

$ 628 62

Respectfully submitted,

JAMES B. STUDLEY,
Superintendent

ROCKLAND ACCOUNT 1938

James Studley, salary	$2 120 00
Louis Litchfield, salary	1 855 00
Harry Holmes, salary	1 855 00
Lawrence Sheehan, labor	1 004 64
Edwin Richardson, labor	982 97
Henry Harris, labor and remittances	971 56
Alice Gammon, office	954 00
Tony Sasso, labor	793 38
Merchants National Bank, interest on standpipe bonds	760 00
Phoenix Meter Corporation, meters and parts	568 02
A. B. Reed, Engineering services	550 00
Corcoran Supply Co., pipe and fittings	539 93
Edward Winslow, labor	320 92
S. W. Baker, services as Commissioner	300 00
E. S. Damon, services as commissioner	300 00
Ralph Fucillo, services as commissioner	300 00
Rensselaer Valve Co., hydrants	289 77
Red Hed Mfg. Co., fittings and supplies	286 04
Dolby's Filling Station, gasoline and repairs	252 93
Boston Pipe and Fitting Co., brass pipe	243 52
N. E. T. & T. Co., service	189 09
John B. Washburn, Registering liens	215 73
National Meter Co., meters and parts	153 40
E. L. LeBaron Foundry Inc., gate boxes and sleeves	151 86

8 00	John R. Parker, P. M., stamps and envelopes	146 98
	E. S. Damon, Insurance	146 22
	William Bell, use of truck (WPA)	142 22
	Abe Wainshalbaum, use of truck, repairs on trucks	124 37
	Johns Mainville Co., transite pipe	122 56
	Rockland Coal & Grain Co., cement and coal	118 73
	Easton Brass Foundry Inc., castings and bolts for meters	118 67
	Mary Dotton, looking up titles on liens	113 50
	A. A. Phelps & Son, Insurance	109 00
	Harry Arena, loam for tank lot	104 00
	George Campbell, gasoline and repairs	92 71
0 00	Warren Woodward, insurance	90 26
5 00	A. Culver Co., Coal and Kerosene	90 00
5 00	William Condon, gravel and use of truck WPA	81 20
4 64	McAuliffe & Burke Co., pipe and fittings	75 36
2 97	L. P. Brown Machine & Tool Co., hydrant valves	74 00
1 56	Bradford Weston Inc., patching material and stone	68 79
00	R. C. Sullivan Co., pipe and couplings	65 17
38	John C. Moore Corp., supplies	61 27
	Neponset Valve Co., hydrant valves	55 50
00	Henry Roache, gravel for tank lot	52 55
02	Sears, Roebuck Co., supplies	51 36
00	Hallamore Machine Co., repairs to hydrants	51 23
93	Brockton Edison Co., service	50 64
92	O. M. Scott, grass seed for tank lot	49 50
00	Mathew O'Grady, labor	49 40
00	George C. Cleaves Jr., sharpening bits	49 08
00	National Foundry Inc., meter covers and rings	47 27
77	Whitehead Metal Products Co., Washers and screws for meters	41 23
04	Dennis O'Connor, insurance	41 15
93	Pittsburgh Testing Laboratory, testing cement	36 00
52	Warren Pipe Co., pipe	34 64
09	Damon Electric, electrical work	33 47
73	P. I. Perkins Co., repairs to compressor	31 76
40	Rockland Standard Publishing Co., printing	31 00
	Douglas Print, printing	30 55

Joseph Sullivan, labor	30 15
C. A. Baker, acetylene gas	29 71
Thompson Durkee Co., brass pipe	29 69
L. Josselyn & Son, laquer and thinner —	27 74
W. J. Dunn Co., rock busters	26 00
H. & B. Machine Co., meter castings	25 35
Francis Geogan, examination of title for tank	25 00
Dunlop Tire Co., tires and tubes for truck	24 83
Hedge & Mathews Co., use of pump	24 50
Gulf Oil Corp., oil	23 86
Parker Danner Co., hammers and hose	21 84
M. F. Ellis Co., rakes	20 58
Hydraulic Developement Corp., hydrotite	20 00
Cambridge Machine & Tool Co., valve	20. 00
Hall & Torrey Co., supplies	19 28
Ingersoll Rand Co., bits for compressor	18 60
Patrick Mahoney, use of truck WPA	17 94
Tovia Jarvinin, use of truck WPA	17 94
Crosby Steam Gage & Valve Co., gages for standpipe	17 92
Charles McGonnigle, labor	17 44
Handlan Inc., Lanterns and globes	16 22
George Caldwell & Co., couplings	15 87
Westinghouse Electric & Mfg. Co., repairs to motor	15 75
Rockland Paint & Hardware, supplies	15 05
Waldo Brothers Co., tile	14 11
Underwood Elliot Fisher Co., repairs to billing machine	13 70
Oaktite Products Co., compound for painting meters	13 58
George N. Beal, repairs and supplies	11 18
P. F. MacDonald Co., supplies	11 04
Chase, Parker Co., supplies	10 37
Old Colony Asphalt & Cement Co., asphalt	10 35
Banker & Tradesman, magazine	10 00
Raymond Martel, chuck and switch	10 00
Jenkins and Simmons, express	9 20

Taunton Lumber Co., cement for tank project PWA	9	00
Ward Stationers, supplies	8	84
Crawford's Service Station, gas and supplies	8	69
A. J. Vargus, batteries and supplies	8	00
John Roth Transportation Co., express	7	76
L. Richmond & Co., supplies	7	27
West Side Grocery, wood and charcoal	7	00
Weymouth Water Department, labor on North ave.	6	96
Old Colony Gas Co., gas	6	82
Pittsburgh Equitable Meter Co., meter parts	6	61
Brown Instrument Co., charts	6	32
N. Y. N. H. & H. R.R., freight	5	39
Indian Head Washer Co., leather washers for meters	5	29
Equipment Co., parts for pump	5	20
Rome Brothers, supplies	5	00
Rockland Transportation Co., express	4	75
Accord Chemical Co., tetrachloride	4	70
National Boston Lead Co., lead	4	15
Burton Finnegan, printing	4	15
Serafino Gentile, dynamiting	3	75
Arthur Casey, use of truck WPA	3	07
Manifold Supply Co., supplies	3	00
Water Works Engineering, magazine	3	00
New England Tool & Steel Co., hammer and handles	3	00
Chandler & Farquhar Co., supplies	2	90
Edwin Shutt, labor	2	88
Thomas Walsh, sharpening picks	2	40
Minneapolis Honeywell Co., supplies	2	24
Bramon Dow Co., oil cans	2	11
Fuller Brush Co., broom	1	99
Paul Nolan, labor	1	92
Frank Bauer, repairs on wrenches	1	80
Blake & Rebhan Co., supplies	1	60
A. S. Peterson, supplies	1	55
J. E. Burns, ribbon	1	00
R. E. Pilling, sighting level	1	00

H. H. Arnold, steel	73
Lamb's Store, supplies	60
N. E. Transportation Co., express	50
Estes Auto Supply Co., paint sprayer	50
C. W. Briggs, file	50
Fred Delay, hydrochloric acid	40
Peerless Motor Express Co., express	35
Western Auto Store, gaskets	20

$19 438 78

½ Joint Works Expense   5 208 63

$24 646 41

Accepted:

SAMUEL W. BAKER,
EVERETT S. DAMON,
RALPH FUCILLO,

Board of Water Commissioners
Town of Rockland

ANNUAL REPORT

OF THE

SCHOOL DEPARTMENT

OF THE

TOWN OF ROCKLAND

For the Year Ending
December 31, 1938

SCHOOL CALENDAR FOR YEAR 1938 - 1939

FALL TERM

Begins Wednesday, September 7, 1938, sixteen weeks; ends Friday, December 23, 1938.

WINTER TERM

Begins Tuesday, January 3, 1939, seven weeks; ends Friday, February 17, 1939.

SPRING TERM

Begins Monday, February 27, 1939, seven weeks; ends Friday, April 14, 1939.

SUMMER TERM

Begins Monday, April 24, 1939, nine weeks; ends Monday, June 19, 1939. Teachers return Tuesday and Wednesday, June 20 and 21, for year-end duties and organization work.

FALL TERM

Begins Wednesday, September 6, 1939, sixteen weeks; ends Friday, December 22, 1939.

HOLIDAYS

October 12, 1938, Columbus Day.
October 28, 1938, Teachers' Convention.
November 11, 1938 Armistice Day.
November 23, 1938, Schools close at noon for remainder of week, Thanksgiving Recess.
April 7, 1939, Good Friday.
May 30, 1939, Memorial Day.

SIGNALS FOR NO SESSIONS OF SCHOOL

Fire Station Siren

A. M.

7:30 - 2 2 repeated: No session of High School.

8:15 - 2 2 repeated: No forenoon session for first six grades.

P. M.

12:45 - 2 2 repeated: No afternoon session for first six grades.

■ The "No School Signal" is used only in extremely stormy weather. The school bus starts on its first trip in the morning ten minutes after seven o'clock in order to collect the children in time for the opening of high school at 8:30 A. M. and the elementary schools at 9:00 A. M. Unless the signal is used before 7:00 o'clock many of the children are already on their way by bus. It is very difficult to determine weather conditions for the day as early as seven o'clock except in cases of severe storms.

People in the outskirts of our town often cannot hear the signal, in which case children appearing in school are disappointed to learn that they must cover the long distance back to their homes, while they may be chilled or wet.

We wish each parent to use his or her best judgment as to whether or not the weather is auspicious for sending their children to school. No penalty is inflicted upon any child for non-attendance on account of severe weather.

Since our teachers are in school and many of the pupils do not hear the signal, it seems wise to use the time to good advantage in warm buildings, whereas during days when the signal may be used many children are out of doors, becoming wet and contracting colds.

Is it not wiser to have them in warm school rooms under supervision, receiving beneficial instruction?

R. STEWART ESTEN,
Superintendent of Schools

January 1, 1939.

School Directory 1938 - 1939

SCHOOL COMMITTEE

DR. BENJAMIN LELYVELD, Chairman   Reed Street
Tel. 16-W. Term expires March, 1940.

MRS. HELEN M. HAYDEN, Secretary 429 Liberty Street
Tel. 454-R. Term expires March, 1939.

DR. WILLIAM A. LOUD   327 Salem Street
Tel. 430. Term expires March, 1940.

MISS M. AGNES KELLEHER   297 Howard Street
Tel. 1484-W. Term expires March, 1941.

DANA S. COLLINS   425 Liberty Street
Tel. 55. Term expires March, 1941.

SUPERINTENDENT OF SCHOOLS

R. STEWART ESTEN   111 Payson Avenue
Office Tel. 1540. Residence Tel. 1250
Office hours every school day from 8:30 to 9:00 A. M. on
Wednesday evenings from 7:00 to 8:00 o'clock.

SCHOOL DEPARTMENT SECRETARY

HARRIET E. GELINAS   241 Myrtle Street
Office Tel. 1540. Residence Tel. 1244

PRINCIPAL OF HIGH SCHOOL

GEORGE A. J. FROBERGER   28 Exchange Street
Office Tel. 1540. Residence Tel. 1302-W

Office hours every school day from 8 to 9 A. M., Mondays
and Thursdays from 3 to 4 P. M. and Wednesday
evenings from 7 to 8 o'clock.

ATTENDANCE OFFICER AND SCHOOL NURSE

LOUISE A. CONSIDINE   69 Webster Street
Office Tel. 1540.
Office hours at the high school every school day from
8:30 to 9:30 A. M.

SCHOOL PHYSICIANS

JOSEPH H. DUNN, M. D.   319 Union Street
Office Tel. 836-W   Residence Tel. 836-R
Office Hours: 2 to 3 and 7 to 8 P. M.

JOSEPH FRAME, M. D.   114 Webster Street
Office Tel. 38-W
Office Hours: 12:30 to 2 and 6:30 to 8 P. M.

DENTAL HYGIENIST

EVELYN DELORY   323 Market Street
Office hours at the McKinley School daily when schools
are in session from 9:00 A. M. to 12 M., and from
1:30 to 3:30 P. M.

DIGEST OF LAWS AND REGULATIONS RELATING
TO SCHOOL ATTENDANCE

Children who are five years and six months of age by the opening of school in September 1939 shall be admitted to the first grade. Those who become five years of age after March 1, 1939, may be admitted after passing a satisfactory mental examination.

Children, otherwise eligible to enter school in September for the first time, are required by law to present at time of entrance either a certificate of vaccination or a certificate of unfitness for vaccination. The school committee and board of health have ruled that certificates of unfitness for vaccination must be renewed each year. Children coming into the school system from other places, whether at the opening of the year in September or during the school year, will be required to produce satisfactory evidence regarding vaccination.

Pupils desiring to enter the first grade must enroll on or before October 1. Otherwise, they will not be admitted.

The school hours for the first grade children, shall be from 9 until 11:30 A. M. The afternoon session shall correspond with other grades, 1:30 P. M. until 3:30 P. M. The ruling, took effect March 6, 1933. An exception is made during the winter months when the afternoon session of the elementary schools concludes at 3:15 P. M. The school hours for the junior-senior high school pupils shall be from 8:30 A. M. until 2:00 P. M.

Pupils who have been absent from school on account of contagious disease must secure a permit from a school physician before re-entering. In cases of doubt, or in cases where there exists a suspicion of contagion, the parents should advise, and the teachers should require that the pupils consult the school nurse, who may refer the case to a school physician for further examination.

Any pupil having a contagious disease or showing symptoms of such a disease may be temporarily excluded from school by the teacher on her own initiative or at the direction of the school nurse or school physician.

Sickness is the only legal excuse for absence from school.

All children between the ages of fourteen and sixteen years must be in school unless they are actually employed under the authority of an employment certificate, a home permit or a special certificate permitting farm or domestic employment.

Any pupil who habitually violates rules of the schools, or otherwise seriously interferes with the proper and orderly operation of the school which he attends, may be temporarily excluded by the teacher or the superintendent of schools or may be permanently expelled by the school committee.

Pupils under seven years of age or over sixteen who elect to attend school must conform to the same rules and regulations as those pupils who are within the compulsory age — from seven to fourteen.

Teachers may require a written excuse signed by a parent or guardian covering any case of absence, tardiness or dismissal.

Whenever a pupil is suspended by a teacher or principal, for any cause for any length of time, an immediate report must be made to the superintendent's office.

Those pupils attending the first eight grades will be transported to and from school if they live in the town of Rockland and reside more than one mile and a quarter from the school where they are authorized to attend.

Those pupils attending the high school, grades nine to twelve, inclusive, will be transported to and from school if they live in the town of Rockland and reside more than two miles from the high school.

Recent Rulings Pertaining to Our Schools

Voted to use the high school building for those activitties which pertain to school work or those carrying on functions for the interest of the schools.

There shall be a Supervisor of Buildings who shall represent the School Committee in charge of all school buildings when they are used by outside organizations (other than school organizations.)

The Supervisor's duties shall be to prevent any damage to school property and to be responsible for proper conduct in and on school property. (Prevent smoking, drinking and unbecoming conduct in the buildings.)

The organization using the building shall be responsible for the expense of such a supervisor.

The supervisor shall receive his instructions from the Superintendent of Schools.

The supervisor shall receive remuneration at the rate of $2.50 until 10:30 P. M., $4.00 if the function continues until 11:30 P. M.; $5.00 after 11:30 P. M.; 75 per hour will be the charge for the building if used before 6:00 P. M. This ruling took effect December 1, 1934.

All work performed by the School Committee shall be

awarded to native born citizens, naturalized citizens, or those who have taken out their first naturalization papers.

The tuition for pupils whose parents reside out of town and wishing to attend the Rockland Schools shall be established as follows: Senior High $100 per year; Junior High $80; elementary grades, $60.

Post-Graduates who are admitted to the Rockland High School, September 4, 1935 or thereafter, shall take a minimum of twenty hours of work per week; shall be satisfactory in conduct; shall be regular in full day's attendance and maintain satisfactory averages in all subjects.

Rulings Regarding Payment of Salaries to Teachers

The teachers of the Rockland Schools shall receive their salaries bi-weekly after two weeks of actual class room teaching—except through July and August when payments shall be made not later than the 15th of each month.

That for each day's absence with the exception of death in the immediate family 1/200 of the yearly salary shall be deducted.

That beginning November 16, 1937, all teachers who are absent on account of illness shall receive the difference between the substitute's pay or its equivalent and the teacher's regular pay.

That a teacher shall receive full pay for five calendar days for death in immediate family. "Immediate" family includes parents, wife, husband, brother, sister or children.

That a teacher absent for more than one half (½) of a session shall lose pay for that entire session.

Visiting schools authorized by the Superintendent of Schools or work pertaining to the schools which has been assigned by the Superintendent may be allowed without loss of salary.

The word "Teacher" in the above ruling applies to Principals, Special Teachers and all class room teachers excepting the Principal of the Junior-Senior High school and the Superintendent of Schools.

REPORT OF ROCKLAND SCHOOL COMMITTEE

To the Citizens of Rockland:

Your School Committee has endeavored to administer the Rockland Schools as economically as possible. We fully realize our obligation in this respect to the taxpayers. We also feel strongly the responsibility placed upon us for the adequate education of our children, for in the final analysis we operate our schools for their benefit.

It has been a source of pleasure to us that the finance committee and the citizens of the town have cooperated in doing all in their power to maintain the schools at a high level.

We are grateful for the fact that sufficient funds were granted us, so that with the utmost economy in other expenditures, we have been able to put into effect a salary schedule embracing all the teachers in our system. We believe this to be a step forward.

The committee is indebted to all organizations and citizens who have contributed their time, effort and money so that pupils might benefit.

We recommend that you read the detailed reports for a complete accounting of our administration.

Again we wish to point out the fine work done by the Superintendent of Schools, the principals, teachers and other school employees. The efforts of this fine group of public servants is the reason for our system maintaining its efficiency.

Respectfully submitted,

ROCKLAND SCHOOL COMMITTEE,
BENJAMIN LELYVELD, Chairman
HELEN M. HAYDEN, Secretary
WILLIAM A. LOUD
M. AGNES KELLEHER
DANA S. COLLINS

FINANCIAL STATEMENT
RESOURCES 1938

General Appropriation $104 373.00

EXPENDITURES

General Expenses	$ 5 102 49
Expense of Instruction	75 974 31
Operation and Maintenance	17 492 56
Auxiliary Agencies	5 200 13
New Equipment	602 84

Total Expenditures $104 372 33

TOWN TREASURER'S RECEIPTS ON ACCOUNT OF SCHOOLS

State Reimbursements:	
Teachers' Salaries	$10 015 00
Tuition and Transportation of Wards	1 143 22
City of Boston for Tuition and Transportation of Wards	563 74
Tuition, Mrs. C. W. Scott	45 00
Materials sold in High School shop	20 65

Total Receipts $ 11 787 61

Net Cost of Schools to Town $92 584 72

RENTAL OF McKINLEY HALL AND SENIOR HIGH GYMNASIUM

Town Appropriation to offset expenses $150 00

Receipts (turned over to town treasurer) 102 00
Expenditures:

Old Colony Gas Company	$ 7 04
J. J. L. DeCosta	21 50
Brockton Edison Company	72 43

Total Expenditures   100 97
                                             ———— $100 97

Balance   1 03
Unexpended Appropriation $49 03

APPROPRIATION TO OFFSET EXPENSE OF W. P. A. PROJECTS HOUSED AT McKINLEY SCHOOL

Appropriation $ 400 00
Expenditures:

Brockton Edison Company	98 56
Albert Culver Company	297 67

Total Expenditures $ 396 23

Unexpended Appropriation $ 3 77

DETAIL OF 1938 EXPENDITURES

Total Resources $104 373 00

GENERAL EXPENSES

Superintendent's Salary	$3 600 00
Other Administrative Expense	1 502 49

EXPENSE OF INSTRUCTION

Supervisors' Salaries	$ 3 162 12
Principals' Salaries	7 096 56
Teachers' Salaries	61 397 03
Text Books	1 778 02
Stationery, Supplies and Miscellaneous	2 540 58

OPERATION AND MAINTENANCE

Janitors' Wages	8 272 04
Fuel	3 946 25
Miscellaneous	2 280 42
Repairs	2 993 85

AUXILIARY AGENCIES

Libraries	52 88
Health	1 898 27
Transportation	1 515 00
Sundries	1 733 98

OUTLAY

New Equipment	602 84
Total Expenditures	$104 372 33
Unexpended Balance	67

FINANCIAL STATEMENT ITEMIZED

SUPERINTENDENT OF SCHOOLS

R. Stewart Esten, Salary	$3 600 00	
		$3 600 00

OTHER ADMINISTRATIVE EXPENSES

Bruce Publishing Co., School Board Journal	$ 6 00
Louise A. Considine, mileage attendance officer	95 49
The Education Digest, Subscription	3 50
Harriet E. Gelinas, salary	1 192 00
John C. Moore Corp., bkkg forms	3 19
N. E. Tel. & Tel. Company, service	109 86

John R. Parker, P. M., envelopes, stamps, cards	75 52
Quincy Visual Projection Co., cans for films	2 40
A. I. Randall, Inc., purchase order books	12 45
Wright & Potter Printing Co., ledger blanks	2 08

Total	$ 1 502 49

EXPENSE OF INSTRUCTION

Supervisors' Salaries	$ 3 162 12
Principals' Salaries	7 096 56
Teachers' Salaries	61 397 03

TEXT BOOKS

American Book Co.	$ 142 76
Arlo Publishing Co.	2 56
American Education Press	2 23
Allyn & Bacon	31 27
The Bobbs-Merrill Co.	21 63
C. C. Birchard Co.	2 50
Bellman Publishing Co.	5 15
Beckley-Cardy Co.	73 95
Edward E. Babb Co., Inc.	25 84
College Entrance Book Co.	11 92
Circle Book Co.	10 36
Dodd, Mead & Co.	3 07
Gregg Publishing Co.	93 47
Ginn & Company	361 72
Houghton Mifflin Co.	147 55
D, C. Heath & Co.	228 08
Harcourt Brace & Co., Inc.	44 01
Informative Classroom Picture Association	4 07
Little Brown & Co.	2 72

M. H. Lewis, Publisher		75
McKnight & McKnight	8	15
Milton Bradley Co.	7	15
Charles E. Merrill Co.	33	92
The MacMillan Co.	103	76
Noble & Noble	4	99
The National Education Association	2	04
The New England News Company	1	90
Thomas Nelson & Son	6	90
F. A. Owen Publishing Co.	10	64
The A. N. Palmer Co.	1	41
Row, Peterson & Co.	33	79
Rand McNally Co.	20	97
The L. W. Singer Co.	1	80
Silver Burdett Co.	50	16
Charles Scribner's Sons	31	51
Scott, Foresman & Co.	99	28
Benj. H. Sanborn & Co.	85	84
O. H. Toothaker	1	26
World Book Co.	2	48
John C. Winston Co.	40	24
Webster Publishing Co.	9	10
The Welles Publishing Co.	5	12

Total $ 1 778 02

SUPPLIES

Automatic Pencil Sharpener Co., blades	$	4 64
The Astrup Co., muslin for stage scenery		13 05
American Type Founders Sales Corp., ink		3 00
Bureau of Publications, tests		10 19
Buck Printing Co., tickets for senior prom		6 37
Brodhead-Garrett Co., materials for manual training		164 53

Boston Music Co., music   51 84
Beaudette & Co., printing guide   3 60
Bates Mfg. Co., wire staples   1 52
E. E. Babb & Co., Inc., schoolroom
  supplies   144 95
Cooperative Test Service, tests   25 04
J. R. Clancy, Inc., materials for
  stage scenery   41 04
Circle Book Co., student assignment
  books   19 36
John S. Cheever Co., schoolroom
  supplies   481 06
Century Laboratories, stencils   5 00
Central Scientific Co., science supplies 69 63´
Dowling School Supply Co.,
  schoolroom supplies   23 95
H. J. Dowd Co., Inc.,
  Schoolroom supplies   30 76
Dept. of Education, film service   15 00
Gregg Publishing Co., notebooks   12 51
Gaylord Bros., bookends, cards   18 25
J. L. Hammett Company, supplies   184 24
W. A. Hall & Son, leather remnants
  for special class   1 10
Jordan Marsh Co., Special class supplies   1 40
Kee Lox Mfg. Co., typewriter ribbons   33 00
Laidlow Bros., arithmetic tablets   1 01
H. B. McArdle, schoolroom supplies   45 74
David Morse, Special Class supplies   1 29
Milton Bradley Co., schoolroom
  supplies   326 28
Geo. M. B. Miller, gas for
  cleaning press   62
National Safety Council, subscription
  For Safety Magazine   1 75
Phillips Ribbons & Carbon Co.,
  ditto carbon   18 00
Phillips Paper Co., mimeograph paper   21 76

A. S. Peterson, schoolroom supplies	9	70
Perry Pictures, Inc., music pictures	1	30
George T. Pascoe Co., schoolroom supplies	12	54
Royal Typewriter Co., typewriter exchanged	22	50
Rome Bros., manual training supplies	20	13
Rockland Coal & Gain Co., manual training supplies	44	76
Rockland High School Cafeteria food classes	34	94
J. A. Rice Co., Special class and Sewing supplies	8	73
Remington Rand, Inc., file folders	4	08
A. I. Randall, Inc., stock for printing	10	10
South Western Publishing Co., Book-keeping supplies	92	79
O. H. Toothaker, schoolroom supplies	52	99
Underwood Elliott Fisher Co., Typewriters exchanged	110	00
World Book Company, tests	35	36
Henry S. Wolkins Co., paper	56	00
Henry J. Winde Co., manual training lumber	19	83
Percy D. Wells, cards	8	54
The Wells Publishing Co., primary drill chart	6	66
John H. Wyatt Co., schoolroom supplies	106	05
Yawman Erbe Mfg. Co., folders and file guides	14	10
Yale University Press Film Service films	30	00
L. C. Smith & Corona Typewriters, Inc., typewriters exchanged	58	00
Total	$ 2 540	58

JANITORS' WAGES

Elmer Dunn, Junior-Senior High	$1 137 34	
Charles Metivier, Junior-Senior High	1 438 32	
Andrew T. Leck, Junior-Senior High and Jefferson	1 074 68	
J. J. L. DeCosta, McKinley	1 305 00	
Mary Davis, McKinley	384 00	
Harold Morse, Jefferson	441 90	
Maurice Mullen, Gleason, Webster and McKinley	548 97	
Ardelle Cushing, Market Street	350 00	
Elizabeth Casey, Central Street	180 00	
Frank Curtis, Lincoln	1 000 00	
Henry S. Marks, Jefferson	142 50	
Frank O'Hara, Gleason and Webster Street	33 33	
Mrs. Frank Hammond, Gleason and Webster Street	236 00	
Total		$8 272 04

FUEL

Abington Coal Corp., coal	$1 252 90	
Albert Culver Co., coal	1 653 85	
Lot Phillips & Co., Inc., wood	8 00	
Rockland Coal & Grain Co., coal	1 001 50	
Daniel J. Reilly, wood	30 00	
Total		$3 946 25

MISCELLANEOUS OPERATING EXPENSES

A. P. W. Paper Company, paper towels	$ 44 00	
Bostonia Products Co., Janitors' supplies	66 50	

Boston Janitors' Supply Co., Inc.,
  miscellaneous supplies   3 30
Beacon Wiper Supply Co., two bales
  cloths for cleaning   14 88
P. & F. Corbin, keys   83
H. J. Dowd, Co., Inc., sweeping
  compound   140 99
C. B. Dolge Co., janitors' supplies   49 94
M. F. Ellis Co., janitors' supplies   8 40
Lester Edwards, labor at high school   6 88
Edison Electric Ill. Co., service   1 220 67
The Floor Treatment Co., floor
  treatment   17 50
L. M. Glover Co., floor treatment   77 03
William M. Horner, floor treatment   18 60
A. C. Horn Co., floor treatment   102 00
John H. Lamb, soap and cleaning
  powder   1 83
Carlton E. McPhee, light bulbs   18 24
Geo. M. B. Miller, gas for cleaning press   1 38
Masury Young Co., floor oil   21 35
Manufacturing Chemists, janitors'
  supplies   16 68
N. E. Tel. & Tel. Co., service   34 64
Old Colony Gas Co., service   32 69
Old Colony Gas Co., light shades   10 00
Rockland Water Department, service   262 51
Rockland Disposal Service, garbage
  removal at McKinley   25
Rockland Hardware & Paint Co.,
  Janitors' cleaning supplies   1 39
Rockland Coal & Grain Co.,
  bone meal for grounds   4 50
Robinson & Co., 12 lbs. drain solvent   2 44
The Swan Co., floor treatment   8 75
State Prison Colony, brushes   48 20
William Thorpe, installing electric
  meters at McKinley   5 00
Taunton Lumber Co., floor treatment   7 75

Union Market, cleaning materials	1 25	
Wadsworth Howland & Co., Inc.,		
floor treatment	29 25	
Hickey Bros., 2 gals. naptha	80	
Total		$2 280 42

REPAIRS

H. H. Arnold Co., belt repaired	$ 2 34	
Stanley A. Ames, repairing		
phonograph	2 50	
Abrasive Products, Inc., process		
paper	7 72	
Burroughs Adding Machine Co.,		
service contract	5 00	
Boston Plate & Window Glass Co.,		
glass	24 60	
Bloom, South & Gurney, Inc., 5 gals.		
red mastic for floors	20 35	
Chester W. Banden, repair work at		
McKinley	82 21	
E. E. Babb & Co., 100 domes		
of silence	2 60	
O. R. Cummings, plastering	79 65	
Corrosion Solvent Eng. Co.,		
McKinley and Lincoln boiler		
systems cleaned	140 00	
P. & F. Corbin, door checks		
repaired	26 71	
Elmer E. Dunn, repair work at schools	7 40	
Luther O. Draper Shade Co.,		
shade cord and pulleys replaced	18 41	
A. B. Dick Co., adjusting		
mimeograph	5 30	
Damon Electric, electrical repairs	37 97	
Thomas Fox, repairing cement walk		
at Jefferson	10 00	
Geo. W. S. Hyde, repairing		
wrenches	1 70	

Hobart & Farrell Plumbing & Heating
Co., labor on school ventilating
and heating systems   191 36
The Halsey W. Taylor Co.,
two fountain heads   17 21
Hall & Torrey, misc. repairs at
schools   184 20
Krohn & Harrington, door closers
repaired   10 15
Carlton McPhee, radio repaired   2 15
J. S. McCallum, plumbing repairs
elementary schools   312 55
Merrick Engineering Co,. labor at
McKinley School   647 00
Mass. Division of the Blind,
pianos tuned   17 00
George C. Norton, removing snow
guard at McKinley   10 00
National Foundry Co., replacing grate   4 62
Forrest L. Partch, electrical repairs   15 53
Rome Bros., materials for repairs   109 18
Harry L. Rome, curtains repaired   18 75
Rockland Welding & Engineering Co.,
chair bases repaired   22 75
Rockland Paint & Hardware Co.,
materials for repairs   30 39
Rockland Coal & Grain Co.,
materials for repairs   73 62
Roberts Numbering Machine Co.,
machine repaired   2 26
Stone Hardware Co., exit bolts repaired 35 96
Standard Electric Time Co., clocks
repaired   102 78
Sloan Valve Co., plumbing materials   6 97
Singer Sewing Machine Co., adjusting
machines   1 45
Edwin Schutt, labor and materials
for repairs   453 20

Geo. V. Tyler, cleaning pipe at Market
    Street school   5 00
Underwood Elliot Fisher Co.,
    typewriters repaired   3 03
Walworth Co., boiler repairs, grate
    rest and bars   195 48
Yale & Towne Mfg Co., liquid
    overhauling refinishing   3 25
Johnson Service Co., adjusting
    thermostats   22 15
Howard E. Bailey, Engineering
    services McKinley School   21 40

       Total $2 993 85

LIBRARIES

Bellman Publishing Co., book $ 3 15
Globe Book Co., book   1 23
McGraw Hill Book Co., book   2 51
Albert Najarian, magazine
    subscriptions   22 00
Vita Specialties Co., magazine covers   13 24
Wilcox & Follett Co., set of ten
    books with globe   10 75

       Total $ 52 88

HEALTH

Louise A. Considine, mileage   95 56
Louise A. Considine, salary   1 416 64
National Education Association,
    class room growth charts   1 07
Rockland Pharmacy, health supplies   22 52
Rockland New System Laundry,
    blankets laundered   1 12
Thomas W. Reed Co., tongue depressors   9 36
Plymouth County Health Association,
    audiometer rental   2 00

Joseph H. Dunn, M. D., salary	175 00	
Joseph H. Frame, M. D., salary	175 00	
Total		$1 898 27

TRANSPORTATION

Howland's Insurance Office, bonds	30 00	
John J. Dwyer, transportation of pupils	1 485 00	
Total		$1 515 00

SUNDRIES

F. J. Barnard Co., rebinding books	$ 57 15
Babson's Statistical Organization, poster service	15 85
Howard E. Bailey, engineering services	175 00
Commissioner of Public Safety, boiler inspection	5 00
Philip S. Collins, insurance	271 87
Douglas Print, high school handbooks	71 96
Everett S. Damon, insurance	85 60
Howland's Ins. Office, insurance	22 80
J. L. Hammett Co., diplomas and covers	76 76
Jenkins & Simmons Express, expressage	23 25
Edward A. Lincoln, administering first grade tests	93 00
Murray Bros., rebinding books	59 10
Maurice Mullen, police service	5 50
N. Y., N. H. & Hartford R. R., freight charges	3 55
James F. O'Connor, insurance	59 84
Pro Merito Society, pins	16 25
Amos A Phelps & Son, insurance	458 14

Rockland Transportation Co.,
  expressage   2 85
Rockland Standard Publishing Co.,
  school reports   65 40
A. I. Randall, Inc., exit signs   2 90
Warren B. Woodward, insurance   96 46
Bernard Carey, census   65 75

    Total $1 733 98

NEW EQUIPMENT

Stanley R. Ames, payment toward
  amplifier for high school $20 00
Mrs. Clarence Bell, extension ladder   7 50
Damon Electric, installing fire alarm
  system in McKinley, Gleason, Lincoln
  and Market Street schools   358 90
Forsberg Electric Co., four holophane
  units   35 88
Jason's phonograph   19 75
Milton Bradley Co., chairs   45 00
Mahoney Chair Co., clamps for
  auditorium seats and intersection
  fasteners   45 00
Yawman & Erbe Mfg. Co.,
  wardrobe and desk tray   41 50
Rockland Coal & Grain Co.,
  lumber for book cases   29 31

    Total $ 602 84

REPORT OF SUPERINTENDENT OF SCHOOLS

To the School Committee of Rockland:

The tenth annual report of my work as Superintendent of Schools is submitted:

To minimize printing expenses, we are presenting the reports of the Superintendent and the High School Principal, along with statistical data, but these reports include general accomplishments and needs of all departments in the entire school system.

The economic situation must be paramount in determining school policies during this chaotic period through which we are passing. An honest effort is being made to reduce the cost of education to a minimum and still maintain a high degree of efficiency commensurate with the expenditure of money until such time as additional funds are vailable.

Our rating as to cost per pupil for education is reported by the Massachusetts State Department of Education (November 1938) as continuing to be seventy-first in our group of eight-three towns. Only twelve of the eighty-three towns spend less per pupil than we do in Rockland. The cost per pupil in our town is $70.20.

DEVELOPMENT OF PROJECTS

The outcome of the professional meetings held the past year in which we discussed the "Superior Teacher" culminated in the formulation of a Code of Ten teacher Tenets for Professional Progress which was distributed to each teacher at the teachers' opening meeting in September. The Code follows:

1. PERSONALITY: The superior teacher dresses appropriately; has excellent posture and carriage; speaks clearly with modulated voice; has poise and confidence.

2. Habits: The superior teacher establishes habits in health conservation, sustained effort, observance of school regulations and obligations.

3. CO-OPERATION: The superior teacher gets the viewpoint of pupil and parent; gains the respect and confidence of the pupil; strives to understand the child's capacity to learn.

4. EQUIPMENT: The superior teacher knows the subject matter; has enthusiasm, patience, adaptability and sympathetic understanding.

5. ATTITUDE: The superior teacher honors his profession; has confidence in his ability; is interested in the welfare of the community which he serves.

6. CULTURE: The superior teacher enriches his experience through advanced study, intelligent social contacts, and travel.

7. CHARACTER: The superior teacher is dependable, courteous, kind, honest and fair.

8. TECHNIQUE: The superior teacher is orderly; has detailed plans; uses helpful methods and devices; approaches new material through the pupils' understanding; has firm discipline; is a friendly adviser.

9. RELATIONS: The superior teacher is a personal friend and counselor to each pupil; inspires the pupil to creative work. He participates in school activities; is loyal to the administration of which he is a valued member; willingly accepts resposibilities as opportunity for professional growth.

10. ACHIEVEMENT: The superior teacher awakens the pupils' active interest in better health, habits of honor and industry, creative activities, and the development of responsible citizenship.

Since the September meeting we have had two outstanding speakers and discussions on fundamental school problems. Dr. Lura Oak of the State Department of Public Health spoke on "The Modern Eye Test in Relation to Other Diagnostic Measures Used in Studying the Reading Problem." Dr. Oak's wide experience and experiments in the field of reading presented many helpful suggestions to teachers both in the elementary grades and high school to assist in diagnosing reading difficulties. The question and answer period proved beneficial to our teachers.

Another vital topic discussed by Mrs. T. Grafton Abbott, Consultant in Parent Education in the Division of Child Hygiene of the State Department of Public Health was "Understanding Human Behavior." A general invitation to the public was presented through the local press. Mrs. Abbott, a very fluent, versatile speaker, who is both a parent and teacher gave a practical discussion of the topic. An expression of opinion on the part of the teachers indicated the effectiveness of these meetings.

DEVELOPMENT OF PROJECTS

JUNIOR RED CROSS

The Junior Red Cross has re-established itself in our elementary schools under the very efficient direction of the town representative, Mrs. Esther Rawson, ably assisted by a teachers committee. The matter was discussed at a teachers' meeting and the consensus of opinion was that we should assist in whatever ways possible by sponsoring activities to render aid to children who needed help to remedy physical defects, requiring teeth repair, tonsil and adenoid removals. In addition to these services the money raised by this organization has been used to purchase shoes, rubbers and an occasional pair of eye glasses for pupils whose economic status would not permit these necessities. The money to finance this program has been raised by the voluntary contributions of pupils who have placed their donations in Red Cross boxes placed in each room with the "Red Cross Lady" Mrs. Rawson, making monthly collections. Some of the buildings sponsored an afternoon health program followed by a tea which raised several dollars for this program. The chief source of money supply came from the receipts received through a "Style Show" presented under the auspices of the Red. Cross Committee by the pupils in the elementary schools. The entertainment was held in the high school auditorium in the fall and was well supported by the public. We are very grateful to Ferber's Specialty Shoppe in town for furnishing the garments and equipment used in the "Style Show." These activities to raise money for the Junior Red Cross are essential in order that the organization may be self-supporting. The chairman of the School Red Cross Committee is to be highly complimented for her earnest and efficient efforts in the work of her committee members and their activities.

MUSIC DEPARTMENT

This past year a somewhat new departure from the usual procedure in this department was attempted by correlating the music with other Social Studies. This has stimulated interest and enthusiasm for both subjects and we believe it will continue. Some new music textbooks were placed in the second grades and we hope that additional books will be forth coming. Our Supervisor of Vocal music is preparing a New Course of Study in Music which will be presented later.

MILK FUND PROJECT

We are indeed grateful to the Rockland Kiwanis Club

for their interest in sponsoring the milk fund which has made it possible for 181 children in our schools to receive a half pint of pasteurized milk along with two graham crackers daily while schools are in session for a period of ninety-three days from November 15, 1937 until April 14, 1938. Those who received this luncheon were the boys and girls of parents who financially were unable to furnish this food to their children. Our weight charts which are posted in each room have proved conclusively that these pupils have benefited greatly from this service. The teachers in our schools assisted the Kiwanis Club in sponsoring the "Movie Queen," to raise money for the milk fund. Through the efforts of the committee assisted by the club members and other interested citizens the function was very successful and resulted in raising six hundred dollars for the fund. The good that is being accomplished by the milk fund from the health standpoint is very much worthwhile and should be continued.

GROUP PIANO LESSONS

We have continued to encourage and provide in our program for group piano lessons although the cost of this specialized program is borne by the parents as no funds in the school budget are available. Miss Maude F. Burnham of Taunton is the instructor in these group lessons which are presented in the Lincoln and McKinley buildings. Miss Burnham has had excellent training at Lasell and Boston University. The course is designed to afford parents an opportunity to ascertain their children's talent in order to determine the advisability of more advanced music training. Also, it teaches the rudiments of piano music and how to play the easier grade selections. The lessons are given in groups and are not intended to take the place of private instruction. Miss Burnham has presented the past two years in June a recital of the work accomplished in her classes. Several parents have spoken with enthusiasm concerning her work with their children.

SCHOOL LIBRARY

The library in our high school has been greatly improved since the books have been recatalogued, additional shelves installed and a system of student librarians introduced. We are grateful to the alumni of our school for the generous contribution of books which they have presented to the high school. Although, with student help we are able to use our library more effectively than before, it is quite essential to have a trained librarian who can give instruction to our pupils on the use and choice of books.

It is hoped that when an additional teacher is added to our staff she may be one who can give some assistance in our library. Those pupils who graduate from our high school are handicapped in going to institutions of higher learning if they have not had instruction in the proper use of books and library methods.

ELIMINATING SCHOOL FAILURES

Whenever a child is not promoted to the next higher grade or in the high school fails in one or more subjects, the cost of educating that pupil increases. Besides the additional cost the personality of the child may be warped by repetition of the work. It is therefore highly desirable that each pupil be carefully placed in order to avoid as many failures as possible. Each child ought to be allowed to progress continually and at a speed normal to him. We are attempting to eliminate school failures as much as possible by the use of a number of different types of tests which may be given individually or in a group, in an attempt to adjust that school work to the mental capacity and achievement of the individual child. The use of these tests of mental ability, achievement, and aptitude tends to clear up many misunderstandings regarding individual children. A given pupil who is doing only fair school work may be shown by the tests to have only fair ability or to be exceptionally brilliant. After interpreting the test results, an attempt is made to discover the specific causes of school failure and to begin a remedial program based on these findings. In no case can the teacher cope with the problem adequately unless she has a knowledge of the facts made available from test results obtained in a scientific manner.

Many times a pupil who is doing unsatisfactory academic work in the Junior High and is therefore more or less a behavior problem shows himself superior in the mechanical line. The past few years this situation has caused our enrolment to increase rapidly in the Weymouth, Quincy and Boston Vocational Schools as we are not able to provide similar training in our high school because of the expensive equipment and additional teaching force which would be necessary. Half of the expense for such training is borne by the town and the other half by the State. In general it is found that some pupils do certain things better than others. They may have abilities in certain fields of endeavor. The school attempts to discover these abilities and to develop them to the best advantage of society and the individual child.

HIGH SCHOOL

It is indeed encouraging to know that the morale in our high school is improving and one can see evidences of responsiveness in our pupils as it grows from year to year. The credit for this improvement goes to the teachers, to the pupils and the principal whose leadership has been intelligent, aggressive and on a high plane.

We are very much concerned about these pupils who are graduating from our high school and who are unable to go on to college because of financial inability or because of scholastic reasons. Industry does not seem to be able at present to absorb them, so many of these pupils find themselves unemployed. Our post-graduate students have increased in numbers the past few years and possibly the solution to this problem will be the establishment of a 13th year. Whenever that is done a planned program of studies for the year should be offered which will parallel the first year's training of a Junior College. In some parts of the country, notably in California there have been established a large number of public junior colleges which extend the work of the high school, two years.

WORKS PROGRESS ADMINISTRATION ACT AS IT AFFECTS SCHOOLS

We have continued our plan of cooperation with the town officials and the federal government in providing suitable quarters for the Recreation and the Sewing Projects of the W. P. A. in the McKinley School Building. Although the citizens of the town in their annual meeting have raised and appropriated $400 to help defray the additional expense of opening the building for these projects the past two years money must also be taken from the school budget to meet this expense.

We have availed ourselves again this year of the opportunity of the National Youth Administration as it operates in schools and colleges throughout the United States. Our quota in Rockland since the opening of schools in September is set at $72.00 per month. We have at present eight high school girls and four boys who are receiving this financial aid of $6.00 per month for which each renders twenty hours of services to our schools. The assistance is clerical or janitor service. The money is given by the government to assist them in paying for school lunches or to purchase necessary clothing in order to continue their attendance in high school.

NURSERY SCHOOL

The Nursery School authorized by the Works Progress Administration has continued to operate throughout the year at the McKinley School. The sessions are held in the gymnasium of that building. The enrolment comprises children from three to five years of age whose parents are on W. P. A. or low income. The unit includes two teachers and a cook. The federal government pays the wages of the employees, the Town and the School Department handle the other expenses of the project. We have twenty-six enrolled at present with an average attendance of twenty-two. The session of the school is from 9:15 A. M. until 2:00 P. M. with a noon luncheon. This project where children are systematically trained and cared for has proved beneficial to both pupils and community.

TEACHER REPLACEMENT

In August of this year Miss Marguerite Croak, for the past five years head of our Commercial Department resigned to be married. Her place as a teacher in the department has been taken by Miss Helen M. Miley of Winchester, Massachusetts. She is a graduate of Boston University with the degree of Master in Education. Miss Miley had two years of teaching experience in New Hampshire before entering our service. The past three summers she has been a Girl Scout leader in a New Hampshire camp.

Miss Constance Tobey resigned in December to be married. She has taught Sewing in the Junior High and Social Science in the Senior High. This combination of subjects is rather unusual and it has been difficult to find a qualified candidate for this opening. At present Miss Marion T. Hall of Morrisville, Vermont, a graduate of the University of Vermont is handling Miss Tobey's classes as a substitute teacher.

During the summer months Miss Isabel Philbrook, our special class teacher resigned to accept a similar position in her home town of Randolph. Her place was filled by the appointment of Miss Rita Kennedy of Newtonville,

Massachusetts. Miss Kennedy graduated from the Salem State Teachers' College and has had a year's experience in special class work in Kingston, Massachusetts.

Miss Helen Kovalchuk, resigned her position as teacher in the upper room at the Gleason School in October. Her place was taken by Miss Catherine M. Reilly of Salem Street, Rockland, a graduate of our local schools and the State Teachers' College in Bridgewater 1936. Miss Reilly had been a teacher in our Nursery school in Rockland for several months and had cadet teaching experience in the Abington grades I-VI.

Miss- Marion Whiting, our Art Supervisor the past eight years resigned in February to accept a teaching position in her home city, Chelsea, Massachusetts. Her place was taken by Miss Eleanor Costa of Revere who had several months of substitute teaching in the Revere High School. Miss Costa was a graduate of Boston University. In October Miss Costa was appointed to a teaching position in the Revere Junior High School and her position as Art Supervisor was filled by the appointment of Miss Nora van der Groen of Needham, Massachusetts. Miss van der Groen, a graduate of Boston University and the Amsterdam Art School had previously supervised art in Grades 1-6 in Needham.

SCHOOL BUILDINGS AND GROUNDS

JUNIOR SENIOR HIGH

Since my last report the drainage system for the high school in accordance with plans outlined by the Special Committee appointed by the town at its March meeting 1936 has been completed. It is my understanding that the sewage line has been hooked into the pipe line carrying the surface water and thus to the seepage bed rather than conducting the sewage line directly to seepage bed apart from the pipe line carrying the surface water as or-, iginally planned by the Special Committee.

In May we received a report from the State Department of Public Safety through the State Building Inspector requiring certain changes and repairs in our school buildings in accordance with Chapter 143 of the General Laws. Several of the requirements necessitated a substantial expenditure of money. The important changes in the Junior Senior High were as follows:

1. Doors in stair towers to open into stair towers.
2. All chairs in auditorium to be secured in place by providing chair clamps.
3. Removal of inflammable scenery.
4. Provide pilot light gas mantles in auditorium lighting system.
5. Provide self-closing device on boiler room door.

The mastic floors in the corridors and toilets have been repaired by our janitors and all wooden floors refinished. Due to the great amount of water which has entered the building since its construction, the window shades have been soaked and over a period of years have rotted so several were of necessity replaced this year. From year to year as these give out they will be replaced. Because of unforseen additional expenses required by the state building inspector's report it was necessary to postpone the major repairs on our mastic floors which must be replaced every four or five years. Likewise we were unable to replace the exit doors in the building that were scheduled for renewal.

Additional physical education equipment will make our program more effective as soon as sufficient funds are available. The Printing and Manual Training Departments need added aquipment and the old Golding printing press should be replaced.

McKINLEY SCHOOL

The drainage of the playground has been inadequate

the past two or three years on account of the additional use of the building by the Nursery, Sewing and Recreation projects. The system being over taxed with additional sewage caused the constant overflow of the cesspools and the additional stagnant water to stand on the surface. This condition was very unhealthful and the■ School Committee engaged the services of an expert Sanitary Engineer, Mr. Howard E. Bailey, who previously had planned the drainage system for the Jefferson School, to prepare plans and specifications for a sewage treatment plant adequate for our present needs. These plans were used as the basis for a W. P. A. project. Work was started very soon after the closing of schools in June and was completed the latter part of September. The situation has improved immensely and sanitary conditions prevail. Roof repairs have been needed and this year we installed copper snow guards to eliminate the hazard of sliding snow. The former guards were rusted and worn out. Several pieces of slate were cracked and these were replaced to prevent leaks in the roof. We may expect a major operation in the replacement of water pipes in the building as they are badly corroded and thus the water pressure is greatly reduced. This past summer the three boilers were thoroughly cleaned internally so that we are getting more efficiency from our heating system this fall than formerly. It was necessary in conjunction with the cleaning to have many of the air valves on the radiators changed.

The state building inspector imposed several requirements upon us in this building. Some of the most important which have been completed are as follows:

1. Provide an automatic fire alarm system with break glass stations on each floor, including basement break glass stations wired in such a manner that the gongs, when the glass is broken will ring simultaneously.

2. Provide floor cleates and clamps to seats in auditorium.

3. Provide metal covered door between basement and boiler room with a self-closing device.

4. Renovate and put in working condition the original ventilating system for the building.

It was further stated in the report that it was doubtful if the slate urinals could be sufficiently cleaned to be useful. Each unit should be ventilated in accordance with the rules and regulations of the department and provided with a vent fan to insure proper removal of air at all times.

LINCOLN

The side walk on Howard Street adjoining the school property has been constructed by the town but there is still need of a cement curb on the West side of the property to prevent drainage on the land of Franklin Avenue residents.

Complying with the request from the State Inspector of Buildings we have installed an automatic fire alrm system for the building, also provided T turn panic bolts on doors leading to fire escapes. In addition we have placed the ventilating system in working order.

This past summer the boilers were thoroughly cleaned and sections of the grates were replaced.

There is need to repaint sections of building on the outside as the paint is badly pealing.

Some of the blackboards in the building have been refinished.

Repairs in the girls' and boys' toilets have been made and the floors treated.

JEFFERSON

A self-closing device, required by the state inspector, has been installed on the boiler room door. The desks, blackboards and floors have been refinished. Repairs were made in the toilets and the boiler grates were replaced.

WEBSTER STREET

The heating unit in this building is very old and presents a dangerous situation. We have had asbestos installed overhead for safety reasons. The ventilating system has been placed in good working order. The blackboards and floors were refinished during the summer months. Additional grading in the yard will improve the limited playground area.

The ventilator on the roof was badly damaged by the hurricane, causing necessary repairs to be made.

GLEASON

We have provided an automatic fire alarm system for this building and placed the ventilating system in good working order.

There is need to repair the outside fire escape from both floors by eliminating a long flight of stairs, which may be accomplished by building an intermediate platform at the first floor level and connecting the two floors to the same stairs, thus eliminating one set of stairs. We should provide hand rails on the inside stairs from the first to the second floors.

The blackboards and floors were refinished. The water bubblers were replaced.

The lighting in this building has been inadequate so new fixtures supplying fifteen foot candles of light for each child has been installed in the lower room. The upper room should have its lighting improved as soon as possible.

CENTRAL STREET

The state inspector is requesting another means of egress from this building at the rear so a door will be installed to comply with these orders.

The bubbler and water pipe systems have had repairs and the blackboards and floors were refinished.

MARKET STREET

The ventilating system has been renovated and placed in working order. Repairs were made in the shed in order to make room for supplies. The hurricane caused some necessary repairs on the roof and also on the shed. The front steps have been repaired.

SPECIFIC NEEDS

In addition to the specific requests of departments listed in my 1937 report there are several other needs not mentioned in that report which are herein listed.

When the main electric service line was installed in the McKinley School building it was located in the boiler room and the switch boxes were not enclosed. Over a long period of years the soot and dust from the soft coal have covered the contacts and caused high degrees of heat. This in turn has caused the fuses to blow and thus leave the building without light and power. This main line entering the building should be enclosed and new equipment installed to prevent this hazardous condition.

A portable piano which could be used in our high school library for club work, especially for small groups, such as glee club would improve our school program greatly.

The circular drive in front of the high school should have a cement curb and be finished with a hard surface. It will greatly improve the appearance of the school building and grounds. At present considerable grit and gravel are tracked into the building on our mastic and wooden floors thus damaging the finish and surface. Undoubtedly the surface of the floors must be refinished more often as a result. Therefore in the long run it will be economically a good project.

The lockers in our boys' shower bath room are inadequate for our present needs and could well be replaced as soon as funds are available. A door cut through the locker room, opening outdoors, will prove advantageous as it will then not be necessary for the boys who are engaged in outside sports such as football, baseball and track to walk through the corridor, down into the gymnasium and thus out onto the field. The wear and tear on our floors will be diminished greatly by this change.

In April 1932 when the drastic cut in the school budget of $32,500 made imperative the discontinuance of several services in our schools, the sick leave formerly granted our teachers was dropped. Before discontinuing the "sick leave" for teachers, five days per year were allowed for personal illness without loss of salary. At present our plan is to allow no "sick leave" with full pay but to allow the teacher the difference between her pay and the substitute's which because of our low scale of salaries amounts to but very little. Many towns and cities in the state have returned the pay cuts and also have "sick leave" and in many cases this is cumulative from year to year. It seems in all fairness to our teachers that serious consideration should be given to the return of the five days per year without loss of salary for illness. I believe many times our teachers who have financial obligations to meet, feel that even though they are not well they should be in school rather than to be subject to the loss of salary. I am sure that most business concerns would not financially distress their salaried employers if absent through a brief period of illness.·

CONCLUSION

I wish to include again the reminder that Rockland children are given our care and instruction only six hours of each day during but five days òf the week and to urge every parent to cooperate in every way to the end that each child may more greatly enrich the community by becoming an intelligent, loyal citizen.

Such an accomplishment is possible only through the concerted effort of parents and teachers. That effort has increased with each year of my service here and evokes my sincere gratitude. My appreciation goeš also to the members of the School Committee, all of whom have given their effort and time unstintingly to the advancement of education in Rockland.

Respectfully submitted,

R. STEWART ESTEN
Superintendent of Schools

REPORT OF THE JUNIOR-SENIOR HIGH SCHOOL PRINCIPAL

Mr. R. Stewart Esten
Superintendent of Schools
Rockland, Massachusetts

My dear Mr. Esten:

My annual report as Principal of the Junior-Senior High School is submitted herein for your consideration.

The total enrollment of the school was about twenty pupils larger on October 1, 1938 than it was on that same date last year. We started this fall with a few less than seven hundred pupils. The enrollment in the Senior High is nearly double that of the Junior High. Again this year some study halls are overcrowded due to a larger enrollment in some courses of study than in others. All rooms are filled to capacity.

The average attendance for the year fell off from last year's good record. This was due to the epidemic which lasted several months. Our record for punctuality was satisfactory and credit should again go to the pupils and parents who cooperated so well in this matter.

More standardized tests were used during the year. The Cooperative Achievement Tests, developed by the American Council on Education, were given last June to test the work in United States History, Mathematics (Algebra and Geometry), Biology, Chemistry, French and Physics. The scores obtained by our pupils were indeed favorable. Some diagnostic tests were also given. From results of the tests given and from reports received from colleges concerning our former pupils, we can be reasonably certain that a high grade of work has been accomplished during the past year.

I feel that the curriculum of the General Course should be broadened to include other worthwhile electives. This is not possible at present for it would require an additional teacher as all of our present faculty are carrying a very full teaching load. However this is worthy of serious consideration for such a broadened curriculum would materially benefit that large group of pupils taking the General Course.

The school library has been much more useful during the last few months. Several factors account for this. First in importance was the receipt of many new books through the generousity of the alumni and the Rockland Woman's Club. Then, we were able to get expert assistance in recataloguing all our books and reorganizing our library. Lastly, a corps of student librarians has been trained to handle ordinary library routine under the direction of the teacher in charge. Nevertheless there still remains the need of a teacher-librarian, one trained in library work, to make our library most efficient and to develop it beyond the good start recently made.

We have been able to extend the use of visual aids in our program beyond the modest start of the previous year. The Yale Chronicles, well-known historical films, are being used this year in connection with the work in our history classes. Several other departments made use of films to supplement their regular work. Another group of boys has been trained to operate the projector. As before this program has been carried on with little cost to the town.

Last Spring an amplification system for the auditorium was purchased through action of the Student Council. It was bought by the students primarily to be used with a phonographic pick-up for entertainments and informal dancing. However, many other educative uses have been found for the system. It enables assembly programs to be heard more clearly; it gives the opportunity for training in speaking before a microphone; and its greatest service comes at the graduation exercises.

Two outstanding projects accomplished during the year are worthy of brief mention. The first Rockland High Handbook made its appearance last June. It contained all necessary and useful information about the school. This Handbook should prove helpful to parents as well as to the pupils of the school, and should be of great worth in helping new pupils get oriented in their new surroundings. The staff and its adviser are to be commended for their fine work in compiling this first Handbook. The other project was the construction of a new set of scenery for the stage of our auditorium. Not only has the set been constructed and painted, but it has also been flameproofed. The Industrial Arts department made the new scenery and it was painted by the Art Department. This fine new scenery will fill a long-felt need of the school.

Progress has been made in our Physical Education program. This is more noticeable in the girls' department chiefly because of the fact that the girls are able to have one more class a week than the boys. The Gym exhibition held last May demonstrated the improvement made in these departments. Physical Education should mean more than a play period. It should assist the pupil in his physical development. A better program will evolve as more equipment is added for use in our classes.

In athletics, the last school year was one of outstanding success. The boys' basketball team won all except from one team of its regular schedule; the baseball team had an undefeated season last spring; this fall our cross-country team also was undefeated; we did very well in track last spring; and improvement was made in girl's basketball and Junior High athletics. Only football lags behind. The reason for this requires special attention and this is being given to the matter. Best of all our school has been commended upon several occasions for the good sportsmanship of its teams and supporters. By this yardstick should the success of our athletic program be measured. It should also be stated that a growing school spirit played no small part in the success of the athletic program. The lack of an enclosed field continues to make the financing of our athletics a difficult matter. We also hope that something may be done very soon to put the running track in condition so that it .may be used. The interest shown in, and the consideration given to some of our athletic teams during the past year, by the local Kiwanis Club, has been most sincerely appreciated by all who have any responsibility in our athletic program.

Our other extra-curricular activities have been expanded. Debating was added as an activity and our teams won two out of their three debates, a very good record for the first year. The good records of the past two years in public speaking were continued. Several of our pupils placed at the district meet, and one of our boys placed third in extemperaneous speaking at the state meet at Fall River. Two more clubs have been organized, a Camera Club and a Dramatic Club. The Commeroff Club enjoyed another successful year.

Pro-Merito is not content with being just an honor society, but has shown that it desires to be a service organization as well. It has assumed the responsibility for furnishing the student librarians. The society has other plans for service for the remainder of the year.

The Student Council has helped in developing school spirit and has done good work in assuming some lavatory supervision. Faster progress in pupil particiation in school government is not being made for pupils overlook an important fact which we as citizens too often fail to recognize—that every privilege or right given obligates us necessarily to corresponding duties. The Council is endeavoring to bring light upon this important matter.

The importance of guidance is accepted by everyone. Yet under our present set-up, very little guidance, especially vocational guidance, can be carried on. To do worthwhile vocational guidance requires special training. It also takes time to study and help the individual pupil. Our home-room teachers have little time for guidance work, and the same is true of all the other members of the faculty. Let us hope that some solution may be found to meet this important need in the immediate future.

Our high school staff lost two of of its members last June. Mr. Elmer E. Dunn, the head custodian, was retired. Miss Marguerite Croak, head of the Commercial Department, resigned to be married. The efficiency and loyalty of both are greatly missed. They both carried with them the best wishes of the entire school.

I conclude this report with an expression of sincere thanks for the cooperation and assistance given to me by the School Committee, the Superintendent, the faculty, parents and pupils.

Respectfully submitted,

GEORGE A. J. FROBERGER,
Principal

REPORT OF SCHOOL PHYSICIANS AND SCHOOL NURSE

Mr. R. Stewart Esten
Superintendent of Schools
Rockland, Massachusetts

My dear Mr. Esten:

We herewith submit our report as School Physicians for the year 1938. We have examined all the pupils in the elementary grades. High School pupils were examined carefully before being allowed to participate in the competitive sports.

The Diphtheria prevention program was carried out during the month of May. We strongly advise that all children over six months of age be given Toxoid as a means of preventing Diphtheria.

We hope for the continuation of the Milk Fund and feel that it has been of distinct value to the under-nourished type of child.

Following is a list of the physical defects found:

Number of physical examinations	818
Number cases of enlarged tonsils and adenoids	92
Number cases cervical glands	12
Number of children given Toxid innoculations	96

CHADWICK CLINIC RESULTS

Number pupils given Von Pirquet	272
Number negative reaction	165

Number positive reaction   115
Number x-rayed by Chadwick Clinic   115
Number found negative after x-ray   99
Number referred for examinatiòn   16
Number found negative after physical examination   4
Number cases to be continued under care of clinic   12

ACTIVITIES OF SCHOOL NURSE

An office hour is maintained each school day at the Rockland High School from 8:30 to 9:30 A. M. and parent or teacher may reach the nurse by telephoning the office of the Superintendent of Schools.

Elementary classrooms are visited twice weekly. Monthly inspections are made in all grade schools. Daily inspections are made if pupils have been exposed to contagious disease.

Pupils are weighed three times during the school year. A steady gain for each pupil is to be desired rather than try to have the child conform to the age, height, weight tables. Emphasis is being placed on the individual gain. To this end weight charts are posted in each elementary classroom.

Number of visits made to classrooms   2081
Number of visits made to homes   609
Number of minor wounds cared for   147
Number of emergency treatments   20
Number of pupils taken home ill   71
Number pupils sent to family physician   5
Number pupils sent to school physician   7
Number classroom inspections   297
Number individual inspections   8482
Number pupils weighed and measured   2034
Number pupils found to have defective hearing   14

All cases of non attendance which have been brought to my attention have been investigated.

We wish to thank all who have co-operated with us.

Respectfully submitted,

JOSEPH H. DUNN, M. D.,
JOSEPH FRAME, M. D.,
School Physicians
LOUISE A. CONSIDINE, R. N.
School Nurse

REPORT OF DENTAL HYGIENIST

My dear Mr. Esten:

I hereby submit my ninth annual report as Dental Hygienist in the Rockland School for the year 1938.

The customary annual dental examination made by the local dentists was again carried out in the first six grades.

Number examined	773
Number in need of temporary extractions	201
Number in need of temporary fillings	197
Number in need of permanent extractions	79
Number in need of permanent fillings	447

PRE-SCHOOL EXAMINATION

Number examined	65
Number temporary defects	40
Number abscessed teeth	3
Number with permanent defects	0
Number with no visible defects	25

CLINIC

Number prophylaxis	854

CLASSROOM

Instruction covered toothbrushes, proper method of brushing, the mouth as a machine, and tooth building foods with particular stress on Vitamin C.

As the above charts clearly indicate, there is great need for dental repair work among the school children.

This past year through the Rockland Teachers' Association and the Junior Red Cross forty-five children received emergency extraction treatment. I wish to thank these two organizations sincerely for their kind interest and generous aid in my particular department.

I hope thesê two organizations will continue their interest so that we may in the future do something really progressive in regard to the control of the most outstanding defect among the school children, namely dental decay.

I earnestly believe that a large percentage of the infected tonsils among the school children can be traced directly to infected teeth. It is also my belief that by focusing corrective attention on the first three grades, or even the first two, for several years, that we could show very definite satisfactory results in regard to both infected tonsils and the control of dental decay.

Respectfully sumbitted,

EVELYN DELORY,
Dental Hygiènist

FINANCIAL REPORT FOR THE ROCKLAND
HIGH SCHOOL CAFETERIA

January 1, 1938 to December 31, 1938

Balance on Hand, January 1, 1938 $ 16 03

Cash Receipts for 1938   5 302 84

Total Cash Receipts $5 318 87

Cash Payments for 1938:

Barnes, W. F.	$ 10	76
Brockton Edison Company	72	00
Berwick Cake Company	183	92
Casey, Arthur	10	50
Chamberlin, E. L.	8	40
Coty's Bakery •	5	52
Cushman's Bakery	120	82
Drake's Bakeries	66	69
Ellis Company, H. F.	78	87
Figlioli Brothers	20	61
Fitts Company, E. V.	370	55
Globe Ticket Company	40	73
Gumpert Company, Inc.	16	50
Gurry, Thomas P.	6	20
Hickey Brothers	877	13
Hostess Cake Company	19	16
Hunt Potato Chip Company	66	94
Jordan Marsh Company	19	48
Linwood Dairy	18	27
Loose-Wiles Biscuit Company	50	32
Nanking Food Products Company	5	80
National Biscuit Company	26	56
Old Colony Gas Company	92	18
Old Colony Service	2	50
Peterson, A. S.	392	16
Plymouth Rock Ice Cream Company	1 197	13

Puritan Cake Company	4	15
Quinn, Margaret	580	00 —
Rice, J. A.	5	67
Rockland Disposal Service	4	50
Rockland New System Laundry	3	65
Rogers, Leroy	11	40
Rome Brothers	2	50
Schuler's Foods, Inc.	28	47
Standard Brands, Inc.	4	95
Stoddard, A. C.	184	46
Traniello, Paul	3	58
Whiting Milk Company	460	02
Wonder Bread Bakery	217	28

Total Cash Payments $5 290 33

Balance on Hand $ 28 54

Respectfully submitted,

ROSE T. MAGADINI
ELEANOR B. LOUD

SCHOOL ENROLLMENT
As of December 23, 1938

Teacher	School	Grade	Pupils
Marjorie Smith	McKinley	1	39
Mary H. Greenan	McKinley	2	38
Mildred Healey	McKinley	3	27
R. Louise Cone	McKinley	4	43
Elva M. Shea	McKinley	5	35
John F. Ryan	McKinley	5	33
Paul Casey	McKinley	6	39
Nellie M. Ford	McKinley	6	39
Rita M. Kennedy	McKinley	Special Class	14
Catherine Coen	Lincoln	1	31
Blanche Thacher	Lincoln	2	29
Harriette E. Cragin	Lincoln	3	33
Miriam Roberts	Lincoln	4	34
Eileen Fitzgibbons	Lincoln	5	31
Margaret McDermott	Lincoln	6	37
Virginia Ford	Jefferson	1 and 2	37
Bertha Campbell	Jefferson	2 and 3	36
Blanche Crowell	Jefferson	4 and 5	35
Annie A. Shirley	Jefferson	5 and 6	34
Madeline Lannin	Gleason	1 and 2	34
Catherine M. Reilly	Gleason	3 and 4	19
Lillian G. Murdock	Webster St.	1, 2 and 3	24
Josephine Lannin	Webster St.	4 and 5	17
Ethel M. Weatherbee	Market St.	1, 2 and 3	24
Margaret Blake	Market St.	4, 5 and 6	26
Alice Murrill	Central St.	1, 2 and 3	22

Total Elementary School Enrollment   810
Junior-Senior High School Enrollment   673

GRAND TOTAL   1483

AGE GRADE TABLE AS OF OCTOBER 1, 1938

Grade	\-	\-	\-	\-	\-	\-	\-	AGE	\-	\-	\-	\-	\-	\-	\-	\-
	5	6	7	8	9	10	11	12	13	14	15	16	17	18	19	Total
1	50	70	15	1												136
2		58	58	11	3	1										131
3			40	57	12		1									110
4				32	56	23	5	3								119
5					58	51	19	9	4	1						142
6						52	64	23	7	4	2					152
7							52	48	20	12	3	2				137
8								43	53	18	2	2				118
9									54	63	16	6				139
10										26	54	11	8	1		100
11											36	50	10	3	1	100
12											2	24	42	15	2	85
P.G.													3	4		7
Ungraded					1	1	3	3	1	1		1	1			12
Total	50	128	113	101	130	128	144	129	139	125	115	96	64	23	3	1488

ROCKLAND HIGH SCHOOL
GRADUATION EXERCISES
Class of 1938

Wednesday Evening, June twenty-second
Rockland High School Auditorium

PROGRAMME

Processional, "Farewell March"   Treaben
R. H. S. Orchestra

Invocation   Rev. Royer H. Woodburn

Honor Essay   "Democracy Through Education"
Gertrude Ilene Mahn

Song—"Prayer of Thanksgiving"   Kresmer
"Venetian Love Song"   Nevin
Rockland High Choristers

Honor Essay — "Facing the World"
Helen Catherine Pike

Chamber of Commerce Prize Essay—"Our Community"
Betty Dunn Stringer

Music — "Operatic Selection"   Julius S. Seredy
R. H. S. Orchestra

Honor Essay — "Let Freedom Ring"
Helen Marie Plouffe

Song — "Kiss of Spring"   Rolfe
"Will You Remember"   Romberg
Soloist- Mary Morgan '40
Girls' Glee Club

Honor Essay — "Those Friends Thou Hast"
Rose Virginia Cifelli

Chamber of Commerce Scholarship
Dr. Joseph E. Lelyveld, President of Chamber

Woman's Club Scholarship
Mrs. Frederic Hall, Chairman of Scholarship Committee

Awarding of other prizes and Presentation of Diplomas
Dr. Benjamin Lelyveld, Chairman of School Committee
Song — "America" Chorus and Audience
Benediction Rev. Royer H. Woodburn

Director of the Chorus Miss Blanche G. Maguire
Director of the Orchestra Mr. Michael Cassano
Accompanist Jean Kierstead, '41

GRADUATES

Thomas Francis Bailey
Virginia Elvira Batson
*Harold Bruce Beal
Dorothy Alice Bell
*Grace Dorella Bombardier
Karl Bradford Burgess
*Rose Virginia Cifelli
Grace Edna Clark
*Walter Johnson Coleman
Joseph Francis Condon
*Kenneth Crawford
William Lloyd Crossman
John Freeman Crowell
Robert Gordon Cuff
Irene Gertrude Cushing
Ernest Gordon Davis
Mary Elizabeth Donovan
Lester Goddard Edwards
Dora Virginia Fange
*William Joseph Foley
*Mary Pauline Gaines
Marion Arlene Hamilton
William Christie Hannigan
Henry Curtis Paul Hines, Jr.
Helen Ann Elizabeth Hoadley
Marilynn Holley Hunter
Joseph William Michael Igna-
· towicz
*Josephine Gloria Jasper
Edward Joseph Keane
Evelyn Elizabeth Keene
*Mary Louisa Lamar
Muriel Elizabeth Leavitt

*Geraldine Rose Mastrodomen-
ico
Ida Marie Mastrodomenico
Sophie Katherine Mazalewski
Helen Kathleen McAuliffe
John Allen McEnroe, Jr.
Leo McIver
John Joseph McMorrow
Catherine McWilliams
Florence Louise Metivier
Rita Anne Morrissey
Ruth Helen Morse
Etta Geraldine Murgida
Richard Arthur Nevens
Edith Nihill
William Henry O'Connell
Francis John O'Hare
*Geraldine Frances Packard
*Edith Eleanor Peabody
Charles Tirrell Phelps
*Phyllis Madelyn Phinney
*Helen Catherine Pike
*Helen Marie Plouffe
Anna Elizabeth Quinn
John Robert Reardon
Daniel Joseph Reilly
*Shirley Elizabeth Roberts
*William Francis Roberts
Charles Irving Robichaud
Ruth Arlene Rose
*Mildred Louise Ryan
*Christine Madelyn Schapelle
*Lilla May Sheldon

Ernest Melvin Libby
Elizabeth Pearson Locke
*Gertrude Ilene Mahn
Eleanor Louise Mahoney
Francis William Mahoney
Alfred Mariani
Marie Agnes Martin
*Antoinette Marie Mastrodomenico

Margaret Louise Smith
Anthony Tony Stankavich
Chester Henry Strefska
*Betty Dunn Stringer
Phyllis Barbara Tisdale
Doris Mary Whitford
Howard Harding Williams
Ila Ruth Wyman
*Walter Joseph Yourell

* PRO MERITO—Honor Society. Average of 85 per cent or over for 4 years.

CLASS OFFICERS

KARL BURGESS — President
PAULINE GAINES — Vice President
JOSEPHINE JASPER — Secretary
WALTER YOURELL — Treasurer

SOCIAL COMMITTEE

Harold Beal   Rose Cifelli   William Roberts

CLASS COLORS

Blue and White

CLASS MOTTO

"Semper Procede" — Ever Onward

CLASS FLOWER

Red Rose

July, and we'll taste freedom, our one dream;
Our first experience with this delight.
But will it be so wonderful that night
When all the celebration's joy supreme
Has died and faded like a candle's beam?
Will light of realism then bring to sight
The straight and narrow path we know is right?
I think that long awaited day will seem
To blend itself into our every plan,
And we won't even know we've crossed the bay

And spanned the gap that separates each man
Among us now from what he is today .
And what he ever hopes and prays he can
Accomplish after graduation day.

Kenneth Crawford, '38

TEACHERS EMPLOYED DECEMBER 31, 1938

Date of
Appointment Salary

Superintendent of Schools

R. Stewart Esten, A. B., Middlebury College,		
A. M., Columbia University	1929	$3600

Junior-Senior High School

George A. J. Froberger, A. B., University		
of Maine, Principal	1935	$2930
Robert C. Healy, A. B., Boston College,		
M. Ed., Boston Univ., Sub-Master, Latin	1919	2480
Katherine S. Burke, Bridgewater Teacher's		
College, Geog., Science	1906	1360
Joseph Cogan, B. S., Bates College, Sciences	1929	1800
Mary D. Costello, Quincy Training School,		
English, Penmanship	1898	1360
Ellen M. Hayes, A. B., University of Wisconsin,		
English	1927	1670
Victoria Howarth, A. B., Radcliffe College,		
English	1925	1800
Emma S. Jewett, Hyannis Teachers' College,		
History	1908	1360
Eleanor Loud, B. S., Simmons College, Household		
Arts	1935	1100
Rose T. Magadini, Bay Path Institute,		
Commercial	1929	1490
Olive H. Mayer, B. S., Boston Univ., A. M.,		
Boston Univ., English	1935	1300
Esther McGrath, B. S. E., Bridgewater Teachers'		
College, Social Sci., Lit.	1918	1360
Helen M. Miley, B. S., Boston University, M. Ed.,		
Boston Univ., Commercial	1938	1200
Helen M. Molloy, Keene, N. H., Normal School,		
Junior Business Training	1930	1270
John B. O'Hayre, A. B., Boston College,		
History	Jan. 1931	1535

Chester J. Poliks, B. S. E., Fitchburg Teachers'
College, B. S., Connecticut, State College,
Physical Ed., Biology   1937   1760
Malcolm L. Pratt, A. B., Dartmouth College,
Mathematics   ·   1933   ·   1500
Leoná W. Sampson, A. B., Boston University,
A. M., Boston Univ., French   Sept. 1937   1550
Frances L. Squarey, Bridgewater Teachers'
College, English, Literature   1921   1360
Robert A. Studley, A. B., Univ. of N. H.,
History   1927   1625
Bertha L. Tenney, Farmington, Maine Normal
School, Sci., Mathematics   1927   1360
Constance Tobey, B. S., University of N. H., Sewing,
History   1936   1200
Earl I. Komarin, B. S. E., Salem Teachers'
College, Commercial   1936   1300
G. William Wilson, B. S. E., Fitchburg Teachers'
College, Manual Training   1937   1250

McKinley School

Nellie M. Ford, High School, Special Courses
Principal, Grade 6   1896 $1490
Marjorie Smith, Bridgewater Teachers' College
Grade 1   1937   1050
Mary H. Greenan, Attended B. U. and Hyannis
Teachers College, Grade 2   1920   1360
Mildred E. Healey, Lesley Normal School,
Grade 3   1930   1100
R. Louise Cone, B. S. E., Boston University,
Grade 4   1930   1265
Elva M. Shea, Bridgewater Teachers' College,
Grade 5   1928   1157.50
John Ryan, A. B., Boston College, B. S. E.,
Bridgewater Teachers' College, Grade 5   1937   1050
Paul Casey, B. S. E., Bridgewater Teachers' College,
Grade 6   1937   1050
Rita M. Kennedy, B. S. E., Salem Teachers' College,
Special Class   1938   1050

Lincoln School

J. Eileen Fitzgibbons, Bridgewater Teachers' College,
Principal, Grade 5   1925   1360
Catherine Coen, Salem Teachers' College,
Grade 1   1930   1270
Blanche Thacher, Wheelock Ktg. School,   Jan.
Grade 2   1930   1225
Harriette Cragin, High School,   Sept.
Special Courses, Grade 3   1910 .   1360
Miriam Roberts, Bridgewater Teachers' College,
Grade 4   '   1934   1100
Margaret McDermott, Hyannis Teachers' College,
Grade 6   1925   1360

Jefferson School

Annie A. Shirley, Bridgewater Teachers' College,
Principal, Grades 5 and 6   1912 $1450
Virginia Ford, B. S. E., Bridgewater Teachers'
College, Grades 1 and 2   1937   1050
Bertha Campbell, Attended Mass. Agr. College,
B. U., Hyannis Teachers' College, Special Courses,
Grades 2 and 3   1923   1360
Blanche Crowell, Framingham Teachers, College .
Grades 4 and 5   1931   1270

Gleason School

Madeline Lannin, Lesley Normal School,
Grades 1 and 2   Jan. 1935 $1100
Catherine Reilly, B. S. E., Bridgewater Teachers'
College, Grades 3 and 4   Oct. 1938   1000

Webster Street School

Lillian G. Murdock, Quincy Training School,
Grades 1, 2 and 3   1922 $1360
Josephine Lannin, Bridgewater Teachers' College
B. S., Hyannis Teachers' College, Grades 4 and 5 1932   1100

Market Street School

Ethel Wetherbee, Symonds Ktg. School, Grades
1, 2 and 3   1928 ' $1360

Margaret Blake, Hyannis Teachers' College,
Grades 4, 5 and 6   1929   1100

Central Street School

Alice Murrill, B. S. E., Bridgewater Teachers'
College, Grades 1, 2 and 3   1937 $1050

Special Teachers

*Blanche Maguire, Attended B. U. and North-
ampton School of Pedagogy, Music   March 1929 $ 900
**Michael Cassano, Virtuoso Music School, Private
School, Private Study in Music, Instructor of
Musical Instruments   Sept. 1928   1200
Louise A. Considine, R. N., St. Eliz. Hospital
Training School, Nurse   1922   1450
Josephine Fitzgibbons, Posse-Nissen, Physical Edu-
cation for Girls   1929   1225
Nora van der Groen, B. S. Boston University,
Art Supervisor   1938   1200

Resignations 1938

Marguerite J. Croak, High School
Isabel Philbrook, McKinley School
Helen Kovalchuk, Gleason School
Eleanor Costa, Drawing Supervisor

Appointments 1938

Helen M. Miley, High School
Rita M. Kennedy, McKinley School
Catherine Reilly, Gleason School
Nora van der Groen, Drawing Supervisor

   *2 days each week
**3 days each week

INDEX
—□—

NUAL REPORT

OF THE TOWN OF

ROCKLAND

1939

SIXTY-SIXTH

ANNUAL REPORT

of the

TOWN OFFICERS

of the

Town of Rockland

For the Year Ending December 31

1939

ROCKLAND STANDARD PUBLISHING COMPANY

ROCKLAND, MASSACHUSETTS

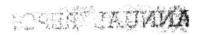

Officers of the Town of Rockland 1939

Town Clerk (elected annually)
RALPH L. BELCHER

Town Treasurer (elected annually)
CHARLES J. HIGGINS

Tax Collector (elected annually)
JAMES A. DONOVAN

Moderator (elected annually)
MAGORISK L. WALLS

men, Board of Public Welfare and Fence Viewers
(elected annually)
HARRY S. TORREY
J. BOWLER   NORMAN S. WHITING

Bureau of Old Age Assistance
(appointed by Board of Public Welfare)
HARRY S. TORREY
J. BOWLER   NORMAN S. WHITING

Supervisor of Old Age Assistance
(appointed by Board of Public Welfare)
MARY L. O'BRIEN

Welfare Investigator
(appointed by Board of Public Welfare)
GERALD A. WHELAND

Assessors
(one elected annually for three years)
IS L. O'CONNOR   Term expires 1942
PH B. ESTES   Term expires 1941
AN J. BEALS   Term expires 1940

School Committee
(for a term of three years)
JOHN T. TROY, JR.   Term expires 1942
DANA S. COLLINS   Term expires 1941
M. AGNES KELLEHER   Term expires 1941
WILLIAM A. LOUD   Term expires 1940
BENJAMIN LELYVELD   Term expires 1940

Park Commissioners
(one elected annually for three years)
PATRICK H. MAHONEY   Term expires 1942
DANIEL H. BURKE   Term expires 1941
CHARLES T. WALLS   Term expires 1940

Water Commissioners
(one elected annually for three years)
JAMES T. SHEA   Term expires 1942
SAMUEL W. BAKER   Term expires 1941
EVERETT S. DAMON   Term expires 1940

Board of Health
(one elected annually for three years)
*EDWARD M. CULLINAN   Term expires 1942
JOSEPH FRAME, M. D.   Term expires 1941
JOSEPH H. DUNN, M. D.   Term expires 1940
HAROLD T. CORCORAN,, appointed Dec. 16, 1939
    to fill vacancy
* Deceased Oct. 24, 1939.

Sewerage Commissioners
(one elected annually for three years)
*FREDERIC HALL   Term expires 1942
GILES W. HOWLAND   Term expires 1940
CHARLES M. HINES   Term expires 1940
* Deceased, Dec. 22, 1939.

Trustees of the Memorial Library
(two elected annually for three years)
BURTON L. CUSHING   Term expires 1942

JOHN B. FITZGERALD   Term expires 1942
EMILY CRAWFORD   Term expires 1941
ANNIE McILVENE   Term expires 1941
EMMA GLEASON   Term expires 1940
FRANCIS J. GEOGAN   Term expires 1940

Auditors
(elected annually)
HAROLD C. SMITH   GEORGE A. GALLAGHER
LEO E. DOWNEY

Tree Warden
(elected annually)
ALFRED T. METIVIER

Highway Surveyor
(elected annually)
RODERICK MacKENZIE

Constables
(elected annually)
*RUSSELL S. HAWES   JOHN H. MURPHY
ADOLPH L. W. JOHNSON   ROBERT J. DRAKE
GEORGE J. POPP
* Resigned Oct. 3, 1939

APPOINTMENTS
(by Selectmen)

Chief of Police
GEORGE J. POPP

Police Officers
(appointed by Selectmen)
*RUSSELL S. HAWES   JOHN H. MURPHY
ADOLPH L. W. JOHNSON   ROBERT J. DRAKE
GEORGE J. POPP
* Resigned Oct. 3, 1939, Samuel J. Cannaway appointed
to fill vacancy.

Special Police Officers
(appointed by the Selectmen)

SAMUEL J. CANNAWAY   GEORGE K. INGLIS
MAURICE MULLEN   ELMER DUNN
EDWARD M. CULLINAN   CHARLES METIVIER
JOHN J. DWYER   BERNARD F. O'HAYRE
CHARLES M. HINES   PERCY ALBEE
FORREST L. PARTCH   THOMAS MAHONEY
JAMES McKEEVER   CHARLES BOUDREAU
JOHN DOYLE   THOMAS FITZGERALD
MICHAEL O'BRIEN   FREDERICK J. PERRY
THOMAS V. MAHON   GEORGE MANLEY
LEE RHODENIZER   THOMAS McDONALD
WILLIAM H. ROBERTS   CLIFFORD ROSE
W. ALTON WHITING   DANIEL C. HINES
EARL WALLACE   BERNARD V. DELORY
LEO E. DOWNEY   GEORGE F. CROSSMAN
HAROLD ANDERSON   JOHN T. TROY, JR.
FRANCIS PATTERSON   JOSEPH P. KEEFE
EARL WYATT   JOHN E. DRISCOLL
FRANCIS T. DWYER

Keeper of the Lock-Up
GEORGE J. POPP

ELECTION OFFICERS

Precinct One   Precinct Two
                Wardens
WILLIAM J. FLYNN   JOHN A. WINSLOW

            Deputy Wardens
ROBERT PARKER   HAROLD C. POOLE

                Clerks
IRVIN E. EMERY   FRED RYAN

                Deputy Clerks
CARL FASS   J. LOCKE LANNIN

Inspectors

JOHN J. PAULIN   ELLIS BLAKE
MATTHEW O'GRADY   CHARLES F. SHIELDS

Deputy Inspectors

ROBERT D. ESTES   FRANCIS L. GAMMON
TIMOTHY WHITE   E. BURTON RAMSDELL
URSULA M. FRENCH   OLIVE C. WHEELER
HELENA W. HUNT   MARY E. LYNCH

Registrars of Voters
(one appointed annually for three years)

ESTHER H. RAWSON   Term expires 1942
THOMAS MORRISSEY   Term expires 1941
ANNIE G. GARRITY   Term expires 1940

Sealer of Weights and Measures
HAROLD J. INKLEY

Measurer of Wood and Bark
GILES W. HOWLAND

Weighers of Hay and Coal — Also Public Weighers

RALPH KEENE   EDITH PETRELL
PERCY JACOBS   ARTHUR PETRELL
MICHAEL D. PETRELL

Agent for Burial of Indigent Soldiers and
Care of Soldiers' Graves
LOUIS B. GILBRIDE

Inspector of Animals and Stables
WILLIAM T. CONDON

Town Physicians for Poor and Soldiers' Relief
JOSEPH H. DUNN, M. D.
NORBERT F. LOUGH, M. D.

Superintendent Gypsy Moth
ALFRED T. METIVIER

Forest Fire Warden
CLYSON P. INKLEY

APPOINTMENTS
(by School Committee)

Superintendent of Schools
R. STEWART ESTEN

APPOINTMENTS
(by Water Commissioners)

Superintendent of Water Works
JAMES B. STUDLEY

APPOINTMENTS
(by Board of Health)

Inspectors of Plumbing
*FREDERIC HALL   J. STUART McCALLUM
* Deceased Dec. 22, 1939

Milk Inspectors
BOARD OF HEALTH

APPOINTMENTS
(by Moderator)
Finance Committee
PAUL I. FLAVELL   Term expires 1942
NORMAN C. POOLE   Term expires 1942
JOHN W. ROSS   Term expires 1942
H. BERNARD MONAHAN   Term expires 1942
DORA B. PATTERSON   Term expires 1942
RUSSELL OSGOOD   Term expires 1941
FREDERICK NUGENT   Term expires 1941

RALPH TEDESCHI	Term expires 1941
PATRICK RYAN	Term expires 1941
WILLIAM G. W. HOLLOWAY	Term expires 1941
WILLIAM KANE	Term expires 1940
WESLEY PIERCE	Term expires 1940
EDWARD RYAN	Term expires 1940
MARY CLANCEY	Term expires 1940
JAMES APPLEFORD	Term expires 1940

Chief of Fire Department

CLYSON P. INKLEY   Tenure of office

Report of the Town Clerk

MARRIAGES REGISTERED IN THE TOWN OF ROCKLAND FOR YEAR 1939

Jan. 2. Michael J. White of Rockland and Marian M. Lawrence of Medford.

Jan. 8. Theodore Florio of Brockton and Rose Marie Umbrianna of Rockland.

Jan. 9. Bronis Frederick Machinski of Brockton and Anna Stankiewicz of Rockland.

Jan. 11. James Albert Tipping and Elizabeth Helen Ferron both of Rockland.

Jan. 14. Clyde Gordon Dunham and Gertrude Rose Mahoney both of Rockland.

Jan. 15. Raymond Patrick Finn of Brockton and Mary Petrine Ralli of Rockland.

Jan. 15. William Briggs Richmond of Weymouth and Theresa Frances Huggett of Rockland.

Jan. 22. Paul Elwin Noland of Rockland and Esther Averill Thayer of Weymouth.

Jan. 29. Wilburn Beach Miller of Brockton and Helen Elizabeth Frame of Rockland.

Feb. 4. Edward McCabe and Mabel A. Fitts both of Rockland.

Feb. 19. Lloyd William Smith of Abington and Vera Marie Mason of Rockland.

Feb. 19. Domenic Joseph Chiminello of Quincy and Lena Elizabeth Ingeno of Rockland.

Feb. 20. Paul William Ryan of Weymouth and Priscilla Bowman of Rockland.

Feb. 21. Charles Bourgault and Rosa Jayal both of West Warwick, R. I.

Feb. 22. John Henry Nelson and Elsie Gilman Whiting both of Hanover.

Feb. 23. William Joseph Duhamel and Grace Edna Clark both of Rockland.

Feb. 25. Warren Alexander Ellis of Rockland and Elsie Rowe Littlefield of Whitman.

March 18. Frederick Austin Chamberlain of Rockland and Susie Ellen Libby of Abington.

March 25. Stanley Mansfield Wood of Rockland and Eleanor Mae Farrar of Norwell.

April 5. Francis Leslie Woodward of Rockland and Alice Ruth Means of Whitman.

April 9. Herbert Francis McLaughlin of Brookline and Mary Louise Cannaway of Rockland.

April 9. Elio Moscardelli of Quincy and Gilda Iannicelli of Rockland.

April 16. Charles Wilson of Cohasset and Catherine Emily Cobb of Rockland.

April 16. Edmund W. Delprete of Rockland and Louise DeGregorio of Braintree.

April 17. Ralph Eugene Arkell of Rockland and Helen Mary Follett of Central Falls, R. I.

April 18. George F. Glidden of Weymouth and Marjorie E. Smith of Rockland.

April 19. Francis L. Gammon of Rockland and Mary J. O'Brien of Charlestown.

April 22. Angelo Costello of Rockland and Evelyn Mary Giardino of Dorchester.

April 23. Francis Edwin Kiernan and Ida Margaret Ralli both of Rockland.

April 26. Thomas M. O'Connor of Rockland and Thelma C. Bigelow of Chazy, New York.

April 29. Reino Saarela and Irene Geloran both of Rockland.

April 29. Robert E. Yourell of Rockland and Margaret Noreen Whittaker of Scituate.

April 30. Anthony James Lukaszewicz of Rockland and Victoria Lena Sadowski of Abington.

May 6. Harold Vincent Mahon and Catherine Florence Fihelly both of Rockland.

May 7. Joseph Francis Hickey of Rockland and Rose Anna Plasse of Whitman.

May 12. Harry Arthur Griffith and Lillian S. Dame (Shurtleff) both of Hanover.

May 18. David Peter DeSimone of Rockland and Marion Palmer of Weymouth.

May 20. Otis Francis Hatch of Hanover and Ruth Sarah Dunn of Rockland.

May 21. Adam P. Landers and Hester U. Harney both of Boston.

May 27. Andrew J. Delano of Duxbury and Florence Lillian Lane (Metcalf) of Rockland.

June 2. George Ezra Anderson and Geraldine Frances Rose both of Rockland.

June 4. Richard Morton Alden of Whitman and Louise Arnold Metevier of Rockland.

June 4. Pasquale Cerce of Brockton and Angelina Theresa Umbrianna of Rockland.

June 4. Fred Atherton Prouty of Hanover and Marjorie Wheeler Marks of Rockland.

June 9. Arthur William Earle and Thelma Mae White both of Rockland.

June 11. Almadose J. Forrand and Elinor Morrill both of Rockland.

June 16. Franklin Henry Still of Brockton and Dorothy Mary Young of Rockland.

June 18. John Francis Jankowski of Rockland and Emily Marguerite Carter of Braintree.

June 27. Reginald Drake Lyon of Pembroke and Dorothy Gledhill Redpath (Buckner) of Rockland.

July 1. Frederick Joseph Micheau of Brockton and Mary Gertrude Gould of Rockland.

July 1. Ralph Oscar Peterson and Ruth Lee Miller both of Rockland.

July 6. Daniel F. Smith Jr. of Rockland and Virginia C. Welch of Abington.

July 14. George Leonard Chamberlin of Schenectady, N. Y., and Helen Kramer of Rockland.

July 15. Kenneth Alden Magoun of Hanover and Esther Stroud of Pembroke.

July 15. Robert Cushing Richards of Rockland and Harriet Frances Brown of Abington.

July 23. Joseph Jeremiah Kelliher of Rockland and Sophie Tekla Danksewicz of Abington.

July 28. Otis Winslow Magoun of Hanover and Phyllis Madeline Phinney of Rockland.

July 29. Charles Forbes Mandell of Rockland and Helen Esselen of Millis.

July 31. George Chauncey Mansfield of Rockland and Edith Catherine Hurley of New Bedford.

Aug. 1. Thomas Ignatious McCue of Rockland and Joyce Marie Fields of Lyndon, Vermont.

Aug. 2. Matthew Peter Bubin of Rockland and Harriet Elizabeth Pepper of Scituate.

Aug. 12. Richard Augustus Roth and Mary Ellen Roberts (FitzGibbons) both of Rockland.

Aug. 12. James Henry Sheridan of Watertown and Gertrude Mansfield of Rockland.

Aug. 13. Joseph William Nihill of Rockland and Shirley Eltona Barnes of Weymouth.

Aug. 17. Edgar Gruver Huntress and Lida May Fisher (Blake) both of Rockland.

Aug. 20. Robert Francis Thomson of Rockland and Isabella Mary Peters of Whitman.

Aug. 27. Francis Abner Beal of Rockland and Fernande Rolande Fafard of Abington.

Aug. 27. Lester Harold Atwood of Hanover and Irene Helen Benoit of Rockland.

Sept. 2. Olof Olson of Brockton and Melinda Estelle Cox (Inglis) of Hanover.

Sept. 3. Peter Q. Norkus of Weymouth and Mary L. Smith of Rockland.

Sept. 3. Michael Cifelli and Loretta Ann Geloran both of Rockland.

Sept. 4. John Joseph Fitzgibbons and Marion Elizabeth Reagan both of Rockland.

Sept. 6. James Butler Studley and Catherine Keane both of Rockland.

Sept. 9. James Henry Cronin and Catherine May Kelliher both of Rockland.

Sept. 12. William Roy Berry Jr., of Rockland and Emilie Anne Vanasse of Weymouth.

Sept. 15. Reginald Gardner Harris of Rockland and Eugenia Ciecinski of Abington.

Sept. 15. William John McGarrey Jr. and Eleanor Mahoney both of Rockland.

Sept. 30. William James Healy and Dorothy Edna Richardson both of Rockland.

Oct. 7. Benjamin Franklin Bowman of Rockland and Diana Manners Gibson of Weymouth.

Oct. 11. Fred Melvin Forbes of Rockland and Alice Mary Rich of Braintree.

- Oct. 12.   John J. Orcutt and Marie E .Damon, both of Rockland.

Oct. 12.   William Daniel Coughlan of Abington and Evelyn DeLory of Rockland.

Oct. 15.   David Poole Torrey and Grace Angelia Jacobs both of Rockland.

Oct. 21.   John Oscar Morgan and Lilian Margaret Glenn both of Whitman.

Oct. 22.   Joseph Harry Arena and Mary Celina Balonis both of Rockland.

Oct. 27.   Henry Arthur Brewster and Mary Blanche Durand both of Rockland.

Oct. 28.   Carl Victor Smith of Hanover and Elizabeth Pearson Locke of Rockland.

Oct. 28.   Fred Albert Arnold Jr., of Rockland and Helen Frances Park of Whitman.

Oct. 29.   Robert Joseph Hafferty of Quincy and Grace Theodora Muti of Rockland.

Nov. 2.   George Leo Dodd and Hazel Marguerite Silvia both of Rockland.

Nov. 4.   Frederick Walter Hussey and Helen Elizabeth Gardner both of Rockland.

Nov. 10.   Lawrence Joseph Whelan of Whitman and Genevieve Agnes Murray of Rockland.

Nov. 11.   James Joseph O'Brien of Whitman and Lucy Ann Rock of Rockland.

Nov. 11.   Edward J. Bogoloski of Rockland and Catherine R. King of Eastham.

Nov. 11. John Zeoli of Weymouth and Catherine Mary Keene of Rockland.

Nov. 11. Armand Philip Girouard of Bridgewater and Mary Frances Cella of Rockland.

Nov. 11. Robert Winthrop Murphy of Abington and Mary Theresa Tobin of Rockland.

Nov. 11. Joseph Cistrao of Rockland and Clara Josephine Ronan of Weymouth.

Nov. 14. Bernard Joseph Mahoney of Whitman and Katherine Joan Mars of Rockland.

Nov. 18. Howard Wilson Allen of So. Weymouth and Geraldine Frances McGlone of Rockland.

Nov. 24. Owen Francis Mahon of Rockland and Virginia E. Vass of Brockton.

Nov. 25. Arthur Charles Tedeschi of Rockland and Jennie Felaccio of So. Braintree.

Nov. 26. John Joseph Winske Jr. of Rockland and Ruth Madeline Torrey of Norwell.

Nov. 29. Adolph A. Marrese of Brockton and Helen Johnson of Rockland.

Nov. 29. Chester Henry Strefska and Alice Bradford Leonard both of Rockland.

Nov. 30. Richard Thomas Mannion of Concord, N. H. and Norma Josephine DeLory of Rockland.

Dec. 2. William Driscoll of Quincy and Kathleen Shields of Rockland.

Dec. 2. Albert Domenic Angie and Vanda Ida Henrietta Anderson both of Rockland.

Dec. 3.   Leo Marshall Nihill of Rockland and Maxine Gertrude Barnes of Whitman.

Dec. 14.   William Chisholm and Ethel Marjorie Salt both of Weymouth.

Dec. 16.   Harold Gouldrup and Edith Victoria Olson both of Rockland.

Dec. 30.   Robert Emmet Shannon of Abington and Kathryn Lucy McGee of Rockland.

Dec. 31.   Byron Arthur Osborne of West Hanover and Mary Alyce Delano of Rockland.

BIRTHS RECORDED IN THE TOWN OF ROCKLAND FOR THE YEAR 1939

Date	Name	Birthplace	Parents
Jan.			
1	Lorraine Grant	Weymouth	Alphonse and Emily T. (Mariani) Grant
4	Ann Marie Vogell	Rockland	Alice D. and Evelyn M. (Quinn) Vogell
5	Caroline Anne Ware	Weymouth	Warren I. and Pauline E. (Lescault) Ware
5	Caroline Avis Dodge	Weymouth	Carroll B. and Dorothy M. (Delano) Dodge
9	George Art Leonard	Brockton	Harold and Mary F. (Fish) Leonard
10	David Hoyt Holway	Weymouth	Lowell H. and Ann C. (Donohew) Holway
22	Janet Rose Derochea	Rockland	John T. and Edna I. (Fisher) Derochea
22	Charlotte Ramsey Chase	Weymouth	Charles M. and Ante L. (Buck) Chase
25	William Torrey Belcher	Smith	Weston B. and Esther (Torrey) Belcher
26	Paul Edward Badger	Rockland	Ralph H. and Mel V. (Snow) Badger
27	Judith Ancy Barron	Boston	Arthur H. and Ethel (Shieber) Barron
27	Sandra Ann Doherty	Weymouth	John J. and Alberta L. (Rowell) Doherty
31	Russell Edmund Lee	Weymouth	Russell E. and Mildred A. (Win) Lee
Feb.			
6	Wayne Keith Baldwin	Weymouth	Robert E. and Emilie I. (Schueller) Baldwin
11	Donald Charles Smith	Brockton	James H. and Helen E. (Wilbar) Smith
11	Helen Gardner Smith	Brockton	James H. and Helen E. (Wilbar) Smith
11	Betsy Ann Morehouse	Brockton	Robert W. and Dorothy (Chamberlain) Morehouse
21	Robert Giles Dunn	Weymouth	Giles B. and Ida E. (Gill) Dunn
23	Carl Frederick Nelson	Brockton	Carl G. and Sylvia (Garfield) Nelson
28	William Henry Smith	Brockton	William V. and Geraldine (Damon) Smith
Mar.			
2	Richard Berry	Brockton	Ralph D. and Meredith (Chase) Berry
3	Ann Marie Ford	Weymouth	John T. and Frances E. (Costello) Crawford
11	Carole Ann Hill	Smith	Louis M. and Marguerite F. (Beal) Hill
12	Robert Francis Bell	Rockland	Cyril F. and Mary T. (McKenna) O'Donnell
13	Norma Dunham	Rockland	Wm F. and Mary (Marchelletta) Dunham
15	Dorothy Pratt	Weymouth	Charles D. and Jennie B. (Curtis) Merritt

BIRTHS RECORDED IN THE TOWN OF ROCKLAND FOR THE YEAR 1939

Date	Name		Parents
31	Gilbert ⬛ Strickland	⬛	⬛rt C. and Pearl M. (⬛ier) Stri ⬛nd
April			
4	Still ⬛m	Rockland	Owen C. and ⬛el G. (Lewis) Damon
8	Esther ⬛ Mary Damon	⬛	⬛w M. ard My ⬛ (⬛) ⬛
9	Patsy Ann ⬛er	⬛th	⬛n S. ard ⬛se E. (⬛t) Ewell
12	⬛d Leroy ⬛l	Brockton	⬛ip L. and My M. ⬛ ⬛) Brown
17	Mary Ann Brown	⬛th	John A. ard Mildred C.
24	Joan ⬛ ⬛le ⬛ni	Brockton	⬛hn ard My ⬛i) Frino
27	Lorraine Frances Frino		
27	Stillborn		
27	⬛cy ⬛e Pilote	Brockton	Edward C. ard Kathryn M. (Hi ⬛ay) Pilote
29	(Male) ⬛w	⬛th	⬛er S. ard Lois P. (Dolan) ⬛w
May			
10	⬛d Francis Stringer	⬛th	⬛les F. and Marion E. ⬛ck) ⬛er
11	Marjorie ⬛ia Burke	⬛th	Everett F. ard ⬛ia A. (Lowney) Burke
13	⬛e ⬛d	⬛th	John V. ard Lilly L. (⬛th) ⬛d
14	Herbert Richard Bowman	⬛h	⬛ir ard ⬛e R. (Vinton) Bowman
19	John ⬛es Gerstle	⬛d	⬛k J. ard Gertrude L. (Holley) Gerstle
26	⬛er Stanley Morehouse	⬛th	Alfred B. and Etta L. (Unwin) Morehouse
26	⬛k Joseph Ryan	⬛d	⬛d E. ard Clara G. (Pratt) Ryan
27	⬛ ⬛d ⬛n	⬛d	⬛nes B. ard Agnes L. (⬛ld) Lonergan
29	Miriam FitzGerald	Brockton	⬛ry K. ard ⬛m (Mulready) ⬛ld
June			
1	John ⬛w ⬛n	Brockton	⬛n T. ard My A. (Mayhew) ⬛n
3	⬛ie Francis ⬛n	Brockton	Lawrence F. ard Irene M. ⬛r) Ryan
4	⬛as ⬛es Pearse	Brockton	John H. ard Ella L. (Billett) Pearse
6	Stillborn		
11	Richard William Lukaszewicz	⬛h	Bronislaw J. ard My M. (Mi ⬛ki) ⬛cz

BIRTHS RECORDED IN THE TOWN OF ROCKLAND FOR THE YEAR 1939

Date	Name	Birthplace	Parents
15	Joyce Thurley Clark	...th	George A. Z. and Marjorie E. (...e) Clk
15	Helena Mary DeLory	...th	Bernard V. and Helena M. (Burns) DeLory
19	John Russell Berryman	Weymouth	Kenneth S. and Virginia F. (Damon) Berryman
19	John Elbridge Mary	Brockton	Arthur C. and Evelyn L. (Cheney) Woodbury
26	Norman Everett Little	Brockton	Norman E. and ...ia W. (Molander) Little
28	Elaine Elizabeth ...ble	Brockton	...n B. and Mel E. (Sylvia) ...le
28	Joan Carol Henrickson	Brockton	...o O. and Florence M. (Dunbrack) Henrickson
29	Charles Francis Benoit	Broc ...n	Arthur ... and ...ssa J. (Richard) Benoit
30	Patricia Ann Hammond	Weymouth	Fran k C. ... M. (Mouchagne) Hammod
July			
3	Walter Lawrence Sunbury	...th	Lawrence I. and Myrtle E. (Starkie) u...bury
5	Stillborn		
6	Mary Lou Clark	Rockland	...ge G. and Agnes E. (...y) Clar k
7	Everett ...t Beale	Weymouth	Minot A. and June N. (Thornton) Beale
9	...es Edward Deegan	Brockton	Leo A. and Emily T. (...ll) Deegan
11	Priscilla Frances Lyon	Brockton	Alton F. and Villa M. (Webber) Lyon
11	Peter Joseph Chiminiello, Jr.	...th	Peter J. and Mary E. (Ingeno) Chiminiello
17	Andrew Hutcheon Merritt	Brockton	Joseph F. and Alice H. (Lamb) Merritt
21	Jeffrey Lane ...re	Weymouth	Harold G. and ...or V. (Stoddard) ...d
25	Averill ...se ...d	Boston	Paul E. and Esther A. (Thayer) ...
Aug.			
3	Sally Derochea	Rockland	Ralph E. and Minnie F. (...t) Derochea
3	Peter Brigham DeMaranville	Boston	Herbert and Valeria (Brigham) DeMaranville
4	Jennie Lee Farrar	Brockton	James E. and ...a L.	...n) Farrar
5	George Michael Hart Jr.	Weymouth	...ge M. and Margaret M. (...u) Hart
6	Sa dran Claire Peachey	Malden	William J. and Virginia F. (Patten) Peachey
7	Marjorie May Hammond	Brockton	Oscar C. and Marjorie C. (Bassett) Hammond
11	Albert Andrew Marcotte	Brockton	Albert J. and Christine K. (...o) Marcotte

BIRTHS RECORDED IN THE TOWN OF ROCKLAND FOR THE YEAR 1939

Date	Name	Place	Parents
17	Stillborn		
18	Ann Eliz bth Shalgian	Ban	Mel P. and Ma M. (Shoe) Halgian
24	George William Wilson Jr.		Gee W. nd Roma F. (Na) Wilson
25	Gil Sandra Kendall	Brockton	Kenneth E. and Phyllis E. (Henshaw) Kendall
26	Stillborn		
31	Joan Aele Mst rno	Wyuth	Iph A. and Aele (Ragni) Mst ranico
Sept.			
1	Hilda at Tyni	Brockton	Unlevi and Mry V. (Pieti)) Tyni
4	Judith Iva Gn	Wbh	Raymond J. nd Dorothy C. (Donovan) Gn
6	Robert Gio Mni	Wbh	Guido J. nd Angie (Felaccio) Mni
7	Stillborn		
8	William Imes Richmond	Brockton	Wm B. and Rosa F. (Hat) mnd
11	Ms Edward Petrosevich	Rockland	Ms E. nd Helen A. (Glinsky) Petrosevich
16	Henry Smith Fraser Jr.	Wbh	Henry S. nd Blanche C. (Holbrook) Fraser
16	Judith Ae Mn	Obh	Md T. and Ana R. (nt) un
20	Wa Mn Salina	Wbh	Joseph J. and Stacia A. (Mileski(Sabina
21	Beverly Ann Eaniri	Wbh	Gald nd Doris H. (Gn) Eaniri
23	Ronald Iph Duhamel	Wbh	William J. and Grace E. (Clark) Duhamel
O.			
4	Patricia Am mBth	I Wbh	Dniel F. and Virginia C. (Wh) mBth
9	David William Mr	Brockton	William H. nd Barbara E. (Clapp) Mvlver
11	Iph Raymond Forrand Mn	Brockton	Ade J. nd Edlor (Morrill) Forrand
11	Richard Abrt Mn	Rockland	John J. and Florence H. (Coe) Mn
15	Vgia Ke Liska	Brockton	Mn L. and Hector N. (Sledge) Liska
15	Maria Lioy	Wbh	William P. ahd Rachel C. (Wheeler) Loy
15	Artur William Casey	Wouth	Mr W. nd Laura T. (Lund) Gl
17	Ted Me Mni	Und	Irving G. and Elfrida M. (Von Beidel) Pennini
18	Angela Maria DelPrete		Joseph and Me (Umbrianna) DelPrete
21	Timothy Francis Twomey	Weym nth	Timothy F. and Dthy M. (Savage) Twomey

BIRTHS RECORDED IN THE TOWN OF ROCKLAND FOR THE YEAR 1939

Date	Name	Birthplace	Parents
22	David Laurence Sargent	ᵃᵗth	Arthur J. ard Florence (Hawes) Sargent
26	Gles Allen aDis	Brockton	les A. ard Margaret G. (Cunningham) Davis
Nv. 8	COia Mastrodomenico	Brockton	Michaeli A. ard Angeline T. (Cerce) Mastrodomenico
11	Gail Carol Ann Wb	Weymouth	Rol et S. and Zaira E. (Golemme) Wb
13	George Vincent Higgins 3rd	Brockton	John T. and Doris M. (Montgomery) Higgins
17	Met Threasa roll	Brockton	Robert E. and Norine M. (Whittaker) Yourell
22	William Alan Schofield	ᵃᵗth	Ralph E. ard Florence A. (Mann) Bold
Dec. 2	l Me) McGarry	ᵃᵗth	William J. ard thor L. My) McGarry
11	les Evans Buckley	Brockton	les H. and Eka M. (Bit) Bdey
12	Margaret Eileen Hayden	Rockland	Robert E. ard Hermina M. (Morehouse) Hayden
14	Ruth Elizabeth Tedesco	Weymouth	als R. ard Lillian A. (Rosenquist) Tedesco
22	Kerry Joan Freeman	ᵃᵗth	Raymond F. ard Joan (Bowman) Freeman
26	Hith Ann Harris	ᵃᵗth	Reginald G. and Eugenia S. (Ciecinski) Harris
30	John Peter Elliott	ᵃᵗth	Edward D. ad Zulina F. (Davis) Elliott
30	Carol Lee Kendall	Htlan	Harold A. and Norma C. (Clark) Kendall
31	te Coppola	Rockland	l to ard Tsa pla

DEATHS REGISTERED IN THE TOWN OF ROCKLAND FOR THE YEAR 1939

Date	Name	Age Y	M	D	Cause of Death	Birthplace
Jan.						
4	Jennie Muriel Tower	79	3	24	Cerebral 1 ...	Rockland
5	William F. Howes	60	3	19	...	...
8	Alice Gertrude Wales	75	3	1	Cardio-Renal Disease	Leed, England
13	Anna ... Kelly	90	3	13	...	Boston
16	... W. ... Jr.	69	3	17	... Esophagus	...
17	... M. Seldon	62		14	Dial ...	...
17	... ...	76		19	Cardio-renal	... Engl and
21	Alice Vernon ...	71	9	1	...	Dartmouth
22	Eliza ...	88	7	1	...	...
25	Arthur ...	73	7	28	... Occlusion	Plymouth
25	Ella ... Osborne	64	10		Broncho 1 ...	Dux l ...
25	... E. Kane	79	9	2	...	Gardiner, ...
29	Annie Reed Pierce	79	1	4	1 ... Heart Disease	Rockland
31	... D. Marshall	6	1			
Feb.						
1	... W. ...	67	2	15	...	Boston
4	Louis Monto	89	5	8	...	Boston
6	James Alton Curtis	80	1	22	...	Rockland
12	Evaline Ermance Fairley	72	5	9	...	...
13	William M. ...	62	5	3	...	New York City
18	Frederick H. Corey	60	2	19	Coronary ...-sclerosis	Charlestown
20	Annie T. Jackson	76	1	4	...	Abington
20	... Eckley Herring	77		8	...	East Lyme, Conn.
23	Paul J. Marshall	10	6	20	Rheumatic ...	E. ..., R. I.
23	Winfield G. Davison	73	10	21	Cerebral Accident	...
24	Harold Archie Davis	14	11	5	Sub-dural Hematoma	Pembroke
25	Mary Jane Kendrigan	81	1	28	Myocarditis	Rockland

DEATHS REGISTERED IN THE TOWN OF ROCKLAND FOR THE YEAR 1939

Date	Name	Y	M	D	Cause of Death	Place
25	r...y Bowser	62	2	12	...y ...s	New Brunswick, Can.
25	...d A. ...ll	1	8	5	...s meningitis	N... ...h
26	Me... ...er	58	6	11	Dia ...s ...is	...o
3	My E. ...y ...n	73	11	17	Bro ...o ...a	Rockland ...d
4	Everett L. ...n	56	6	18	Bro ...o ...a	...n
11	...y	53	3	12	...ar ...a	...d
15	...r C. Dill	61	2	—	...s	...d
16	...et G. Melville	29	—	—	r...a of larynx	Ireland
19	...s F. ...h	82	—	21	...a ...s	...nd
26	William ...n Loud	62	1	13	...ditis ...onia	...eld
30	...a ...g	91	1	13		
4	...t ...ell Bole	86	8	16	...o ...s	...eld
4	Ellis W. ...d	81	11	25	...al r ...e	...n
9	Nil A. ...t	67	2	1	...s	P. E. I. C ...a
10	...e I. ...p ...y	72	10	3	...y r ...sis	...er
13	...n Franklin ...itt	78	4	6	...o scl ...s	Abington
26	Stillborn	75	5	27		Duxbury
27	Ruth ...n Denham	83	6	—	Cerebral ...ppl...y	...d
29	...y Irving ...s	58	1	13	...s	..., Me
29	...n F. ...n	77	2	14	...s	...d
29	...es F. Horan Ir.	10	6	2	...d skull	...h
3	...s F. Riordan	73	1	9	Cerebral Hemorrhage	...d
3	...th An ...y	71	5	7	...a of r ...h	...d

DEATHS REGISTERED IN THE TOWN OF ROCKLAND FOR THE YEAR 1939

Date	Name	Age Y	Age M	Age D	Cause of Death	Birthplace
4	Fred Grant Holbrook	68	9	2	Myocarditis	Weymouth
4	Abel Merriam Poole	79	—	4	Arterio sclerosis	Rockland
10	John P. Tyler	81	8	29	Uremia	Rockland,
12	Martha McCurda	84	6	22	Chr. ...is	Rockland
14	Na Ethelyn Johnson	40	4	9	Hodgkins disease	Braintree
15	...er E. ...in	33	8	—	Hodgkins disease	Boston
19	...la F. Spafford	34	—	26	Carbon monoxide poisoning	Burlington, Vt.
19	Henry Giza	24	—	—	...l on monoxide poisoning	...a
23	Philip A. Shinn	53	5	17	Cerebral hemmorrhage	Portland. Maine
June 3	Leon ...k Thompson	43	11	5	...te Coronary ...	Millis
5	...er Lincoln ...ne	79	7	25	Carcinoma of Esophagus	...nd
6	Stillborn					
7	...se A. Hill	70	5	—	Cerebral Arterio-sclerosis	Boston
12	Joseph Saunders Gardner	79	4	25	...io ...is	Rockland
12	Timothy W. Ryan	81	2	14	...al	Ireland
14	Mary E. Collins	82	—	—	Myocarditis	Boston
17	...n Franklin Hawes	57	10	12	Bacterial Endocarditis	Rockland
21	...is Howard ...te	84	10	8	Myocarditis	No. Wrentham
30	...ip P. ...lie	60	7	7	Myocarditis	...ll
July 1	Marion E. O'Brien	58	10	19	...a of B...st	Rockland
2	Frederick Stephen Currie	37	4	—	Suicide	New Brunswick, Can.
5	Stillborn					
18	Agnes G. Carney	65	6	2	Cardio-renal disease	Rockland
19	...ne ...e	78	3	—	Cerebral hemorrhage	Italy
27	Raymond S. ...ns	38	7	28	...h by suspension	...ill
Aug.						

DEATHS REGISTERED IN THE TOWN OF ROCKLAND FOR THE YEAR 1939

Date	Name	Age Y	M	D	Cause of Death	Birthplace
3	Joseph D. McGee	77	2	8	Arterio sclerosis	Ottawa, a&ada
10	Elizal eth Connelly	59		7	Heart de	Rockland
18	Millie Z. Boudreau	48	11	7	dto scl eⁿis	Canada
18	Stillborn					
26	Stilll oⁿn					
30	Margaret Elⁱeth Stiles	72	5	26	Chr. itis	Col ml ns, Ohio
St.						
7	Stillborn					
10	Ruth M. kesworth	24		1	Compound	Rockland
11	la A. ey	71		26	Corinary l s	Baldwinsville
20	William H. ee	84	6	20	al s	Rockland
29	Emeline Hut r	87	7	12	al r ge	er
29	as P. ld	75	6	15	Arterio sclerosis	
Oct.						
5	s Albert Tipping	29	3	19	Bacterial	l o
8	Mary J. Wherity	71	11	10	to s	Rockland
8	Dora A. Metivier	64	1	7	al	Norwell
10	Elizabeth L. Smith	90	8	24	Arterio s	So. Weym th, M.
11	Olive Ann ne	64	7	24	to e	So. Orrington, n, N. H.
13	John Baptiste u	57	2	5	a of Pancreas	Townsend
14	Ae Holbrook Hutchinson	77	11	17	y thrombosis	Somerville
14	Ellen Catherine McCarthy	85	1		Arterio sclerosis	Ireland
16	Margaret E. Foley	51	2	17	Myocarditis	Leicester, En d
16	Frank Rol t W er	42	8	24	a of Colon de	Cambridge
19	Edward M. h	59	1	17	Hypertensive t	Rockland
24	Fannie A. s	70	1	24	G. Fibroid pthisis	N.
26	Warren Ashton Vinton	63	6	4	Chr. is	h
29				13	Myocarditis	Rockland

DEATHS REGISTERED IN THE TOWN OF ROCKLAND FOR THE YEAR 1939

Date	Name	Age Y	M	D	Cause of Death	Birth Place
30	Arthur S.	51	10	2	philia	
30	Eliz beth Adelia Inglis	79	1	1		
Nov.						
18	Eliott L. Poole	81	2	16		Italy
20	W. Go	61		3	Diabetes	
26	as W.	72	7	17		
28	N. Flynn	63	11	10		
30		89	11	11	Chr.	Boston
Dec.						
3	Frances Pearl Vinton	51	9	11		Pembroke
6	er S.	71	5	16		
13	a E.	71	9	12		, Ill.
20	George Winthrop ey	66	7	4	ry	
22		81	6	6	Arterio-sclerosis	
25	t S.	76				Ireland
25	Irma F.	35		17	ry of Uterus	
26	Florence Herbert	62	10	7		
27	David W.	65	9	19		Weymouth

Report of the Records for the Year 1939

Pursuant to the foregoing warrant a meeting was held in the Rockland Opera House, beginning at 7:30 o'clock P. M. and the following votes were passed and action taken.

The meeting was called to order at 7:30 P. M. by the Moderator, Magorisk L. Walls.

The warrant and Constable's return of service thereof was read by the Town Clerk.

Article 1. Voted to accept the reports of the various Town Officers and Committees as published in the Town Report.

Article 2. Voted to raise and appropriate the following amounts for the purposes named:

School Department	$105 200 00
State Aid	600 00
Soldiers' Relief	9 000 00
Care of Soldiers' Graves	150 00
Memorial Library and Dog Fund	4 400 00
Street Lighting	8 898 00
Highway Surveyor	1 350 00
Tarvia and Road Binder	3 000 00
Highway Repairs	1 800 00
Sidewalks	500 00
Cleaning Union Street	1 200 00
Clean-Up-Week	75 00
Guide Boards and Signs	100 00
Fire Department	11 080 00

Police Department	8 955	00
Forest Fires	750	00
Board of Health	6 000	00
Inspection of Animals	150	00
Park Department	2 800	00
Old Age Assistance	55 000	00
Moth Department	300	00
Tree Warden	900	00
Town Officers	7 700	00
Office Rent	1 800	00
Sealer of Weights and Measures	400	00
Elections	1 000	00
Compensation Insurance	1 928	71
Mass. Industrial School	1 800	00
Town Report and Poll Book	1 585	00
Support of Poor and Infirmary	51 000	00
Mother's Aid	9 500	00
Town Notes and Interest	36 000	00
Assessors	2 500	00
Snow Removal	9 500	00
Reserve Fund	4 000	00
Miscellaneous Assessors	1 550	00
Miscellaneous Treasurer	800	00
Miscellaneous Clerk	350	00
Miscellaneous Selectmen	120	00
Miscellaneous Registrars	650	00
Miscellaneous Sealer	190	00
Miscellaneous Collector	1 450	00
Miscellaneous Unclassified	1 100	00

Total amount raised under this article $357 131 71

Under Article No. 2. Meeting of March 6, 1939.

Amendment to raise and appropriate $103,300.00 for the School Department was not agreed to.

Voted to pass over appropriations for the following:

Military Aid, Massachusetts Hospital School and Burial of Indigent Soldiers.

Under Article No. 2 Adjourned Meeting March 13, 1939

Voted to return to Article No. 2 and to reconsider the amount pertaining to Snow Removal.

Voted to raise and appropriate the sum of $9,500.00 for Snow Removal, which amended the amount of $7,000.00 raised and appropriated at the meeting of March 6.

Article 3. Voted to authorize the Town Treasurer, with the approval of the Selectmen, to borrow money from time to time in anticipation of the revenue of the financial year beginning January 1, 1940 and to issue a note or notes therefor, payable within one year, and renew such note or notes as may be given for a period of less than one year in accordance with Section 17, Chapter 44, General Laws.

Article 4. Voted to raise and appropriate the sum of fifteen hundred dollars ($1,500.00) to be spent under the direction of the Selectmen for the part payment of a Visiting Nurse.

,Article 5. Voted to approprate the sum of twenty-nine thousand five hundred dollars ($29,500.00) for use of the Water Department the same to be taken from the Water Revenue.

Artcile 6. Voted to raise and appropriate the sum of two hundred eighty-eight dollars ($288.00) to be spent under the direction of the Selectmen for the purpose of renting quarters for the use of the Veterans of the Spanish-American War.

Article 7. Voted to raise and appropriate the sum of four hundred dollars ($400.00) to be spent under the di-

rection of the Selectmen for the observance of Memorial
Day.

Article 8. Voted to raise and appropriate the sum of
sixty dollars ($60.00) for the care of the Town Cemetery.

Article 9. Voted to raise and appropriate the sum of
nine hundred dollars ($900.00) to be spent under the di-
rection of the Selectmen for the purpose of renting quarters for the use of the Rockland Post No. 147 of the American Legion.

Article 10. Voted to pass over the raising and appropriating of a sum of money for the use of the Plymouth
County trustees for County Aid to Agriculture and the
choosing of town director as provided in Sections 41 and
45 of Chapter 128, General Laws.

Article 11. A motion to raise and appropriate the sum
of $100.00 for the purposes of carrying out this article
not agreed to .

Voted to raise and appropriate $150.00 to be used by
the School Committee to pay for the expense of heating,
lighting, and Casualty Insurance of Junior-Senior High
and McKinley School Buildings as well as additional expense for janitors when the buildings are used by individuals and associations for educational, recreational and
like purposes under the provision of Chapter 71, Section
71 of the General Laws.

Article 12. Voted to raise and appropriate the sum of
one hundred dollars ($100.00) for criminal cases in court.

Article 13. Voted to raise and appropriate the sum of
two hundred ninety-two dollars and fifty cents ($292.50)
to insure the Firemen of the Town of Rockland that they
might receive compensation in case of accident when on
duty.

Article 14. Voted to raise and appropriate the sum of six thousand dollars ($6,000.00) to be spent in conjunction with the State and County to rebuild West Water Street from the Abington line to Union Square.

Article 15. Motion to pass over this article not agreed to.

Voted to raise and appropriate the sum of fifteen hundred dollars ($1500.00) to employ a "Visitor" to administer Public Welfare. This "Visitor" to be selected by the Board of Public Welfare from qualified applicants subject to standards recommended by the State Public Welfare Department.

Article 16. Voted to pass over the raising and appropriating the sum of four thousand three hundred dollars ($4300.) for the material cost and contributory expenses to rebuild Exchange Street from Union to Liberty street, a distance of 1800 feet, the labor to be furnished by the W. P. A.

Article 17. Voted to pass over the raising and appropriating of the sum of one hundred dollars ($100.00) to help defray the expenses of Christmas lighting on Union Street.

Article 18. Voted to raise and appropriate the sum of forty four hundred twentyseven dollars and thirty-five cents ($4427.35) for the maintenance of the Plymouth County Hospital.

Article 19. Voted to establish a Planning Board under the provisions of General Laws, Chapter 41, Section 81A, and amendments thereof, the board to consist of five members and at the annual election in 1940 to elect one member for a term of five years, one member for a term of four years, one member for a term of three years, one member for a term of two years, and one member for a term of one year, and thereafter to elect each year one member for a term of five years, also that the Moderator be instructed to appoint a committee of five to continue as a Planning Board Committee and prepare a map showing the proposed zoning of the town to be submitted to the next annual meeting.

Committee appointed: Arthur P. Wilcox, Chairman, James A. Cody, Francis L. Gammon, Joseph Lelyveld, and Carl G. Fass.

Article 20. Voted to raise and appropriate the sum of nine hundred dollars ($900.00) for the maintenance of traffic beacons and signals.

Article 21. Voted to raise and appropriate the sum of five hundred dolars ($500.00) for the cleaning of catch basins and drains.

Article 22. Voted to appropriate the sum of four hundred fifty dollars ($450.00) from the amount raised by bond issue under Article 13, of the Special Town Meeting of August 8, 1938 for materials to resurface the sidewalk on the westerly side of Union Street between Vesper's Garage and the property of Maria Jenkins, a distance of 900 feet, the labor to be furnished by the WPA.

Article 23. Voted to raise and appropriate the sum of eight hundred seventy-five dollars ($875.00) for materials, for revising, indexing and filing of all Vital Statistics records of the Town of Rockland in conformity with Federal requirements, all labor to be performed by the WPA.

Article 24. Voted to pass over the raising and appropriating of the sum of six hundred dollars ($600.00) to pay for material for repairs at G. A. R. hall, the labor to be taken from the W. P. A.

Article 25.   Voted to install a Street light on Forest Street, near the residence of Charles Rose and raise and appropriate the sum of fifteen dollars ($15.00) for the same.

Article 26.   Voted to pass over the raising and appropriating of the sum of five hundred dollars ($500.00) to repair and resurface Beal Street Extension from East Water Street easterly a distance of approximately 430 feet.

Article 27.   Voted to pass over the raising and appropriating of the sum of four hundred six dollars and sixty-eight cents to pay bill of E. Worthington, Sanitary Engineer, for work in preparing sewage plans for the town.

At adjourned meeting of March 13, a motion to reconsider this article not agreed to.

Article 28.   Voted to pass over the raising and appropriating of a sum of money to build a sidewalk and curb on the north side of Belmont Street from the residence of Charles McGonagle a distance of 225 feet.

Article 29.   Voted to pass over the installing of a water main on Weymouth street, a distance of 1225 feet, and raising and appropriating the sum of $1750.00 for material for same.

Article 30.   Voted to appropriate the sum of six hundred dollars ($600.00) from the amount raised by bond issue under Article 13, of the Special Town Meeting of August 8, 1938 for materials to install a sidewalk and curb on the south side of Reed Street from the residence of Patrick Mahoney to Plain Street, the labor to be furnished by the W. P. A.

Article 31.   Voted to raise and appropriate the sum of

five hundred dollars ($500.00) to pay the expense of foreclosing tax titles in the Land Court and cost of sale of land of low value acquired by the town by tax sales without foreclosure.

Article 32.   Voted to raise and appropriate the sum of twelve hundred dollars ($1200.00) to be spent for the cost of material and general expenses under the W. P. A.

Article 33.   Voted to authorize the selectmen to lease, for use as town offices, the store and basement in the building on the corner of Union Street and Taunton Avenue, for a term of not more than five years, at a rental not exceeding eighteen hundred dollars per annum, provided the owner will install a vault and suitable office partitions.

Article 34.   Voted to raise and appropriate the sum of twenty-four hundred dollars ($2400.00) as part payment for Sewing Material used in the Sewing Unit of the W. P. A.

Artcile 35.   Voted to raise and appropriate the sum of five hundred and fifteen dollars, and eighty-seven cents ($515.87) to pay in part for administration expenses for Federal Commodity Distribution.

Article 36.   Voted that the Moderator appoint a committee of nine to act in conjunction with the Tri-Town observance of Armisice Day and raise and appropriate the sum of four hundred dollars ($400.00) for the same.
Armistice Day Committee: Fred Martin, Chairman; James P. Kane, Frank H. Dixon, Harold R. Morse, Warren B. Hamilton, Horace L. Crossman, William F. Watson, J. Rufus Chilton, Ray Bradbury.

Article 37.   Voted to raise and appropriate the sum of four hundred dollars ($400.00) to pay for the expense of heating, lighting, gas and removal of garbage in the

McKinley School building when the building is used by the Nursery, Sewing and Recreational projects of the Works Progress Administration.

Article 38. Voted to raise and appropriate $37.00 to provide suitable lights at the entrance to the drive in front of the high school and also at the Taunton Avenue entrance to the high school building.

Article 39. Voted to appropriate the sum of eight hundred eighty-five dollars ($885.00) from the amount raised by bond issue under Article 13, of the Special Town Meeting of August 8, 1938 for materials for a curbing and hard surface for the circular walk in front of the high school on Taunton avenue, the labor to be performed by the W. P. A.

Article 40. Voted to pass over the raising and appropriating of a sum of money to complete the running track in Memorial Park.

Article 41. Voted to pass over the raising and appropriating a sum of money to complete the tennis courts in Memorial Park.

Article 42. Voted to pass over the raising and appropriating of a sum of money for a fence to enclose the athletic fields at Memorial Park.

Article 43. Voted to pass over the raising and appropriating of a sum of money for materials, to install a sidewalk and curb on the north side of Reed street from Division to Plain street, the labor to be taken from W. P. A.

Article 44. Voted to appropriate the sum of seven hundred dollars ($700.00) from the amount raised by bond issue under Article 13, of the Special Town Meeting of August 8, 1938 for materials to rebuild the sidewalk on the west and south side of Prospect street from West

Water street to Highland Street, the labor to be furnished by the W. P. A.

Voted to take up articles 45, 46 and 47 collectively.

Article 45. Voted to raise and appropriate the sum of two hundred seventy-five dollars ($275.00) for new tires for the combination truck of the Fire Department.

Article 46. Voted to pass over the raising and appropriating of the sum of eighty-five hundred dollars ($8500.00) to purchase a triple combination pump for the use of the Fire Department.

Article 47. Voted to pass over the purchasing of a triple combination pump for the use of the Fire Department and raising and appropriating of the sum of two thousand five hundred dollars ($2500.00) in the year 1939, and authorize the treasurer to borrow the sum of six thousand dollars ($6000.00) for such purpose, and to issue bonds or notes of the town to be payable in five years, under the provisions of Chapter 44, Section 7, of the General Laws (Tercentenary Edition).

Article 48. Voted to pass over the raising and appropriating of the sum of thirty-five hundred dollars ($3500.-00) to purchase pipe and material to connect 12 inch water mains from North Avenue to Rice Avenue the labor to be furnished by the W. P. A.

Article 49. Voted to adopt the following By-Law:— At any special town meeting no appropriation of money shall be made unless ten percent (10%) of the registered voters of the town are present at said meeting.

Unanimous Vote

Article 50. Voted to raise and appropriate the sum of twenty-five dollars ($25.00) for materials to reopen the former drain pipes at Wright's Brook on Webster Street near Liberty Square and install curb recessed opening type drain with catch basin top, the labor to be performed by the W. P. A.

Article 51. Voted to pass over the raising and appropriating of a sum of money to install an electric light on the south side of Webster Street between East Water Street and Hingham Street.

Article 52. Voted to pass over the raising and appropriating of the sum of thirteen hundred fifty dollars ($1350.00) to build a sidewalk and curb on the south side of Prospect Street, from West Water Street to Highland Street, a distance of 1350 feet.

At 10:00 P. M. Voted to adjourn until March 13, 1939 at 7:30 P. M.

Article 53. Voted to appropriate the sum of five hundred dollars ($500.00) from the amount raised by bond issue under Article 13, of the Special Town meeting of August 8, 1938 for materials to build a sidewalk and curb on the west side of Myrtle Street from Bigelow Avenue to Summit Street, a distance of 1200 feet, the labor to be furnished by the W. P. A.

Article 54. Voted to raise and appropriate the sum of fifty dollars ($50.00) to repair the bridge on Emerson Street, the labor to be furnished by the W. P. A.

Article 55. Voted to pass over the accepting of the provisions of Chapter 31, Section 48, of the General Laws relative to placing members of the Police Department under Civil Service Laws.

Article 56. Voted to pass over the accepting of the provisions of Chapter 31, Section 49, of the General Laws relative to placing the Chief of Police under Civil Service Laws.

Actile 57. Voted to authorize the Police Department to exchange the present police car and purchase a new cruising car and to raise and appropriate the sum of four hundred dollars ($400.00) for the same.

Article 58. Voted to pass over the raising and appropriating of a sum of money to build a sidewalk and curb on west side of Monroe street from West Water to Grove Street.

Article 59. Voted to pass over the taking of any action regarding the office hours of the Town Treasurer.

Article 60. Voted to pass over having printed in the next annual report the full assessment of all property within the town as assessed for the year 1939.

Article 61. Voted that the Moderator appoint a committee of five to revise and redraft the by-laws of the town of Rockland, said redraft to be presented to the town at the next annual town meeting for its acceptance.

Committee: Francis J. Geogan, Chairman; Harry S. Torrey, Ralph L. Belcher, James P. Kane, Dennis L. O'Connor.

Article 62. Voted to appropriate the sum of three hundred dollars ($300.00) from the amount raised under Article 32, for General W. P. A. purposes, for materials, for a drain and two catch basins on the easterly side of Concord street starting at the end of the present drain near the residence of Dominic DelPrete and running a distance of 300 feet southerly, the labor to be furnished by the W. P. A.

Article 63. Voted to pass over the raising and appropriating of a sum of money to build a sidewalk on the west side of Franklin Avenue, from the corner of Church street to the corner of School Street.

Article 64. Voted to raise and appropriate the sum of three hundred fifty dollars ($350.00) for Reed's Pond.

Article 65. Voted to pass over the raising and appropriating of one thousand five hundred dollars ($1500.00) to rebuild Carey Court and install a curb and sidewalk starting at Reed Street and continuing toward North Avenue until money is exhausted, work to be done by WPA.

Article 66. Voted to pass over the taking of land and buildings on Taunton Avenue known as the Friary property and the adjacent land through to Reed street known as the Gleason property, with the buildings thereon, said land after removal of buildings to be used for parking purposes, and to raise and appropriate a sum of money to take that property.

Article 67. Voted to pass over the authorizing of the Real Estate Board to sell the buildings on the Friary and Gleason Lots, as described in the above article, same to be removed from the land.

Article 68. Voted to pass over the raising and appropriating of a sum of money to grade and asphalt the Friary-Gleason lots, as described in Article 66, and to mark the same for parking purposes.

Article 69. Voted to pass over asphalting and marking the School Street lot for parking purposes, and to raise and appropriate a sum of money for same.

Article 70. Voted t opass over the raising and appropriating of a sum of money to police the School Street parking lot.

Article 71.   Voted to pass over the raising and appropriating of a sum of money to purchase or erect signs to direct autoists to the School Street parking lot.

Article 72.   Voted to pass over the establishing of a school of shoemaking, for this year only, to be operated under the direction of the Superintendent of Schools and to raise and appropriate a sum of money for same.

Article 73.   Voted to pass over the authorizing of the Selectmen to appoint a committee to conduct a Fourth of July celebration, and to raise and appropriate for this purpose a sum of money not to exceed one thousand dollars ($1,000.00).

Article 74.   Voted to accept the legacy of one thousand dollars ($1000.00) which was bequeathed to the Town of Rockland under the will of William J. Grace, late of San Francisco, California.
Unanimous vote.

Article 75.   Voted to pass over the raising and appropriating of the sum of three hundred fifty dollars ($350.-00) to gravel the extension of Rice Avenue, from Douglas Street west a distance of approximately 400 feet the labor to be furnished by the W. P. A.

Article 76.   Voted to raise and appropriate the sum of one hundred dollars ($100.00) to gravel Dexter Road Extension a distance of about 75 feet.

Sense of Meeting Votes:
Voted that each Department head furnish the Finance Committee with an itemized monthly statement of their expenditures.
Unanimous vote.

Upon motion of George J. Popp, Chief of Police, the meeting stood for a period of thirty seconds in tribute to the memory of Cornelius J. McHugh, former Police Officer.

A Subsequent Meeting for the election of Town Offic-ers was held in the Rockland Opera House, Savings Bank Building, Monday, March 13th, 1939. The Moderator, Magorisk L. Walls, formally opened the polls at 5:45 o'clock in the forenoon and they were closed at 4:00 o'clock in the afternoon as provided in the warrant for the meeting.

The following Ballot Clerks and Tellers were sworn to the faithful performance of their duties by the Town Clerk.

BALLOT CLERKS

Lavinia Condon   Mary Lynch
Evelyn Whiting   Olive Wheeler
Elizabeth Crane   Ralph McVein
Joseph Feeney   William O'Neil
Robert Parker   Jeremiah Shea

TELLERS

Carl Fass   John Winslow
Robert Estes   Angelina Ball
Matthew O'Grady   Josephine Gammon
Kathryn Tobin   John Paulin
Timothy White   Ellis Blake
Louise Hussey   Philip Murphy
Archie Minnis   James McPartland
Marion Tobin   Herbert Gardner
Anna Anderson   Helen Morrissey
John Dillon   George O'Donnell
John White   Lillian Rainsford

Before the opening of the polls, cards of instructions and cards containing abstracts of the laws imposing pen-alties upon voters and specimen ballots were posted as required by the laws of the Commonwealth relating to the

"Conduct of Elections" and all other provisions of law complied with.

At the opening of the polls the ballot boxes were publicly opened and shown to be empty; and they registered 0000.

The ballot boxes were opened and ballots taken therefrom for counting before the close of the polls upon the order of the Moderator and Town Clerk.

Upon the closing of the polls the ballot boxes registered

Ballot Box No. 1   1569
Ballot Box No. 2   1676
                    ————
                    3245

Total Three thousand two hundred forty-five (3245)

The total number of names of voters checked of the Voting Lists:

At Box No. 1   Men   840   Women   729   1569
At Box No. 2   Men   897   Women   779   1676
                      ————   ————   ————
Total names checked 1737   1508   3245

The total number of ballots cast were:
Three thousand two hundred and forty-five (3245)

At 8:10 o'clock P. M. the Town Clerk publicly announced the result of the voting as follows:

Total number of Ballots Cast   3245
    which included 24 Absentee Voting Ballots

MODERATOR—One Year

    Magorisk L. Walls   2505

Burton L. Cushing	1
Blanks	739

TOWN CLERK—One Year

Ralph L. Belcher	2691
Blanks	554

TOWN TREASURER—One Year

Nathaniel S. Groce	456
Charles J. Higgins	2553
Walter C. Fihelly	2
Blanks	234

TAX COLLECTOR—One Year

James A. Donovan	2686
Blanks	559

SELECTMEN, BOARD OF PUBLIC WELFARE, AND FENCE VIEWERS—One Year

John J. Bowler	1781
George E. Mansfield	1510
Fred Stevenson	794
Harry S. Torrey	1581
Norman S. Whiting	1974
James Fitzgibbons	1
Blanks	2094

HIGHWAY SURVEYOR—One Year

William Bell	1365
Roderick MacKenzie	1800
Blanks	80

ASSESSOR—Three Years

Dennis L. O'Connor	2479
Blanks	766

AUDITORS—One Year

Leo E. Downey	2136
George A. Gallagher	2331
Harold C. Smith	2102
Blanks	3166

SCHOOL COMMITTEE—Three Years

Emmie P. Black	553
Dorothy M. Kavka	879
John T. Troy, Jr.	1565
Blanks	248

WATER COMMISSIONER—Three Years

Ralph Fucillo	1062
James T. Shea	2033
Blanks	150

BOARD OF HEALTH—Three Years

Edward M. Cullinan	1696
Domènico DelPrete	424
Thomas Fox	818
Blanks	307

LIBRARY TRUSTEES,—Three Years

Burton L. Cushing	2115
John B. Fitzgerald	2224
Blanks	2151

PARK COMMISSIONER—Three Years

Elwin E. Gould	939
Patrick H. Mahoney	1921
Blanks	385

SEWER COMMISSIONER—Three Years

Frederic Hall	2133

Blanks   1112

TREE WARDEN—One Year

Wililam C. Greene, Sr.   191
Charles L. Hunt   1010
Alfred T. Metivier   1740
Blanks   304

CONSTABLES—One Year

Carl D. Benham   367
Samuel J. Cannaway   1422
Clarence S. Damon   337
Robert J. Drake   1942
William A. Gardner   103
Russell S. Hawes   1508
Adolph L. W. Johnson   2194
Matthew J. Lioy   272
Edward H. Lynch   283
John H. Murphy   1879
Bernard F. O'Hayre   668
George J. Popp   1635
Charles M. Scott   360
Blanks   3255

The Moderator declared the following persons duly elected to the offices named and the terms specified: Moderator, one year, Magorisk L. Walls; Town Clerk one year,
Ralph L. Belcher; Town Treasurer, one year, Charles J.
Higgins; Tax Collector, one year, James A. Donovan; Selectmen, Board of Public Welfare and Fence Viewers,
one year, John J. Bowler, Harry S. Torrey, Norman S.
Whiting; Highway Surveyor, one year, Roderick Mac-
Kenzie; Assessor, three years, Dennis L. O'Connor; Auditors, one year, Leo E. Downey, George A. Gallagher, Harold C. Smith; School Committee, three years, John T.
Troy, Jr.; Water Commissioner, three years, James T.
Shea; Board of Health, three years, Edward M. Cullinan;

Library Trustees, three years, Burton L. Cushing, John B. Fitzgerald; Park Commissioner, three years, Patrick H. Mahoney; Sewer Commissioner, three years, Frederic Hall; Tree Warden, one year, Alfred T. Metivier; Constables, one year, Robert J. Drake, Russell S. Hawes, Adolph L. W. Johnson, John H. Murphy, George J. Popp.

At 8:15 o'clock P. M. Voted to adjourn.

A true copy, Attest:

RALPH L. BELCHER
Town Clerk

AMOUNTS RAISED AND APPROPRIATED
ANNUAL TOWN MEETING MARCH 6, 1939

School Department	$105 200 00
State Aid	600 00
Soldiers' Relief	9 000 00
Care of Soldiers Graves	150 00
Memorial Library and Dog Fund	4 400 00
Street Lighting	8 898 00
Highway Surveyor	1 350 00
Tarvia and Road Binder	3 000 00
Highway Repairs	1 800 00
Sidewalks	1 500 00
Cleaning Union Street	200 00
Clean-up Week	75 00
Guide Boards and Signs	100 00
Fire Department	11 080 00
Police Department	8 955 00
Forest Fires	750 00
Board of Health	6 000 00
Inspection of Animals	150 00
Park Department	2 800 00

Old Age Assistance	55 000	00
Moth Department	300	00
Tree Warden	900	00
Town Officers	7 700	00
Office Rent	800	00
Sealer of Weights and Measures	400	00
Elections	1 000	00
Compensation Insurance	1 928	71
Mass Industrial School	1 800	00
Town Report and Poll Book	1 585	00
Support of Poor and Infirmary	51 000	00
Mothers Aid	9 500	00
Town Notes and Interest	36 000	00
Assessors	2 500	00
Snow Removal	9 500	00
Reserve Fund	4 000	00
Miscellaneous Assessors	1 550	00
Miscellaneous Treasurer	800	00
Miscellaneous Clerk	350	00
Miscellaneous Selectmen	120	00
Miscellaneous Registrars of Voters	650	00
Miscellaneous Sealer Weights and Measures	190	00
Miscellaneous Tax Collector	1 450	00
Miscellaneous Unclassified	1 100	00
Part Payment Visiting Nurse	1 500	00
Quarters Veterans Spanish-American War	288	00
Observance of Memorial Day	400	00
Care of Town Cemetery	60	00
Quarters Rockland Post No. 147 American Legion	900	00
Expense of heat, light, casualty Insurance Jr.-Sr. High and McKinley School, prov. Chap. 71 Sec. 71 Gen. Laws.	150	00
Criminal Cases in Court	100	00
Compensation Insurance for Firemen	292	50
Rebuild West Water Street (Chapter 90)	6 000	00
Employ "Visitor" Public Welfare Dept.	1 500	00
Maintenance Plymouth County Hospital	4 427	35
Maintenance Traffic Beacons and Signals	900	00
Cleaning catchbasins and drains	500	00

Material expense W. P. A. Vital Statistics		
Project	875	00
Install Street Light, Forest St. (near res.		
Chas. Rose)	15	00
Foreclosing Tax Titles in Land Court	500	00
Cost of Materials and General Expense W.P.A.	1 200	00
Materials Sewing Unit (W. P. A. project)	2 400	00
Administrative expense Federal		
Commodity Distribution	515	87
Tri-Town observance of Armistice Day	400	00
Heat, light, gas and garbage removal		
McKinley School when used by W.P.A. projects		
	400	00
Install lights Taunton Ave. entrance to		
High School	37	00
Tires for Combination Truck, Fire Department	275	00
Materials for curb recessed opening type		
drain Webster Street at Wright's Brook		
labor W. P. A.	25	00
Materials to Repair Bridge Emerson St.,		
labor W. P. A.	50	00
Exchange Police Car	400	00
Reeds Pond	350	00
Gravel Dexter Road Extension	100	00

Total amount raised and appropriated	$381 692	43
APPROPRIATION, from Water Revenue		
For use of Water Department	29 500	00
	$411 192	43

A true copy, Attest:

RALPH L. BELCHER,
Town Clerk

APPROPRIATIONS FROM AVAILABLE FUNDS
ANNUAL TOWN MEETING, MARCH 6, 1939

*From Bond Issue provided by Article No. 13, Special Town Meeting, August 8, 1938.

Art. No. 22. Materials to resurface sidewalk west side of Union St. from Vespers Garage to property of Maria Jenkins, Labor W. P. A. $450 00

Art. No. 30. Materials for sidewalk and curb south side of Reed Street from residence of Patrick Mahoney to Plain street, labor W. P. A.   600 00

Art. No. 39. Materials for curb and hard surface circular walk in front of High School labor W. P. A.   885 00

Act. No. 44. Materials rebuild sidewalk of west and south side Prospect Street from West Water to Highland St., labor W. P. A.   700 00

Art. No. 53. Materials for sidewalk and curb on west side of Myrtle Street from Bigelow Ave. to Summit St., labor W. P. A.   500 00

       $3 135 00

From amount raised for General Expense W. P. A. Art. No. 32 Annual Town Meting, March 6, 1939

Art. No. 62. Materials for 2 catch basins east side of Concord Street near residence of Dominico DelPrete running 300 feet southerly, labor W. P. A.   300 00

                                                      $3 435 00

SPECIAL TOWN MEETING
SEPTEMBER 18, 1939

Pursuant to the foregoing warrant a meeting was held in the Rockland Opera House, beginning at 7:30 o'clock P. M. and the following votes were passed and action taken.

The meeting was called to order at 7:30 P. M. by the Moderator, Magorisk L. Walls.

The warrant with Constable's return of service thereof was read by the Town Clerk.

The chairman of the Finance Committee, Harold B. Monahan, reported that the committee had approved the article.

Article 1. VOTED that the terms "laborers, workmen and mechanics" as used in Section 69 to 75 inclusive, under Chapter 152, General Laws, Ter. Ed. as amended, shall include such employees, except members of the police and fire department regardless of the nature of their work, as may be employed on work to be done under contracts with the Commonwealth.

Voted to adjourn at 7:38 P. M.

A true record of the doings of the meeting.

RALPH L. BELCHER
Town Clerk

SPECIAL TOWN MEETING
DECEMBER 29, 1939

Pursuant to the foregoing warrant a meeting was held in the Rockland Opera House, beginning at 7:30 o'clock P. M. and the following votes were passed and action taken.

The meeting was called to order at 7:30 P. M. by the Moderator Magorisk L. Walls.

The warrant with Constable's return of service thereof was read by the Town Clerk.

Mr. Holloway, of the Finance Committee, reported that the Finance Committee approved of the articles in the warrant.

Article 1. VOTED: that the sum of Three Thousand dollars ($3000.00) be transferred, from the unexpended balance raised at a Special Town Meeting, August 8, 1938 under Article 13 for the building of Sidewalks and Curbs under the W. P. A., to a general fund for the administration and local contribution of W. P. A. Projects, or take any other action thereon.

Article 2. VOTED: to permit Mt. Pleasant Cemetery Association to use for burial purposes a lot of land containing one and three tenths acres which it has recently purchased from Josephine P. Guyette lying southeasterly of other land of said Association, the location of which has been approved in writing by the Board of Health of the Town of Rockland under the provisions of Chapter 114, Section 34 of the General Laws, Ter. Ed.

Voted to adjourn at 7:34 P. M.

A true record of the doings of the meeting.

RALPH L. BELCHER,
Town Clerk

Commonwealth of Massachusetts

Office of the
Commission To Establish Representative Districts
In the County of Plymouth
Authorized by Chapter 467 of the Acts of 1939
Commissioners:
FREDERIC T. BAILEY, Chairman
719 Country Way, North Scituate
Tel. Scituate 60
MAGORISK L. WALLS, Secretary
82 Webster St., Rockland
Tel. Rockland 300
MARY B. BESSE
120 Main St., Wareham
LOUISE B. CLARK
5 Library Place, Bridgewater
ANTHONY KUPKA
232 Main St., Brockton

Town Clerk and Board of Board of Registrars:
Town of Rockland
Dear Sir:
December 2, 1939
The special commission appointed under authority of Chapter 467 of the Acts of 1939, by his excellency, the governor, have held public hearings and executive sessions, and have unanimously apportioned the representative districts of Plymouth County, and have assigned representatives thereto, as follows:

District 1 — Plymouth, Kingston, Halifax, Plympton, Carver, with 7686 voters, and with meeting place in Plymouth, and having one representative.

District 2 — Scituate, Marshfield, Duxbury, Pembroke, and Hanover, with 7217 voters, and with meeting place at Marshfield, and having one representative.

District 3— Hull, Hingham, Cohasset, Norwell, with 7815 voters and with meeting place at Hingham, and having one representative.

District 4 — Rockland, Hanson, Abington, having 8393

voters, with Rockland as the meeting place, and having one representative.

District 5 — Whitman, East Bridgewater, West Bridge- water, and Bridgewater, having 9952 voters, with Bridge- water the meeting place and having one representative.

District 6 — Wareham, Middleboro, Marion, Lakeville, Rochester and Mattapoisett, having 9939 voters, with Middleboro the meeting place, and having one representa- tive.

District 7 — Wards three and four of the City of Brock- ton, having 8432 voters with Brockton as the meeting place, and having one representative.

District 8 — Wards one, two and five of the City of Brockton, having 12,511 voters with Brockton as the meeting place, and having two representatives.

District 9 — Wards six and seven of the City of Brockton, having 8904 voters, with Brockton as the meet- ing place and having one representative.

FREDERIC T. BAILEY, Chairman
MAGORISK L. WALLS, Secretary
ANTHONY KUPKA,
LOUISE B. CLARK,
MARY B. BESSE,

Annual Report

of the

SCHOOL DEPARTMENT

of the

Town of Rockland

For the Year Ending December 31, 1939

SCHOOL CALENDAR FOR YEAR 1939-1940

FALL TERM

Begins Wednesday, September 6, 1939, sixteen weeks; ends Friday, December 22, 1939.

WINTER TERM

Begins Tuesday, January 2, 1940, seven weeks; ends Friday, February 16, 1940.

SPRING TERM

Begins, Monday, February 26, 1940, seven weeks; ends Friday, April 12, 1940.

SUMMER TERM

Begins Monday, April 22, 1940, nine weeks; ends Wednesday, June 19, 1940. Teachers return Thursday and Friday, June 20 and 21, for year-end duties and organization work.

HOLIDAYS

October 12, 1939, Columbus Day. Closing of schools on Wednesday night and reopen Monday, October 16, 1939.

October 27, 1939, Teachers' Convention.

November 29, 1939, Schools close at noon for remainder of week, Thanksgiving Recess.

March 22, 1940, Good Friday.

May 30, 1940, Memorial Day. Closing of Schools on Wednesday night and reopen Monday, June, 3, 1940.

SIGNALS FOR NO SESSION OF SCHOOL
Fire Station Siren

A. M.

7:30 — 22 repeated: No session of Junior-Senior High School.

8:15 — 22 repeated: No forenoon session for first six grades.

P. M.

12:45 — 22 repeated: No afternoon session for first six grades.

The "No School Signal" is used only in extremely stormy weather. The school bus starts on its first trip in the morning ten minutes after seven o'clock in order to collect the children in time for the opening of high school at 8:30 A. M. and the elementary schools at 9:00 A. M. Unless the signal is used before 7:00 o'clock many of the children are already on their way by bus. It is very difficult to determine weather conditions for the day as early as seven o'clock except in cases of severe storms.

People in the outskirts of our town often cannot hear the signal, in which case children appearing in school are disappointed to learn that they must cover the long distance back to their homes, while they may be chilled or wet.

We wish each parent to use his or her best judgment as to whether or not the weather is auspicious for sending their children to school. No penalty is inflicted upon any child for non-attendance on account of severe weather.

Since our teachers are in school and many of the pupils do not hear the signal, it seems wise to use the time to good advantage in warm buildings, whereas during days when the signal may be used many children are out of doors, becoming wet and contracting colds.

Is it not wiser to have them in warm school rooms under supervision, receiving beneficial instruction?

R. STEWART ESTEN,
Superintendent of Schools
January 1, 1940

SCHOOL DIRECTORY 1939 - 1940

SCHOOL COMMITTEE

DR. BENJAMIN LELYVELD, Chairman   Reed Street
Tel. 16-W.   Term expires March, 1940

DR. WILLIAM A. LOUD   327 Salem Street
Tel. 430.   Term expires March, 1940

MISS M. AGNES KELLEHER   297 Howard Street
Tel. 1484-W.   Term expires March, 1941

DANA S. COLLINS   425 Liberty Street
Tel. 55.   Term expires March, 1941

JOHN T. TROY, Jr.   563 Liberty Street
Term Expires March, 1942

SUPERINTENDENT OF SCHOOLS

R. STEWART ESTEN   111 Payson Avenue
Office Tel. 1540   Residence Tel. 1250
Office hours every school day from 8:30 to 9:00 A. M. and
on Wednesday evenings from 7:00 to 8:00 o'clock.

SCHOOL DEPARTMENT SECRETARY

HARRIET E. GELINAS   241 Myrtle Street
Office Tel. 1540   Residence Tel. 1244

PRINCIPAL OF HIGH SCHOOL

GEORGE A. J. FROBERGER   28 Exchange Street
Office Tel. 1540   Residence Tel. 1302-W
Office hours every school day from 8 to 9 A. M., Mondays and Thursday from 3 to 4 p. m. and Wednesday evenings from 7 to 8 o'clock.

ATTENDANCE OFFICER AND SCHOOL NURSE

LOUISE A. CONSIDINE, R. N.   69 Webster Street
Office Tel. 1540
Office hours at the high school every school day from 8:30 to 9:30 A. M.

SCHOOL PHYSICIANS

JOSEPH H. DUNN, M. D.   319 Union Street
Office Tel. 836-W   Residence Tel. 836-R
Office Hours: 2 to 3 and 7 to 8 P. M.

JOSEPH FRAME, M. D.   114 Webster Street
Office Tel. 38-W
Office Hours: 12:30 to 2 and 6:30 to 8 P. M.

DENTAL HYGIENIST

ETTA MURGIDA   131 Reed Street
Office Tel. 1357   Residence Tel. 1313-W
Office hours at the McKinley School daily when schools are in session from 9:00 A. M. to 12 M., and from 1:30 to 3:30 P. M.

DIGEST OF LAWS AND REGULATIONS RELATING TO SCHOOL ATTENDANCE

Children who are five years and six month of age by the opening of school in September 1940 shall be admitted to the first grade. Those who become five years of age after March 1, 1940, may be admitted after passing a satisfactory mental examination.

Children, otherwise eligible to enter school in September for the first time, are required by law to present at time of entrance either a certificate of vaccination or a certificate of unfitness for vaccination. The school committee and board of health have ruled that certificates of unfitness for vaccination must be renewed each year. Children coming into the school system from other places, whether at the opening of the year in September or during the school year, will be required to produce satisfactory evidence regarding vaccination.

Pupils desiring to enter the first grade must enroll on or before October 1. Otherwise, they will not be admitted.

The school hours for the first grade children, shall be from 9 until 11:30 A. M. The afternoon session shall correspond with other grades, 1:30 P. M. until 3:30 P. M. The ruling, took effect March 6, 1933. An exception is made during the winter months when the afternoon session of the elementary schools concludes at 3:15 P. M. The school hours for the junior-senior high school pupils shall be from 8:30 A. M. until 2:00 P. M.

Pupils who have been absent from school on account of contagious disease must secure a permit from a school physician before re-entering. In cases of doubt, or in cases where there exists a suspicion of contagion, the parents should advise, and the teacher should require that the pupils consult the school nurse, who may refer the case to a school physician for further examination.

Any pupil having a contagious disease or showing symptoms of such a disease may be temporarily excluded from school by the teacher on her own initiative or at the direction of the school nurse or school physician.

Sickness is the only legal excuse for absence from school.

All children between the ages of fourteen and sixteen years must be in school unless they are actually employed under the authority of an employment certificate, a home permit or a special certificate permitting farm or domestic employment.

Any pupil who habitually violates rules of the schools, or otherwise seriously interferes with the proper and orderly operation of the school which he attends, may be temporarily excluded by the teacher or the superintendent of schools or may be permanently expelled by the school committee.

Pupils under seven years of age or over sixteen who elect to attend school must conform to the same rules and regulations as those pupils who are within the compulsory age — from seven to sixteen.

Teachers may require a written excuse signed by a parent or guardian covering any case of absence, tardiness or dismissal.

When ever a pupil is suspended by a teacher or principal, for any cause for any length of time, an immediate report must be made to the superintendent's office.

Those pupils attending the first eight grades will be transported to and from school if they live in the town of Rockland and reside more than one mile and a quarter from the school where they are authorized to attend.

Those pupils attending the high school, grades nine to twelve, inclusive, will be transported to and from school if they live in the town of Rockland and reside more than two miles from the high school.

Recent Rulings Pertaining to Our School

Voted to use the high school building for those activities which pertain to school work or those carrying on functions for the interest of the schools.

There shall be a Supervisor of Buildings who shall represent the School Committee in charge of all school buildings when they are used by outside organizations (other than school organizations.)

The Supervisor's duties shall be to prevent any damage to school property and to be responsible for proper conduct in and on school property. (Prevent smoking, drinking and unbecoming conduct in the buildings.)

The organization using the building shall be responsible for the expense of such a supervisor.

The supervisor shall receive his instructions from the Superintendent of Schools.

The supervisor shall receive remuneration at the rate of $2.50 until 10:30 P. M., $4.00 if the function continues until 11:30 P. M.; $5.00 after 11:30 P. M.; 75 cents per hour will be the charge for the building if used before 6:00 P. M. This ruling took effect December 1, 1934.

All work performed by the School Committee shall be awarded to native born citizens, naturalized citizens, or those who have taken out their first naturalization papers.

The tuition for pupils whose parents reside out of town and wishing to attend the Rockland Schools shall be established as follows: Senior High $100 per year; Junior High $80; elementary grades $60.

Post-Graduates who are admitted to the Rockland High School, September 4, 1935 or thereafter, shall take a minimum of twenty hours of work per week; shall be satisfactory in conduct; shall be regular in full day's attendance and maintain satisfactory averages in all subjects.

Classes in the high school of less than ten in any subject shall be discontinued unless two classes can be combined.

Pupils between the ages of twelve and sixteen who engage in street trades, selling newspapers, magazines, etc., must secure a badge from the Superintendent of schools or his duly authorized agent.

Rulings Regarding Payment of Salaries to Teachers

The teachers of the Rockland Schools shall receive their salaries bi-weekly after two weeks of actual class room teaching — except through July and August when payments shall be made not later than the 15th of each month.

Five days of personal "sick leave" shall be allowed teachers without loss of salary in any school year. This ruling became effective September 7, 1939.

A teacher shall receive full pay for five calendar days for death in immediate family. "Immediate" family includes parents, wife, husband, brother, sister or children.

For each day's absence, with the exception of the two reasons mentioned above, 1/200 of the yearly salary shall be deducted.

A teacher absent for more than one half (½) of a session shall lose pay for that entire session.

Visiting schools authorized by the Superintendent of Schools or work pertaining to the schools which has been assigned by the Superintendent may be allowed without loss of salary.

The word "Teacher" in the above ruling applies to Principals, Special Teachers and all class room teachers excepting the Principal of the Junior-Senior High school and the Superintendent of Schools.

REPORT OF ROCKLAND SCHOOL COMMITTEE

To the Citizens of Rockland:

The School Committee herewith submits its annual report:

We wish to point out the following statistical fact: Of the twenty-seven towns in Plymouth County, ROCKLAND SPENDS LESS for the INDIVIDUAL CHILD than any of the other towns in this group. Rockland has the lowest PER PUPIL COST in Plymouth County.

You will note by the school budget a request for a large increase over last year's appropriation. The major part of this increase is due to the fact that a large number of five year insurance premiums must be paid during the coming fiscal year.

We recommend that you read the Superintendent's report and the detailed Financial Statement for a complete account of our administration.

The committee wants to thank the Superintendent of Schools, the principals, teachers and school employees for their cooperation.

The continued help of the Rockland Woman's Club in offering its annual scholarship, and the Kiwanis Club in sponsoring the Milk Fund is greatly appreciated by the Committee.

Your School Board makes special mention of the help given it through the intelligent study of its problems by the Finance Committee.

Respectfully submitted,

BENJAMIN LELYVELD, Chairman
JOHN T. TROY, JR., Secretary
WILLIAM A. LOUD
M. AGNES KELLEHER
DANA S. COLLINS

FINANCIAL STATEMENT
RESOURCES 1939

General Appropriation		$105 200 00

EXPENDITURES

General Expenses	$5 144 29	
Expense of Instruction	77 155 32	
Operation and Maintenance	17 826 74	
Auxiliary Agencies	4 803 52	
New Equipment	269 52	
Total Expenditures		$105 199 39
Unexpended Balance		.61

TOWN TREASURER'S RECEIPTS
ON ACCOUNT OF SCHOOLS

State Reimbursements:		
Teachers' Salaries	$10 285 00	
Tuition and Transportation of Wards	978 15	
City of Boston for Tuition and Transportation of Wards	304 64	
Sale of furnace grates and battery lead	2 55	
Sale of stencils and paper	2 30	
Articles sold in Special Class	2 95	
Articles sold in High School Shop	32 60	
Sale of old books	39 00	
Total Receipts		$11 647 19

NET COST OF SCHOOLS TO TOWN	$93 552 20

RENTAL OF McKINLEY HALL AND SENIOR HIGH GYMNASIUM

Town Appropriation of offset expenses		$150 00
Receipts (turned over to town treasurer)	$160 00	
Expenditures:		
Brockton Edison Co.	$86 30	
J. J. L. DeCosta	23 35	
Maurice Mullen	23 35	
Rockland Water Department	17 00	
Total Expenditures		$150 00

APPROPRIATION TO OFFSE EXPENSE OF W. P. A. PROJECTS HOUSED AT McKINLEY SCHOOL

Appropriation		$400 00
Expenditures:		
Albert Culver Company,coal	$164 48	
Rockland Water Dept., service	17 33	
Old Colony Gas Co., service	12 05	
Brockton Edison Co., service	131 12	
Abington Coal Corp.,	69 02	
Dominic DelPrete, Garbage removal	6 00	
Total Expenditures		$400 00

DETAIL OF 1939 EXPENDITURES

Total Resources	$105 200 00

GENERAL EXPENSES

Superintendent's Salary	$3 600 00
Other Administrative Expense	1 544 29

EXPENSE OF INSTRUCTION

Supervisors' Salaries	3 312 28

Principals' Salaries	7 275	50
Teachers' Salaries	62 742	06
Text Books	1 383	08
Stationery, Supplies and		
Miscellaneous	2 442	40

OPERATION AND MAINTENANCE

Janitors' Wages	8 383	10
Fuel	4 529	62
Miscellaneous	2 389	55
Repairs	2 524	47

AUXILIARY AGENCIES

Libraries	42	69
Health	1 965	77
Transportation	1 500	00
Sundries	1 295	06

OUTLAY

New Equipment	269	52

Total Expenditures	$105 199	39

Unexpended Balance	.61

FINANCIAL STATEMENT ITEMIZED

SUPERINTENDENT OF SCHOOLS

S. Stewart Esten, Salary	$3 600 00

OTHER ADMINISTRATIVE EXPENSES

Administrative Process Seminar,		
Charts	$	3 00
Beaudette & Co., stencils		2 05

Bruce Publishing Co., Subscription School Board Journal	6	00
Louise A. Considine, mileage at- tendance officer	95	08
Douglas Print, contracts printed	12	00
Emerson & Co., stamp pad and ink	1	30
Mittag & Volger, carbon paper	5	00
N. E. Tel. & Tel. Company, service	108	24
John R. Parker, P. M., envelopes, cards and stamps	42	76
The School Executive, magazine renewal	3	00
Wright & Potter Printing Co., ledger blanks	4	16
John H. Wyatt Company, vivid roll, stencils	19	70
Harriet E. Gelinas, salary	1 242	00

Total $ 1 544 29

EXPENSE OF INSTRUCTION

Supervisors' Salaries	3 312	28
Principals' Salaries	7 275	50
Teachers' Salaries	62 742	06

TEXT BOOKS

Allyn & Bacon	52	95
American Book Company	24	81
American Education Press	2	00
Arlo Publishing Co.	6	14
Edward E. Babb & Co., Inc.	11	09
Banks, Upshaw & Co.	16	56
Beckley-Cardy Co.	25	60
Bobbs-Merrill Co.	2	55
Boston Music Co.	13	46
Bruce Publishing Co.	1	85
Character Building Publications	22	50

Circle Book Co.	4 67
Cooperative Study of Secondary School Standards	90
Carl Fischer, Inc.	9 75
Ginn & Company	247 99
D. C. Heath & Co.	158 09
Henry Holt & Co.	8 31
Houghton Mifflin Co.	45 04
Iroquois Publishing Co.	38
Johnson Publishing Co.	11 76.
Jr.-Sr. High Clearing House	5 00
The Macmillan Company	80 59
Charles E. Merrill Co.	48 77
National Conservation Bureau	13 60
National Education Association	1 00.
Thomas Nelson & Sons	5 13
Newson & Company	14 22
The Orthovis Company	1 20
The A. N. Palmer Company	1 70
Prentice-Hall, Inc.	30 30
Row Peterson & Co.	17 97
Scott Foresman & Co.	234 43
Charles Scribner's Sons	7 99
Silver Burdett Company	16 13
The L. W. Singer Co.	59 17
South-Western Publishing Co.	54 65
Stephen Daye Press	61
O. H. Toothaker	20 81
Treasurer of United States	1 00
Webster Publishing Co.	15 04
John C. Winston Co.	83 37
World Book Company	4 00

Total $1 383 08

STATIONERY, SUPPLIES AND MISCELLANEOUS

American Type Founders Sales
Corps., Shop materials   23 10

Automatic Pencil Sharpener Co.,
    blades   4 64
Edward E. Babb Co., schoolroom
    supplies   93 08
Beckley-Cardy Co., clock dial   1 07
Brodhead-Garrett Co., shop lumber
    sandpaper   286 52
Central Scientific Co., science
    supplies   30 44
John S. Cheever Co., paper   653 43
Cooperative Test Service, tests   24 35
Douglas Print, report cards   22 25
H. J. Dowd Co., schoolroom
    supplies   37 90
Dowling School Supply Co., paper   2 20
Educational Guild of N. E., schoolroom
    supplies   9 70
Educational Test Bureau, tests   4 81
Ginn & Company, class record books   24 00
J. L. Hammett Company, schoolroom
    supplies   113 27
Charles W. Homeyer & Co., Inc., music 19 86
Informative Classroom Teacher,
    schoolroom supplies   2 97
H. B. McArdle, schoolroom supplies   50 78
Milton Bradley Co., schoolroom sup-
    plies   352 82
National Committee for Art Appreci-
    ation, pictures   5 50
The A. N. Palmer Co., pencils   18 47
George T. Pascoe, schoolroom sup-
    plies   21 92
A. S. Peterson, notebook, fillers, ink   3 00
Remington Rand, Inc., typewriter   40 00
J. A. Rice Co., supplies for sewing
    classes   9 55
R. H. S. Cafeteria, food classes   39 18
Rockland Coal & Grain Co., shop
    materials   25 79

Rome Bros., shop materials	30	49
Royal Typewriter Co., typewriters		
replaced	225	00
School Arts Magazine, subscription	3	00
School Products Bureau, schoolroom		
supplies	5	54
Singer Sewing Machine Co., needles		56
South Western Publishing Co.,		
bookkeeping sets	46	89
State Department of Education,		
film service	22	50
O. H. Toothaker, pencils, maps	93	80
Walberg & Auge, music supplies	1	15
Henry J. Winde Co., shop materials	22	55
F. W. Woolworth Co., special class		
materials	2	30
World Book Co., tests	35	64
John H. Wyatt Co., stencils and ink	9	05
Yale University Film Service,		
film services	16	97
Joseph G. Zifchock, colored tickets	6	36

Total $2 442 40

JANITORS' WAGES

Charles Metevier, Junior-Senior		
High	$1 620	32
Andrew T. Leck, Junior-Senior high	1 349	92
J. J. L. DeCosta, McKinley	1 174	50
Maurice Mullen, McKinley	988	31
Harold Morse, Jefferson	926	24
Frank O'Hara, Gleason and Web-		
ster Street	753	31
Frank Curtis, Lincoln	1 000	00
Elizabeth Casey, Central Street	180	00
Ardelle Cushing, Market Street	350	00
Mary Davis, Helper at McKinley	40	50

Total $8 383 10

FUEL

Abington Coal Corporation	$2 918	61
Albert Culver Company	980	18
Rockland Coal & Grain Company	613	83
Roderick MacKenzie	17	00
Total	$4 529	62

MISCELLANEOUS

Arrow System, gym mat cleansed	18	00
Atlas Products Co., light bulbs	10	32
Ralph F. Bass, paper toweling	42	50
Boston Janitors' Supply Co., sweeping compound	67	52
Brockton Edison Company, service	1 247	22
Arthur M. Buckley, janitors' supplies	62	59
Arthur M. Condon, cleaning powder	22	75
Continental Car-Na-Var Corporation, floor wax	6	30
P. & F. Corbin, keys		63
F. H. Crane & Sons. Inc., spangles	7	90
Albert Culver Co., lawn seed	4	50
Dominic DelPrete, garbage removal at McKinley School	11	50
C. B. Dolge Co., disinfectant	65	27
H. J. Dowd Co., sweeping compound	35	00
M. F. Ellis & Co., sweeping compound	8	75
Flexoid Products, Inc., boiler treatment	3	00
Gilbert Howe Gleason Co., cleaning sewage pump at Jefferson	7	75
L. M. Glover Co., floor wax	40	76
Hickey Bros., cleaning fluid		30
A. C. Horn Company, floor wax	78	15
William M. Horner, Janitors' supplies	11	25
Lamb's Store, Janitors' supplies		45

Carlton E. McPhee, light bulbs	25	71
Patrick H. Mahoney, loam for high school grounds	32	00
Market St. Garage, gas for cleaning printing press	1	35
Masury-Young Company, floor oil	52	31
Alfred T. Metivier, clearing poison ivy at Jefferson	10	00
Geo. M. B. Miller, gas for cleaning printing press		92
N. E. Tel. & Tel. Co., service	121	54
Old Colony Gas Co.	22	82
Raynham Bleachery, cleaning cloths	18	70
Rockland Coal & Grain Co., fertilizer for grounds	5	70
Rockland Water Department, service	273	12
Rome Bros., lawn seed	2	50
The Swan Company, wax and wool pads	41	10
The Tropical Paint & Oil Company, Janitors' supplies	6	68
Wadsworth Howland & Co., Inc., Janitors' supplies	20	50
West Disinfecting Company, rust polish paste	2	19

Total $2 389 55

REPAIRS

Abrasive Products, Inc., process paper	8	97
Stanley R. Ames, repairing high school amplifier	2	00
H. H. Arnold Co., Inc., materials for repairs	1	77
Waldo W. Atwood, labor digging pipe line at Central St., school	16	50
E. E. Babb Co., Inc., window shades		

repaired	90	25
Joseph H. Baker, clocks repaired	5	50
George N. Beal, water pipe repaired, welding rod	1	25
E. J. Beary, flush repaired at McKinley school	1	00
Bloom, South & Gurney, mastic flooring	40	00
Boston Plate & Window Glass Co., glass	22	81
Burke & James, Inc., two paper cutter springs		41
Burroughs Adding Machine Co., service contract	5	00
W. D. Cashin Co., valve spud		44
C. & D. Plumbing & Hardware Supplies, materials for repairs	24	77
Chase, Parker & Co., Inc., shovels replaced	6	38
Commonwealth Electric & Radio Co., sanding machine parts	6	10
Corrosion Solvent Eng. Corp., boiler treatment	16	00
Albert Culver Co., cement repairing high school steps	9	80
Orrin R. Cummings, plastering repairs	177	70
Damon Electric, electrical repairs	14	15
A. B. Dick Co., mimeograph cylinder	3	50
Luther O. Draper Shade Co., replacing shade cord	12	64
Flexoid Products Co., materials for cleaning boilers	56	00
General Electric Co., printing press motor repaired	22	75
Harry I. Granger, fire extinguishers repaired	4	50
Hall & Torrey, materials for repairs	145	86

J. D. Harris & Co., concrete floor covering	15	97
Hobart-Farrell Plumbing & Heating Co., materials for repairs	163	14
William M. Horner, materials for repairs	61	85
Geo. W. S. Hyde, two furnace hoes repaired	3	00
International Eng. Works. Inc., paint for lockers	12	02
Johnson Service Co., 1 valve body complete	3	00
Leonard Valve Co., valve repaired for H. S. heating system	50	95
J. S. McCallum, plumbing repairs at McKinley and Jefferson	68	83
Mass. Division of the Blind, pianos tuned and repaired, chairs caned	42	30
A. L. Measures, painting at high school	55	20
Merrick Engineering Co., replacing slates at McKinley in place of snow guards	17	00
Alfred Metivier, sand for repairing high school steps	2	00
Forrest L. Partch, electrical repairs	70	68
Louis A. Reardon, labor on high school sewerage system	120	10
Richardson & Boynton Co., grate for high school boiler	10	75
Rockland Coal & Grain Co., materials for repairs	57	79
Rockland Paint & Hardware Co., materials for repairs	34	25
Rockland Water Dept., repairs at Central St., and High school	146	16
Rockland Welding & Engineering Co., printing press welded	4	00
Rome Bros., materials for repairs	244	44

Harry L. Rome, curtains repaired	10	25
Roscoe Laboratories, cement		64
William B. Savage Co., auditorium cur-		
tains relined	106	25
Edwin Schutt, misc. repairs at		
schools	324	86
Singer Sewing Machine Co., adjusting		
machines		60
Sloane Valve Co., valves for plumbing		
system		99
L. C. Smith & Corona typewriters		
Inc., machines repaired	4	20
W. A. Snow Co., Inc., grates	7	00
Sphinx Chair Glide Co., glides for		
cafeteria stools	67	50
Standard Electric Time Co., clock		
repairs	43	50
Stone Hardware Co., door closers		
repaired	22	29
Telescope Folding Furniture Co., cot		
covers Nursery school	14	00
William Thorpe, electrical repairs	21	00
W. H. Turbayne, repairing Golding		
press	18	44
Welsbach Co., mantles replaced	1	47
The White-Warner Co., one door		
frame	2	00

Total $2 524 47

LIBRARIES

American Book Company, books	1	84
Ginn & Company, books	1	75
Houghton Mifflin Company, books	3	48
McGraw Hill Book Company, books	2	43
Arthur E. Tarbell, books	19	34
Time, magazines	8	00
O. H. Toothaker, two atlases	3	80

Macmillan Company, books 2 05

Total $ 42 69

HEALTH

Bemis Drug Co., supplies		6 24
Louise A. Considine, salary	1	466 72
Louise A. Considine, mileage		95 09
Fred S. Delay, supplies		30 81
Joseph H. Dunn, M. D. salary		175 00
Joseph Frame, M. D. salary		175 00
Horace Partridge Co., soccor ball		4 05
Plymouth County Health Association audiometer rental		2 00
Thomas W. Reed Co., tongue de-pressors		10 86

Total $1 965 77

TRANSPORTATION

John J. Dwyer $1 485 00
Howland's Insurance Office, bond 15 00

Total $1 500 00

SUNDRIES

Frank S. Alger, advertising bids	12 00
Babson's Statistical Organization, poster service	14 00
F. J. Barnard Company, books re-bound	140 02
Brockton Transportation Co., expressage	75
Buck Printing Co., "Senior Prom" tickets	6 37
Phillip S. Collins, insurance premium	92 24

Commissioner of Public Safety, boiler
    inspection   .   5 00
Everett S. Damon, insurance
    premium   154 00
Josephine Fitzgibbons, requested to
    attend conference at B. U.   1 50
Francis J. Geogan, legal services   50 00
J. L. Hammett Co., diplomas   77 99
Howland's Insurance 'Office, insur-
    ance premium   116 21
Jenkins & Simmons Express, expres-
    sage   37 71
Dr. Edward A. Lincoln, administer-
    ing tests for first grade entrance   60 00
McCarthy Freight System, Inc.,
    expressage   1 10
Charles E. Morgan, census enumer-
    ation   64 10
Nemasket Transportation Co.,
    expressage   50
N. Y., N. H. & Hartford R. R.,
    freight charges   3 14
James F. O'Connor, insurance
    premium   63 00
John B. O'Hayre, requested to at-
    tend Course given at B. U.   12 00
Amos A. Phelps, insurance
    premiums   260 28
Chester J. Poliks, requested to at-
    tend conference at B. U.   1 50
Pro Merito Society, pins   13 00
Quincy Patriot Ledger, advertising
    bids   5 10
A. I. Randall, printing school
    reports   73 80
Rockland Standard, advertising   6 50
Rockland Transportation Co.,
    expressage   1 35

Warren B. Woodward, insurance
premium   21 90

Total $1 295 06

NEW EQUIPMENT

J. L. Hammett Co., desk and chair
units   252 00
Rockland Coal & Grain Co., lumber
for music cabinet   7 52
Singer Sewing Machine Co., second hand machine for Sp. class   10 00

Total $ 269 52

REPORT OF SUPERINTENDENT OF SCHOOLS

To the School Committee of Rockland:

The eleventh annual report of my work as Superintendent of Schools is submitted.

To minimize printing expense, we are following the plan of the past few years by presenting the reports of the Superintendent and the High School Principal, along with statistical data. These reports include general accomplishments and needs of all department in the entire school system.

In 1931 our school budget was $128,500 and this past year it has been $105,200 which represents a reduction of $23,300 or 18%. In 1931 we had an enrollment of 1498. Of this number 813 were elementary pupils and 685 Junior-Senior High pupils. In 1939 our total enrollment came to 1483 and of this number 778 were in the elementary schools and 705 in the Junior-Senior high.

The gross cost of educating a pupil in the elementary school in 1939 was $65.66 whereas the cost in the Junior Senior High in 1939 was $76.77 indicating that high school education is more expensive due to more costly equipment and higher salaries paid to the teaching personnel. It is also true that school costs have increased the past two years from 10 to 25%. This condition has necessitated a great deal of careful planning in order to reduce the cost of education to a minimum and still maintain a high degree of efficiency commensurate with the expenditure of money until such time as additional funds are available. I am convinced that we have spent only in the wisest manner, for the greatest good and without waste or extravagance. Economy has been practiced and savings effected in many instances.

DEVELOPMENT OF PROJECTS

Tardiness Record

The principal of the high school and the teachers in the elementary schools by continuous effort on their part and the cooperation of the parents have maintained a very satisfactory record of tardiness for the past school year. In 1928-1929 the number was 1882 whereas in 1938-1939 the number has been reduced to 991 with an enrollment of 1483. This policy of being punctual is fundamental in the life of boys and girls who will need to be prompt in their business and social relationships upon leaving school. May we urge continued support on the part of parents so that our present record may be improved.

Junior Red Cross

The Junior Red Cross is continuing its excellent work in our schools under the direction of the town representative, Mrs. Esther Rawson, ably assisted by a committee of teachers. Activities have been sponsored to raise money by teachers and pupils to remedy physical defects, requiring teeth, tonsil and adenoid removals. In addition to these services the money raised by this organization has been used to purchase shoes, rubbers and an oc-, casional pair of eye glasses for children whose economic status would not permit these necessities.

Music Department

A new Course of Study in Music, prepared by the Supervisor of Vocal Music, has been adopted by the School Committee for the elementary schools and it becomes effective as of January 1940. This Course has been prepared to accompany the music series which we are now using. This course is worked out by calendar months so that appropriate music will be taught monthly.

Milk Fund Project

We continue to be grateful to the Rockland Kiwanis Club for their interest and effort in sponsoring the milk fund which has made it possible for 150 children in our schools to receive each a half pint of pasteurized milk along with two graham crackers daily while schools are in session for a period from November 14, 1938, until April 14, 1939. Those who received this luncheon were the boys and girls of parents who financially were unable to furnish this additional food to their children. The Club raised the money this year by public subscription, by donations of money placed in milk bottles in the business houses of the town and from receipts of an Old Timers Baseball game as well as a Soft Ball game. It requires from five to seven hundred dollars annually to meet this expense depending upon the number of boys and girls assisted. The money raised for the milk fund renders invaluable aid to the children of our town from the standpoint of health. Weight charts which are kept in the elementary schools prove conclusively that these pupils are physically benefited.

Group Piano Lessons

Another year has passed and we continue to encourage and foster group piano lessons for those pupils who have musical interest. The course is designed to afford parents an opportunity to ascertain their children's talent in order to determine the advisability of more advanced music training which is usually supplied by private instruction. The actual cost of the instruction of this specialized program is borne by the parents. Miss Maude F. Burnham of Taunton has been the instructor since the inception of the project three years ago. Miss Burham has presented in June a recital of the work accomplished in her classes and only words of highest praise have been spoken for her work.

Character Education

For the past two years a teachers' committee has been working on a Course of Study in Character Education for our elementary grades. It has been adopted and is now effective in grades 1 to 6. The challenging job of the parent and the teacher is to help the child meet his life situations, that is, his tasks, duties, and conflicts, manfully and successfully. Left unaided and unguided, the child would, in many instances, no doubt, respond in ways that are wholesome and that develop such traits as industry, self-reliance, honesty, self-confidence, patience, and foresight. But in far too many instances the clash between impulsive desires and duty is disastrous, devoloping such traits as loss of self-control, attitudes of failure, inferiorities, selfishness, sullenness, dishonesty, laziness, indifference, and poor judgment. These maladjustments make the child a misfit in group living. He is said to be abnormal. He is doomed to failure and unhappiness. Guidance, then, at all those points in his experiences where wrong choices are likely to be made is the child's birthright. It is evident, then, that character training has a two-fold aspect: (1) Prevention, that is, helping the child learn to make wholesome adjustments to his daily life situations so that he will emerge out of every conflict stronger physically, intellectually and emotionally; and (2) Cure, that is, helping the child overcome certain maladjustments or bad habits by supplanting these with good habits. Unfortunately character training too often has to spend its best energies upon the latter aspect-uprooting the bad habits.

HIGH SCHOOL

The increased enrollment in our Junior-Senior high makes it rather imperative to add at least one additional teacher this year. We need to do more with a guidance program than we have been able to do in the past. It is alarming to realize the large percentage of students who graduate from high school and college and then never pursue the work for which they are trained. It is evident that more attention must be given to the individual guidance of our pupils. This is not possible at present as our teachers have full programs and no instructor is released for this important function in our school.

It is gratifying to know that the graduates of our high school who are undertaking advanced training in higher institutions of learning are doing a very creditable piece of work as indicated by the reports we are receiving from the various colleges and schools of nursing. I am very much pleased with the excellent reports we have received from the testing service of the American Council of Education referred to in the principal's report which indicate that we are doing a high grade of work in our school.

Although our student librarians are doing well, there is still great need of a teacher librarian so that the library may be opened to our students throughout the school day and after school hours. Our pupils need instruction in library methods and the use and selection of books. We are indeed grateful to all organizations who are generously assisting us in building up our library. Pupils who go to college find themselves greatly handicapped if they have not had instruction in the use of a library. If we had an additional teacher or two we might be able to extend the use of our library to more pupils.

As a large percentage of our students do not receive any formal education beyond the high school it is desirous that they receive the utmost attention while in high school. This will necessitate the broadening of our General Course which at present includes a large percentage of college preparatory and commercial subjects with a very few offerings in the Practical Arts such as advanced work in Clothing, Cooking, Home Making, Woodworking, Printing, Drawing, etc. It is impossible to add these subjects to our curriculum on account of a now over-loaded personnel and the expense of equipment.

Recognizing the importance of good English speech in school and especially in after life I wish to quote directly from the report of the Head of our English Department to which I subscribe 100 percent. "The Crying Need of our English department is for correct and clear speech at all times and in all places. Upon examination it is always found that pupils know how to speak correctly, but are unwilling to do so. Because of poor speech heard and practised outside of class, they are inclined to regard correct speech as weak, effeminate and undesirable. We must, at least, insist on good English everywhere within the school building if we are to accomplish what we know to be vital for the future progress of our pupils."

WORKS PROGRESS ADMINISTRATION AS IT AFFECTS THE SCHOOLS

We still continue our plan of cooperation with the town officials and the federal government in providing suitable quarters for the Sewing and Recreation projects of the W. P. A. in the McKinley School Building. It is necessary to keep this building open throughout the entire year to accommodate these projects which is an added expense for light, heat, power and janitor service, although this is partially met by the citizens of the town in their annual meeting when they raise and appropriate $400 to help defray this additional expense of opening the building for these two projects. During the month of December we had an electric bill amounting to $53.00. The gymnasium is in use practically every afternoon and evening until 9 to 9:30 o'clock.

. We have availed ourselves again this year of the opportunity of the National Youth Administration as it operates in schools and colleges throughout the United States. Our quota in Rockland since the opening of schools in September is set at $90.00 per month, an additional $18.00 over last year's quota. We have at present seven boys and eight girls who are receiving this financial aid of $6.00 per month for which each renders twenty hours of service to our schools per month. Two of the boys are engaged in janitor service at the McKinley building whereas the others are rendering clerical or janitor service at the high school. The six dollars per month is given by the government to assist these students in paying for school lunches or to purchase necessary clothing in order to continue their attendance in high school.

The Nursery School authorized by the Works Progress Administration continues to operate although it was closed from the middle of June until about October first by order of the federal government. The sessions are held as formerly in the gymnasium of the McKinley building. The enrollment comprises children from three to five years of age whose parents are on W. P. A. or low income. The unit includes at present one teacher and a cook but until the first of December we had two teachers and a cook. At the present time we have a requisition for an additional teacher. The federal government pays the wages of the employees, the Town and the School Department handle the other expenses of the project. We have twenty-five enrolled at present with an average attendance of twenty. The session of the school is from 9:15 A. M. until 2:00 P. M. with a noon luncheon. This systematic care and training of children has proved beneficial to both pupils and community and should be continued, if possible.

TEACHER REPLACEMENT

In June Miss Marion T. Hall of Morrisville, Vermont and a graduate of the University of Vermont was appointed a regular teacher to handle Miss Tobey's classes in Clothing and Social Science. Miss Hall had substituted in those classes since Miss Tobey resigned in January to be married.

Miss Helen Molloy, for nine years a teacher in our Junior High resigned in June to be married. Mr. John Ryan for the past two years a teacher of one of the fifth grades at the McKinley School was transferred to the Junior High to take Miss Molloy's place. Mr. Ryan is a graduate of Boston College and Bridgewater Teachers' College.

The vacancy in the fifth grade at McKinley caused by the transfer of Mr. Ryan to the Junior High was filled by the appointment of Mr. John Metevier of Rockland, a graduate of the Bridgewater State Teachers' College in 1939.

Miss Marjorie Smith, teacher of the first grade at the McKinley School resigned in April to be married. As it was unwise to change teachers in the first grade so late in the school year she was asked to substitute for the remainder of the term. In September Miss Madeline Lannin who had taught the lower room at Gleason was transferred to the McKinley to fill the vacancy made by Miss Smith's resignation. Miss Alice Murrill, for two years a teacher at Central Street school was transferred to the Gleason School. Miss Geraldine Crowell, a graduate of Bridgewater Teachers College, who had substituted in various schools during the past year was appointed to fill the vacancy at the Central Street School.

In December Miss Helen M. Miley, a teacher in our Commercial Department resigned to accept a position in Lasell Junior College. She is remaining with us until her place is filled.

SCHOOL BUILDINGS AND GROUNDS

Junior Senior High

A very much needed improvement to our school grounds was made during the past summer by the installation of a cement curbing and black top to the circular drive in front of the high school building. At the annual town meeting money was appropriated to pay for the material cost and a W. P. A. project provided the labor. Much less gravel and dirt are now brought into the school via the front entrance. It will be highly desirable to install a hard top in the parking area and drive at the rear of the building whenever funds are available.

The mastic floors in the corridors and toilets have been repaired by our janitors and wooden floors filled and waxed. Major repairs on our mastic floors will soon be necessary. We have found it necessary to replace several window shades in the building due to the fact they have been soaked and over a period of years have rotted. Several more will need to be replaced each year as they become torn and inadequate.

In order to stop the rapid deterioration of the large exit doors in the gymnasium and auditorium as well as the entrance doors to the building, galvanized sheet metal has been installed to hold them together and to make them water tight. It will undoubtedly prolong the life of these doors several years and provide a definite saving as these doors are very expensive.

Domes of silence have been placed on all the stools in the high school cafeteria. These have been very much needed since the opening of the building twelve years ago as stools are very noisy when being moved about on a cement floor by more than 400 pupils. This improvement will reduce greatly the noise and thus the confusion while pupils are eating their luncheon.

Although the leaks in the outside walls of the building

have been greatly diminished the past eleven years nevertheless due to the fact that they lack air spaces to dry them when moisture does enter, repairs on the plastered walls have been necessary. It was therefore essential to redecorate some of the walls after they were replastered.

The linings of the drapes in the auditorium were torn and ragged on the south side so it was necessary to reline them. The water from the metal window frames had entered along with very strong sun over a period of several years and as a result had rotted the linings. The drapes on the north side will need to be relined this year or next.

On account of the natural drainage of the Rockland hill we seem to have large quantities of rust in our water pipes and system so it is only a question of a short period of time before many of our water pipes will need to be replaced. In several cases already small pieces of pipe and unions have rusted to the leaking point making replacement necessary. We are using a solution in the water of the heating plant to prevent and retard the accumulation of rust. We have noticed great improvement in our results of heating the building.

Repairs have been made on locks, door checks, bubblers and furniture by our janitors and in some cases the services of a carpenter. A small cabinet has been constructed to store the music of the orchestra and band. This is located back of the stage.

McKinley School

On account of the danger from sliding snow, guards have been placed on the roof to prevent that hazard.

I should like to call attention to the fact that it is just a question of a short time before the insurance inspectors will condemn the water tube boilers in this building. The inside shell of each boiler is becoming very thin and so this makes a fire hazard. As soon as possible one sectional boiler should be installed and this one used except in the very cold weather when one of the two water tube boilers could be used in conjunction with the sectional boiler for a month or two. The water pipes are so corroded that the pressure is greatly reduced and major repairs will be necessary almost any minute. The ventilating system has been renovated and repaired so we are getting a larger degree of efficiency from our heating system.

It is evident that conductor pipes should be installed on the rear side of the building to improve drainage conditions on the grounds. The school yard is flooded during the wet season, due to a large amount of drainage water from the roof. Dry wells would remedy this condition.

The stone and brick work of the building needs repointing. Last spring we tried to secure a W. P. A. project to make these necessary repairs but to date have been unsuccessful. This work is imperative.

Two additional lights have been installed in the lobby of the building to assist in reducing the danger of small children leaving their rooms at the close of school during the dark months.

The office has been connected by a doorway with the classroom occupied by the principal to make more efficient the administration of the school. This improvement has been needed for several years.

The gymnasium in the basement needs renovation. It has not been redecorated for more than twenty years and now that it is used constantly by the Nursery School these repairs are most desirable.

On account of insufficient funds in our budget we have been unable to install the new light fixtures that are very much needed in the building. This should be done as soon as funds are available.

Several of the blackboards, desks and floors have been
.refinished, as well as many minor repairs made in the
building.   The auditorium floor has been filled with a
preparation which makes dancing on the floor much better than heretofore when floor oil was used.   The cement
floors in the boys' and girls' toilets have been treated so
they are cleaner than formerly.

Lincoln School

The heating plant in this building is very old and it is
only a question of time before new equipment will be
necessary. We are using a fluid in the boilers to prevent further corrosion which is improving the heating
efficiency of the building.

One or two portable book cases have been placed in the
classrooms of this building.

There is need to repaint sections of the building on the
outside as the paint is badly peeling.   Because of possible
danger the fire escape platforms were recovered.

Some of the blackboards in the building have been refinished as well as some of the desks and chairs.   Other
repairs of locks and door checks have been made.

The hurricane of a year ago had caused considerable
damage to the ventilators on the roof of the building so
repairs were made as well as the installation of wire mesh
over the openings of the ventilators to prevent the entrance of pigeons which had caused considerable commo-
tion.

Jefferson

Repairs were made on the roof of the building.   The
desks and floors have been refinished.   Some repairs
were necessary in the toilets as well as several panes of
glass replaced.

Webster Street School

The heating unit in this building has outlived its usefulness. It should be replaced as it is very difficult to heat the building properly during very cold weather. There should be a cellar under the building and the foundation walls repaired.

The small motors used to throw the heat into the toilets have given out and will need to be replaced.

The floors have been refinished and the desks revarnished. Other minor repairs have been made.

Gleason School

There is still need to repair the outside fire escape from both floors by eliminating a long flight of stairs, which may be accomplished by building an intermediate platform at the first floor level and connecting the two floors to the same stairs, thus eliminating one set of stairs. Hand rails must be provided on the inside stairs from the first to the second floors.

The blackboards and floors have been refinished. The coal bin has been repaired and improved.

We have not found it possible to secure sufficient funds to improve the lighting system on the second floor but this should be done as soon as possible.

Market Street School

The heating unit in this building is very old and inadequate and the same suggested data for the Webster Street School applies to this building. Minor plumbing repairs have been made and repairs to the outhouse which is now used for storage of supplies.

Central Street School

On account of a greatly increased enrollment in this building additional desks and chairs have been installed. We now have 36 in this one room building. Repairs to the heating system and plumbing have been made.

A new water service for this building was imperative last fall as the pipes from Central Street were loaded with rust so we received insufficient water for the bubblers and toilets. Although we used Welfare help with a foreman to do the digging of the trench, the expense of these repairs came to approximately one hundred dollars. The Water Department furnished the pipes at a cost of $77.20 and supervised the installation.

SPECIFIC NEEDS

The enormous increase in the number of bicycles brought to high school the past few years has developed a problem of housing these vehicles as no provision was made in the building for them. At present we are parking the bicycles in the basement corridors but as the number has increased to more than thirty and therefore a hazardous situation prevails, it will be necessary for us to install a rack outside of the building in the rear of the school this spring where all bicycles will henceforth be parked.

The large increase in the enrollment of the 7th and 8th grades of the Junior High school the past few years has made inadaquete the equipment in the sewing classes for the girls. We are in need of one or two additional sewing machines and if possible we should have the more modern type, the electric machines.

I wish to call attention again to the fact that the lockers in the boys' shower bath room are inadequate for our present needs and should be replaced as soon as funds are available. I wish to suggest that we install one new section of twelve or fifteen a year until they are all replaced. It is hoped that we can cut a door through the locker room, opening outdoors, so that our boys who are engaged in outside sports such as football, baseball and track will not find it necessary to walk through the corridor, down into the gymnasium and thus out on to the field. It is even more necessary now since the locker room is being used by other than school organizations for football and outdoor sports. The wear and tear on our gymnasium floor will be greatly diminished.

. We have a Golding Printing Press in our print shop that was second hand when we purchased it twelve years ago and it should be replaced by a more modern press. Safety devices are available on the newer machines and although we are still using the press it is quite inadequate so that our printing department is seriously handicapped. A first class second hand machine with safety equipment will cost from $300 to $400. Several new fonts of type should be purchased as soon as possible.

Because the wear and tear on the shop tools are so great and very few have been bought the past two years it is necessary to replace and repair the tools to keep them in first class condition. Additional machines are very much needed.

SALARY SCHEDULE

It is highly desirable in any school system, no matter how small, to have a salary schedule which outlines professional requirements of its personnel with the corresponding salary payments in order to maintain the esprit de corps of the faculty and a scholarship level worthy of a Class A School System. With this in mind a schedule has been established by the School Committee a copy of which is herewith printed. This became effective at the opening of schools in September 1938. From time to time educational and economic conditions may necessitate changes in the schedule.

The return to the policy in September 1939 of allowing teachers a "sick leave" of five days during the school year for "personal illness" without loss of salary is in line with the practice in most cities and towns in the state and a ruling that was effective in Rockland in 1931. More interest in the activities of the school is evidenced by the personnel as a result of this judicious practice.

SCHEDULE

	Minimum	Maximum
Supt of Schools		3600
Secetary to Supt of Schools and School Committee		1400
Junior-Senior High School Principal		3000
*Junior-Senior High School Sub-Master		2500
Senior High School Teachers holding Bachelor's Degree	1100	1700 (women)
Senior High School Teachers holding Bachelor's Degree	1100	1800 (men)
Senior High School Teachers not holding Bachelor's Degree	1100	1600
Junior High School Teachers holding Bachelor's Degree	1100	1600 (women)
Junior High School Teachers holding Bachelor's Degree	1100	1700 (men)
Junior High School Teachers not holding Bachelor's Degree		1400
Elementary School Teachers	1000	1400
Principal of McKinley Building		1600
Principal of Lincoln Building		1500
Principal of Jefferson Building		1450
Supervisor of Music (2 days per week)		900
Orchestra and Band Instructor (3 days per week)		1200
Supervisors of Art and Physical Education holding Bachelor's Degree		1800
Supervisors of Art and Physical Education not hold Bachelor's Degree		1700
School Nurse and Attendance Officer		1700
School Physicians		175

Janitors — To receive maximum salaries paid in 1937

. All new school employees must successfully pass a tubercular examination before accepting a school position.

All teachers who are not receiving the maximum salary shall receive a yearly increment of $50 until the maximum is reached.

. All teachers who hold a Master's Degree will be eligible for a super-maximum of $100 additional salary.

All regular teachers in the Junior-Senior High school and elementary schools are required to have at least four years of training beyond high school to be eligible for appointment.

All teachers who have reached the maximum salary and who do not hold a Master's Degree will be required to take at least 4 points of degree credit within a period of three years.

. * The maximum salary of the High School Sub-Master elected before 1937 shall be $2500 and elected after 1937 shall be $2200.

CONCLUSION

The education of our boys and girls is Rockland's biggest and most important enterprise. To keep the spark glowing, to illumine the minds of our youth, to build and strengthen the character of each individual is big business and demands the earnest support and cooperation of every parent.

My appreciation and thanks go continually to our entire staff of teachers and to the members of the Rockland School Committee who work diligently for the advancement of local education, without remuneration and often without the thoughtful understanding cooperation which should be part of the investment every parent puts into the fine business of his child's education.

Respectfully submitted,

R. STEWART ESTEN,
Superintendent of Schools

REPORT OF THE JUNIOR-SENIOR
HIGH SCHOOL PRINCIPAL

Mr. R. Stewart Esten
Superintendent of Schools
Rockland, Massachusetts

My dear Mr. Esten:

My report as Principal of the Junior-Senior High
School is submitted below.

Since 1935 the enrolment of the school has gradually
increased. This fall it reached a total of seven hundred
and five pupils which was the second largest enrolment
in the history of the school. This increase is quite even-
ly distributed between the Junior and Senior High.
Therefore some home rooms in the Junior High and all
study halls in the Senior High are overcrowded while all
other rooms are filled to capacity.

The average attendance and the record for punctuality
were satisfactory for the year and again indicate the co-
operation of parents and pupils in this matter.

Authoritative reports have been recently received
from the testing service of the American Council on Education, indicating that from the scores obtained by our
pupils on standardized achievement tests, the medians of
our groups were above the national medians in all subjects
tested. Favorable reports have also been received concerning the work of some of our recent graduates now attending such institutions as Boston College, Boston University, Bates, Brown, Carnegie Institute of Technology, Harvard, University of Maine, Bridgewater Teachers College, and several training schools for nurses. From
the above it is reasonable to assume that our high scholastic standards have been maintained.

Again do I call attention to the need for broadening the

General Course curriculum. The majority of that large group of pupils who do not go on to other educational institutions, take this course, and they are limited to college preparatory or commercial subjects. If we could offer them some practical subjects, we would be able to meet better the needs of this large group. As all of our present faculty are carrying a full teaching load, this is not possible without an additional teacher. This matter merits serious consideration.

Because a sufficient number did not elect to take third-year French, we could not offer the subject this fall. Although three years of French are necessary for college entrance only under certain conditions, nevertheless a sense of mastery comes only after more than two years' study of a language. It is to be hoped that we may be able to offer the third year of French again next fall.

As a part of the campaign for highway safety, the Registrar of Motor Vehicles and the Commissioner of Education have requested the public schools to incorporate a course in automobile driving into the curriculum. With the approval of the School Committee, a member of our staff took a week's intensified training in the conduct of such a course. We will now introduce the pre-driving part of the course as a unit in our Problems of Democracy classes. The full program, which includes teaching pupils to drive, can only be undertaken in our school when the necessary equipment is available and, more important, when we have additional help so that a teacher may be relieved to carry on this program which requires nearly full time for the year. When we consider that every boy and girl is a potential driver of the future, the necessity of the whole course appears evident.

In my opinion, our printing course offers much of vocational value. However, we are seriously handicapped in this department because of the condition of the press. It is old and really beyond repair. Operating our present press involves risks for which it would be unfair to hold us responsible. A new press — or at least a second-hand one in first class condition — should be obtained immediately.

During the past year serious thought was given to the establishment of the so-called P. F. I. (Physical Fitness Index) system in our program of Physical Education. In brief, this system endeavors to find out the exact physical condition of each individual pupil and then attempts to correct any weaknesses disclosed by the tests and physical examinations. However, we found that we could not set up such a system under present conditions because, being a program dealing with individuals, much more time would have to be devoted to physical education by the instructors. Under the existing conditions these teachers cannot be relieved from teaching other necessary subjects. I am sure it will be agreed that the best system of Physical Education is the one which can do the most for each indivilual pupil.   As physical fitness is of the utmost importance, the establishment of some such system in our school is vital to the community.

As a result of action by the last Legislature, Massachusetts high schools were allowed to join with those from other New England states in underwriting athletic injuries. Our school was immediately enrolled in the plan and we were able to offer it to our athletes this fall. At the rates charged, it is readily understood that this plan is not complete insurance coverage. It is a step forward, however, and I am sure it will be appreciated more and more by the parents of our athletes, especially as the coverage is broadened from time to time.

For a number of years, only a relatively small group of boys has gone out for football. It has been understood that many boys did not go out because their parents were fearful of injuries with the resulting expenses. However the coverage plan did not seem to make much difference in the number reporting for football this fall, as we had a squad of less than thirty boys who stayed out the whole season. Nevertheless, I feel that this plan will help the football situation in the immediate future.

Our athletic teams have fared well during the past year with the exception of football. We had exceptionally fine teams in cross-country and boys' basketball, the latter winning the Brockton Y. M. C. A. South Shore Tournament. Baseball enjoyed a good season, while the track team did well considering the fact that our track is not in a useable condition for practice purposes. Girls' basketball is on the upgrade and it should receive as much attention as the other teams since it is the only athletic activity for the girls. We may expect better football teams for the next two or three years as most of this year's team were Freshmen and Sophomores. A well-organized program of athletics for both boys and girls has been carried on in the Junior High. Due almost wholly to the loyal support of the pupils to their Students' Association we have been able to pay all past debts and carry on seven varsity teams in spite of the handicap of an uninclosed athletic field.

Very worthwhile accomplishments were made in other extra-curricular activities. In forensic work we entered debating teams and speakers in the district meet, winning several places. We also placed three winners at the state forensic meet. One of our boys, Freeman Rawson, won the right to attend the national meet in California. This he did last June at his own expense and thereby brought honor to his school and community. There is so much educational value in this activity that I hope much more may be done in the future.

Four additional clubs were organized during the year: the Art, French, Personality and Stamp Clubs. These, together with the Camera, Dramatic, and Commercial Clubs previously established, serve to develop further the varied interest of our pupils.

Pro Merito, our honor society, has continued its service to the school. Last June, the chapter presented a large felt banner for the school's use. Again it has assumed the responsibility for furnishing the student librarians who perform a much-needed service in the library.

The library has been much more useful since we received the new books over a year ago. We acknowledge with thanks another donation for library books by the Woman's club. The student librarians have catalogued all new books and have efficiently handled the library routine. A teacher-librarian is still needed, however, in order to have the library service necessary for a modern school.

I conclude this report with a couple of miscellaneous items worthy of note. Several of our faculty attended schools last summer and others have been taking professional courses during the fall term. With pride I report that upon several occasions our school has been complimented for the good sportsmanship of our teams and their supporters.

My thanks is extended to the School Committee and the Superintendent for their encouragment and support and to the faculty for their efficient cooperation.

Respectfully submitted,

GEO. A. J. FROBERGER,
Principal

REPORT OF SCHOOL PHYSICIANS AND SCHOOL NURSE

Mr. R. Stewart Esten
Superintendent of Schools
Rockland, Massachusetts

My dear Mr. Esten:

We herewith submit our report as School Physicians for for the year 1939. We have examined all the pupils in the elementary grades. High School pupils were carefully examined before their participation in the competitive sports. We have also made an inspection of the classrooms whenever the pupils had been exposed to contagious disease.

In May we carried out our Diphtheria Prevention Program. We advise that all children over six months of age be given the Toxoid Inoculations.

We feel that the Milk Fund carried on by the Kiwanis Club is a very worthwhile project in which the underprivileged child benefits greatly. We suggest its continuance.

The Junior Red Cross has accomplished a great deal in furnishing surgical and dental care for children.

Following is a list of physical defects found:
Number of physical examinations   964
Number of cases of enlarged tonsils and adenoids   84
Number of cases of cervical glands   16
Number given Toxoid Inoculations   96

ACTIVITIES OF SCHOOL NURSE

An office hour is maintained each school day at the High School from 8:30 to 9:30 A. M. and parents or teachers may reach the nurse by telephoning the office of the Superintendent of Schools.

Elementary classrooms are visited twice weekly. Monthly inspections are made in all grade schools; these inspections are made daily by the nurse if the pupils have been exposed to contagion.

Pupils were weighed three times during the school year. A steady gain in each pupil is the aim rather than trying to have the child conform to any specific age, weight table. Weight Charts are posted in all the classrooms.

Number of visits to classrooms	1904
Number of visits to homes	542
Number of minor wounds dressed	103
Number of emergency treatments	9
Number of pupils taken home ill	43
Number of pupils sent to family physician	8
Number of pupils sent to school physicians	1
Number of classroom inspections	82
Number of individual inspections	2297
Number of pupils weighed and measured	979
Number of pupils found to have defective hearing	14
Number of pupils found to have defective vision	33

Industrial conditions still being poor in Rockland, much social and relief work is required by the nurse. She has been able to carry on this additional work only by the splendid cooperation of the teachers and the financial assistance of the Rockland Teachers' Association. I think the attitude of the teaching group is most admirable.

All cases of non-attendance which have been reported to me have been investigated.

Respectfully submitted,

JOSEPH H. DUNN, M. D.
School Physician
JOSEPH FRAME, M. D.
School Physician
LOUISE A. CONSIDINE,
School Nurse

REPORT OF DENTAL HYGIENIST

To the Superintendent of Schools:

I hereby submit my report for the year ending December 31, 1939.

The results of the annual dental examinations in grades 1-6 are as follows:

Number examined	865
Number with cavities in temporary teeth	269
Number needing temporary extractions	231
Number needing permanent extractions	289
Number of cavities in permanent teeth	368
Number of children having no defects	106

The results of the pre-school examinations:

Number examined	92
Number of temporary defects	63
Number of permanent defects	3
Number with no defects	29

Sixty-eight per cent of the number examined had visible defects.

During the year 775 oral prophalaxis were given and children received individual tooth brush instruction at the clinic.

In the classroom instruction the proper method of brushing the teeth, the structure of the tooth, and tooth building foods were taken up.

Several extraction clinics were held the funds for which were provided by the Junior Red Cross and the Rockland

Teachers' Association. Eighty-six children were cared for by the Junior Red Cross and three by the Teachers' Association.

I sincerely believe that the work which has been done by these two organizations is beginning to show results. I should like to extend by appreciation to them with the hope that they will continue this work.

Respectfully submitted,

ETTA MURGIDA,

December 22, 1939   Dental Hygienist

FINANCIAL REPORT FOR THE ROCKLAND HIGH SCHOOL CAFETERIA

January 1, 1939 to December 31, 1939

Balance on Hand, January 1, 1939	$ 28 54
Cash Receipts for 1939	5 443 79
Total Cash	$5 472 33

Cash Payments for 1939:

Barnes, W. F.	$ 9 57
Berwick Cake Company	191 24
Brockton Edison Illuminating Co.	72 00
Chamberlain, E. L.	8 12
Condon, Lavina	9 00
Cook, Hubert	27 01
Coty's Bakery	44 08
Cushman's Bakery	100 43
Drake's Cake Company	83 73
Ellis Company, H. F.	70 47
Figlioli Brothers	95 52
Fitts, Company, E. V.	348 34
Fitts, Welcome	15 00
Globe Ticket Company	26 75
Gumpert S., Inc.	20 63
Hickey Brothers	758 43
Hostess Cake Co.	32 64
Hunt Potato Chip Co.	55 30
Loose-Wiles Biscuit Company	52 24
Lovell, Arthur M.	37 68
National Biscuit Company	19 23
Old Colony Gas Company	86 50
Old Colony Service Company	7 80
Paul's Spa	1 25
Peterson, A. S.	450 06
Plymouth Rock Ice Cream Co.	1 187 90

Rockland Disposal Service	15 00
Rockland New System Laundry	2 93
Rockland Water Department	10 00
Rome Brothers	24 50
Schulers Foods, Inc	3 94
Standard Brands, Inc	6 75
Stoddard, A. C.	43 21
Quinn, Margaret	614 00
Weatherbee, Charles N.	186 87
White Brothers Milk Company	414 52
Whiting Milk Company	113 93
Williamson, Anita	23 38
Wonder Bread Bakery	176 34

Total Cash Payments $5 446 29

Balance on Hand $ 26 04

Respectfully submitted,

ROSE T. MAGADINI,
ELEANOR B. LOUD

SCHOOL ENROLLMENT

As of December 22, 1939

Teacher	School	Grade	Pupils
Madeline Lannin	McKinley	1	39
Mary H. Greenan	McKinley	2	32
Mildred Healey	McKinley	3	38
R. Louise Cone	McKinley	4	28
Elva M. Shea	McKinley	5	29
John Metevier	McKinley	5	29
Paul Casey	McKinley	6	38
Nellie M. Ford	McKinley	6	35
M. Rita Kennedy	McKinley	Special Class	13.
Catherine Coen	Lincoln	1	32
Blanche Thacher	Lincoln	2	29
Harriette Cragin	Lincoln	3	32
Miriam Roberts	Lincoln	4	31
Eileen Fitzgibbons	Lincoln	5	33
Margaret McDemott	Lincoln	6	34
Virginia Ford	Jefferson	1 d 2	36
Bertha M. Campbell	Jefferson	2 d 3	37
Blanche Crowell	Jefferson	4 and 5	33
Annie A. Shirley	Jefferson	5 and 6	34
Alice Murrill	Gleason	1 and 2	33
Catherine Reilly	Gleason	3 and 4	29
Lillian G. Murdock	Webster St.	1, 2 d 3	15
Josephine Lannin	Webster St.	4 d 5	18
Ethel Wetherbee	Market St.	1, 2 d 3	18
Margaret E. Blake	Market St.	4, 5 d 6	18
Geraldine Crowell	Central St.	1, 2 and 3	35

Total Elementary School Enrollment   778

Junior-Senior High School Enrollment   690

Grand Total   1468

AGE TABLE AS OF OCTOBER 1, 1939

Grade	5	6	7	8	9	10	11	12	13	14	15	16	17	18	19	20	Total
1	49	75	11	1													136
2		44	66	6													116
3			53	64	14	8	2										141
4				41	54	9	3	1									107
5					41	64	8	6	3								122
6						62	48	18	10	2	1						141
7							38	78	19	6	3	2	1				147
8							1	51	46	25	7	2					132
9									45	49	21	4	2				121
10									2	46	62	18	3				131
11											26	46	11	3			86
12												31	45	8	1	1	86
P. G.													1	1			2
Ungraded			1		1	3	2	3	3	1	1						15
Total	49	119	131	112	110	146	100	156	128	129	121	103	63	12	1	1	1483

ROCKLAND HIGH SCHOOL

GRADUATION EXERCISES

Class of 1939

In The Auditorium

Wednesday Evening, June 21, 1939

Rockland High School

PROGRAMME

Processional — "For Ever"   J. Schrammel
Rockland High School Orchestra

Invocation   Rev. George A. Riley

Honor Essay —   "The Future of Young America"
John Simmons Allison

Song — "Come to the Fair"   Martin-Salter
Rockland High Choristers

Honor Essay —   "Fighting the Enemies to Growth"
Dorothy Richardson

Chamber of Commerce Prize Essay —
"Our Community"
Edith Isobel Jukes

Music — "Selection"   Arr. by L. Cocuben
Rockland High School Orchestra

Honor Essay —   "A Salute to Our Commanders"
Virginia Anne Shalgian

Song — "Dream of Summer"   Lehar
Girls' Glee Club

Honor Essay — "New Fields to Conquer"
Allen Edwards Martin

Woman's Club Scholarship Mrs. Horace Studley
Chairman of Scholarship Commmittee

Awarding of other prizes and
Presentation of Diplomas
Dr. Benjamin Lelyveld
Chairman School Committee

Song — "America" Chorus and Audience

Benediction Rev. George A. Riley

Director of the Chorus - Miss Blanche G. Maguire

Director of the Orchestra - Mr. Michael Cassano

Accompanist - Jean Kierstead, '41

GRADUATES

*John Simmons Allison
Vanda Ida Anderson
*Marjorie Olva Bromley
*Jeanne Meredith Bryant
Richard Merritt Burbank
*Natalie Parlow Burrows
Anita Elizabeth Callahan
Leo Francis Carreaux
Louise Mary Carreaux
Mary Evelyn Chamberlain
Elsie May Cookson
Robert Edward Crane
Ruth Louise Crovo
Dorothy Delfino Dondero
*Francis Andrew Donnellan, Jr.
Alice Virginia Downey
*Joseph Alton Dunn
Dorothy Jean Essery
Daniel John Flavell
Irving Charles Fletcher
LeRoy Edward Gardner
Alexander Hugie Gillis
Agnes Treasa Glinsky

*Olive Ferguson MacLeod
Mary Annie MacLeod
Mildred Mary Mahoney
*Allen Edward Martin
Rosalie Agnes Martin
*Beatrice Patricia Mastrodomenico
Marie Stetson McCaw
Francis Joseph McKenna
Josephine Louise Mileski
Michael Joseph Mileski
*Dorothy Miller
Conrad Charles Morris
Joseph Murgida
Rita Carmella Nastasi
Marjorie Louise O'Brien
Paul Henry O'Brien
Eleanor Ann O'Connell
Marguerite Frances O'Neil
Roland Turner Phillips
Ralph Joseph Porrazzo
*Freeman Leigh Rawson, Jr.
Irma Phyllis Rhodes
*Dorothy Richardson

Elizabeth Gertrude Grant
Thomas Lawrence Haggerty
Fredericia Frances Hartmann
Dorothy Marguerite Higgins
Corine Virginia Hill
Florence Deane Hirtle
*Mary Elizabeth Ignatowicz
Margery Lucille Inglis
*Edith Isobel Jukes
*Charles Kent Lane, Jr.
Robert Joseph. Ledwell
Eleanor Beatrice Leighton
Alice Bradford Leonard
Doris Mabel Lonergan
Ralph Joseph Lordi
Vincent John Lordi
Beatrice Mary Loring

Regina Rose Rock
Mary Margaret Ryan
*Alfred Joseph Sciarappa
*Virginia Anne Shalgian
Elbridge Franklin Simmons
Eva Elvira Spera
Jean Margot Sweet
Clyde Dustin Turner
Mary Teresa Walls
James Henry Walsh
John Joseph Ware
Fred John Wendt
Joseph Michael Williams
Judith Meriam Williams
Mary Celina Wilmot
Louise Maybelle Wright
Emma Margaret Ziegler

* Pro Merito — Average of 85% or above for four years.

CLASS OFFICERS

President JOHN ALLISON

Vice President ELEANOR LEIGHTON

Secretary ELIZABETH GRANT

Treasurer ALFRED SCIARAPPA

SOCIAL COMMITTEE

Olva Bromley   Paul O'Brien   Virginia Shalgian

CLASS COLORS

American Beauty Red and Silver

CLASS MOTTO

Carpe Diem — Seize the Opportunity

CLASS FLOWER

Red Rose

CLASS ODE

Into a world of trouble and of strife,
  Into a world of turmoil we must go.
We must accept the challenge of this life,
  Although each vic'try will be pained and slow.
Let's not, like stupid creatures, groan and cry,
  Because we have not hit a happier age,
But upward pull and strain and try.
  By trial only, we our strength may gauge!
Thus, we are fortunate to be alive,
  To bear the brunt of man's long past mistakes,
To try our best to make the day arrive
  When no man o'er his brother 'vantage takes.
We thank God for the age where we belong,
  'Tis toil, not ease, that makes men brave and strong!

Freeman L. Rawson, Jr., '39

SUPERINTENDENT OF SCHOOLS

	Appointment	Salary
R. Stewart Esten, A. B., Middlebury College, A. M., Columbia Univ.	Sept. 1929	$3600

JUNIOR-SENIOR HIGH SCHOOL

	Appointment	Salary
George A. J. Froberger, A. B., Univ. of Maine, Principal	1935	2980
Robert C. Healey, A. B., Boston College, M. Ed., Boston Univ., Sub-Master, Latin	1919	2500
Katherine S. Burke, Bridgewater Teachers' College, Geog., Science	1906	1400
Joseph Cogan, B. S., Bates College, Sciences	1929	1800
Mary D. Costello, Attended Quincy Training School, English, Penmanship, Special Courses	1898	1400
Marion T. Hall, B. S., University of Vermont, Sewing, History	1939	1100
Ellen M. Hayes, A. B., University of Wisconsin, English	1927	1700
Mia Howarth, A. B., Radcliffe College, English	1925	1800
Emma S. Jewett, Hyannis Teachers' College, History	1908	1400
Eleanor Loud, B. S., Simmons College, Household Arts	1935	1150
Rose T. Magadini, Bay Path Institute, Commercial	1929	1540
Joe H. Ayer, B. S., Boston Univ., A. M., Boston Univ., English	1935	1350
Esther McGrath, B. S., E., Bridgewater Teachers' College, Social Sci., Lit.	1918	1400
Helen M. Miley, B. S., Boston University, M. Ed., Boston Univ., Commercial	1938	1250
John B. O'Hyare, A. B., Boston College, History	Jan. 1931	1585
Chester J. Poliks, B. S., E., Fitchburg Teachers' College B. S., Connecticut State College, Physical Education, Biology	1937	1800
Malcolm L. Pratt, A. B., Dartmouth College Mathematics	1933	1550
John Ryan, A. B., Boston College, B. S. E., Bridgewater Teachers' College, Junior Bus. Training	1937	1200
Leona W. Sampson, A. B., Boston University, A. M., Boston University, French	Sept. 1937	1600
Frances L. Squarey, Bridgewater Teachers' College, English, Literature	1921	1400
Robert A. Studley, A. B., Univ. of N. H., History	1927	1675
Bertha L. Tenney, Farmington, Maine Normal School, Sci., Mathematics	1927	1400

TEACHERS EMPLOYED, DECEMBER 31, 1939

Name and Qualifications	Year	Salary
Earl I. Komarin, B. S. E., Salem Teachers' College, Commercial	1936	1350
G. William Mson, B. S. E., Fitchburg Teachers' College, Manual Training	1937	1300

McKINLEY SCHOOL

Name and Qualifications	Year	Salary
Nellie M. Ford, High School, Special Courses, Principal, Grade 6	1896	1540
Madeline Lannin, Lesley Normal School, Grade 1	1937	1150
My H. Greenan, Attended B. U. and Hyannis Teachers' College, Grade 2	1920	1400
Mildred E. Healey, Lesley Normal School, Grade 3	1930	1150
R. Louise Cone, Boston University, M. E. D., Grade 4	1930	1365
Elva M. Shea, Bridgewater Teachers' College, Grade 5	1928	1207.50
John Metevier, B. S. E., Bridgewater Teachers' College, Grade 5	1939	1000
Paul Casey, B. S. E., Bridgewater Teachers' College, Grade 6	1937	1100
M. Rita Kennedy, B. S. E., Salem Teachers' College, Special Class	1938	1100

LINCOLN SCHOOL

Name and Qualifications	Year	Salary
J. Eileen Fitzgibbons, Bridgewater Teachers' College, Principal, Grade 5	1925	1410
Catherine Coen, Salem Teachers' College, Grade 1	1930	1320
Blanche Thacher, Buck Ktg. School, Grade 2	Jan. 1930	1275
Harriette Cragin, High School, Special Courses, Grade 3	Sept. 1910	1400
Miriam Roberts, Bridgewater Teachers' College, Grade 4	1934	1150
Margaret McDermott, Hyannis Teachers' College, Grade 6	1925	1400

JEFFERSON SCHOOL

Name and Qualifications	Year	Salary
Annie A. Shirley, Bridgewater Teachers' College, Principal, Grades 5 and 6	1912	1450
Virginia Ford, B. S. E., Bridgewater Teachers' College, Grades 1 and 2	1937	1100
Bertha Cambell, Attended Mass. Agr. College, B. U., Hyannis Teachers' College, Special Courses, Grades 2 and 3	1923	1400
	1931	1320

GLEASON SCHOOL

Name and Qualifications	Year	Salary
Blanche Crowell, Framingham Teachers' College, Grades 4 and 5		
Alice Murrill, B. S. E., Bridgewater Teachers' College, Grades 1 and 2	1937	1100

TEACHERS EMPLOYED, DECEMBER 31, 1939

Catherine Reilly, B. S. E., Bridgewater Teachers' College, Grades 3 and 4 — 1938 — 1050

WEBSTER STREET SCHOOL

Lillian G. █k, Quincy Training School, Grades 1 2 and 3 — 1922 — 1400
█n, Bridgewater Teachers' College, B. S. E., Hyannis e█chers' College, Grades 4 and 5 — 1932 — 1150

MARKET STREET SCHOOL

Ethel Wetherbee, Symonds Ktg. School, Grades 1, 2 and 3 — 1928 — 1400
Margaret Blake, Hyannis Teachers' College, █des 4, 5 ard 6 — 1929 — 1150

CENTRAL STREET SCHOOL

Geraldine █well, B. S. E., Bridgewater Teachers' College, █des 1, 2 and 3 — 1939 — 1000

SPECIAL TEACHERS

* Blanche Maguire, Atte █d B. U. █d Northampton School of Pedagogy, Music — March 1929 / Sept. — 900

█ael Cassano, Virtuoso Music School, Private Study in █ic, █ r of █al Instruments — 1928 — 1200
█ise A. █le, R. N., St. █s Hospital Training School, School U█se — 1922 — 1500
Josephine Fitzgibbons, Posse-Nissen, █al Education for Girls — 1929 — 1275
█a van der █, B. S., Boston University, Art Supervisor — 1938 — 1250
* 2 days per week
** 3 days per week

RESIGNATIONS 1939

Helen M. █y, Junior High School
Constance Tobey, Senior-Junior High School
█ie Smith Glidden, McKinley School

APPOINTMENTS 1939

Marion T. Hall, Junior-Senior High
John █, McKinley School
Geraldine Crowell, Central St. School

Sixty-sixth Annual Report Of The Selectmen

STATE AID

Paid under Chapter 19, Revised Laws and Amendments thereto.

Total amount of State Aid Paid		$460 00
Appropration	$600 00	
Under appropriation	140 00	

CARE OF TOWN CEMETERY

Paid:

W. E. Vining, services		$60 00
Appropriation		$60 00

MILITARY AID

Paid: Relief Under Military Aid	$210 00
Amount from Reserve Fund	$210 00

SOLDIER'S RELIEF

Paid for Relief		$8 993 44
Appropriation	$9 000 00	
Under appropriation	6 56	

CARE OF SOLDIERS' GRAVES

Paid:

C. S. Tilden, care of lots	$55 00	
W. A. Whiting, care of lots	15 00	
W. F. Hunt, care of lots	15 00	
Warren B. Hamilton, care of lots	5 00	
James Maguire, care of lots	5 00	
Louis B. Gilbride, services	50 00	
		$ 145 00
Appropriation	$150 00	

| Expended | 145 00 |
| Under appropriation | $5 00 |

CLEAN UP WEEK

Paid:

William C. Greene, labor	$54 00	
Rockland Standard Pub. Co., Adv	1 50	
Quincy Patriot Ledger, Adv.	1 00	
Expended		$56 50
Appropriation	$75 00	
Under	$18 50	

CRIMINAL CASES IN COURT

Paid:

Leroy Phinney, prisoners to		
Plymouth	18 80	
George J. Popp, prisoners to		
Plymouth	29 00	
Robert J. Jackson, services	7 00	
		$54 80
Appropriation	$100 00	
Expended	54 80	
Under appropriation	45 20	

STREET LIGHTING 1939

Paid:

Brockton Edison Co., Service		$8 894 03
Apppropriation	8 898 00	
Appropriation install light		
Forest Street	15 00	
Appropriation install light		
High School	37 00	
	$8 950 00	
Expended	8 894 03	
Under appropriation	55 97	

HIGHWAY SURVEYOR

Paid:
Roderick MacKenzie, Salary $1 350 00·
Appropriation $1 350 00·

TARVIA AND ROAD BINDER

Paid:—
William Condon, 135 loads gravel $ 67 50
The Barrett Co., tarvia   802 13
C. H. Swift, kerosene   1 00
Market St., Garage, storage   97 65
Southeastern Con. Co., supplies   70 86
Rockland Coal and Grain Co., supplies   80 48
Bradford Western Inc., concrete   323 22
M. F. Ellis & Co., supplies   47 59
A. Culver Co., supplies   10 75
Rockland Motors Inc., repairs   14 78
Rome Bros., supplies   48 54
E. L. LeBaron Foundry Co., grates   3 68
Buffalo-Springfield Co., Repairs   6 79
Brockton Welding Shop   49 40
Payroll, labor ——— -   1 374 59
Total $ 2 998 96·
Appropriation $3 000 00
Expended   2 998 96·
Under   1 04

List of Payroll Tarvia and Road Binder
George Tyler $ 417 00
William Condon   94 50
Raymond LaCombe   24 75
Lawrence Cull   33 00
Arthur Smith   56 82
Arthur Deacon   3 38
Joseph Daley   41 63
John McQuaide——— ··   28 41
Joseph Kelliher   1 13
Frank O'Hara   1 41
John White   1 13

J. J. Dwyer	45 75
Patrick Mahoney	3 00
A. DelPrete	2 25
Vincent Lee	11 25
Edward Tobin	43 31
Michael Murphy	27 00
George Beverly	120 37
Paul McDonnell	13 50
John Ricca	18 00
Russell Chandler	13 50
Carl Nelson	9 00
Joseph Costello	7 00
Donald Baker	7 56
William Cannaway	4 75
Edward Lynch	23 50
Dominic DelPrete	56 75
Fred Dill	2 25
Daniel Smith	2 25
Fred Walls Jr.	2 25
Leo McAuliffe	4 50
John Capelice	6 75
George Umbrianna	4 50
Joseph Walls	2 25
Harold Dill	4 50
Dominic DePrete Jr.	2 25
Fred Wall Sr.,	6 75
Raymond Rainsford	6 75
Jerry Frino	6 75
Charles Roberts	6 75
Joseph Shoughrow	18 00
James Maliff	9 00
Foster Chute	9 00
A. Wainshilbaum	5 00
Thomas Bailey	63 00
Michael Bowen	6 75
Melvin Gay	25 00
Lyle Tibbetts	1 69
J. B. Parmenter	9 00

————————$ 1 374 59

HIGHWAY REPAIRS

Paid:—

Roderick MacKenzie, gravel	$ 35 00	
Market Street Garage, storage of tractor	20 00	
Gideon Studley, use of cellar for storage	75 00	
George W. S. Hyde, repairs	105 00	
Roderick MacKenzie, use of car	250 00	
M. F. Ellis & Co., supplies	58 52	
The Barrett Co., tarvia	197 57	
Payroll, labor	726 61	
Rockland Disposal Co., removal of rubbish	50 00	
Bradford Weston Inc., bit. concrete	327 59	
N. E. Metal Culvert Co., supplies	40 31	
Rome Bros., supplies	63 74	
Raymond Finn, damage to tire	17 85	
Southeastern Con. Co., supplies	9 99	
E. L. LeBaron Foundry Co., grate	2 00	
Rockland Water Dept., service	10 00	
Gordon Mann, rent of pit	37 50	
Hall & Torrey Inc., supplies	22 32	
Expended		$ 2 049 00
Appropriation	$1 800 00	
Reserve Fund	250 00	
Total available		$ 2 050 00
Under appropriation		1 00

List of Payroll Highway Repairs

Paid:—

Lea Cull	$ 13 50
J. J. Dwyer	69 00
George Tyler	102 00
Charles Clark	23 63
Joseph Casey	24 75
Joseph Kelliher	24 75
Augustine Yourell	21 38

Thomas Bailey	30 38
Thomas Bennett	21 94
William Green Jr.	9 00
John White	20 25
George Umbrianna	9 00
Richard Hussey	9 00
Carl Nelson	9 00
Russell Chandler	9 00
Paul McDonald	4 50
Dominic DelPrete	64 50
Patrick Mahoney	54 00
George Beals	30 00
Arthur Casey	24 00
Raymond LaComb	36 00
Michael Murphy	3 38
Burton Norman	3 38
Joseph Daley	4 50
Edward Tobin	4 50
Arthur Deacon	3 38
Arthur Smith	3 38
John Ricca	3 38
Jerry DelPrete	3 38
John McQuaide	6 75
Frank O'Hara	6 75
Joseph Shoughrow	4 50
Joseph Costello	6 75
Thomas DeSimione	4 50
Warren Hamilton	4 50
Louis Roche	9 00
William Cannaway	4 50
George Beverly	22 50
William Condon	18 00

$726 61

WEST WATER STREET, CHAPTER 90

Paid:—

Payroll, labor and trucks	$3 202 12
Hume Pipe Co., pipe	428 06
Roderick MacKenzie, gravel	7 90

Crystal Concrete Co., concrete	1 144 58	
Northern Steel Co., steel	149 13	
Rockland Coal & Grain Co.,		
Lumber and supplies	504 71	
C. M. White Iron Works, pipe fence	180 00	
M. Agnes Kelliher, gravel	42 72	
A. Culver Co., cement	2 80	
State Prison Colony, iron pipe	139 84	
Edward T. Dwyer, gas shovel	111 75	
Independent Coal Tar Co., tar	85 79	
Expended		$ 5 999 40
Transfer Reserve Fund		$1 500 00
Received from Com. of Mass.		2 217 06
Received from County of Plymouth		1 108 53
Total		$4 825 59
Due from Commonwealth of Mass		
and County of Plymouth		$1 174 41

List of Payroll, Labor and Trucks

Leo Cull	$ 393 00
John Ricca	67 49
Russell Chandler	51 46
Lyle Tibbetts	18 83
Louis Roche	54 25
Joseph Arena	8 43
Wm. Duhaine	96 95
Wm. Condon, truck	229 50
George Tyler, truck	66 75
Michael Bowen, truck	70 59
Donald Baker	167 51
John J. Dwyer, truck	55 50
Thomas Bailey	29 31
Timothy Mahoney	64 12
Arthur Smith	21 66
Philip Murphy	21 66
George Beverly	327 59
Albert Boynton	78 65

Crystal Sand & Gravel Co. pump	16 50	
Thomas Bailey Jr.	22 21	
Ernest McNutt	48 37	
Alex Weatherbee	135 30	
Wilbur Adams	92 40	
Joseph Casey	51 46	
Bernard Cull	33 46	
Joseph Dailey	6 18	
Wm. Cannaway	8 15	
J. B. Parmenter	6 18	
Oscar Lincoln	6 18	
Thomas Bennett	38 53	
Carl Nelson	4 50	
Tovia Jarvinen, truck	31 50	
Patrick Mahoney, truck	36 75	
Joseph Golemme, truck	30 75	
Dominic DelPrete, truck	31 50	
Edward J. Rourke, roller	93 75	
Arthur Casey, truck	20 25	
William Bell, truck	21 00	
Paul McDonald	18 56	
John Gillis	4 50	
Clarence Damon	4 50	
Lawrence Cull	4 50	
John White	4 78	
Fred Kane	16 03	
Fred Ferron	4 78	
Charles Hunt	13 50	
Waldo McPhee	17 72	
Roderick MacKenzie	6 00	
E. Dwyer, gas shovel	549 12	
Total ,	—————	$ 3 202 12

EAST WATER STREET CONSTRUCTION 1939
Paid:—

Payroll, labor	$	4 50
Bradford Weston Inc., stone and stone dust		3 352 07
Comm. of Mass:, road markers		43 20

Trimount Bit Products Co., asphalt   212 72
Expended   ——————$ 3 612 49
Balance 1938 Appropriation $1 808 11   —
Received County of Plymouth   601 46
Received Comm. of Mass.   1 202 92
Total available   ——————$ 3 612 49

REBUILDING WEST WATER STREET

Appropriation Article 14, 1939 $6 000 00
Unexpended balance $6 000 00

SOLDIERS' MEMORIAL LIBRARY

Paid:—
Lida A. Clark, salary $1 200 00
Natalie F. Holbrook, salary   600 00
Elida T. Butler, salary   600 00
W. G. Holbrook, Janitor   300 00
Edwin H. Totman, janitor   600 00
Brockton Edison Co., service   102 14
A. S. Peterson, supplies   23 56
N. E. Tel. & Tel. Co., service   39 96
Rockland Water Dept., service   5 00
J. F. Barnard Co., supplies   1 66
A. Culver Co., Coal and supplies   96 97
Junior Literary Guild, books   56 27
Lida A. Clark, miscellaneous supplies   7 60
New Eng. News Co., Books   403 87
Damon Electric, new wiring   67 80
American Library Ass'n. subscription   5 00
American Rescue League, subscription   60
H. W. Wilson Co., books   21 20
Chester A. Hickman, expense on roof 131 90
Pioneer Store, supplies   68
Ward Stationers, labels   22 50
O. H. Toothaker, book   1 90
Gaylord Bros., Inc., supplies   14 48
Dr. B. F. Beck, book   3 00
H. R. Huntting, supplies   8 06

Personal Book Shop Inc., book	3 85	
Amos A. Phelps & Son, insurance	160 76	
American News Co., subscriptions	102 15	
Jean Kass, Books	13 90	
Rockland Standard Pub. Co., printing	6 25	
W. A. Wilde Co., book	11 88	
Rockland Hardware Co., supplies	2 26	
American Book Co., book	76	
A. Wainshilbaum, labor	7 00	
Edward Metivier, labor	5 00	
Hall & Torrey Co., supplies	2 80	
Library of Congress, supplies	1 26	
Rome Bros., supplies	23	
Educational Guild of N. E., supplies	1 82	
Rockland Coal & Grain, coal	66 50	
Martin Murray Co., book	9 00	
Douglas Print, 1000 index cards	4 25	
Careful Moving Co., 1 show case	3 00	
A. I. Randall Inc., supplies	5 25	
R. R. Bowker Co., supplies	60	
L. A. Wells Library Binding, ref. books	35 82	
Allen R. Holbrook, 8 venetian blinds	57 00	
Expended		$4 815 49
Appropriation	$4 400 00	
Dog Fund	415 50	
		$ 4 815 50
Under appropriation		01

SIDEWALKS 1939

Paid:—

J. S. McCullum, supplies	$ 3 88	
Bradford Weston Co., bit. concrete	159 87	
A. J. Vargus, supplies	34	
George N. Beal, repairs	4 25	
Payroll, labor	326 55	
Expended		$ 494 89
Appropriation	$500 00	
Under appropriation	5 11	

List of Payroll

Lawrence Cull	$ 2 25
George Beverly	140 62
Earl Wallace	4 50
George Tyler	42 00
James Mailiff	4 50
Thomas Bailey	64 12
William Condon	20 75
Joseph Arena	3 38
Donald Baker	7 59
Michael Bowen	9 84
Joseph Dailey	4 50
J. B. Parmenter	22 50
Total	———— $ 326 55

AMERICAN LEGION POST No. 147

Paid:

American Legion Building Association	$900 00
Appropriation	$900 00

PETER A. BOWLER CAMP, No. 63
SPANISH WAR VETERANS

Paid:

Old Colony Post Building Association rent	$288 00
Appropriation	$288 00

CLEANING UNION STREET

Paid:

Thomas J. Higgins, labor		$1 197 00
Appropriation	$1 200 00	
Expended	1 197 00	
Under appropriation	3 00	

INSPECTION OF ANIMALS AND STABLES

Paid:

Williams T. Condon, Inspector	$150 00
Appropriation	$150 00

SEALER OF WEIGHTS AND MEASURES

Paid:

Harold J. Inkley, services	$400 00
Appropriation	$400 00

FIRE DEPARTMENT MAINTENANCE

C. P. Inkley, balance 1938 salary	$ 146	00
J. Barry, balance 1938 salary	100	00
G. W. Clark, balance 1938 salary	33	37
Call Men, balance 1938 pay	313	50
C. P. Inkley, Chief, salary	1 500	00
J. P. Barry, Dep. Chief, salary	200	00
G. W. Clark, Supt. Fire Alarm	400	00
James Fitzgibbons	1 731	60
William Parker	1 638	00
J. Mulready, sub driver	120	00
Engine Co. No. 1 payroll	1 608	75
Ladder Co. No. 1 payroll	1 388	35
C. P. Inkley, use of auto	250	00
A. Culver Co., fuel	58	75
Rockland Coal Co., fuel	75	06
Edison Light Co., electricity	179	45
Telephone Co., service	69	32
Old Colony Gas Co.	4	05
Water Dept.	13	78
W. Woodward, insurance	52	74
A. A. Phelps, insurance	3	38
Columbia Electric Co., wire	171	08
Mass. Gas & Elec. Co., wire	16	20
Gamewell Fire Alarm Co., parts	21	81
Albert Clark, labor on fire alarm	58	00
Hyle Cook, labor on fire alarm	48	00
F. Metivier, labor on fire alarm	63	00
W. Pratt, labor on fire alarm	2	00
G. W. Clark, extra labor on fire alarm	40	00
Estes Auto Supply Co., parts	2	73
Crawford Gas Station, parts	5	39
American LaFrance Co., parts	37	43

R. W. Hyde, labor and material	1 50	
J. Riordan, spark plugs	1 20	
Bailey Motor Co., battery	33 85	
Damon Electric Co., labor	2 00	
P. Ouelette, labor	10 00	
H. B. Vesper Co., gasoline	10 60	
Bailey Motor Co., gasoline	49 90	
A. J. Vargus Co., gasoline and		
·. supplies	100 30	
Tyler Oil Co., oil	41 25	
American Chemical Co., polish and		
supplies	11 05	
M. F. Ellis & Co., supplies	29 91	
Gorham Fire Equipment Co., supplies	184 40	
H. Grayson, pyrene	4 50	
C. M. Warner, Ladder	9 00	
J. C. McCallum, supplies	7 45	
Hall & Torrey, supplies	5 70	
Rome Bros., supplies	28 68	
J. S. Cheever & Co., toilet supplies	22 51	
Pioneer Stores, supplies	5 99	
Roger & Co., supplies	6 66	
J. A. Rice Co., supplies	5 40	
C. H. Batchelder, flag	6 01	
Heaney Mfg. Co., supplies	42 00	
J. & S. Express Co.,	1 40	
Henry Condon, truck Hire	7 00	
Douglas Print	3 50	
Brewer & Co., express paid	50	
C. P. Inkley, telephone and expense	93 62	
Total	————$11 078 03	
Appropriation	11 080 00	
Under appropriation	$ 1 97	

FOREST FIRE DEPARTMENT

Gorham Fire Equipment Co., supplies	$26 50	
Brewer & Co., supplies	24 92	

Payroll	698 00	
Total		$ 749 42
Appropriation	$750 00	
Transfer Reserve Fund	12 42	
Total		762 42

Under appropriation $ 13 00

NEW TIRES FOR FIRE DEPARTMENT

| Crawford's Gas Station | $ 225 76 |
| Appropriation | 275 00 |

Under appropriation $ 49 24

POLICE DEPARTMENT
EXPENDITURES FOR 1939

George J. Popp, service	$1 924 00
John H. Murphy, service	1 444 00
Robert J. Drake, service	1 424 80
Russell Hawes, service	747 62
Samuel Cannaway, service	677 18
Adolph Johnson, service	1 424 80
George J. Popp, use of auto	250 00
John H. Murphy, use of auto	10 00
Samuel Canaway, service	53 15
Maurice J. Mullen, service	267 95
Michael J. O'Brien, service	10 00
Thomas J. Fitzgerald, service	7 50
John J. Dwyer, service	2 00
Forest L. Partch, service	15 00
Thomas Mahoney, service	15 00
Charles Boudreau, service	12 00
James McKeever, service	9 00
John J. Troy, Jr., service	4 00
Bailey Motor, oil and gasoline	54 69
H. B. Vesper, police car expense	1 76
George N. Beal, police car expense	29 98
Spurr & Tedeschi, police car expense	15 21

A. J. Vargus, police car expense   26 36
Whiting Service, police car expense   15 08
Socony Service, police car expense   13 65
Wainshilbaum Bros., police car expense 13 23
Miller's Store, police car expense   9 94
A. Wainshilbaum, police car expense   19 65
A. Wainshilbaum police car
    expense (1938)   32 36
Matt's Radio, police car radio
    repairs   13 00
George Crawford, insurance police car   55 50
Amos Phelps, insurance police car   4 80
Brockton Edison Co., lights, (station)
    traffic   64 92
N. E. T. & T. Co., telephone service   84 41
George Fourlas, food for prisoners   21 45
Rockland Coal & Grain Co.,
    fuel station   87 80
Rome Brothers, supplies   16 60
Becker Co., supplies   10 85
Reed Lumber Co., supplies   4 48
Hancock Paint & Varnish Co., paint   5 55
Ralph Measures, labor   7 20
Toiva Jarvinen, labor   4 00
Rockland Disposal, removal rubbish   2 00
Rockland Water Dept., water service   16 25
Edward Meara, painting signs   2 00
Iver Johnson Co., equipment   37 53
Charles Menchin, labor   5 00
Charles Hines, killing and burial 33 dogs 39 00
Austin Print, letterheads   4 00
George J. Popp, expense stamped
    envelopes   3 00
Police service at Keith, Keith, McCain
    factory   72 00
A. Wainshilbaum, police car expense   20 63
    Total   —————$ 9 111 88
    Appropriation $8 955 00

Reserve Fund 157 50
——————$ 9 112 50
Expended 9 111 88

Under appropriation 62

BOARD OF HEALTH

Paid:—
Evelyn DeLory, services $ 866 72
Etta Murgida, services 333 28
Plymouth County Hospital, patients 1 398 80
Dr. Joseph H. Dunn, investigations
and vaccinations 93 00
Charles Hyland, burying dogs and cats 26 50
Mass. Memorial Hospital, care or
patients 94 00
Elbert Chamberlin, supplies 1 75
City of Malden, care of patient 112 00
Rome Bros., supplies 4 83
Various persons, burying dogs and cats 9 00
Hall & Torrey, supplies 67 47
Dr. F. H. Corey, services 27 00
Roland Poole, glasses 5 00
Dr. J. B. Gallagher, services 85 00
Rockland Paint and Hardware Co.
supplies 10 03
McGregor Instrument Co., supplies 9 09
Thomas McDonald, cement blocks 4 68
George Ingalls, care of dump 139 50
Rockland Coal & Grain Co., supplies 15 27
Edw. Cullinan, salary 40 78
Ever Ready Cupply Co., supplies 23 53
Rockland Standard Co., printing 14 25
P. Lanzolotta, bulldozer at dump 35 00
George W. S. Hyde, sharpen tools 4 95
Mass Gen. Hospital, care of patients 168 15
Howland & Howland, surveyong dump 41 15
John J. Gallagher, tile 2 64

A. Wainshilbaum, use of truck	6 00	
George Beverly, labor at dump	4 50	
John Hood Co., supplies	2 45	
Woodman Dental Depot, supplies	15 95	
A. Culver Co., supplies	29 40	
Dr. D. H. Burke, dental services	10 00	
Bemis Drug Co., 27 fumigations	17 55	
Dr. Joseph H. Dunn, salary	50 00	
Payroll, labor	2 050 81	
H. F. Gardner, oil	1 80	
Gerald Wheland, services	2 00	
Dr. Joseph Frame, services	100 00	
Dr. Joseph Frame, fumigations	36 00	
Dr. Joseph Frame, miscellaneous expenses	5 50	
George Bolling, services	3 00	
		$ 5 968 33
Appropriation	$6 000 00	
Expended	5 968 33	
Under appropriation	31 67	

List of Payroll, Board of Health

Thomas Bailey	$ 380 81
Louis Roche	13 53
Edward Cullinan	504 00
Joseph Sullivan	9 00
Joseph Meade	87 75
George Inglis	27 00
Felix Carreaux	9 00
Edward Corcoran	20 25
Frank Boudreau	51 75
Paul Noland	2 25
John J. Dwyer	252 50
Abe Wainshilbaum	18 00
Robert Badger	6 75
Harold Corcoran	87 19
Samuel Cannaway	9 00
James Shortall	22 50

Michael Murphy	47 25
William Smith	40 50
Frank Hibberd	11 50
Lawrence McAuliffe	9 00
John Kelly	60 75
Tovia Jarvenin	3 00
John Gillis	82 68
Royal Horton	9 00
Thomas Bailey Jr.	12 75
Angus McLeod	9 00
Fred Kuster	13 50
Edward Tobin	49 78
Loring Inglis	38 25
William Martin	4 50
George Beverly	29 25
Henry Roche	24 75
James Smith	4 50
Lawrence Haggerty	10 69
Phillip Murphy	15 19
John Sullivan	9 00
William Santry	22 50
William Morrison	4 50
Stephen McNamara	4 50
Albert Wood	15 19
James Carreaux	13 50
Frank Callahan	4 50

———————$ 2 050 81

PARK DEPARTMENT

Paid:

Rockland Hardware Co., supplies	$ 19 09
Rome Bros., supplies	6 80
A. Wainshilbaum, supplies	14 20
Patrick Mahoney, use of truck	45 50
J. S. McCallum, supplies	1 24
J. D. Mahoney, repair mower	75 95
Kenneth Kemp, sharpen mower	1 50
A. Culver Co., supplies	7 70

M. Vincent Fitzgibbons, insurance   26 20
Hall & Torrey Co., supplies   9 03
Hickey Bros., supplies   4 15
Thomas Murrell, gravel   2 00
Rockland Water Dept., services   5 00
Payroll, labor   2 579 66
    Total   ————$ 2 798 04
    Appropriation $2 800 00
    Expended   2 798 04
    Under appropriation   1 96

List of Payroll

Peter Hickey $686 26
Joseph Meade   677 26
James Mahoney   695 26
John Burke   520 88
    Total   ————$ 2 579 66

OBSERVANCE OF MEMORIAL DAY

Paid:—
Rockland Post American Legion Band.
    services $100 00
Rockland High School band, services   35 00
Old Colony Post Junior Drum Corps
    services   35 00
Harold Tilden, flowers   10 00
Warren Hamilton, 250 dinners   100 00
S. P. Bruinsma, 525 wreaths   63 00
Chas. E. Staples, 7 gross flags   52 50
Burton Finegan, setting grave stones 4 00
    Expended   ———— $ 399 50
    Appropriation $400 00
    Under appropriation   50

MOTH DEPARTMENT

Paid:
Sherwin Williams Co., Creosote $ 13 50
Jenkins & Simmons, express   1 75

Frost Insecticide Co., Creosote 14 58
Rockland Trans. Co., express 1 56
Payroll, labor 268 61
   Expended ————— $ 300 00
   Appropriation $ 300 00

List of Payroll
John White $ 40 50
John Doucette 40 50
Harold Beaupre 40 50
Alfred Metivier 120 11
Charles Heath 27 00
————— $ 268 61

PLYMOUTH COUNTY MAINTENANCE
Paid:
Treasurer of Plymouth County $4 427 35
Appropriation $4 427 35

COMPENSATION TO FIREMEN 1939
Paid:
George H. Crawford, insurance $259 65
Phillip S. Collins, insurance 25 11
   Expended ————— $ 284 76
   Appropriation $292 50
   Under appropriation 7 74

TREE WARDEN
Paid:
Horace I. Stickney, sharpen tools 3 50
Acme Rubber Co., spray hose 108 78
Frost Insecticide Co., suplies 4 33
C. & D. Hardware Co., supplies 3 60
Sherwin & Williams Co., arsenate
  of lead 96 06
Rome Bros., tools 12 28
Samuel Cabot, 50 gal. creosote 13 50
Rockland Trans. Co., express 1 50

Frank H. Albee, supplies   21 00
Payroll, labor   635 45
                                  ───────── $ 900 00
        Appropriation $900 00
        Expended   900 00

List of Payroll

John White $ 45 00
Joseph Kelliher   18 00
Alfred Metivier   383 45
John Doucette   18 00
Russell Shea   27 00
Benedict DeYoung   4 50
Leo McKeever   96 75
Edward Lynch   6 75
Charles Heath   36 00
                                  ───────── $ 635 45

TOWN OFFICERS

Harry S. Torrey, Chairman and Clerk
    Board of Selectmen, Board of Public
    Welfare, Board of Old Age
    Assistance $1 980 00
Norman S. Whiting, Member Board of
    Selectmen, Board of Public Welfare,
    Board of Old Age Assistance   300 00
John J. Bowler, Member Board of
    Selectmen, Board of Public Welfare,
    Board of Old Age Assistance   300 00
Charles J. Higgins, salary as
    Treasurer   1 350 00
James A. Donovan, salary as
    Tax Collector   1 500 00
Ralph L. Belcher, salary as
    Town Clerk   700 00
Ralph L. Belcher, salary as Registrar 300 00
Esther Rawson, salary as Registrar   300 00

Thomas Morrissey, salary as
Registrar   300 00
Annie Garrity, salary as Registrar   300 00
Leo Downey, salary as Auditor   100 00
Harold Smith, salary as Auditor   110 00
George Gallagher, salary as Auditor   100 00
Magorisk L. Walls, salary as moderator 50 00
                                          ————————$ 7 690 00
    Appropriation $7 700 00
    Expended   7 690 00
    Under appropriation   10 00

RENT OF TOWN OFFICES

Paid:
Rockland Savings Bank, rent $ 723 33
Crowley Bros., rent   20 00
John J. Bowler, rent   135 00
A. W. Perry, Inc., rent   750 00
    Total   ————————$ 1 628 33
    Appropriation $ 1 800 00
    Expended   1 628 33
    Under appropriation   171 67

ELECTION 1939

Paid:—
John J. Bowler, rent, Nov. 8 $ 100 00
John J. Bowler, rent, March election   150 00
Rockland Standard Pub. Co., printing and
    adv.   319 65
Bemis Drug Co., dinners   19 45
George Fourlas, dinners   45 90
John J. Lannin, dinners   6 50
Italian Women's Club, dinners   1 00
Chinese Restaurant, dinners   1 50
Payroll of Tellers at Election   356 00
    Expended   ————————$ 1 000 00
    Appropriation $1 000 00

TOWN NOTES AND INTEREST

Paid:

Rockland Trust Co., Interest on School Bonds	$ 3 825 00	
Rockland Trust Co., Payment on School Bonds	16 000 00	
Merchants' National Bank Interest on Relief Loan	522 00	
Merchants' National Bank Payment Union St. Notes	4 000 00	
Merchants' National Bank Interest Union St. Notes	500 00	
Merchants' National Bank Interest Fire Station	776 25	
Rockland Trust Co., Payment Plymouth County note	1 000 00	
Merchants' National Bank Payment on Relief Loan	4 800 00	
Merchants' National Bank Payment on Fire Station	2 137 40	
Merchants' National Bank Premium on Fire Station	362 60	
Albert W. Rice, Interest on Hospital Note	75 00	
Rockland Trust Co., Discount on Notes	405 21	
Director of Accounts, certifying notes	24 00	
		$34 427 46
Appropriation	$36 000 00	
Premium Fire Station Bonds	362 60	

	$36 362 60
Expended	$34 427 46
Under appropriation	$ 1 935 14

COMPENSATION INSURANCE

Paid:

Amos A. Phelps & Son., insurance	$1 928 71
Appropriation	$1 928 71

TOWN REPORT AND POLL BOOK

Paid:

Lester Rose, delivery of town reports	9 00	
Ralph Measures, delivery and car of town reports	29 00	
Earl Wallace, delivery of town reports	9 00	
A. I. Randall Inc., 2500 copies Town Report	1 137 50	
A. I. Randall Inc., balance poll book 1938	23 77	
Rockland Standard Pub. Co. 650 Poll Books	376 73	
		$ 1 585 00
Appropriation		$ 1 585 00

McKINLEY SCHOOL SEWAGE W. P. A.

Paid:

Payroll, labor	$ 6 13	
Rockland Coal & Grain, cement	42 80	
Depot Service Station, gas	3 18	
William Condon, sand, etc.	15 50	
		$ 67 61
Transfer from 1938	$94 30	
Expended	67 61	
Unexpended balance	$ 26 69	

MASSACHUSETTS INDUSTRIAL SCHOOL

Paid:

City of Boston, vocational school	$ 360 36	
City of Quincy vocational school	193 86	
Norfolk County Agri. School	68 00	
Weymouth Vocational School	1 095 74	
County of Plymouth	70 57	
		$ 1 788 53
Appropriation	$1 800 00	
Expended	1 788 53	
Under appropriation	11 47	

SNOW REMOVAL 1939

Paid:

Payroll, labor and trucks	$8 877 84	
George W. S. Hyde, repairs	43 90	
Market St., Garage storage and repairs	194 74	
Lot Phillips Co., supplies	6 50	
Rockland Welding Co., repairs	81 40	
A. Weatherbee, repairs	13 00	
William A. Condon, sand	49 50	
Rockland Motor Co., repairs	1 00	
George N. Beal, repairs	11 00	
Reed Lumber Co., supplies	2 50	
The Neil Co., parts for plow	8 00	
McCarthy Co., express	50	
Hallamore Mach. Co., labor	27 50	
Gideon Studley, storage of sand	75 00	
Central Welding Co., repairs on plows	42 00	
Inter-state Steel Co., plow blades	62 17	
Expended		$ 9 496 55
Appropriation	$9 500 00	
Under appropriation	3 45	

ASSESSORS 1939

Paid as Salary:

Joseph B. Estes	$1 440 00	
Dennis L. O'Connor	530 00	
Norman J. Beal	530 00	
Expended		$ 2 500 00
Appropriation		$ 2 500 00

MISCELLANEOUS CLERK

Paid:—

J. Emmett Sullivan, death returns	$ 6 75
C. L. Rice and Son, death returns	8 75
Murry Bros. Co., Binding Rockland Standard	7 30

A. S. Peterson, supplies	2	50
Warren B. Woodward, clerk's bond	7	50
Ralph L. Belcher, postage etc.	1	94
J. Frank Curtain, birth returns		75
Arthur W. Barron, birth returns		75
Herbert J. Hulse, birth returns	2	00
Norbert F. Lough, birth returns	1	50
Becker & Co., supplies	2	80
Douglas Print, 500 certificates	5	75
Rockland Standard, Adv. By-law	9	00
Rockland Standard, Adv. dog notices	7	50
Hall & Torrey Co., 1 waste paper basket	1	00
Ralph Stoddard, repairs	1	50
Rockland Coal & Grain, supplies	2	56
L. J. Peabody Office Co., 1 book case	31	00
Jenkins & Simmons, express	1	35
Ralph L. Belcher, expense Clerk's convention	5	50
Ralph L. Belcher, Vital Statistics	239	00
H. C. Metcalf, repair typewriter	3	00

Expended $ 349 70

Appropriation $350 00

Under appropriation   30

MISCELLANEOUS SELECTMEN

Paid:

A. I. Randall Inc., Selectmen's Ledger and Warrants	$ 32	10
U. S. Post Office, envelopes	57	68
Harry S. Torrey, expense Selectmen's meeting	4	40
Plymouth County Selectmen's Association, dues	6	00
A. S. Peterson, supplies	1	05
Harry S. Torrey, expense to Boston	2	00
Hobbs & Warren Inc., supplies	5	13
Hall & Torrey, supplies	2	08
Harriet Anderson, services at hearing	2	50

Rockland Hardware & Paint Co.,
supplies   1 75
Rockland Standard Pub. Co.,
Adv. of Hearing   3 50
Expended   ——————— $ 118 19
Appropriation $120 00
Under appropriation   1 81

MISCELLANEOUS SEALER WEIGHTS AND MEASURES

Paid:
W. & L. E. Gauley, weights and
supplies $ 94 18
Amos A. Phelps & Son, insurance   16 96
Harold J. Inkley, expense to convention 6 00
Harold J. Inkley, miscellaneous expense 7 20
Harold J. Inkley, use of auto   65 00
Expended   ——————— $ 189 34
Appropriation $190 00
Under appropriation   66

MISCELLANEOUS REGISTRARS

Paid:
The Douglas Print, index cards $ 18 50
Thomas Grown Co. Inc., binders and
files   26 45
U. S. Post Office, envelopes   16 60
Ralph L. Belcher, express   1 25
Ralp L. Belcher, Absentee Voters
expense   1 86
A. S. Peterson, supplies   79
Rockland Standard Pub. Co.,
Adv. and Printing   19 50
Esther Rawson, auto expense   50 00
Annie Garrity, auto expense   50 00
Mary E. Dolton, service   150 00
Mass. Reformatory, table and chairs   24 76
Yarman & Erbe, supplies   4 00

John O. Donovan, supplies   9 75
Expended   ———————— $ 373 46
Appropriation $650 00
Under appropriation   276 54

MISCELLANEOUS ASSESSORS

Paid:
Mary E. Dolton, service $ 780 00
L. E. Muran, loose binders   49 44
Nat. Ass'n. Assessing, dues   10 00
Brockton Trans. Co., express   35
L. E. Muran, cards and poll sheets   32 03
A. S. Peterson, supplies   2 95
H. C. Metcalf, repairs on machines   3 75
George A. Barnstead Son Co., tax cards   1 00
Sergeant of Arms, Legislative reports   2 00
Damon Electric, repairs   1 00
Alton F. Lyon, transfer cards
and service   105 00
Alton F. Lyon, deeds and abstracts   25 00
Edison Electric Co., lamps   2 05
Amos A. Phelps, insurance   10 00
A. I. Randall Inc., printing and cards 28 45
N. E. Tel. & Tel. Co., service   66 41
U. S. Post Office, envelopes   30 00
Banker & Tradesman, subscription   10 00
Dennis L. O'Connor, auto expense   60 90
Hobbs & Warren, binders   30 52
Douglas Print, letter heads and blanks 21 00
Speed Key Mfg. Co., Rubber typewriter
keys   4 00
Joseph B. Estes, school of instruction   6 00
Davol Printing House, printing   11 25
Joseph B. Estes, auto expense   115 70
Norman J. Beal, auto expense   76 50
Austin Print, filing cards   9 13
Hall & Torrey, supplies   6 47
Dennis L. O'Connor, school of
instruction   12 00

Rome Bros., supplies   90
Warren B .Woodward, insurance   9 04
Appelate Tax Board, reports   3 00
Norman J. Beal, school of instruction 12 00
Joseph B. Estes, postage   2 86
James F. O'Connor, insurance   8 94
    Expended   ————————$ 1 549 64
    Appropriation $1 550 00
    Under appropriation   36

MISCELLANEOUS TREASURER

Paid:
The Todd Co., checks and supplies $116 36
A. S. Peterson, supplies   1 85
U. S. Post Office, envelopes   103 52
L. E. Muran Co., files   6 30
Annette White, services   200 00
Hobbs & Warren Co., supplies   14 15
Ward Stationer, supplies   3 50
Chas. J. Higgins, expenses to Boston   10 57
Amos A. Phelps & Son., bond   206 50
Amos A. Phelps & Son, insurance   25 42
H. C. Metcalf, repairs   3 00
Becker & Co., supplies   4 36
Rome Bros., supplies   30
John Renagh, ½ cost adding machine   42 50
John O. Donovan, file   17 95
A. E. Martell Co., cash book   12 87
Chas. J. Higgins, postage and mailing   30 36
    Expended   ———————— $ 799 51
    Appropriation $800 00
    Under appropriation   49

MISCELLANEOUS TAX COLLECTOR

Paid:
Douglas Print, tax bills   23 00
Amos A. Phelps & Son, bond   403 00
Amos A. Phelps, burglar insurance   25 42

Ralph L. Belcher, service	200 00	
Commercial Supply Co., forms	17 28	
U. S. Post Office, envelopes	305 60	
Austin Print, tax bills	29 25	
Warren B. Woodward, deputy bond	10 00	
Annette P. Write, service	3 00	
Becker & Co., transfer files	14 75	
Hobbs & Warren Inc., supplies	40 05	
Rockland Standard Pub. Co.		
Adv. Tax Sale	52 00	
Francis J. Geogan, Service tax sale	173 00	
A. I. Randall Inc., tax bills	43 30	
A. S. Peterson, supplies	1 00	
Edison Electric Co., lamps	90	
John H. Renagha, ½ cost adding machine	42 50	
James A. Donovan, expenses to Boston	12 00	
Wh. H. Sperry, supplies	2 00	
James A. Donovan, postage and wire	43 68	
Expended		$ 1 441 73
Appropriation	$1 450 00	
Under appropriation	8 27	

MISCELLANEOUS UNCLASSIFIED

Paid:

Francis J. Geogan, legal advise 1938	$130 00	
Rockland Standard, Adv.		
Thompson property	13 50	
Rockland Standard Adv. lost man	7 85	
County of Plymouth, layout West Water Street	3 00	
A. I. Randall Inc., Printing warrants	27 50	
L. E. Muran Co., files	6 90	
N. Y., N. H. & H. R. R. freight	55	
Town Finance Com. dues	10 00	
John H. Renaghen, rep. adding machine	4 95	
Damon Electric, repairs	1 00	

A. S. Peterson, supplies	2	10
Paul Eisenhardt, supplies	2	00
Franklin & Perkins, paper towels and supplies	18	00
Brockton Trans. Co., express		35
Becker & Co., supplies	5	50
Hobbs & Warren Inc., supplies	6	05
Payroll, guarding fire boxes	11	00
Dion Hafford, supplies	1	00
Henry A. Whiting, extra keys	3	60
Howard Clock Pro. Inc., repair town clock	80	00
Reed Street Lunch, elections dinner	4	50
Becker & Co., supplies	3	25
Donald Loud, labor on floors	3	50
Alton F. Lyon, settlement Chas, Rose accident	461	30
Raymond Rainsford, extra work	2	00
Rockland Standard Pub. Co., Jury lists	12	75
Bristol County House of Correction 1 mat	5	55
Herman Rome, 18 used chairs	28	00
Reformatory for Women, 1 flag	3	54
H. C. Metcalf, repair machine		75
Norman S. Whiting, services Town report	106	00
Charles Hines, janitor services	140	00
Roland Poole, care of town clock	53	25
Hall & Torrey Co., supplies	7	59
Douglas Print, printing	11	00
Edison Electric Co., lamps	4	80
John J. Dwyer, putting out flags	52	50
Rockland Standard Co., Advertising	1	25
Rome Bros., supplies	4	65
Harry W. McKinnon, supplies	3	75
Harry S. Torrey, purchase Miscellaneous supplies	2	54

Harry L. Rome, 12 yds, rubber
matting   5 88
Charles Hines, killing 12 dogs   24 00
Rockland Hardware Co., supplies   35 16
Edison Electric Co., lamp town clock   4 60
Hobbs & Warren Inc., license blanks   2 60
Dr. Joseph H. Dunn, expense in law
cases   13 00
Hall & Torrey Co., supplies   10 60
Edward C. Holmes, record easements   6 10
Comm. of Public Safety, license books   2 10
Emma W. Gleason, storage of flags   24 00
Raymond Rainsford, janitor service 276 00
Edison Electric Co., service   177 83
New Eng. Tel. & Tel. Co., service   124 63
Total   ———————$ 1 953 82
Appropriation $1 100 00
Reserve fund   861 30
                                   ———————$ 1 961 30
Expended   1 953 82
Under appropriation   7 48

BEACONS 1939

Paid:
Damon Electric Co., care of Stop and
go lights $125 00
Edison Electric Ill. Co., service   143 50
Traffic Equipment, care of beacons 559 33
Abe Wainshilbaum, moving beacon   5 00
Expended   ——————— $ 832 83
Appropriation $900 00
Under approriation   67 17

VISITING NURSE

Paid:
Mrs. Harry W. Burrill, Treasurer $ 1 500 00
Appropriation $ 1 500 00

GUIDE BOARDS AND SIGNS

Paid:

Ralph L. Measures, labor	47 55	
Rome Bros., paint	2 40	
Chas. A. Vaughn, clamps	1 00	
Expended		$50 95
Appropration	$100 00	
Under appropriation	49 05	

W. P. A. STREETS

Paid:

Alice Hannigan, gravel	$ 12 50	
Rockland Coal & Grain, supplies	4 93	
The Edson Corp., hose and coupling	24 25	
Expended		$41 68.
Transfer from 1938	$1 148 49	
Unexpended balance	$1 106 81	
Transferred to W. P. A.		

W. P. A. EXPENDITURES

Paid:

M. Warren Wright, services	$1 196 00
Fred M. Ryan, services	1 248 00
Rome Bros., supplies recreation project	9 16
Rockland Pharmacy, medical supplies	10 37
John J. Bowler, use of car commod.	66 00
John J. Dwyer, use of truck commod.	71 00
Roderick MacKenzie, ice nursery project	15 80
James G. Lamb, provisions nursery project	159 62
Charles Weatherbee, milk nursery project	55 57
Peter's Grocery, supplies, sewing	8 00
A. S. Peterson, office supplies	14 61
Fred M. Ryan, gas for car	18 75
John J. Bowler, rent of offices	120 00

Norman Crosby, transportation etc.	19	50
Sport Shop, supplies, recreation		
project	38	28
Franklin Perkins, bags, commodity	18	00
New Eng. Tel & Tel., services	136	07
Crowley Bros., rent	20	00
John Cheever, drinking cups	33	50
Singer Sewing Machine Co., repairs	7	20
Lois Williams, expense convention	5	00
H. C. Metcalf, supplies	3	75
Stall & Dean, supplies recreational		
project	20	75
N. Y., N. H. & H. R. R., crossing tracks		
Sewage project	197	96
William H. Sperry, supplies	1	50
M. Warren Wright, expenses to Boston	8	00
Rockland Standard, printing	9	35
Helen Purcell, expense convention		
sewing	5	00
John J. Dwyer, trans. machines	2	00
Gerald Wheland, expense to Boston	2	40
Fred M. Ryan, expense to Boston	12	00
Horace Partridge, supplies		
recreational	13	19
Ruth Shea, expense convention		
Nursery	5	00
Cora Johnson, expense convention		
Nursery	5	00
Dorothy Arkell, expense convention		
Nursery	5	00
Brockton Edison Co., lamps	4	35
John S. Triggs, warehouse expense		
Brockton	4	00
Yawman & Erbe Co., 2000 folders	14	00
Douglas Print, 500 letterheads	4	00
J. A. Rice Co., patterns, sewing		
project	1	35
Expended	$ 3 589	03

Appropriation 1939	$1 200 00	
Transfer 1938	1 211 47	
Transfer Vital Statistics	30 00	
Transfer Engineering project	45 00	
Transfer W. P. A. Sidewalks		
special meeting	3 000 00	
Transfer W. P. A. Streets	1 106 81	
Total Amount Available	————$ 6 593 28	
Unexpended Balance	3 004 25	

PAYSON AVENUE SIDEWALK W. P. A.

Paid:

Payroll, trucks	$ 59 07	
Quincy Oil Co., supplies	5 43	
Expended		$64 50
Transfer 1938 Article	$65 37	
Unexpended balance	87	

GEORGE STREET SIDEWALK, W. P. A.

Paid:

Payroll, trucks	$41 57	
Thomas Murrill, sand	3 50	
Mary E. Farrar, stone	4 25	
Expended		$49 32
Transfer 1938 Artcile	$50 88	
Unexpended balance	1 56	

ASSESSORS MAP W. P. A.

Paid:

H. J. Dowd Co. Inc., supplies	$15 20	
James FitzGerald, auto mileage	6 00	
Spaulding Moss Co., supplies	116 92	
Payroll, labor	280 50	
Expended		$ 418 62
Transfer 1938	$623 81	
Unexpended balance	$205 19	

UNION STREET SIDEWALK, W. P. A.

Paid:

Payroll, trucks	$ 61 26	
Rockland Coal & Grain, lumber	11 69	
Hall & Torrey, supplies	49 00	
Bradford Weston Inc., bit. concrete	328 05	
Expended		$ 450 00
Transfer General Sidewalks Article 22		$450 00

HOWARD STREET SIDEWALK W. P. A.

Paid:

Payroll, trucks	$ 70 88	
Bradford Weston Inc., bit. concrete	112 95	
William Condon, gravel	12 25	
Rockland Coal & Grain Co., supplies	10 40	
A. Culver Co., cement	17 50	
Michael Bowen, hay	3 00	
Expended		$ 226 98
Transfer 1938		$ 226 98

EMERSON STREET SIDEWALK W. P. A.

Paid:

Payroll, trucks	$ 62 13	
Depot Service Station, gas	3 47	
Bradford Weston Inc., bit. concrete	143 07	
Thomas Murrill, sand	4 00	
William Condon, gravel	7 50	
Chris Tompkins, gravel	2 00	
Thomas Mahoney, use of mixer	24 75	
Rockland Coal & Grain Co., supplies	24 54	
A. Culver Co., cement	74 65	
Expended		$ 346 11
Transfer 1938	$474 35	
Unexpended balance	128 24	

PLAIN STREET SIDEWALK 1939

Paid:

Bradford Weston Inc., Bit. Concrete	$142 02
William Condon, sand and gravel	35 64

Payroll, trucks	138 26	
Rockland Coal & Grain Co.,		
Cement and supplies	39 36	
A. Culver Co., cement	29 32	
Arthur Casey, use of mixer	19 00	
Expended	————	$ 403 60
Transfer 1938		$ 403 60

DIVISION STREET SIDEWALK
(W. P. A. Labor)

Paid:

Bradford Weston Inc., Bit. Concrete	$133 62	
Trimount Bit. Concrete Co., Bit		
Concrete	90 76	
Expended	————	$ 224 38
Transfer 1938	$237 99	
Unexpended balance	13 61	

LIBERTY STREET SIDEWALK
(W. P. A. Labor)

Paid:

Bradford Weston Inc., Bit. Concrete	$234 58	
Expended	————	$ 234 58
Transfer 1938		$ 234 58

ENGINEERING PROJECT W. P. A.
Under Chapter 58

Paid:

Alden W. Blanchard, use of car	$ 18 39
Rome Bros., supplies	55
Spaulding Moss Co., supplies	74 07
Payroll, labor	46 69
Buff & Buff Mfg. Co., use of	
equipment	76 00
Transfer W. P. A., rent	45 00
A. S. Peterson, supplies	2 27
Ralph E. Snell, 2 special tripods	60 50
Haywood & Haywood, blue prints	1 16

James P. FitzGerald, labor 4 50
  Expended   ————— $ 329 13
  Transfer 1938 $510 55
  Unexpended balance $181 42

EAST WATER STREET LAND DAMAGE

Paid:
Almerta Goodfellow, damage   9 75
Fred L. Ferron, damage   13 50
Ernest W. Parquette, damage   12 50
Albert Culver Co. damage   16 50
  Expended   ————— $52 25
  Transfer 1938 $118 05
  Unexpended balance   65 80

REED POND IMPROVEMENT

Paid:
Payroll, labor $463 65
A. Culver Co., supplies   50 00
Hall & Torrey Co., Inc., supplies   57 39
Fred S. Delay, supplies   3 31
Rockland Coal & Grain Co., supplies   83 13
Henry A. Whiting, padlocks   3 45
George W. S. Hyde, repairs   1 25
McManus Box Co., slabs   23 25
Rockland Hardware & Paint Co.
  supplies   79
Brockton Edison Co., service   12 76
C. A. Paulding, gas   2 00
Patrick Mahoney, labor   12 25
Rockland Water Dept. repairs   3 11
Rome Bros., supplies   3 63
Charles S. Beal, cedar   15 00
  Expended   ————— $ 734 97
  Transfer 1938 $ 1 197 79
  Unexpended balance   462 82

LAND COURT TAX TITLES AND
PROPERTY OF LOW VALUE

Paid:

Francis J. Geogan, services and foreclosures	$161 25	
Dennis L. O'Connor, insurance	33 30	
Rockland Coal & Grain Co., supplies z	9 59	
Joseph B. Estes, postage paid	3 99	
Edward S. Burbank, auction (2) properties	10 00	
James F. Shanahan, auction (2) properties	10 00	
Rockland Water Dept. service and supplies	33 25	
Land Court, tax titles	170 00	
Payroll, labor	60 91	
Expended		$ 492 29
Appropriation	$500 00	
Under appropriation	7 71	

FIRE STATION HOUSING

Paid:

Bailey Motor Sales Inc., rent	$ 355 00
Hub Building Wrecking Co., Demolition of station	160 00
Standard Oil Co., rent, of land	1 00
Joseph Reardon, oil	26 80
National Foundry Inc., casting	16 00
Amos A. Phelps & Son, insurance	52 70
J. A. Rice Co., Inc., blankets and supplies	63 68
Harry L. Rome, 4 mattresses	78 00
George W. N. Clark, labor on moving	15 00
Estes Auto Supply, battery charger	39 50
Jenkins & Simmons, moving	17 00
Morris Gordon & Sons. Inc., cutlery	4 30
Morris Gordon & Sons Inc., dishes and supplies	81 00

Expended		$ 910 01
Transfer 1938	$987 11	
Unexpended balance	77 10	

ERECTION OF FIRE STATION

Paid:

Norman J. Beal, clerk of works	$1 300 00	
N. E. Inspection Bureau, tests	33 75	
Carilli Construction Co., payments	51 917 69	
J. William Beal & Son., services	2 009 64	
Carilli Cons. Co., toll calls	23 10	
J. William Beal & Son, travel expense	16 35	
Charles L. Callanan, Adv. Boston Globe	37 60	
Banker & Tradesman, Adv.	13 25	
Norman J. Beal, toll calls	8 50	
Amos A. Phelps & Son, insurance	92 86	
Harry L. Rome, 22 Shades	39 50	
Rockland Standard Pub. Co., Adv.	10 00	
O. P. Killan & Son, furniture	432 72	
Contract Sales Co., refrigerator, etc.	285 90	
Francis J. Geogan, legal service	20 00	
Director of Accounts, certifying notes	2 00	
McCarthy Bros., furniture	171 56	
J. W. Beal & Son, blue prints and specifications	175 43	
Expended		$56 589 85
Transfer 1938	$30 869 78	
Received from Federal Gov. 1939	21 000 00	
Due from Federal Gov.	5 535 93	

PARK DEPARTMENT W. P. A.

Paid:

Payroll, removing stumps	$ 78 00	
Payroll, trucks and derrick	183 95	
Expended		$ 261 95
Transfer 1938	$862 40	
Unexpended balance	$600 45	

REPAIRS AT INFIRMARY

Paid:

Chester S. Clark, painting	$55 00	
C. & D. Hardware Co., supplies	30 86	
Rome Bros., supplies	4 90	
Expended		$90 76
Unexpended balance 1938	$96 28	
Unexpended balance	5 52	

SEWING PROJECT W. P. A.

Paid:

Treasurer of United States, payment on material		$2 380 00
Transfer 1938	$360 00	
Appropriation 1939	2 400 00	
Total		$ 2 760 00
Unexpended balance		$ 380 00

FEDERAL COMMODITY DISTRIBUTION

Paid:

Treasurer of United States	$515 87
Appropriation	$515 87

VITAL STATISTICS PROJECT W. P. A.

Paid:

H. C. Metcalf, sales, repairs and rent typewriters	35 75	
Transfer, 3 months rent to W. P. A.	30 00	
Leo E. Downey, transportation	3 50	
Murry Bros Co., binding and index	16 00	
Ralph E. McVein, expense to convention	5 00	
Rockland Standard Pub. Co., printing	1 00	
Yawman & Erbe Mfg. Co., supplies	123 50	
Expended		$ 214 75
Appropriation	$875 00	
Unexpended balance	660 25	

W. P. A. GENERAL SIDEWALKS

GENERAL EXPENSE

Paid:

Rome Bros., supplies	$182	58
Hall & Torrey, Inc. supplies	123	74
Rockland Hardware & Paint Co., supplies	55	13
A. M. Eaton Paper Co., paper cups	3	00
E. M. Fisher, repairs	1	25
William Condon, gravel	92	00
A. L. Postman, drinking cups	16	50
Rockland Coal & Grain Co., supplies	1	00
Hedge & Matthews, repairs	1	35
Rockland Water Dept., use of compressor	9	00
C. W. Briggs, repairs	11	15
C. & D. Hardware Co., supplies	3	65
Rockland Pharmacy, supplies	15	09
John S. Cheever Co., drinking cups	33	10
Fred S. Delay, supplies	10	32
H. H. Arnold Co., steel bars	16	30
George N. Beal, repairs	18	87
Earl Wallace, repairs	1	50
M. F. Ellis Co., supplies	7	05
N. E. Tel. & Tel. Co., service	14	18
Earle & Blake, repairs	7	50
Douglas Print, printing	3	50
Elliott Magoun, repairs		75
Miller Garage, repairs	15	85
Fred M. Ryan, use of auto	112	75
Total General Expense	$ 757	11

SUMMARY OF EXPENSE ON SIDEWALKS

Webster St., from Union	$1 419	03
Myrtle Street	61	85
Grove Street	340	39

Pacific Street	742	92
Belmont Street	147	32
Liberty Square	400	83
Emerson Street	80	01
Summit Street	594	47
Union Street from Summit	515	54
Arlington Street	241	28
Central Street	15	75
Concord Street	1 062	21
Webster St., E. Water to Hanover line	185	71
Stanton Street	329	19
Franklin Avenue	108	65
Beal Street	666	05
Hingham Street	188	84
Crescent Street	185	04
Dexter Road	220	53
Howard Street	411	13
Linden Street	325	27
Monroe and Maple Streets	690	74
Plain Street	1 243	08
Church Street	468	25
Union St., from Bigelow Ave.	406	66
Everett Street	273	10
Liberty Street	353	89
Green Street	480	17
Reed Street	429	56
East Water Street	790	50
West Water Street	156	67
Albion Street	386	40
Hartsuff Street	230	55
Exchange Street	993	68
Custer Street	571	55
Union from Salem Street	591	39
Total	———$16 308	20

Balance of Article 13, Voted Aug. 8, 1938 $26 555 44
    Deductions Voted March 1939
        Union Street $450 00

Myrtle Street	500 00	
Reed Street	600 00	
Prospect Street	700 00	
Junior & Senior High school drive	885 00	
Market Street	1 779 99	
Total Deduction	——————$	4 914 99
Transfer Dec. 29, 1939 meeting		3 000 00

		$ 7 914 99
Amount Available		$26 555 44
Transfer		7 914 99
Expended		17 065 31
Unexpended balance		$ 1 575 14

Concord Street Drain voted but not approved by W. P. A.

MARKET STREET SIDEWALK
Under General Sidewalks

Paid:

Payroll, trucks	$ 995 43	
C. A. Paulding, gas and oil	36 74	
Edward Casey, use of mixer	195 00	
Arthur Casey, use of mixer	195 00	
Fred M. Ryan, use of car	2 50	
William Condon, 2756 cubic yds gravel	342 32	
Lucius Burgess, labor	12 00	
Expended	——————$	1 778 99
Transfer from General Sidewalks	1 779 99	
Unexpended balance	1 00	

CLEANING CATCH BASINS AND DRAINS
Paid:

Payroll, labor	$ 498 00	
Appropriation		$500 00
Under appropriation		2 00

LIST OF PAYROLL
Paid:

Augustine Yourell	$ 9 00

Wm Cannaway	27 00	
Warren Hamilton	22 50	
Albert Norman	9 00	
Joseph Costello	27 00	
Michael Murphy	27 00	
Edward Tobin	27 00	
Joseph Daley	27 00	
Jerry DelPrete	27 00	
Arthur Smith	27 00	
Arthur Deacon	27 00	
Louis Roche	27 00	
Frank O'Hara	24 75	
Joseph Shoughrow	27 00	
Raymond LaCombe	9 00	
John Ricca	27 00	
George Tyler	24 00	
Dominic DelPrete	15 00	
John J. Dwyer	13 50	
John McQuaide	15 75	
Burton Norman	18 00	
Wilbur Adams	9 00	
Peter Hickey	13 50	
Thomas DeSimone	18 00	
Total	———————	$ 498 00

LIBERTY STREET W. P. A.

Paid:

Trimount Bit. Products Co., asphalt	$ 287 18
Transfer 1938	287 18

PURCHASE POLICE CAR

Paid:

George N. Beal, purchase of car	$400 00
Appropriation	$400 00

DEXTER ROAD

Paid:

Payroll, labor	$ 89 34

Roderick Mackenzie, gravel   8 00
  Expended   ———— $97 34
  Appropriation $100 00
  Under appropriation   2 66

LIST OF PAYROLL
Paid:
Lawrence Cull $ 13 50
William Cannaway   9 84
Arthur Smith   4 50
Joseph Costello   4 50
Arthur Deacon   4 50
Joseph Daley   4 50
Arthur Casey   24 00
William Condon   24 00
  Total   ———— $89 34

CONCORD STREET SIDEWALK W. P. A.
Paid:
Bradford Weston Inc., Bit. Concrete $26 86
Transfer 1938 $26 86

RESERVE FUND 1939
Transfer to:
Police Dept. car insurance $ 55 50
Highway Repairs   250 00
Military Aid   210 00
Unclassified Miscellaneous   461 30
Highway Dept. W. Water St.
  bridges   1 500 00
Police Dept., special strike
  duty   77 00
Police Dept. Traffic paint   25 00
Unclassified Miscellaneous
  moving expense   400 00
Forest Fires   12 42
Public Welfare   1 008 78
  Transfer $ 4 000 00
  Appropriation $ 4 000 00

REEDS POND ARTICLE No. 64

Paid:

Payroll, labor	$291 25	
Forest L. Partch, electric repairs	7 75	
Thomas T. Harvey, boat and oars	37 50	
Brockton Edison Co., Service	2 00	
Chas. E. Meara, lettering boat	2 50	
Rome Bros., supplies	7 98	
Expended		$ 348 98
Appropriation	$350 00	
Under appropriation	1 02	

HIGHLAND STREET SIDEWALK W. P. A.

Paid:

Payroll, truck	$ 21 00
Transfer 1937-1938	$ 23 91
Unexpended balance	$ 2 91

MYRTLE STREET SIDEWALK W. P. A.

Paid:

Payroll, trucks	$ 113 32	
Rockland Coal & Grain Co.,		
Cement and supplies	103 72	
Whiting's Service Station, gas	1 48	
P. Hart, gas	2 82	
Bradford Weston Inc., Bit. Concrete	258 03	
Expended		$ 479 37
Transfer Gen. Sidewalks	$500 00	
Unexpended balance	20 63	

REED STREET SIDEWALK W. P. A.

Paid:

Payroll, trucks	$155 75
Arthur Casey, use of mixer	15 50
Thomas Mahoney, use of mixer	6 00
Clyde Dunham, use of mixer	1 50
Rockland Coal & Grain Co.,	
Cement and supplies	89 98

William Condon, Sand and gravel   23 25
Quincy Oil Co., gas and oil   8 18
Bradford Weston Inc., Bit. Concrete   279 30
   Expended   ———— $ 579 46
Transfer Gen. Sidewalks $600 00
Unexpended Balance   20 54

SCHOOL STREET SIDEWALK W. P. A.

Paid:
Payroll, trucks $ 7 00
Bradford Weston Inc., Bit. Concrete   15 69
J. L. Milberry, stone   6 50
   Expended   ———— $29 19
Transfer 1938 $29 96
Unexpended balance   77

MYRTLE STREET SIDEWALK

Paid:
Guy Baker, stone $ 6 75
Payroll, trucks   42 00
   Expended   ———— $48 75
Transfer Article No. 25 1938 $69 45
Unexpended balance   20 70

PROSPECT STREET SIDEWALK W. P. A.

Paid:
Payroll, trucks $ 140 01
Rockland Coal and Grain Co., lumber   8 17
A. Culver Co., cement   94 50
Depot Service Station, gas   1 00
William Condon, gravel   7 00
Edward Casey, use of mixer   35 00
Bradford Weston Inc., Bit. concrete   443 79
   Expended   ———— $ 729 47
Transfer 1938 $ 38 96
From Gen. Sidewalks   700 00
   Total   ————   738 96
Unexpended balance   9 49

OBSERVANCE OF ARMISTICE DAY

Paid:

Fred L. Martin, postage	$ 5	00
Rockland Women's Club 1 prize	25	00
Knight of Pythias, 2nd prize	15	00
Vets of Foreign Wars, 3 rd prize	10	00
Rockland Red Cross, prize	5	00
Abington Legion Post, prize	15	00
Rockland Boy Scouts, prize	5	00
Rockland High School, prize	15	00
Rockland Girl Scouts, prize	5	00
Francis Harrington, prize	10	00
Anne Lincoln, prize	5	00
Helen Holmes, prize	2	50
Whitman Legion Band, services	50	00
Whitman High School Band, services	10	00
Abington High School Band, services	10	00
Rockland High School Band, services	10	00
Charles Metivier, janitor	7	00
Andrew Leck, janitor	7	00
Maurice Mullen, police	5	00
Joseph Magsamen, speaker	10	00
John J. Dwyer, bus and car	16	00
Gately Dec. Co., decorating office	5	00
Lannin Lunch, 56 dinners, Co. K	28	00
Hotel Thomas, 30 Dinners Marines	15	00
Rockland Standard Pub. Co., printing	5	00
Mildred Martin, 862 lunches	90	00
Helen Kane, expenses	14	50
Expended	$ 400	00
Appropriation	$ 400	00

JUNIOR-SENIOR HIGH SCHOOL DRIVE

Paid:

Payroll, trucks	$ 70	00
Rockland Coal & Grain Co., lumber	14	32
A. Culver Co., cement	94	50
Clyde Dunham, use of mixer	3	00

William Condon, gravel 5 75
Bradford Weston Inc., Bit. Concrete 630 00
A. Wainshilbaum, gas and crane 7 56
    Expended ——————— $ 825 13
Transfer from Gen. Sidewalks $885 00
Unexpended balance 59 87

BLOSSOM STREET SIDEWALK W. P. A.
Paid:
Payroll, trucks $ 21 00
Transfer Article 61, 1937-1938 $27 39
Unexpended balance 6 39

GLENN STREET SIDEWALK, W. P. A.
Paid:
William Condon, sand and gavel $ 89 00
Transfer Article 83, 1938 $89 26
Unexpended balance 26

EAST WATER STREET SIDEWALK W. P. A.
Paid:
Payroll, truck 24 50
Bradford Weston Inc. Bit. concrete 21 10
    Expended ——————— $45 60
Transfer Article 81, 1938 $48 57
Unexpended balance 2 97

EMERSON STREET BRIDGE
Paid:
Burrell & DeLory, supplies $8 85
    Expended $ 8 85
Appropriation Article 54, 1939 50 00
Under Appropriation 41 15

SUMMIT STREET SIDEWALK W. P. A.
Paid:
Chris Tompkins, gravel $ 4 50
George J. J. Clark, stone 2 25

Agnes Kelliher, gravel	4 50	
Patrick Mahoney, stone	75	
Gilbert West, stone	1 50	
Expended		$13 50
Transfer from 1937	$14 39	
Unexpended balance	89	

WILLIAM STREET SIDEWALK W. P. A.
Paid:

Queen Ann Nurseries, sand	$ 5 00	
Alice Hennigan, gravel	17 25	
Expended		$22 25
Transfer Article No. 88 1938	$22 94	
Unexpended balance	69	

WESTER STREET CATCH BASIN
Paid:

Payroll, truck	$ 7 00	
E. L. LeBaron Foundry, frame and grate	13 20	
William Condon, gravel	4 75	
Expended		$24 95
Appropriation	$25 00	
Under appropriation	05	

RECAPITULATION OF AMOUNTS AVAILABLE AND EXPENDITURES

(*) Denotes Unexpended Balances Dec. 31, but Available in 1940

	Previous Year	Raised March 1939	Expended	Under
School Department		$105 200 00	$105 199 39	61
State Aid		600 00	460 00	140 00
...e of ...wn		60 00	60 00	
Military Aid (Trans. Reserve Fund $210.00)			210 00	
...e of Soldiers Graves		150 00	145 00	5 00
...an Up Week		75 00	56 50	18 50
Criminal ...es in ...rt		100 00	54 80	45 20
...eet Lighting (App. $8,898.00 Forest St. $15, High School $37.00)		8 950 00	8 894 03	55 97
Highway Surveyor		1 350 00	1 350 00	1 04
Tarvia and Road Binder		3 000 00	2 998 96	1 00
...y Repairs ($1800 App. Reserve Fund $250 00)		2 050 00	2 049 00	01
Soldiers ...al Library (App. $4400. Dog Fund $415.50)		4 815 50	4 815 49	5 11
Sidewalks		500 00	494 89	
Rent, Quarters ...an Legion		900 00	900 00	
Rent, Spanish War ...ts		288 00	288 00	
Cleaning Union Street		1 200 00	1 197 00	3 00
Fire Department		11 080 00	11 078 03	1 97
Forest Fires (App. $75 0 Reserve Fund $12.42)		762 42	749 42	13 00
Police Dept. (App. $8,955. Reserve $157.50)		9 112 50	9 111 88	62
Inspection of ...ls and Stables		150 00	150 00	
Sealer of Weights ...ard Measures		400 00	400 00	
Board of Health		6 000 00	5 968 33	31 67
Park Department		2 800 00	2 798 04	1 96
Observance of ...orial Day		400 00	399 50	50

RECAPITULATION OF AMOUNTS AVAILABLE AND EXPENDITURES

(*) Denotes Unexpended Balances Dec. 31, but available in 1940

	Available Previous Year	Raised March 1939	Expended	Amount Under
Health Department		300 00	300 00	
Plymouth uty Maintenance		4 427 35	4 427 35	
Compensation to Firemen		292 50	284 76	7 74
Tree Warden		900 00	900 00	
Town Officers		7 700 00	7 690 00	10 00
Rent of Town Offices		1 800 0	1 628 33	171 67
Elections		1 000 00	1 000 00	
Town Notes and Interest (App. $36,000 Prem. in bond $362.6)0		36 362 60	34 427 46	1 935 14
Town Report and Poll Book		1 585 00	1 585 00	
Compensation Insurance		1 928 71	1 928 71	
McKinley School Sewage W. P. A.	94 30		67 61	*26 69
Massachusetts Industrial School		1 800 00	1 788 53	11 47
Snow Removal		9 500 00	9 496 55	3 45
Assessors		2 500 00	2 500 0	
Miscellaneous Clerk		350 0	349 70	30
Miscellaneous Selectmen		120 00	118 19	1 81
Miscellaneous Sealer		190 00	189 34	66
Miscellaneous Registrars		650 00	373 46	276 54
Miscellaneous Assessors		1 550 00	1 549 64	36
Miscellaneous Treasurer		800 00	799 51	49
Miscellaneous Collector		1 450 00	1 441 73	8 27
Miscellaneous Unclassified (App. $1100 Reserve $861.30)		1 961 30	1 953 82	7 48
Beacons		900 00	832 83	67 17

RECAPITULATION OF AMOUNTS AVAILABLE AND EXPENDITURES

(*) De ntes Unexpended Bal nes Dec. 31, but Av lable in 1940

	Available Previous Year	Raised March 1939	Expended	nt Under
Visiting Nurse		1 500 00	1 500 00	49 05
He Boards and Signs		100 00	50 95	
W. P. A. Streets (Trans. $1106.81 to W. P. A.)	1 148 49		41 68	
W. P. A.		1 200 00		
ms. from 1938	1 211 47			
Trans from W. P. A. Streets	1 106 81			
ms. fom Rent Acc.	75 00			
ns. fom W. P. A. Sidewalks	3 000 00		3 69 03	*3 004 25
W. P. A. Sidewalks	18 640 45		17 065 31	*1 575 14
Less mt. voted at March ming 4914.99				
Less mt. ted at Dec. meeting $3000. 0				
Reed's Pond Improvement	1 197 79		734 97	*462 82
Payson Avenue Sidewalk	65 37		64 50	87
George Set Sidewalk	50 88		49 32	1 56
ors Map	623 81		418 62	*205 19
n St. Sidewalk (ns. Gen. Sidewalks)		450 0	450 0	
Howard Street Sidewalk	226 98		226 98	
Emerson Street Sidewalk	474 35		346 11	*128 24
Plain Street Salk	403 60		43 60	
Division Street Salk	237 99		224 38	*13 61
Liberty Street Sidewalk	234 58		234 58	
Engineering Project W. P. A.	510 55		329 13	*181 42
East Water St, Land Damage	118 05		52 25	*65 80
d Court, Tax Titles te.		500 00	492 29	7 71

RECAPITULATION OF AMOUNTS AVAILABLE AND EXPENDITURES

(*) Denotes Unexpended Balances Dec. 31, but Available in 1940

	Available Previous Year	Raised March 1939	Expended	Amount Under
Fire Station Housing	987 11		910 01	*77 10
Erection of Fire Station	30 869 78	56	589 85	4 720 07D
Reimbursed from Fed. Gov't 1939 (Due $5535.93)	21 000 00			
Park Department W. P. A.	862 40		261 95	*600 45
West Water Street Construction	1 808 11		3 612 49	
Received State aid utility	1 04 38			
Repairs at Ferry	96 28		90 76	5 52
Sewing Project W. P. A.	360 00	2 400 00	2 380 00	*380 0
Federal City Distribution		515 87	515 87	
Vital Statistics Project W. P. A.		875 00	214 75	*660 25
Market Street War Set		6 000 00		*6 000 00
Gig Catch Basins and Drains		1 779 99	1 778 99	1 00
Liberty Street W. P. A.	287 18	500 00	48 00	2 00
Purchase of Police Car		400 00	287 18	
Dexter Road		100 00	97 34	2 66
Concord Street Sidewalk	26 86		26 86	
Reed's Pond No. 640	23 91	350 00	348 98	1 02
Highland St. Sidewalk			21 00	2 91
Myrtle St. Sidewalk, (trans. Gen. Sidewalks)		500 00	479 37	*20 63
Reed St. Sidewalk, (trans. Gen. Sidewalks)		600 00	579 46	*20 54
School Street Sidewalk	29 96		29 19	77
Myrtle Street Sidewalk	69 45		48 75	*20 70
Dext St. Sidewalk, (trans Gen. Sidewalks $700)	38 96	700 00	729 47	9 49

RECAPITULATION OF AMOUNTS AVAILABLE AND EXPENDITURES

(*) Denotes Unexpended Balances Dec. 31, but Available in 1940

	Available Dec. 31	Raised 1939	Expended	Over Under
Care of the Day		400 00	40 00	*59 87
Junior-Senior School Drive (trans. Gen. Sidew lks)		885 00	825 13	6 39
Blossom Street Walk	27 39		21 00	26
Glenn Street lk	89 26		89 00	
East War Street Sidewalk	48 57		45 60	2 97
Emerson Street Bridge		50 00	8 85	*41 15
West Water St. Chap. 90 (From Reserve Fund $1,500.			5 999 40	
State and County $3325.59, due $741)			13 50	89
Summit Street Sidewalk	14 39		22 25	69
William Street Sidewalk	22 94	275 00	225 76	49 24
Tires For Fire lk		25 00	24 95	05
War Street h Basins		00 00		6 56
Soldiers' Relief		9 00 00	8 993 44	

ANNUAL REPORT

OF THE

WATER COMMISSIONERS

TOWN OF ROCKLAND

MASSACHUSETTS

1939

JOINT WATER BOARD OF ABINGTON
AND ROCKLAND

H. C. WITHERELL, Chairman

S. W. BAKER, Secretary

GEORGE GRAY   E. S. DAMON
F. L. MERRILL   JAMES T. SHEA

LEWIS E. WHEELER, Water Registrar

WATER BOARD OF ROCKLAND

S. W. BAKER, Chairman

E. S. DAMON   JAMES T. SHEA

JAMES B. STUDLEY, Superintendent

Regular meeting of the Board every
Thursday evening at 7:30

Main and Superintendent's Office 96 E. Water St.

Open 8-12 A. M. — 1-5 P. M.   Telephone 901

Collection Office, Gladstone Block

Open 9-12 A. M.   2-5 P. M.

Friday Evenings 7-9 P. M.   Saturday 9-12 A. M.

Telephone 940

Water Commissioners Report

The Water Commissioners herewith submit their fifty-fourth annual report.

A Ross 8″ double acting altitude control valve has been installed at the Beech Hill Standpipes, also a similar type valve, 12″ Ross, at the Abington Standpipe for the same purpose. This will allow a continuous pumping period from the morning start until all standpipes and tank are full. As the Beech Hill standpipes are nearest to the pumping station they will fill first, then the altitude valve will close and allow all water to go into the towns; then the Lincoln Street Standpipe, North Abington, will fill and the altitude valve will close and allow all the water to go into the Rockland tank. The Rockland tank fills last on account of it being located in a thickly settled area, where the demand for water is greater.

When the tank fills a signal rings at the fire station and the pumping station is so notified. It is planned to fill all storage twice a day. By this arrangement all gates between the towns are open at all times. The three standpipes and tank are in the same level, total capacity when all are filled over 2,600,000 gallons.

The joint board has been unable to agree with the management of the Sandy Bottom Bog Co., operators of a cranberry bog adjacent to Great Sandy Bottom Pond, and a bill in equity has been filed in the Superior Court of Plymouth, which action is now pending.

The Inhabitants of the Town of Pembroke brought an action in the same court against the Inhabitants of the Town of Abington and the Inhabitants of the Town of Rockland. By agreement with the Selectmen we defended the action against the Inhabitants of the Town of Abington by obtaining the services of Mr. John R. Wheatley, Attorney-at-law. The Inhabitants of the Town of Rockland were represented by Judge Francis J. Geogan. Both attorneys filed demurrers which were argued on December 20, 1939, before Hon. Paul C. Kirk at Brockton, who took the matter under advisement. On December 22, 1939, the court sustained the demurerrs which ends the case. The actions sought to require Abington and Rockland to find a new water supply and abandon Great Sandy Bottom Pond on the grounds that the sanitary rules damaged the value of adjacent property.

The source of Supply, Great Sandy Bottom Pond in Pembroke should be improved by diverting or purifying the inlet from Little Sandy Pond; vegetable growth should be removed from the pond bottom; land should be obtained around the pond to better protect it from pollution; the shores should be walled up in many places, a pier should be built out to the end of the intake pipe and a screen installed. The pumping equipment consists of a steam pump purchased in 1896 and an electric gasoline pump purchased in 1923. These will need replacement before many years. The 5 miles of 16-inch force main from the station to the Beech Hill standpipes has accumulated a lining of rust formation that now gives it the friction of a new 10-inch pipe which wastes power and makes it unsafe to pump through at the full capacity of the pumps. Cleaning will restore its capacity for a time. The two standpipes on Beech Hill have seen considerable service. The steel standpipe was built in 1886 and the concrete standpipe in 1910. Whenever these fail they will have to be replaced with others at the same or some other location.

Services in Rockland   1964
Services in Abington   1537
Services in Joint Works   128

New Services in Rockland   11
New Services in Abington   1

Water rates received by Abington $22 448 38
Water rates received by Rockland $24 906 97
Water rates received by Joint Works   2 608 80

                                          $49 964 15

JOINT ACCOUNT 1939

Edison Electric Ill. Co., services $3 717 12
William Brown, salary   ₤ 120 00
Lewis Wheeler, salary   696 00
A. Culver Co., coal and paint   319 07
Abington Coal Corp, coal   283 79
N. E. T. & T. Co., service   194 21
W. Scott Osborne, labor on standpipe   177 50
Town of Pembroke, taxes for 1939   167 05
John R. Wheatley, legal services   165 20
Williard Nickerson, labor   **132 77**
Monsanto Chemical Co., chlorine and sulphate   132 05
C. J. Higgins, services as treasurer   100 00
Harrison Witherell, services as chairman   100 00
S. W. Baker, services as secretary   100 00
Walworth Co., Pipe and supplies   98 71
Lawrence Sheehan, labor   87 76
Skinner & Sherman, Analysis   80 00
Abington Water Department, installations
    and repairs   64 70
Keith Oil Corporation, gasoline   63 12
Curry Brothers Oil Co., supplies   52 75
E. S. Damon, services as Comm.   50 00
George Gray, services as Comm.   50 00
Frank Merrill, services as Comm.   50 00
Collins Packing Co., supplies   44 80
K. E. Richardson, Electrical work   43 06
J. T. Shea, services as Comm.   39 58

Douglas Print, printing and supplies	35	61
National Meter Co., meters and repairs	32	29
Rockland Water Department, repairs and supplies	28	81
A. W. Chesterton Co., supplies	26	85
James Thibeault, labor	24	75
Ashton Valve Co., material for valve	22	98
B. L. Herrick, labor and supplies	21	91
Robert Welch, labor	20	54
Robert Porter, labor	19	69
Leslie Brown, labor	19	69
Hohman Flowers, loma-lawn mower	19	30
Peter DeSimone, labor	18	57
Poss Peters, labor	18	00
Benjamin Lang Co., supplies	16	47
Ira Richards, labor	15	00
Edwin Richardson, labor	14	06
Goulds Pump Inc., supplies	12	12
Sears, Roebuck Co., Batteries and burner	11	96
Reed Lumber Co., lumber and supplies	10	95
Ralph Fucillo, services as Comm.	10	42
Builders Iron Foundry, charts	10	16
Commissioner of Public Safety, inspection of boiler	10	00
Amos Phelps & Son, insurance	10	00
Tony Sasso, labor	9	56
Herbert Hunter, labor	8	25
C. and D. Hardware Co., supplies	8	19
Crosby Steam Gage & Valve Co., charts	7	74
E. M. White, labor and supplies	7	10
W. E. Kingsbury, Gravel	6	50
Philip LaPoint, labor	5	06
Stearns Express, express	4	95
Hayes Pump & Machinery Co., chemicals	4	74
Rockland Paint & Hardware Co., batteries	4	75
William Brown, postage	4	75
John Condon, labor	4	50
Lawrence Cardarelli, labor	4	50
Mathew O'Grady, labor	4	50

John Foster Lumber Co., supplies	4 00
Edward Whitmarsh, labor	4 00
General Electric, Oil	3 92
Rockland Transportation Co., express	3 70
Terry McKeon, labor	3 38
Albert Doherty, labor	3 38
Frank Hovey, labor	2 45
Wallace & Tiernan Co., supplies	2 34
Hall & Torrey Co., rake	1 25
A. S. Peterson, supplies	85
Rome Brothers, wire and tape	59
Railway Express, express	51

$10 674 83

Rockland one-half $ 5 337 42

REPORT OF SUPERINTENDENT

OF THE JOINT WORKS

To the Joint Board of Water Commissioners
of Abington and Rockland:

Gentlemen:

I hereby submit my report as Superintendent for the year ending December 31, 1939.

The usual analysis of water from Big Sandy and Little Sand Pond has been made by the State Board of Health. Also samples of water from Big Sandy Pond were mailed each month, from March to November inclusive, to Lawrence Experiment Station for bacterial examination.

All hydrants were tested during the year.

The brick wall on south side of Station was repaired.

The shores of the pond and the cottage owners proper--ty are in good condition.

The new control valves, recently installed at Beach Hill and Abington stand-pipes, enables us to fill all four reservoirs to full capacity.

Three new services were added, and one renewal from Main to street box, and two service leaks repaired.

The Financial Report of the Joint Works will be found under the Report of the Water Registrar.

Respectfully submitted,

WILLIAM H. BROWN,
Joint Superintendent.

Month 1939	Hours Pumping h m	Daily Average h m	Gallons	Daily Average	lbs. Coal Consumed	Gal Daily Ave.	Avg. height in Reservoir	Gal. Pumped per lb Coal	Gal. Pumped per K. W. H.
January	296 35	9 34	17 932 000	578 452	20 21	652	97.2	356	727.2
February	262 40	9 23	16 058 000	573 500	16 816	672	97.2	360	722.6
March	304 00	9 48	17 331 000	559 065	19 623	633	95.7	359	704
April	293 30	9 47	16 615 000	553 833	13 770	459	96.5	358	710.2
May	343 05	11 04	19 308 000	622 839	10 912	352	97.4	360	707.0
June	395 00	13 10	22 152 000	738 400	6 930	231	97.0	357	705.5
July	501 10	16 10	28 262 000	911 678	2 387	77	97.0	358	705.7
August	482 00	15 33	27 670 000	892 581	None		97.0		713.0
September	380 00	12 40	22 263 000	742 100	6 490	283	97.2	360	720.2
October	364 15	11 45	21 432 000	691 355	10 323	333	97.0	359	720.4
November	328 00	10 56	19 081 000	636 033	13 264	442	97.2	360	715.0
December	335 25	10 49	19 419 000	626 420	15 097	457	96.8	359	711.6
Totals	4285 40		247 523 000		139 824				
Average	357 08		20 626 000		11 652		96.9		713.9

Average Static Head 218.9. Average Dynamic Head 282. Maximum weekly used July 18 to July 24 7,980,000 gallons. Maximum daily used July 22, 1,319,000 gallons. Coal on hand 1939 - 164,100 lbs. Coal on hand Jan. 1, 1940 - 47,072 lbs. Gallons pumped via electricity 246,134,000 gallons. Gallons pumped via steam 7,900 gallons. Gallons pumped via gasoline engine 592,000 gallons. Gasoline on hand Jan. 1, 1940 - 835 gallons. Duty one in foot lbs per 100 lbs of coal 86,238,440. Gallons pumped per gal. of gasoline 4460.

WILLIAM H. BEAN, Chief Engineer

REPORT OF WATER REGISTRAR

To the Joint Board of Water Commissioners
of Abington and Rockland

Gentlemen:
I herewith submit my report as Water Registrar for
the year ending December 31, 1939.

Water Rates	$2 448 71	
New Services	75 13	
Total Amount Collected		$ 2 523 84
Water Rates Due	$176 21	

Three new accounts

Respectfully submitted,

LEWIS E. WHEELER,
Water Registrar

SUPERINTENDENT'S REPORT

To the Board of Water Commissioners:
Gentlemen:

I herewith submit my report of the Water Department for the year ending December 31, 1939.

Receipts from Water Rates	$24 906	97
Receipts from Installations	1 306	45
Receipts from Small Jobs	476	61
Receipts from Meter Repairs	116	45
Receipts from Water Liens	896	04
Receipts from ½ Joint Works	1 304	40
	$29 006	92

SERVICES

New service installations	11
Renewal of services	27
Renewals to property line	5
Meter Pit Installations	3
Services Cleaned	4
Corporations disconnected	2
Bleeders installed	5

HYDRANTS - GATES - BOXES

Hydrants repaired	5
Hydrant gates added	6
Hydrants replaced	5
Hydrants located inside curb	10
Gates packed	5
Service boxes adjusted	84
Gate Boxes adjusted	20

LEAKS

12 Leaks were repaired during the year.

MAINS

Norman Street Extension

75 ft. of 6" transite pipe was added on Norman Street. This completes the main as far as the street has been accepted by the Town.

UNION STREET

1672 ft. of 12" transite pipe was purchased by the Department to connect the 12" main at the corner of Union Street and North Avenue, with the 16" main on Rice Avenue. This will bring the delivery of water in the business section for Fire Protection over the requirements of the New England Insurance Exchange. Labor is being furnished by the W. P. A.

GENERAL

150 ft. of 6" water main on West Water Street was lowered 2½ feet to clear one of the new bridges.

Two wires have been installed between the tank on Rice Avenue and the Fire Station, providing for the installation of an alarm gong in the Fire Station.

A faucet for the benefit of the users of the Park at Reed's Pond was installed.

1172 service calls were taken care of during the year.

A report of the recent survey of water rates in New England listed Rockland as one of the lowest.

The approximate footage of main in service today; 16" 1600 ft. 12" 7800 ft. 10" 3300 ft. 8" 17,700 ft., 6" 158,400 ft. 4" 200 ft.

LOCAL REPORT OF EXPENSES

The following expenditures are included in the total expenditures of $23,661.31.

UNION STREET MAIN, (1939)

1672 ft. transite pipe	$2 580 65
Freight	127 17
	$2 707 82

NORMAN STREET

75 ft. pipe	$ 48 75
Labor	49 50
1-6" Sleeve	4 60
	$102 85

Respectfully submitted,

JAMES B. STUDLEY, Supt.

LOCAL ACCOUNT

Merchants National Bank, bonds and interest	$2 720 00
Johns Mansville, pipe and fittings	2 635 12
James Studley, salary	2 080 00
Louis Litchfield, salary	1 820 00
Harry Holmes, salary	1 670 37
Corcoran Supply Co., pipe and supplies	994 66
Henry Harris, labor and remittances	953 79
Alice Gammon, office	936 00

Tony Sasso, labor	836	82
Edwin Richardson, labor	747	97
Lawrence Sheehan, labor	733	26
Phoenix Meter Corp., meter parts	530	18
A. B. Reed, Engineering services	400	00
Boston Pipe & Fittings Co.,		
brass pipe and fittings	310	54
J. R. Parker, P. M., envelopes and postage	304	92
S. W. Baker, services as Commissioner	300	00
E. S. Damon, services as Commissioner	300	00
Rensselaer Valve Co., hydrants	279	17
Red Hed Mfg. Co., fittings	250	80
J. T. Shea, services as Commissioner	237	50
National Meter Co., meters and parts	224	17
S. F. Doane Co., supplies	221	01
George Campbell, gasoline and oil	212	37
E. L. LeBaron Foundry Co., service boxes and		
fittings	198	38
A. Wainshalbaum, truck repairs and supplies	185	85
N. E. T. & T. Co., service	176	73
George Caldwell Co., fittings and supplies	166	91
Sears, Roebuck Co., stoker and supplies	164	85
Rockland Coal and Grain Co., coal and lumber	150	33
N. Y., N. H. & H. R. R., freight	139	18
George W. N. Clarke, wiring and installation	112	00
L. P. Brown Machine & Tool Co., valves	110	00
Amos Phelps & Son, insurance	101	80
Warren Woodward, insurance	89	78
Lawrence Cardarelli, painting hydrants	88	00
Stuart McCullum, repairing goosenecks	85	44
Philip Murphy, labor	78	20
Edward Holmes, Register, registering liens	72	10
E. S. Damon, insurance	71	40
Brockton Coal & Ice Co., coal	70	65
A. J. Vargus, Gas and Oil	68	91
Douglas Print, printing and supplies	67	90
Walworth Co., pipe and supplies	66	48
Dunlop Tire Co., tires and tubes for truck	65	84

Crawford's Service Station, tires and tubes for truck	63	86
Ralph Fucillo, services as Commissioner	62	50
Mary Dotton, checking lien titles	62	00
Brockton Edison Co., service	61	96
McAuliffe & Burke Co., brass pipe	60	94
Harry Arena, loam for standpipe	58	00
M. F. Ellis Co., shovels and lanterns	50	40
Underwood Elliot Fisher Co., typewriter	50	00
Columbia Electric Supply Co., electrical supplies	46	40
William Carey, labor	42	77
Easton Brass Foundry, castings	42	51
Bradford Weston Inc., stone	42	43
John J. Duane Co., shoring and planks	41	54
Damon Electric, electrical work	40	85
Edward Keane, labor	40	51
Dennis O'Connor, insurance	40	34
R. Winslow Lloyd, blinds	37	50
Hallamore Machine Co., labor on hydrants	37	15
Cambridge Machine & Valve Co., valve	36	65
Sherwin Williams Co., paint	34	12
C. A. Baker, gas and oxygen	31	76
P. I. Perkins Co., pneumatic hammer	30	35
George C. Cleaves & Son, sharpening drills	28	20
Pittsburgh Meter Co., meters and bolts	26	50
Whitehead Metal Products Co., rods and screws	25	74
Hayden, Harding, & Buchanan, furnishing elevations	25	00
A. I. Randall Inc., printing	22	80
Chase, Parker & Co., supplies	22	49
Boston Blue Print Co., cloth and tracing paper	22	03
Rockland Hardware & Paint Co., supplies	21	67
Hydraulic Development Corp., hydrotite	20	00
Gulf Refining Co., Oil	17	10
Hall & Torrey Co., supplies	16	29
Fred Ferron, repairing garage doors	16	19
Hobart Auto Supply Co., gas and oil	15	58
Blake & Rebhan Co., office supplies	15	45

C. & D. Hardware Co., supplies	14	17
William Santry, labor	14	06
Edson Corp., supplies	13	63
John C. Moore Corp., office supplies	13	10
Joseph Baker, stop watch and clock repairs	13	00
Homelite Corp., impeller for pump	12	00
Joseph Daley, labor	11	82
Frank O'Hara, labor	11	82
O. M. Scott & Son, Grass seed and mixture	11	75
William T. McCarthy, envelopes	11	50
James Thibeault, labor	10	97
Farnan Brass Works, supplies	10	46
Old Colony Gas Co., gas	10	38
Boston Lead Co., lead wool	9	31
P. F. McDonald, crow bars	9	00
Morse Twist Drill & Machine Co., dies	8	76
Rockland Standard, printing	8	25
Jenkins & Simmons, express	7	25
George N. Beals, repairs	7	10
L. Josselyn & Son, laquer and thinner	7	05
Indian Head Washer Mfg. Co., meter washers	6	55
Becker & Co., journal	6	03
Brown Instrument Co., charts and ink	5	17
Hickey Brothers, wood	5	00
Chandler & Fraquhar, cabinets	4	75
George Inglis, labor	4	50
Joseph Poole, labor	4	50
Manifold Supply Co., Carbon Paper	4	50
W. J. Dunn Co., sharpening bits	3	86
Brockton Sporting Goods Co., supplies	3	85
Edward Farrar, labor	3	80
Fred Kane, labor	3	38
L. Richmond Co., floor oil	3	36
Standard Modern Printing Co., carbon paper	3	30
C. W. Briggs, blacksmith work	3	28
West Side Grocery, wood	3	20
Dr. Joseph Dunn, examination	3	00
H. H. Arnold Inc., steel	2	70

Greene's Service Station Oil	2	50
Rome Brothers, supplies	2	50
Ward's Stationers, office supplies	2	50
Ellis Smith, stamp pad	2	25
Commonwealth Stationery Co., paper	2	00
James Haggett, labor	1	97
Ira Richards, labor	1	97
Lester Rose, labor	1	97
Charles Fucillo, labor	1	97
William Bailey, labor	1	97
Addressograph Co., Addressograph ribbons	1	94
Industrial Machine, supplies	1	60
Rockland Transportation Co., express	1	55
Lamb's Store, oakite	1	47
Market St., Garage, cutting threads	1	25
Brockton Trans. Co., express		81
A. S. Peterson, tape		60
John E. Dowming, repairing tape		50
Reynolds Brothers, express		50
Estes Auto Supply, No. 45 reducer		45

Total	$ 23	661	31
½ Joint Works	5	337	42
	$ 28	998	73

Accepted:

SAMUEL W. BAKER,
EVERETT S. DAMON,
JAMES T. SHEA,
Board of Water Commissioners,
Town of Rockland

Report of Board of Health

The Board of Health herewith submits its annual report for 1939.

Cases of reportable diseases reported to the board:

Measles 29
Scarlet Fever 9
Whooping Cough ....
Lobar Pneumonia 6
Chicken Pox 1
Dog Bite 5

The health of the town has been good for the year. The common cold is always with us and gives rise to more trouble then perhaps anything else. A few days off is the best cure in the long run.

For a very few we may say that the public dump on Pleasant street is the only dump recognized as the proper place for the disposal of refuse. Invitations to fill in excavations or swamp holes near residences always lead to complaints.

JOSEPH FRAME,
HAROLD T. CORCORAN,
JOSEPH H. DUNN,
Board of Health

Auditors Report

Jan. 26, 1940

The books of the various departments of the Town have ben audited and verified. The audit included the books of the Treasurer which showed all disbursements in accord with warrants furnished him by the different departments. His receipts were verified with vouchers filed and they were found to be correct. His bank balance was reconciled with statements furnished by the banks.

The audit also included the books of the water and school departments, the town clerk and sealer of weights and measures and they were found to be correct in every respect.

The accounts of the tax collector were examined and a verification of unpaid accounts revealed no discrepancies.

Respectfully submitted,

HAROLD C. SMITH, Chairman
GEORGE A. GALLAGHER,
LEO M. DOWNEY,
Auditors

ESTIMATES OF APPROPRIATIONS FOR THE YEAR
1940 BY HEADS OF DIFFERENT DEPARTMENTS
AND AMOUNTS RAISED IN 1939

	Raised 1939	Est. 1940
School Department	$105 200 00	$113 795 68
State Aid	600 00	500 00
Soldiers' Relief	9 000 00	9 000 00
Care of Soldiers' Graves	150 00	150 00
Memorial Library and	4 400 00	4 650 00
Dog Fund ($407 04)		
Street Lighting	8 898 00	9 400 00
Highway Surveyor	1 350 00	1 350 00
Tarvia and Road Binder	3 000 00	3 775 00
Highway Repairs	1 800 00	5 250 00
Sidewalks	500 00	1 000 00
Cleaning Catch Basins and Drains	500 00	1 000 00
Cleaning Union Street	1 200 00	1 200 00
Clean Up Week	75 00	75 00
Guide Boards and Signs	100 00	200 00
Fire Department	11 080 00	11 800 00
Police Department	8 955 00	9 100 00
Forest Fires	750 00	1 700 00
Board of Health	6 000 00	6 000 00
Inspection of Animals	150 00	150 00
Park Department	2 800 00	3 475 00
Old Age Assistance	55 000 00	57 000 00
Moth Department	300 00	500 00
Tree Warden	900 00	1 300 00
Town Officers	7 700 00	7 800 00
Office Rent	1 800 00	2 914 00
Sealer of Weights and Measures	400 00	400 00
Elections	1 000 00	1 800 00
Compensation Insurance	1 928 71	1 900 00
Mass. Industrial School	1 800 00	2 300 00
Town Report and Poll Book	1 585 00	1 635 00
Support of Poor and Infirmary	51 000 00	58 000 00
Mothers' Aid	9 500 00	9 500 00

Town Notes and Interest	36 000 00	32 700 00
Assessors	2 500 00	2 500 00
Snow Removal	9 500 00	12 000 00
Reserve Fund	4 000 00	4 000 00
Misc. Assessors	1 550 00	1 590 00
Misc. Treasurer	800 00	950 00
Misc. Clerk	350 00	350 00
Misc. Selectmen	120 00	220 00
Misc. Registrars	650 00	650 00
Misc. Sealer	190 00	105 00
Misc. Collector	1 450 00	1 450 00
Misc. Unclassified	1 100 00	1 000 00
Visiting Nurse	1 500 00	1 500 00
Beacon	900 00	800 00
Military Aid		300 00
Burial of Indigent Soldiers		200 00
Care of Town Cemtery	60 00	60 00
Observance of Memorial Day	400 00	500 00
Rent, Quarters, American Legion	900 00	900 00
Rent, Quarters, Spanish War	288 00	288 00
Criminal Cases in Court	100 00	100 00

Financial Report of Public Welfare

The report of the Board of Public Welfare for the year 1939 is hereby submitted:

BUREAU OF OLD AGE ASSISTANCE

Town Physicians, services	$	700 00
Paid Other Towns		903 71
Expended for cases		53 386 74
Total		$54 990 45
Appropriation	$55 000 00	

Expended   54 990 45
Under appropriation   9 55

Received from Federal Funds:
Balance Jan. 1, 1939 $ 4 693 76
Credited to cases   49 584 30

                              $54 278 06

Expended from Federal Funds   50 893 66

Balance Jan. 1, 1940 $ 3 384 40

Received from Federal Funds for Administration:
Balance Jan. 1, 1939 $ 625 05
Credited for Administration   1 652 76

Total $ 2 277 81
Expended   1 707 31

Balance Jan. 1, 1940 $ 570 50

List of Expenditures Under Bureau of

Old Age Assistance Administration

Paid:
Mary L. O'Brien, salary and car $856 00
Harriet Anderson, clerical   260 00
Annette White, clerical   104 00
Katherine McGee, sub clerical   10 00
Yawman & Erbe Co., supplies   25 53
A. S. Peterson, supplies   70
Hobbs & Warren Inc., forms   23 24
U. S. Post Office, envelopes and postage   181 08
Mary L. O'Brien, special service   8 00
Douglas Print, forms   6 25
The Todd Co., checks   55 03
Becker & Co., folders   8 25

H. C. Metcalf, clean typewriters		2 00
Expense to Boston		2 90
Yawman & Erbe, 1 desk		74 58
H. C. Metcalf, 1 adding machine		58 00
Shaw and Walker, folders		31 75

$1 707 31

Total amount expended from Town
and Federal Funds $105 884 11

MOTHER'S AID

Expended under Chapter 118, General Laws:
Expended from Town Funds $8 645 45
  Appropriation $9 500 00
  Expended   8 645 45

Under appropriation $ 854 55

Received from Federal Grant $2 557 37
Expended   1 142 00

Balance Jan. 1, 1940 $ 1 415 37

Federal Reimbursement for Administration $ 264 50
Expended   44 00

Balance to Jan. 1, 1940 $ 220 50

Total Expenditures from Town and Federal
  Funds $ 9 787 45

INFIRMARY

Paid:—
Kate Kelly, maid $ 376 00
Annie Stewart, maid   502 00
Harold Mock, bread   50 26

E. L. Murrill, meats	162 47
New Eng. Tel. & Tel. Co., service	53 59
Earl & Blanche Wyatt, salary	1 020 00
Brockton Edison Co., service	101 83
Burrell & Delory, shoes	9 26
Fred S. Delay, medical supplies	129 57
A. Fiaschetti, provisions	142 92
Handschumacher & Co., curing hams	7 61
Comm. of Mass., supplies	23 18
Coty's Bakery, bread	15 12
John H. Lamb, provisions	121 55
Levitan & White Inc., clothing	13 80
Rockland Coal & Grain Co., coal	391 80
McManus Box Co., supplies	42 20
W. F. Barnes, fish	105 43
Comm. of Mass. State Prison	
supplies	27 43
George Morrison, bread	13 12
J. A. Rice Co., supplies	5 62
A. Culver Co., feed	245 68
A. Culver Co., coal	264 50
Pacific Street Market, provisions	123 42
Edith Estes, maid	30 00
W. H. Clayton, shoeing Horse, etc	36 65
Rockland Water Dept. service	88 41
Rockland Pharmacy, medical supplies	68 14
Daniel J. Reilly, wood	14 00
A. S. Peterson, tobacco and supplies	87 04
E. L. Chamberlin, supplies	40 30
Lot Phillips & Son., supplies	15 70
M. Y. Clements, meats	132 88
Charles Blanchard, killing hogs	3 50
Hall & Torrey Co., repairs and	
supplies	102 75
Rockland Coal & Grain Co., supplies	28 82
George Tyler, clean cesspool	12 00
John V. Hoadley, repairs	25 40
Alice Holbrook, extracts	10 50

Tracey's Store, provisions	105	11
Roland Poole, glasses	4	50
William T. McCarthy, sign	6	25
Harry L. Rome, shades	3	75
Old Colony Co., repairs	30	25
Rockland, Hardware & Paint Co., Supplies	39	12
Market Street Grocery, provisions	113	60
H. I. Stickney, sharpening tools	4	30
Rockland Shoe Repair Co., shoes	1	25
C. A. Paulding, supplies	1	33
John S. Cheever, supplies	17	35
H. F. Gardner, provisions	142	69
A. Culver Co., supplies and flour	75	80
Goodco Sanitary Co., deoderant	29	50
Ferber's Store, supplies	3	90
W. E. Trufant, supplies	22	95
Dominic DelPrete, plowing	21	75
Herman Rose, harness	14	00
Comm. of Mass. inspection boiler	5	00
P. T. Manter, provisions	157	01
City Ag. Congress, supplies	1	00
Pioneer Store, provisions	108	41
Lelyveld Shoes, shoes	5	45
Dennis O'Connor, shoes	6	75
A. Tedeschi, provisions	130	33
Dr. Benj. Lelyveld, services	2	00
Dr. John M. Young, services	2	00
T. M. Fucillo, repairs	6	40
I. G. Miller, provisions	131	18
S. T. Howland, vac. horse	7	50
Royt Sanitary Co., supplies	7	00
Ralph C. Briggs, services	6	00
Rockland N. S. Laundry, services	3	80
Donald Robbins, repairs	7	25
James G. Lamb, provisions	74	95
Henry Manoli, provision	63	72
C. & D. Hardware Co., supplies	20	21

Annie Capelis, provisions	110 74	
J. S. McCallum, repairs	26 89	
Ranney's Store, clothing	32 95	
Howland's Ins., Office, insurance policy	43 65	
Everett C. Ford, chicks	4 80	
Michael Ryan, provisions	118 36	
Hickey Bros., provisions	107 22	
J. A. Rice Co., supplies	19 48	
Total	————$	6 491 70

EXPENSES OF OUTSIDE POOR

Hospitals — Paid:

Brockton Hospital	$ 548 57	
Weymouth Hospital	349 29	
Mass. General Hospital	334 09	
Mass. Eye and Ear Infirmary	44 40	
Palmer Memorial Hospital	94 00	
Goddard Hospital	24 15	
	————$	1 394 50

Administration — Paid:

Harriet Anderson, salary	$676 00	
Hobbs & Warren Inc., blanks and forms	36 98	
John J. Dwyer, trans. CCC	16 00	
E. W. Jones, services	4 00	
John J. Dwyer, ambulance and trans. to Hospitals	36 00	
Harry S. Torrey, Expense and trans. CCC	2 90	
Franklin & Perkins, supplies	13 30	
Douglas Print, forms	20 50	
H. C. Metcalf, repair typewriter	1 00	
Gerald Wheland, transportation	17 22	
	————$	823 90

Transportation of WPA to Out of Town Projects
Paid:—
Carey Motor Service, trans.

to Hingham	$ 470 00	
Lovell Bus Lines Inc., trans.		
to Hingham	1 564 50	
John J. Dwyer, trans. to Abington	162 00	
Payroll to State Projects	199 05	
		$ 2 395 55

SALARY WELFARE AGENT

Paid:—
Gerald Wheland, services (yearly $1,500.) $ 1 067 08

Administration of Commodity Distribution
Paid:—

John J. Bowler, trans. goods to		
Brockton	246 00	
John J. Dwyer, trans. of commodities	246 50	
Franklin & Perkins, paper bags	72 28	
John S. Triggs, warehouse expense	28 00	
Crowley Bros., rent	10 00	
James G. Lamb, paper bags	33	
Clerical Expense	20 00	
		$ 623 11
Paid Other Towns		437 22

Provisions Orders	$3 571 49	
Rents	3 724 75	
Medical (including hospital to State		
and Other Towns	3 371 34	
Fuel	1 804 24	
Boarded cases	1 222 50	
Clothing	177 45	
Burials	587 00	
Misc. Items	229 00	
Cash	25 591 73	

                         $40 275 50

Total $53 508 56

Appropriation	$51 000 00
Welfare Agent	1 500 00
Transfer from Reserve Fund	1 008 78
	$53 508 78
Expended	53 508 56
Under appropriation	22

SUMMARY OF EXPENDITURES OF PUBLIC WELFARE

Expense at Infirmary	$6 491 70	
Paid for Hospitals (town cases)	1 394 50	
Paid for Administration	823 90	
Trans. for Outside Projects	2 395 55	
Expense Commodity Distribution	623 11	
Salary of Agent	1 067 08	
Paid Other Towns	437 22	
Expense of Outside Poor	40 275 50	
		$53 508 56

CREDITS

Received From

Other Towns, temporary aid	$ 5 306 59
Other Towns, Old Age Assistance	1 610 13
Comm. of Mass. Old Age Assistance	35 234 42
Comm. of Mass., sick state poor	671 95
Comm. of Mass., Mother's Aid	1 423 33
Comm. of Mass., temporary	8 740 71
Personal Fefund, temporary aid	34 59
Personal Refund, Old Age Assistance	669 00
Board at Infirmary	539 38
Refund Mass. Hospital School	26 57
	$54 256 67

Due From:

Other Towns for board at infirmary	$ 1 962 02

Federal Funds Mother's Aid, Nov and Dec.	414	66
Federal Funds Old Age, Nov. and Dec.	8 719	50
State Temporary Aid	5 007	64
Other Towns, Temporary Aid	4 260	63
State Mother's Aid	5 193	61
State Old Age Assistance	27 680	80
Other Towns, Old Age Assistance	1 754	15
State Sick State Poor	206	25
State Dangerous Disease	138	00

$55 337 26

Report of Board of Public Welfare

The Board of Public Welfare herewith submits its annual report from Jan. 1 to Dec. 31, 1939.

The Board is again pleased to report a decrease in expenditures of Public Welfare and Infirmary costs for the second year in succession amounting to $4,785.01 in Public Welfare and $1,608.30 in Infirmary expenses over 1938 and a saving of $13,504.74 over 1937.

This indicates that we are slowly returning to normalcy in Welfare costs.

Under a vote of the Town the Board of Public Welfare were instructed to employ a visitor for the Department with the qualifications required by the State Department. After interviewing several applicants it was decided to employ Mr. Gerald Wheland for this position. The Board feels that the choice was a very fortunate one and the town has benefited not only financially, but a more thorough investigation of cases and better care of our needy poor has been conducted.

Two items were added to the expenses under Welfare this year, that had been previously entered under other headings. The Commodity Distribution amounting to $623.11 and Transportation of out of Town Projects, under WPA which increased the cost of the Department $2,395.55.

We feel confident that a greater gain could have been obtained if the WPA could be conducted in a more stable manner. The WPA rule that all employees could not be employed more than 18 months without a lay off of at least 30 days, which often extended over a period of a number of months before returning to work, increased our Welfare costs.

Also the rule of WPA that all Projects must carry a 25% local contribution to be eligible. This eliminated many projects such as open drains, fire lines and of many others that were of small local cost and others that we did not have available local funds to operate the project.

The Civilian Conservation Corps for young men helps their families to the extent of $22.00 per month, which has been a benefit to many families. Also the Youth program connected with the WPA allows young people to supplement from $15 to $20 the earnings of their families.

The distribution of food and clothing to needy families continues as in past years. The following table shows amount received and distributed in Rockland the past year:

30,000 lbs.	Corn Meal	33,882 lbs.	Butter
14,602 lbs.	Wheat Cereal	5,445 lbs.	Carrots
60,730 lbs.	Wheat Flour	6,686 lbs.	Cabbage
14,945 lbs.	Graham Flour	8,500 lbs.	Prunes
27,788 lbs.	Grape Fruit	11,165 lbs.	Sweet Potatoes
5,775 lbs.	Dry Peaches	19,655 lbs.	Oranges

33,210 lbs. Apples	2,930 lbs. Squash
6,200 lbs. Rice	1,008 lbs. Tomatoes
3,150 lbs. Roll Oats	16,416 cans Grapefruit
24,900 lbs. Dry Beans	8,640 cans Evap. Milk

There was 37, 320 yards of cloth issued to our town, and 19,312 pieces of clothing issued to the town for distribution.

We wish to thank Mrs. Lauretta Bresnahan, State Selecting Agent, in connection with CCC enrollments. The various departments and visitors from the State Dept. of Public Welfare, the local churches, Red Cross, Fraternal and Patriotic Societies that have assisted us in our work, also the Town Physicians, Dr. Joseph H. Dunn and Norbert Lough, and Miss Miriam Dexter our Visiting Nurse for their co-operation.

We have at present on Relief Rolls:

15 Mother's Aid cases.
3 Child Boarded cases.
75 Families on Outside Relief.
72 Single persons on Outside Relief.
22 Families on Soldiers' Relief.
14 Single Persons on Soldiers' Relief.
318 Old Age Assistance Cases.
14 At Infirmary.

HARRY S. TORREY,
JOHN J. BOWLER,
NORMAN S. WHITING,
Board of Public Welfare

List of Jurors

As prepared by the Selectmen of the Town of Rockland under General Laws of Massachusetts, Chapter 234, Section 4.

July 1, 1939

Name Street and Number	Occupation
Bacon, Paul, 48 Williams	Salesman
Ball, Percy, 770 Union	Shoe Worker
Beal, George, 739 Market	Weaver
Bell, William, 558 Liberty	Truck Driver
Briggs, George E., 139 Exchange	Machinist
Burrell, H. Chester, 340 Liberty	Shoe Operative
Burbank, Edward, 25 Hartsuff	Shoe Operative
Cahill, Joseph W., 104 West Water	Shoe Worker
Callanan, Charles, 7 West Water	Reporter
Caplice, James H., 108 Howard	Shoe Operative
Crosby, Norman, 80 Market	Instructor
DeLory, Bernard, 168 Myrtle	Clerk
Dill, Percy E., 136 North Ave.	Shoe Operative
Dolan, Edward, 865 Union	Shoe Operative
Dondero, Joseph, 412 Webster	Shoe Operative
Donovan, Daniel H., 117 Liberty	Machinist
Easton, Carrol, 858 Union	Salesman
Ednie, John, 520 Market	Painter
Estes, Joseph B., 305 Liberty	Town Assessor
Fass, Carl G., 377 North Ave.	Draftsman
Feeney, James, 171 North Ave.	Chef
Fitzgerald, Thomas F., 51 North Ave.	Shoe Operative
Ford, Patrick J., 542 Liberty	Salesman
Gammon, Frank L., 644 Market	Manager
Garrity, Peter, 162 North Ave.	Janitor
Greenan, James, 39 East Water	Retired
Harney, Edmund F., 66 Church	Shoe Operative

Hawes, Fred M., 88 Howard	Salesman
Hayden, Robert E., 40 Summit	Laborer
Higgins, Thomas S., 32 Belmont	Laborer
Holmes, Harry O., 248 Central	Meter Reader
Howland, Giles W., 181 Webster	Civil Engineer
Hunt, Charles L., 36 Belmont	Chauffeur
Hunt, Lester A., 224 Myrtle	Shoe Operative
Inkley, Harold J., 230 Greenwood	Shoe Operative
Johnson, Clarence B., 266 Plain	Teamster
Kramer, Charles F., 39 Grove	Shoe Operative
Leighton, Ellis, 233 Liberty	Electrician
Lelyveld, Benjamin, 129 Pacific	Podiatrist
Lewis, Willard A., 69 Hartsuff	Shoe Operative
Locke, Louis F., 30 Reed	Webbing
Loud, Fred, 28 Myrtle	Bookkeeper
Lovel, Jasper, 4 Maple	Box Cutter
Mahon, Thomas, 31 Summit	Janitor
Main, William H., 161 Exchange	Shoe Operative
Mastrodominico, Joseph, 355 Union	Shoe Operative
McCarthy, Michael J., 22 School	Shoe Operative
McKeever, James, 199 Webster	Clerk
Measures, Ralph, 251A Union	Painter
Morrison, Arthur J., 68 Custer	Shoe Operative
Mullen, William, 865 Union	Shoe Operator
Murphy, Philip M., 231 West Water	Laborer
Najarian, Arthur, 112 Webster	Laborer
Newhall, Otis A., 186 Howard	Shoe Operative
Niles, George R., 137 Pacific	Carpenter
Phillips, Roland P., 61 Stanton	Manager
O'Brady, Matthew, 108 Belmont	Laborer
O'Hayre, Bernard F., 278 Reed	Shoe Operative
Orr, Charles E., 67 Stanton	Salesman
Orvitt, Frank D., 185 Crescent	Sales manager
Partch, Forest L., 115 Webster	Electrician
Poole, Norman C., 580 West Water	Salesman
Phelps, Edward J., 119 Myrtle	Insurance
Ransom, Roger T., 31 Hartsuff	Engineer
Reardon, Thomas, 101 Summit	Clerk

Rose, John A., 516 Union	Repairman
Rose, Lester E., 348 Liberty	Laborer
Ross, John W., 127 West Water	Salesman
Ryan, Patrick C., 122 Myrtle	Shoe Operative
Scott, Charles N., 91 Pacific	Clerk
Sears, Clifford H., 22 Blanchard	Shoe Operative
Sheehan, Eugene, 39 Pacific	Shoe Worker
Sheehan, Maurice, 101 Prospect	Shoe Operative
Shields, Charles T., 42 Franklin Ave.	Shoe Operative
Smith, Bartholomew J., 35 Stanton	Shoe Operative
Smith, Leslie G., 30 Everett	Bus Driver
Tedeschi, Ralph D., 95 Belmont	Clerk
Toothaker, Oliver H., 618 Market	Salesman
Umbrianna, Michael, 35 Salem	Shoe Operative
Vargus, Antone J., 215 Crescent	Auto Supplies
Walker, Samuel C., 10 Sunnybank	Mechanic
Walls, Magorisk, 82 Webster	Inspector
Wallace, Earl, 231 Myrtle	Foreman
Wheeler, Walter S., 54 Beal	Mechanic
White, John S. Jr., 273 Reed	Laborer
Whiting, W. Alton, 455 Webster	Shoe Operative
Wilcox, Arthur P., 58 Union	Real Estate
Williams, Howard D., 188 Central	Salesman

HARRY S. TORREY,
NORMAN S. WHITING,
NOHN J, BOWLER,
Selectmen of Rockland

Report of Fire Department

To the Honorable Board of Selectmen:
Gentlemen:

I hereby submit my report as Chief of the Fire Department for the year 1939.

On June 30, 1939, the Fire Department moved into its new quarters. I wish at this time in my report to thank the Fire Station Building Committee for the splendid building erected under their supervision. I know they put much time and thought into this building which is a credit to the town, both in appearance and usefulness. I also in behalf of myself and members of the Fire Department wish to thank the Selectmen, the Finance Committee, and all others for the assistance given in securing and constructing the Fire Station. We at the Station take pride in his building and are only too glad to have the public inspect it at almost any time.

The number of fire alarms is still increasing each year. During 1939 we had 252 calls which shows an increase over 1938 of thirty-seven. There were eighty-three bell alarms, one hundred sixty-five verbal and telephone alarms and four ADT calls. Unfortunately we had twenty-eight false alarms. I do not believe the people who pull the false alarms realize the danger of pulling an alarm for nothing at all. The apparatus and men answering the alarm are either apt to get smashed up, or run into somebody else and some one might be killed or sent to the hospital. Also while answering a false alarm another alarm for a real fire might come in, where some one's life would be in danger to say nothing of the possible loss of property before the arrival of the Department.

Perhaps the public does not realize besides answering fire alarms the Department had seven calls for the Inhalator in the year 1939 and was successful in their efforts to save the lives of the patients. We used fifteen small tanks and three large tanks of oxygen in the endeavor to preserve life. Altho not using the Inhalator all the time we stood watch over one patient for about forty-eight hours ready at any time to give oxygen.

The Department laid during the year 9750 ft. of 2½" hose; 4650 ft. of 1½" hose, and 9050 ft. of chemical hose. We also used 987 gallons of soda and acid, 12½ gallons of foam, 9 quarters of Pyrene, besides chimney compound and the small pump cans which were used in 121 fires.· Another part of the fireman's duty today is to save as much property as possible from water and falling plaster by the use of salvage covers. These covers were used very effectively on the Savings Bank Block fires thereby saving many dollars worth of property. Also the portable lights were used to great advantage a number of times.

FIRE ALARM SYSTEM

Much work was done during 1939 in clearing up the Fire Alarm System after the hurricane, and in about another year this system should be in good condition.

With the new Fire Alarm equipment which is installed in the new station, we are able to divide the Fire Alarm System into four circuits instead of the two we formerly had. This means should repairs be necessary, only a small portion of the town would be without Fire Alarm service.

A number of the old boxes which were installed in 1889 should be replaced at once as it is impossible to secure parts for these boxes.

Much of the expense of this Department is caused by the necessary erection of new poles by the Telephone or

Light companies, which means the changing over of our system.

NEW APPARATUS

We were fortunate during 1939 that no large repairs were necessary on any of the apparatus. I have not changed my mind in regard to the Combination which was purchased in 1912. I expect almost any time to have to bring it back to the Station and lay it up for repairs. I recommend that a new 750 Gallon Triple Combination be purchased in the year 1940 to replace the present combination.

Ontside of the tires on the Pump car the apparatus appears to be in good condition. The tires have been on six years and should be replaced.

RECOMMENDATIONS

For the year 1940 I recommend an appropriation of $11,800 for Fire Department Maintenance.

CONCLUSION

In concluding this report I wish to thank the Finance Committee for their co-operation, the Board of Selectmen, Board of Water Commissioners and their employees, and the Chief and Members of the Police Department for the help and co-operation given the Fire Department. I also wish to express my appreciation to the officers and members of the Fire Department, and to all others who have assisted me in the performance of my duty as Chief of the Fire Department.

Respectfully submitted,

CLYSON P. INKLEY,
Chief Rockland Fire Department

Report of Police Department

To the Honorable Board of Selectmen:

I herewith submit my report for the Police Department of the Town of Rockland for the year ending December 31st, 1939.

NUMBER OF ARRESTS

Year 1939   190

SUBDIVISION

	Male	Female
Assault and Battery	4	
Assisting Gaming Nuisance	1	
Breaking and entering (night-time)	4	
Breaking an entering (day-time)	4	
Drunkenness	104	2
Disturbing the peace	2	
Insane persons	7	3
Keeping a building for gaming purposes	2	
Lewd and lascivious person	1	
Larceny (less than $100)	11	
Maintaining gaming nuisance	1	
Motor vehicle violations	25	
(1) Operation under the influence	9	
(2) Operating uninsured car	2	
(3) Operating unregistered car	2	
(4) Operating after revocation	3	
(5) Operating so as to endanger	3	
(6) Operating not being licensed	3	
(7) Operating unreasonable speed	1	
(8) Leaving scene of accident	1	
(9) Manslaughter	1	

Non-Support   5
Promoting a lottery   3
Present where gaming impliments are   7
Transcient vendor not being licensed   1
Violation Pure Food Law   2

Total   185   5

Males 185
Females 5

Total 190

MISCELLANEOUS

Automobile thefts investigated   2
Automobiles recovered   5
Automobile accidents investigated   78
Complaints investigated   812
Miles traveled by Police cruiser   12,624
Persons reported missing   4
Persons located for out-of-town Police departments   9
Number arrests for out-of-town departments   14
Stores found unlocked   40
Persons lodged for the night   15
Number of autos stopped for license etc   400
Electric lights reported out   12
Summons served for out-of-town police   56
Telegrams (emergencies) persons notified   18
Reported defects on Highway   8
Police cruiser used to convey persons to hospital   2

Crime in Rockland for the year ending December 1939 was of a minor nature; persons convicted for operating a motor vehicle under the influence of intoxicating liquors decreased from 11 in 1938 to 9 in 1939; Larceny increased from 6 in 1938 to 11 in 1939; persons arrested for drunkenness decreased from 143 in 1938 to 106 in 1939.

The police cruiser purchased in April 1939 has traveled a distance of approximately 13,000 miles during the nine months covering the entire town mostly on the night patrol; officers are instructed to be ever watchful for fires in homes during the night patrol; fortunately no fires had to be reported during the past year.

In the annual report as compiled by the Massachusetts Safety Council Rockland's standing was 17th on the list of 48 towns approximately the same population of our town. Last year Rockland was fortunate in not having a fatal accident; this year we regret to list that one fatal accident occured and for this reason we were placed from seventh to seventeenth position on the Mass. Safety Council's list.

Labor trouble for the first time in many years was witnessed in our town; this department was summoned to police the vicinity of the factory which was being picketed; this department is gratified to report that no signs of violance; disorder; property damage; or arrests were made during the period of the labor trouble. The officials of the Union and the owners of the factory co-operated with the local police.

The parking problem in Rockland has for many years been of a serious nature, especially Friday and Saturday nights; the Selectmen with this department have certain recommendations which they have investigated and expect that changes will be made to remedy this situation to some extent.

Again I take pleasure in giving the thanks of the entire department to the Town and County officials and to the many citizens who have given valuable assistance when at an opportune time. As Chief of this department I am appreciative of the excellent work of the regular and special officers, all of whom have labored to give the finest service; and to the Finance committee who after consideration approved of the appropriation asked for by this department.

Respectfully submitted,

GEORGE J. POPP,

Chief of Police

Report of Forest Fire Warden

To the Honorable Board of Selectmen:
Gentlemen:

I hereby submit my report as Forest Fire Warden for the year 1939.

The Forest Fire Department answered 103 calls for fires during the year 1939. On August 13, 1939 we had a very serious fire on the corner of Forest and Weymouth Streets, which was caused by carelessness, and cost the town a considerable amount of money to extinguish.

Many people are having out-of-door fires without permits, which they are required to secure according to law.

For the year 1940 I recommend an appropriation of $1,700.00 in order to take care of the balance of the payroll due the Firemen for the year 1939.

Respectfully submitted,

CLYSON P. INKLEY,

Forest Fire Warden

Report of W. P. A. Sponsor Agent

To the Board of Selectmen:

The W. P. A. has closed the year 1939 with completions of all work voted by the town in its annual meeting which the regulations would permit.

Due to the application of many changes enacted into law by the last session of Congress there have been slight interruptions in the operation of W. P. A. work at various times making it all-in-all a somewhat hectic year.

The invoking of the eighteen months continuous assignment law being the cause for dismissal was undoubtedly the most sweeping and least understood. The impression was given that the workers would be laid off for a period of thirty days, in reality it was a discharge and the worker was obliged to go through the complete procedure of a new case. On account of this law there are persons in Rockland who were laid off in August and have not been reassigned as yet by Boston Headquarters. This in itself has been the cause of increasing the town welfare burden for which purpose it has been generally understood the W. P. A. was operated to reduce.

Another change in the operation of the W. P. A. the past year is in the assignment of persons to work which is now carried on direct from Boston Headquarters without local request and is the cause of furthur complications.

Another new law is the increase of sponsor contributions to a minimum of twenty-five percent of the total project which has eliminated the availability of many former worth while projects and curtailed the source for new projects. It is hoped that the new Congress will enact or amend the present legislation to overcome these handicaps in the efficient operation of the W. P. A. from the federal and local angle.

The largest project operated in 1939 was a continuation of the installation of permanent sidewalks. The program adopted in 1938 of the cement curb and bituminous walk on at least one side of practically every street in town and both sides of streets leading from the business section was continued. Installation has been made upon forty-three streets in the town the past year making a total of 7 2/3 miles at a cost to the town of $19,512. The federal government has contributed for sidewalks 1500 bags of cement with a value of $1,018.75.

Other projects operated during the year included Vital Statistics, High School Sewer, Water Mains, Emerson Street Bridge, Wright's Brook Drain, Hurricane Cleanup, High School Drive, Engineering Survey, Reed's Pond Improvement, Pre-School Unit, Sewing, Housekeeping Aide, Recreation and Commodity Distribution. With the exception of the Pre-School, Sewing, Housekeeping Aide, Recreation and Commodity Distribution, which expenses have been carried by W. P. A. General Fund, the sponsor expense has been very near $7,000.00.

The year 1939 opened with 354 on W. P. A. payrolls and closed with 289. The smallest number to receive W. P. A. checks was the week of August 23, to 30, 1939 when 207 persons were on the payroll. The largest number working was the week ending March 15, when 393, were employed. The largest W. P. A. weekly payroll was $6,659.44. The payroll for the year was in excess of $200,709. This figure brings the total pay checks in Rockland since August 1, 1934, when the federal emergency relief act went into operation, in excess of $980,559 close to a million dollars.

Last August the W. P. A. Headquarters were moved to the Gladstone Block with the Town Offices. This has worked to advantage as it has centralized all inside projects with added working room and more accessible to the public.

During the past year the W. P. A. has been called upon for volunteers· for blood transfusions and the response has been very gratifying. Over fifty men have been charted for "type of blood," and fifteen men have given transfusions.

In common with municipalities throughout the state· the Recreation Project under the supervision of Norman Crosby has made rapid progress in attendance and in scope. Particularly noticeable is the interest manifested by the young people which will undoubtedly have an influence on their social standing in the years to come.

The Housekeeping Aide Project under the supervision of Miss Lois Williams and Miss Meredith O'Hara, has given 12,240 work hours assistance to families in Rockland. This is one of these projects that does a world of good that cannot be publicized.

The sewing Unit in McKinley School Building under the supervision of Miss Helen Purcell has continued its good work and has made a variety of garments totaling 12,931 peice which includes nearly five thousand girl's dresses and three thousand men's shirts, that have been distributed to the needy.

The Commodity Distribution division, in charge of Mr. John J. Bowler assisted by Mrs. Lillian Ransford, has operated smoothly and more expediously in its new quarters in the basement of the Gladstone block. It has distributed 19,312 pieces of clothing and 25,056 cans and 314,563 pounds of food articles to Rockland families.

It is with regret that I understand that Mr. Roderick MacKenzie will not be our Higway Surveyor in 1940, as I will greatly miss his advice and cooperation. His assistance has been a vital factor in the operation of out-door projects.

In meeting the many sudden changes and new laws in relation to the operation of the W. P. A., I am deeply indebted to Mr. John M. Brennan, Mr. Loring Jacobs and Mrs. Muriel Godfrey, district Federal supervisors, for their co-operation and assistance.

For the coming year I would suggest a continuance of the permanent sidewalk program that has proved so beneficial. Also the widening of many streets by the treating of the gutters on each side with bituminouus surfacing giving about eight feet of additional travelled way. The rebuilding of Exchange Street should be included for the program for 1940 to safe-guard the town from damages.

Respectfully submitted,
FRED M. RYAN,
Sponsor W. P. A. Agent for Rockland

Report of Highway Surveyor

To the Honorable Board of Selectmen

I wish to report that all of the work covered by the various appropriations granted to the Highway Department has been completed.

This work included making necessary repairs to various streets, putting on tarvia, and cleaning out catch basins and drains. During the year a number of sidewalks were completed in various sections of the town as W. P. A. projects.

Two bridges were constructed on West Water street in co-operation with the state and county.

RODERICK MacKENZIE,
Highway Surveyor

Report of Trustees of Memorial Library

The trustees of the Memorial Library submit the following report for 1939:

Two improvements were made in the interior of the building. Lighting in the north reading room being insufficient, three new lights with 500 watt bulbs were installed. The librarian's office was fitted with Venetian blinds.

Of interest to the patrons of the library were the exhibits. The excellent one of the art department of the schools was noteworthy, as was Mrs. Joseph Lelyveld's collection of dolls.

The continuing interest of the Rockland Woman's club in the library was shown by its gift of five dollars and a membership card. The trustees thank the club, and also the Garden Club and others who have contributed books.

By the death of Mr. W. G. Holbrook a vacancy occurred in the position of janitor. This was filled by the election of Mr. E. H. Totman, who had been substituting with entire satisfaction during the illness of Mr. Holbrook.

Income from the trust funds was paid out as follows:

Hattie Curtis Fund	$ 13 67
Zenas M. Lane Fund	15 00
Alice L. French Fund	12 26
Everett Lane Fund	2 32
Charles Edwin Vinal Fund	25 16
Mary A. Spence Fund	12 70
Sarah J. Spence Fund	7 74
John W. Rice Fund	10 06
John A. Martin Fund	3 15
Mothers' Mutual Improvement Society Fund	1 33
	$103 39

These withdrawals left on deposit in the Rockland Savings Bank, December 31, 1939:

Hattie Curtis Fund	$500	20
Zenas M. Lane Fund	500	56
Alice L. French Fund	500	32
Everett Lane Fund	100	25
Charles Edwin Vinal Fund	1 000	15
Mary A. Spence Fund	500	25
Sarah J. Spence Fund	300	51
John W. Rice Fund	400	18
John A. Martin Fund	100	16
Mothers' Mutual Improvement Society Fund	50	11

The terms of Francis F. Geogan and Emma W. Gleason expire in 1940.

An appropriation of $4650 plus the dog refund of $407.04 is recommended for 1940.

FRANCIS J. GEOGAN,
JOHN B. FITZGERALD,
BURTON L. CUSHING,
EMMA W. GLEASON,
ANNIE E. McILVENE,
EMILY F. CRAWFORD,
Trustees

Librarians Report

To the Trustees of the Rockland Memorial Library:
The sixty-first report of this library is herewith submitted.

A total of 60516 books and magazines have been loaned for home use.

The average monthly circulation, 5043. The average

daily circulation 206.   Largest number delivered in one day, 387. Smallest numbered delivered in one day, 69.

Received for fines, reserved books, sale of cook books, subscriptions from non-residents, old   magazines   and books, $356.

Number of books added by purchase (including replacements), 421.   Number of books presented, 35. Number of books worn out and missing 120.   Number of books rebound, 48.   Number of books in library December 31, 1939, 21,436.

Character of books loaned: Literature 4 per cent; history and travel 4 per cent; biography, 3 per cent; miscellaneous (adult) 6 per cent; fiction (adult) 53 per cent; fiction (juvenile), 15 per cent; miscellaneous (juvenile), 6 per cent; magazines 9 per cent.

The Public Library has doubtless meant more to many of our people, the past year, than ever before.   It is useful to so many different people in so many different ways. The very process of reading, through the impetus it gives the mind, enriches the quality of public thought and adds to the sturdiness of the town character.   However, it is sometimes hard to make the public realize this and thus give the support that should go with it.

One of the greatest pleasures of writing reports is the opportunity for recording the library's thanks for the generosity of its friends during the year.   Outstanding was the specialized books on gardening from the Rockland Garden Club, and the generous amount of money from the Rockland Woman's Club from which we purchased one of the highlights of the year, "Masterpieces of Art."

We also make acknowledgement of and express cordial thanks for other books and pamphlets of value to the library.

The public demands bring about changes in our periodicals, and from our point of view a more scholarly quality is in demand.

All the latest books are not available nor are even a small part of them on hand exactly when we wish them, but the reserve priviledge is well patronized, and we borrow from neighboring libraries if the demand warrants.

Our reference department has increased its demands, and many of the reserved books for reference are kept in the stack room. From here we search through the books, with the student, showing him the best technique in locating references with the least, possible expenditure of time. Also in the children's room the reference work has been busy, and very often all the chairs about the tables will be filled with boys and girls from the Junior High school busily working on school assignments.

During book week the Library puts forth an effort to become better acquainted with its patrons and to present to them at least a few new books of the season. An exhibit somewhat different from those we have had in former years was the display of dolls, loaned by Mrs. Joseph Lelyveld. Coming from all over the world fitted in well with the theme for book week, "Around the world with books."

Displays of various kinds for young and old create an atmosphere of informality. Our Bethleham scene at Christmas was noted, the "World's Fair" posters and especially the splendid exhibit of the art department of the schools, which could hardly be credited to pupils of their age.

We also gave the new books a chance to prove their worth against old time favorites by having an exhibit of the latter from time to time, since these books have not so good a shelf location as we might wish.

Magazine files have been used more than ever before

to answer questions on government, legislation and foreign and domestic political affairs. With political, economy and social history being made daily, current material plays a much greater part in reference work than writings of the past. In these times of fast moving and momentous world events the demands of the general reader as well as of the student require all the reference knowledge that can be gathered.

Many favorable comments have been passed upon our new lights in the north reading room. This room now is in a condition to attract and serve the public in increasingly better manner.

Early in the year Girl Scouts visited the library in connection with one of their projects, learning the system of classification, cataloguing, and use of reference books. Later your librarian visited the High School library to offer a few suggestions to the new student workers. We were also glad to have one of the grade schools visit our library, with their teacher. Many of these children had never before been to the library, but since their visit many have taken out cards and become regular borrowers.

Our whole demand for books is affected by what is happening today at home and abroad, and our library must attempt to be an impartial provider on as many new questions and problems, now before the public, as possible. Our citizens are concerned with government and the library should do much to foster that interest.

I have tried to give all a voice in the library's policy, and I have felt that each one considered that the maintenance of the good name of the library is a part of his responsibility.

Respectfully submitted,

LIDA A. CLARK,
Librarian

Assessors Report 1939

The Assessors have assessed the sum of $318,987.90 upon the Polls and Property subject to taxation in the Town of Rockland and have committed said sum to the Collector for collection.

Number of Polls assessed		2691
Value Real Estate assessed	$5 647 855	
Value Land assessed	1 540 045	
Total Value Real Estate including land	$7 187 900	**00**

VALUE PERSONAL PROPERTY

Value of Stock in Trade	$ 172 640	00
Value of Live Stock	14 755	00
Value of Machinery	34 225	00
Value of all other Personal	447 781	00
Total Value Personal Property	669 401	00

Total Valuation Real and Personal Property 7 857 301 00

Town Appropriations	406 765	08
Appropriations from Available Funds	79 715	91
State Tax	24 660	00
Underestimate 1938 State Tax	12 330	00
County Tax	14 518	60
Underestimate County Tax 1938	30	90
Hospital Tax	60	00
State Parks and Reservations	452	62
Overlays	15 216	23
Auditing Municipal Accounts	454	54
State Parks and Reservations Underestimate 1938	27	32

Tuberculosis Hospital   4 427 35

            $558 658 55

ESTIMATED RECEIPTS

Income Tax	25 410	62
Corporation Taxes	12 259	69
Motor Vehicle Excise	15 872	33
Licenses	5 190	00
Fines	124	80
General Government	335	50
Health and Sanitation	645	00
Charities	24 071	49
Old Age Assistance	30 898	08
Schools	2 602	88
Libraries	340	00
Water Department	29 500	00
Tax Costs	284	83
Interest	6 940	36
Veterans Exemptions	241	78
Refund Compensation Policy	527	90
Chapter 504 Acts 1939	13 737	94
Poll Taxes	5 382	00
Appropriations from Available Funds	85 715	91

Total Estimated Receipts $260 081 11

Total amount to be raised on Property   298 577 44

Tax Rate Per Thousand $38.00

Number of Motor Vehicles and Trailers assessed	2519
Value of Motor Vehicles and Trailers	$488 945 00
Number Persons assessed on Personal Estate only	197
On Real Estate only	1812
On both Personal and Real Estate	110
Total Number of Persons assessed	2119
Number of Dwellings	1887

Number of Cows   82
Number of Horses   14
Number of Yearlings, Bulls, etc.   8
Number of Swine   101
Number of Fowl   7450
Number of Acres   5745

AMOUNTS COMMITTED TO COLLECTOR

Real and Personal $298 577 44
Water Liens   741 84
Poll Tax   5 382 00
December Assessments on Polls   12 00
Excise Tax   14 274 62

Total $318 987 90
Respectfully submitted,
NORMAN J. BEALS,
DENNIS L. O'CONNOR,
JOSEPH B. ESTES,
Board of Assessors

Report of Committee to Revise and Re-draft By-Laws of the Town of Rockland

Your committee appointed to revise and re-draft the By-Laws of the Town of Rockland has been in correspondence with towns of comparable population and has secured copies of the By-Laws of said towns.

We find in all but one of the towns contacted, that like ouselves, there has been no revision of By-Laws for the past thirty years or more.

In that one town, Ludlow, Mass., a special committee made a most exhaustive study and presented to their town in 1937 a very complete and up-to-date set of By-

Laws which up until the present time have failed of acceptance by the voters of that town.

Because of the detail and study necessary to properly
present to the town By-Laws which would be adequate
and acceptable to the voters we respectfully request that
we be given further time to prepare our re-draft and revision to be reported at some future town meeting.

Respectfully submitted,

FRANCIS J. GEOGAN, Chairman
HARRY S. TORREY,
DENNIS L. O'CONNOR,
JAMES P. KANE,
RALPH L. BELCHER, Secretary
Committee

Report of Infirmary

To the Honorable Board of Selectmen
Gentlemen:

I hereby report the activities which have taken place
during the year 1939.

We have taken care of twenty-seven inmates during the
year, the youngest being four months and the oldest
eighty-nine.

Three deaths have taken place, all men.
At the present time we have fourteen inmates, twelve
men and two women.

Respectfully submitted,

EARL W. WYATT,
Supt. of the Infirmary

Report of the Board of Sewer Commissioners for the Year 1939

The State Board of Health still keeps bringing to our attention the fact that the Town of Rockland should have a System of Sewerage and their engineers have from time to time called on this Board in furtherance of this fact.

Early in the year Sanitary conditions at the Junior-Senior High school building were not satisfactory and Plans of the system as approved for installation were furished the School Committee at its request.

Mr. E. Worthington of Dedham, the Engineer who assisted in securing the Federal Grant for Sewer System here in 1938-1939 has not yet been paid for his services in that connection and has requested us to bring this to the attention of the town.

When he presented his bill to the Town a year ago, the Selectmen had no specific funds for this project and upon consultation with Town Counsel notified him that they could not pay this bill. This Board feels that Mr. Worthington is entitled to his pay as it was largely due to his services and suggestions that we received the Federal Grant of One Hundred and Sixty-Two Thousand Dollars ($162,000.00) Altho the Town refused this grant, Mr. Worthington was successful on his part for the town. "The laborer is worthy of his hire."

Again in October conditions were such at the Junior-Senior High School building that at the request of the School Superintendent, the State Board of Health was asked for advice and suggestions to help us care for unsatisfactory conditions. The State Board sent us their Regional Engineer, Mr. Doggett. He, with Mr. Brennan, Regional Federal Engineer, made examination of premises, filter bed, etc. They were to take up the matter with the State Board of Health.

On Dec. 22nd, last, we lost our esteemed fellow member and friend Chairman Frederick Hall who had served as chairman of the Board for fifteen years. His death was a personal loss to use and to the entire community as well. A man, of integrity and ability, a willing worker and a faithful friend, we hold his memory in higest esteem.

At a joint meeting of the Sewer Commissioners and Board of Selectmen, Neal J. Lioy was chosen to act as Sewer Commissioner until his successor be chosen at the March Meeting.

Respectfully submitted,
GILES W. HOWLAND,
CHARLES M. HINES,
NEAL J. LIOY,
Sewer Commissioners.

In Memoriam

FREDERICK HALL

Chairman of Sewer Commissioners

A faithful and capable town officer, an upright and valuable citizen. We regret his passing and honor his memory.

Board of Sewer Commissioners

Sealer of Weights and Measures

To the Honorable Board of Selectmen
Gentlemen:

I have with my standard weights and measures tested and sealed all weighing and measuring devices which I have jurisdiction over also several scales for private use.

Inspections and weighing of merchandise which is put up for sale and delivery were also made, also all gas meters were retested. The inspection and resealing of these measuring devices is an important item after sealing.

Frequently inspections of all stores in town that have measuring devices are made. Computing scales need attention as in most cases they are found to be incorrect. I see to the fact that the pedlers and transient vendors laws are enforced and make sure all are properly licensed. The town receives the fund from these licenses.

The oil meters on oil trucks are another item which have to be checked more carefully on account of the increasing sale of oil.

I have co-operated sincerely all year with the Division of Standards and Necessities of Life.

The duties of a Sealer of Weights and Measures increase yearly and I am on call at all times. My duties are under State and Town regulations.

Following is an itemized account of the work I have performed for the year 1939:

	Adjusted	Sealed	Not Sealed	Condemned
Scales over 10,000 lbs.	3	4		
Platform over 5000 lbs.				
Platform 100 to 5000 lbs.	19	40	2	
Counter 100 lbs or over	1	3		
Counter under 100 lbs.	6	34		
Beam 100 lbs. or over		1		
Beam under 100 lbs.		1		
Spring 100 lbs. or over	4	9		
Spring under 100 lbs.	14	46	2	
Computing 100 lbs. or over				
Computing under 100 lbs.	20	57		
Personal Weighing	1	11		
Prescription		4		

WEIGHTS

Avoirdupois	8	319
Apothecary		48
Metric		42

CAPACITY MEASURES

Liquid	58	4
	5 Liquid over 1 gal.	

AUTOMATIC MEASURING DEVICES

Oil Meters	1	7	1
Gasoline Pumps		4	3
Gasoline Meters	8	63	2
Kerosene Pumps		10	1
Oil Measuring Pumps		19	19
Quantity Measure on Pumps	4	58	

Cloth Measuring Device 2
Yard Sticks 32
Molasses Measuring Devices 1 1

TOTAL UNITS SEALED

Total units sealed 878
Weighing and measuring devices adjusted 89
Weighing and measuring devices condemned 10
Weighing and measuring devices not sealed 35

Sealing fees returned to Town Treasurer $114 52
Due to Treasurer 20

REWEIGHING AND REMEASURING

Number correct 213
Number tested 254
Over wight 5
Under weight 36

Respectfully submitted,

HAROLD J. INKLEY

Report of
Inspector of Animals and Stables

To the Honorable Board of Selectmen:
Gentlemen:

I herewith submit my report as Inspector of Animals and Stables, for the year ending December 31, 1939.

Number of Stables inspected 36
Number of Cows inspected 123
Number of Swine inspected 403
Number of Goats inspected 6

Number of Sheep inspected	1
Number of visits made in inspections	111
Number of Dogs quarantined	15
Number of visits made to premises of quarantined animals	75

Respectfully submitted,

WILLIAM T. CONDON,
Inspector of Animals and Stables

Report of Supervisor of Old Age Assistance

There is at present 320 recipients of the Old Age Assistance in the Town of Rockland. The majority are living in their own homes, with some six or seven in Rest Homes.

When an applicant applies for Assistance they should have with them their birth record, all marriage records, proof of citizenship, proof of 5 years residence in Massachusetts out of the last nine years, and all insurance policies. An applicant may have $300 in the Bank, and an equity of $3000 in property, on which they must reside. If they own property in excess of $3000, a bond may be given to the Town for the difference on which no interest has to be paid.

The State Bureau of Old Age Assistance recently changed their set up, and where we were under the Boston district, we now are under the jurisdiction of Brockton, with weekly visits from Supervisors, so that cases will be handled more quickly and once accepted will be final, unless the financial situation of the recipient changes.

Many cases have to be disallowed because of the earnings of children, who should contribute to the support of parents, and we were advised by recent State and Federal auditors, that if children refuse this responsibility, the case should be taken into court.

It must be remembered by applicants whose cases have been denied, that while the local Board may be disposed in their favor, if rejected by the State, there is nothing we can do until the present status is changed.

I wish to express my appreciation to the Board of Public Welfare for their co-operation during the past year.

Respectfully submitted,

MARY L. O'BRIEN

Report of Collector of Taxes

Taxes of 1936

Outstanding, January 1, 1939	$ 810 91
Collected during year	$ 810 91

1936 Motor Vehicle Excise

Oustanding January 1, 1939	$ 221 65
Collected during year	$ 221 65

Taxes of 1937

Outstanding January 1, 1939	$67 070 18
Collected during the year	66 325 72
Outstanding January 1, 1940	$ 744 46

1937 Motor Vehicle Excise

Outstanding January 1, 1939	$ 1 608	66
Collected during year	1 021	74
Outstanding January 1, 1940	$ 586	92

Taxes of 1938

Outstanding January 1, 1939	$113 470	62
Collected during year	47 252	01
Outstanding January 1, 1940	$ 66 218	61

Water Liens added to 1938 Real Estate Taxes

Outstanding January 1, 1939	$ 1 401	40
Collected during year	308	78
Outstanding January 1, 1940	$ 1 092	62

1938 Motor Vehicle Excise*

Outstanding January 1, 1939	$ 659	67
Collected during year	287	46
Outstanding January 1, 1940	$ 372	21

Taxes of 1939

Amount committed to Collector	$278 534	20
Collected during year	174 173	75
Outstanding January 1, 1940	$104 360	45
Water Liens added to 1939 Real Estate Taxes	$ 741	84
Collected during year	104	82
Outstanding January 1, 1940	$ 637	02

1939 Motor Vehicle Excise

Amount committed to Collector	$14 274	62
Collected during year	13 317	29
Outstanding January 1, 1940	$ 957	33

1939 Personal Tax

Amount committed to Collector	$25 437	24
Collected during year	20 071	17
Outstanding January 1, 1940	$ 5 366	07

Water Liens

Outstanding January 1, 1939	756	95
Amounts committed during year	402	84
Total	1 159	79

Amounts re-committed with 1939 Real Estate
   Taxes   741 84
Total of Water Liens not yet added
   to Real Estate Taxes   417 95
Paid during year to collector $113 16
Payments made direct to Treasurer   49 04
       $ 162 20

Outstanding January 1, 1940 $ 255 75

Respectfully submitted,

JAMES A. DONOVAN,

Collector of Taxes

Report of Town Treasurer

Treasurer's Report of the Receipts and Disbursements for the year 1939.

January 1, 1939, cash on hand $130 749 63

RECEIPTS

Anticipation Tax Notes	$250 000 00
Taxes, Real Estate, Personal	
and Poll	291 038 48
Taxes, Excise	14 008 39
Taxes, Interest	6 562 18
Taxes, Costs	343 10
Tax Titles Redeemed	6 341 84
Licenses, Liquor, etc	4 718 00
Licenses, Miscellaneous	675 00
Trust Funds (Cemetery)	1 437 10
Dog Licenses	496 40
Water Department	27 702 52
Joint Water Department	7 946 22
Memorial Library	356 00
Sealer of Weights	114 52
School Department	239 40
Court Fines	385 90
City of Boston, Tuition	304 64
Unearned Comp. Ins. premium	415 40
Fire Department, sale building	40 00
Miscellaneous, Infirmary,	
Highway	69 61
Sales and rents, R. E. owned	
by town	1 383 50
Loan, Anticipation Fire	
Station Grant	6 000 00
Loan, Anticipation Funds	
West Water Street, Cons.	4 000 00

Federal Grant, Fire Station   21 000 00

$645 578 20

COUNTY TREASURER

Dog Dividend	$	415 50
E. Water St., Construction		601 46
W. Water St., Construction		1 108 53

2 125 49

$778 453 32

Welfare and Old Age Assistance
Towns and Cities $ 8 356 58

State Treasurer

Old Age Assistance	$35 037 98
Temporary Aid	9 021 36
Aid to Schools	641 35
Tuition of Children	978 15
Public Health	1 531 29
Aid to Dependent Mothers	1 423 33
State Aid	514 00
Military Aid	100 00
Mass Hospital School	26 57
Income Tax	24 687 32
Corporation Tax	8 458 56
Veteran's Exemption	211 86
U. S. Grant Old Age Assistance	51 237 06
U. S. Grant Aid to Children	2 822 51
Chap. 232 Highway Fund	13 737 94
E. Water St. Construction	1 202 92
W. Water St., Construction	2 217 06

$153 849 26

$940 659 16

PAYMENTS

Selectmen's Warrants	$185 869 38	
Public Welfare and Mother's aid	61 814 01	
School Department	105 199 39	
Old Age Assistance	54 990 47	
Old Age Assistance, U. S. Grant	50 893 66	
Old Age Administration, U. S. Grant	1 707 31	
Water Department Warrant	23 661 31	
Joint Water Dept. Warrant	10 674 83	
Town Abington, Joint Rates	1 304 40	
Tax Refunds	384 11	
Aid to Dependent Mothers',		
U. S. Grant	1 142 00	
Cemetery Trust Funds	1 437 10	
Anticipation Tax Notes	275 000 00	
McKinley School appropriations	550 00	
Fire Station	57 499 86	
Mothers' Aid Administration		
U. S. Grant	44 00	
		$832 171 83

County Treasurer		
County Tax	14 518 60	
Dog Licenses	493 40	
		15 012 00
		$847 183 83

Commonwealth of Massachusetts		
State Tax	24 660 00	
Care C. W. Veterans	105 00	
Auditing Accounts	454 54	
State Parks	405 87	
		25 625 41

Cash on hand, December 31, 1939   67 849 92

$940 659 16

OUTSTANDING INDEBTEDNESS

Anticipation
Revenue Notes $100 000 00
Federal Grant Fire Station   6 000 00
State and County Funds
  W. Water St.   4 000 00

$110 000 00

PERMANENT LOANS

Junior Senior School Bonds
3¾% Maturing $10,000
annually 1940-1943   40 000 00
3¾% Maturing $6,000
  annually 1940-1948   54 000 00
                                                  94 000 00
Plymouth County Hospital Note
5% maturing $1000 1940   1 000 00
Union Street Construction Notes
2% maturing 1940-1946   23 000 00
Water Tank Construction
2% maturing 1940-1956   34 000 00
Municipal Relief, Loan Chap. 58
1½% maturing 1940-1948   30 000 00
Fire Station Notes
2¼% maturing 1940-1958   32 000 00

FIRE STATION DOCKET 1440

Jan. 1, 1939 Balance $32 253 99
Federal Grant   21 000 00
Temporary Loan   6 000 00

$59 253 99

Payments	57 862 46

Unexpended balance, Dec. 31, 1939	$ 1 391 53

JOINT WATER DEPARTMENT

Receipts

From Joint Rates etc	$	608 80
From Abington ½ Maintenance		337 42
From Rockland ½ maintenance	9	337 41

	$13 283 63

Payments

Warrants	$10 674 83
½ Joint Rates to Abington	1 304 40
½ Joint Rates to Rockland	1 304 40

	$13 283 63

WATER DEPARTMENT

Receipts

Rates, Construction etc	$27 702 52
½ Joint Rates	1 304 40

	$29 006 92

Payments

Warrants	23 661 31
½ Cost Joint Maintenance	5 337 41
Receipts over payment	8 20

	$29 006 92

ASSETS

Accounts Receivable:

Cash		$ 67 849 92
Taxes 1937	744 46	
Taxes 1938	66 218 61	
Taxes 1939	104 360 45	
		171 323 52
Motor Excise		
1937	586 92	
1938	372 21	
1939	957 33	
		1 916 46
Water Liens		1 985 39
Tax Titles and Real Estate Owned		11 704 48
		$254 779 77

LIABILITIES

Anticipation Revenue Loans	$100 000 00
Anticipation Federal Grant	6 000 00
Unexpended Balances	11 806 13
Real Estate Fund	5 190 00
War Tax Fund	4 021 70
Surplus Revenue	127 761 94
	$254 779 77

CEMETERY TRUST FUNDS

Bequest	Cemetery	Balance Jan. 1, 1939	Deposited During 1939	Income	Expended	Balance Dec. 31, 1939
Jeremiah Hy	St. Patricks	$100 00		$ 2 51	$	$102 51
Mary Spence	St. Patricks	404 28		10 16		414 44
Margaret Smith	St. Patricks	100 00		2 51		102 51
Patrick McCaffrey	St. Patricks	107 52		2 68		110 20
James H. O'Connell	St. Patricks	101 11		2 53		103 64
Gallagher-Driscoll	St. Patricks	233 13		5 86		238 99
John Ford	St. Patricks	473 93		11 89		485 82
Mary Gallagher	St. Patricks	101 11		2 53		103 64
Catherine McIntyre	St. Patricks	202 26		5 07		207 33
Daniel Sullivan	St. Patricks	101 11		2 53		103 64
Patrick Cullinan	St. Patricks	75 08		1 88		76 96
George Hatch	St. Patricks	101 11		2 53		103 64
James Crowley	St. Patricks	101 11		2 53		103 64
Margaret D. Quinlan	St. Patricks	202 26		5 07		207 33
Daniel Crowley	St. Patricks	101 11		2 53		103 64
Bridget Conway	St. Patricks	110 75		2 77		113 52
Patrick O'Hern	St. Patricks	50 04		1 24		51 28
Daniel H. Lynch	St. Patricks	101 11		2 53		103 64
Nicholas Dell	St. Patricks	101 11		2 53		103 64
James Maguire	St. Patricks.	101 11		2 53		103 64

CEMETERY TRUST FUNDS - Continued

Bequest	Cemetery	Balance Jan. 1, 1939	Deposited During 1939	Income	Expended	Balance Dec. 31, 1939
Ellen Sullivan	St. Parks	50 04		1 24		51 28
Mary J. Coughlin	St. Patricks	101 06		2 53		103 59
Katherine E. Crowley	St. Patricks	202 26		5 07		207 33
Nel Sullivan	St. Patricks	101 11		2 53		103 64
Wm Mth	St. Patricks	100 82				1 0 82
James Tangney	St. Patricks	202 26		5 07		207 33
Catherine E. O'Brien	St. Patricks	101 11		2 53		103 64
Thas Russell	St. Patricks	101 11		2 53		103 64
Timothy Kelliher	St. Patricks	151 18		3 79		154 97
Mary J. Samuels	St. Patricks	202 26		5 07		207 33
William B. Burke	St. Patricks	50 54		1 25		51 79
Henry Lyons	St. Patricks	101 11		2 53		103 64
Sarah J. Spence	St. Patricks	404 53		10 16		414 69
William Fitzgerald	St. Patricks	101 11		2 53		103 64
Thas J. Fin	St. Patricks	101 11		2 53		103 64
John Leahy	St. Patricks	202 26		5 07		207 33
John Parker	St. Patricks	85 98		2 14		88 12
Thas J. Lynch	Holy Family	125 14		3 13		128 27
Fah Santry	Holy Family	202 26		5 07		207 33
Ana B. Rogers	Holy Family	100 11		2 51		102 62

CEMETERY TRUST FUNDS - Continued

Bequest	Cary	Balance Jan. 1, 1939	Deposited During 1939	Income	Expended	Balance Dec. 31, 1939
John T. Ford	Holy Family		300 00	3 13		300 00
Mary Clancey	Holy Family	125 08		3 13		128 21
John W. Cullinan	Holy Family	125 14		2 53		128 27
Mary E. Kelley	Holy Family	101 11		2 73		103 64
Frederic Dill	Mt. Pleasant	109 47		2 65	4 00	108 20
Ernest M. Paine	Mt. Pleasant	106 11		2 61	2 00	106 76
Guy L. Keene	Mt. Pleasant	104 11		2 63	4 00	102 72
Wallace Damon	Mt. Pleasant	105 33		5 83		107 96
Collins-Branson	Mt. Pleasant	232 77		3 42	4 00	234 60
Elvira S. Holmes	Mt. Pleasant	141 67		2 08	10 00	135 09
C. A. Johnston	Mt. Pleasant	83 51		6 06	2 00	83 59
Henry Chase	Mt. Pleasant	241 26		1 51	4 00	243 32
Emma Hutchinson	Mt. Pleasant	60 54		6 13	2 00	60 05
A. Hilton Studley	Mt. Pleasant	246 26		2 88	8 00	244 39
William G. Perry	Mt. Pleasant	115 27		2 51	2 00	116 15
Gardner-Damon	Mt. Pleasant	100 00		2 51	2 51	100 00
Charles H. Poole	Mt. Pleasant	100 00		3 47	2 51	100 00
Howard Carr	Mt. Pleasant	138 83		2 99	2 00	140 30
Charles G. Turner	Mt. Pleasant	119 95		2 58	2 00	120 94
Eric Shaw	Mt. Pleasant	103 64			2 00	104 22

CEMETERY TRUST FUNDS - Continued

Bequest	Cemetery	Balance Jan. 1, 1939	Deposited During 1939	Income	Expended	Balance Dec. 31, 1939
Kie Man	Mt. Pleasant	100 76		2 50	2 00	101 26
Burrell-Douglas	Mt. Pleasant		100 00	1 04	1 04	100 0
Soranus Holbrook Lot	Mt. Pleasant		150 00	31		150 31
Reveire-Briggs	Mt. Pleasant		100 00	1 04		101 04
J. H. Lot	Mt. Pleasant		150 00	1 56		151 56
McManus-Horne	Mt. Plant	51.85		1 28	1 00	52 13
A. A. Crooker	Mt. Plant	135 77		3 39	2 00	137 16
Frank P. Lewis	Mt. Pleasant	53 13		1 32	3 50	50 95
James J. Donaldson	Mt. Plant	328 04		8 25	4 00	332 29
Henry G. Multon	Mt. Plant	554 98		13 93	4 00	564 91
Marsena Lovell, Heirs	Mt. Pleasant	128 77		3 22	2 00	129 99
E. W. Whiting	Mt. Pleasant	156 69		3 92	4 00	156 61
Fidelia Estes	Mt. Plant	310 15		7 79	7 00	310 94
Emma L.	M Pleasant	104 80		2 62	2 00	105 42
Abbie F. Merrill	Mt. Pleasant	206 60		5 18	4 00	207 78
Eben P. Everett	Mt. Pleasant	88 02		2 21	2 00	88 23
Frank, Geo. Lawrence	M. Plant	176 94		4 36	6 00	175 30
Thomas-Litchfield	Mt. Plant	232 56		5 83	10 00	228 39
Andw Me	Mt. Pleasant	115 33		2 88	2 00	116 21
Edward Crane	Mt. Pleasant	181 60		4 51	3 00	183 11

CEMETERY TRUST FUNDS - Cont'nal

Bequest	Cemetery	Balance Jan. 1, 1939	Deposited During 1939	Income	Expended	Balance Dec. 31, 1939
L. Evelyn Dill	Mt. Pleasant	130 90		3 27		134 17
Reuben Ellis	Mt. Pleasant	109 93		2 74	2 00	110 67
H. J. Cushing	Mt. Pleasant	107 53		2 68	2 00	108 21
Harold B. Vesper	Mt. Pleasant	100 81		2 52	2 00	101 33
Alvin G. Bates	Mt. Pleasant	00 0		1 66	1 66	100 00
Samuel M. Watts	Mt. Pleasant		100 00			100 00
Fannie H. Turner	Mt. Pleasant	318 52		7 99	6 00	320 51
Easton Lot No. 249	Mt. Pleasant	107 58		2 68	2 00	108 26
Henry D. Smith	Mt. Pleasant	100 00		2 51	2 00	100 51
Francis Soule	Mt. Pleasant	100 00		2 51	2 00	100 51
George T. Poole	Mt. Pleasant	317 95		7 97	6 00	319 92
Dl- hap	Mt. Pleasant	215 78		5 40		221 18
Elias A. Burrell	Mt. Pleasant	102 95		2 57	2 00	103 52
John Stoddard	Mt. Ple asnt	76 88		1 91	2 00	76 79
Emma M. Gy	Mt. Pleasant	104 22		2 61	2 00	104 83
L. Wilfred Poole	Mt. Pleasant	103 82		2 55	3 00	103 37
Mary H. Breck	Mt. Pleasant	106 10		2 65	2 00	06 75
Uuie Linton	Mt. Pleasant	106 31		2 65	2 00	106 96
Thompson-Whiting	Maplewood	122 53		3 07	2 25	123 35
J. M. He-C. bat	Maplewood	345 66		8 67	12 18	342 15

CEMETERY TRUST FUNDS - Continued

Name		Balance Jan. 1, 1939	Deposited During 1939	Income	Expended	Balance Dec. 31, 1939
Phillips-Goodspeed		101 26		2 53	2 25	103 79
Aha	Maplewood	129 65		3 24		130 64
Flora		50 00		1 24	2 25	51 24
W. Harris	Maplewood	130 51		3 27	2 25	131 53
Leander Torrey	Maplewood	125 27		3 13		126 15
A. Beal	Maplewood	100 03		2 51		102 54
allis	Mapl		150 00			150 00
Edgar L. Hps	Mapl		150 00			150 00
Hopkins-Damon		100 82		2 52		103 34
I. tz		10 13		2 75		112 88
ta Son		556 97		13 82	17 50	553 29
William T. r	Maplewood	104 55		2 61	4 25	102 91
leitt	Mapl	101 25		2 53		103 78
Stoddard-Loud	Maplewood	166 65		4 17		170 32
Phillips	Mapl	50 33		1 24		51 57
Davis	Mapl	345 10		8 67	3 00	350 77
Mrs. Elbridge Whiting	Mapl	120 17		3 01	2 25	120 93
D. W. cobs		166 20		4 17	2 25	168 12
Wing	Maplewood	70 30		1 75	2 25	69 80
niel Hps		163 26		4 09	3 00	64 35

CEMETERY TRUST FUNDS — Continued

Bequest	City	Balance Jan. 1, 1939	Deposited during 1939	Income		Balance Dec. 31, 1939
... Everson	Maple ...	101 25		2 53		103 78
... A. Baker	Spring Lake	100 00		2 51	2 51	00 00
...os A. Reed	Spring Lake	150 00		3 74	3 74	150 00
...ie Doane	Spring Lake	102 21		2 55	4 00	00 76
Zenas	Spring Lake	110 95		2 77	4 00	109 72
	Spring Lake	152 56		3 82	3 82	152 56
... I. Burgess	Spring Lake	125 00		3 13	3 13	125 00
Elbridge Payne	Mill	331 36		8 31		339 67
Betsey Battles	Beal	246 68		6 14	9 00	243 82
Wm J. ...	Assinippi	109 22		2 73		11 95

CHARLES I. HIGGINS,

INDEX

Lightning Source UK Ltd.
Milton Keynes UK
UKHW041338111218
333787UK00011B/1474/P